The Building Blocks of Meaning

HUMAN COGNITIVE PROCESSING is a forum for interdisciplinary research on the nature and organization of the cognitive systems and processes involved in speaking and understanding natural language (including sign language), and their relationship to other domains of human cognition, including general conceptual or knowledge systems and processes (the language and thought issue), and other perceptual or behavioral systems such as vision and non-verbal behavior (e.g. gesture). 'Cognition' should be taken broadly, not only including the domain of rationality, but also dimensions such as emotion and the unconscious. The series is open to any type of approach to the above questions (methodologically and theoretically) and to research from any discipline, including (but not restricted to) different branches of psychology, artificial intelligence and computer science, cognitive anthropology, linguistics, philosophy and neuroscience. It takes a special interest in research crossing the boundaries of these disciplines.

Editorial address

Jan Nuyts, University of Antwerp, Dept. of Linguistics (GER),
Universiteitsplein 1, B 2610 Wilrijk, Belgium.
E-mail: jan.nuyts@ua.ac.be

Volume 13

The Building Blocks of Meaning: Ideas for a philosophical grammar
by Michele Prandi

The Building Blocks of Meaning

Ideas for a philosophical grammar

Michele Prandi

Bologna, Italy

John Benjamins Publishing Company

Amsterdam / Philadelphia

The paper used in this publication meets the minimum requirements of American National Standard for Information Sciences – Permanence of Paper for Printed Library Materials, ANSI Z39.48-1984.

Library of Congress Cataloging-in-Publication Data

Prandi, Michele, 1949-
The building blocks of meaning : ideas for a philosophical grammar / Michele Prandi.
p. cm. (Human Cognitive Processing, ISSN 1387–6724 ; v. 13)
Includes bibliographical references and index.
1. Semantics. 2. Grammar, Comparative and general. 3. Language and languages--Philosophy. I. Title. II. Series.

P325.P639 2004
401'.43-dc22 2004049426
ISBN 90 272 2365 3 (Eur.) / 1 58811 526 7 (US) (Hb; alk. paper)

John Benjamins Publishing Co. · P.O. Box 36224 · 1020 ME Amsterdam · The Netherlands
John Benjamins North America · P.O. Box 27519 · Philadelphia PA 19118-0519 · USA

Table of contents

Acknowledgments

Lapis quem reprobaverunt aedificantes
factus est in caput anguli (Psalm 118)

At the source of this book lies an idea which is as old as my academic life. As a graduate in Philosophy, interested in both the conceptual background of human language and the linguistic framing of thought, I was reading Chomsky with Husserlian glasses when I came across the question of conflictual complex meanings. Beyond such artificial examples as *Colorless green ideas sleep furiously*, I immediately thought of the documents of conceptual creativity offered by real texts: *The silver moonbeam pours her ray* (Shelley), *The green woods laugh with the voice of joy* (Blake), *And Winter pours its grief in snow* (E. Brontë), *Shadows – hold their breath* (Dickinson). What irresistibly attracted me, however, was not so much the aesthetic appeal of conflicts as the occasion they offer to take apart the competing factors governing the connection of complex meanings, that is, formal syntactic constructions and shared, long-lasting conceptual architectures. My first course in General Linguistics, held in Geneva in 1980, was about the construction of conceptual conflicts through linguistic forms. During my teaching on the shores of Lac Léman, I wrote *Sémantique du contresens* (1987), where conflictual meanings, discarded by both philosophers and linguists as pseudo-sentences, are systematically explored as "a privileged point of observation upon the inner framing of complex meanings". This book takes a further step along the same path.

The ideation, realisation and revision of this monograph took me twelve years, during which my academic life underwent some significant changes. When the main ideas of this book began to take shape, I was taking up teaching duties in Genoa, at the Faculty of Modern Languages. When remembering the first tentative drafts, I see myself in a bright room opening onto a courtyard closed by a nympheum and filled with orange trees set against a metallic winter sky. I had already drawn up the overall plan and written some chapters when, in 1995, I was called to join the Department of Linguistics at the ancient University of Pavia. Since its foundation by Paolo and Anna Ramat, this

Department has been a regular meeting point for scholars, students and visitors of academic excellence, open to stimulating exchange and discussions. Finally, when the first draft was coming to an end, in 2000, I was engaged by the Faculty of Translation and Interpreting of the University of Bologna, located in Forlì, where the flat land corrugates into pleasant hills and approaches "la marina dove 'l Po discende", loved and depicted by Dante. A deep longing for my own native mountains, their steep terraced vineyards, dark woods and icy peaks has followed me throughout this time and in all these places.

Writing this book in English was a difficult but rewarding challenge for me. When shaping, reshaping and chaining sentences and paragraphs together, I became aware of a feeling so well illustrated by the great Italian writer Beppe Fenoglio: for a native speaker of Italian, to write in English really amounts to carving up one's thoughts. But if a long cherished project has become a readable book, it is thanks to the friendly help of Ian Harvey and Peter Mead, who both not only corrected my mistakes, but above all introduced me step by step to the secrets of their mother tongue.

I am grateful to my students, pupils, colleagues and friends who helped me with their ideas and feelings. In particular, I would like to thank for concrete help Jane Agrò, Guy Aston, Annalisa Baicchi, Franco Bertaccini, Remo Bracchi, Cristiano Broccias, Silvia Bruti, Anna Cardinaletti, Sonia Cristofaro, Pierluigi Cuzzolin, Hanna Flieger, Fabrizio Frasnedi, Chiara Frigeni, Cristina Grasseni, Gaston Gross, Elzbieta Jamrozik, Elisabetta Jezek, Bernd Kortmann, Francesca La Forgia, Giovanni Massidda, Marco Mazzoleni, Salah Mejri, Simona Negruzzo, Malvina Nissim, Adriana Orlandi, Maria Pavesi, Maribel Peñalver, Rachel Pearce, Jan Rijkhoff, Micaela Rossi, Mette Rudvin, Francesco Sabatini, Laura Salmon, Leo Schena, Giuseppe Sertoli, Fiachra Stockman, Jennifer Varney, Federica Venier, Jean-Christophe Verstraete. Many valuable suggestions have come to me from the anonymous referees of the first submitted version.

Chapter 1 is a substantially revised version of "Meaning and Indexicality in Communication", in H. Parret (ed.), *Pretending to Communicate*, Berlin / New York: De Gruyter, 1994. With kind permission from the publisher.

Cristiana De Santis was my magical helper for the final formatting of the text. Bertie Kaal was a reassuring guide through the publication process.

My wife Giuliana and my sons Giulio and Guglielmo were always at my side, supporting me with the discrete strength of real life.

This book is dedicated to the memory of Maria-Elisabeth Conte and Jérôme Lindon.

Foreword

The idea of philosophical grammar

Quis dabit mihi pinnas columbae ut volem et requiescam
Ut procul abeam et commorer in deserto? (Psalm 54)
Super pectus tuum gradieris
Et terram comedes cunctis diebus vitae tuae (Genesis)

An array of simple meaningful expressions itself forms an expression, on condition that it has a unitary meaning. But on what conditions does an array of meaningful expressions have a unitary meaning? These few words put in a nutshell the most basic semiotic question that can be applied to a complex linguistic expression — the question of significance. The aim of this book is to engage in a reflection about the general question of significance and the consequences its clarification might have upon the synchronic description of complex linguistic expressions and meanings.

A first, rough and ready formulation of the question regarding significance could be the following: does the successful ideation of complex meanings stem from a unitary, unifying, well-formed grammatical structure, or does it depend on the accessibility of a consistent content matching a shared conceptual model? In other words, do linguistic structures really *construct* a network of connections between atomic concepts by virtue of their formal properties, or do they simply *bring to expression* autonomous networks of connections founded in the structure of the expressed concepts?[1] If the sentence *The farmer kills the duckling* is successful in depicting a state of affairs, for instance, is it thanks to its well-formed syntactic structure, which is capable of bringing together the atomic concepts in precisely this way, or is it because the atomic concepts are ready to match the structure of a consistent action owing to their independent content?

These alternative answers to such a question circumscribe the two competing paradigms that have inspired both theoretical reflections about language and field research in linguistics in the last few decades — namely, the formal paradigm and the functional paradigm.[2]

According to the formal paradigm, linguistic structures are autonomous both from their conceptual content and from the social functions of real utterances.[3] According to the functional paradigm, linguistic forms are instruments at the service of conceptual contents and social functions, shaped by them.

Both the functional and the formal paradigm have provided deep insights into the nature of language and its cognitive and social functions. We are indebted to both of them for allowing increasingly detailed empirical analysis of the most disparate linguistic facts and for building up an impressive body of empirical knowledge about language. Almost everything we know and understand about the structure of complex meaningful expressions comes from either one tradition or the other. But precisely the fact that two opposite paradigms are equally able to provide deep insights and to build up positive knowledge about one and the same phenomenon suggests that this phenomenon is too complex to be grasped by either. Both formalism and functionalism are partial perspectives, neither of which is capable of fully grasping the complex interplay between a grammar of forms and a grammar of concepts in the ideation of complex meaningful structures.

Strict formal theories envisage language as a closed system displaying a pure inner form free of any functional constraint, and engaged in shaping a shapeless conceptual purport which offers no resistance at all. To this idea we can apply Kant's allegory against the idealist abuse of formal categories outside the strict limits imposed on them by the hard experience of things: "The light dove cleaving in free flight the thin air, whose resistance it feels, might imagine that her movement would be far more free and rapid in airless space". But in the void there is no freedom — there is only death. Like all things human, language can only fly to the extent to which its wings are supported by socially shared functions.

The functional idea of language is opposite in orientation but equally limited. As they are supported and ultimately justified by socially shared functions, linguistic forms are anchored to the flat ground of independent concepts and experiences. If the formal idea of language evokes a flight in the void, the functional idea seems to make no room for flight, as if language, like the snake in the Bible, were condemned to crawl without ever looking up at the sky.

Though opposite in their issues, both paradigms share a common presupposition — namely, the presupposition that one — and only one — factor governs the ideation of complex meanings. This presupposition is a particular instance of what could be named Thales' prejudice, according to which one sole first principle lies at the basis of any complex phenomenon.

If this presupposition is right, the question about significance has a polar form and its answers are mutually exclusive. Either linguistic forms are responsible for the construction of complex meanings, or complex meanings are in fact complex concepts accessible irrespective of linguistic forms: *tertium non datur*. In the former case, it is implied that concepts have no independent structure outside linguistic expression; in the latter, the implication is that linguistic forms are nothing more than instruments of expression at the service of independent structures. If the presupposition is wrong, however, the polar question about significance simply dissolves. If the ideation of complex meanings does not rest on a first principle, it makes no sense to ask whether it is a formal principle or a functional principle that lies at the basis of significance — whether complex meanings are really constructed or simply expressed by linguistic forms.

In a sense, our line of argument simply seeks to challenge Thales' prejudice in the field of significance. The idea is that the ideation of complex meanings is neither the exclusive achievement of formal grammatical connections, nor the simple transference into expression of independent conceptual structures, but the outcome of a complex interaction between a formal principle and a functional principle. Instead of excluding each other, the two factors compete in performing a common task. Instead of stating a first principle once and for all, we make room for a rich and heterogeneous typology of forms of interactions.

The leading idea of this book has been inspired by a careful observation of conflictual complex meanings. Traditionally disregarded by both linguists and philosophers as deviant expressions, and left aside from the mainstream of linguistic description and reflection, conflictual complex meanings provide the best point of observation upon the roots of significance (Prandi, 1987).

Whenever an interaction takes place, one admitted outcome is co-operation, and the other is conflict. Conversely, both co-operation and conflict require the presence of autonomous and competing factors. The methodological advantage of conflict over co-operation is that the former, unlike the latter, makes these competing factors perfectly visible. The meaning of a sentence like *The farmer kills the duckling* is consistent. The network of connections imposed on the atomic concepts by the syntactic structure of the sentence perfectly matches an independent conceptual model. The competition between formal linguistic modelling and conceptual structures remains in the shadow. Marinetti's invitation to *kill the moonlight*, on the contrary, linguistically constructs a conflictual complex meaning devoid of any independent conceptual counterpart. The competing factors of meaningfulness are brought to full light.

A conflictual complex meaning is above all a linguistic meaning whose inner structure succeeds in unifying the parts into a whole. In our example, the moonlight takes on the role of patient of an act of killing because it is the direct object of the verb *kill*. However reluctant on conceptual grounds, the moonlight cannot escape this role. The formal possibility of conflictual complex meanings shows beyond any doubt that linguistic forms have the strength to impose a formal mould on concepts. This, however, does not imply that the mould is imposed on a shapeless conceptual purport. On the contrary, the conflict is in itself proof that concepts are independently organised in complex and consistent networks. In fact, the formal possibility of conflict shows that both complex linguistic expressions and complex concepts have an independent syntax of their own, and that two opposite and complementary principles interact in connecting complex meanings.

An inquiry in the field of conflictual complex meanings proves that language is neither a purely formal system insensitive to conceptual purport nor a mere instrument at the service of independent concepts and social functions. Language is both a formal system and an instrument of ideation and communication. Once the competing factors of significance have been isolated thanks to the observation of conceptual conflicts, the same style of enquiry can be applied to consistent complex meanings. Though conflicting in one case and co-operating in the other, the same competing factors are involved in both cases.

If these remarks are true, the observation of conflictual complex meanings pushes towards a change of paradigm — namely, towards the construction of a paradigm which goes beyond the narrow alternative between a formal and a functional idea of language.

Within this paradigm, the question about significance cannot be put in the form of a polar yes-no question, but must take the form of a graded question: to what extent and within which limits are complex meanings shaped by an independent linguistic mould, and to what extent and within which limits do they simply coincide with the structure of independent concepts? Or, to put it in a different way, to what extent and within which limits are linguistic structures autonomous from their contents, and to what extent and within which limits is their form motivated by the structure of independent concepts? Each complex expression displays a peculiar equilibrium between linguistic shaping and passive expression. While the relevant factors can be isolated once and for all, the outcomes of their competition form a potentially endless set.

This paradigm makes room for a grammar of forms, on the assumption that linguistic structures have a form and a shaping power which are, to a given extent, independent of both conceptual contents and functional purposes. But it also makes room for a grammar of concepts, on the assumption that the concepts brought to expression by linguistic forms have an autonomous structure, which is largely accessible independently of linguistic expression.

Insofar as it focuses on the active and creative role of autonomous grammatical structures, the project contains a pure grammar, that is, a grammar ready to undertake "the great task [...] of investigating that *a priori* system of the formal structures which leave open all material specificity of meaning, in a formal theory of meaning" (Husserl, 1901(1970: 511)).

Insofar as it describes and clarifies independent long-lasting conceptual structures, it circumscribes a province of "descriptive metaphysics", that is, of a philosophical analysis of shared concepts whose object is "the actual structure of our thought about the world" (Strawson, 1959(1964: 9)).

A label which fits this paradigm, underlining its twofold nature of grammatical and conceptual analysis, is the old label of philosophical grammar. The main insight of a philosophical grammar is very simple: the ideation of complex meanings is the outcome of a variable interplay of language-specific formal structures and consistent conceptual structures. Developed consistently, however, this simple idea has far-reaching consequences. If we assume that a manifold and variable interaction between forms and concepts lies at the basis of significance, the very idea of linguistic coding and its relationship to linguistic expression are called into question.

On the one hand, coding is a vector which can run in two opposite directions, that is, either from expression to content, imposing on the connected concepts a formal mould drawn by a network of grammatical relations, or from concepts to forms, using linguistic forms to mark independent concepts and conceptual relations. The twofold orientation of coding will be dealt with thanks to the opposition between a relational and a punctual way of coding.

On the other hand, coding is in competition with inferencing, that is, with a form of natural reasoning that provides an independent access to consistent conceptual models of things and situations.

Once more, both formal and functional paradigms are equally insensitive towards the heterogeneous springs of meaning. According to the formal paradigm, coding is reduced to a unilateral imposition of form on a shapeless conceptual purport. According to the functional paradigm, coding is a purely expressive device, which leads to expression and makes intersubjectively accessible independent conceptual structures. According to both, inferencing is not a true partner of coding in connecting meanings, but a residual device devoid of semantic import and confined within the realm of pragmatics.

The idea of philosophical grammar represents a challenge to all of these assumptions. Both forms of coding are relevant to the study of significance, because a complex meaning is neither a pure linguistic construction nor a pure expression of independent concepts. Up to a certain point, atomic concepts are unified into a complex meaning because a syntactic structure imposes a mould on them. Within these limits, linguistic coding draws an active shaping power from its formal roots. Beyond this point, atomic concepts are unified into a complex meaning to the extent that independent conceptual structures are accessible through linguistic expressions. Within these limits, coding is a marking device at the service of independent concepts.

When engaged in the ideation of complex meanings, inference is not a residual pragmatic device based on contingent contextual data, but a systematic resource at the disposal of language users based on long-lasting conceptual structures. If inference is defined in this way, it is nothing other than the most direct way open to independent concepts to take part in the connection of meanings. Its territory is the same as that occupied by the punctual form of coding: the complex conceptual structures that directly motivate inferencing are the same as those brought to expression by a punctual and instrumental form of coding.

The previous remarks cast new light on the relation between linguistic forms and functions. A formal approach and a functional approach to the structure of meaningful sentences would be really incompatible if both viewpoints were applied to the same facts. If they can be seen as compatible, and even inseparable, it is because they cover different territories within the structure of meaningful sentences. In order to make room for both paradigms, one has not to attenuate their most radical implications. Instead, one has to circumscribe the area of relevance of each and, within these limits, assume the most radical implications of each. Within the strict limits of relational coding, a radical formal stance is required. Within the area circumscribed by the interaction between punctual coding and inferencing, an equally radical functional stance is required.

The dividing line between the area of autonomous forms and the area of instrumental functions is marked on the ground, so to speak, within the structure of each meaningful sentence.

Each sentence has a core whose formal architecture cannot be justified by outer instrumental functions, for its only function is to build up a solid network of purely grammatical relations, devoid of any substantive content and ready to receive many. Like the structural skeleton of a building, the core of a sentence has to stand firm irrespective of its changing functional destinations. The expressions belonging to the peripheral strata, on the contrary, are integrated into a unitary structure insofar as they are endowed with an instrumental function, and put at the service of a given substantive content.

The core of the sentence is the realm of a purely grammatical kind of lawfulness, the elective territory of a "grammar of rules" (Halliday, 1978: 4). The peripheral structures form a system of options at the service of outer, instrumental functions, and in the first place of the expression of independent concepts. They belong to the realm of a "grammar of options" (Halliday, 1978: 4). Within the realm of a grammar of rules, grammatical forms and constructions are the primitive terms, to be taken just as they are and described through internal, formal criteria. Within the realm of a grammar of options, one has first to identify a set of conceptual structures and describe each in autonomous conceptual terms. It is only at this point that it makes sense to circumscribe sets of heterogeneous grammatical resources as alternative means for bringing a given concept to expression.

Almost any structure that is both instrumental, endowed with a substantive content and submitted to option can be specified inside the sentence structure as well as displaced outside it, in a textual dimension. This implies that when it is purely instrumental grammatical connection is itself an option, competing with textual strategies directly based on conceptual consistency, textual coherence and cohesion, both in simple (see Chapter 9, §3) and complex sentence (see Chapter 10, §2). When engaged in instrumental expression, grammar is no longer a pure grammar of forms, but a repository of means at the service of an underlying grammar of concepts.

A last step to be made before developing our research programme is to make its scope explicit. In particular, the reader who has just gone through the preceding pages may wonder whether the present study is about a single language — namely, English — a group of languages, or language in general. In a sense, this book is about human language in general. In another sense, this book is mainly about English, and occasionally about some familiar European languages.

First and foremost, it is about language in general. The main questions and insights focused on in the book concern some structural properties, functions and conditions any symbolic form (in the broad sense defined by Cassirer (1923(1953)) has to share in order to be considered a human language, irrespective of changing historical and typological manifestations.

All human languages must provide a set of grammatical structures and lexical resources for constructing significant expressions. Besides owning some kind of immanent structure designed for this inner function, all human languages are rooted in a given conceptual background, and each of them is compelled to interact with this background in a non-trivial way. In particular, a language is expected to project its active forms on concepts and shape them up to a given point, while yielding to their pressure and reflecting their structure to some significant extent. Moreover, all living human languages are constantly used as serviceable instruments in contingent and unpredictable acts of communication. On any occasion, each and every language is compelled to run the risk of placing its complex repertoire of long-lasting and shared structures and options, all independent of any particular act, at the service of individuals and their occasional aims.

Each human language, at each different stage of its historical life, may reasonably be expected to find out a peculiar way of performing its functional tasks and to attain a specific equilibrium between the inner organisation of its complex and long-lasting formal architectures, the pressure of an equally complex and long-lasting system of concepts and the daily functional engagement at the service of individual occasional purposes. The focus of the present study, however, is not the typological variety of issues open to such a complex interaction, but its general conditions and general factors. Each language, so to speak, has its peculiar story to tell in this regard. But while each story develops and ends in a peculiar way, the initial conditions that set things in movement and the essential steps of the plot can be expected to be largely shared, if not universal, among languages.

If each language interprets in a specific way a general plot starting from a general set of initial conditions, however, the observation of a single language can provide an adequate way of access to the most general topics and questions. This reference language, of course, cannot be any language whatsoever. Access to it cannot be limited to the reception of descriptive data from outside, but has to be possible from within the linguist's direct experience. Husserl's idea of an original experience that "*presents itself in 'intuition' in primordial form*" (Husserl, 1913(1931: 92)) refers to this point. So could the classical opposition between indirectly acquired *knowledge* and direct *acquaintance* (Russell, 1912), had the concept of knowledge not been extended in recent years (almost since Chomsky, 1965) to cover precisely the sense of direct acquaintance.

The most obvious candidate reference language is naturally the linguist's mother tongue, or a language that underlies a significant part of his life. If one goes through the best known classical works, one realizes that most useful insights about language in general are based on a careful observation of the linguist's mother tongue, or of a language that plays a significant role in his living experience. Both Sapir and Bloomfield carve out the basic structure of sentences by analysing English expressions, and the same can be said of Chomsky. Most of the inspiring insights to be found in Saussure's learning come from the observation of French data, while Trier and Porzig's seminal works on lexical semantics are based on German. The observation of one's mother tongue sends back data which are limited in their empirical variety but telling in their value and implications, so that insights inspired by a very narrow data base can prove relevant on a larger scale, and be successfully tested across a large sample of typologically different languages.

As far as the present research is concerned, however, English is neither my mother tongue nor the language of my professional life, as French was when I wrote my previous books during my years in Geneva. English is simply a language I have been struggling with for many years to give shape to my thoughts and to make them accessible to other human beings with other minds and feelings. Yet, I could not use my mother tongue, Italian, as a reference language while thinking in English and addressing English-speaking people. The only option available to me was a compromise. I had to take the risk of directly exploring a foreign territory with limited insight, striving to balance a bold course with awareness of my limits, and to borrow sharpness of sight from outside.

This book contains three sections. The first section seeks to clarify the semiotic bases of the ideation of complex meanings, and above all of the meaning of simple sentences. The meaning of a simple sentence is defined as a structural object independent of the messages an utterance is ready to carry in contingent situations of use. Its constitutive formal and conceptual factors, that is, relational coding, punctual coding and inferencing, are isolated and described in general terms.

The second section deals with the different kinds of conceptual structures that are relied upon in inferencing, and thus take part in the connection of complex meanings. The relevant conceptual structures form a layered system, which is independent of language-specific lexical structures. A relatively shallow layer is formed by shared cognitive models of things and situations, which are by definition consistent. A deeper layer is formed by the conceptual constraints that circumscribe the area of consistent concepts, or consistency criteria. According to our hypothesis, consistency criteria are neither lexical nor cognitive structures. If they govern the consistency of cognitive and lexical structures, it is only insofar as they are practically presupposed by consistent human behaviour.[4]

The third section studies in greater detail the interaction, both co-operative and conflictual, between grammatical structures and conceptual structures in the ideation of both simple processes and interclausal links. Conflictual interaction lies at the roots of the so-called figures of meaning, and in particular of those figures of conceptual conflict which are traditionally called oxymoron, synecdoche, metonymy and metaphor. A philosophical grammar considers them not only as kinds of semantic structure, which can be described as any semantic structure can, but first and foremost as the outposts of linguistic creation, which both make visible the shaping power of linguistic structures upon concepts and disclose for observation the autonomous syntax of concepts. For all these reasons, the study of figures is the natural end-point of a philosophical grammar.

Part I: The semiotic background

Coding and inferencing in the ideation of complex meanings

Introduction

The focus of this section is a tentative clarification of the general semiotic principles underlying the ideation of complex meanings, and above all of the meaning of simple nuclear sentences.

When digging out the roots of complex meanings, nothing can be taken for granted — everything has to be called into question.

It is a truism that complex linguistic expressions are used by individual persons for communicating messages. Yet, the meaning of complex expressions cannot be reduced to the content of individual messages. Individuals entrust to linguistic expressions the content of contingent intentions. In order to achieve their occasional aims, however, individuals rely on long-lasting and systematic linguistic and conceptual structures, which are only given insofar as they are shared. The meaning of a complex expression is torn, so to speak, between its inner systematic structural conditions and its outer contingent functions. Accordingly, the meaning of a complex expression has to be defined both from the outside and the inside. It is defined from the outside when it is taken apart from, and yet connected with, the content of occasional messages. It is defined from the inside when the shared constitutive factors involved in its ideation are analytically identified and described.

In our direct experience, linguistic meanings are phenomenologically inseparable from messages which circulate in communication, but do not coincide with the contents of these messages (Chapter 1).

A message is the occasional content of an occasional speech act performed by a person, and is essentially based on contingent factors. A complex meaning is the content of an expression, and has an inner structure which is essentially based on systematic factors, both formal and conceptual. According to our hypothesis, the relationship between meanings and messages in communication is indexical, and thus contingent: a person uses a meaningful expression to draw the attention of an addressee to an intended message on a given occasion. Conversely, the content of a given meaningful expression and its being uttered on a particular occasion are taken by a cooperative addressee as an index of a given message and, if necessary, as a starting point for inferring it.

Complex meanings can be considered structures on condition that the aptitude of expressions to receive the most unforeseeable communicative values can be justified on independent grounds. The hypothesis of an indexical relation between meanings and messages secures both the structural stability of linguistic meanings against the drift of occasional messages and the autonomy of communication with regard to symbolic lawfulness. The indexical relation allows us to describe communication as a form of human interaction governed by autonomous ethical principles and maxims, while the meaning of complex linguistic expressions can be described as a structure on the basis of its systematic factors.

To carry a message during occasional communicative acts is a functionally relevant but contingent property of expressions. To have a meaning — to be significant — is the constitutive property of linguistic expressions (Chapter 2).

It is a truism that a language is a coding device. Yet expression cannot be reduced to coding. If considered from the inside, the structure of a complex meaning can be seen as the outcome of an interaction between two main factors: coding, which is internal to linguistic structures, and inferencing, which is external to it. Inference, for its part, is not necessarily a pragmatic device. It belongs to pragmatics when it rests on contingent data accessible from within the boundaries of an occasional act of communication. But it does not when it rests on such long-lasting and systematic shared conceptual structures as general cognitive models and consistency criteria. If coding relies on systematic language-specific structures of the formal order, inferencing relies, to a significant extent, on systematic data of the conceptual order, which are shared far beyond the borders of a given linguistic community. Accordingly, systematic inferencing is not a pragmatic strategy but a resource of semantics.

The meaning of a simple nuclear sentence, which can be considered as the paradigmatic case of complex meaning, can be defined as a process, that is, a disposition of arguments and marginal roles around a predicator. Its inner form is shaped by the interplay of two organising factors: grammatical forms of linguistic expressions and independent conceptual structures (Chapter 3). Up to a certain point, the structure of the process is the result of the shaping power of linguistic expressions, irrespective of their conceptual contents. In this case, we can say that linguistic forms really construct their meanings. Beyond this point, the structure of the process simply reflects a network of complex relations among the concepts involved independently of linguistic forms. In this case, we can say that linguistic forms simply express their meaning.

Construction and expression are each bound to a distinct way of coding, that is, relational coding and punctual coding respectively.

Relational coding is based on the formal relational properties of syntactic structures. Punctual coding is essentially based on the content of linking words or expression. Thanks to an autonomous network of grammatical relations, relational coding constructs semantic structures which are independent of conceptual lawfulness, as is proved by the availability of inconsistent complex meanings. Punctual coding expresses independent conceptual structures, whose configuration is faithfully mirrored by the structure of the expression. As the semantic structures it constructs are insensitive to conceptual lawfulness, relational coding is incompatible with inferencing. Insofar as it is based on the meaning of linking words, punctual coding is inherently gradable, and ranges from undercoding to full coding and overcoding. In the case of undercoding, the function of coding is systematically taken over by inferencing. This is the reason why expression, unlike costruction, does not reduce itself to coding but includes inferencing.

In the presence of punctual coding, the content of the roles is immediately coded by the expression. In the presence of relational coding, what is immediately coded is a network of grammatical relations, whereas the content of each role stems from the main predicator according to the relevant grammatical relation. Within a strictly functionalist approach, grammatical relations are reduced to an instrument of perspective. The distinction between relational and punctual coding highlights their active role in the construction of complex meanings.

CHAPTER 1

Meanings and messages

> A language is not the property of any particular nation,
> and obviously it belongs to all who can speak it
> (India's Official Language Commission, 1956)

Human sciences may be defined as those sciences which study facts, behaviours and ideas shared by human beings. Even when the available data seem to project indisputable objectivity, this is no more than an effect of their being shared.

The most significant example of this can be drawn from language, and even from its apparently most solid structures — that is, phonological structures. If we consider that the sounds which provide words with a body are objective data — acoustic or articulatory facts — they resemble a Babelic constellation of material differences which cut across not only countries and regions, but also villages and families, and even the different moments of an individual life. None of these differences, however, does anything to affect the institutional, shared function of linguistic sounds — namely, their ability to keep distinct different words with different meanings. The distinction and the identification of linguistic sounds do not rest on their elusive physical body, but on the fact that they are perceived by the members of a linguistic community as distinct units performing a shared function. A common language exists as long as a community of speakers is ready to grasp, beyond the variable nebula of physical sounds, a basis of shared structures at the service of shared functions.

If such a remark is true, the relevant distinction to be drawn in the field of human sciences is not between objective structures independent of people's changing behaviour and structures that are simply shared by a group of persons, but between different domains, objects and ways of sharing structures. There are structures whose general sharing is taken *a priori* as a condition for use: for instance, phonological, lexical and grammatical patterns of language, as well as the essential conceptual structures familiar to a given cultural community, which the members of the community rely upon with the same confidence as a walker relies on solid ground. And there are, at the opposite end of the scale, such realities as happen to be shared in the form of contingent aims of contingent acts. It is in this sense, for instance, that two persons may come to share a feeling at a given moment of their lives. Verbal communication — the process that leads two people to share a message carried by a meaningful expression — owes its peculiar structural complexity and epistemological interest to the fact that it involves both these ways of sharing.

This insight is a first step along the path that leads to a definition of the manifold bases of linguistic meaning, for it will help to draw a preliminary distinction between the meaning of linguistic expressions and the messages exchanged in verbal communication. Verbal communication entrusts occasional messages to meaningful expressions. Meaning is a systematic property of linguistic expressions which is essentially based on grammatical, lexical and conceptual structures shared *a priori* by the members of a linguistic community. A message is a contingent content which happens to be shared on a given occasion by the subjects of a contingent speech-act.

1. Meaningful expressions as signals of message

1.1 From shared meanings to the sharing of messages

> Nous pouvons contre-passer des gens à cheval venant vers nous
> […] et les hommes qui nous suivent
> peuvent crier qu'on nous arrête.
> Ceci voulait dire: Rechargez vos armes (Stendhal)

The cleavage between meanings and messages is such a platitude as to escape notice, but it remains the essential fact about communication. Let us take an example. A friend I am talking to looks at his watch, picks up his briefcase with a worried look on his face and says: "It's noon". The meaning of the expression is clear to me, for my friend and I speak the same language and share the same conceptual background. But it is equally clear to me that the speaker is not just informing me about the time — really, he is reminding me that it is time to take him to the station. This is the message I am invited to share. In order to grasp this message, on the other hand, it is not enough for me to speak the same language and rely on the same long-lasting concepts as my friend. What I am called upon to do, is to share the contingent plans and intentions of the person who speaks to me. Interpreting a message amounts to identifying, beyond the content of a given expression, the motive of its being uttered.

Such an overt dissociation between the meaning of the expression and the message it carries under given circumstances may appear to be an extreme case. In fact, it is simply a revealing case, which casts light on the terms of the question. If we look without prejudice at our experience as communicators, two facts are evident: the contingent message differs, *de jure* if not always *de facto*, from the meaning of the expression which carries it, while the signal embodies a constellation of data which is likely to go far beyond the structural properties of the linguistic expression.

The meaning of the expression is no more than a starting point on the path towards the message. Interpreting a message is not just decoding an expression, but looking for the sense of a human action, for its motives and purposes. Interpretation of messages transfers us from the realm of long-lasting structures into the realm of contingent acts. Between the meaning of an expression and the occasional message entrusted to it there is an essential cleavage, which is made visible by the active construction of coherence in discourse. In the example of my friend's utterance *It's noon*, such an answer as *Thank you, I have already set my watch* would not be perceived as coherent with the communicative background, that is, as co-operative, while an answer like *I'll take you to the station at once* would be appropriate. The coherent, co-operative answer is not an answer to the meaning of the expression, but to the contingent message I have interpreted from the speaker's words in these particular circumstances.

The signal which forms the input of a communication act, on the other hand, cannot be identified with the *signifiant* of the linguistic expression. It includes in the first place the meaning of the expression, along with a contingent, unforeseeable constellation of such non-linguistic factors as gestures, bodily attitudes and expressions, affective tenor, and even the edges of silence which surround expressions. In our example, the fact that the speaker grabs his briefcase with a worried look on his face is certainly a relevant component of the signal, which significantly affects the interpretation of the message. The relevance of such non-verbal features of the signal for the interpretation is overtly a contingent fact, which has to be evaluated by the addressee on any particular occasion at his own responsibility.[5]

1.2 The natural attitude towards language

Though essential, the cleavage between meanings and messages tends to escape observation and systematic analysis. The main reason for this is the fact that the two orders of reality appear to coincide perfectly from the natural standpoint of language users.

Our spontaneous experience of language is the experience of actors directly involved in communicative events. This internal perspective tends to afford a peculiar image of communication and its chief instrument — language. To those involved in it, communication appears as a transaction defined by two parallel devices: a speaker encodes a definite communicative intention through a linguistic utterance; a receiver, by decoding it, identifies the intended message.

Seen in this way, language reduces itself to a helpful tool at the service of the speaker, devoid of structural autonomy. Individual acts of communication are assumed to succeed on the grounds of an obvious transparency of the signs, whose meanings conform perfectly to the communicative intentions of the speakers and accurately transmit them to the occasional addressees. To understand the meaning of an utterance and to identify a given communicative intention are taken as one and the same process. Our natural attitude towards linguistic facts is faithfully mirrored by the expressions we actually use to describe our dealings with utterances. The use of the verb *mean*, in particular, covers a large conceptual area, ranging from the intention of a subject — communicative or not — to the *signifié* of complex linguistic expressions and individual words. We normally speak of utterances which carry messages and of nouns which identify objects in the same way as we speak of keys which open doors or hammers which drive in nails.

Looked at from a theoretical point of view, the natural standpoint is antithetic to any genuinely cognitive approach. While knowledge requires us to question phenomena beyond received conceptual frames, natural attitude leads us to ignore problems as long as they receive a practical solution. Its aim has nothing to do with a disinterested analysis of phenomena in their structural complexity. If it builds up an image of the object, it is not in order to explore its mysterious depths, but in order to account for its working on the most familiar terms.

Looked at from an ethical point of view, on the other hand, the idea of an inherent transparency of signs relieves the communicator from personal responsibility, giving him the illusion that the aim of his acting — the success of communicative exchanges — is automatically granted by the objective properties of his instrument. Quite obviously, such an idea does not actually prevent subjects from acting ethically; it simply conceals the essentially ethical nature of communicative processes.

Taken literally, natural attitude is intrinsically contradictory. On the one hand, the responsibility for communication is transferred from the subject to the language: the communicative subject sees himself as engaged in a sort of purely technical performance, as if communication were merely a matter of encoding and decoding signs correctly. On the other hand, language itself is seen as no more than a useful tool available to the subject, and therefore devoid of any autonomous structural value.

In spite of its misleading theoretical and ethical implications, natural attitude does not reduce itself to a sort of delusion deceiving the subject. Rather than being simply wrong, natural attitude reflects a limited standpoint. If it encapsulates an illusion, it is, in a sense, a necessary illusion,[6] determined as it is by the real position of communicators in living experience. For the partners in a communicative event, language is really taken and correctly relied upon as a transparent tool which makes it possible to communicate,[7] just as the sun is correctly taken and relied upon as rising and setting in our everyday life. If it keeps the specific structural properties of language in the shade, the natural standpoint faithfully documents the psychological reality of its functional subservience to communication — it encapsulates a functional view of language.[8]

Given the twofold character of linguistic expressions, their structural complexity and their instrumental function, an accurate and exhaustive analysis of verbal communication goes beyond the natural standpoint to pursue two complementary aims. It promotes a disinterested investigation of the internal, autonomous structures of language, without disregarding the obvious, familiar fact that language not only works, but can also unfold towards knowledge, mainly in communication.[9]

1.3 The indexical nature of verbal communication

> The silence which had fallen on his last words
> had lasted for five minutes or more.
> What did it mean? (Conrad)

The idea of an autonomous linguistic structure and the idea of an instrumental function of language in communication are not as such incompatible. They look incompatible against the background of a supplementary assumption, that is, the assumption that messages are directly encoded in linguistic utterances. If we drop this assumption, both linguistic patterns and communicative events may be consistently seen as autonomous from each other on structural grounds, and yet essentially connected at a functional level. The best way to untangle this knot of problems is to dissociate the meaning of expressions from the occasional messages they are ready to convey when used by persons. Our hypothesis is that meaningful linguistic utterances work in communicative events as indexes of occasional messages, or, to look at things from the other side, that occasional messages are inferred from the content of linguistic utterances.

Indexes are objects or events that, under occasional circumstances, are capable of drawing someone's attention on something else. In the simplest cases, an index draws the addressee's attention on a visible object. This happens, for instance, if I point my finger towards a book within a perceptual space shared by the addressee. In the most complex cases, which are relevant for our present topic, an index is taken by an addressee as a premise from which a given conclusion can be drawn through an act of inference.[10] In this case, inference and indexicality are two sides of one and the same relation: if *q* is inferred from *p*, then *p* is taken as an index of *q*.

The indexical relation and its inferential development are not specific discursive phenomena. Rather, they are more general semiotic and cognitive strategies which are ready to be transferred into the field of verbal communication. As a matter of fact, both the content of an utterance taken as true and the direct perception of a state of affairs may equally be interpreted as indexes of something else and therefore trigger an inferential process. If I notice that John's shutters are wide open, for instance, I can be led to infer that he has come back home exactly as I would do, under the same circumstances, if someone drew my attention to this fact, or told me about it.[11]

The idea that linguistic expressions are used as indexes of contingent messages during communication is explicitly formulated by Husserl. In his *Logical Investigation I*, he first distinguishes between expressions and indexes. Linguistic expressions, like symbols in the Aristotelian and Peircean tradition, and signs in Saussure's semiotics,[12] are characterised by the property of carrying a meaning irrespective of any occasional communicative use. Indexes, on the other hand, are either objects or facts that can be taken as signs only insofar as they actually draw the attention of an occasional addressee to something else. Such a theoretical distinction, however, does not hold as a criterion for classifying instances of signs in reciprocally exclusive sets. Taken in this way, it would obviously fail. If examples of pure indexes abound in our everyday experience — a pointed finger, for instance — we cannot normally find pure expressions. In our actual communicative experience, the only expressions we meet are expressions working as indexes: "all expressions in *communicative* speech function as indications. They serve to the hearer as signs of the 'thoughts' of the speaker, i. e. of his sense-giving inner experiences, as well as of other inner experiences which are part of his communicative intentions"[13] (Husserl, 1901(1970: 277)).

The fact that expressions actually work as indexes is not an argument for dismissing the distinction between indexes and expressions. Rather, the opposition has to be reinterpreted as a relevance criterion for distinguishing, within the complex phenomenon of expression, between essential properties and occasional ones: between what happens to an expression in given circumstances and what an expression is in itself. According to such a hypothesis, the fact that they hold as indexes of occasional messages is a real but occasional property of linguistic utterances. The fact of having a meaning, on the other hand, is an essential structural property of linguistic expressions, independent of any occasional communicative event they may take part in. Whilst experience offers us expressions which work as indexes, this criterion allows us to see, beyond the immediate evidence of the indexical function, the essential property of expressions: their significance. While the indexical function is, however effective, a purely occasional function expressions share with non-linguistic indexes, significance is the essential and exclusive property of linguistic expressions. An out-of-work index is no longer an index; an out-of-work expression is still an expression. Its significance is not ruled out by the loss of the context of an occasional use.[14]

This remark opens up two intertwined paths to analysis. The principal aim of the present project is to study the significance of complex linguistic expressions and its systematic bases, shared *a priori*. In order to do so, however, it is essential to understand that the occasional sharing of messages relies on autonomous principles of practical import. After all, the exchange of messages is not a structural relation between expressions and meanings, but a kind of purposeful human action that uses meaningful expressions as instruments for attaining contingent aims.

2. The inner space of communication: Literal and non-literal interpretation

Littera enim occidit,
Spiritus autem vivificat (St. Paul)

When the message happens to coincide with the meaning of the expression involved, it is only too easy to share the main assumption of natural standpoint and think that the message *is* this meaning — that there is no structural gap between them. The identity of meaning and message is assumed in this case to be the paradigmatic form of communication — an assumption which is at the basis of the idea of literal meaning.

According to our hypothesis, on the contrary, the most revealing form of communication is not the coincidence between meaning and message, but their radical divergence. It is in this case, when the message has an autonomous content, connected with the meaning of the expression by a contingent link, that communication openly displays its indexical nature. In the light of such a hypothesis, the coincidence between meaning and message can no longer be taken as a structural property of some kind of meaning, but reveals itself as the occasional outcome of an essential cleavage between a contingent intended message and the long-lasting linguistic meaning of the utterance designed for its expression. Accordingly, it is the observation of non-literal expression and interpretation that makes it possible to analyse the essential feature of communicative interactions, that is, the contingent link between meanings and messages.

The idea defended here is that such predicates as *literal* and *non-literal* cannot be consistently applied to the meaning of complex expressions. Taken as such outside a communicative use, that is, as a network of structural relations between the contents of atomic expressions, the meaning of a sentence may be consistent, inconsistent or contradictory, fully determined, indeterminate or ambiguous, but cannot be defined as either literal or non-literal. Instead, the two predicates consistently apply to a double-way relation that involves a complex meaning as one of its terms, that is, to the expression of an intended message thanks to a meaningful utterance and to the interpretation of a meaningful utterance as the signal of a contingent message. What can be consistently defined as literal or non-literal is once more the contingent indexical relation between a given meaning and a given message.[15] An intended message can either coincide with the meaning of the expression used to convey it or go far beyond. In the former case, the expression is literal; in the latter, it is non-literal. Conversely, an act of interpretation can either take the meaning of the utterance as the relevant message or move far away from it by following a complex inferential chain. In the former case, the interpretation is literal; in the latter, it is non-literal. On the assumption that literal interpretation ideally matches literal expression and vice-versa, in the following paragraphs we shall focus on the interpretative side of the indexical link, first of all because the addressee's standpoint highlights the practical and ethical nature of communicative interactions.

2.1 The message takes the meaning as its content: The literal interpretation

> There comes a time when the world
> is but a place of many words and man appears
> a mere talking animal not much more wonderful than a parrot
> (Conrad)

Literal interpretations are above all interpretations.[16] The coincidence between meaning and message, documented by literal interpretations, is not an essential property of the expression, as the idea of literal meaning suggests, but an occasional issue of an interpretative device whose structure does not differ from the structure of non-literal interpretations. The reasons which, on some occasions, lead an addressee to a literal interpretation — that is, to the conclusion that the meaning of a given utterance needs no further development to become a message — are the same as those which, under different circumstances, lead him to a complex inferential development — namely, an evaluation of the uttered content against the background of a given context. A literal interpretation is contextually justified if this evaluation gives a positive answer; in the opposite case, one has to draw adequate inferences in order to obtain a contextually relevant message. The identity of meaning and message is a particular case of their indexical connection.

If these remarks are true, literal and non-literal interpretations can be seen as opposite issues of the same process. The gap between a literal interpretation and an inferential development is only a contingent difference. If there is an essential gap, it is located between a linguistic meaning — a network of relations essentially resting on systematic structures of the linguistic and conceptual order — and a message — the outcome of a contingent act of interpretation aimed at identifying the contingent communicative value of an expression. The link between a meaning and a message, be it the result of literal interpretation or of a long chain of inferences ending far away from the meaning of the expression, is always a contingent relation of the indexical order, defined by a contingent co-occurrence of contextual factors answering to a criterion of coherence. The role played by contextual data and coherence is as essential in the case of literal interpretation as in the case of non-literal interpretation.[17]

Once these points have been made clear, however, one cannot help feeling that only one side of the question has been clarified. If it is true that non-literal interpretation enjoys the epistemological privilege of highlighting the indexical link between meanings and messages, literal interpretation certainly enjoys the practical privilege of being the favourite option in many real communicative acts.

The use of linguistic expressions for communicative purposes — and in particular during face-to-face interactions — is systematically associated with a strong implication, according to which the message tends to be interpreted as coinciding with the meaning of the expression until proven otherwise.[18] This sound insight, which is rooted in natural attitude and provides the idea of literal meaning with its intuitive ground, can consistently be formulated in terms of literal and non-literal interpretation. Literal interpretation is the favoured option for the addressee of an act of communication, while non-literal interpretation is as naturally taken into account if literal interpretation turns out not to be coherent with co-textual and contextual data.

At the other end of the scale, the idea of a direct expression of thought in words, that is, of an expression meant to be interpreted literally, has an indisputable regulating value in scientific and philosophical texts. This of course implies neither that indirect formulation is banished from science and philosophy nor that there is no room left for non-literal interpretation in such texts. It simply means that two parallel maxims of direct expression and sober interpretation tacitly regulate the communicative contract in scientific and philosophical speech (see Chapter 11, §3.1).

In any case, to express one's thought literally remains a speaker's option, though highly praised and practically preferred by the addressee in most kinds of interaction. Accordingly, literal expression is not an empirical property of utterances but a value of the practical order. It is within these limits that the idea of literal meaning can be considered as the wrong way of expressing a correct insight.

2.2 The message has an autonomous content: The non-literal interpretation

> He had spoken the very truth,
> and transformed it into the veriest falsehood (Hawthorne)

Our experience as language users makes us familiar with a rich typology of conflicts between the meaning of an expression and contextual data, which push the quest for coherence away from the meaning of the expression towards a non-literal option. In this case, the message loses any predictable link with the meaning of the expression, and takes on an autonomous content, connected with the meaning by a contingent chain of context-dependent inferences. By way of illustration, we shall examine some of the more overt and significant cases from this standpoint.

A traditionally favoured case of cleavage between meaning and message is provided by tropes, and chiefly by metaphor.

The most paradigmatic instances of metaphor are provided by inconsistent utterances, which are characterised, as in the following example, by an overt conceptual conflict:[19]

> The moon, like a flower,
> In heaven's high bower,
> With silent delight
> Sits and smiles on the night (Blake)

What is peculiar about inconsistent utterances is the fact that no contingent information is required in order to detect the conceptual conflict, which is based on systematic linguistic and conceptual structures holding *a priori*, as the quoted example shows. On the one hand, *The moon* is the subject of *smile* according to English syntax; its referent must thus be the agent of smiling. On the other hand, our shared conceptual structures do not allow a heavenly body to smile. If an inconsistent expression generally prompts a non-literal interpretation, this is certainly owing to its conflictual meaning, which cannot be immediately taken as a true message. One tempting conclusion of this is that what requires a non-literal interpretation is not the contingent inclusion of the expression in a contingent context, but a systematic property of its very meaning, that is, inconsistency. Such a conclusion, however, is incorrect.

The first point to be stressed is that an inconsistent utterance allows a literal interpretation if it refers to an alien world. In this case, the content of the utterance, however conflictual, cannot be considered as metaphorical. The conflict is no longer between the meaning of the utterance and the structure of our world, governed according to a shared ontology, but between the world it refers to when it is interpreted literally, ruled by a peculiar ontology, and our shared world. This is the case, for instance, with Phaedrus' fables, which consistently depict an alien world inconsistent with ours:

> Calumniari si quis autem voluerit,
> quod arbores loquantur, non tantum ferae,
> fictis iocari nos meminerit fabulis

Under such circumstances, the alternative between literal and metaphorical interpretation of a conflictual meaning depends on a supplementary piece of information, that is, whether the utterance is about our shared world or not.[20] Such information is certainly a contingent one.

A second relevant point is that an inconsistent utterance about our world — that is, a true metaphor — is not necessarily bound to result in a consistent non-literal interpretation. In other words, a metaphor is not necessarily received as the inconsistent signal of a consistent message. Of course, many metaphors — and most "metaphors we live by" (Lakoff & Johnson, 1981) — enjoy such an ephemeral life. But this is, once more, a contingent fact. The value of the most interesting metaphors, indeed, lies more in the open, virtually endless conflicts they shape than in any of their possible, contingent solutions. A metaphor lives, in a sense, as long as the possibility of a literal, conflictual interpretation is kept open (see Chapter 11, §5).

Finally, even when a conceptual conflict is expected to be resolved in a definite, consistent interpretation, its value as a message may be identified only within the boundaries of a given context of utterance. For all these reasons, what is relevant to the life of the metaphor, that is, to its value as a message, is not so much the systematic properties of the inconsistent meaning as the contingent properties of the context which directs its use.[21]

Of course, a consistent utterance is *de facto* more likely to receive a literal interpretation, which takes the content of the utterance as the relevant message, than an inconsistent one. This circumstance, however, is far from implying that literal interpretation is written into the structure of consistent meaningful expressions. One cannot deduce the unpredictable communicative values an utterance is ready to take from its structural properties — once more, the last word is said when the expression is used as an index in a given context. Let us consider some paradigmatic cases.

Unlike analytical falsity, or contradiction,[22] empirical falsity is a property of consistent utterances. A false statement cannot carry a relevant message without being taken as the vehicle of a true content — that is, without receiving a non-literal interpretation that connects it to an independent content. We may imagine two ways of using a false statement in order to communicate a true message: in the first case, the falsity of the statement is overtly displayed, so that the addressee is explicitly invited to draw appropriate inferences; in the second case, it is hidden, on the assumption that contextual information will naturally lead the interpreter to identify the correct message.

A well-known case of displayed falsity is hyperbole: *I'm dead*, for instance, or *Nobody lives in Padua* (Lodge). Hyperbole is traditionally described as a figure which "enhances or reduces things to an excessive degree, presenting them well above or well below what they really are, with a view not so much to misleading as to pointing towards the truth and, by stating the incredible, establishing what must really be believed" (Fontanier, 1968: 123). As Fontanier correctly argues, the truth is not in the words — it is in the intended thought. But this implies that the thought has an independent content of its own, which has to be inferred from the words under the pressure of contextual data.[23]

A good example of the second case is provided by Sperber & Wilson (1986a: 18–19):

> Suppose that Marie lives in Issy-les-Moulineaux, fifty metres outside the Paris city limits. At a cocktail party in London, she meets Peter. He asks her where she lives, and she answers: "I live in Paris". Literally speaking, Marie's answer is not true, but under ordinary circumstances it is not misleading. Peter can infer a large amount of true or plausible information from her statement — that Marie spends most of her time in the Paris area, that she knows Paris, that she has an urban lifestyle, that he could try and meet her when he next visits Paris, and so on.

At a purely interactional level, the distance between overt and hidden falsehood could not be wider. By overtly displaying the falsehood, the speaker offers the addressee the key for a correct understanding and shares with him the communicative responsibility. By keeping the falsehood hidden, on the contrary, the speaker takes the full responsibility for a unilateral breaking of the communicative contract. If he behaves as a co-operative speaker, however, he makes his choice on the assumption that there is enough shared contextual information to lead the addressee to draw a set of true and relevant inferences.

The most obvious and familiar reason why a consistent and true utterance requires a complex inferential development is its lack of coherence with co-textual or contextual information. Let us imagine a homely scene: Mary asks about the cat, and John answers: *The window is open.* The piece of information is true but ostensibly non-relevant, for it is not about the assumed topic. However, Mary knows that the open window is a favoured escape route for the cat, and easily infers from the utterance about the window that the cat is likely to have gone out through it. Within the borders of this shared situation, the incoherent statement about the window is taken as an index of a coherent and relevant message about the cat. Topic continuity, which is a strong condition for coherence, is attained in the absence of any punctual anaphoric thematisation of the relevant referent — of the cat.[24]

A widely studied kind of utterance which, though both consistent and coherent, generally requires a peculiar contextual development in order to become a message is the approximate utterance. According to Austin (1962(1975: 143–144)), an approximate utterance is not an utterance with an approximate meaning, but a meaningful utterance which gives too "rough" a picture of a state-of-affairs to be correctly understood — for instance, to be received as a true or false statement. "Consider the constative, 'Lord Raglan won the battle of Alma', remembering that Alma was a soldiers' battle if ever there was one and that Lord Raglan's orders were never transmitted to some of his subordinates. Did Lord Raglan then win the battle of Alma or did he not?".

Asked in this form, the question is pointless. If, as Wittgenstein (1922(1961: 4.024)) suggests, "to understand a proposition means to know what is the case if it is true", an utterance with insufficient content to provide a basis for guessing "what is the case" cannot be understood, still less can be considered true or false. It is only against the background of a definite context that the content of the utterance could be processed, thanks to some appropriate inference, into a fully understandable picture of some possible state of affairs.[25] In the context of a schoolbook, for instance, the sentence would simply suggest, probably, that Raglan was the commander-in-chief of the army which won the battle, and would therefore be taken as true. In the context of a scholarly historical research paper, on the contrary, it would probably suggest that the victory was due mainly to Raglan's own orders and decisions, and would therefore be taken as false. What is in fact checked against experience is not immediately the content of the utterance, but a cognitively exhaustive picture of a given state of affairs obtained by way of inference against the background of a given context.

3. The interpretation of messages

3.1 The interpretation field: Structure and functions

> Obviously, it would be something very simple
> — the simplest impossibility in the world; as, for instance,
> the exact description of the form of a cloud (Conrad)

An expression can be identified and decoded independently of its uses because its being an expression depends to a significant extent on its belonging to a complex encoding system. The meaning of an expression is essentially understood on the basis of systematic data, irrespective of any occasional speech situation.

Unlike the meaning of an expression, a reference made with an index — for instance, a pointed forefinger — is not governed by a network of systematic structures independent of the occasional conditions of use — that is, by a code

— but depends on the occasional and fortuitous co-occurrence of a set of unpredictable factors in a complex configuration. Its identification, therefore, demands on any occasion a contingent act of interpretation, which takes into account a set of contextual factors. To the extent that an expression works as an index of a given message, its communicative value rests on a similar set of conditions. Unlike a linguistic meaning, a message is not encoded in the signal, but simply connected to it through a contingent linkage. Therefore, a message is not decoded by the receiver on the grounds of systematic properties of the expression, but interpreted, like any other index, on the grounds of shared co-occurring information.

When it is interpreted as an index of a message, the meaning of an expression is not taken in isolation, but as part of a set of cooccurring data, which are neither necessarily nor typically framed in words, and it is this contingent network as a whole that holds as a premise for further inferencing. In the cat and window scene discussed above, for instance, the circumstance that the window is open justifies the conclusion that the cat has escaped on the condition that it is connected with the shared piece of information that the window is a favourite escape route for the cat.

When an utterance is used to convey a message, the signal is taken within a complex configuration of cooccurring data which shapes the contingent indexical relation in the same way as linguistic structures shape the coded relation between expression and meaning. Under such conditions, the shared situation in which the transient link between an utterance and a message takes shape is no longer to be considered a passive appendix of the linguistic realm, that is, a set of accessory data we take into account when a purely linguistic description fails to account for the content of an expression. Once it is involved in the game of communication, a linguistic meaning is no longer to be considered as the centre of gravity of the communicative event. Along with any essential or contingent property of the expression, it becomes a constituent of a complex relational structure, and it is this structure that actively confers its communicative value on the meaningful expression.

A widespread prejudice restricts the label of structure to the paradigms — the sets of units competing *in absentia* — or at best to the configurations *in praesentia* resting on underlying paradigmatic structures. A paradigm — for instance, a lexical field — is certainly a structure, for its members receive a value on the basis of their correlations with competing units. A complex disposition of expressions *in praesentia* — a sentence, for instance — is not simply a chain of words but a structure because it confers a value and a function on its constituent parts. Given a sentence like *The girl is offering hyacinths*, for instance, the noun phrase *The girl* is the subject because it is the noun phrase which holds as immediate constituent of the sentence. The same phrase would have neither the same value nor the same function outside this syntactic relationship.[26]

What is really difficult to make room for is the idea that a fortuitous disposition of elements, devoid of any systematic underlying rule, may hold as a structure. The essential property of a structure, however, is not so much its outer shape or its resting on systematic grounds, but its being capable of unifying many elements into a whole and of conferring on the constituent parts a specific value they would not possess outside the configuration. Given this premise, even a fortuitous disposition has to be considered a structure if it is capable of unifying its parts into a whole and conferring a value on each. This is precisely the case with the complex, contingent co-occurrence of data within which a linguistic expression receives its value as a message. Such a configuration does not resemble a structure of the canonical order, for its shape is as ephemeral and fleeting as the shape of a cloud. However, it is precisely within such an ephemeral and fleeting configuration that an expression becomes the vehicle of a message. Outside this peculiar, contingent configuration, the same expression would not receive precisely this peculiar value as a message; outside a structure of this kind, the same expression would not convey any message at all.

In order to characterise such a structure in a positive, non-residual way, the notion of context seems inadequate. As we shall see later on (Chapter 2, §1.2), the idea of context is the outcome of a progressive and rather uncontrolled accumulation of heterogeneous elements performing different functions and sharing the purely negative property of being extra-grammatical facts. As a result, the notion of context does not identify a well-defined and active structure characterised by a precise function or set of functions, but a shapeless and passive container of any kind of extragrammatical data. What is needed in order to account for the interpretation of meaningful expressions as indexes of messages, on the contrary, is an active structure capable of conferring a value on its elements. For our purpose, we can turn to a valuable, though largely underexploited concept: the concept of field, defined by K. Bühler[27] in order to describe the occasional referential function of indexes in communication. All we have to do with this notion is to fit it into a more complex, though not essentially different function, performed by far more complex indexes — namely, complex linguistic expressions engaged in communication.

3.1.1 *From indexical field to interpretation field*

> The classification of the constituents of a chaos, nothing less is here essayed (Melville)

The indexes Bühler has in mind in connection with his notion of field are the atomic indexical expressions of language — for instance, pronouns like *I* or *you* and adverbs like *here* or *now* — which encapsulate in their very meaning the reference to the speech situation they occur in. What is interesting about these expressions is that they illustrate paradigmatically, although in its simplest, most rudimentary terms, the possibility for an expression to be a symbol within the linguistic system while working as an index when used in texts and discourses — a property which characterises, according to our hypothesis, the whole set of linguistic expressions used in communication. As linguistic symbols, indexical atomic expressions like *I*, *you*, *here* and *now* carry an arbitrary meaning coded within the English language. Unlike non-indexical atomic expressions like *dog* or *beautiful* or *run*, which give access to an independent and long-lasting concept, the meaning of indexical atomic expressions contains the instruction to interpret them as indexes in a shared field, coinciding with the speech situation itself.[28]

At this stage, the difference between pure symbols and indexical expressions seems very deep. But if we consider complex saturated expressions,[29] namely noun phrases like *The dog* or sentences like *The dog is running*, it is easy to note that they are ready to be put into use as indexes, and therefore to share the twofold nature of atomic indexical expressions. In a given text or discourse, the noun phrase *The dog* may be used to point to a given, individual dog, while the sentence *The dog is running* may be used to convey a peculiar message. Which dog is actually referred to, and why this dog is actually said to be running, are relevant questions an occasional addressee has to be able to answer.[30]

The most straightforward use of indexical expressions is the deictic use: the immediate reference to an entity physically given in the surrounding perceptual space. In the case of the deictic use of indexical expressions, the field shared by the speaker and the addressee is essentially the same as that which governs gestural indication — Bühler's *demonstratio ad oculos*. The success of a deictic act of reference to a given book by means of an indexical expression like *This book*, for instance, requires the presence of the book within the visual field shared by the interlocutors, just like its gestural indication. But indexical expressions are not necessarily put to deictic use. Definite noun phrases and third person pronouns allow for anaphoric or cataphoric use. During anaphoric indication, the expression remains the same, but the field undergoes a change. The expression does not typically refer to an individual physically given in the perceptual field, but necessarily refers to an entity previously or subsequently named within the same discourse or text:[31] *I'm reading* a paper *on cataphora. I find* it (this paper) *interesting.*

The observation of anaphoric indication allows us to submit the notion of field to a first development in the direction of a more complex notion, capable of accounting for the interpretation of messages. Beyond the referents physically given in the discourse situation, the indexical expression is able to refer to any kind of entity — present or absent, existent, non-existent or even absurd.[32] As a consequence, the indexical field underlying anaphoric reference stretches far beyond the physical borders of a given communicative situation. Anaphoric reference dissociates indication from the deictic situation, opening the indexical field to all kinds of purely symbolic entities.

This, however, is only a first step. While anaphoric reference depends on the identification of real or symbolic entities directly or indirectly introduced into the text or the discourse by a linguistic expression and located within a narrow range, an interpretation field includes any kind of long-term knowledge and occasional information, assumptions and expectations not overtly connected with the uttered content. Unlike the set of entities referred to in a text or discourse, knowledge and information at the disposal of the receiver during a communication act form an open and mobile constellation whose extent and internal perspective are not previously planned with this particular speech act in mind. In order to interpret an utterance correctly, its receiver must be ready to reorganize this constellation of data each time — namely, to foreground relevant pieces of information and to background irrelevant ones. The occasional shaping of the field critically depends on a relevance criterion.[33] This relevance criterion, however, is itself occasional and devoid of any structural necessity.

The last point makes an obvious difference with regard to more simple indexical fields. The interpretation field is no longer to be considered as the object of a passive reception and becomes, to a variable extent but effectively, the object of an active construction for which the interpreter is responsible. The structure of the field can be justified in prospective rather than retrospective terms, that is, in view of an intended interpretative end rather than on the basis of a previously given set of objective contextual data. This, however, implies that the interpreter, when interpreting a given utterance, has at his disposal a plurality of potentially relevant fields, each consistent with an interpretative purpose, which in turn allow for a plurality of potentially coherent interpretations. The interpretation of a message eventually results from a choice, for which the interpreter takes responsibility, among an open set of possible interpretations, each solidary with a different field. Let's take an example from Virginia Woolf's *To the Lighthouse*. To interpret correctly his mother's utterance about next day's bad weather as transmitting a message like «We won't sail to the lighthouse», little James must take into account a totally autonomous topic — the planned trip — and connect it with the content of the utterance. This piece of information, however, is not previously connected in a relevant way to the received utterance. On the contrary, it has to be foregrounded at the expense of other pieces of potentially relevant information present on the stage, for instance, the plan to cut pictures or his mother's sadness. If one of these topics had been foregrounded, the interpreted message would have proved very different.

3.1.2 *Situational and constructed dimensions of interpretation fields*

When one looks for signs, one finds them (Maalouf)

As our example shows, interpretation fields vary along two complementary dimensions: an external one, immediately connected with the variety of speech situations, and an internal one, connected with the composition and perspective of the constructional side of the field. The first, more obvious dimension is evident from the observation of oral face-to-face interactions, while the second and more interesting dimension is underlined by the interpretation of written texts.

If one imagines a continuum including all possible kinds of communicative signal, oral face-to-face interaction and the long-lasting written text are two extremes, while a rich variety of mixed forms occupy the middle ground between the two. Of course, each of these different kinds of signal undergoes a more or less different interpretative process. According to our hypothesis, however, what differentiates each kind of process is not its essential structure, that is, its dependence on a field, but rather a different balance between the different factors contributing to the construction of a relevant field. These factors are roughly the following: situational data and constructed components of the field, the (presumed) intentions of the speaker, his (possible) assent, the direct responsibility of the interpreter, the weight of the non-linguistic features of the signal.

During the interpretation of oral face-to-face interactions, the context of utterance is the centre of gravity of the whole field, which can be seen as a sort of endocentric expansion of it. In this case, a certain balance is ensured between the given and constructed data of the field. As a consequence, the plurality of possible interpretations for a single utterance seems essentially connected with the uncontrollable plurality of discourse situations.[34] If Mary's utterance *It's raining* is to be interpreted today as a hint to bring in the washing, the utterance of the same sentence by John can be interpreted tomorrow as the realisation that a planned trip has to be cancelled.

A written text of the ideal type — that is, a text intended for long duration — dissociates emission and reception, splitting the utterance situation. As a consequence the interpretative field, uprooted from the contingencies of the discourse situation, takes the text itself as its centre of gravity.

Looked at from the standpoint of the systematic structures of language, a text is no more than the unforeseeable outcome of the fortuitous co-occurrence of expressions in a linear sequence. In spite of this, a text appears to its reader as if it were an orderly microcosm. It appears as a complex structure governed by a sort of inner necessity, and capable as such of conferring a peculiar value on its constituents, from the content of each simple utterance down to the most idiosyncratic arrangement of words and sounds.[35] The model of such a structure is certainly not the systematic structure of language, with its paradigms of values insensitive to contingent facts, but the contingent structure of a field. Being constructed as a field, the text itself forms the core around which wider and more complex and rich interpretation fields may be constructed out of extra-textual data.[36]

Under such conditions, the balance between the different factors of an interpretation field is upset, to the advantage of the constructional side. The author's intentions and his possible approval are taken as irrelevant. If they are available, for instance on philological evidence, they are considered no more relevant, in principle, than other data of the field. A literary text is received less as the expression of a subject's intentions than as an autonomous construction fully open to wide-ranging explorations. The content of the interpretation, thus, depends essentially on the preliminary choices made by the interpreter — namely, on his decision to include in the field a given constellation of relevant data and to assume as relevant some features of the signal.

In a famous passage of Torquato Tasso's poem *Gerusalemme liberata* (*Jerusalem Delivered*), a tree, struck by Tancredi's sword, suddenly bleeds. The reason is that the tree harbours the soul of Clorinda, the warrior girl loved and unwittingly killed by Tancredi. What does this episode mean exactly? The editor of the text interprets it as an instance of the *topos* of a tree sheltering a soul and bleeding from an unconscious stroke, against the background of a rich intertextual tradition including Virgil, Dante and Ariosto.[37] Evaluating it against a radically different constellation of data and hypotheses, Freud interprets the same passage as a poetic transfiguration of a conflictual drive — as an instance of repetition compulsion, which urges human beings to act out the same game again and again against their will.[38] What is interesting here is that the traditional sources, which are obviously relevant for the philologist, would be misleading for the psychoanalyst, for all of them miss the crucial point, that is, the unconscious repetition of an unintentional act. The two interpretations, so different from each other, are nonetheless each coherent with a field, whose structure only provides a justification for them. Incidentally, there is nothing shocking about this. It simply underlines a constitutive property of literary texts, that is, their being open to different interpretative hypotheses, each coherent with a given field whose structure and composition are open to intersubjective examination.[39]

The gap between the interpretation of an oral message during a face-to-face interaction and the interpretation of a literary text could not be wider. In spite of this, the essential structure of the interpretative process remains unchanged. In both cases, to interpret a message is to identify the value of an index within a field — that is, to establish a relation *in praesentia* between a structurally firm signal and a contingent message against a field whose structure can vary according to different parameters.

What the interpretation of a literary text underlines is the main question of interpretation, which is somehow hidden by its being practically solved in direct, face-to-face communication — namely, the essential link between the constructional side of the field, the virtual plurality of admitted interpretations, and the responsibility of the interpreter. As the interpretation of literary texts shows, essential differences in interpretation are not necessarily connected with a correlative variation in situational data, but depend on the constructional side of interpretative fields. But if a given interpretation is justified in connection with a consistent field, and this field is to a given extent a constructed structure, perhaps intentionally built up with this peculiar interpretation in mind, a circular link is formed between a given interpretation, the construction of a particular interpretative field, and the responsibility of the subject engaged in it. A question naturally arises at this point: is interpretation an absolutely open task — are there absolutely no limits imposed on it?

3.2 The limits of interpretation

> Signs are small measurable things,
> but interpretations are illimitable (G. Eliot)

During successful, non-traumatic communicative events, the actors involved are not aware of the plurality of messages a single utterance is able to communicate within different fields. Generally, it is in connection with traumatic experiences that one becomes familiar with the possibility of plural interpretation. Accordingly, from a natural standpoint the plurality of interpretations is seen as a pathological accident, due to the intervention of external factors troubling the inherent transparency of signs. Within our framework, the potential plurality of interpretations is to be considered as a structural property of communication, the direct consequence of the mutual autonomy of significance and indexicality and of the wide margin left to the interpreter for the construction of relevant fields. It is the success of communication that seems to become a kind of mystery, or miracle. As a matter of fact, the potential plurality of interpretations and the success of communication in normal circumstances are not conflictual realities — they are both basic data of our experience. What is needed in order to reconcile these two data is a supplementary assumption — that is, the assumption that some kinds of restriction are *de facto* imposed on interpretation, so as practically to narrow the wide margin virtually open for it. Against such a background, the essential question about communication becomes the question about the limits of interpretation.[40]

In order to answer such a question, two main lines of argument may be followed. According to the first line, the limits of interpretation belong to the theoretical and empirical order — that is, they are structures or data open to empirical enquiry. According to the second, the limits of interpretation belong to the practical order — they are grounded on principles and maxims that govern the responsible behaviour of free human beings.

The theoretical line of argument tries to secure, so to speak, the solid rock of objectivity against the potential drift of interpretation: what constrains the work of interpretation is some external structure or datum. These objective limits, in turn, may be located either in the structure of the expression, or in the intentions of the speaker. In the first case, the dam against the drift of interpretations is the idea of literal meaning; in the second, it is the idea of authentic interpretation — of a kind of interpretation which assumes the communicative intention of the speaker as its leading criterion.

3.2.1 *Communicative intentions*

Forgive me, my dear, if my words are confused.
The thread is in my heart (from a love letter)

As we have already argued, the idea of literal meaning is either an inconsistent notion, or has to be taken as referring to a specific issue of an interpretative process. If taken this way, the idea contains the sound insight that the meaning of an expression offers itself, *prima facie*, as if it were the real message. Insofar as it is a kind of interpretation, however, literal interpretation does not rest on some structural privilege of the expression, but is the outcome of an evaluation of its content against a consistent field. If literal interpretation springs, so to speak, out of meaning, it is not with the absolute strength of a structural bond, but only with the relative strength of a favoured option open to the responsible choice of the interpreter. In other words, if the idea of literal meaning is inconsistent, the idea of literal interpretation refers to a practical kind of bond.

The notion of authentic interpretation seems, at first sight, as inconsistent as the idea of literal meaning. In order to be effective as a limit on interpretation, the communicative intention of the speaker should be accessible independently of the expression that conveys it. But the only available access to a communicative intention is its expression, which in turn does not reduce itself to a transparent tool serving a given intention, and has to be interpreted, and so on *ad infinitum*. But this argument, however correct, is beside the point.

The point about communicative intention is not so much its more or less direct accessibility as its relevance — and it is a plain fact that communicative intention is the relevant aim for the interpretation of many kinds of oral and written messages. In direct face-to-face communication, for instance, the aim of our interpreting activity is the 'true' intentions of the speaker. Even when they are difficult to grasp, they nevertheless remain relevant, a circumstance which pushes the co-operative interpreter to make every effort to penetrate them.[41] The most striking manifestation of this interest in understanding people is our willingness to correct our interpretations when they are not shared by the speaker, and, more generally, to negotiate them with him. As trained subjects of communication, we all share the feeling that a tendential approximation to the speaker's intention is the criterion that, silently but severely, guides the interpreter. On these grounds, we are inclined to blame deviations from this criterion as instances of underinterpretation or overinterpretation, or, in the popular sense, of 'interpretation'.

Agreement about communicative intentions, the negotiations which sometimes lead to it, and the pathological character recognised in both underinterpretation and overinterpretation all give practical confirmation of the interpreter's success in identifying the speaker's intention. Looked at from this standpoint, however, the communicative intentions of the speaker can no longer be seen as an outer bound imposed on interpretation. Communicative intentions are not directly accessible as empirical data — they can only be pursued as an ideal aim. Even in face-to-face communication, therefore, the intentions of the speaker effectively hold as limits on interpretation only insofar as the interpreter is ready to take them as the relevant criterion.

As far as its structure is concerned, the interpretation of oral discourses turns out to be potentially as open in itself as the interpretation of written texts. In both cases, the subject is potentially allowed to justify many different interpretative choices by constructing coherent interpretative fields. The difference between interpreting a text and understanding a person is not structural but practical. In one case, the subject decides to exploit the whole range of possibilities offered by an inanimate text; in the other, he makes a sober, controlled choice, ideally oriented towards the speaker's intentions. The question about the limits of interpretation becomes at this point a practical question: why does the addressee of an oral message decide not to exploit the entire range of options potentially open before him?

4. The practical nature of communicative interactions

4.1 Relevance and interest

> 'Tis only when a character is considered in general,
> without reference to our particular interest,
> that it causes such a feeling or sentiment,
> as denominates it morally good or evil (Hume)

A possible answer to the question is the following: because it is rational for him to do so. Such a question and such an answer, however, presuppose that the focus has been displaced from external to internal constraints — that is, from constraints imposed on the interpreter by independent structures and facts to constraints to which he freely decides to submit his behaviour.

This Copernican revolution in communication is mainly due to Grice's work. According to Grice, the "logic of conversation" and its coherence are not rooted in the structural properties of the exchanged utterances but in the rational behaviour of the actors of communication: "one of my avowed aims is to see talking as a special case or variety of purposive, indeed rational behaviour" (Grice, 1975: 47). The Gricean perspective focuses on the speaker, but his conclusions may easily be extended to the behaviour of the interpreter, for the former can act rationally only on the assumption that the latter also does, and vice versa. The inferences contextually drawn by an interpreter from what is said — or "conversational implicatures", in Grice's own terminology — can be motivated only on the assumption that the speaker acts according to the "co-operative principle".[42] On the other hand, if a speaker is ready to entrust his messages to any kind of indirect expression requiring non-literal interpretation and inferencing, it is on the basis of a symmetric assumption about the interpreter. Against the background of such mutual assumptions, the observance of the co-operative principle is in the interest — a rational kind of interest, indeed — of both speaker and interpreter: "I would like to be able to show that observance of the C[o-operative] P[rinciple] and maxims is reasonable (rational) along the following lines: that any one who cares about the goals that are central to conversation/communication (e.g. giving and receiving information, influencing and being influenced by others) must be expected to have an interest, given suitable circumstances, in participation to talk exchanges that will be profitable only on the assumption that they are conducted in general accordance with the CP and the maxims" (49).

The Gricean idea of rational communicative behaviour receives more precise content within the framework of Sperber & Wilson's relevance theory. According to Sperber & Wilson, co-operative behaviour in communication is motivated by the "mutually manifest" assumption that both speaker and addressee pursue "optimal relevance" as a shared aim: "The level of relevance that will be presumed to exist takes into account the interest of both communicator and audience. Let us call it a level of optimal relevance [...] Every act of ostensive communication communicates the presumption of its own optimal relevance" (Sperber & Wilson, 1986: 157–158). On the basis of this assumption, the rational interest of a speaker is to send his partner such a signal as to make his communicative intentions optimally manifest under the circumstances. The rational interest of the addressee, on the other hand, lies in interpreting the signal in such a way as to achieve an optimal balance between effort and cognitive gain.[43] Thus, on the presupposition that the speaker acts rationally, the optimal interpretation is the interpretation that tries to make out the communicative intentions of the speaker.

So far, the argument appears to be a description of an empirical fact — the fact that most people behave in a given way. In fact, the model of rational communicative behaviour sketched by Grice and developed by Sperber & Wilson does not describe how people normally behave, but how people ought to behave in order to achieve optimal mutual understanding. The rationality of communicative behaviour does not rest on the empirical fact that most people behave in that way, but on the shared assumption that people ought to do so and, consequently, are expected to do so until it is proved that they do not. The rationality of communication is not a fact but a value, which works as long as it is assumed as a shared ideal goal in practical behaviour. This ideal side of the communicative model is explicitly stressed by Grice (1975: 48): "I am, however, enough of a rationalist to want to find a basis that underlies these facts, undeniable though they may be. I would like to be able to think of the standard type of conversational practice not merely as something that all or most do in fact follow but as something that it is reasonable for us to follow, that we should not abandon". This is the reason why the co-operative principle and its maxims do not take the indicative mood — "People normally behave in such and such a way" — but the imperative: "Behave in such and such a way".

Such a shift from the descriptive to the prescriptive mood should not be undervalued, for it is nothing less than the signal of a practical turn imposed on the whole discussion. If rational behaviour cannot be grounded on empirical facts, it is because rational behaviour is not a fact but a value, and Grice is enough of an empiricist to know, along with Hume and Kant,[44] that values cannot be grounded in facts. Besides being a classical topic in moral philosophy, the dissociation of the empirical and the ideal dimension has an immediate intuitive import. According to our shared moral feeling, one may ground a choice of immediate interest, but not a moral choice, in empirical criteria. In the name of what kind of empirical criterion is it rational to make an effort towards understanding a person? In the name of what balance of effort and gain is it rational to help a handicapped person to live his life? As Sperber & Wilson (1986: 55) observe, "when a drowning man calls for help, his only chance is that some passer-by will find it morally preferable, however physically inconvenient, to help him".

4.2 The ethical grounds of communication

> Si linguis hominum loquar et angelorum,
> caritatem autem non habeam,
> factus sum velut aes sonans
> aut cymbalum tinniens (St. Paul)

> No one could make out what he said but Kitty;
> she alone understood. She understood
> because she was all the while mentally keeping watch
> on what he needed (Tolstoy)

Coming back to the question of why the subject of an oral interaction decides not to exploit the full range of options potentially open to him, I see only one answer. The subject of an oral interaction acts as a responsible ethical subject. He knows that before him he does not have a text, the petrified work of a remote person, but a person in whom he is ready to recognise the same ethical dignity he claims for himself. He is not interested in dissecting his speech, but in understanding his thoughts and feelings. No objective structure, be it grammatical or cognitive, is strong enough to bind him to such a choice. The only relevant bond is the bond of reciprocity, which rests upon the free, responsible agreement of free, responsible subjects: when I try to understand you, I make the same effort I expect and hope you will make in order to understand me.

If communicative interaction were annexed to the realm of theoretical reason, the drift of potential interpretations and the role played by the subject would appear as a serious disruption of the structural order. If, on the other hand, we restore the communication event to its essentially practical dimension, the wide room left for the subjects no longer looks as a puzzling, menacing prospect, but seems a normal, reassuring aspect of the general human condition. The human being engaged in communication is only a particular case of the human being interacting with his fellows, while mutual understanding reveals itself to be a precious value we are called upon to promote with our responsible and sympathetic behaviour. Mutual understanding is a value precisely because it is not a warranted fact, but the frail result of unpredictable human behaviour.

If we regard things in this way, we realise that communicative interaction is governed by the same criteria which apply to our interpersonal behaviour in general. This remark holds particularly for these basic ethical categories which, before being analysed by philosophers, form a shared heritage of schemes and models familiar to everybody's direct experience. Respect for persons is one of these categories.

Free, unconditional respect — a balance between sympathy and distance[45] — is intimately bound up with an almost potential condition of reciprocity, and one cannot help seeing that communication provides us with an ideal setting for exercising such an attitude. The reversibility of roles in communication is a model of reciprocity — of how identification meets separateness to become respect. While trying to understand him, I naturally respect the speaker as a separate being, playing a separate role which is likely to become my own role, and I expect from him, when he becomes my addressee, the same attitude.[46]

The disruption of the balance between sympathy and distance leads to violence. Just like any other form of interpersonal interaction, communication is open to violence in both its aspects, as lack of sympathy and as lack of distance.

If I am not able to understand another person, for instance, I dismiss what he is saying as nonsense. By doing so, I am hiding my unwillingness to understand him behind a claimed objective fault of his utterance. Understanding a person, however, goes far beyond decoding an utterance. Our everyday experience shows that opaque messages are often entrusted to perfectly significant utterances, while a positive effort to collect missing data and connect them into a coherent field can make a clear message out of confused speech. Maybe my interlocutor addresses a truly meaningless utterance to me. But even in this case the signal is not absolutely void of sense: such extrasemantic features as tone of voice or bodily expression may be more relevant to the message than utterance meaning itself. Even silence is able, in given circumstances, to carry a loud message.[47]

If lack of sympathy is an obvious source of violence, lack of distance has its dangers too. Someone speaks to me with a sad voice. Struck by this, I bypass the meaning of his utterance as irrelevant. Maybe, I understand his 'true' intentions better than himself, but it is possible that I simply put a mask that I have drawn myself on the face of another person. Just as it may end in sympathy, the active construction of a field may also end in violence. Just like violence in general, violence in communication can always be justified on empirical grounds; if it is bad, it is so on moral grounds.

Chapter 2

The ideation of complex meanings

Coding and inferencing

Linguistic meanings and messages exchanged in communication are heterogeneous kinds of object, defined on the basis of autonomous relevance criteria. The meaning of a complex expression is the end point of a process of ideation, while a message takes shape when a constructed meaningful expression is used by a speaker in order to achieve a contingent communicative aim and interpreted by an addressee against the background of a shared field. The interpretation of messages from meaningful expressions was the subject of the first chapter. In Chapter 2 and 3, we shall turn to the other side of the question, that is, to the ideation of complex meanings.

As the interpretation of messages from meaningful expressions is the outcome of a process of inferencing, it is tempting to project the distinction between inferencing and coding onto the distinction between ideation and interpretation, and jump to the conclusion that the ideation of complex meanings is the exclusive outcome of linguistic coding. If the structure of complex meanings is observed without any pre-conceived idea, however, it is clear that ideation does not reduce itself to linguistic coding, but is completed to a significant extent by a process of inferencing based on extra-grammatical data. This leads us to re-examine both the nature of inferencing and the content of semantic description.

If it is considered in its full range of action, inferencing is a rather more complex process than appears at first sight.

On the one hand, two different layers of inferencing have to be taken into account, each bearing a different relationship to the encoded meaning: an external layer, which connects meaningful expressions to occasional messages, and an internal layer, which plays an active role in the ideation of complex meanings, taking over where linguistic coding leaves off (§1). The role played by internal inferencing does not challenge the strategic boundary between ideation of complex meanings and interpretation of messages, but it challenges the idea that ideation coincides with coding. Insofar as it provides any complex expression with a core meaning, coding is what defines a linguistic expression as such. But when coding proves unable to articulate the whole structure of a complex meaning, inferencing is ready to take over (§2).

On the other hand, inferencing is not necessarily a pragmatic kind of process, as it is traditionally assumed. This idea is certainly true for external inferencing, connecting meaningful expressions and occasional messages, which is essentially motivated by the contingent configuration and the occasional content of a field. But it is just as certainly misleading for internal inferencing, engaged in the ideation of complex meanings. The most qualified bases of internal inferencing are not provided by contextual information of pragmatic import, but are formed by a system of long-lasting conceptual structures shared regardless of any contingent act of communication. This holds, in particular, for the inferential enrichment of encoded meanings at the level of both simple sentences and interclausal links (§3).

The double nature of inferencing — contingent, based on contextual information, and systematic, based on long-lasting conceptual structures — challenges the traditional boundary between semantic description and the realm of pragmatics.

The boundary between semantics and pragmatics does not coincide with that between coding and inferencing, for inferencing co-operates with coding in the ideation of complex meanings. Nor does it coincide with the boundary between external and internal inferencing, since internal inferencing is based to a given extent on contingent data bound to occasional speech situations. The relevant boundary of semantic description is internal to internal inferencing, and coincides with the borderline between systematic inferencing, based on long-lasting conceptual structures, and occasional inferencing, based on contingent contextual data.

One side of this critical boundary is occupied by a semantic description of sentence meaning, based both on linguistic coding and systematic internal inferencing. The other side of the boundary, which coincides with the realm of pragmatics, does not form a coherent territory, but is occupied by a *continuum* ranging from the contextual determination of utterance meaning by contingent inferencing to the inferential development of contingent messages out of meaningful expressions. Utterance meaning, in particular, marks the transition between the ideation of complex meanings and the interpretation of messages. Utterance meaning certainly belongs to ideation, insofar as it is the end point of an inferential determination of the encoded meaning that is preliminary to interpretation. At the same time, as it depends on contingent information, it can only be determined in connection with a given interpretation field, just like the interpretation of contingent messages (§3.3).

Our analysis has a double implication for semantic description. On the one hand, a purely linguistic semantics, exclusively based on immanent coding devices, is not adequate for an exhaustive description of complex meanings. On the other hand, the extra-linguistic components of this description do not reduce themselves to a set of contingent data of pragmatic import, but include long-lasting conceptual structures, which are no less systematic than linguistic structures. This opens the door to a semantic description that reaches far beyond coding without dissolving into pragmatics, because it is both open to substantial conceptual contents and systematic. According to this premise, the topic of this chapter is not just linguistic coding but the whole process of ideation, and therefore the interaction between coding and inferencing, with particular regard to systematic inferencing.

1. Meaning beyond coding

A significant obstacle we meet when trying to clarify the complex relations between expression and meaning, meaning and messages, coding and inferencing, linguistic structures and context, semantics and pragmatics, is the fact that such key-notions as *inference*, *interpretation* and *context* are not used consistently. The terms *interpretation* and *inference* are used to denote any kind of natural reasoning giving way to any kind of content that spreads beyond coded meaning. As a consequence, their use covers two distinct conceptual territories. Sometimes they refer to a process of contextual determination or enrichment of the meaning of an expression; at other times they refer to the act of developing a contingent relevant message out of a meaningful expression. The *context*, accordingly, is generally seen as a composite repository of extra-grammatical data and structures, partly contingent and partly long-lasting, which sometimes plays a role in the ideation of complex meanings, and sometimes motivates the interpretation of a contingent message from a meaningful expression.

In the following paragraphs, we shall maintain that interpretation is the path towards any content located beyond coding, and that inferencing is its instrument, and simply draw a further distinction between an internal and an external kind of interpretation and inferencing (§1.1). The notion of context, for its part, will undergo a more radical deconstruction, in order to identify the different strata of structures and data, some contingent and some systematic and long-lasting, that are traditionally gathered under this label (§1.2).

1.1 Internal and external inferencing

If encoded meaning has to be decoded, meaning which goes beyond coding has to be interpreted, that is, inferred by an addressee against a given set of extra-grammatical data. Given this premise, however, the critical threshold which keeps apart the ideation of complex meanings and the identification of contingent messages does not coincide with the threshold between coding and inferencing, but is internal to inferencing. In order to identify it, therefore, we must look deeper into the process of inferencing, and make explicit the conditions, orientations and relevance criteria which govern it in either case.

Inferencing interacts with verbal communication at two distinct levels. It can act either outside the expression, connecting its form and meaning to an occasional message, or inside it, taking part in drawing the network of relations that form a complex meaning. Owing to the function they perform, we can distinguish an external and an internal kind of inferential interpretation.

Internal and external inferencing are complementary devices. The interpretation of an expression as the signal of a message presupposes a process of decoding and, in most cases, of internal inferencing. Like decoding, internal inferencing belongs to ideation, and is a preliminary step towards the contextual definition of a message. The question underlying internal inferencing is 'What is the content of this expression?' The question underlying external inferencing is 'What does the speaker mean when using this expression?' or, more generally, 'What is the value of this expression within this particular text or context?'. The model of external inferencing is Black's "meaning formula", which is in fact an interpretation formula: "When Caesar said '*Veni, vidi, vici*', he meant that he had won the battle"[48] (Black, 1962a: 17).

Internal inferencing is required when the meaning of an expression is taken as inadequate for use: when the expression is ambiguous, or leaves open a paradigm of alternative inferential issues, or when it codifies a link which does not attain coherence in the light of its conceptual contents. External inferencing is open to any expression that happens to be used in communication to convey a contingent message.

When it takes part in the ideation of a complex meaning, inferencing may be defined as an endocentric process: though depending on extra-grammatical factors, the content it develops takes the coded meaning of the expressions as its core. When an ambiguous meaning is disambiguated, a choice between an invited inference and its admitted counterpart is made, or a coded link is enriched through inference,[49] inferencing simply takes over from linguistic coding at the point the latter stops working. When it connects a meaning to an independent message, inferencing becomes an exocentric process: the content of the interpreted message does not necessarily take the meaning of the expression as its core. Even though it may in practice coincide with it, the content of the message remains in principle an independent object.

An essential continuity is maintained between internal inferencing and coded meaning. A given interpretation of an ambiguous expression selects one of the readings authorised by the expression. An invited inference forms a paradigm with an alternative option, and either this paradigm or one of the competing options is opened up by the encoded meaning of the expression. An enriching inference encapsulates the coded link it improves. For an expression to be taken as an occasional message, on the contrary, no continuity in content is required.[50]

1.2 Beyond context

A sharp theoretical distinction between the inferential determination of a linguistic content and its inferential interpretation as the vehicle of a contingent message is made difficult by the following circumstance: both internal and external inferencing rely on roughly the same constellation of data and structures, which we are accustomed to gather under the label of context. In both cases, inferencing depends on a set of extra-grammatical data, partly occasional, partly long-lasting and systematic, evaluated by a responsible subject ready to co-operate and capable of decision. The object of linguistic analysis, however, is not rough data, but relevant structures and functions. Accordingly, a set of background data taking part in the ideation of complex meanings and a configuration of similar data which justifies the interpretation of a meaningful expression as the vehicle of a contingent message form different kinds of structure. These structures perform different functions and are revealed by different relevance criteria.[51]

A message is a value that a meaningful utterance is ready to acquire once it is integrated as a constituent into a structure of a higher level. When one speaks of context in order to justify the interpretation of a meaningful expression as the vehicle of an occasional message, one makes reference to a higher level structure which incorporates it. What is relevant at this stage is not the content of the context, which is variable according to different parameters,[52] but the peculiar form taken by the occasional configuration of the co-occurring data, that is, the fact that they form a structure capable of conferring a contingent communicative value on a meaningful expression.

The meaning of a sentence is a structure that integrates into a network of relations a set of elements belonging to a lower level without belonging as such to a higher level structure. When one speaks of context in order to justify the structure of a complex meaning, one does not make reference to an active structure, but to a passive repository of extra-grammatical data and structures ready to motivate a given relation among atomic meanings. What is relevant at this stage is not the occasional configuration formed by the fortuitous co-occurring data and structures in a contingent speech situation, but the essential properties of each different layer of data and structures involved in inferencing — namely, the fact that some are contingent and others not, that some are empirical while others, like grammatical patterns, are *a priori* structures.

The first step towards an analysis of the relation between coding, inferential improvement of complex meanings and interpretation of messages out of meaningful expressions, therefore, is to analyze the hybrid idea of context into more specialised notions, displaying different structures and performing different functions.

Since it was first formulated by Malinowski (1923(1952)) and elaborated by Firth (1950(1957: 182)), the notion of "context of situation" went on growing by simple accumulation, until it became too composite and elusive to be consistently used.

A strategic step on this path was the inclusion of any kind of long-lasting, non-contingent extra-grammatical structures and data independent of any speech situation. According to Lyons (1963: 83): "The context of utterance must be held to include, not only the external objects and the actions taking place at the time, but the knowledge shared by the speaker and hearer of all that has gone before. More 'abstractly', it must be held to comprehend all the conventions and presuppositions accepted in the society in which the participants live, insofar as these are relevant to the understanding of the utterance". Halliday's (1978: 29) "general types of situation" refer in fact to such cognitive models which are generally considered as "schemata" (Fillmore, 1977; Rumelhart, 1980) or "scripts" (Shank & Abelson, 1977), whose long-lasting structure outlive individual speech acts and situations. At the end of the path, one easily imagines that "'context' can be the whole world in relation to an utterance act"[53] (Pinkal, 1985: 36, quoted by Quasthoff, 1994: 733), that is, everything and nothing. Unless one believes that the structure of the world is reshaped at any utterance act, such an idea of context represents a true epistemological obstacle towards the analysis of both complex meanings and contingent messages.

The more traditional layer of the notion of context, that is, the contingent configuration of relevant data responsible for the interpretation of an expression as signal of a message, is better described and understood with the help of a specific notion — namely, the notion of interpretation field. The idea of field inherits the contingent nature of the traditional idea of context as defined by Malinowski and Firth. Unlike the latter, however, it highlights two qualifying properties, which play an essential role in interpreting messages. First, a field is explicitly defined as a peculiar kind of structure rather than a simple a constellation of random data. Its forming a structure and its capabilitity of conferring a value to its constituent parts are more relevant than its material content. Secondly, a field does not reduce itself to an external background, but contains a more or less significant constructed part.

The more recent layer acquired by the notion, that is, the composite universe of long-lasting extra-grammatical data and structures which take part in the ideation of complex meanings, has to be analysed into the different factors it contains. In particular, contextual information in the traditional, narrow sense — that is, contingent information bound to the utterance situation — has to be kept apart from long-lasting conceptual structures shared independently of the utterance situation. In particular, it has to be kept apart from consistency criteria and shared cognitive models. Together with an independent foundation of communicative interaction on autonomous principles of practical import, an accurate analysis of long-lasting and systematic conceptual structures involved in inferencing is an essential step in securing the study of complex meanings against an irreversible pragmatic drift and paving the way to a philosophical grammar. While contingent inferencing, based on contingent data, is a pragmatic fact, systematic inferencing based on long-lasting conceptual structures is a grammatical fact — a fact that relies on a true grammar of concepts.

Once these points have been made clear, a restricted and well defined idea of context is certainly useful to grasp the composite area of contingent data that form both the given, non-constructed part of an interpretation field and the most shallow, situation-bound layer of factors contributing to the ideation of complex meanings. In some cases, moreover, it can also be useful to split this generic notion of context into two more specific co-hyponyms: a co-text, made up by co-occurring linguistic expressions, and a context in a narrow sense, restricted to the extra-linguistic components of the hyperonym concept.

2. Complex meanings: Coding and inferencing

At first sight, the coded component of a complex meaning might seem to coincide with what is explicitly asserted, and the inferred component with what remains implicit. The relationship between the different layers of a complex meaning, however, is actually far more intricate.

Of course, what is explicitly asserted is necessarily coded. Equally, what is inferred is necessarily not explicitly asserted. This, however, implies neither that any piece of non-explicit content is inferred, nor that any piece of inferred content is implicit. On the one hand, non-explicit components are open to coding, and as such associated with complex meaning as non-detachable parts. On the other hand, when non-explicit components of meaning are inferred, they are neither necessarily nor even typically implicit. When it activates an implicit component within a complex meaning, inferencing simply actualises one among a set of virtual options left open by coding. When inferencing really goes beyond coding, as in case of enriching and bridging inferences, its content can by no means be considered an implicit component of the encoded meaning. In such cases, inferencing is not simply a residual integration of coding, but a truly creative device. Creative inferencing, which introduces into the expression a non-implicit component of meaning, is the most typical kind of inferencing.

On the following pages, we shall examine the most revealing cases of the relation between coding and inferencing: coding and its failures (fragmentary expressions and ambiguity. §2.1); invited inferences and their encoded counterparts (§2.2.1); enriching inferences, which improve coding, and thus can be considered as creative inferences of the most typical kind (§2.2.2); bridging inferences, which operate outside the territory of coding (§2.3).

2.1 Coding and its failures

2.1.1 *Explicit and implicit encoded meaning*

In the complex sentence *The fields are dry because it never rains*, the relationship of consequence[54] is both coded by the conjunction *because* and explicitly asserted. It is coded because its expression survives a conflict with conceptual content: the expression *The fields are dry because it rained heavily* is odd precisely because a relationship of consequence is actually coded by the conjunction despite its conflicting contents. It is explicitly asserted because the content of the interclausal link — the relationship of consequence — exactly coincides with the overt meaning of the conjunction.

In the complex sentence *Although it rained heavily, the fields are dry*, encoded meaning and explicit meaning no longer coincide, for the former stretches far beyond the latter. The complex sentence does not explicitly assert that the state-of-affairs q, which actually took place, is the opposite of the expected outcome of p: because of heavy rain, the fields should be green. However implicit, this piece of content is at the same time essential for the ideation of a concessive link and encoded by the conjunction *although*. In Grice's words, the non-explicit component of meaning carried by *although* is a conventional implicature: "In some cases the conventional meaning of the words used will determine what is implicated, besides helping to determine what is said" (Grice, 1975: 44).

Being part of the coded meaning, a conventional implicature is insensitive to the conceptual contents of the connected clauses. If conflicting information is provided by these contents, the implicature is not cancelled. An utterance like *Although it rained heavily, the fields are wet*, for instance, cannot escape a concessive interpretation, in spite of its challenging our shared assumptions about the effects of rain.

2.1.2 *The reconstruction of fragmentary utterances*

When the word *sentence* is used in a pre-theoretical sense, it has a twofold range of denotation. In one of its senses, instantiated by such expressions as *You've not finished your sentence*, it refers to a type of grammatical pattern meeting specific structural requirements. In other cases, the same word refers to a token that may be found in a given text, or discourse, or communicative interaction: *The news was given in the opening sentence of the report.*

In the first case, the sentence is focused on as a complex expression that integrates expressions of a lower rank — words and phrases — within a unitary configuration ruled by syntactic patterns. In the second case, the sentence is considered a module integrated within a structure of a higher rank — a text, or a direct communicative interaction. These different ways of categorising the pre-theoretical datum are kept distinct within the descriptive metalanguage by such oppositions as *sentence* vs *utterance* or *system-sentence* vs *text-sentence.*[55]

If they are compared with the structural models provided by system-sentences, text-sentences display a revealing property: they may hold as signals of messages, that is, as functional equivalents of sentences, without being structurally complete as system sentences should be.[56] Textual modules may drop essential constituents — *Ieri* $Ø_i$ *ho visto Giovanni.* $Ø_{ii}$ *ha appena comprato un'auto nuova* ($Ø_i$ *saw John yesterday.* $Ø_{ii}$ *has just bought a new car*) — or even be reduced to a single fragment, without losing their function as sentence equivalents:

> 'What do you do all day?' she asked hastily.
> 'Nothing' (K. Mansfield)

When it lacks essential parts, and even more so when it is fragmentary, an utterance looks like a challenge to coding, for it does not have the strength to code a process with its own structural means. If it were taken in isolation, it would not be able to perform its elective function. But at the very moment it is charged with a function, an utterance cannot stand in isolation — the concept itself of an utterance in isolation is contradictory. At this point, what is not provided by the inner structure can by definition be recovered from outside.

When placed within its co-text, for instance, the utterance *Nothing* regains its place within a sentence frame with the function of direct object — it is interpreted as if it were a functional equivalent of the complete sentence *I do nothing all day.* Starting from such obvious remarks, it is only too easy to jump to the conclusion that both the missing constituents of an incomplete sentence and the missing frame of a fragmentary expression are provided by contextual data. In fact, contextual information, however essential, does only a part of the job. If it is a plain fact that the context provides the (contextually) relevant missing contents, it is equally clear that these contents are integrated or even organised into syntactic patterns which are accessible independently of contextual data. If an utterance is correctly interpreted as subjectless, or an isolated noun phrase is integrated into a sentence frame as a direct object, for instance, it is because underlying structural models of sentences are available to the interpreter and relied upon by him. Incomplete and fragmentary utterances are received as functional equivalents of sentences and decoded with reference to systematic models, just as a head above a hedge is not taken as a walking head but as the visible part of a hidden person.[57] Thanks to structural models, coding regains its control over the ideation of sentence meanings.

2.1.3 *Ambiguity and coding*

Ambiguity can be defined as a local failure of a given coding device. Lexical ambiguity is a local failure of coding due to the presence of polysemous lexemes. The sentence *Professor Lodge has left the University*, for instance, admits at least two readings: either Professor Lodge has gone out of the university building, or he has given up university teaching. Constructional ambiguity is a local failure of a syntactic structure to code a grammatical relation.[58] The disposition of words in the French sentence *J'ai fait écrire une lettre à Paul*, for instance, neutralises the distinction between subject and indirect object, which is generally encoded in sentence structure: *I made someone write a letter to Paul* and *I made Paul write a letter to someone.*

In the case of ambiguity, the ideation of meaning does not achieve the level of functional adequacy. What is coded is not one definite meaning ready to be used, but an unresolved paradigm of alternative options. Owing to this, the expression is not fit for use until the meaning is somehow determined. At the very moment of use, however, the determination of meaning generally takes place: the context of utterance provides enough relevant information to select the relevant reading: for instance, Professor Lodge has actually given up teaching to become a professional writer; the letter has been written to Paul.

Insofar as it is a failure in coding, ambiguity presupposes coding. Either below or beyond coding, it makes no sense to speak of ambiguity. In case of undercoding, there is indetermination or vagueness (see Chapter 5, §4.1.1.3). Outside the territory of coding, the manifold indexical relation between meaningful expressions and messages cannot be reduced to a case of ambiguity.

One immediate outcome of the confusion between ideation of meanings and interpretation of messages is that the plurality of messages an expression is ready to take on when used is seen as a form of ambiguity. Starting from this premise, all the possible messages an expression is able to convey are considered as if they were implicitly contained within its meaning, and their interpretation is seen as a form of contextual selection: "the readings that a speaker attributes to a sentence in a setting are a selection from among those that the sentence has in isolation. It is clear that, in general, a sentence cannot have readings in a setting which it does not have in isolation"[59] (Katz & Fodor, 1963: 177).

The phenomenon that really corresponds to a contextual selection, however, is not the interpretation of messages out of a meaning, but the contextual determination of an ambiguous meaning, which is a preliminary move towards the interpretation of a message. Once an ambiguous meaning is determined, whether it coincides or not with the relevant message is a separate question, which can only be answered within a given field.

2.2 Inferencing beyond coding

2.2.1 *Invited inferences*

At first glance, an invited inference seems to be as directly activated by the expression as a conventional implicature. Unlike a conventional implicature, however, an invited inference is sensitive to conceptual content, and therefore does not survive a conceptual conflict.

The clearest example of invited inference is provided by conditionals. A well-known and rather puzzling piece of natural logic is the common tendency to "perfect conditionals to biconditionals" (Geis & Zwicky, 1971: 562), that is, to interpret simple conditionals as if they contained an implicit component of biconditionality. A conditional like *If it hails, the harvest will be lost*, for instance, is normally taken as implying not only that the second fact will happen if the first takes place, but also that the second will not happen if the first does not take place: if it does not hail, the harvest will not be lost.

Owing to this implicit component, the conditional practically conveys the same content as the corresponding biconditional: *The harvest will be lost* only *if it hails.* In spite of this, the implicit component of biconditionality — if it does not hail, the harvest will not be lost — is not expressed under the same conditions. When the biconditional is used, the implicit is coded as a conventional implicature; when the simple conditional is used, it is activated as an invited inference. This difference can be detected on the basis of a different behaviour with regard to conceptual conflict.

If a biconditional is used in a conflicting conceptual environment, as in the example *The harvest will be lost only if it hails, and the same will happen if it does not rain,* the implicit component of biconditionality is not cancelled, and the whole expression becomes incoherent. This is the proof that the implicit is coded.

If a simple conditional is used out of context or in a coherent environment, the implicit component of biconditionality is automatically activated, and is practically as effective as a conventional implicature. But if it is used in a conflicting environment, as in the example *If it hails, the harvest will be lost, and the same will happen if it does not rain*, the implicit component is dropped. This makes way for an alternative option, which is simply admitted, that is, activated under the pressure of the conceptual environment.[60] In this case, the conditional is interpreted as a material implication: if the premise becomes real, the consequence will take place; if the premise does not materialise, nothing can be predicted about the consequence. If it does not hail, nothing can be predicted about the harvest. Its sensitivity to consistency is the proof that the implicit component of biconditionality is not coded but inferred.

The invited inference is maybe the clearest case of a component of meaning whose activation is bound to the fact that the expression is used against the assumption that the speaker's communicative behaviour is consistent. The semantics of conditionals looks very different depending on whether the expression is observed as a kind of linguistic structure regardless of use — as a sentence — or is received as a signal during a real act of communication — as an utterance. A person reflecting about conditionals by the fireside would certainly conclude that what is coded by a conditional is no more than a relation of material implication. As a matter of fact, one and the same effect can have many different causes. But it is hard to imagine the same person interpreting a conditional in the same way when playing the role of addressee during a real act of communication. It is clear that the very act of uttering a conditional would be functionally unjustified, and therefore inconsistent as a speech act, if the premise were really held to be irrelevant to the consequence. Thus, the plain fact that a conditional has been uttered justifies the addressee's assumption that the premise is not just a sufficient condition among others for the consequence to take place, but rather a necessary — or at least salient — condition. The addressee may be ready to drop this assumption, but only if he is explicitly given proof to the contrary.[61] In the case of invited inference, the relationship between inferencing and its conceptual background is thus reversed. An ordinary inference can be drawn only under the active pressure of a consistent conceptual background. An invited inference, on the contrary, is directly activated when the expression is used. What the conceptual background can do is to dismantle it in case of conflict, making room for the admitted option.

Invited inference and its admitted counterpart form an asymmetrical paradigm of alternative options, which is implicitly contained in the meaning of the sentence. In spite of this, the alternative is not encoded as such, because what is encoded is no more than the admitted option, while the invited inference is ready to be activated only if the expression is used. Thus, the correlation between invited and admitted inference is rather paradoxical. Once the expression is put into use, the encoded meaning — the value as material implication — is challenged by a competing inference: the biconditional value. At this point, the inferred content becomes the preferred interpretation, while the encoded meaning is reduced to the rank of admitted option.

2.2.2 *Inferential Enrichment*

Enriching inferences (König & Traugott, 1988; Hopper & Traugott, 1993: 74) take as their starting point the coded meaning of a linguistic expression, onto which they graft, so to speak, a specific, creative contribution.

Unlike invited inferences, enriching inferences are in no way implicitly contained in the meaning of the expression, and are even less in competition with the coded base. Coding and inferential improvement actually take turns in the same process of ideation as complementary factors. Such a complex sentence as *John decided to buy a new car after his old one was seriously damaged in an accident* is normally interpreted as if the damaging of the old car had not only preceded the purchase of a new one, as the conjunction *after* conventionally means, but was also the motive for it. This kind of motive is not incompatible with the coded relationship of temporal sequence — on the contrary, the former encapsulates the latter as a necessary condition. At the same time, the motive is neither implicitly contained in a temporal sequence nor alternative to it — it moves a step farther along the same conceptual path.

The most widely studied domain of inferential enrichment is interclausal linkage, but its role is equally pervasive, and its observation probably more revealing, at the level of simple sentence.

Within the structure of a simple sentence, inferential enrichment is ready to contribute to any kind of peripheral meaning connection. In particular, it takes part in the ideation of the peripheral roles of the process at sentence level and of the relations between head nouns and complements at noun phrase level.

In the sentence *John drove the nail with a stone*, the prepositional phrase *with a stone* is interpreted as expressing the peripheral role of instrument. The prepositional phrase, however, does not encode an instrumental relationship, but simply puts the referent of the complement noun and the action into an almost empty relation, whose full content can be determined only by inference: a stone is ready to be used as an instrument for driving nails. If the noun *care* were used, as in the example *John drove the nail with care*, the same prepositional phrase would be interpreted as expressing a different relation, that is, manner (see Chapter 3, §2.5.3).

A complex noun phrase such as *The church of the village* is interpreted as referring to a church located in a village, while *The arrival of my father* refers to the action of arriving performed by my father. The genitive link encodes neither relation. Once more, what is coded is an almost empty relationship, which can be improved by inference into a heterogeneous and potentially open range of different substantive relations (see Chapter 5, §4.1).

At the level of interclausal linkage, inferential enrichment is in competition with both absence of coding, that is, bridging inferencing (see below, §3), and full coding, that is, absence of inferencing. However strategic, therefore, inferential enrichment is not an inescapable step for the expression of any link. The following structures, for instance, express the same interclausal relationship with different means. In (1), the concessive connection is fully encoded; in (2), it is fully inferred; in (3) it is encoded up to a certain point and inferred from that point onwards:

(1) Though I wrote three letters to him, John didn't answer
(2) I wrote three letters to John. He didn't answer
(3) After I wrote him three letters, John didn't answer

At the level of intraclausal structures, on the contrary, a whole layer of meaning relations systematically combines a weak degree of coding and inferential enrichment. The genitive link between a head noun and a complement is the best example of this. A genitive link is systematically undercoded, and thus structurally designed for inferential enrichment. If it were not provided with a content through inference, a genitive link would be absolutely empty, and thus useless at the functional level. At the same time, a language which fully encoded the whole set of relations open to a genitive link would be not only of unthinkable complexity but actually inconceivable, for the set of inferrable relations is as open as the unforeseeable combinations of concepts. Language as it really is, the instrument of expression we rely upon in everyday life, based on a wonderful equilibrium between accuracy of coding and open flexibility of inferencing, would not be the same if expression were reduced to coding and if inferential enrichment were not a familiar and essential resource for shaping meaning connections.

2.3 Inferencing instead of coding: Bridging inferences

A form of interaction between coding and inferencing which is located at the opposite end of the scale to full coding is bridging inference (Van Dijk & Kintsch, 1983). Whereas full coding systematically activates a conceptual link irrespective of both connected contents and contextual information, a bridging inference constructs a link exclusively motivated by conceptual contents in a total void of coding.

Bridging inferences operate at the level of interclausal connection, and it is thanks to them that the mere juxtaposition of independent utterances, devoid of any grammatical connection, is taken as expressing a link between two processes. Such a juxtaposition as *John cannot study law. His parents are too poor*, for instance, would not normally be taken as containing two independent assertions about unrelated topics. On the contrary, a co-operative interpreter would infer from their being spoken in sequence that the juxtaposed contents are somehow connected, and from an evaluation of the expressed processes that they are connected by a causal relationship: roughly, *John cannot study law* because *his parents are too poor*. Whereas an enriching inference improves the conventional content of a grammatical link or, in extreme cases, imposes a definite conceptual profile on a void grammatical link, a bridging inference is alternative to coding. It builds a conceptual bridge between two utterances in the absence of any unifying syntactic frame.

The expression of a conceptual link between two independent utterances makes sense only on the preliminary assumption that the juxtaposed utterances are meant to convey a unitary message. Insofar as they are based on assumptions about the communicative intentions of the speaker, bridging inferences mark the transition from internal to external inferencing — from the expression of meaning connections to the interpretation of messages out of meaningful expressions. Unlike enriching inferencing, bridging inferencing is a phenomenon of the textual order, which is based on the coherence of a complex message.

3. The bases of inferencing

Our overview of the interaction between coding and inferencing clearly shows that the basis for inferencing cannot be reduced to contextual information shared by the actors of communication within the limits of the contingent speech situation. Accordingly, inferencing cannot be reduced to a purely pragmatic process. In some cases, inferencing actually proves to be supported by contingent contextual information. This happens, for instance, when an ambiguous meaning is determined, or when an invited inference is dropped in favour of its coded counterpart. In the case of enriching and bridging inferences, however, inferencing is mainly based on long-lasting conceptual structures, shared irrespective of any contingent speech situation. This point is relevant in particular for enriching inferences, the only kind which really interacts with coding in the ideation of complex meanings.

Invited and bridging inferences cannot be considered as true partners of coding, because for different reasons both are alternative to it: invited inferences because they replace a coded option, bridging inferences because they operate in the absence of coding. Enriching inferences operate on the same territory as coding — they erect a creative edifice, so to speak, on coded foundations. If coding and inferencing are the two main paths towards expression, they take turns in the case of enriching inferences.

Enriching inferences can be found everywhere coding is at work, while the radius of action of invited and bridging inferences is very restricted. Bridging inferences are limited to interclausal links, and invited inferences of the kind examined here, that is, competing with an encoded option, are almost exclusive to conditional structures.[62] This means that the kind of inference which relies mainly on systematic conceptual structures, that is, enriching inferencing, is also the only kind which can be considered as a true partner of coding, a complementary strategy interacting with it. This circumstance calls into question many common assumptions about the bases of inferencing.

The fact that the ideation of complex meanings is not exclusively the result of coding is commonly accepted. If the role played by inferencing is nevertheless either undervalued or misunderstood among linguists, the main reason is the widespread tendency to reduce conceptual data and structures to contextual data, and inferencing to a pragmatic strategy. If we want to dig out the roots of complex meanings, both grammatical and conceptual, the first step is to go beyond context and look more deeply into the heterogeneous constellation of data and structures it precludes from analysis.

3.1 Contingent data and conceptual structures

When dealing with enriching inferences, linguists almost automatically think of conversational implicatures as a proper model (see for instance Hopper & Traugott, 1993; König & Traugott, 1988), and are therefore inclined to take them as "context-dependent readings"[63] of expressions. An immediate corollary of this attitude is the tendency to consider any extra-grammatical factor involved in the ideation of complex meanings as being of pragmatic import. Beyond coding, in other words, everything belongs to pragmatics. Kortmann (1997: 203), for instance, speaks of "pragmatic processes of interpretative enrichment", while Hopper & Traugott (1993) consider that the activation of enriching inferences ends in "pragmatic polysemy".[64] Such a view is generally not argued for — it is simply assumed.

At the root of such consensus is the fact that successful inferencing requires the sharing of a set of background assumptions by speaker and addressee. As the actual sharing of them during a communicative exchange is a pragmatic fact, the assumptions themselves are normally referred to as "pragmatic presuppositions" (Stalnaker, 1970; 1973; 1974). But what is really pragmatic about pragmatic presuppositions?

The structure of a pragmatic presupposition is the structure of an intentional relation (Husserl, 1901(1970: *V Research*)). An intentional relation can be analyzed in two parts: on the one hand, there is an attitude on the part of a subject; on the other hand, there is an independent content of this attitude. In the case of presuppositions, there is a shared attitude of presupposing and a shared content. Now, the term *presupposition* is actually used to refer both to the attitude and to its content. On the one hand, "presupposition is a propositional attitude. More specifically, it is an attitude of accepting something to be true" (Stalnaker, 1973: 450). The subject of the presupposition "does act as if he takes the truth of the presupposition for granted, and as if he assumes that his audience recognizes that he is doing so" (451). On the other hand, "a presupposition is *like* an item of presumed common knowledge, or what is taken to be a shared belief" (450). Owing to the ambivalence of the term *presupposition*, the adjective *pragmatic*, correctly applied to the contingent attitude, is extended to the content.

The crucial fact about intentional structures, however, is that the intentional content is not necessarily homogeneous with the intentional act. Therefore, the properties which can be applied to the act do not necessarily apply to the content. Fearing, for instance, denotes a psychological attitude; people or things one happens to fear, however, are not psychological entities, but hard counterparts of them — "the fear of snakes is not identical with snakes", as Searle (1983) puts it. The same holds for presuppositions. The act of presupposing — the fact that two people happen to (assume that they) share more or less the same set of relevant contents — is certainly a contingent, and therefore pragmatic fact. But what they happen to share is not necessarily a contingent, and therefore a pragmatic fact. A piece of information occasionally shared within the limits of a given speech situation is a contingent and pragmatic fact. A long-lasting conceptual structure shared independently of any speech situation is neither.

If we examine in the light of such remarks a significant case of enriching inference, that is, the interpretation of genitive links, we easily realise that contingent contextual information is neither the exclusive nor the most significant source of inferencing.

A noun phrase like *John's dream*, for instance, refers to a dream dreamt by John, while *A midsummer night's dream* is interpreted as referring to a dream which has taken place in summer. The two different inferential improvements of the same encoded link are motivated by a layer of basic conceptual structures holding as consistency criteria. According to our shared consistency criteria, a human being can be consistently thought of as the experiencer of a dream, while a stretch of time may only provide someone's dream with a temporal frame. Consistency criteria are shared by the members of a cultural community regardless of any occasional speech situation. Far from being pragmatic data, they constrain the form and the content of any possible empirical fact, including the subset of empirical facts which form the object of pragmatics.

The noun phrase *The wall of my garden* refers to a wall surrounding my garden thanks to a shared cultural model predicting with reasonable reliability the expected form and content of typical empirical facts. In other cases, the ground for inferencing is provided by a corpus of positive, long-standing knowledge about empirical facts of the natural or cultural order: *Juda's tree* is the tree on which Judas hanged himself; *The tree of liberty* is a tree planted to honour liberty during the French Revolution. Both cognitive schemes of empirical facts and stored up cognitive data are accessible *de iure*, if not shared *de facto*, regardless of any occasional speech situation.

The noun phrase *The hyacinth girl* is interpreted as denoting a girl who is given hyacinths, rather than a girl who grows, or sells, or offers hyacinths, only once it is integrated into its co-text, that is, T. S. Eliot's poem:

> "You gave me hyacinths first a year ago;
> They called me the hyacinth girl".

In such cases, and only in such cases, one can say that a meaning connection is shaped under the pressure of contingent contextual information, accessible within the limits of an occasional context — in our case the immediate co-text.

3.2 From a pragmatics of inference to a grammar of concepts

The ground of inference is neither necessarily nor even typically formed by contingent data shared within a given speech situation, but forms a continuum ranging from contingent data to essential conceptual structures. Contingent, situation-bound data are certainly pragmatic and contextual facts. Such solid and long-lasting conceptual structures as consistency criteria and shared cognitive models are not.

Insofar as they hold as *a priori* conditions for experience, including pragmatic experience, shared cognitive models, and *a fortiori* consistency criteria, are grammatical rather than pragmatic structures. Consistency criteria form a true grammar of concepts which governs our consistent access to experience and, in the case of linguistic experience, consistent expression. Cognitive models form the bulk of the lexical definition of most concepts. If these structures are reduced to contextual data, their essential structural properties are trivialised and their function undervalued, while the real functions performed by true contextual information, both in shaping complex meanings and in drawing messages out of meaningful expressions, remain in the shadow.

Overloaded as it is under the pressure of increasingly complex descriptive and explicative tasks, the notion of context is stretched beyond reasonable limits. On the one hand, the traditional narrow notion of context of situation as the contingent environment of a given utterance act, which is undoubtedly coherent, becomes more and more inadequate insofar as the analysis of complex meanings goes beyond the study of marginal adjustments. On the other hand, the most elaborate notions may be rich enough to provide significant insights into the ideation of complex meanings, but they are so heterogeneous as to become incoherent. As a concoction made up of the most surprising ingredients, the notion of context is an undifferentiated mix of contingent data and essential structures, structures holding *a priori* and empirical information about beings, ephemeral and permanent. While all these heterogeneous data may be relevant to meaning connection, there is no reason to put them in a single overall category, a move which obscures the essential properties of each.

Starting from this premise, the notion of context will be restricted to the set of contingent data accessible from within a given speech situation that take part in the ideation of complex meanings, that is, for disambiguation, selection between invited inferences and their admitted counterparts, and contingent inferential enrichment. The long-lasting conceptual structures shared independently of a given speech situation, on the other hand, will be analysed and described as they are, that is, as the systematic conceptual counterpart of systematic linguistic structures engaged in a common task — the ideation of the complex meanings of sentences.

3.3 Sentence meaning and utterance meaning

The cleavage between contextual data and conceptual structures provides a solid basis for the distinction between sentence meaning and utterance meaning.

A (system) sentence is defined on the basis of its structure, and so is its meaning. A sentence is a sentence only insofar as it has a meaning, or at least a potential for meaning, in isolation, irrespective of any actual use and of the very fact of ever being used. The structure of this meaning is by definition independent of any kind of contingent datum connected with a given context of utterance, and integrally depends on systematic data. It depends on linguistic structures as far as coding is concerned, and on long-lasting and generally shared conceptual structures as far as inferencing is concerned.

The specific component which qualifies the meaning of an utterance is grafted onto the meaning of the corresponding sentence thanks to contingent inferencing, based on occasional data accessible within the same speech situation which confers on it a given message value. Utterance meaning is a functional rather than structural object. An expression can be used as an index in communication only if its meaning has been ideated in its essential parts. In spite of this, some components of meaning which are required only if the expression is actually used, and can easily be inferred at the very moment of use, have not necessarily to be either encoded or inferred outside the contingent speech situation.

In such a sentence as *John prepared a pie with the hyacinth girl*, for instance, coding tells us that John is the agent ad the pie the result of the process. The fact that the hyacinth girl is a coperformer rather than an instrument is the outcome of systematic inferencing, based on long-lasting conceptual structures shared independently of the occasional speech situation. At this point, the construction of sentence meaning stops: as in some old maps of the New World, some unknown details shade into vagueness. Only at the very moment the sentence turns into an utterance in use will it be possible to draw the exact relationship between the girl and hyacints. In a similar way, the ambiguity of such a sentence as *John left the university* can only be resolved in the presence of contingent data belonging to an occasional communicative field, and therefore at the level of utterance meaning.

At the level of the utterance, expression is coding plus systematic and occasional inferencing. The presence of a layer of contingent inferencing documents the functional application of linguistic expressions to contingent use.

At the level of the sentence, expression is coding plus systematic inferencing. The presence of a systematic inferential layer in sentence meaning documents the fact that linguistic expressions are deeply rooted in a shared cognitive and conceptual ground.

Though based to a certain extent on inferencing, sentence meaning can be isolated from utterance meaning and protected from a pragmatic drift insofar as it is grounded in systematic structures and is independent of true contextual data. If coding rests on a grammar of forms, systematic inferencing is grounded in a grammar of concepts and therefore belongs to semantics. Accordingly, a careful analysis of long-lasting shared conceptual structures makes it possible to describe sentence meaning as a kind of grammatical structure in a broad sense — in the sense that its bases, both formal and conceptual, are in any case systematic.

Chapter 3

At the roots of complex meanings

The object of philosophical grammar

An expression is ready to carry, on any contingent occasion, a contingent message, which has to be interpreted on the basis of its coherence with a contingent field. But an expression is an expression only to the extent that it is significant, that it is assumed to have, irrespective of any particular use and even of its ever being used, if not necessarily a definite and full meaning, the aptitude to carry a meaning. Significance — the shared presumption of meaningfulness — is the essential property of expressions.

Simple expressions — roughly, words — are significant in a tautological way: they form part of a shared stock of forms whose meaningfulness is taken for granted and relied upon by the members of the speech community, and in some cases registered in dictionaries. Complex expressions, on the other hand, do not as such form part of a shared heritage of structures, but are constructed by arranging simple meaningful expressions according to creative grammatical patterns. The significance of complex expressions, therefore, cannot be assumed as a fact — it must be questioned. A complex arrangement of simple expressions is significant insofar as the meanings of its constituent parts are linked with each other to form a network of connections, that is, a unitary structure of a higher order. This implies that significance is a question of form, but does not imply that the formal skeleton of a complex meaning is the exclusive achievement of the formal grammatical structures of the expression. To ask what significance means, thus, amounts in a sense to asking what kinds of structure are responsible for the formal framework of a unitary meaning, besides the formal grammatical structure of the expression.

The relevant question about significance can also be framed as a question about construction and expression — namely, to what extent the structure of a complex meaning is constructed by a complex linguistic form, and to what extent it is simply expressed by it. Roughly, a complex meaning is constructed when its inner form is shaped by the formal properties of the expression, and is expressed when its inner form mirrors the independent structure of a complex concept.

The distinction between construction and expression is connected in a revealing way not only to the distinction between coding and inferencing, which was examined in the last chapter, but also to a more subtle distinction between a grammatical-relational, or simply relational kind of coding, directly based on the purely formal grammatical properties of sentence structures, and a punctual kind of coding, based on the content of more or less specialised linking words and expressions.

Our enquiry about the conditions of significance will be made mainly within the boundaries of simple sentence. Among the different kinds of functionally relevant complex expressions, that is, noun phrases, simple and complex sentences, and texts, it is the simple sentence that is traditionally considered as the paradigmatic case of meaningful complex expression. The traditional point of view is fully justified from the standpoint of an enquiry into the roots of significance, for it is within the simple sentence that we find the optimal balance between coding and inferencing and between the different kinds of coding — relational and punctual — and the different kinds of inferencing — systematic and contingent.

The meaning of noun phrases is closed to relational coding. Being typically undercoded, moreover, it depends in an essential way on inferencing, both systematic and contingent, a circumstance which hides the real strength of formal syntactic connection. At the opposite end of the scale, a text is to be seen as a coherent chain of contingent messages put together to form a unitary message, rather than as a complex meaningful expression. Complex sentences cannot be considered indispensable tools for their ideational function, as simple sentences are, because they are to a significant extent interchangeable with alternative linking devices based on textual coherence and cohesion rather than on grammatical connection.

1. The meaning of the sentence

The meaning of a sentence, or process,[65] is a hierarchical network of different kinds of relations among different kinds of roles such as agent, patient, instrument, location, goal, and so on. As Tesnière (1959(1966: 103)) points out, "The verbal node […] establishes a small-scale drama in its entirety. Like a drama, it necessarily involves a process, and generally actors and circumstances […] Shifted from the dimension of drama to that of structural syntax, the process, actors and circumstances become the verb, arguments [*actants*] and circumstantial expressions [*circonstants*]". A typical action, for instance, necessarily includes a main predicative term, or predicator,[66] typically a verb, which encapsulates a schematic draft of the whole process, and in particular the essential roles required by its valency: for instance, an agent and a patient. It may be further enriched by such peripheral roles as instrument or purpose, and located at some point in space and time.

While the term *process* denotes the meaning of a sentence, the term *state of affairs* is meant to refer to an independent conceptual structure, by definition consistent, which is accessible through inference independently of any specific linguistic expression. This use is inspired by Dik (1989(1997: 105)), according to whom a state of affairs, the *designatum* of a "predication", is defined as "a conceptual entity", and therefore neither as something "said to exist in the real world" nor in the first instance as the specific meaning of a sentence. A process and a state of affairs are structures of a different kind. Inside the network of grammatical relations, the two structures are logically independent: for a sentence to be meaningful, it is not required that it depicts an autonomous state of affairs, as is shown by the ideation of inconsistent meanings. Outside this area, the structure of the process mirrors the structure of an independent state of affairs.

A process is a complex conceptual and formal object, which puts substantive conceptual roles into a complex network of relations belonging to different layers. Two questions naturally arise in connection with such a definition: what does the structure of a process look like, and what is responsible for the construction of this complex network of relations, that is, for the identification of the relevant roles and relations.

The first question circumscribes the specific object of semantic description at the level of sentence structure. The second is a more basic question, which goes beyond the boundaries of linguistic semantics: it is the question of significance. This concerns not the actual form of a complex meaning, but its formal possibility: under what grammatical and conceptual conditions a handful of simple meaningful expressions is unified by a hierarchical network of relations into a complex whole.

To answer the first question amounts to drawing a map of the process. The different roles bear different relations with one another and with the whole process. Some of these roles are essential, in that they are arguments of the main predicator, while others are not. The valency of the main predicator governs the presence (actual or latent) and the conceptual content of its arguments, but its control on their formal properties is restricted to the predicate. Essential roles are by definition internal to the process. Among non-essential roles, some are internal and some external. Each internal role, moreover, displays a peculiar degree of closeness to the ideal centre of gravity of the process — to the main predicator.

Answering the second question amounts to digging out the formal and conceptual roots of significance, and defining the role played by each and its limits. An enquiry into the bases of significance aims at establishing to what extent the structure of a process is constructed by linguistic forms, to what extent it mirrors the independent configuration of a complex concept which is simply expressed by linguistic forms, to what extent it is coded and in which way, to what extent it is inferred, and thanks to what kinds of conceptual structures and data.

The two questions and their answers are intertwined, in the sense that asking the first question presupposes an explicit or implicit answer to the second. In order to describe the structure of a process, in particular, one has to know whether one is describing the formal configuration of syntactic structures, the content of linking words or expressions, or the structure of an independent complex concept — of a state of affairs. In fact, any semantic description of complex expressions necessarily contains an implicit philosophical grammar. All we are trying to do is to make explicit its main questions and to give them some tentative answer.

1.1 Formal syntactic coding and ideation of complex meanings

An enquiry into the roots of significance is, in the first instance, an enquiry into the relevance, the power and limits of formal syntactic coding in connecting complex meanings. There are syntactic structures that are designed for the construction of processes, and syntactic structures that are not. This is true from a double perspective.

First, some structures are not involved in the ideation of processes because they are designed for other functions, particularly textual and interpersonal (Halliday, 1970). The textual function, connected with the functional sentence perspective, is the most illuminating for our present discussion.

On the other hand, some structures, however involved in the ideation of processes, do not construct meaning connections because they simply express independent conceptual structures. In other words, if the function of sentence structures does not reduce itself to the ideation of processes, ideation does not reduce itself to construction, but includes expression.

The distinction between ideation of processes and putting them into perspective is a question of the typology of sentence structures. There is a type of sentence structure which can be considered nuclear (Chomsky, 1957), or basic (Keenan, 1976), because it is integrally and exclusively designed for the ideation of processes.[67] And there are different kinds of sentence structures which can be considered non-nuclear, or derived, because they are called upon to provide the language user with different ways of giving processes a communicative perspective in texts and discourses (§1.2). As the imposition of a given perspective on a process presupposes its ideation, the structure of non-nuclear sentences presupposes, and can only be described with reference to, the structure of nuclear sentences.

The distinction between construction and expression is not a question of the typology but of the topography of sentence structures. The nuclear type of sentence structure, which is functionally designed for the ideation of processes, contains a solid formal core surrounded by a weaker periphery. Thanks to formal syntactic coding devices, the core actively constructs meaning connections, imposing an independent mould on the organized contents, while peripheral syntactic structures transfer onto the expression plane a network of relations whose structure is independently justified on conceptual grounds. The constructed part of a complex meaning is mainly the outcome of a relational kind of coding based on the formal syntactic properties of the expression. The expressed part is the outcome of a punctual kind of coding, based on the content of linking words and expressions, improved to a variable extent by inference (§2).

1.2 Ideation and perspective

The distinction between ideating a process and imposing a given perspective on it — between nuclear and non-nuclear sentences — defines the focus of our enquiry from outside. Its clarification is a preliminary step towards the study of significance.

A nuclear sentence contains all and only the syntactic structures that are designed for connecting the constituents of a process into a whole. In other words, the syntactic structures of a nuclear sentence can be wholly justified with reference to the ideational function.

In non-nuclear sentences, on the other hand, the syntactic means engaged in the construction of the process coexist with, and their observation is to a variable extent disturbed by, a surplus of syntactic structures which are justified on the basis of independent functions. By way of illustration, we shall focus on the syntactic structures whose function is to impose a marked communicative perspective on a given process without affecting its ideational structure.

Let us compare the nuclear sentence (1) with the left dislocation (2) and the cleft sentence (3):

(1) The farmer killed the duckling
(2) The duckling, the farmer killed it
(3) It's the farmer that killed the duckling

The three sentences shape the same process. In all cases, the farmer is the agent of the killing, and the duckling is the patient. Each of these sentences, on the other hand, is characterised by a peculiar communicative perspective. Sentence (1) is about the farmer, while sentence (2) is about the duckling. Sentence (3) highlights the agent as a marked focus, which is treated as a sort of communicative peak against a flat background.

The different communicative perspectives are not imposed on the process under the same conditions. Sentences (2) and (3) contain peculiar syntactic devices, which are specifically designed to express a marked communicative perspective, whereas the perspective of nuclear sentence (1) is not due to the presence of specific syntactic means. More generally, the communicative perspective of a nuclear sentence is no more than a by-product of the syntactic construction of the process. The topic of a nuclear sentence necessarily coincides with the subject, and its comment with the predicate, while the focus, the climax of the communicative progression internal to the comment, is the last constituent on the right.[68]

Insofar as its communicative perspective is not due to the presence of special grammatical means, the structure of a nuclear sentence can be studied as if its only relevant function were the ideational function.[69] Conversely, it is at the level of nuclear sentence structure that it makes sense to study the ideation of processes.

2. Construction and expression

Throughout this book, the terms *construction* and *expression* (of complex meanings) will be used in a technical sense. Construction is taken to denote the active shaping of complex meanings by linguistic forms, thanks to autonomous formal relational properties; expression refers to the instrumental use of linguistic forms at the service of independently accessible complex concepts.

Our use of these terms is reasonably intuitive, and perfectly compatible with the shared lexicon of linguistics. Both *construction* and *expression* are polysemous words, which can denote either a static object or a dynamic process. The traditional use of both terms in linguistics mainly takes on the static sense: an *expression* is either a linguistic sign or a significant array of linguistic signs; a *construction* is a significant syntactic pattern. The term *construction*, in particular, is used in this sense in construction grammars (Fillmore, 1985; 1988; Goldberg, 1995; Croft, 1999; 2001). In the present research, the two terms are also used in the dynamic sense, to denote two kinds of ideational process with distinct and different aims. When *expression* is used, the complex content is seen as an *objectum affectum*, which can be conceived of independently of its linguistic body. If a grimace expresses pain, for instance, the latter is given independently of the former: even an enduring Stoic feels pain. When *construction* is used, the complex content is seen as an *objectum effectum*, brought into existence by the ideational process itself.

As it will become clear in the course of this chapter, the static and the dynamic use of the term *construction* are deeply interrelated. In particular, the idea of construction in the dynamic sense and the connected idea of relational coding presuppose the logical priority of constructions (in the static sense) over constituent parts in the core of sentence structures (see §2.3).

2.1 Relational coding and punctual coding

The distinction between construction and expression puts under focus the relationship between the formal syntactic structure of the sentence and the structure of the process. Roughly, a process is constructed to the extent that its content is based on the formal grammatical properties of the expression. A process is expressed to the extent that its content mirrors the autonomous structure of an independent complex concept.

The distinction between construction and expression overlaps the distinction between coding and inferencing, but does not coincide with it: while construction necessarily requires coding, expression is open to both coding and inferential enrichment. The relevant distinction to be taken into account is a subtler one, internal to coding — namely, the distinction between a relational way of coding the roles of the process and a punctual one.

Relational coding depends on the presence of an independent network of grammatical relations.[70] In the presence of relational coding, a given phrase —

for instance, a noun phrase — encodes a given role — for instance, the agent — not in isolation, but as a term of a grammatical relation — typically, as subject or object.

Punctual coding operates outside the network of grammatical relations. In the presence of punctual coding, a given expression is connected to a given role not as a term of a grammatical relation but in isolation. The statement has to be taken in its strongest sense. In the area of punctual coding, the formal structure of the sentence is not autonomous, but is only justified insofar as it mirrors the structure of an independent complex concept. This in particular implies that a given phrase — typically, a prepositional phrase — does not as such bear any purely grammatical relation with the formal syntactic structure of the sentence. On the contrary, it is connected to the structure of the sentence only insofar as it is decoded or interpreted as the expression of a given role — for instance, instrument or beneficiary.[71] This role, in turn, bears a definite relationship with the independent conceptual structure of a consistent state of affairs.

The switch from relational to punctual coding deeply affects the relation between expression and content.

Expressions belonging to the network of grammatical relations are ready to take a content within the framework of a given process, but are as such devoid of inherent content and, above all, are identified irrespective of any content. The content a subject takes within a given sentence, for instance, neither belongs to the subject as such nor contributes to its definition and identification, but is rooted in the whole structure. The general profile of the role is controlled by the main predicator. The subject of a verb like *fell*, for instance, expresses the force that causes the process: *John felled the tree*; *The wind felled the tree.* A more precise definition of this profile, however, can be affected by the content of the predicate, and in particular by the presence of modifiers or non-argumental roles closer to the main predicator than the subject itself.[72] For instance, if the predicate contains an instrument, the subject is bound to express a fully intentional agent: *John felled the tree with an axe.* This means that for an expression belonging to the network of grammatical relations the question about the content can be asked only within the whole structural network. In this case, a given expression is said to receive a *relational content of role.*[73]

Expressions located outside the network of grammatical relations, on the contrary, are both defined, identified and connected to the syntactic structure of the sentence thanks to their association with a substantive content of role. A given expression of the form *with + NP*, for instance, can only be defined, identified and connected to the whole once it has been interpreted as the expression of a given role, for instance the instrument or the co-performer. It is not the identification of a structural network that makes possible the identification of a role, but the identification of a role that makes possible the identification of a structural link. In this case, the expression is said to have an *inherent content of role.*

2.2 Degrees of punctual coding

Owing to the priority of networks of grammatical relations over contents in the presence of relational coding, it is tempting to conclude that the area of relational coding coincides with that of construction, while the area of punctual coding circumscribes expression. Though not altogether false, however, this statement is not sufficiently accurate.

On the one hand, it is true that relational coding implies construction (see §2.5.1). This point is made clear by the formal possibility of constructing inconsistent processes, that is, purely semantic structures which by definition do not mirror the structure of independent complex concepts[74] (see §2.5.2).

On the other hand, punctual coding does not reduce itself to expression, but leaves some residual room for construction.

In the area of punctual coding, in the absence of formal grammatical relations, the aptitude of an expression to code a role critically depends on the content of the linking word — typically, a preposition — which may perform its function with greater or lesser accuracy. The consequence is that punctual coding is inherently a matter of grading. A given role, in particular, may be either fully encoded, or undercoded, or overcoded by a linking word. While undercoding and full coding are confined within the area of expression, overcoding makes room for construction.

In the case of full coding, the linking word performs its task of identifying a role as a serviceable tool is expected to do, no more and no less. Actually, it is not easy to find a preposition that would code no more and no less than one given role within a sentence structure. For instance, there is no preposition that would code no more and no less than the instrumental relation. One could be inclined to think that *by means of* is such a preposition, owing to the fact that it encapsulates the very term *means.* There are many uses, however, which could hardly be considered instrumental in a narrow sense, for instance *It is most unwise to compare the effectiveness of hospital units* by means of *crude, unadjusted perinatal mortality rates* (British National Corpus). This strengthens the insight that in the area of punctual coding some degree of inferential enrichment (or adjustment) is in any case required.

In the case of undercoding, the profile of a role is the outcome of an interaction between coding and inferencing. The more the content of the linking word or expression is defined and specialised, the more accurate the coding, and the less room is left for inferencing. The more this content is vague and unspecialised, the less accurate the coding, and the more room is left for inferencing.[75] When it is expressed by a prepositional phrase introduced by *with*, for instance, the role of instrument is undercoded and can be attained only by inferencing (see §2.5.3). Undercoding is the most revealing form of punctual coding, because what is relevant in this case is the whole range of the inner properties of the involved expression — namely, the content of the linking word as a ground for coding and the conceptual content of the complement noun phrase as a ground for inferencing.

In the case of overcoding, the linking word both encodes a given role, whose relational content is defined with reference to the conceptual structure of a consistent state of affairs, and grafts on it a finer semantic profile. This specific profile is really constructed by the linguistic expression, for it is the work of a specific form of coding and is barred to inference.[76] A good example of overcoding is provided by the ideation of such spatial relations as location, goal and spatial circumstances (see §2.5.4).

2.3 The structure of the sentence and the structure of the process: The structural gap

According to a widely held idea, explicitly formulated by Wittgenstein (1922(1961)), the relationship between the syntactic form of the sentence and the structural skeleton of the process is a diagrammatic relationship, that is, an iconic relation between two isomorphous networks of connections.[77] A nuclear sentence, in this view, may be defined as a cluster of nominal and prepositional phrases, each of which directly expresses a conceptual role of the process drafted by the predicator. However, to the extent that a syntactic construction codes the core of the process as a whole, as it is the case in the area of relational coding, this sort of diagrammatic isomorphism is not at all required. In fact, if we compare the structure of a nuclear English sentence and the structure of a simple process, we easily realize that their relationship is by no means so direct, a circumstance that recalls into question the relationship between coding and iconic motivation.

Considered in its essential conceptual structure, irrespective of linguistic expression, the core of a process is a monocentric structure, formed by a predicator surrounded, like the sun in the Copernican system, by a cluster of controlled arguments.

The syntactic structure of the nucleus of a sentence is an exocentric and hierarchical structure.[78] The immediate constituents of a nuclear sentence — noun phrase and verb phrase, or, in functional terms, subject and predicate — are both essential components of the sentence structure; therefore, the main predicative term cannot be considered as its centre. Moreover, this general scheme circumscribes the essential syntactic structure of the English sentence in general — it provides an autonomous formal mould for any kind of process, irrespective of the number of its arguments and even of the nature of the predicator. If the process involves more than one argument, only one of them — the role identified by the subject — is expressed by an immediate constituent of the sentence structure, while the rest are entrusted to expressions which form the verb phrase together with the main predicative term. Thus, the different arguments of a monocentric process are entrusted to phrases that occupy different layers of a hierarchical formal structure.[79]

The gap between the conceptual structure of the process and the syntactic structure of the sentence is made visible by the different conditions under which the main predicator controls its arguments. The monocentric structure of the process justifies the fact that the content of the subject is controlled by the predicator as well as the content of any other argument. The exocentric structure of the sentence justifies the fact that the verbal control over the form of the arguments is limited to the predicate. In formal terms, the subject cannot be reduced to the expression of a given argument. Being an immediate constituent of the sentence structure as such, it has a form of its own, which is independent of the inner structure of the predicate, and *a fortiori* of the specific properties of the predicator, both formal and conceptual.

The gap between the nuclear sentence structure and the structure of the process is a challenge to the diagrammatic hypothesis. In particular, the distribution of the roles of the process among different layers of an autonomous formal syntactic hierarchy is the proof that the nucleus of a sentence structure enters into relation with the core of the process as a whole, that is, as a network of grammatical relations grounded in the formal syntactic structure of the sentence.[80] This implies that, in the presence of purely grammatical relations the whole — the structure of the sentence nucleus — is logically prior to its constituent parts. Croft (1999: 73) provides a powerful argument for considering complex grammatical structures as primitive with regard to their constituents. Such categories as subject and object are defined by their position within the nuclear sentence. If this is true, however, it is circular to assume that constituent categories, and not complex constructions, are primitive terms: "there is a fundamental theoretical conflict between the distibutional method and the assumption that the categories and relations defined by constructions are the syntactic primitives [...] Constructions are used to define categories — this is the distributional method. But then categories are taken as primitives which define constructions — this is the standard syntactic model of representation".[81]

The idea of a diagrammatic relationship between roles and phrases correctly describes the kind of coding which is at work among the peripheral strata of the process, in the absence of independent grammatical relations. In this area, the whole that is logically prior to its constituent parts is not syntactic but conceptual in nature — it is not a grammatical construction but a consistent state of affairs, and this is the reason why the sense of coding is reversed. A given prepositional phrase is connected to a complex syntactic structure only insofar as it is decoded or interpreted as the expression of a conceptual constituent — of an instrument, for instance — belonging to a consistent state of affairs. Looked at from a grammatical standpoint, a connection that is motivated from outside cannot be seen as a whole logically prior to its parts. Instead, the parts, that is, a sentence nucleus and a prepositional phrase filled with a given content, are prior to the whole, which is the outcome of their connection.[82]

The above remarks provide solid grounds for the distinction between relational and punctual coding. Coding is relational when the relationship between phrases and roles is mediated by a whole network of abstract grammatical relations, that is, by such functional categories as subject or object which can be identified independently of any conceptual content. Coding is punctual when the roles of the process are immediately mapped onto phrases, so that no pure grammatical link can be detected irrespective of a given conceptual content. In the presence of relational coding, a network of grammatical relations codes a complex concept as a whole; in the presence of punctual coding, an isolated expression becomes a part of a grammatical whole insofar as it expresses a part of a conceptual whole.

Let us consider, by way of illustration, a simple transitive action including the roles of agent, patient, instrument and time: *After dinner, my son cut the firewood with an axe.* If the noun phrase *my son* expresses the agent, it is because it is the subject of the sentence; if the noun phrase *the firewood* expresses the patient, it is because it is the direct object of the main verb. On the other hand, the prepositional phrases *After dinner* and *With an axe* directly express temporal circumstances and the instrument respectively. There is no pure grammatical relationship comparable to subject and object, independent of conceptual content, to mediate the link between prepositional phrases and roles:

After dinner	my son	cut	the firewood	with an axe
PrepPh	NP		NP	PrepPh
Ø	Subject		Object	Ø
Time	Agent		Patient	Instrument

What is relevant to relational coding is the position of a given expression in the network of grammatical relations. The conceptual content of the expression is not relevant to identify such functional categories as subject or object, which are made directly visible by the constituent structure of the sentence. Conversely, the formal grammatical properties of the expression do not directly encode a conceptual content such as that of agent, but an empty grammatical relation, which in turn is compatible with a broad sample of heterogeneous roles. What is relevant in the case of punctual coding, on the other hand, is the inner properties of the expression, both formal and conceptual, and in particular the content of the linking word — typically, a preposition — which makes it more or less capable of expressing a given conceptual role — for instance, that of instrument.

2.4 Relational coding, punctual coding and iconism

One consequence of the previous remarks is that the question about the iconic motivation of syntactic structures can be correctly dealt with: iconic motivation is in fact restricted to the area of punctual coding. Within these limits, the question is relevant at two stages.

A punctually coding expression is iconic in a global and relational sense, that is, diagrammatic, since the relation it bears to the structure of the sentence mirrors the independent structure of a complex concept. The diagrammatic form of iconism holds in the presence of both undercoding, full coding and overcoding, for a given phrase is in any case integrated into the structure of a complex expression insofar as it identifies a role belonging to an independent conceptual structure.

A punctually coding expression can also be iconic in a local and inherent sense: to the extent that it requires inferential enrichment, the identification of a given role is not integrally based on the conventional meaning of a linking word but depends on the conceptual content of the whole expression. As it requires inferencing, this punctual form of iconism is relevant to undercoding but excluded from both full coding and overcoding.

In the presence of relational coding, it is pointless to speak of iconism in both its relevant senses. As shown by the formal possibility of conflictual complex meanings, a network of grammatical relations shapes the core of the process irrespective of the structure of any independent concept. Being independent of the content of the organised expressions, on the other hand, the construction of the process is barred to inferencing, and thus to punctual conceptual motivation. Owing to its absolute blindness towards the organized contents, relational coding can be considered the most qualified kind of coding, which offers a good illustration of the power of formal grammatical patterns over concepts.

2.5 Coding, construction and expression: Some paradigmatic cases

In order to analyse in greater detail the relevant differences between punctual and relational coding with regard to the distinction between construction and expression, we shall examine some paradigmatic cases: the construction of the agent in the area of relational coding, the expression of the instrument in the area of punctual coding, and the construction of language-specific determinations for spatial circumstances, location and goal in the area of punctual coding.

2.5.1 *Construction in the area of relational coding: The agent as subject*

The agent of an action framed by a nuclear sentence structure is necessarily expressed by the noun phrase that occupies the position of subject. However, the identification of the subject within the syntactic structure of the sentence is logically prior to, and independent of, the identification of the agent. The identification of the subject is supported by formal criteria, and is independent both of the conceptual structure of the process and of the content of the involved noun phrase. The identity of the subject, in other words, is strictly formal and relational (See Chapter 9, §1.2).

Functional categories and roles are both relational categories. Unlike roles, however, functional categories are not functions of the conceptual structure of the state of affairs, but functions of the hierarchical constituent structure of the sentence. Functional categories simply make the constructional and relational side of syntactic structures explicit. Accordingly, the fact that a given noun phrase identifies the functional category of subject is not a sufficient condition for determining the role attributed to its referent within the process. This role can only be identified when the content of the predicator is known. Once the content of the predicator is known, however, the network of functional categories governs the distribution of the roles as a rigid formal mould. Each functional category lays a formal claim to the role of its referent, whose rank is bound to the position of the expression within the hierarchy of constituents. As an immediate constituent of the sentence, the subject is bound to express the most pre-eminent role in the process. If the main predicative term is a verb of action, for instance, the subject expresses the agent. In the presence of a verb of affection, it expresses the experiencer, and so on.[83]

The content of the noun phrase is irrelevant both to the identification of the subject and to the assignment of a role to it. In particular, an inconsistent content cannot prevent a noun phrase that possesses the formal properties of a subject either from standing as a subject, or from taking the role assigned to the subject within the framework of the process. Given a sentence framing the process of kissing, for instance, the referent of the noun phrase displaying the formal properties of the subject cannot avoid taking the role of agent, irrespective of whether its conceptual profile is consistent with this role — *John kissed Mary* — or inconsistent: *Then Sunrise kissed my Chrysalis* (Dickinson). These are precisely the conditions under which a process can be considered a constructed kind of structure.

2.5.2 *Inconsistent complex meanings as revealing data*

When it is coded by a network of grammatical relations, the formal skeleton of a complex meaning is insensitive to conflict — it cannot be undone by conflicting conceptual contents.[84] The formal possibility of inconsistent complex meanings is the most powerful argument for the idea that the core of the process is really constructed, rather than simply expressed, by formal grammatical relations. It is owing to the autonomous strength of a grammatical mould that linguistic expressions can ideate such kinds of complex meanings as do not mirror the structure of independent complex concepts.

Since it puts under focus the significance of complex expressions, our programme not only demands that inconsistent complex meanings be included within the scope of semantic description, but also confers on them the role of a strategic vantage point. This does not strictly imply that inconsistent meanings are the only, or the principal object of enquiry. It simply implies that the constitutive factors involved in the ideation of complex semantic structures can only be grasped on the condition that inconsistent expressions are kept in focus as fully significant complex expressions.

Consistent expressions are silent on the point of significance. When a consistent meaning is framed, the different factors which take part in its ideation — formal grammatical connections and independent connections between concepts — define exactly the same structural skeleton. If we consider a sentence like *John poured the wine into Mary's glass*, for instance, it is impossible to establish whether the responsibility for the connection of the process lies with the syntactic structures, which make *John* the subject and *wine* the object of the sentence, or it is the categorisation of John among human beings and of wine among liquid substances that makes the former the agent and the latter the patient of the action of pouring. Under such conditions, the shaping power of grammatical relations remains absolutely hidden. All grammatical relations seem to do is to mirror solid and independent relations among concepts.[85]

If we take into account inconsistent meanings, the relationship between linguistic forms and conceptual structures becomes clear. The actual network of connections projected onto concepts by grammatical relations and the virtual network of connections drawn by shared conceptual structures no longer coincide, but enter into conflict. As a consequence, each factor of significance can be observed separately, and the power of each may be exactly determined. Given a sentence like:

> And Winter pours its grief in snow
> When Autumn's leaves are lying (E. Brontë)

it is clear beyond any reasonable doubt that the connection between the action of pouring and grief does not mirror the structure of an independent complex concept, but results from the projection of a network of autonomous grammatical relations upon the atomic concepts. More generally, an inconsistent process can be conceived only insofar as it is the meaning of a complex expression. It is conceivable as a constructed semantic structure without being conceivable as an expressed conceptual structure. It is in this sense that the core of a process can be considered a constructed kind of structure. Even when it actually mirrors the structure of an independent complex concept, as in the case of consistent processes, its formal possibility is not subject to this condition.

Inconsistent meanings are the best argument for the autonomy of nuclear grammatical relations, but also the best argument for the autonomy of conceptual structures. The conflict that splits inconsistent complex meanings both highlights the shaping power of nuclear syntactic structures and betrays the resistance of conceptual structures to an alien mould.

The observation of inconsistent meanings raises the question about significance in the right terms. The relevant question is not whether syntactic structures have the power to shape concepts, which is indisputable, but what are the limits of this power, that is, to what extent syntactic structures construct complex meanings independently of the organised concepts, and to what extent they simply express autonomous conceptual structures. Once the competing factors underlying the connection of complex meanings have been isolated, the analysis can quit the restricted field of conflictual meanings, for the same factors which have been focused on thanks to conceptual conflicts are capable of cooperating when consistent meanings are constructed. These are the reasons why an enquiry into inconsistent meanings can lay down the theoretical basis for a philosophical grammar — for a grammar which complements a formal analysis of linguistic structures with a substantive analysis of conceptual structures in order to account for the power and limits of both.[86]

2.5.3 *Expression in the field of punctual coding: Instrument*

In the realm of punctual coding, a given expression is not taken as a constituent of an autonomous sentence structure, but works as an instrument at the service of an independent conceptual structure. The most relevant feature of a role like that of instrument, for instance, is the fact that it is assigned to a phrase — typically, a prepositional phrase of the form *with + NP* — which as such does not bear any purely grammatical relation to the sentence structure. A role like that of instrument, in other words, does not belong to a meaningful connection by virtue of the formal integration of the prepositional phrase within the syntactic structure of the sentence. If the prepositional phrase finally enters into a meaningful expression, it is only because it is taken as expressing the role of instrument, which bears a definite relation to the conceptual structure of a consistent state of affairs. This is the main reason why, in the presence of punctual coding, the relation between phrases and roles can be considered iconic: the position of the phrase within the sentence structure is justified by the position of the role within the state of affairs.

Under such conditions, the orientation of the analysis needs to be reversed, that is, the analysis of the structure of the expressions must be subordinated to the analysis of the conceptual structure of the state of affairs. The conceptual profile of the role is the constant, while both the form of the expression and the accuracy of coding are variable. Once the instrumental relation is defined on conceptual grounds, for instance, it makes sense to ascertain how many ways of expressing it are available within a given language, and what are the relevant properties and limits of each. This move marks the passage from a grammar of rules, focused on autonomous networks of expressions governed by rigid formal patterns, to a grammar of options (Halliday, 1978: 4), where expressions are taken as instruments at the service of independent concepts, belonging as such to paradigms of interchangeable means at the disposal of the speaker.

2.5.3.1 *The conceptual structure of the instrument*

The role of instrument is not an atomic but a relational concept, which can be defined only within the structure of a state of affairs. However substantive, therefore, the definition of instrument is necessarily relational: an instrument is an entity, as a rule an inanimate one, which may be consistently imagined in the hands of an agent that uses it to perform a purposeful action.

Such a relational concept of instrument may be defined in two senses: a weak one and a strong one. In a weak sense, any object can have access to the role of instrument provided that it is used within the framework of an appropriate action.[87] A stone, for instance, is not an instrument as such, but is ready to take on this role if used by an agent for performing an action: *John knocked the nail in with a stone.* The difference between a stone and an instrument in the strong sense — a hammer, for instance — is that the latter is not only used as an instrument, but has been purposefully shaped in order to be used as an instrument. Before being instrumentally engaged in a purposeful action, it is itself the result of a purposeful action. A stone is an occasional instrument, an object possessing an independent structure which happens to be used as an instrument within the confines of an occasional action, while a hammer keeps its functional destination for action permanently inscribed within its essential structure.

The process that involves an instrument is necessarily an action, performed by an intentional and responsible agent — for instance, *John killed the snake with a stick.* If the process is not an action in this strong sense, the prepositional phrase is not interpreted as expressing the instrument:[88] *The falling tree hit John's car with a branch.* Strong agentivity, which is relevant to instrumentality, is a responsible (Palmer, 1994: 25–26) and purposeful kind of causation. If causation is not purposeful and responsible, no instrument can be consistently associated with it. Within our natural ontology, for instance, the wind is conceived of neither as a responsible agent[89] nor as an instrument in the hands of an agent,[90] but as a non-responsible force (Fillmore, 1977a: 71). While it may cause something to happen, it cannot consistently use an instrument to do it: *The wind felled the tree* (**with an axe*).

2.5.3.2 *The expression of instrument: Coding and inferencing*

> The Sun is freed from fears,
> and with soft grateful tears
> ascends the sky (Blake)

Once the conceptual structure of a role such as that of instrument is independently defined in conceptual-relational terms, it makes sense to ask which linguistic means can be used to express it. When the coding is punctual, as in this case, the relevant properties of the coding expression are not grammatical-relational, but inherent, and essentially based on the conventional content of the linking word or expression — typically, of the preposition. Insofar as this content weakens, punctual coding shades into inferencing.

The most typical form of instrumental expression — a prepositional phrase of the form *With + NP* — does not attain full coding. The meaning of the preposition *with* is very weak, and simply suggests that something is connected with something else in some way. As a consequence, the instrumental relation can only be established by way of inferential enrichment, evaluating the connected contents against the background of shared conceptual models. The prepositional phrase is interpreted as expressing the role of instrument if — and only if — it is associated with an action and its referent meets the conceptual conditions required for an instrument within the framework of this action. If the main process is not an action, or the content of the prepositional phrase does not meet the appropriate conceptual conditions, the prepositional phrase is assigned another role or, in extreme cases, its role remains indeterminate.

Given a sentence like *John felled the tree with an axe*, for instance, the prepositional phrase is interpreted as the expression of the instrument: an axe is an object which can be consistently used as an instrument, and is an appropriate instrument for felling trees.

In a sentence like *John cut his finger with an axe*, the axe cannot be interpreted as an instrument because the main process is not an action.

In a sentence like *John felled the tree with Robert*, the main process is an action, but the referent of the prepositional phrase does not meet the appropriate conceptual conditions for instrumentality. As a consequence, it is assigned another role, compatible with his ontological status of responsible human being — the role of "co-performer of the action" (Foley & Van Valin, 1984: 84).

According to the content of the complement noun phrase, the coded content of the preposition *with* is open to the most heterogeneous paths of inferential enrichment, and is thus able to express such relations as manner —

Ann wrote her report with great accuracy — cause — *Metal contracts with cold* — and any kind of outer circumstances: *She greeted him with a smile.* In Flaubert's novel, M.me Bovary despises her husband because *He strolls around with a knife, like a peasant.* Of course M. Bovary does not use a knife for strolling around. He simply holds a knife in his pocket when doing so. As is the rule in the area of punctual coding, different roles bear different relationships to the structure of the process according to the content of each.[91]

Since the linguistic coding is very weak, when the contents of the involved expressions do not univocally match a definite conceptual scheme the relation between a prepositional phrase and the process it is associated with is open to indeterminacy and even to vagueness. In the first case, the structure is compatible with many paths of inferential enrichment; in the second, no definite relation can be inferred at all.[92]

An expression like *He sits down with holy fears* (Blake) probably associates a background circumstance with the process, but an exact profile of it is not easy to draw. An expression like *John answered with a sigh*, on the other hand, may be interpreted as containing either a circumstantial background to the action or its metaphorical instrument, or both. The same holds for the next passage, where the instrumental interpretation, though inconsistent, is encouraged by the co-text:

> Their marble tombs I built with tears,
> and with cold and shuddering fears (Blake)

Different roles belonging to this continuum, even expressed by different forms, may be coordinated, as if grammar frankly admitted that a fringe of vagueness inevitably surrounds them: *She spoke these last words with a smile and softness inexpressible* (Fielding); *I had walked about in the greatest security, and with all possible tranquillity* (Defoe); *He answered me in his pleasant quiet voice and with a faint, slightly wistful smile* (Conrad).

2.5.4 *Construction in the area of punctual coding: The semantic shaping of spatial relations*

A most typical domain of overcoding is provided by the language-specific ideation of such spatial relations as location, goal and spatial circumstances.

Spatial relations display a layered profile, that is, a general relational profile and an inherent profile. The general profile of these roles is defined on the basis of their position with regards to the structure of consistent processes. Goal and location are arguments of specific kinds of process — of state and motion respectively. Spatial circumstances, for their part, are ready to circumscribe from outside any kind of actualized process. These different functions, on the other hand, are open roughly to the same sample of expressions, each of which draws a given spatial relation thanks to its inherent content. O*n the top of a hill*, for or instance, one can both *live* (location), *go* (goal) and *meet some friends* (spatial circumstance).

The inherent content of each spatial relation cannot be reduced to an independent concept brought to expression by a linguistic form. One can certainly imagine a conceptual core, but this core is bound to receive a language-specific shaping, whose extent and limits depend on the inherent properties of the available coding devices — on their aptitude to draw more or less fine-grained spatial relations. In order to perform this task, each language has at its disposal a specific supply of linguistic means — locative prepositions and adverbs — distributed along language-specific relevant dimensions.[93] Accordingly, the inner profile of spatial relations is typically overcoded in a language-specific way, which in turn implies that it cannot be inferred — either it is coded or it is not accessible at all.

In my native dialect, which is spoken in a south-facing mountainside village in Valtellina, in the Italian Alps, one cannot simply say, for instance, *sum ən'daːtʃ a sy'raːnə.* ("I went to Surana", a small hamlet lying about a hundred meters farther up). Instead, one has to say *sum ən'daːtʃ 'sa* (*sy+a*) *sy'raːnə* ("I went *up* to Surana"). *sum ən'daːtʃ a sy'raːnə* is an ill-formed sentence, just as *I went Canterbury* in English. When describing the goal of a motion, the speaker is compelled to specify not only the end point — for instance, *a sy'raːnə* — but also some relevant features of its relation to the location of the speaker, or deictic *origo*:[94] for instance, *sy*. The same holds when the location of an object is described — for instance, *gɔ 'nbryːʎu sa sy'raːnə* ("I've got an orchard *up* at Surana") — or a process is provided with a local frame: *ɔ 'trwat la ma'riːə sa sy'raːnə* ("I met Mary *up* at Surana). In such expressions, the prepositional phrase — *at Surana* — and the deictic adverb — *up* — perform two distinct functions. The prepositional phrase draws a given objective relation between an individual or process and a place. The adverb — hence named *positional adverb* — defines the position of the place from the speaker's standpoint. Performing different functions, the positional adverb and the preposition cannot conflict even if their inherent content is opposite. In the sentence *əl 'pa lɛ fint* (*fø+int*, "outside" + "inside") *əl 'praː*, the father is said to be *inside* a meadow, which in turn is located *outside* from the speaker's standpoint.

The obligatory expression of the speaker's standpoint implies that the description of any spatial relation necessarily contains a deictic component. This already makes a non-trivial point, but the most intriguing issue has to do with the nature of the deictic *origo*, which is not assumed to be mobile but fixed in the space. When a language is spoken over a large territory, the field of spatial orientation is like a mobile galaxy. Each speaker, at each different moment of time, makes his contingent position the centre of the field — the *origo* follows the speaker like a snail's shell. But for a dialect spoken in a very small territory with a marked landscape, the *origo* is liable to be treated as if it were fixed in a given point of the territory — typically, in the middle of the village — turning the field into a sort of Copernican universe revolving around a fixed centre. This is precisely what happens in my native dialect, where the association between toponyms and positional adverbs is typically frozen, irrespective of the speaker's contingent location. A person finding himself in a place above Surana, for instance, typically identifies the *origo* with the village he normally lives in, and defines Surana's position with regard to it: *gɔ ˈnbryːʎu sa syˈraːnə* ("I've got an orchard *up* at Surana").[95] At first sight, the determination of the *origo* seems connected with the phenomenon described by Bühler (1934: Chapter 2, §8) as "*deixis am Phantasma*": the speaker behaves as if he actually were in the village. The case in point, however, is very different: the gap between the actual location of the speaker and the assumed *origo* is not a free option of the speaker, but a social fact shared by the speech community. This gives birth to a very special case of spatial deixis, ground-oriented rather than speaker-oriented, whose function is not to express the speaker's contingent point of view but to impose on the surrounding territory a long-lasting social mark.[96]

The positional adverbs are organized thanks to a handful of relevant dimensions. The vertical dimension — *sy* ("up") vs *dʒu* ("down") — is rather obvious, but combines with other more idiosyncratic. The opposite terms *int* and *fø* not only mean "inside" and "outside" with reference to such closed spaces as houses, woods or waterpools, but also "upstream" and "downstream" with reference to the two lateral valleys delimiting the municipality,[97] and "mountainside" (*int*) as opposite to "riverside" (*fø*) along the main valley. The opposition between *viːə* (roughly "away") and *fø* is rather elusive, but has a clear main value. Imagining the village as if it were a person standing against the northern mountainside and looking southwards, the opposition divides the space roughly located on a level in two halves: *viːə* is relevant to the left one (East to South) and *fø* to the right one (West to South). Here are some combinations of positional adverbs and prepositional phrases: *sa* (*sy+a*) *syˈraːnə* ("up at Surana"); *s int* (*sy+int*) *i ˈrunk* ("up inside *i runk*", a vineyard); *fa* (*fø+a*) *mun'taːɲə* ("outside at Montagna", a nearby village, west); *int al 'tʃatts* ("inside at the Piazzo", a part of the village); *dʒa (dʒu+a) 'sundrə* ("down at Sondrio", the main town of the valley); *dʒint (dʒu+int) iŋ'ʃɛrən* ("down inside the Inferno, a vineyard"); *va (viːə+a) trə'zif* ("away at Tresivio", a nearby village, east).

Such roles as goal, location and spatial frame can be saturated by both prepositional phrases and adverbs, which are in turn completed by the same positional specifications. The adverb *la'sy*, for instance, combines a distal component *la-* and a positional component *sy*. Like the prepositional phrase, the distal component *la-* cannot occur in isolation.

An adverb like *la'sy* exactly corresponds to a prepositional phrase like *sa sy'raːnə*. In the latter case, a deictic location centred on the speaker's socially assumed position — the positional component *sy* — is combined with the expression of an objective spatial relation involving a toponym: *a sy'raːnə*. In the former case, the same positional component is combined with a further deictic expression to form a multidimensional deictic adverb. Unlike the positional component, this last deictic expression belongs to the familiar proximal — distal paradigm. It is not anchored in a ground-oriented, and therefore fixed *origo*, but in a speaker-oriented, ad therefore mobile one. Thus, the two kinds of deixis coexist in multidimensional locative adverbs, and so do their functions: the distal component *la-* organizes the surrounding space from the speaker's contingent standpoint, whilst the positional component underlines a long-lasting social map of the territory.[98]

In my native dialect, the formation of multidimensional deictic adverbs is severely restricted. The proximal deictic adverb *ki'lɔ* ("here") is incompatible with any positional component, so that forms such as **kilɔ'sy* or **kilɔ'dʒu* are not allowed. The distal adverb *'la-* ("there"), for its part, can receive no more than one positional determination, chosen among the forms *sy*, *dʒu*, *int*, *fø*, *viːə*. Accordingly, only five bi-dimensional adverbs are allowed — *la'sy* ("there up"); *la'dʒu* ("there down"); *la'int* ("there inside"); *la'fø* ("there outside"); *la'viːə* ("there away") — whereas such forms as **lafø'sy* ("there outside up"); **lafø'dʒu* ("there outside down") do not occur. Most dialects spoken in nearby villages, however, are more liberal. At Faedo, for instance, one finds such three-dimensional combinations as *laite'sy* ("there inside up"), *lafe'sy* ("there outside up") and *lafi'dʒɔ* ("there outside down"). At Montagna, one can both build up multidimentional forms containing the proximal deictic component *kwa-* and cumulate up to two positional determinations. The combination of the two strategies gives birth to two parallel series of adverbs, both bi- and three-dimensional, opposed on the distal vs proximal dimension:

Proximal:	*kwaˈsy* ("here up")	
	kwaˈdʒu ("here down")	
	kwaˈint ("here inside")	
	kwaˈfø ("here outside")	*kwaføˈsy* ("here outside up")
		kwaføˈdʒu ("here outside down")
	kwaˈviːə ("here away")	*kwaviˈsy* ("here away up")
		kwaviˈdʒu ("here away down")
Distal:	*laˈsy* ("there up")	
	laˈdʒu ("there down")	
	laˈint ("there inside")	
	laˈfø ("there outside")	*laføˈsy* ("there outside up")
		laføˈdʒu ("there outside down")
	laˈviːə ("there away")	*laviˈsy* ("there away up")
		laviˈdʒu ("there away down")

In the dialect of Grosio, the wealth and almost free accumulation of spatial dimensions leads to a paradigm of deictic locative adverbs including no less than sixty-eight items (Bracchi, 1995: 124; see also Bracchi, 1994: XLVI-XLVII). Two significant examples of four-dimensional adverbs are *kulain'su* ("there inside upside, in a distant, not well defined place, including the other side of the lateral valley"), and *kulainˈdʒɔ* ("as above, downside").

The theoretical import of such forms of categorisation is discussed by Levinson (1997; see also Bickel, 1997). As Levinson correctly remarks, such a fine-grained and highly specific regimentation of spatial relations cannot be reduced to the structure of independent concepts, but can only be attained thanks to the availability of language-specific coding devices. Therefore, it is not a matter of conceptual import, and even less of pragmatic import,[99] but really a matter of semantic import. When overcoding is at work, language is none the less at the service of thinking. Not in the sense that language provides independent thinking with a serviceable means of expression, however, but in the sense that it makes possible a given way of thinking by shaping a set of specific semantic categories. "The conceptual coding […] appears to mirror the structure of the linguistic coding", as Levinson (1997: 38) underlines.

In some of the cases examined, the language-specific categorisation of spatial relations achieves a degree of exactness that appears as almost obsessive in the eyes of the average European speaker. But at this level even historically and typologically related languages of the Average European type normally display significant differences in imposing fine-grained distinctions on spatial relations. For a native speaker of Italian, for instance, such oppositions as *on* vs *over* vs *above*, *under* vs *below*,[100] or *between* vs *among* are far from being self-evident. In order to express such spatial relations correctly, a learner of English as a second language must first adapt his way of framing them in thought — he has to train himself in "thinking for speaking", to put it in Slobin's terms.[101]

3. The function of functional categories

3.1 Construction and expression of processes: Functional core and periphery of the sentence

The twofold distinction between relational and punctual coding and between construction and expression of processes marks a critical threshold which divides the functional core of the sentence from a periphery devoid of an autonomous grammatical organisation, which simply mirrors the structure of the expressed concepts.

Within the functional core, the relation is from form to content. A given expression receives a role on the basis of its formal grammatical properties, irrespective of its conceptual content. Functional categories are the instruments through which the formal structure of the sentence controls the distribution of the main roles of the process. To put it in Jespersen's terms, functional categories "Janus-like, face both ways, towards form, and towards notion" (Jespersen, 1924: 56). Thanks to functional categories, the formal grammatical structure imposes on the process a strong formal mould, independent of the conceptual properties of the connected terms. As a consequence, the syntactic well-formedness of the expression is a sufficient condition for significance, as is documented by the availability of inconsistent complex meanings.

Along the periphery, the relation is from content to form. A given phrase — typically, a prepositional phrase — which has no definite position within the syntactic structure of the sentence, expresses a role which bears a definite relation to the conceptual structure of a consistent state of affairs. As a consequence, the distribution of phrases within linguistic expressions is controlled by the conceptual structure of a consistent state of affairs. In the area of punctual coding, moreover, prepositional phrases are not necessarily up to coding a definite role, so that coding is relayed to a significant extent by inferencing. Under such conditions, syntactic well-formedness is not necessarily a sufficient condition for significance. To the extent that the linking word is not definite enough to identify a role univocally, a given expression is successfully integrated into a unitary meaning on the supplementary condition that its content fits a consistent conceptual mould. A purely formal grammar is complemented by a grammar of concepts within the framework of a philosophical grammar.

Our distinction between functional core and periphery is not to be confused with the distinction between core and periphery inherited from Tesnière's tradition. When differentiating core and periphery, Tesnière takes as a relevant criterion the conceptual structure of the process. Accordingly, the roles that are essential for framing a given process — which are controlled by the valency scheme of the main predicative term — are separated from the roles which are not.[102] Our definition focuses on the conditions of significance, that is, on the relationship between syntactic structures and processes, and takes as a relevant criterion for circumscribing the core the presence of a relational kind of coding involving functional categories.[103] In this sense, our definition is closer to Fillmore's definition of "the nuclear system of grammatical relations" (Fillmore, 1977a: 77), whose relevance criterion is neither the conceptual structure of the process nor the syntactic obligatoriness of the expressions, but the role played by functional categories in shaping the process: "I will refer to the elements that are brought into perspective — the elements that appear as subjects and direct objects — as NUCLEAR ELEMENTS in the sentence" (Fillmore, 1977a: 75). The remaining elements, which are located outside the network of grammatical relations, form the periphery of the sentence structure.

3.2 Are functional categories "perspectival functions"?

The role played by functional categories is entirely lost — or, at least, is sorely underestimated — if syntactic structures are considered as a means for expressing, rather than constructing, complex meaning connections. If the meaning of a sentence is immediately described as a cluster of roles mirroring the structure of a state of affairs, such functional categories as subject and object seem literally inoperative, or at least confined to a marginal function, connected with the textual presentation of the process. This is precisely what happens within the framework of functional grammars. According to Givón (1984: 135), subject and object "are of a different kind from all other — semantic — case-roles. To begin with, they co-exist with semantic case-roles [...] Clearly then, both 'subject' and 'direct object' are grammatical/syntactic categories coding *another* functional level in language, that of discourse-pragmatics, and more specifically the complex system which codes the clausal topic". In Dik's opinion (Dik, 1989(1997: 27), "the notions Subject and Object [...] will be regarded as having their own contribution to the semantics of the expression, a contribution consisting in defining different perspectives over the State of Affairs designated by the predication. For that reason, 'perspectival functions' might be a better term to cover their essential nature". According to Halliday (1976: 16), "Even such an apparently 'grammatical' function as 'subject' is clearly relatable to language use (in fact the notion of a 'purely grammatical' function is absurd)".

In order to grasp the real import of functional categories, two points must be evaluated. First, the concept of perspective is currently used and defined in two different ways. Only one of them is directly connected with the role of functional categories. Second, in order to justify the functional categories in terms of perspective, the kind of perspective connected with the distribution of functional categories should form a distinct level of analysis, autonomous from the ideation of the process.

3.2.1 *Message perspective and process perspective*

The traditional concept of perspective, which was first defined by the linguists of the Prague School, has to do with the variable contribution made by the different constituents of an utterance to its "communicative dynamism". The unequal distribution of communicative weight within the sentence is captured by such categories as theme (topic), rheme (comment) and focus. This kind of perspective may be defined as communicative perspective, or perspective of the message. The examples discussed above — *The farmer killed the duckling*; *The duckling, the farmer killed it*; *It's the farmer that killed the duckling* — impose different communicative perspectives on the same process. When Givón (1984: 135) connects the distribution of functional categories to the coding of the clausal topic, he certainly has in mind the shaping of communicative perspective within the simple nuclear sentence, whose topic coincides with the grammatical subject.

A more recent definition of perspective, put forward within the framework of functional and cognitive linguistics, takes into account the relative salience the different roles of the processes are given on the basis of their association with functional categories, and in particular with subject and object.

According to Fillmore (1977), the meaning of a sentence — a process — is a cognitive invariant — a "scene" — taken into a specific perspective. A raw cognitive invariant may be looked at from different standpoints, each of which is provided by a different sentence structure. Two features of the expression are relevant on this account, and both have to do with grammatical relations: first, which roles are located within the network of grammatical relations and which are not, and second, which role is associated to the subject and which to the direct object. The first point is illustrated by the behaviour of such verbs as *hit*, which allow for more than one valency scheme: "The verb *hit* — for instance — fits scenes in which something comes into abrupt contact with something else, including those in which some agent manipulates the first of these objects. In the three-elements hitting scene, the agent or causer of this event appears as the subject, but apparently either of the other two entities can be realized in the direct object position. That is, we can say either 'I hit the cane against the fence' or 'I hit the fence with the cane'" (Fillmore, 1977: 96). The second is illustrated by the alternative between a pair of converse verbs — *Harry sold a puppy to John* and *John bought a puppy from Harry*, for instance — which associate different roles with the grammatical subject. In Fillmore's examples, the role expressed by the direct object, which is included within the network of grammatical relations, is more salient for the structure of the process than the role expressed by the prepositional phrase, while the role associated with the subject is more salient than the role associated with the direct object.

Clearly, what is at issue in such cases is not immediately the distribution of communicative weight among the constituents of the process. In all the quoted examples, the most salient element in terms of communicative perspective is neither the subject nor the direct object, but the focal prepositional phrase. What is at issue is in fact a hierarchy imposed on the roles by a network of grammatical relations, and therefore the language-specific internal configuration of the process itself as a sentence meaning. Accordingly, this kind of perspective may be called the perspective of the process, or ideational[104] perspective. It is in this sense that two sentences such as *I hit the cane against the fence* and *I hit the fence with the cane* impose different perspectives on a raw cognitive invariant.

The metaphor of perspective is justified for both ideational and communicative perspective, for what takes place in both cases is a figure-ground relation. Moreover, ideational and communicative perspective are intertwined in actual utterances: the reasons which induce a speaker to impose a given ideational perspective on a state-of-affairs have mainly to do with the consequences of this option on communicative perspective.[105] In spite of this, the two phenomena are independent, and should not be confused.

Ideational perspective is a static property of the inner form of the process: the roles associated with functional categories are more salient than the peripheral ones, while the role associated with the subject is given first rank. The different ranks imposed on the roles of the process may be compared with the different ranks — main character or second lead, for instance — of the different actors involved in a play. These different ranks, of course, are not correlated with the contingent position of the actors on the stage, but are defined once for all by the structure of the plot.

Communicative perspective, on the other hand, is a dynamic property of the message carried by an utterance, which is interconnected with, but structurally independent of, the inner form of the process. In particular, the communicative weight of the different roles is not measured on the basis of the salience of each in the structure of the process, but on the basis of the contribution each gives to the communicative progression of the ongoing discourse.[106] The different weight imposed on the constituents of the process in terms of communicative perspective may be compared with the different positions occupied by the different actors on the stage — upstage or downstage, in the spotlight or in the shadows — at a given point during the play. This position, of course, is independent of the rank each actor is given within the structure of the plot.

If the metaphor of perspective is coherently developed, the criteria of ideational and communicative perspective conflict precisely in the presence of nuclear and passive sentences, that is, of those sentence types where the shaping of communicative perspective is strictly connected with ideational perspective, and therefore with functional categories. In nuclear and passive sentences, the most salient role in terms of ideational perspective — the role identified by the subject — coincides with the topic, that is, with the role that is upstage in terms of communicative dynamism.[107]

3.2.2 *Process perspective and construction*

Clearly, it is not communicative perspective but ideational perspective that is immediately connected with the distribution of roles among functional categories. In order to evaluate the weight of functional categories in shaping the process, therefore, one has to grasp the exact nature of ideational perspective.

Within the functional and cognitive paradigm, the distribution of roles among functional categories and the ideational perspective in which it results are assumed to be a matter of choice on the part of the speaker. According to Fillmore, for instance, "the decision to include things in the sentence nucleus is the decision to take a particular perspective on a scene" (Fillmore, 1977: 97). This way of putting things, however, is rather misleading, for the room left for individual choice is in fact very narrow in sentence nuclei. Some margins of real choice are left when two competing valency schemes admit an alternation of forms for the same role — *Janine climbed the mountain*; *Janine climbed up the mountain* (Hopper & Thompson, 1982) — or entrust different roles to the same form — typically, to the direct object of a transitive verb and to the subject of an intransitive verb: *John loaded the hay on the truck*; *John loaded the truck with hay*; *Bees are swarming in the garden*; *The garden is swarming with bees* (Waltereit, 1999). Beyond these peculiar cases,[108] the relevant choice is logically prior to the linguistic shaping of the process: it is the choice of the main predicator — typically, of the main verb — and its diathesis. Once this choice is made, the main roles are at the same time identified and given a rank by a rigid network of grammatical relations: *Mary gave a book to John*; *Mary presented John with a book*; *John was presented with a book by Mary.*

If this is true, the language-specific shaping of the process and its ideational perspective are in fact the same thing. The question that becomes relevant at this point is whether the language-specific shaping of a process is reduced to the imposition of a perspective on an independent cognitive structure, or whether it coincides with the construction of a semantic structure. In the former case, the formal possibility of the process requires the accessibility of a consistent state of affairs independent of further linguistic shaping.[109] In the latter, the formal possibility of the process lies in its language-specific construction, and ideational perspective is just another name for it; if functional categories play a role in ideational perspective, it is insofar as they play a role in the construction of the process.

Once more, the crucial argument in favour of the second hypothesis is the formal possibility of inconsistent processes. Inconsistent processes cannot be conceived as peculiar perspectives imposed on independent conceptual structures. They can only be conceived as purely semantic structures — as meanings of linguistic expressions — devoid of any independent conceptual counterpart. This is possible, in turn, because a network of grammatical relations has the strength to impose a rigid mould on the organized concepts — that is, to construct processes rather than simply expressing them. The construction of inconsistent processes simply pushes towards its limits and makes visible the most qualifying structural property of nuclear syntactic structures: the form of the core of a process is not governed by the form of the state of affairs it describes, but by the formal properties of the core of its linguistic expression.

If this idea is true, ideational perspective is not an autonomous level — it is simply another name for the construction of the process. A level that is really autonomous from construction, on the other hand, is communicative perspective. Unlike ideational perspective, communicative perspective is not necessarily a by-product of construction, because it has at its disposal specific syntactic and phonological means for breaking the biunivocal association of perspectival categories with functional categories. The most significant example of this is the relationship between subject and topic. If this association were as rigid as the association between subject and first rank role, communicative perspective would in turn be reduced to a simple by-product of construction. In fact, this happens only in nuclear and passive sentences, where the subject is at one and the same time the first rank role and the topic,[110] but neither in non-nuclear sentences other than passives nor in nuclear sentences with marked intonation.

In the case of non-nuclear sentences, specialised syntactic means dissociate perspectival categories and functional categories — in particular, topic and subject — without affecting the association between roles and functional categories, and therefore without affecting the construction of the process and its ideational perspective. A dislocated object, for instance, becomes a topic without becoming a subject. A cleft subject becomes a focus though remaining a subject. The same holds, *a fortiori*, when the perspective is modified through the intervention of phonological means.

If these remarks are true, the idea that functional categories are perspectival functions draws a false conclusion from two true premises. It is true that communicative perspective forms an autonomous structure, whose organisation is a matter of choice made by the speaker among a set of different — syntactic and phonological — options. It is also true that functional categories play an essential role in shaping ideational perspective, for ideational perspective is only another name for the construction of the process. But it is false that functional categories are perspectival categories, for they are diagnostic when perspective is a simple by-product of construction, and non-diagnostic when perspective forms an autonomous level.

3.3 The methodological dilemma

The idea that nuclear syntactic structures form a system of options functionally designed to express independent conceptual structures, which implies an underevaluation of functional categories, is the ruling idea of typological research. In order to attain typological adequacy, linguistic description has to be grounded on a system of categories so as to be independent of the different language-specific forms of expression, and therefore capable of providing the typological comparison with a neutral *tertium comparationis.* Such a requirement is actually attained at the level of the conceptual structure of the process, defined as a cluster of arguments controlled by a main predicative term.[111]

Of course, the task of providing typological comparison with a common ground cannot be performed by the network of functional categories mediating the relation between nuclear grammatical structures and roles of the process. Although widespread among human languages, functional categories are formal-relational categories, which by definition depend, for their relevance as well as for their formal profile, on the peculiar grammatical structures of a given language.[112] Any attempt to give a general definition of functional categories, therefore, is bound to "have to eliminate from the definition [...] the most characteristic features, reducing it to a notion so general as to convey very little" (Ramat, 1984: 65).

This point is well illustrated by the attempts to formulate a general definition of the category of subject. If it remains within the limits of a given language, a definition of the subject can rely on a definite set of exclusive formal properties — of necessary and sufficient conditions of the formal order.[113] If it aims at generality, on the other hand, a definition of the subject is compelled to rely on extragrammatical correlations of the conceptual and discursive order — that is, to correlations between subjecthood and agentivity, topicality and referential autonomy — which are no more than probabilistic.[114] Keenan's universal definition of the subject, for instance, is based on a list of "pragmatic, semantic, or syntactic" properties which tend to be "characteristic"[115] of subjects across languages (Keenan, 1976: 311–312). As the true obstacles towards a generalisation of the category of subject are not its characteristic functions but its language-specific grammatical form, however, it is no wonder that Comrie's definition (1981: 101) cuts the Gordian knot by dropping any reference to grammatical properties: "the prototype of subject represents the intersection of agent and topic, i. e. the clearest instances of subjects, cross-linguistically, are agents which are also topics" (Comrie, 1981: 101).

Once more, the typological approach tends to highlight general conceptual and discursive functions at the expense of language-specific grammatical structures, for the good reason that the function is constant while the grammatical form is variable. But it is none the less true that a strictly functional perspective, if it is adequate in the area of punctual coding, misses the essential point about the language-specific construction of the process in the area of relational coding. More generally, it leaves aside the question of significance, that is, the question about the extent and limits of the shaping power of language-specific grammatical structures. If we shift our attention from typological comparison to the question of significance, the critical variable is precisely the presence and firmness of a language-specific network of grammatical relations. In order to answer the relevant question about significance — to what extent a complex meaning is constructed and to what extent it is simply brought to expression by grammatical structures — one has to identify, for any language, a core of grammatical relations which are at one and the same time grounded in formal grammatical structures and independent of the conceptual properties of the organised contents. Insofar as the conditions of significance are at issue, therefore, a functional category such as the subject is relevant only to the extent that it is univocally identified, for a given language, within autonomous networks of grammatical relations.[116]

From such a perspective, general definitions of functional categories like Comrie's are inadequate. The problem with such definitions is not so much their being multi-factor and prototypical,[117] as the fact that probabilistic extra-grammatical criteria miss the essential point about functional categories — the shaping force they draw from their formal roots. On the other hand, a purely formal characterisation of functional categories, if it justifies their effective power of shaping concepts, is by definition language-specific, if not even construction-specific (see Croft, 2001: 46), and eludes generalization: generalisation is certainly possible, but only *a posteriori* and across typologically similar languages.

Thus, as far as the general question of the form-meaning relation is concerned, a sort of complementarity principle governs linguistic description. If the question of significance is at issue, what is needed is a finely tuned description of the conditions under which a given language — or a group of similar languages — builds up a nuclear network of autonomous grammatical relations. A deep insight into the ideation of meanings is attained at the expense of cross-linguistic generalisation. Typological comparison, on the other hand, requires a previous, independent definition of extra-grammatical functions, a move which naturally tends to reduce the language-specific grammatical structures to the passive role of instruments of expression, underestimating their constructive power. Wide-ranging cross-linguistic comparison is attained at the expense of an accurate definition of the conditions of significance.

Two perpendicular perspectives appear at first sight to be incompatible. In fact, this is not really the case. If the form and the extent of the functional core are language-specific data, we can reasonably hypothesize that any language has at its disposal the formal means for constructing a core of independent grammatical relations capable of shaping independent meaning connections. The fact that this aim is achieved by precisely such categories as subject and object is a language-specific datum, restricted to a given group of languages. But the fact that a network of functional categories has the function of providing the construction of processes with a strong mould is possibly a general fact about languages whose extent and formal properties are open to cross-linguistic examination. If the aptitude to shape processes through grammatical relations is recognised as a real function of language, an explicit enquiry into the conditions of significance, beside its general interest for a "philosophy of symbolic forms" (Cassirer, 1923(1953)), opens up a new frontier to typological comparison (see Chapter 12, §2).

4. Digging out the roots of meaning: The idea of philosophical grammar

> Then it will no longer be necessary to speak of 'philosophical problems'
> for one will speak philosophically concerning all problems,
> that is: clearly and meaningfully (Schlick)

Though involving linguistic structures and having important implications for linguistic description, the question about significance has a typically philosophical flavour, due to its content and, above all, to its method.

Though playing an essential role in the ideation of the meanings of complex linguistic expressions, the systematic bases of inferencing are not language-specific structures, but general conceptual structures. Though typically refined and modulated by language specific forms of expression, the very core of our basic conceptual equipment is not the property of any particular speech community, but is shared by many. Its elucidation is not the task of linguistic description but forms the object of a philosophical analysis. For this reason, a grammar that includes significance within its scope is a philosophical grammar, that is, a grammar that integrates the descriptive tools of formal grammar with an explicit grammar of concepts.

On the other hand, philosophy is characterised not so much by a specific subject matter as by a specific style of enquiry. Philosophy is firstly defined by a habit of thought — the habit of challenging the hidden assumptions that lie at the root of cognitive and practical enterprises. In the specific field of significance, it is the task of philosophy — and of the philosophical component of a philosophical grammar — to call into question the tacit assumptions about the form-meaning relationship. What we propose to call philosophical grammar, thus, is not a new model of grammar launched onto an overcrowded market. It is a way of analyzing complex expressions and their complex meanings explicitly centred on the question of significance, that is, the question about the formal and conceptual conditions for complex meanings, and their actual ideation thanks to the complex interplay of formal grammatical structures and shared conceptual structures.[118]

The rich and changing interaction between the structures of linguistic expressions and concepts which lies at the root of complex meanings is not normally focused on and analysed in linguistic research, but simply made the object of tacit assumptions.

The relationship between language-specific syntactic structures and conceptual structures is traditionally considered by linguists as a one-way relationship between an active domain and a passive domain. The active domain displays and constructs specific and autonomous structures, and shapes the configuration of the passive one. Once this premise is taken for granted, only two issues are left: either linguistic forms are taken as primitive and autonomous structures which shape a conceptual purport devoid as such of any independent structure, or conceptual structures are taken as primitive and autonomous, and assumed to be simply brought to expression and put into perspective by instrumental linguistic forms.

Even when they are treated as primitive and autonomous structures, moreover, conceptual structures are generally reduced to cognitive structures, that is, to simplified models of empirical things and situations — to "distillations"[119] of empirical data.

The guiding idea of the present study is that both these assumptions are wrong, and impose heavy limitations on semantic description. On the one hand, the ideation of complex meanings cannot be reduced to a unilateral imposition of form, be it on the part of grammatical structures or on the part of conceptual structures, but is the outcome of a variable interaction between two autonomous orders of structures, each characterised by its own form and capable to a given extent of imposing a form. Conceptual structures, on the other hand, are formed by different layers, and cognitive models are only one of these layers, albeit a significant one. Not any concept and conceptual structure is so because it is a cognitive content. In particular, we shall see that consistency criteria cannot be defined as cognitive contents in any sense. They are not known in the everyday sense of the word, but silently relied upon in practical behaviour.

The continuation of the present work is planned according to this guiding idea.

Part II can be considered the *pars destruens* of the project. It aims at differentiating the non-linguistic factors of significance, that is, the heterogeneous layers of conceptual structures involved in the ideation of complex meanings, both from each other and from language-specific grammatical and lexical structures.

Part III is designed to form the *pars construens*. Once conceptual structures have been carefully differentiated and defined, we are ready to analyse the rich and manifold functional interaction, both co-operative and conflictual, between all the different factors which are engaged in a common task — the ideation of complex meanings — at the level of simple and complex sentence structures.

4.1 *Pars destruens*: from lexical and cognitive structures to consistency criteria

According to our hypothesis, conceptual structures cannot be reduced to cognitive models — to simplified schemes of things and processes founded on experience. A careful analysis identifies at least two layers of conceptual structures, which can easily be differentiated on the basis of their nature and functions.

Cognitive structures, which define the typical profile of things and processes, are certainly the most familiar kind of conceptual structures. Providing general and occasional knowledge with its organising principles, they form the conceptual skeleton of our direct experience. Both contingent cognitive contents and general cognitive structures, however, are by definition consistent. Now, the consistency of cognitive structures and contents is not simply a matter of fact — it is a question of lawfulness, and therefore depends on a more basic layer of conceptual structures holding as consistency criteria.[120]

The layman confidently applies this tacit system of conceptual categories and relations that secure conceptual lawfulness, and takes consistency as a self-evident fact. An exhaustive conceptual analysis, however, cannot be satisfied with describing consistent concepts as they are commonly assumed in everyday life. It has to question their consistency, make explicit the system of restrictions on which it is based and, above all, clarify their exact nature and functions.

4.1.1 *Consistency and well-formedness*

One of the leading ideas of the present research is that consistency plays in the content plane the same role as well-formedness in syntax. Accordingly, consistency criteria form the most systematic and "grammatical" kind of conceptual structures — the true counterpart of formal syntactic structures in the field of concepts.

Both consistency and well-formedness are attributed to a complex object against the background of a system of restrictions shared *a priori*. In the latter case, this system of restrictions belongs to a grammar. In the former, according to our hypothesis, it belongs to a shared natural ontology. Just as grammar is the very domain of formal lawfulness, natural ontology governs a substantial-conceptual kind of lawfulness, and can therefore be considered a true syntax of concepts. Just as formal syntax imposes a set of restrictions on the combination of forms, natural ontology imposes a set of restrictions on the combination of concepts. Just like an intuitive judgement of well-formedness, an intuitive judgement of consistency is easily accessible to any competent subject. In both cases, however, a full account of its basis requires the accurate and explicit description of a complex system of categories and relations.

Consistency is a property of either a piece of behaviour or the content of a complex expression — typically a sentence. It refers to the absence of contradiction, or more generally of conflict, in it. Though attributed to an object in isolation, consistency and its negative counterpart, that is, conflict, are not inherent properties of this object, but relational properties that qualify this object with reference to a system of external constraints. A piece of behaviour or the content of an expression are consistent if they meet these restrictions, inconsistent if they do not. According to our shared natural ontology, for instance, a person addressing another person behaves consistently, whereas a person addressing a being of the inanimate world — a tree, a rock, the moon, for instance — behaves inconsistently. The same system of restrictions tells us which linguistic expressions frame a consistent content and which do not. The content of *John kissed Mary*, for instance, is consistent with our natural ontology, while *The Sunrise kissed my Chrysalis* (Dickinson) is not.

4.1.2 *Consistency and coherence*

The relational nature of consistency — its relying on an independent system of restrictions — can better be grasped through a comparison with the cognate concept of coherence.[121]

If consistency is a relational property of an object in isolation — a piece of behaviour or an expression — against the background of an external system of criteria, coherence is the property of a relationship that rests on immanent principles. Coherence can apply either to the relationship between an atomic message and its context, or, more typically, to the relationship between the co-occurring utterances intended to form a unitary text. Unlike the consistency of a sentence meaning, the coherence of an act of utterance or a text does not depend on a set of *a priori* external requirements, but on purely internal criteria, which are as contingent as the textual configuration itself. A text is not coherent because it fits some kind of grammar holding independent of it, but because its parts fit one another, that is, can be interpreted as co-operating in attaining a unitary communicative goal.[122] Insofar as it requires the evaluation of a complex meaning against an external system of criteria, consistency presupposes meaningfulness, and therefore cannot be considered a necessary condition for the significance of expressions. An inconsistent expression is none the less a significant expression (on this point, see Chapter 4, §2). Though relying on immanent and contingent conditions, coherence is an essential property of texts. An incoherent array of utterances is not a text. Coherence "is not a *qualitas* of texts, but their *quidditas*, the property which constitutes their textuality" (Conte, 1988: 29).

4.1.3 *What are consistency criteria?*

However central in our spontaneous thought, consistency criteria are by far the least known layer of conceptual structures. Traditionally, consistency criteria have always been reduced, both by linguists and philosophers, either to linguistic — syntactic or lexical — structures, or to cognitive models. In both cases, consistency criteria are not analysed, but simply assumed as known. In both cases, an essential property of consistency criteria gets lost: in the first case, their substantial nature; in the second, their forming a system of non-empirical structures that hold *a priori.*

Though substantial like the former and holding *a priori* like the latter, consistency criteria are neither cognitive nor linguistic structures. According to our hypothesis, consistency criteria form the core of a natural ontology — of a system of shared conceptual categories and structures of practical import which silently govern our consistent behaviour. They circumscribe the consistent conceptual domain of conceivable things and processes, open to both language-specific lexical organisation and cognitive modelling and processing. The *pars destruens* of this study is thus mainly concerned with identifying and locating consistency criteria. A complete map of the manifold factors of significance, both language-specific and conceptual, can be drawn only after a rigorous definition of the structure and role of consistency criteria with regard to both language-specific and cognitive structures.

4.2 *Pars construens*: The interplay of syntactic structures and conceptual structures

The essential question about significance may be framed in two ways. The first takes the form of an absolute alternative: is the connection of complex meanings the achievement of formal syntactic structures, or of autonomous conceptual structures brought to expression by linguistic forms? The second is a matter of degree, and the answer is open to a variable balance between the two factors: to what extent is the structure of a complex meaning the outcome of the shaping power of autonomous syntactic structures, and to what extent is it an autonomous conceptual structure brought to expression by linguistic forms?

The second form of the question rests on precisely the presupposition that the first denies. The inner form of a complex meaning is seen as a composite object, which is the product of grammatical structures up to a given point, and reflects the structure of complex concepts from this point onward. This, in turn, is conceivable only if each factor of significance, be it formal or conceptual, is assumed to be fully autonomous. Structural autonomy is the *conditio sine qua non* of functional interaction. It is on this point that the project of a philosophical grammar calls into question the assumptions of both formal and functional paradigms.

Within a formal paradigm, the autonomy of syntax is generally proclaimed at the expense of the autonomy of concepts. The most striking example of such an attitude is early generative grammar, which opposes the creative power of syntactic structures to a shapeless conceptual purport. Chomsky's statement that "grammar is autonomous and independent of meaning" (Chomsky, 1957: 17) is to be taken in its strongest sense. Besides forming an autonomous linguistic level, independent of the organized contents, syntactic structures are fully responsible for the organization of complex meanings:[123] the syntactic structure of a sentence "*uniquely* determines its semantic interpretation" (Chomsky, 1966: 5). As a consequence, no significant information about the structure of complex meanings may be gathered from an independent analysis of conceptual data. The relationship between syntactic structures and complex meanings is a one-way relationship, which "can only be studied after the syntactic structure has been determined on independent grounds" (Chomsky, 1957: 17, note 4).

This assumption of the formalist paradigm — the idea that concepts have no structure independent of linguistic shaping, and therefore conceptual content plays no active role in connecting complex meanings — is supported by arguments that are drawn exclusively from the observation of the nuclear layers of sentence structures, where the shaping power of syntactic structures is really insensitive to the organised conceptual contents. But the specific form of interaction between syntactic forms and concepts which takes place within the nuclear layers cannot be generalised to cover the whole structure of the sentence. Outside the functional core organised by grammatical relations, the autonomous structure of concepts plays an active role in the connection of complex meanings, for it governs the structural configuration of the expression and motivates the inferential enrichment of undercoded connections.

The extreme formalism of early generative grammar raised an antithetical reaction of comparable intensity. If thirty years ago the two opposing fronts were occupied essentially by the two main tendencies of generative grammar, the place of generative semantics has been taken over by functional and cognitive linguistics.[124] Within a functional and cognitive paradigm, linguistic expressions are conceivable only as instruments for expression and communication. According to Dik (1989(1997: 8)), "Semantics is regarded as instrumental with respect to pragmatics, and syntax as instrumental with respect to semantics. In this view there is no room for something like an 'autonomous' syntax. On the contrary, to the extent that a clear division can be made between syntax and semantics at all, syntax is there for people to be able to form complex expressions for conveying complex meanings, and such meanings are there for people to be able to communicate in subtle and different ways". Cognitive grammar, for its part, "takes the radical position that grammar *reduces* to the structuring and symbolization of conceptual content and thus has no autonomous existence at all" (Langacker, 1993: 465). The structure of complex meanings, accordingly, is not shaped by linguistic structures, but iconically mirrors the autonomous configuration of complex conceptual structures. In Halliday's view, the grammatical structure of the sentence can only be defined on the basis of the structure of the process it expresses: it "represents a configuration of roles, or syntactic functions, a configuration which is not arbitrary since it represents very clearly the meaning of the sentence as a set of options in the semantic system" (Halliday, 1978: 45).

In spite of such emphatic statements, the functional position on syntax is in fact less extreme than the formalist position on concepts. From a formalist standpoint, concepts are assumed to be shapeless, and *a fortiori* devoid of shaping power. Functional and cognitive linguists cannot go so far as to deny the reality of syntactic structures which, being language-specific, are by definition autonomous, at least to a certain extent. This point is well illustrated by Durie (1995: 282): "there can be a temptation to think that in exposing the links between grammar and discourse constraints we have done away with grammar altogether, that a relatively distinct module 'syntax' has simply ceased to exist". Such an extreme move, however, is much more than is required by the functional paradigm: "It is quite possible for a formal structure to have a relatively independent and self-contained existence as a structure, to be subject to formal analysis and representation, and yet to be significantly constrainded over time by functional factors".[125]

The concept of autonomy is a complex one, which can be defined in many ways and with many different implications (see for instance Croft, 1995; Newmeyer, 1998: Chapter 2). Grammar in general, and syntactic forms in particular, can be considered autonomous either from the structure of concepts — from the "semiotic function" in Croft's terms — or from the socially shared functions of language, or "external function". Autonomy, in turn, may be conceived of either in a loose way, implying that grammar contains "isolated examples of arbitrary syntactic patterning" (Newmeyer, 1998: 29), or in a stricter sense, implying that syntax forms an immanent system whose form is motivated neither by the structure of concepts nor by language's social functions. As Newmeyer (1998: 31) puts it, "the question is whether the relationship between purely formally defined elements is so systematic that a grammar should accord a central place to formalizing the relationship among these elements without reference to their meanings or functions".

More or less radical versions of the autonomy principle are certainly compatible with a functional stance. According to Durie (1995) and Newmeyer (1998), it would not be inconsistent for a functionalist to endorse even the strictly interpreted version of autonomy.[126] Looked at from the standpoint of significance, however, the question of autonomy acquires a further dimension. One has to ask not only what is autonomous, from what and to what extent, but also with what implications for the interaction between linguistic forms and concepts when complex meanings are actually shaped in sentences. What is really at issue at this point is not so much whether expressions have an autonomous form, and even a systematic autonomous form, but the consequences of this form upon the articulation of complex meanings.

Now, the concept of form may be conceived of in two different ways, either passively, as a static disposition of elements, or actively, as a shaping power — either as *ergon* or as *energeia*, in Humboldt's terms.[127] To admit that syntactic structures have a static form, and even an autonomous and systematic static form, does not amount to admitting that they have the power to impose their form on concepts. It is precisely on this issue that the functional paradigm fails: all autonomous syntactic structures are allowed to do is to express the structure of states of affairs defined in conceptual terms, and impose a given perspective on them.

If it is systematically connected to significance, autonomy appears in a new light. Traditionally, the question of autonomy is dealt with in relation to the virtual grammatical system: "The central question, of course, is *how* grammar can be both autonomous and externally motivated" (Newmeyer (1998: 366–67). Put in these terms, the opposition between formal autonomy and conceptual motivation seems absolute. If it is displaced into the structure of actual meaningful sentences, however, the static opposition turns into a dynamic competition.[128] When engaged in the ideation of complex meanings, autonomous syntactic patterns have to face the pressure of organised concepts. The natural outcome of this competition for form is some point of equilibrium between the tendency of syntax to mould concepts and the pressure of independent concepts towards expression.

In order to be effective as shaping forms, syntactic structures have to be autonomous *qua* structures, in the sense that their formal architecture has to be sheltered from the pressure of the organized concepts. Conversely, however, syntactic structures need autonomy only to the extent that they really impose a mould on concepts, that is, in a limited, though qualified core of sentence structures. Outside this core, the terms of the question are reversed, and it is at this point that the question about the autonomy of forms becomes inseparable from the parallel question about the autonomy of concepts. Just as nuclear syntactic forms shape concepts, peripheral syntactic structures are shaped by autonomous conceptual structures. This implies that concepts can work as a mould for forms just as forms can work as a mould for concepts.

When we speak of autonomy for both grammatical and conceptual structures, we not only assume that each structural domain has its peculiar static form — its peculiar syntax. We also assume that each has its own shaping power — that is, each plays an active role, within its own limits, in the ideation of the inner form of processes. The structure of a complex meaning is the outcome of an interaction — either co-operative or conflictual — between two competing forces, that is, a formal syntax and a syntax of concepts. The peculiar outcome of this contest may be empirically determined for each kind of structure and for each particular language, but its general conditions can be assumed as a universal manifestation of the twofold identity — both formally self-contained and functionally engaged — of language.

Part II: The conceptual factors of significance

Consistency criteria, lexical structures, cognitive models and data

Introduction

This section opens with an intuitive presentation of consistency criteria, followed by a brief survey of the treatment consistency criteria have received within philosophical and linguistic thinking (Chapter 4).

This sketch seeks to draw the reader's attention to a significant cleavage between the role played by consistency criteria in organizing our consistent behaviour and the place accorded to them within philosophical and linguistic analysis. Most philosophers and linguists agree in restricting the relevance of consistency criteria to the field of language. On such a premise, consistency criteria are traditionally described as kinds of syntactic or semantic structure. When the essential link with linguistic structures is called into question, however, consistency criteria tend to be confined within cognitive structures and data. According to our hypothesis, all these approaches neglect the role of consistency criteria as a system of tacit background assumptions — a natural ontology — which underlies consistent behaviour, and thus consistent discourse and knowledge.

The analysis of the complex relationship holding between consistency criteria and grammatical structures — and, above all, syntactic structures — takes the form of a critical discussion of Carnap's conception of consistency criteria as a fine-grained kind of syntactic structure (Chapter 5).

The result of our analysis is to highlight the formal skeleton of natural ontology, whose structure is not conceivable without taking into account its systematic correlation with the essential syntactic structures of noun phrases and sentences. An accurate definition of the formal side of natural ontology, for its part, leaves its conceptual content completely aside. The organisation of natural ontology into such categories as concrete and abstract entities, animate and inanimate beings, human and non-human creatures, is independent of its formal skeleton and, hence, independent of the syntactic structures of a given language or group of languages.

When the substantive content of consistency criteria is taken into account, there is an almost inevitable tendency to think of the lexicon as its natural home. Before discussing the relationship between consistency criteria and lexicon, however, we first need to clarify the notion itself of lexicon (Chapter 6).

If it is examined more closely, the concept of lexicon splits into two structurally heterogeneous, though functionally complementary objects. On the one hand, the lexicon may be seen, along with phonological and grammatical structure, as a formal, language-specific structure. Considered from a functional point of view, on the other hand, the lexicon appears to be a repository of substantive definitions, whose structures and cognitive content are largely independent of language-specific lexical structures.

The content of this chapter fits in with our project at two different levels — a local one and a general one.

The study of the relationship between lexical structures and lexical information is in itself a relevant topic for a philosophical study of language. At the level of lexical analysis, the general question of philosophical grammar takes the specific form of a question about the formal and cognitive roots of atomic concepts. What is focused on is to what extent the structure of atomic concepts is shaped by the language-specific formal organisation of lexical paradigms and lexical solidarities, and to what extent it rests on an independent cognitive categorisation. Or, to put it another way, to what extent lexical structures can be considered as means of expression of independent cognitive structures, and to what extent they really construct specific concepts.

At the same time, the clarification of the relationship between lexical structures and cognitive categories is only a preliminary step towards a careful exploration of the conceptual roots of significance, and in particular of the nature and functions of consistency criteria. Once lexical structures and cognitive structures have been carefully distinguished, and their interaction made explicit, we can go back to the general question of consistency criteria and formulate it more precisely: are consistency criteria a kind of lexical structure, or a kind of cognitive structure, or neither? There are many arguments for concluding that consistency criteria belong neither to lexical structures nor to lexical definitions, but circumscribe from the outside the territory of consistent concepts occupied by both lexical structures and lexical definitions (Chapter 7).

If consistency criteria are neither linguistic nor cognitive structures, but rather autonomous conceptual structures, what exactly is their nature? Consistency criteria can be described as a set of background assumptions underlying our shared natural attitude towards the world, which provide consistent behaviour with its conceptual frame (Chapter 8).

Looked at from this general point of view, natural ontology displays a meaningful analogy with grammar. Natural ontology imposes conceptual restrictions upon our practical and theoretical acts of categorisation in order to ensure consistency, just as grammar imposes formal restrictions upon our production of linguistic utterances in order to ensure grammaticality. On these grounds, natural ontology can rightly be defined as a grammar of concepts. Natural ontology cannot be reduced to a given cognitive picture of the world, just as grammar cannot be reduced to a given text or discourse. Natural ontology is the canvas outside whose frame no consistent picture of the world can be painted.

Chapter 4

Consistency criteria within philosophic and linguistic reflexion

1. The natural experience of consistency criteria

How does one kill fear, I wonder?
How do you shoot a spectre through the heart,
slash off its spectral head, take it by its spectral throat?
[...] An enterprise for a dream, my master! (Conrad)

Our everyday behaviour is governed by a complex system of restrictions — by a natural ontology — according to which it can be considered either consistent or non-consistent. Looked at from within our shared ontology, for instance, a person addressing another person behaves consistently, whilst a person addressing the moon behaves inconsistently. According to the same criteria, the content the expression *John kissed Mary looks consistent, whilst The Sunrise kissed my Chrysalis* (E. Dickinson) does not.

These guiding rails of our everyday life lie so deep in our spontaneous behaviour as to escape expression and even notice. Consistency criteria perform their duty in silence. Their content is seldom brought to expression, and if so only occasionally, and in particular circumstances: for instance, one may imagine an adult explaining to a child that a piece of wood does not feel pain when he cuts it.

This lack of expression is not just an empirical fact about consistency criteria, but an essential condition for their function. Consistency criteria are effective insofar as they are relied upon without being called into question, and expression is the first step towards doubt, enquiry, proof or argument. The path from doubt to proof or argument is the typical path of positive knowledge and disputable beliefs. But positive knowledge and disputable beliefs are part of our experience, the consistency of which depends on the solidity of underlying, unquestioned criteria.

1.1 The observation of consistency criteria in linguistic expressions

As consistency criteria escape direct experience, the only way to analyse them is to pay attention to the effects of their silent work, that is, to focus on instances of transgression that ignore, or intentionally break, essential conceptual boundaries. Among these instances, inconsistent linguistic expressions enjoy an indisputable privilege.

Inconsistent expressions are a very familiar landmark of our symbolic landscape, both in ordinary speech and in literary texts. The most typical examples of figures of content, and above all metaphors, are first of all instances of inconsistent utterances, and both ordinary speech and poetic texts are crowded with inconsistent entities and inconsistent processes:

> Sunk are the turrets of cloud into the ocean of dreams;
> While in a haven of rest my heart is riding at anchor,
> Held by the chains of love, held by the anchors of trust
> (Longfellow)

Experience of inconsistent expression is obviously more wide-ranging than experience of inconsistent behaviour. Direct experience of inconsistent behaviour is accessible only when human beings are involved. As subjects of ontological categorisation, human beings can behave inconsistently as well as consistently. A man, for instance, can take his stool for a horse ready for a ride, or his toothbrush for a barking dog; he can ask the moon a question, just as he can a friend:

> Che fai tu, luna, in ciel? dimmi, che fai,
> Silenziosa luna? (Leopardi)

But this does not hold for the universe of non-human beings. As passive objects of ontological categorisation, non-human beings cannot transcend the bounds of consistency in their observable behaviour: the moon, for instance, cannot answer a poet's question. It is only when we cross the borders of symbolic experience, and in particular of linguistic expression, that inconsistent behaviour is open to the whole universe of beings, and the foundations of consistency can be explored in their full depth. The direct experience of a speaking stream, for instance, is out of reach; but nothing prevents us from describing such behaviour in words:

> But the little stream would not be comforted, and still kept telling its unintelligible secret of some very mournful mystery that had happened — or making a prophetic lamentation about something that was yet to happen — within the verge of the dismal forest (Hawthorne)

Apart from being incomparably richer, our experience of inconsistency in the field of linguistic expression differs in quality from our experience of it in human behaviour. Whereas inconsistent human behaviour is generally seen as pathological, our contact with inconsistent utterances is indissolubly bound up with our most stimulating cognitive and aesthetic experiences.[129] For all these reasons, a systematic analysis of a wide sample of inconsistent utterances provides the most straightforward access to the structure and content of consistency criteria encapsulated within our shared natural ontology.

1.2 Consistency criteria and linguistic expression: Calling into question an essential link

The observation of inconsistency in linguistic expressions and the occasion it provides for a wide-ranging exploration of consistency criteria show once more that the links between consistency, natural ontology and linguistic expression are very close, so that it is very difficult even to imagine either our linguistic expressions uprooted from natural ontology or vice-versa. But this circumstance may easily lead to a misleading conclusion — namely, to the conclusion that consistency criteria, besides having deep and essential links with linguistic structures, are themselves a kind of linguistic structure. This is precisely what happens in linguistic and philosophical analysis.

If we compare the role played by consistency criteria in our general experience with their prevailing treatment by linguists and philosophers, we cannot help seeing a huge disproportion. From the layman's point of view, it would be natural to expect the enquiry about consistency criteria to have taken the form of a description, aimed at analysing the most basic conceptual structures and relations, at elucidating the way they actually work in shaping and orienting our practical and symbolic behaviour, and, finally, at clarifying their complex intertwining with such connected fields as linguistic structures, verbal communication and empirical knowledge. In fact, the enquiry about consistency criteria narrows its scope to the linguistic field, taking the form of a question about the relation between consistency, grammaticality and significance of complex linguistic expressions.

A problem of conceptual analysis, with interesting and essential links with linguistics and philosophy of language, becomes a technical problem of philosophy of language and linguistics and, within these restricted domains, of lexicology or syntax: how to provide a descriptive device — a generative grammar, or a logical grammar — with a set of rules capable of describing the whole set of well-formed sentences while ruling out both grammatically ill-formed strings of words and inconsistent complex meanings. Besides implying a severe underestimation of the role played by consistency criteria in governing our form of life, such a restrictive attitude contains a logical mistake. Contiguity in experience does not entail structural inherence. The fact that natural ontology and linguistic expression are so deeply connected does not imply that consistency criteria belong to linguistic structures. The fact that many Greek vases were found when excavating the Etruscan site of Spina, to take a similar case, certainly shows how deep the links between the two peoples were, but would not be taken by any professional archaeologist as an argument for concluding that the vases are Etruscan. In both cases, the question remains fully open to investigation.

As we shall see later (Chapter 8, §2.4), the prevailing attitude among linguists and philosophers can be justified on historical grounds. The study of the connection between consistency criteria and language is a chapter in the history of the linguistic turn in philosophy — of the project of grounding the propositions of philosophy, mathematics and empirical sciences in shared linguistic structures, rather than in independent structures of thought undermined by psychologism. Given such a premise, the inclusion of consistency criteria among linguistic structures has to be interpreted as an attempt to secure them from an empirical and psychological drift.

2. Philosophy of language: Significance and consistency

> Exsurge psalterium et cithara
> exsurgam diluculo (Psalm 107)

The question about consistency makes its entry into the philosophy of language in close connection with the problem of significance, that is, of the formal and conceptual conditions a string of words has to fulfil in order to form a meaningful linguistic expression. The framework of such an enquiry about the bounds of sense, moreover, is not a general reflection about language as a symbolic system as such, with its specific structures and its full range of heterogeneous functions and actual uses, but about language restricted to one of its most specialized and peculiar uses — language as the elective tool for constructing and communicating empirical knowledge. In order to be an adequate means for encoding contents of knowledge, a linguistic utterance must have the property of carrying a proposition that can be empirically tested — either verified or falsified. This in turn requires consistency.

The very narrow scope of these philosophical discussions is frustrating for a linguist interested in the wide-ranging, real uses of language, and naturally leads one to ask whether the whole matter is really worth considering. In spite of this, I find two arguments for doing so. First, the connection between significance and conceptual consistency, which is a central issue of the present research, was first focused on in precisely these terms. Second, and above all, a widely shared common-sense view about the whole matter is still constrained by the turn imposed on it during the first half of the last century. To give only one example of this widespread attitude, the question of conflictual complex meanings is seen in a strikingly similar way from two totally opposite fronts. Both Chomsky (1957; 1965) and the rhetoricians of the Groupe μ (1970(1982)) consider metaphors as violations of linguistic rules, passively inheriting Carnap's (1932) view of inconsistency as a form of grammatical deviance.

2.1 Schlick: significance and verifiability

The upgrading of the restricted, though respectable, function of language as a vehicle of empirical knowledge is well illustrated by Schlick (1936). Schlick identifies significance — the aptness of a complex linguistic utterance to carry any meaning whatsoever — with verifiability — the aptness of a linguistic expression to carry a proposition open to empirical control: "Stating the meaning of a sentence amounts to stating the rules according to which the sentence is to be used, and this is the same as stating the way in which it can be verified (or falsified). The meaning of a proposition is the method of its verification" (Schlick, 1936: 341). Under such a condition, if a sentence is not verifiable, it is *ipso facto* meaningless.

Verifiability is not a factual property a given utterance happens to possess for contingent reasons, but an essential property resting on systematic, structural grounds: "Verifiability means possibility of verification" (347); "possibility of verification which is relevant to meaning cannot be of the empirical sort; it cannot be established *post festum*. You have to be sure of it before you can consider the empirical circumstances" (349). "Verifiability, which is the necessary and sufficient condition of meaning, is a possibility of the logical order; it is created by constructing the sentence in accordance with the rules by which its terms are defined" (351). Conversely, "logical impossibility" — i. e. failure in verifiability — is due to "a discrepancy between the definitions of our terms and the way in which we use them" (350).

This last statement connects verifiability with consistency. Verifiability does not entirely coincide with consistency, first of all because the structural grounds of verifiability include the syntactic criteria of well-formedness. What is certain, however, is that consistency is a prerequisite of verifiability — that verifiability presupposes consistency.[130] Looked at from within such a theoretical framework, inconsistent utterances can only be taken as meaningless utterances, as instances of nonsense. Their use in discourse deserves a philosophical, and even a moral censure. If they are taken seriously, inconsistent utterances are the most effective Trojan horse for smuggling metaphysics into the field of philosophy and science.

2.2 Carnap: Inconsistency as meaninglessness

An explicit connection between significance and consistency, designed for protecting linguistic use from metaphysical slides, is made by Carnap (1932).

The topic of Carnap's paper, which is representative of a whole intellectual tradition, is the explication of logico-linguistic criteria for discriminating significant strings of words and phrases which form true, meaningful sentences, from apparently similar non-significant strings, which do not. Two possibilities of meaninglessness are taken into account by Carnap: a string can be meaningless either if it lacks, so to speak, raw material — if it contains one or more meaningless words — or if it lacks form — if it arranges meaningful words in an incorrect way. While the first family of meaningless sentences could encourage the idea that the meaningfulness of single words is a sufficient condition for the significance of complex sentences, the second draws attention to the essential role played by structural arrangements of words and phrases into sentences.

A first, obvious structural factor of significance is the syntactic organization of complex strings of words: a lack of syntactic organization can only end in meaninglessness. A casual array of words which violates the syntactic rules on co-occurrence of words belonging to distinct grammatical classes obviously fails in constructing a meaningful sentence. Carnap's example is a string of words which fills with a conjunction a slot fit for a noun phrase: *Caesar ist und* (*Caesar is and*).

According to Carnap, however, syntactic well-formedness is a necessary but not sufficient condition for meaningfulness, for the syntax of natural languages is too generous in certifying significance. In particular, natural syntax ends by smuggling into the realm of significance the whole family of inconsistent strings of words and phrases which violate the rules of conceptual agreement between the constituent parts. In spite of the disposition of their constituents, which gives them the appearance of true sentences, inconsistent sentences are considered meaningless by Carnap: "The word sequence 'Caesar is a general', e. g., is formed in accordance with the rules of syntax. But, now, the word sequence (2) [*Caesar is a prime number*] is likewise syntactically correct, for it has the same grammatical form as the sentence just mentioned. Nevertheless, (2) is meaningless. "Prime number" is a predicate of numbers; it can be neither affirmed nor denied of a person" (Carnap, 1932(1959: 67–68)).

According to Carnap, conceptual inconsistency destroys signifiance to the same extent as syntactic ill-formedness. Moreover, while syntactically incorrect strings of words honestly show their naked meaninglessness, inconsistent sentences hide it under a syntactically faultless disguise: "It may happen that such a sequence of words looks like a statement [*Satz*] at first glance; in that case we call it a pseudo-statement [*Scheinsatz*]"[131](61).

In order to avoid the construction of meaningless utterances, and protect philosophical and scientific thought from nonsense and metaphysics, Carnap suggests improving the syntax of natural languages — "*grammatische Syntax*" — by what he calls a "logical syntax" — "*logische Syntax*". A logical syntax is sensitive not only to the distribution of grammatical categories — nouns, verbs, adjectives, prepositions, and so on — but also to the distribution of conceptual categories — such categories as "human" or "numeral". The most immediate way of doing so is to subcategorise predicative terms — nouns, verbs, adjectives — on the basis of their compatibility with certain sorts of arguments: "If, e.g., nouns were grammatically subdivided into several kinds of words, according as they designated properties of physical objects, of numbers etc., then the words `general' and `prime number' would belong to different word-categories, and (2) [*Caesar is a prime number*] would be just as linguistically incorrect as (1) [*Caesar is and*]" (68).

Such a "logical" complement to syntax turns out to be, in fact, a sort of grammar of concepts, sharing with linguistic grammar the status of a system of *a priori* restrictions governing the construction of sentences. If actually built up, a syntax of concepts would, in spite of the narrowness of its purported scope, perfectly coincide with an analytical description of the whole network of conceptual categories and relations — solidarities and incompatibilities —

which form natural ontology. Within this programme, natural ontology is thus virtually open to philosophical analysis.

If Carnap's project leaks somewhere, it is at the stage of preliminary assumptions about language and significance. The subordination of significance to consistency, and its direct consequence — the meaninglessness of inconsistent utterances — are not supported by our shared, direct experience of texts and discourses. Literary texts, ephemeral speech acts, and even scientific texts are packed with inconsistent sentences. Looked at from a purely linguistic and semantic point of view, most metaphors and other figures of meaning are in fact instances of inconsistent complex meanings. Inconsistent utterances are not generally received as if they were instances of nonsense, but as if they were altogether meaningful. If our linguistic behaviour encapsulates an implicit philosophy of symbolic forms, it certainly holds inconsistency, along with consistency, as one outcome of significance — of the successful connection of various atomic meanings to form a complex one.

In spite of this, Carnap's idea of digging out the grammar of concepts governing the construction of consistent complex meanings does not entail the strict association of consistency and significance which actually led to it. On the contrary, the analysis of consistency criteria is perfectly compatible with — and is in fact no less strategic within — the hypothesis of a strong dissociation between significance and consistency. The theoretical framework for such a dissociation was set up by E. Husserl (1901).

2.3 Husserl: Counter-sense and nonsense

In his *Logical Inquiry IV*, Husserl sharply distinguishes between significance and consistency. Significance and consistency are independent properties of expressions, resting on independent orders of lawfulness and requiring independent analysis.

Significance rests on purely formal grounds, and coincides with a successful formal linkage of significant parts to form a meaningful whole, or "unified meaning" ("*einheitliche Bedeutung*"). Insofar as the formal connection of significant parts is the elective task of syntactic structures, significance depends ultimately on the syntactic well-formedness of sentences, that is, on a network of distributional restrictions imposed by syntax on formal classes of words and phrases. "Where nominal material stands, any nominal material can stand, but not adjectival, nor relational, nor completed propositional material. But where we have materials from such other categories, other material of the same kind can be put, i.e. always material from the same category and not from another" (Husserl, 1901(1970: 511–512)).

If based on the correct distribution of formal syntactic categories within the framework of a "pure grammar", significance is independent of the conceptual content of the connected meaningful parts. Accordingly, the realm of sense is open to contradictory and inconsistent meanings, grouped by Husserl under the label of counter-sense (*Widersinn*): "In such free exchange of materials within each category, false, foolish, ridiculous meanings [...] may result, but such results will necessarily be unified meanings, or grammatical expressions whose sense can be unitarily realised. When we transgress the bounds of categories, this is no longer true" (512). For instance, from a well-formed sentence like *This tree is green* we can obtain, by substitution of the noun phrase, a sentence like *This algebraic number is green.* However inconsistent, the content of the latter sentence is as well-connected as the content of its model. In both cases the meaningful parts are unified into a meaningful whole thanks to a well-formed syntactic structure — the correct distribution of syntactic categories[132] among the different syntactic positions.

Counter-sense shares with consistent meaning the aptitude to impose a unifying structure on atomic meanings. Along with consistent meaning, it contrasts with nonsense, which fails to unite atomic meanings into a whole: "one must not confound the senseless (or 'nonsensical') with the absurd (or 'counter-sensical'), though we tend to exaggerate and call the latter 'senseless', when it is rather a sub-species of the significant" (516–517). Meaninglessness — failure to join atomic senses into a molecular one — has nothing to do with conceptual lawfulness. It only depends on the collapse of syntactic structure. A string like *This but is green*, for instance, is necessarily meaningless. If nonsense is a true failure of significance — the co-occurring meaningful parts do not succeed in linking themselves into a meaningful linguistic expression — an inconsistent meaning is but an accident of successful linkage, and thus of significance.

Once inconsistency is dissociated from meaninglessness and included within the realm of meaningfulness, consistency criteria do not lose their relevance at all. Within a Husserlian framework, consistency criteria are no longer to be seen as a logical appendix to the syntactic structures of an ideal language engaged in narrowing down the set of admitted sentences. Rather, they form a system of shared conceptual categories and relations engaged in telling apart consistent and inconsistent meanings of significant sentences. Though confined within the borders of the linguistic field, a substantial step is made towards a clarification of the effective functions performed by consistency criteria.

3. Linguistics: Distribution, sense and nonsense

The approach to consistency criteria within linguistic analysis shares some essential features with their philosophic treatment. In both fields, consistency criteria are generally seen as essentially connected with linguistic structures, and their analysis overlaps, to a variable extent, the analysis of significance conditions. There is one Carnapian assumption, in particular, which linguists seem to share unanimously: consistency criteria are annexed to linguistic structure as one of its constitutive components.

The problem of consistency becomes critical within a distributional approach to sentence structure. If we share the basic idea of distribution as the relation holding between a given syntactic construction and classes of expressions fit to occur in its different positions, a question naturally arises in connection with consistency: are inconsistent environments relevant when defining the distribution of a word or phrase? To take a popular example by Chomsky, is the inconsistent co-occurrence with the noun *idea* relevant when defining the distribution of the verb *sleep*? One way of reading the history of distributional syntax is to see it as a series of tentative answers to such a question.

3.1 Early distributional syntax: Distribution and selection

The early distributional study of syntactic structures, as documented by such seminal works as Harris (1946) and Wells (1947), is essentially grounded on a classification of words and expressions into the main formal grammatical categories — partly coinciding with traditional parts of speech (noun, verb, adjective, preposition, and so on) and partly with more complex expressions (noun phrase, verb phrase, and so on) — on the basis of the syntactic environments open to each of them. If it is a necessary condition for accounting for the distributional structure of grammatically well-formed sentences, however, the classification of words and expressions into such purely grammatical categories soon proves insufficient for ensuring grammaticality. As a consequence, the distributionalist programme is very soon compelled to cope with a further subdivision of categories of words and expressions into finer subcategories, sharing common distributional properties.

Subcategorisation, however, is a complex phenomenon, involving heterogeneous criteria, partly grammatical and partly conceptual. The nouns *tree* and *idea*, for instance, can be put into different subcategories for two different reasons. On the one hand, *idea*, but not *tree*, can receive a clause as a complement — *The idea of making a long journey* vs *The tree of making a long journey*; on the other hand *tree*, but not *idea*, can be modified by a colour adjective: *A green tree* vs *A green idea*. The first distinction, formulated in terms of the syntactic environment of the head noun, aims essentially at well-formedness, and thus at formal conditions of significance; the second, formulated in terms of the conceptual environment of the noun, aims at consistency.

Realising this, Harris (1946: 178) distinguishes distribution in a narrow sense, which deals with formal categories and subcategories accounting for syntactic well-formedness, from selection, which deals with conceptual subcategories accounting for consistency. On the one hand, there are formal distributional patterns, that is, "*formulae*" which "give us the limitations upon the freedom of occurrence of morphemes in the language". On the other hand, "there are further limitations of selection among the morphemes, so that not all sequences provided by the *formulae* actually occur. Individual limitations of selection cannot be described in these *formulae*; at best, the most important among them can be stated in special lists or in the dictionary". It is as a label for consistency criteria that the phrase "selection restrictions" has become popular among linguists.

3.2 Generative grammar: Two roots of nonsense

In his seminal work, Chomsky (1957) takes up the distinction between the syntactic well-formedness of a sentence and the conceptual consistency of its meaning. As far as formal syntactic rules are concerned, an inconsistent string of words like *Colorless green ideas sleep furiously* is as well-formed as a consistent sentence like *The book seems interesting*. Inconsistency, accordingly, should not be confused with ill-formedness. Such a specimen of inconsistency as *Colorless green ideas sleep furiously*, for instance, should be distinguished from a true specimen of ill-formedness like *Furiously sleep ideas green colorless.*

This perspective upon the relationship between grammaticality, significance and consistency bears, at first sight, some resemblance to the Husserlian distinction between nonsense, a failure in grammatical connection, and counter-sense, an inconsistent issue of grammatical connection. Rather surprisingly, however, Chomsky places both ill-formed and inconsistent sentences

— non-connected meanings and connected conflictual meanings — in the realm of nonsense. The distinction between grammatical well-formedness and conceptual[133] consistency does not affect the question of significance. As Jakobson (1959(1971: 494–495)) immediately points out, this perspective on form and meaning betrays a severe underestimation of the structural strength of autonomous syntactic forms. While a well-shaped syntactic form is capable of unifying within a complex meaning even the most conflictual concepts, "actual agrammaticalness deprives an utterance of its semantic information".

However connected as complementary criteria of significance, syntactic well-formedness and conceptual consistency are none the less ascribed by Chomsky (1965) to different kinds of relevant subcategorisation: the so-called "strict subcategorisation", relevant to purely formal syntactic rules, and the system of "selection restrictions", relevant to the consistency of well-formed sentences.

Strict subcategorisation divides the main lexical categories into subclasses characterised by a specific syntactic environment. A transitive verb like *eat*, for instance, which can have a direct object, is distinguished from *like*, which requires one. *Give* and *elect* can each take two complement noun phrases, but the second, unlike the first, requires agreement between them. A verb like *know*, which can take a clause as a direct object, is distinguished from *eat*, which only accepts a noun phrase. Equally, a noun like *idea* falls into a distinct subcategory because of its taking, unlike nouns like *tree* or *gold*, a clause as a complement.

In order to state selection restrictions, nouns are subcategorised on the basis of such inherent features as "± animate", "± human", whose positive or negative value is specified by the matrix associated with each lexical item. Relational lexical categories like verbs and adjectives are in turn subcategorized in terms of contextual features, that is, of inherent features of the nouns which can occur within their immediate environment: transitive two-places verbs, for example, are classified according to the nature of their consistent subjects and objects. In line with this suggestion, a verb like *frighten* can take any kind of subject but demands an animate object; *drink*, on the other hand, requires an animate subject and an instance of concrete liquid mass as object. An adjective like *green* modifies a noun referring to any concrete object presenting an extended surface, while *deep* can modify both concrete and abstract nouns.[134]

Strict subcategorisation is obviously a matter of syntax. When looking for a proper place for selection restrictions within a generative grammar, Chomsky annexes them to syntax too, as if the grammar of natural language incorporated a natural ontology, and its generative model a sort of Carnapian logical grammar.

3.3 Generative semantics: Selection and meaning

Within the theoretical framework set up by Chomsky (1965), consistency criteria — selection restrictions — are isolated once and for all from true distributional restrictions, and a recognised borderline is irreversibly drawn within the complex and confused constellation of co-occurrence limitations. Once this has been done, linguists' attention turns towards a definition of the exact nature — syntactic or "semantic" — of consistency criteria and of their field of application.

According to McCawley, selection restrictions are not syntactic restrictions on well-formedness but conceptual conditions imposed by the meaning of atomic lexemes on the "semantic well-formedness" of molecular meanings: "If it in fact turns out that the 'selectional restrictions' of all lexical items are predictable from their meanings, then they are not restrictions on how lexical items may be combined but rather restrictions on how semantic material may be combined, i.e. restrictions on 'possible message'" (McCawley, 1970 (1971: 218)).

An argument for this hypothesis is the possible neutralisation of inconsistency within appropriate contexts: "Many so-called selectional restrictions are actually no real restrictions, since 'violations' of them are quite normal in reports of dreams, reports of other people's beliefs, and science-fiction stories" (219). To the instances quoted by McCawley, we can add negation[135] — *Papa was not a rock* (G. Eliot) — certain modalities — *Youth should be a wild rose* (K. Mansfield) — counterfactual contexts —

> It seemed to argue so wide a diffusion of her shame, that all nature knew of it; it could have caused her no deeper pang, had the leaves of the trees whispered the dark story among themselves, — had the summer breeze murmured about it, — had the wintry blast shrieked it aloud! (Hawthorne)
>
> S'i' fosse foco, arderei 'l mondo,
> s'i' fosse vento, lo tempesterei;
> s'i' fosse acqua, i' l'annegherei
> s'i' fosse Dio, mandereil'en profondo[136]
> (Cecco Angiolieri)

— and, last but not least, the creation of fictive worlds ruled by a peculiar conceptual lawfulness:

> Calumniari si quis autem voluerit,
> quod arbores loquantur, non tantum ferae,
> fictis iocari nos meminerit fabulis[137]
> (Phaedrus)

McCawley's remarks make a good case against the syntactic nature of selection restriction. While an inconsistent connection may be incorporated into a consistent utterance, no ad hoc context is able to incorporate an ungrammatical string of words — *Know you this book*? or *It depends you*, for instance — into a grammatical sentence. All we can do is to report it as a quotation within a metalinguistic context: *Bob, you can't say "It depends you"*, for instance. To state that selection restrictions do not belong to syntax, however, is not yet to define their nature in a positive way. To state their semantic nature, on the other hand, is a void claim, since the word "semantic" can refer either to the lexical structures of a given language or to more general conceptual and cognitive structures, independent of a given language (see Chapter 6).

Another line of criticism against the treatment of selection restrictions by Chomsky focuses not on their nature but on their field of application. Analysing the connection between subject and main verb, Lakoff points out that, in order to prevent inconsistency, the verb is not immediately sensitive to the inherent "syntactic properties of the head noun" in subject position, but to the "semantic" properties attributed to its potential referents by the subject noun phrase as a whole (Lakoff, 1971: 330). Making a nest, for instance, is one of the most typical actions of birds, but a dead, stuffed bird cannot possibly perform it: *Uccelli impagliati nidificavano dentro due campane di vetro* (Fogazzaro: *Stuffed birds were nesting in two glass cloches*).

Beyond its local value, such a remark casts light upon the conditions under which consistency is attained. What is at issue when consistency is checked is not the aptness of some words to occupy some syntactic positions according to some kinds of co-occurrence restriction, but the aptness of some kinds of beings to fit some kinds of roles in a process according to a shared system of conceptual restrictions.

On the one hand, the conceptual profile of a being is drawn by the whole noun phrase referring to it. Going back to the example *Stuffed birds were nesting*, what is actually at issue is not so much whether the noun *bird* has such an inherent feature as "animate", but whether the virtual referents of the subject noun phrase are animate or inanimate beings, capable or incapable of performing the action of nesting consistently. The presence of such a modifier as *stuffed* is obviously critical in defining the profile of the intended referent.

On the other hand, the consistency of a being engaged in a role depends on its position within the whole network of functional and conceptual relations which form the process. The consistency of a complex meaning is built up, and therefore at stake, at any node of its hierarchical inner structure, starting from the main nuclear connections — the only ones to be taken into account within generative grammars — right down to the most peripheral relations.

If it is true that an intransitive verb is sensitive to the whole content of a subject noun phrase, as Lakoff points out, the selectional partner of a subject is not, as a rule, the main verb, but the whole predicate, including not only the nuclear complements of the verb, but also such non-nuclear constituents as verb modifiers, instrumental or purpose expressions. A stone, for instance, can kill a man, but cannot to do so intentionally, or with a knife, or in order to steal his money. A direct object, in turn, is not immediately selected by the main verb, but is sensitive to the contribution of its modifiers: if we can hit any concrete body, for instance, we can deal a mortal blow only to animate beings.[138] What could appear prima facie as a matter of lexical selection turns out to be a global evaluation of complex and highly hierarchical meaning structures on the background of general conceptual models.

3.4 Cognitive semantics: the empirical and psychological drift

When speaking of referents and their properties, it is only too easy to think immediately of a set of empirical, factual properties of beings attained by way of knowledge. Moreover, the sort of evaluation a complex meaning undergoes for its consistency to be checked is so similar to an act of verification as to clearly suggest that it possibly involves similar criteria, namely its matching either a kind of empirical evidence or some consolidated cognitive models predicting how things normally go.

An example of precisely this kind of treatment is to be found within the framework of cognitive semantics, where selection restrictions tend to be defined as kinds of co-occurrence constraints imposed on the constituents of complex meanings by the structure of prototypical schemata of actions and events which language users acquire by way of experience. Within the cognitive framework, selection restrictions are included in lexical information, which in turn is reduced to a network of cognitive structures and empirical contents activated by the use of words. Fillmore (1977: 130), for instance, defines selection restrictions in terms of compatibility among cognitive models of events, or schemata, and linguistic frames which bring them to expression.[139]

In this way, the cognitive perspective dissociates consistency criteria from linguistic structures and is ready to analyse them as autonomous conceptual structures. This turn, however, is taken at the price of an empirical stance, which in turn implies the risk of losing sight of an essential property that consistency criteria share with linguistic structures: consistency criteria are not cognitive contents acquired by way of experience, but a system of *a priori* conditions imposed on experience. What gets entirely lost is the idea that consistency criteria form an order of lawfulness as effective in the field of conceptual consistency as grammatical lawfulness is in the field of well-formedness.

At this point, the analysis of consistency criteria seems to involve a dilemma: either they are to be considered a system of *a priori* structures, forming an order of conceptual lawfulness, and, as such, included within linguistic structures, or they are to be considered a system of conceptual structures independent of language, and therefore reduced to structures of the empirical order. Our hypothesis is that neither of these ideas is adequate: consistency criteria can both be defined as autonomous conceptual structures, independent of language, and considered, along with linguistic structures, a system of *a priori* conditions of consistent experience. In other words, conceptual structures do not reduce themselves to cognitive contents, but include a deeper layer of structures holding *a priori.*

Chapter 5

The formal framework of natural ontology

In Carnap's view, an adequate grammar should incorporate a set of consistency criteria limiting the construction of complex meanings, which amounts to saying that consistency criteria are a part of the grammatical structure of each language. If this were the case, our shared ontology would be both a formal and language-specific ontology.

Such an extreme position is hardly tenable, since the main categories involved in consistency are neither formal nor language-specific. Such categories as concrete and abstract, or animate and inanimate, or human and non-human are not formal but substantial. They are thus autonomous from the grammatical structures of a given language, and shared far beyond the borders of a given linguistic community. What may at first seem absurd, however, is often a good idea whose limits of application have been pushed too far. This is precisely the case with Carnap's idea. The idea of a formal ground for natural ontology becomes worth investigating in greater detail if one tries to clarify its limits. In particular, it makes sense to ask whether natural ontology embodies a formal kind of categorization and, if so, to what extent and within which limits this formal framework is rooted in formal grammatical categories and structures. These questions mark a first step towards a satisfactory analysis of the complex links between linguistic and conceptual structures. The hypothesis defended in this chapter is that the answer to the first question is yes, while investigating the second makes it possible to identify a deep-lying relationship between formal ontological categorisation and grammar.

Our shared ontology actually embodies a formal classification of entities based on formal kinds, independent of the substantial conceptual properties subsequently attributed to these. According to our hypothesis, the formal skeleton of natural ontology contains at least the following relevant formal kinds of entities: individuals and classes of individuals, masses and instances of masses, which can be considered as first-order entities, or entities *stricto sensu*; properties of individuals and instances of masses, and processes involving individuals and instances of masses, which can be considered as higher-order entities.[140]

The structure of this formal skeleton seems significantly connected with some basic grammatical structures, suggesting that a common ground of formal categorization underlies both our shared natural ontology and the main grammatical structures of at least the languages belonging to the Standard Average European type (Whorf, 1941), or European mainstream (Kortmann, 1997). A careful examination of English constructions, in particular, provides evidence for a deep-lying correlation between the grammatical structure of noun phrase and the formal profile of first-order entities, and between the grammatical structure of sentence and the formal profile of second order entities. It is an essential requirement for our line of argument that the formal skeleton of natural ontology, like its substantive content, should not be language-specific, but should be shared far beyond the limits of a given linguistic community. It is not required, however, that either the formal skeleton or the substantive content be universal, though further investigation of this point seems promising.[141]

1. Formal kinds of being

1.1 Things and concepts

A preliminary question when dealing with ontology is to what extent one can speak of kinds of beings without implicitly assuming familiar concepts. Like the boundary between perception and categorisation, the boundary between formal kinds of being and formal kinds of concept is not clear-cut. Typical individuals certainly offer themselves to perception as ultimate beings. A tree one bumps one's head against, for instance, offers itself as an immediate, rough counterpart of perception. But what can reasonably be classed as perceptual rather than conceptual in a familiar loaf of bread? Typical processes are as certainly concepts — one cannot see an act of giving in the same sense as one sees its actors. But what about such perceptible processes as fire or sounds (see for instance Strawson, 1959: Chapter 2)? To give a reasonable answer to such questions goes far beyond the limits of the present study. But the questions, at least, have to be kept in the background.

Masses and classes are certainly concepts, and more exactly punctual concepts, that is, criteria for subsuming first order entities under categories:

individuals are grouped into classes such as persons, dogs, trees, and instances of shapeless stuff are subsumed under mass concepts like water, sand or bread.

First order entities are identified as objects at the perceptual level: a person, a dog, a tree; a pool of water, a heap of sand, a loaf of bread, for instance, can be seen and touched. This, however, does not necessarily imply that the identification of instances in perception is logically prior to conceptual categorisation. The most typical kinds of individuals — persons, dogs, trees — offer themselves to perception in an immediate way. They can be directly pointed to as individuals in a way that is reasonably independent of further grouping into categories, and this is confirmed, in some privileged cases, by the use of proper names. The status of instances of masses as objects of perception is more intricate: there is nothing obvious in seeing a pool of water or a loaf of bread rather than, for instance, a 'small water' or a 'small bread'.[142] The form of mass instantiation familiar in Western cultures is rooted in the structure of quantified noun phrases prevailing in Standard Average European, so that it is difficult to disentangle our perception of individual instances from the effects of language-specific categorisation — merely seeing from "seeing for speaking", in a sense. As Whorf (1941(1956: 141)) points out, "Our language patterns often require us to name a physical thing by a binomial that splits the reference into a formless item plus a form".

The relationship between identity, individual *Gestalt* and concept is clearly not the same for individuals and instances of mass. The most qualifying property of individuals, that is, shape, is documented by each single instance, whereas the most qualifying property of masses, that is, homogeneity, is captured at the level of the general concept.[143] Each individual is characterised by a specific *Gestalt*, which is reasonably stable across time and contributes in an essential way to its identity. The shape of an instance of mass, on the contrary, is both extrinsic and contingent, so that its identity is rooted in the long-lasting homogeneous mass concept rather than in the volatile shape of the individual instance. As a consequence, individuals are naturally dealt with as if they were prior to classes. For the most typical instances of individuals, like persons, animals, trees, one has the feeling that individuals are grouped into classes. Individual instances of masses, on the contrary, are dealt with as if mass concepts were prior to instances. For the most typical instances of mass, like water, milk, sand, one has the feeling that instances can be conceived as such and referred to only as particular cases of a general concept.

Second order entities, that is processes and properties, see the light as concepts, and more exactly as relational concepts. One cannot see a relation or point to it in the same sense as one sees or points to a tree. One can identify instances of a given relation in actual experience to the extent that one is provided with the relevant relational category. If I see a man moving his arm in a given way, I realise that he is saying goodbye to a friend if — and only if — I am familiar with the relational category "saying goodbye". A Bororo looking at the performance of two chess players would hardly *see* an instance of playing chess, perception of which requires conceptual glasses.

The formal skeleton of our shared natural ontology can thus be described as a hierarchy of formal kinds of concepts and beings. The distinction between punctual and relational concepts is the highest in the hierarchy. Punctual concepts classify individuals and give access to instances of masses, while relational concepts give access to properties of individuals and instances of masses, as well as to processes involving individuals and instances of masses. All these nuclear categories provide natural ontology with an independent formal framework, which circumscribes the relevant formal kinds of entity and relation underlying any further conceptual classification and connection. The classificatory component of natural ontology can draw its substantial conceptual boundaries only within the borders of such formal kinds of entities as countable individuals and amorphous masses. The relational component, in turn, can restrict only to given classes of individuals or kinds of masses the consistent domains of application of such relational categories as processes or qualities.

In order to describe the formal skeleton of natural ontology, we shall first examine the opposition between punctual and relational concepts (§1.2). After a brief survey of the ontological commitment of parts of speech (§2), we shall analyse the formal kinds of being that can be considered instances of punctual concepts against the background of the noun phrase (§3), and the formal kinds of relational concepts against the background of sentence structure (§4).

1.2 The basic framework: Punctual and relational concepts

Punctual concepts are concepts that subsume instances of beings under categories. Relational concepts are concepts that impose relations on instances of beings. The most direct means of access to the distinction between punctual and relational concepts is the observation of conflictual complex meanings.

In some cases, conceptual conflict affects the primary classification of beings. A being belonging to a given category is identified with a being belonging to another, incompatible, category: a spinner is *a living stone* (D. H.

Lawrence); the wind is *the breath of heaven* (Marlowe); the memory is *that great thorow-fare of the brain* (Defoe); a smile is *the real sunshine of feeling* (C. Brontë).

In other cases, beings are classified in a consistent way, but the qualities or processes attributed to them are not consistent with their conceptual identity:

> And Winter pours its grief in snow
> When Autumn's leaves are lying (E. Brontë)
> Shadows — hold their breath (E. Dickinson)

The two ways of attaining inconsistency show *en filigrane* the two basic, perpendicular dimensions of natural ontology: a paradigmatic, classificatory dimension, and a syntagmatic, relational dimension. Thanks to the classificatory component, the relevant kinds of being are kept apart from one another on the basis of inherent essential properties: concrete from abstract, animate from inanimate, human from animal and vegetable. Thanks to the relational component, properties and processes are characterised by the kinds of being they can take as consistent arguments. Speaking, for instance, is restricted to human beings, while feeling and expression are also associated with animals; birth and death are restricted to animate beings, while colour can be attributed to any concrete being. In formal ontological terms, the paradigmatic dimension of natural ontology presupposes the availability of punctual classificatory concepts, while the syntagmatic component requires the accessibility of relational concepts. Like many other natural conceptual structures relied upon in everyday life, the distinction between classificatory and relational concepts has been made explicit and clarified in its ontological import by Aristotle (*The Categories*, 5, 2a).

Aristotle opposes such concepts as "man" or "horse", which classify or subsume individuals ("first substances, *tode ti*"), to such concepts as "white" or "walk", which can be applied to individuals in a non-classificatory, relational way. The critical difference is drawn by Aristotle thanks to a test based on the transitivity of definitions. When a classificatory concept is applied to an individual, the definition of the former is also applied to the latter. Each individual horse, for instance, inherits the definition of "horse": it can be consistently defined as "a large animal which people ride". When a relational concept is applied to an individual, on the contrary, the definition of the former cannot be applied to the latter. An individual white horse does not inherit the definition of "white": a white horse cannot be consistently defined as "the lightest colour that there is, the colour of milk and snow"[144] (*Collins Cobuild*).

Strawson (1959: 168) draws a similar distinction between "sortal" and "characterising" universals, or concepts: "A sortal universal supplies a principle for distinguishing and counting individual particulars which it collects. It presupposes no antecedent principle, or method, of individuating the particulars it collects. Characterising universals, on the other hand, whilst they supply principles of grouping, even of counting, particulars, supply such principles only for particulars already distinguished, or distinguishable, in accordance with some antecedent principle or method". A verb like *dream*, for instance, not only applies to individuals, but even supplies a principle for grouping individuals — for keeping individuals to which it applies apart from individuals to which it does not. This relational kind of classification, however, presupposes a prior punctual classification of individuals into distinct kinds according to inherent criteria.

1.3 Saturated and unsaturated expressions

The two dimensions of natural ontology are connected in an essential way to the grammatical distinction between saturated and unsaturated expressions. Punctual concepts, which group kinds of beings, are meanings of saturated expressions — typically nouns — while relational concepts, which draw processes and properties, are meanings of unsaturated expressions — typically verbs and adjectives. While the ontological distinction between punctual and relational concepts goes back at least to Aristotle, the distinction between saturated and unsaturated expressions was first drawn by Frege (1891) and transferred into linguistic analysis by Tesnière (1959).

If we look at the structure of a simple process, it is clear that it contains at least two kinds of expression, displaying distinct grammatical properties and performing two complementary functions: a predicator and one or more arguments. The predicator — typically a verb — draws the plan of the whole structure; the arguments — typically noun phrases — bring the participant roles into the structure. In a sentence like *The farmer killed the duckling*, for instance, the verb *kill* provides the relational scaffolding of the whole action, whereas the two noun phrases *the farmer* and *the duckling* fill this purely virtual scaffolding with two actual participant roles, turning it into the picture of a definite kind of action.

The predicator forms the active part of a complex relational structure in which the noun phrases are passively involved. In spite of its privilege of rank and function, or better because of it, however, the predicator is not capable of performing its task on its own. A verb, for instance, contains *in nuce* the plan of a process, but it is not a process as such until it is completed by an appropriate number of arguments. Since Frege and Tesnière, such a property of predicators has been referred to as non-saturation, with a telling metaphor drawn from chemistry. Verbs are the most typical instances of non-saturated expressions.

An argument performs a function of a lower level: it does not provide the structural framework for a process, but can identify referents ready to take roles in any kind of process. Though humbler in rank, this function can be performed by a noun phrase alone, without the help of any other expression. For this reason, a noun phrase is considered a saturated expression, whose function is to fill the empty positions opened by non-saturated terms. The clear-cut examples of referential noun phrase, verb and sentence provide a more general criterion for distinguishing non-saturated and saturated expressions. An expression is saturated when it is able to perform its function without being completed by another expression. A noun phrase is thus a saturated expression, because it can be used as a referential expression as it is. At a higher level, a nuclear sentence is also a saturated expression, because it is capable of framing a process. An unsaturated expression, on the other hand, has to be completed in order to perform its function. A verb, for instance, is an unsaturated expression, because it can frame a process on condition that its free positions are saturated by appropriate arguments.

The distinction between saturated and non-saturated expressions is closely related to the immanent structure — either classificatory or relational — of the involved concepts, and coincides neither with the distinction between nouns and verbs, nor with that between referential and predicative position. On the one hand, many nouns are unsaturated terms, and therefore are used as pivots of processes and even of sentence structures[145] (see §4). Such a noun as *description*, for instance, contains the plan of a process just as much as a verb like *describe*. The noun phrase *John's description of the city* and the sentence *John gave a description of the city* frame a process just as much as *John described the city*. On the other hand, both kinds of term may be found in either predicative or referential position: *This nightingale*; *This bird is a nightingale*; *John smokes heavily*; *Smoking is dangerous*. *John gave a careful description of the city*; *John's description of the city was careful*.

2. Parts of speech

La rotondità calva del monte
color cenere (Gadda)

A first hint at the formal relevance of nuclear ontological categories is offered by a simple survey of the main grammatical categories of lexemes, or parts of speech, within the languages belonging to the European mainstream. According to the traditional view, there is an essential link — a sort of elective affinity — between names and individuals, between nouns and classes of individuals or amorphous masses of substance, between adjectives and qualities ascribed to entities, between verbs and processes involving entities. In other words, the main grammatical boundaries between lexemes also identify a nuclear classification of formal kinds of entities.

The difficulty with the traditional idea is that there is no direct correspondence between lexical classes and formal ontological categories. Among the words of a language, we find many instances of hybrid items, which associate the distributional and morphological properties of one class with the conceptual status of another.

Among verbs and adjectives, the lack of correspondence between the formal class and its ontological content can be considered rather marginal. It is devoid of any true functional relevance, and does not deeply affect the elective ontological specialisation of each formal category.[146] Among nouns, however, the lack of correspondence is both widespread and functionally relevant.

Besides the formal distinction between masses and classes of individuals within the area of punctual concepts, the category of nouns neutralizes the basic distinction between punctual and relational concepts. Besides denoting classes and masses, nouns are systematically fit to express processes and qualities, in an almost unrestricted way: from a purely grammatical point of view, such lexemes as *sin*, *beauty* or *death*, in spite of their relational content, are no less nouns than *dog* or *water*.

From a functional point of view, the nominal categorisation of qualities or processes is to be considered a systematic device for promoting the access of second-order entities to the most typical nominal position — the position of discourse topic. As it is systematically open to any kind of ontological content, the grammatical class of nouns has an ontologically unspecialized range of denotation.

An immediate way out of this impasse is not difficult to find. Each main grammatical category can be described as containing an ontologically relevant core surrounded by a non-homogeneous periphery whose range of denotation is not ontologically relevant. The most critical category, that of nouns, contains a core formed by nouns denoting classes of individuals and mass concepts, surrounded by others denoting processes and qualities. The parts of speech can thus be defined by two non-isomorphous and complementary criteria. Each part of speech is defined by a grammatical criterion in relation to effective membership, while ontological criteria circumscribe the nuclear, ontologically relevant subset.

Grammatically speaking, this solution has its own merits. The sharp dissociation of the competing criteria for class membership theoretically bridges the gap between the results given by each, removing the risk of inconsistency which has threatened the analysis of parts of speech since its origins.[147] As far as our question is concerned, however, such a solution is of no use. The use of ontological criteria for nuclear membership presupposes a firmly established formal ontological classification of entities, so that it assumes as independently grounded the same nuclear ontological categorisation which should, according to our hypothesis, belong to a common formal ground. A theory of parts of speech, in other words, is either ontologically neutral or committed to a previous, independent ontological classification. Our pursuit of a common ground of formal categorisation shared by ontological and linguistic structures must therefore leave lexical classification aside and turn to syntactic patterns — namely, to noun phrases and sentences.

3. Individuals, classes and masses: The structure of noun phrases

If the structure of the noun phrase is taken as a relevance criterion, English distinguishes three main formal classes of nouns.

Nouns belonging to the first class — proper names — take only the singular form and cannot, as a rule, be used with any article or determiner: *John*, **Johns*, **the John*, **a John*, **some John*.[148]

Unlike proper names, common nouns accept, and typically require a determiner in order to form a noun phrase. According to the possible or necessary form of determination, common nouns are further distinguished into two main classes. A first class of common nouns includes those behaving like *book*, which demand a determiner, can take the plural form and refuse singular quantification: **book*, *books*, *the book*, *a book*, **some book*, *some books*. A second class includes nouns that behave like *water*, which allow singular quantification but are incompatible with either plural form or indefinite article: *water*, **waters*, *the water*, **a water*, *some water*, **some waters*.

The above classification of nouns, strictly based on the formal properties of the related noun phrases, coincides exactly with the formal ontological distinction between countable individuals, classes of countable individuals, and shapeless masses. Proper nouns are meant to refer, when used, to unclassified individuals — to individuals taken as such.[149] Common nouns like *book* denote classes of countable individuals. The function of the determiner within the corresponding noun phrase is connected with the specific way of instantiating class-concepts — namely, the selection of one or more individuals taken as members of the class. Common nouns like *water* denote shapeless masses. The specific way of instantiating a mass, connected with the use of determiners, consists in selecting a given portion out of the mass, and sometimes in imposing a shape or a container on it.[150]

The categories of individual, class and mass are sharply distinguished on the basis not only of the distinct forms taken by the corresponding noun phrases[151], but also of the specific interaction between each kind of noun and each shared determiner.

In English, the most characteristic example is the interaction between the generic quantifier *some* and the grammatical number of the noun: *some* occurs with the plural of count nouns and with the singular of mass nouns. This has clearly to do with the different form taken by instantiation in each case — namely, the taking apart of a given plural set of individuals from a class, and of a given singular quantity from a mass.

Italian is less accurate than English in formally distinguishing mass and count nouns. Both mass and count nouns, for instance, freely allow a singular definite article — *il gatto*, *l'acqua* — and each definite noun phrase allows two interpretations, one referring to a given instance, the other to the general category. The two interpretations, however, are not equally favoured. For each class of nouns, one of these interpretations is invited, and is immediately activated in the absence of specific contextual obstacles or out of context, while the other is simply admitted under the pressure of a specific context. With a mass noun, the invited interpretation is the reference to the general category; with a count noun, it is the reference to a given instance. The noun phrase *l'acqua*, for instance, refers first to the whole mass — like *water* — and residually to a given instance: *L'acqua è sul tavolo* (*The* (*glass of*) *water is on the table*), while *il gatto* refers first to a given instance — like *the cat* — and residually to the whole class:[152] *Il gatto è un animale socievole* (*The cat is a sociable animal*).

Both the distribution of determiners and their interaction with the different kinds of nouns prove that the distinction between countable individuals, classes and masses is both ontologically relevant and strictly formal. The distinction is ontologically relevant because it provides natural ontology with a very general and highly schematic distinction between two ways of governing the relationship between general notions and particular instances. At the same time, this distinction is strictly formal because it is in itself conceptually neutral, though prior to any substantial conceptual categorization. This point is well illustrated by a comparison with a substantial conceptual opposition — the opposition between concrete and abstract entities.

The formal distinction between individuals and masses cuts across the substantial distinction between concrete and abstract entities. Just as we can conceive of concrete individuals, like *books* or *cats*, and masses, like *water* or *sand*, we can conceive of abstract entities — *ideas* and *remarks* — and masses — *music* and *courage*. What the entities belonging to the same formal category have in common is not some substantive feature, but simply the way of connecting general notions with particular instances — the fact that a book and an idea are both taken as countable individuals out of a class, while an instance of courage and a glass of water are both taken as a part out of a mass which is in itself absolutely shapeless.[153]

Conversely, the opposition between concrete and abstract entities has no formal basis — it is not related to any significant restriction on the form of expressions. As far as the nuclear structure of noun phrases is concerned, the nouns denoting abstract entities behave, like their concrete counterparts, as either count nouns or mass nouns. *Idea* behaves like *book*: **idea, ideas, the idea, an idea, *some idea, some ideas*; *Courage* behaves like *water*: *courage, *courages, the courage, *a courage, some courage, *some courages.*[154]

The distinction between countable individuals, classes and shapeless masses can be seen as formal in a double sense: because it is deeply rooted in the formal structures of expressions, irrespective of the substantial properties of the involved concepts, and because it provides natural ontology with a formal framework, which is in turn independent of, and preliminary to, any further conceptual characterisation.

4. Formal kinds of relations: The structure of the sentence

4.1 The formal possibility of processes

A process is a kind of structure that relates one or more individuals or instances of masses. The most immediate way of expressing a process is a sentence that connects a predicative term with its arguments:

(1) My father has arrived

In purely functional terms, however, an adequate complex noun phrase — a noun phrase containing an unsaturated noun as its head and one or more complements providing its arguments — appears as a true alternative to the sentence structure as a way of expressing a process:

(1) My father has arrived
a. The arrival of my father
(2) My father has a doubt
a. My father's doubt

Given such examples, one is encouraged to conclude that the sentence and the noun phrase are two alternative tools available to the speaker for performing the same task in different textual or discursive conditions. Unlike the noun phrase, the sentence actualises, so to speak, the process, giving explicit expression to such dynamic categories as tense, aspect and mood. The noun phrase, on the other hand, counterbalances the radical stylisation it imposes on the ideation of the process by its free accessibility to nominal positions, which in turn allows for easy topicalisation or focalisation of a process within a simple sentence. Thanks to their peculiar structural properties, the sentence and the noun phrase seem fit for complementary functional specialisations. Owing to its accuracy in framing the relevant features of the process, the sentence appears to be the favourite tool for first introducing a process into the discourse. Owing to its distributional flexibility, the noun phrase can be seen as the favourite tool for referring back to a previously introduced process, a function which does not require ideational accuracy.

However natural it may seem, such a view rests on a previous assumption which is not self-evident: the assumption that a process is not essentially the counterpart of a specific linguistic form, but a conceptual structure that can be conceived as such irrespective of any form of expression, and can thus be expressed by many.

In my view, the formal possibility of a process depends on the shaping power of the sentence structure. Looked at from this point of view, the structural difference between sentence and noun phrase is far more than a matter of gradual transition along such functional parameters as ideational accuracy and textual flexibility. The noun phrase can be considered as a tool for expressing a process, whereas the sentence is to be seen as the proper tool for conceiving and formally constructing a process. On the following pages, we shall examine some arguments supporting this claim.

4.1.1 *The first argument: The formal specificity of the process*

4.1.1.1 *First Type: 'The arrival of my father'*. Within noun phrases, processes have no exclusive formal means of expression at their disposal. The expression of the participant roles of a process within a noun phrase is the work of one or more complements of the head noun, whose form and distribution share, as a rule, the form and distribution of normal complements. In spite of the very different kinds of connection they frame on the semantic level, the phrases (1a) and (3), (2a) and (4) share the same syntactic structure. In other words, their structure as noun phrases bears no relation to their different content:

(1) a. The arrival of my father
(3) The wall of my garden
(2) a. My father's doubt
(4) My father's book

It is only within sentence structures that the construction of a process relies on a specific formal frame:

(1) My father has arrived
(2) My father has a doubt

The aptness to express a wide range of heterogeneous conceptual connections by means of undifferentiated syntactic structures is the most characteristic property of noun phrases, independent of their involvement in framing processes. As an instrument of ideation, the noun phrase systematically acts as a weak mould[155] that, as a rule, lacks the strength to impose a given connection on its terms. The formal frame of a noun phrase simply suggests that a relevant connection holds between its terms, but says nothing about its content.[156] If a definite connection can ever be framed and identified, it is not owing to linguistic coding, but thanks to supplementary inferential enrichment based on non-formal criteria, partly systematic and partly occasional. Within the borders of noun phrase, the presence of a well-formed syntactic structure is not a sufficient condition for the formal articulation of meaning connections, which ultimately depends on inferencing.

The critical difference between a noun phrase expressing a process and a noun phrase denoting an individual is a conceptual one, and lies entirely in the content of the head-noun. In the first case — *The arrival of my father*, for instance — the head noun is the unsaturated pivot of a relation. In the second case — *The wall of my garden* — the head noun is a saturated classificatory noun, which denotes one of the terms of an unnamed relation with the complement noun. According to their different conceptual content, the two kinds of noun offer the interpreter of the noun phrase two different kinds of instruction.

When the head noun does not frame a relation, the instruction is, roughly, the following: there is a relevant relationship between the head noun and the complement; try and infer its content on the basis of conceptual structures, cognitive schemes and contextual information. Given a noun phrase like *The tent of secret sins* (Blake), for instance, the favoured interpretation would be a consistent one: "The tent where someone sins". Other interpretations compatible with the form — for instance, a tent belonging to sins — are normally ruled out. Within the field of consistency, the choice tends to be narrowed down to the most natural options. According to general cognitive criteria, for instance, a compound noun like *windmill* would be interpreted as referring to a mill driven by the wind rather than to a mill which produces wind.[157] When different consistent and cognitively appropriate interpretations are open to inferencing, and especially when there are so many as to threaten the identification of the link itself, the final criterion is coherence[158] with co-textual or contextual information. A significant case of systematic dependence on co-textual information is provided by titles. The noun phrase *The Volcano Lover*, for instance, is the title of a novel by Susan Sontag. In order to understand the relationship between the person and the volcano, one has to know the content of the story.

When the head noun is the pivotal term of a connection, the instruction it sends out sounds different: the head noun contains a valency scheme which frames a process; try and discover which participant or peripheral role of the process is expressed by the complement noun. As the valency scheme of the head noun is purely notional, devoid of any specialised formal counterpart, the role is identified by inference, based once more on conceptual structures, cognitive schemes and contextual information.

The first datum to be taken into account is that some nouns of process are decidedly oriented towards a given role, which is activated by an invited kind of inference. *Victory*, for instance, is agent-oriented — *The victory of our fleet* — while *defeat* is patient-oriented — *The defeat of our fleet.* Most nouns, however, are indifferent on this point: if *Cook's explorations* are made by Cook, *The explorations of Australia* aim at discovering Australia. *Gutenberg's invention* is made by Gutenberg; *The invention of the press* brings the press into existence.

The activation of participant roles is generally invited by the unsaturated content of the pivotal noun. As the expression of roles is both unspecialized and optional, however, their activation is subject to a conceptual filter. As a consequence, any complement of the head noun that turns out to be conceptually unfit for a participant role is ready to be interpreted as expressing a peripheral one. If *John's dream* describes a dream dreamt by John, for instance, *A midsummer night's dream* is a dream which takes place during a midsummer night; *Three days' sorrow* is sorrow which lasts three days and *The joys of night* are joys caused by something which happens during the night:

> Are not the joys of morning sweeter
> Than the joys of night? (Blake)

When many consistent connections are conceivable between a noun of process and a complement, a further selection can be made on the basis of general cognitive criteria, but the last word is left once more to co-textual and/or contextual coherence.

When two nouns of process are linked, the interpreter is called upon to infer a relevant relationship holding between them, just as in the case of two nouns of thing.[159] *A cry of fear*, for example, is in the first instance a cry caused by fear. When several relations are possible, the choice is normally based on coherence with co-textual and contextual information: *A song of joy*, for instance, may be a song caused by joy, or made in a joyful way, or meant to give joy. Of course, it is not always easy, and sometimes seems pedantic, to identify a relevant relation, even within a given text or context. For instance, what exactly is the content of such a phrase as *The ecstasy of consummation*?

> Meanwhile, on the length of the mountainridge, the snow grew rosy-incandescent, like heaven breaking into blossom [...]. In the rosy snow that shone in heaven over a darkened earth was *the ecstasy of consummation* (D. H. Lawrence).

4.1.1.2 *Second type: 'The murder of the spy by the police'.* The articulation of the process is appreciably more precise if a nominal form expresses only and all the participant roles, which in this case tend to receive differentiated expressions. In such strings as *John's order to Mary*; *John's gift of a book to Mary*; *The murder* *of the spy by the police*, the process looks almost as carefully constructed as in the related sentences. Before jumping to hasty conclusions about the formal *régime* of such nominals, however, we need go more deeply into the question.

The first point to be stressed is that even the full expression of a process does not benefit from exclusive syntactic structures. Expressions (5) and (6), for instance, are formally identical. Yet (5) frames a process, while (6) describes an object:

(5) The murder of the spy by the police
(6) The wall of the garden by the railroad

In addition, it is not certain that such nominal forms as *The description of the city by Paul* or *John's order to Mary* are true noun phrases. What is at issue, in particular, is the nature of such expressions as *by Paul* and *to Mary*, which have the same form they would take if the head noun were used as the main predicative term in a sentence structure: *John gave an order to Mary*; *The description of the city was given by Paul.* My hypothesis is that such expressions are not constituents of the noun phrase, but are inherited, so to speak, from the corresponding sentence structure.

If the main predicative term of a sentence is an unsaturated noun, it cannot perform its function unless it is supported by a sort of auxiliary verb — a support verb.[160] In *John gave an order to Mary*, for instance, *give* has such a function. A support verb does not contribute to the content of the process, which is entirely defined by the predicative noun. Its function is to convey such grammatical determinations as mood, aspect, tense and person, the specification of which requires a verbal form.

The diagnostic criterion for detecting support verbs is their behaviour under nominalisation. Unlike predicative verbs, support verbs are dropped in case of nominalisation:

(7) Luc gave Paul an order
(8) Luc gave Paul a book
(7) a. Luc's order to Paul
(8) a. *Luc's book to Paul

Whereas form (7a) can be considered as a nominal expression of process (7), form (8a) is not interpretable as a process, a circumstance that deprives the prepositional phrase *à Paul* of a clear function. If we cut out this prepositional phrase, on the other hand, the expression becomes fully interpretable as the description of an object: *Luc's book.* In (7a), the process is framed by the predicative noun *order*, which maintains the function of main predicator that it has in the corresponding sentence. The verb can be dropped, because its content takes no part in framing the process, while the purely grammatical information conveyed by it becomes textually irrelevant. In (8a), on the contrary, the absence of the verb destroys the process, which can receive a nominal expression only if an appropriate predicative noun is available to take over the verb, as in (8b):

(8) b. The gift of a book to Paul

This proves that in (8) the verb *give* is the predicator, whereas in (7) the same verb simply supports the predicative noun. The function of support verbs in sentence structures is to allow a predicative use of relational nouns, and thus, in a sense, to "conjugate predicative nouns" (Giry-Schneider, 1987: 1).

Against this background, the sequence (7a) — *Luc's order to Paul* — does not have the structure of a single noun phrase formed by a head noun controlling two complements. The head noun only controls the form of the genitive *Luc's*, which forms with it the noun phrase *Luc's order*, whereas the prepositional phrase *to Paul* is inherited from the structure of the corresponding sentence with a support verb:

(7) Luc gave Paul an order
b. The order Luc gave to Paul
a. Luc's order to Paul

In a similar way, the prepositional phrase *by Paul* in such an expression as *The description of the city by Paul* is inherited from the passive sentence with a support verb:

(9) The description of the city has been given by Paul
a. The description of the city which has been given by Paul
b. The description of the city given by Paul
c. The description of the city by Paul

Given that the form of the nominal expression partly depends on the form of the corresponding sentence containing a support verb, a further question becomes relevant: to what extent does the form of the sentence depend on the formal properties of the support verb.

The presence of the form *by + NP* is independent of the properties of a specific class of support verbs, for it is inherited from a general type of sentences, that is, passive sentences.

The case of the form *to + NP* is more complex. In some cases, the presence of an indirect object is clearly required by the valency scheme of the support verb. Though behaving as a support verb in (7) and as a predicator in (8), *give* requires the same valency-scheme in both sentences:

(7) Luc gave Paul an order
(8) Luc gave Paul a book

In other cases, the indirect object can be justified only in connection with the predicative noun. The difference between (10), (10a) and (10b), for instance, depends on the relational properties of the head noun:

(10) John made a present (of a book) to Mary
a. John made a journey to London (around the world, in East Africa)
b. John made a mistake

In both cases, the indirect object can easily be justified from within the corresponding sentence form containing a support verb. In (6) and (7), the indirect object stems from the valency scheme of the support verb *give*.[161] In (10) the phrase *make a present* behaves as a predicator requiring an indirect object. In neither case does the indirect object in the nominal string imply that predicative nouns have a syntactic valency-scheme of their own, beyond the genitive complement they share with any kind of noun.

If our analysis is correct, the apparent strength of such nominal expressions as *The description of the city by Paul, The present of a book to Mary by John* or *Paul's order to Mary* is no more than a legacy from the formal *régime* of the corresponding sentence. If we cancel from our expressions the constituents inherited from the corresponding sentences, on the other hand, we are led back to the simple, unspecialised and indeterminate kind of noun phrase we first took into account: *The description of the city; Paul's order; Paul's gift of a book.*[162]

4.1.1.3 *The nominal expression of processes: Indetermination or ambiguity?*

> I matemi e le quadrature di Keplero
> che perseguono nella vanità degli spazî senza senso
> l'ellisse del nostro disperato dolore (Gadda)

The systematic weakness of noun phrases as moulds for meaning raises an intriguing question: is the indetermination of noun phrases a kind of constructional ambiguity?[163] Many arguments suggest that the answer is negative.

Constructional ambiguity can be considered as an occasional collapse of a structure which is designed, as a rule, to encode a given meaning connection.

Ambiguity, in other words, presupposes coding. As we have already observed, the French sentence *J'ai fait écrire une lettre à Paul* can be considered ambiguous, in that it neutralizes a distinction that is generally encoded by French syntactic structures — namely, the distinction between subject and indirect object: *I got someone to write a letter to Paul* and *I got Paul to write a letter to someone.* The indetermination of noun phrases, on the contrary, is not due to an occasional collapse of coding, but is the outcome of a systematic undercoding, systematically open to many paths of inferential enrichment.[164]

As an occasional accident of coding, ambiguity circumscribes a finite set of options, which can easily be selected when the expression is actually used in context. As the outcome of a structural weakness of coding, indetermination virtually allows an indefinite set of options, which are not necessarily open to reduction, either because inferencing goes beyond a univocal content or because it stops before it. The first case is that of indetermination in the strict sense: a set of potential options, instead of excluding one another, simultaneously coexist. The second case is that of vagueness: no precise, positive connection can ultimately be attained.

The structural difference between ambiguity and indetermination has a significant functional counterpart. As it threatens the main articulations of a complex meaning, structural ambiguity is seen as an obstacle to the coherent use of the expression in a text or discourse, and is designed for reduction in real communication. The addressee of our French example, for instance, cannot ultimately remain in doubt as to whether Paul receives or writes the letter. Indetermination, on the contrary, is not normally felt as an obstacle to the use of the expression, and is neither necessarily nor even typically designed for reduction. It would be pedantic, for instance, to wonder whether *A song of joy* is a song caused by joy, or made in a joyful way, or meant to give joy to the hearer. Probably, it is all these things, and in any case it can be all of them.[165]

It has often been said that poetry loves ambiguity.[166] Maybe it does sometimes, but it is more likely that the halo of semantic density that surrounds poetic texts is due to an intense, systematic valorisation of undetermined and vague structures. What we commonly find within poetic texts are not so much ambiguous sentence structures, as sentence structures that connect indeterminate or vague nominal constituents in a non-ambiguous way. In such cases, the solidity of the grammatical core secures the main predicative links, while many potential meanings of indeterminate noun phrases coexist in semantic density. The following sentence, for instance, shapes a non-ambiguous process — it is absolutely clear who gave up what in exchange for what. At the same time, its nominal constituents express indeterminate conceptual relations:

Thou gavest the tears of pity away
In exchange for the tears of sorrow (Blake).

The following passage is a striking example of the link between indetermination and density:

Sweet dreams, form a shade
O'er my lovely infant's head;
Sweet dreams of pleasant streams
By happy, silent, moony beams (Blake).

The last two lines, in particular, form an inextricable network of possible connections whose interaction *in praesentia* draws a dense labyrinth of sense: the streams can be the content of the dreams, but also their local setting, or even their metaphorical subjects, and in fact all these alternatives coexist; the "moony beams" can be part of either the setting or the content of the dream, or both.

Poetry proves a good field of observation for such linguistic facts. On the one hand, the densest tangles of possible senses are compatible with the most solid architecture of nuclear connections. On the other hand, we are faced with the plain fact that a noun phrase can remain forever devoid of any definite content, even within a narrowing context. The vagueness of noun phrases is not a specific feature of poetry, but a general property of these linguistic structures. Poetry simply highlights vagueness, pushing it towards the limits of nonsense: who could ever tell what is the exact meaning of such expressions as *The voice of the shuttle* (Sophocles), *The narrow path of twilight* (D. H. Lawrence) or *Der Tisch aus Stundenholz*[167] (P. Celan: *The table out of hourwood*)?

4.1.2 *The second argument: Linking a process to a noun*

A noun of process and a sentence can both be linked to a head noun, but not under the same formal conditions. Consider the following examples:

(11) The idea of living (that he live)
a. *The tree of living (that he live)
b. The tree of life
(12) La joie de vivre (qu'il vive)
a. *La planche de vivre[168] (qu'il vive)
b. La planche de la vie (de sa vie)
(13) La voglia di sognare (che egli sogni)
a. *L'acqua di sognare (che egli sogni)
b. L'acqua dei sogni[169] (dei suoi sogni)

As our examples show, a process framed by a sentence can be linked only to a restricted set of relational nouns. When the process is expressed by a noun, on the contrary, no such syntactic restriction apply. The reason is already known: syntactically speaking, the behaviour of a noun phrase expressing a process is closer to a non-specialised noun phrase than to a specialised formal frame of process — to a sentence. Here, the difference between the noun phrase and the sentence is not a matter of conceptual content: the content of the given processes — life, dream — is exactly the same. Neither is it a matter of formal ontological compatibility: in both cases, a process is linked to an individual, non-relational entity. The question is clearly a formal syntactic one: the distribution of sentence structures is governed by strong formal restrictions, which do not hold for the corresponding noun phrases.

In fact, there is a significant correlation between the presence of strong distributional restrictions for a given syntactic structure and its autonomous shaping power. When a linkage is syntactically constrained, grammatical well-formedness is a sufficient condition for the connection of a complex meaning. When a complement sentence is linked to a noun, a strong mould is gained through distributional rigidity. When a linkage is syntactically weak, grammatical well-formedness is just a preliminary, non-sufficient condition for the connection of a complex meaning. Under such conditions, a meaning connection only takes place if some conceptual link between the concrete thing and the process can be inferred: for instance, the tree symbolises life, or houses living creatures; life is seen as a board, or a board as an instrument for saving life, or something else is metaphorically seen as a board for saving life; water is the content of the dream, or its local setting, or something which causes someone to dream, and so on. A weak mould is the price to be paid for distributional flexibility.[170]

4.1.3 *The third argument: The formal possibility of inconsistent processes*

An inconsistent process cannot, by definition, rest on autonomous conceptual structures, which are by definition consistent. The formal possibility of conceiving of an inconsistent process, therefore, strictly depends on the active shaping power of an autonomous syntactic mould.

As an inanimate being, the moon cannot smile according to our shared conceptual structures. The only way to conceive of a smiling moon is to construct a sentence containing the noun phrase *the moon* as the grammatical subject of the verb *to smile*:

The moon, like a flower,
In heaven's high bower,
With silent delight
Sits and smiles on the night
(Blake)

Under such conditions, the moon inevitably takes on the role of experiencer.

The syntactic structure of a noun phrase is not strong enough to construct a meaning connection independent of the connected contents. Instead of imposing a network of connections on them, a noun phrase tends to adapt its inner connections to the content of its constituents. Owing to this, the expression *A midsummer night's dream* is immediately interpreted as a dream which has taken place during a midsummer night, and not as a dream made by a midsummer night. In the expression *Sweet dreams of pleasant streams*, the streams are more probably the content of dreams than their experiencers.

The above remarks do not imply that inconsistent connections are actually banished from noun phrases. Actually, the noun phrase is one of the favourite grammatical locations for any kind of metaphor: *The eyes of sorrow* (G. Eliot); *The deep fountains of affections* (G. Eliot); *The walls of an aching heart* (E. Brontë); *Time's troubled fountains* (Blake). But this is beside the point. When it is expressed by a noun phrase, an inconsistent meaning is not, as it is within the sentence, the result of a formal construction, but the outcome of an act of interpretation.

One reason which can induce an interpreter to identify an inconsistent connection is the lack of consistent and plausible alternatives. In such examples as *The knees of my heart* (Brothers Wedderburn), *The colour of my mind* (E. Brontë), *Thunders of thought, and flames of fierce desire* (Blake) or *The fenceless fields of air* (Longfellow), inconsistency is the last resource against nonsense. In most cases, however, what prompts a metaphorical interpretation is not the lack of consistent alternatives, but its coherence either with a familiar cognitive landscape whose categorization largely relies on metaphor, or with co-textual or contextual information.[171] In the latter case, textual coherence prevails over conceptual consistency.

An expression like *The curtains of the night* (Blake) allows a consistent interpretation. In spite of this, the average reader would probably take it as a metaphorical characterisation of obscurity, which hides light as curtains do. As metaphorical categorisation of such familiar objects of experience as light and darkness forms part of our familiar cognitive landscape, to see the darkness as a sort of curtain is a more immediate move than to think of real curtains somehow connected with the night.[172] The co-text of the expression supports this interpretation: [...] *the holy light/ Had just removed the curtains of the night.* Out of context, the expression *The valley of humiliation* (G. Eliot) could easily be interpreted as consistently referring to a valley where an instance of humiliation has taken place. In fact, the co-text supports an inconsistent metaphorical interpretation — the humiliation has to be passed through as if it were a valley. Similarly, *The walls of an aching heart* (E. Brontë) are part of the heart itself;[173] in *Romeo and Juliet, Nights candles* are the stars.

The fact that inconsistent meanings can be expressed by noun phrases does not mean that noun phrases have the strength to construct inconsistent concepts. It simply means that we are ready to conceive of inconsistent concepts and, if necessary, to express and identify them by means of noun phrases. If inconsistent concepts form part of our familiar conceptual landscape, on the other hand, it is owing to the active power of sentence structures, which have irreversibly brought them into the horizon of expectancy shared within our form of life.

If our analysis is correct, we can conclude that the formal condition of possibility of such relational entities as processes lies within the syntactic structure of the sentence. This remains somehow hidden within the field of consistent meanings, which are perfectly conceivable as independent complex concepts, and is highlighted by the observation of inconsistent meanings.

At the same time, careful observation of inconsistent meanings also reveals the limits of the formal articulation of processes. The essential semantic property of an inconsistent complex meaning is the dissociation between the formal possibility of the process — its being successfully connected as a network of relations — and its conceptual possibility — its consistency. Insofar as it is independent of any kind of conceptual lawfulness, the formal possibility of a complex meaning says nothing about its conceptual conceivability. So far, the strongest argument for the autonomy of syntax — its aptness to impose an independent mould on concepts — becomes the most convincing proof of its limits — of its conceptual neutrality. Just as in the field of individuals, classes and masses, formal categorisation calls for a conceptual counterpart. Formal ontology calls for substantial ontology.

4.2 Sentence and noun phrase: The attribution of qualities to beings

The attribution of a quality to a being — its qualification — is open to two alternative structures: the attributive link within a noun phrase, and the predicative link within a sentence. Both the noun phrase *This red apple* and the sentence *This apple is red*, for instance, ascribe the colour red to the apple. As in the case of processes, the question is to ascertain whether the alternative available structures are equally effective in shaping the formal connection. My hypothesis is that a strong formal mould for qualification is provided only by sentence structure, which is insensitive to inconsistent contents, while the noun phrase is ready to negotiate the connection with the connected concepts.

If we take conceptual conflict as a test, both the sentence and the noun phrase seem strong enough to oppose a formal mould to organized concepts. Both the noun phrase *This blond hill* and the sentence *This hill is blond*, for instance, ascribe to the hill the conflicting quality of blondness. On closer examination, however, it turns out that noun phrases do not always behave in this way. Under the pressure of conflicting contents, in particular, the attribution of a quality is ready to shift from the inconsistent syntactic partner of the adjective to a consistent entity in some way connected to it. The expression *Blonde ambition* (a headline in *The Guardian*), for instance, would not normally be taken as metaphorically attributing blond hair to ambition. In fact, it is the ambitious person referred to who is qualified as blonde. What is meant to be crimson in the following passage is the bed — a metaphorical bed indeed, but this is beside the point:

> O rose, thou art sick!
> The invisible worm
> That flies in the night,
> In the howling storm,
>
> Has found out thy bed
> Of crimson joy (Blake)

In the examples above, the result of conflict is a shifted or oblique modification — a relationship of modification whose final objective falls outside its syntactic framework. The final target of a shifted modification may be: (1) connected to the syntactic partner of the adjective within the same expression — *The indistinct* grey *movement of — perhaps — a* rat (G. Greene); (2) inferred from its content — *Blonde ambition*; (3) retrieved within a larger context — *Una stanca strada* (Fenoglio: *A tired road*) is a road walked by tired people.[174]

Oblique modification is not totally incompatible with sentence structure, as the following example shows: *Once more Ralph dreamed, letting* his skilful feet *deal with the difficulty of the path. Yet here* his feet seemed less skilful *than before* (Golding). In actual fact, however, oblique modification tends to avoid sentence form, whose assertive character is more akin to direct, metaphorical attribution.[175] The least we can say is that in the case of conceptual inconsistency the attributive use of adjectives is weak enough to allow a shift in modification, whereas the predicative use tends to be strong enough to impose a qualificative metaphorical interpretation.

The advantage of the sentence over the noun phrase, which is a matter of elective affinity in the case of inconsistent qualification, becomes a sharp difference when the adjective is not used to qualify a noun, that is, if we take into account non-qualificative uses of qualificative adjectives and non-qualificative adjectives.

When applied to an agent noun, a qualificative adjective does not normally modify its referent. Instead, it tends to characterise the involved action, or, more exactly, the specific way the action is habitually performed by the agent. A heavy smoker, for instance, is someone who smokes heavily; a good dancer is someone who dances well. This shift in modification from individual to process is blocked by the predicative position, which is restricted to the qualification of beings. The sentence *This smoker is heavy* attributes heaviness to the subject as an individual, not as a smoker. This subtle point dates back to Aristotle: "Though a man is a cobbler and good, yet we cannot combine them together and pronounce him also 'a good cobbler'".[176]

Relational adjectives[177] share some critical morphological properties of adjectives but do not behave as true adjectives. In their elective use, relational adjectives do not ascribe a quality to the *designatum* of the head noun, but connect it with another entity. A rural policeman, for instance, is a policeman who works in the countryside (lat. *rus*); the nervous system is a system made of nerves.[178] When the head noun is a noun of process or quality, the most striking function of relational adjectives is to express not a property of the process or quality, but an argument or circumstance of the process, or the bearer of the quality. The expression *The Indian war* may refer to a war involving Indians or India. A *monosyllabic preoccupation* (Hardy) is a preoccupation expressed in monosyllables. In the expression *Une blancheur animale* (Mallarmé: *An animal whiteness*), the adjective refers to the bearer of the quality expressed by the head noun.[179] In the following sentence, the adjective *watery* brings into the text the subject of desolation — a surface covered with water: *The wide area of watery desolation was spread out in dreadful clearness around them* (G. Eliot).

These non-canonical uses of adjective are all ruled out by sentence structure, which proves to be a more exclusive, almost intransigent formal mould for qualification than the noun phrase. A sentence like *The policeman is rural* is at least unnatural,[180] for the predicate can hardly be applied to the subject as a true quality. The same holds for such sentences as *The desolation was watery*, *This war is Indian*, *Cette blancheur est animale*. If both noun phrase and sentence can be used to frame the attribution of a quality to a being, the privilege of the sentence lies in its tendency to filter out the wide range of non-qualificative uses of adjectives which are open to noun phrase. The difference in behaviour of sentence and noun phrase is a particular case of the more general distinction between a relation kind of coding and a punctual one, systematically open to undercoding and therefore sensitive to conceptual consistency. If the previous remarks are correct, the rigid formal framework of the sentence structure proves to be more relevant for the attribution of qualities than the availability of a specialized class of adjectives.[181]

5. Formal ontological categorisation: Structure and limits

Such general categories as countable individual, class of individuals, mass and instance of mass, quality and process can be considered formal in two senses: because they provide natural ontology with its formal frame, and because they are connected in a significant way to such formal linguistic structures as the noun phrase and the sentence. The two senses of the adjective *formal* are logically independent. The fact that natural ontology actually has a formal skeleton neither implies nor excludes that its structure is connected in a significant way to some formal linguistic pattern. The existence of such a deep connection is thus an empirical question. If this connection were documented, formal ontological categorisation could be seen as a bridge between basic linguistic structures and natural ontology. If it were not, the function of formal categorisation in providing natural ontology with its basic formal scaffolding would not be disputed. Before turning to the connection between formal ontological categorisation and its substantial filling (§5.2), let us spend some words about the connection between formal ontology and linguistic forms.

5.1 Formal ontology and linguistic forms

The connection between formal ontological categorization and grammatical structures is traditionally interpreted in two ways: either the basic formal categories which frame natural ontology depend on the grammatical structures of a given group of languages (as claimed by Whorf, 1941(1956)), or they are universals of human thought ready to surface in linguistic forms (see for instance Wierzbicka, 1988: 501–503). Put in absolute terms, the alternative is probably beyond any rational approach, first of all because there are many layers of formal categorisation, some of which are language-specific and some more general, and possibly universal. But a point remains relevant in both cases, that is, the idea that formal ontological categorisation could form a common ground shared to some extent by some widespread linguistic structures and natural ontology. If so, it would be as if one and the same kind of seed — the seed of formal categorisation — had developed into a family of distinct but intertwined kinds of plants. A largely shared ontological categorisation would be ready both to surface in very general grammatical structures and to be refined into highly language-specific ways of "thinking for speaking". Whether and to what extent such a common ground is actually shared among human languages is an empirical question, which can be examined only in field research. In the following lines, I shall simply put forward some general remarks.

The first point to be stressed is that different formal kinds of being and concept can surface to a different extent and in different ways among the grammatical structures of different languages. Moreover, the fact that a given language does not provide overt grammatical marking for some kind of formal category does not imply that these categories are not accessible to the speakers as independent concepts. The fact that a given language does not share the Western grammar of mass instantiation, for instance, does not imply that such formal kinds as individual or mass are not active as conceptual categories. The lack of overt coding is logically compatible with the independent salience of a concept as well as with its absence.

The distinction between punctual and relational concepts can reasonably be expected to be as universal as the correlative distinction between saturated and unsaturated terms.

For the same reason, the category "process" is likely to belong to a universal common ground of formal categories, insofar as it is difficult to imagine a human language devoid of specialised grammatical means for connecting processes, that is, of unsaturated predicators and saturated argumental terms.

To remain at the level of sentence structure, the case of qualities is less trivial, owing to the fact that the category "adjective", which typically encodes qualities in Standard Average European, cannot be simply assumed as universal.[182] Before jumping to hasty conclusions, however, it should be observed that formal categorisation, as it is argued in this research, does not rely so much on specialised word classes as on the availability of specialised syntactic patterns. If the relevant construction for the attribution of qualities is not attribution but predication, no formal obstacle prevents the encoding of qualities by either noun-like or verb-like lexemes instead of adjectives. Provided that these lexemes can occur as predicators in sentence structure, the formal roots of qualification are secured.[183] An extreme example is Lango (Noonan, 1992: 103, quoted by Rijkhoff, 2002: 134): "there is no grammatical construction in Lango which is attributive and does not involve embedding. To translate an attributive adjective from English to Lango, it is necessary to resort to a relative construction, i.e. adjectives are always predicates in Lango".

The most controversial issue is certainly the formal ontological status of kinds of beings, that is, individuals and masses, and in particular their connection with the grammatical distinction between count and mass nouns. Though widespread among human languages, this distinction is probably not universal.

Starting from Rijkhoff's (2002: Chapter 2) classification of nouns, the languages of the world can roughly be grouped into three major types in this respect.

Some languages have distinct classes of nouns overtly marked for individuals and masses. Nouns for individuals can be further divided in two groups — singular object nouns and set nouns — according to the priority of either individual or class. Singular object nouns, familiar in Standard Average European, "are obligatorily marked for plural number when modified by a free numeral higher than 'one'" (Rijkhoff, 2002: 34): *Three dogs*. Set nouns "are unmarked for number when modified by a free numeral" (39), as Basque *Hiru neska*, (Three girl, "Three girls").

Sort nouns, attested in languages like Mandarin Chinese, Korean, Vietnamese and Thai, are not overtly marked as distinct from mass nouns. Sort nouns "purely denote *concepts* and, for this reason, are incompatible with direct quantification" (Hundius & Kölver, 1983: 166, quoted by Rijkhoff, 2002: 47). Both sort and mass nouns can only be determined in the presence of classifiers, which are ready to take over the relevant distinction. Sortal classifiers apply to sort nouns for individual instantiation, as in Thai *Pèt hâa tua* (duck five classifier: body; "Five ducks"). Mensural classifiers apply to mass nouns for mass instantiation, as in Thai *náamtaan sǎam thǔai´* (sugar three cups, "Three cups of sugar") (Hundius & Kölver, 1983, quoted by Rijkhoff, 2002: 48).

Some languages, finally, have "general nouns", which conflate individuals and instances of mass. The Yucaltec Maya noun *Há'as*, for instance, can be translated with either "banana entity", including "banana fruit(s), banana tree(s), banana leaf or leaves, bunch of bananas", or "banana 'stuff' (i.e. the mass)" (Rjikhoff, 2002: 146, after Lucy 1992: 74). According to Lucy, general nouns combine with classifiers which are in turn blind to the "' sortal' versus 'mensural' distinction":

	a/one — Classifier	banana	
(a)	*un-tz'íit*	*há'as*	one/a 1-dimensional banana (i.e. the fruit)
(b)	*un-wáal*	*há'as*	one/a 2-dimensional banana (i.e. the leaf)
(c)	*un-kúul*	*há'as*	one/a planted banana (i.e. the plant/tree)
(d)	*un-kúuch*	*há'as*	one/a load banana (i.e. the bunch)
(e)	*un-p'íit*	*há'as*	one bit banana (i.e. a bit of the fruit)

The conclusion is that in Yucaltec Maya "there is no clear distinction between *sort nouns* and *mass nouns*" (Rijkhoff, 2002: 49). More generally, if a language has only general nouns, the distinction between individual and mass has no grammatical counterpart, which implies that it does not belong to a common ground shared by grammatical patterns. Whether the formal ontological distinction is also lost, is an independent empirical question.

5.2 Natural ontology: Formal framework and substantial filling

The categories of class, individual and mass provide a formal framework for the classificatory component of natural ontology. This means that a given conceptual classification is conceivable only within the boundaries of formal categories, that is, as a classification which applies substantive labels to kinds of individuals and masses. One cannot think of a concrete or abstract being without conceiving of it as an individual or an instance of mass; one cannot think of a living or human being without conceiving of it as an individual. Water, for instance, is a concrete mass, whereas fear is an abstract one. An idea is an abstract individual, while a book, a cat and a lawyer are concrete individuals. A book is an inanimate individual, while a cat is an animate one and a lawyer a human one.

The categories of quality and process provide a formal framework for the relational component of natural ontology. Processes and qualities enter into relation with, or create a relationship between, first-order entities. The task of the relational component of natural ontology is to specify what substantive kinds of individuals and masses each process or quality is allowed to enter into relation with, or to create relationships between. A process like killing, for instance, is consistent if its targets are animate individuals, while hitting is consistent with concrete ones, both animate and inanimate. A property like virtue is consistent with human beings, while colour is consistent with concrete individuals and instances of masses, and depth with both concrete and abstract entities.

However essential for the structural organisation of natural ontology, formal categorisation neither affects consistency nor is affected by inconsistency.

Formally speaking, an individual is no more than an individual. A man who is said to be a bird, for instance, is an inconsistent entity. Nevertheless, it remains an individual:

> [...] the drowsy cry of Watchmen
> (those hoarse unfeather'd Nightingales of Time!)
> (Coleridge)

When pity is said to be poured in someone's breast, it is treated as a concrete mass. However inconsistent, it remains a mass:

> And can he who smiles on all
> Hear the wren with sorrow small,
> Hear the small bird's grief and care,
> Hear the woes that infants bear,
>
> And not sit beside the nest,
> Pouring pity in their breast
> (Blake)

In the same way, a process remains a process even if it is performed by inconsistent beings:

> When the green woods laugh with the voice of joy,
> And the dimpling stream runs laughing by:
> When the air does laugh with our merry wit,
> And the green hill laughs with the noise of it
> (Blake)

And a quality remains a quality, irrespective of the conceptual properties of its support:

> The gentle wind, a sweet and passionate wooer,
> Kisses the blushing leaf (Longfellow)

Natural ontology certainly contains a formal framework. Consistency, however, does not depend on formal categorization but on its substantive filling. Even if it were proved that the formal skeleton of natural ontology has solid roots in grammar, therefore, consistency would nevertheless be governed by a conceptual rather than a grammatical form of lawfulness.

Once grammar is put aside, it is all too easy to think of the lexicon, which is traditionally considered as a repository of concepts and conceptual structures, as a proper home for consistency criteria. Accordingly, it is no wonder that consistency criteria, which are a kind of conceptual structures, are traditionally located among lexical structures. This premise shapes our next question — namely, what is the relationship between consistency criteria, lexical structures and lexical information.

CHAPTER 6

Lexical structures and lexical information

The question about the nature of consistency criteria has been of great interest ever since the publication of Chomsky's *Aspects* (1965), when generative linguists were torn between two opposite schools, one claiming that selection restrictions are part of syntactic structures, the other arguing for their "semantic" nature (see Graffi, 1975). After several years of angry exchanges, the whole matter was then buried in oblivion. It is now normally agreed that selection restrictions are semantic structures, which find their place among lexical data, and this is the way introductory books to semantics treat the topic (see, for instance, Leech, 1974; Palmer, 1976; Lyons, 1977).

This unanimous identification of consistency criteria with a kind of semantic structure, however, is more a way of denying the formal syntactic character claimed for selection restrictions by Chomsky than the premise for a true elucidation of their nature and functions.

The adjective "semantic" is not used by linguists in a consistent way. In some cases, it is used without specific reference to any linguistic system, and holds as an equivalent of "conceptual", or "notional" in Jespersen's (1924: Chapter III) sense. This is the use to be found among generative semanticists, cognitive and functional linguists. According to Lakoff (1987: 539), for instance, "the meanings are concepts in a given conceptual system".[184] In these cases, to say that selection restrictions are semantic structures roughly means that they are a kind of conceptual or cognitive structure. In other cases, the term is used in a language-specific sense, with an explicit reference to the language-specific formal articulation of the content plane. This use, which can be traced back to Saussure, exerts a deep influence on structuralism and, more generally, on European linguists. According to Lyons (1963: 37), for instance, "Each language must be thought of as having its own semantic structure, just as it has its own phonological and grammatical structure". In these cases, to say that selection restrictions are semantic structures amounts to saying that they are a kind of language-specific lexical structure.

To claim that selection restrictions are semantic data generally implies that their study pertains to lexical description. But the concepts of lexicon and lexical description are no less elusive than the concept of semantics. On the one hand, the lexicon is assumed to be, along with phonology and grammar, a part of linguistic structure. Looked at from such a formal, immanent point of view, the lexicon is seen as a complex network of correlations and relations among lexemes whose formal configuration is specific to a given language and therefore, in principle, different from the formal configuration it receives within other linguistic systems. On the other hand, the lexicon is taken as a sort of repository of positive information about any aspect of word content — from shared concepts to encyclopaedic information — which is likely to become relevant when words are used for the construction and cognitive elaboration of complex meaning expressions. Looked at from such a functional point of view, the lexicon cannot be considered as a language-specific structure, for the mass of information it is assumed to contain, though distributed among words in a language-specific way, is not necessarily a language-specific reality in itself. As a matter of fact, functionally relevant information is largely shared independently of the borders of a given linguistic community — far beyond these borders in the case of widespread, common concepts, or far above in the case of idiosyncratic, highly specific matters.

For all these reasons, any statement about the semantic or lexical nature of selection restrictions is devoid of content until one makes clear in which sense these concepts are to be taken. Thus, a correct analysis of the relationship between consistency criteria and lexical facts requires a previous clarification of the concept itself of lexicon.

1. The formal structure of the lexicon

> Par un progrès ultérieur et révolutionnaire,
> les femmes en sont venues à s'habiller
> sans se vêtir (La Harpe)

The idea that the lexicon of a language has a specific formal structure can be traced back to the seminal work of Ferdinand de Saussure (1916). In his opinion, while the diachronic study of linguistic forms gives the image of a chaotic accumulation of idiosyncratic facts,[185] the synchronic description of a given linguistic state relies on the idea that a language is a compact system, a network of relations involving phonic and conceptual units which imposes on both a specific shape.

Both phonic and conceptual purport are conceived of by Saussure as shapeless masses: "Without language, thought is a vague, uncharted nebula. There are no pre-existing ideas, and nothing is distinct before the appearance of language" (Saussure, 1916(1974: 112)). The same holds for the phonic purport out of which distinct linguistic signifiers are built up within a given language: "Phonic substance is neither more fixed nor more rigid than thought; it is not a mold into which thought must of necessity fit". It is only when these two heterogeneous and amorphous realities meet that a linguistic structure takes shape: "Linguistics then works in the borderland where the elements of sound and thought combine; *their combination produces a form, not a substance*". According to this premise, neither sounds nor concepts can be conceived independently of each other; they can only be conceived as "values emanating from the system" (117). In particular, the lexicon of a given language is defined as a system of conceptual values, which takes a specific shape thanks to its relation with linguistic expression.

As with any other values to be found within the field of social sciences, linguistic values are characterised along two complementary dimensions. The first dimension involves two heterogeneous orders of entities, one of which is located outside the system: the value of a given unit is defined on the basis "of a *dissimilar* thing that can be *exchanged* for the thing of which the value has to be determined". The second dimension involves entities of the same order, all belonging to the system: the value of a given unit is defined on the basis "of similar things which can be compared with the thing of which the value is to be determined".[186]

"When we speak of the value of a word — in particular — we generally think first of its property of standing for an idea". According to Saussure, this attitude is not wrong, for "this is in fact one side of linguistic value", but unilateral. If the external side of value is exclusively taken into account, the language system is reduced "to a simple naming-process" (114–115), that is, to a list of labels applied to independent concepts. But no independent concept can be conceived of outside linguistic expression, for each language cuts out its concepts in a specific way: "If words stood for pre-existing concepts, they would all have exact equivalent meanings from one language to the next; but this is not true. French uses *louer* (*une maison*) 'let (a house)' indifferently to mean both 'pay for' and 'receive payment for', whereas German uses two words, *mieten* and *vermieten*; there is obviously no exact correspondence of values". This implies that the identity and conceptual content of a word cannot be defined without taking into account its correlations with the competing values belonging to the same conceptual area of the system: "Within the same language, all words used to express related ideas limit each other reciprocally; synonyms like French *redouter* 'dread', *craindre* 'fear', and *avoir peur* 'be afraid' have value through their opposition: if *redouter* did not exist, all its content would go to its competitors" (116).

The language-specific and immanent turn imposed by Saussure on the identification of lexical values inevitably raises the question of arbitrariness. If the content purport is in itself devoid of any shape, the only shape to be found in meanings stems from within the linguistic system itself, which amounts to saying that the linguistic cutting up of concepts is arbitrary.

Arbitrariness is a complex notion, which has to be defined at two distinct levels, that is, both within and outside the structure of the sign.

Within the structure of the sign, to say that the relationship between *signifiants* and *signifiés* is arbitrary amounts to saying that the phonic body of words is not motivated by the properties of the expressed concepts — that the *signifiant* is not an icon of the corresponding *signifié*. This is the most obvious dimension of arbitrariness — a dimension nobody could seriously challenge.[187]

The really interesting dimension of arbitrariness is the one located outside the sign, which involves the relationship between linguistic meanings and the realm of inner and outer experience. To say that the relationship between linguistic *signifiés* and things is arbitrary amounts to saying that the structure of concepts is not motivated by the independent properties of a common experience, but is ultimately justified by a network of correlations with competing values within the linguistic system. If they are considered arbitrary in this sense, linguistic meanings are not positively characterised by a conceptual content, but negatively differentiated as competing values in a relational network. According to Saussure, "in language there are only differences *without positive terms*".

The ideas that lexical structures form an immanent system of pure differences «*without positive terms*», that language-specific lexical structures shape a shapeless purport, and that the linguistic shaping of experience is arbitrary form an interdependent constellation. If one of these ideas is called into question, the whole system has to be readjusted.

As we shall see later on (§2), a formal approach is justified and illuminating insofar as it focuses on the immanent, language-specific configuration of lexical structures. Besides displaying a purely differential side, however, lexemes are used and relied upon by speakers as if they had a substantive content, whose roots lie outside the closed linguistic system, in the realm of outer and inner experience. This implies that a formal approach to lexical structures calls for a complementary functional approach to substantive lexical contents.

Once a substantive side of lexical contents is admitted, the idea that linguistic structures shape a shapeless purport is in turn called into question. In fact, the attribution of a language-specific form to the content of signs does not require *a priori* that the conceptual purport be as such devoid of any shape. The question whether language has a specific, autonomous structure and shaping power on concepts is an empirical question, logically independent of the question whether and to what extent inner and outer experience has a structure of its own, independent of language-specific forms. Just as a sculptor can carve his figures out of shaped as well as out of rough stone, so linguistic structures can carve lexical values out of a shaped as well as out of a shapeless purport.

Finally, if one admits that linguistic structuring operates on structures, the idea of arbitrariness cannot be retained in its strongest sense, but has to be reformulated. If a conceptual and cognitive purport which already has a form of its own undergoes further language-specific shaping, it is clear that the range of action open to this further shaping is significantly limited. In particular, if lexical values shape a conceptual purport which has an independent structure and content of its own, the structure of the purport is likely to motivate to a given extent the formal articulation of lexical values. This does not prevent us from considering arbitrariness the qualifying property of linguistic signs. What becomes untenable is the idea that arbitrariness is an absolute property of signs, incompatible with any kind of motivation. But if arbitrariness is seen as a gradable property, the presence of some degree of conceptual motivation stops looking like a logical obstacle and becomes an empirical question. As we shall see later on (§ 2.2.3), the content of each sign displays a variable and specific balance between arbitrariness and motivation — between its attitude to cut out language-specific lexical values and the pressure of independent conceptual contents and structures towards expression.

1.1 Lexical paradigms

Saussure's idea of the internal value of lexical units can be developed along two paths. On the one hand, one can try to define the relevant domain involved in the immanent determination of lexical values. This domain is not the whole lexicon, but a limited set of lexemes expressing "related ideas", that is, organising a homogeneous conceptual area. The meaning value "good", for instance, is not limited by the meaning "green", but by the related meanings "bad", or "excellent". On the other hand, the lexemes belonging to a homogeneous area are involved in different kinds of relations. Saussure cites the relation of synonymy, but other relevant relations can be identified. The first point has been developed by Trier, the second by Lyons.

1.1.1 *Lexical fields*

Trier's interest in the Saussurean approach to lexical structures arises out of a difficulty he finds when studying the evolution of German vocabulary in the field of intellectual skills through the Middle Ages. Trier's inherited methodological model for historical semantics is the onomasiological perspective, based on the previous identification of independent concepts or things working as *tertium comparationis* for the study of different languages or different historical stages of a given language. When the object of inquiry is the expression of material things, whose experience is largely independent of linguistic categorisation (say, a natural kind of plant, or a very common tool), the way open to onomasiological research is relatively straightforward. Once the thing is identified, words will follow. The task becomes difficult, however, when the object is a constructed abstract concept, the experience of which is essentially bound to its language-specific shaping. According to Trier, "conventional onomasiological enquiries are helpless in the face of non-material contents. There is no history of the sign for cleverness [*Klugheit*] as there can be a history of the sign for a sickle " (Trier, 1932(1973: 98)). It is at this point that Saussure's idea becomes valuable.

According to Saussure, the value of a given lexeme is better determined through its relation with the competing lexemes than on the basis of its notional content. In Trier's own words, "The value of a word is only recognised when it is set off against the value of neighbouring and opposing words. It has meaning only as part of a whole; meaning only exists in a field" (Trier, 1931(1973: 45)). If a lexeme has no definite value outside a whole, however, the whole which determines its value does not coincide with the totality of lexical structure, but with a given area of it: "There are, namely, organisational units that exist between the language as a whole and individual words and forms" (Trier, 1932(1973: 94)). The most strategic of these hierarchical lexical strata are "the groups of semantically connected words" known since as lexical fields (*sprachliche Felder*). As single words, lexical fields are members of paradigmatic structures of a higher order; as the whole lexicon, they include units of a lower order: "Fields are living realities intermediate between individual words and the totality of the vocabulary; as parts of a whole they share with words the property of being integrated in a larger structure, and with the vocabulary the property of being structured in terms of smaller units" (Trier, 1934(1973: 148)). The lexical field is not regarded as a mere conceptual area, but as the specific way a given conceptual area is linguistically organised: "a field is an area of meaning seen in terms of its linguistically organised representation in a word group" (Trier, 1932(1973: 95)).

1.1.2 *Sense relations*

If lexical structure is conceived of as a hierarchy of fields, and lexical fields as networks of relations among lexemes, the most immediate task open to analysis is the identification of the different kinds of relations holding among the lexemes included within the same lexical field or located in hierarchically related fields.

Lyons' work on lexical relations is based on the hypothesis that each language has "its own semantic structure" (Lyons, 1963: 37), which consists of a network of relations among meaning units, or "sense relations": "I propose to define the notion of 'semantic structure' in terms of certain relations that hold between the items in a particular semantic subsystem". These relations can be distinguished between equal relations, internal to a given field, and hierarchical relations, holding among lexemes belonging to different levels of articulation. Equal relations are opposition (for instance, "dead" vs "alive"), antonymy, or graded opposition (for instance, "cold" vs "lukewarm" vs "warm"), synonymy (for instance "murmur" vs "mutter"), and converseness (for instance "sell" vs "buy"). Hierarchical relations are hyponymy and hyperonymy:[188] "flower", for instance is the hyperonym of the whole series including "rose", "violet" and "hyacinth", all of which are co-hyponyms of "flower".

According to Lyons, sense relations, in spite of their being "generally treated by semanticists in terms of a prior notion of 'meaning', independently defined" (57), are the primitive terms of a semantic theory focusing on lexical structures: "meaning is to be regarded as a function of these several relations, rather than the reverse". A good example of the import of such a change of perspective in semantic description is the analysis of synonymy.

Synonymy is generally treated as a relation of identity of meaning.[189] Such a definition, however, raises two problems: it rests on a previous definition of meaning, and associates synonymy to an identity of meaning which, intuitively, is never absolute. A relational definition of synonymy avoids both difficulties.

If they are located within the lexical structure, synonyms can be identified without any reference to a previous concept of meaning, let alone of identity of meaning. Synonyms can be found as competing terms located on one and the same side of a lexical opposition: "bad" and "evil", for instance, are both opposite of "good". Or they are competing co-hyponyms of a given lexeme located on the same side of a given oppositive dimension: "murmur" and "mutter", for instance, are both hyponyms of "speak" denoting quiet and indistinct speech, in opposition to "shout" or "scream". Or they jointly hold as determinant terms of a lexical solidarity[190] as a single lexeme would do: "cat" and "pussy", for instance, jointly determine "mew" as "lion" determines "growl".

The fact that the meaning of synonyms is never absolutely the same is not a difficulty from an immanent and formal point of view. On the contrary, the fact that two lexemes are competing for a given position involves by definition a difference in meaning, however slight or difficult to catch. On the basis of their synonymy, for instance, we can predict within which limits "pussy" and "cat" do not have the same meaning: "pussy" is affectively marked, whereas "cat" is not. As Lyons points out, a lexeme "*a* is not synonymous with *b* because of its meaning; the fact of their synonymy is part of their meaning" (58). More generally, "the meaning of a given linguistic unit is defined to be a set of (paradigmatic) relations that the unit in question contracts with other units of the language [...] without any attempt being made to set up 'contents' for these units"[191] (59).

1.2 Differential articulation of lexical meaning: the formal relevance criterion

Trying to substantiate the idea of a language-specific "content form", Hjelmslev puts forward the hypothesis that this form is not limited to the construction of language-specific paradigms of semantic values — of fields — and their articulation according to given sense relations. If the conceptual purport, assumed to be in itself shapeless, is moulded by a language-specific form to become a shaped content-substance, it must be possible to read, so to speak, the traces of this process written in conceptual letters within the very substance of content. According to Hjelmslev, the differentiation among the meaning values included in a given lexical paradigm — that is, in a field — is based on strategic, linguistically relevant conceptual oppositions. For each lexical paradigm, there is a network of minimal conceptual differences systematically related to differences in expression. One task of a semantic description is to make explicit the conceptual oppositions which differentiate the lexical meanings, and to identify the "content entities" involved in them.

The model of such an analysis of the content plane is the phonological analysis, which dissolves the complex phonic structures — words and syllables — into simple constituent units. The same method "is then to be applied to the content plane in just the same way as in the expression plane. If, for example, a mechanical inventorying at a given stage of the procedure leads to a registration of the entities of content 'ram', 'ewe', 'man', 'woman', 'boy', 'girl', 'stallion', 'mare', 'sheep', 'human being', 'child', 'horse', 'he', and 'she' — then 'ram', 'ewe', 'man', 'woman', 'boy', 'girl', 'stallion', and 'mare' must be eliminated from the inventory of elements if they can be explained univocally as relational units that include only 'he' or 'she' on the one hand, and 'sheep', 'human being', 'child', 'horse' on the other" (Hjelmslev, 1943(1961: 70)). The items of the second series — 'sheep', 'human being', 'child', 'horse' — each identify the common root meaning of the paradigms, while the first couple — 'he', 'she' — identifies the oppositive dimension organising each paradigm,[192] that is, the sex.

Unlike its phonemic body, however, the meaning of a lexeme takes the form not of a syntagmatic chain of overt constituents, which can be isolated by segmentation, but of a simultaneous bundle of covert components. As Lounsbury (1956: 162) points out, a paradigm of lexical components — or "content entities" — " differs from the paradigms with which we are traditionally acquainted inasmuch as no component is ever represented overtly in the segmental structure of the forms. The structure of the set is entirely one of covert categories". According to this premise, a good phonological model of a lexical meaning is not the chain of phonemes identifying the lexeme itself — the word — but the minimal phonic segment of it — the phoneme. According to Jakobson (1949: 8), "the phoneme, like a chord in music, can be broken up into smaller simultaneous components", so that it can be seen "as a set [...] of distinctive features (Saussure's *éléments différentiels*). For example, the French phoneme *b* can be substituted (in such a series of words as *bu, pu, vu, mu*) by phonemes *p, v, m*, etc.; and it is voiced in contrast to *p*, plosive in contrast to *v*, oral (non-nasal) versus *m*, etc. Analysing in this way the differential value of the French phoneme *b* we establish its linguistic content: voicing, plosivity, orality, etc. All differences in phonemes in any language can be resolved into simple and indecomposable binary oppositions of distinctive features".[193]

Since they are not characterised by overt marking, covert categories cannot be found directly, by segmentation, but only indirectly, by substitution and commutation. Hjelmslev (1943(1961: 73)) defines commutation as a substitution in one linguistic plane — for instance, in the content plane — correlated with a substitution in the other plane — for instance, in the expression plane: "A correlation in one plane, which in this way has relation to a correlation in the other plan of language, we shall call a *commutation*".

Just as the commutation with the content plane is the relevance criterion for analysing a minimal discrete expression unit — a phoneme — into its covert distinctive features,[194] the commutation with the expression plane is the relevance criterion for analysing the meaning of a minimal meaningful expression unit — of a lexeme — into its covert differential features, that is, the features which are called upon to differentiate its meaning from the meanings of the competing lexemes. In the content plane, "as in the expression plane, the criterion is the exchange test, by which a relation is found between correlations in each of the two planes. Just as exchanges between *sai*, *sa*, and *si* can entail exchanges between three different contents, so exchanges between the content-entities 'ram', 'he', and 'sheep' can entail exchanges between three different expressions. 'Ram' = 'he sheep' will be different from 'ewe' = 'she-sheep', just as *sl* will be different from, say, *fl*, and 'ram' = 'he sheep' will be different from 'stallion' = 'he-horse', just as *sl* will be different from, say, *sn*. The exchange of one and only one element for another is in both cases sufficient to entail an exchange in the other plane of language" (Hjelmslev, 1943(1961: 70)).

1.3 Lexical solidarities

Lexical structures do not reduce themselves to paradigmatic correlations — such as the correlation between "bark" and "mew" — but also include syntagmatic relations, or lexical solidarities — for instance, that between "bark" and "dog". The terms of a correlation are admitted as alternative options in order to fill a given slot within a structure, and are thus connected in terms of the "either-or" function. The terms of a relation actually occur as simultaneous constituents of the same construction, and are thus connected in terms of the "both-and" function.[195] Porzig opens his seminal paper on lexical solidarities with the following remark: "Part of the concept or essence of walking [*gehen*] is that is requires human feet, because a dog doesn't walk over the road, a cat doesn't walk along a wall: the German verb would be *laufen*. These sense relations [*Bedeutungsbeziehungen*] between words, that is, the fact that one is implicitly posited by the other, are very frequent in language" (Porzig, 1934: 70).

A lexical solidarity is an asymmetrical kind of relation. As Coseriu (1968: 15) points out, "In a solidarity, there is always one term which determines and another which is determined". The determined term is an unsaturated term, which imposes language-specific restrictions on its range of arguments.[196] The determinant term is the (set of) admitted argument(s) which circumscribe(s) the value of the determined term. Given the solidarity between "bark" and "dog", for instance, the verb is the determined term. It demands a dog as a subject — the determinant term — and its relation with the dog characterises its lexical value.

Lexical solidarities are language-specific structures, not to be confused with syntagmatic associations justified by the independent structure of our experience: "This is obviously not simply consociation in Sperber's sense of the word, that is to say, the idea that one word comes to mind easily when thinking of another; it is rather a relationship that is founded in the essence of the intended meanings. For this reason I call them essential sense relations [*wesenhafte Bedeutungsbeziehungen*]" (70). The word "essential" (*wesenhaft*) is used here in a narrow, technical sense: it means non-empirical, structural. An essential fact does not belong to the order of phenomena, but holds as *a priori* condition of phenomena. According to this premise, lexical solidarities are not a product of linguistic use, but a rule imposing conditions on linguistic use. The proof that lexical solidarities are not mere empirical affinities but essential lexical structures is the fact that they are effective when they are not realised, or even violated, by actual use. If the determinant term is not specified in actual speech, for instance, it is entailed by the use of the determined term. If the verb *bark* receives an empty subject (*It barks*), this subject is automatically interpreted as referring to a dog. If it receives a non-solidary subject (*John barks*), the actual subject conflicts with the latent determinant term, creating a specific form of metaphor: the man conflicts with the dog, which is applied to the man as a model. As Porzig points out, "for each word there is a sphere of use, where it is at home, where it belongs. A word can be used outside this sphere, but this gives rise to a stylistic effect produced by the tension between the actual meaning of the word and the stranger meaning into which it is incorporated" (77–78). The conflict is the best proof that the solidarity is encapsulated within the content of the determined term.

Looked at from the point of view of lexical structures, lexical solidarities turn out to be peculiar kinds of oppositive dimensions — namely, relational oppositive dimensions. Relational oppositive dimensions perform the same function as inherent oppositive dimensions — they play a strategic role in shaping the inner structure of the paradigms to which the determined terms of the solidarity belong. Inherent oppositive dimensions are extracted directly from the content of the opposite lexemes. The meanings of *shout* and *murmur*, for instance, are differentiated through an inherent oppositive dimension, which focuses on an inner characteristic of the opposite processes. Relational oppositive dimensions, on the contrary, ground the differentiation of the meanings of two or more lexemes in an external link — in a relation with a connected term. An example involving synonyms is the differentiation among the set of adjectives denoting age in Latin: "In Latin, to indicate advanced years, there are the three adjectives *senex*, *vetulus* and *vetus*. They can be opposed to one another — *senex* for people, *vetulus* for animals and plants, *vetus* for things" (Duchacek, 1965: 58).

If lexical solidarities are a kind of oppositive dimension, the relevance criterion at work in analysing them is the same as holds for inherent oppositive dimensions — namely, the commutation with the expression plane. The verb *bark*, for instance, denotes a kind of cry determined by its solidarity with a given subject — a dog. The change of subject — for instance, its replacement with "horse" — results in a change of expression: *bark* is replaced by *neigh*.

The commutative relevance criterion may appear too severe, for it disregards a large number of syntagmatic relations among contents which are clearly relevant on conceptual grounds. Coseriu, for instance, criticises Bally for treating the associations raised by the concept "boeuf" ("ox") as if they were a network of lexical relations involving the French word *boeuf*: "The word *boeuf* evokes: 1) *vache*, *taureau*, *veau*, *cornes*, *ruminer*, *beugler*, etc., 2) *labour*, *charrue*, *joug*, etc., *viande*, *abattoir*, *boucherie*, etc.; finally, it can — and, in French, does — trigger associations with the concept of strength, endurance, patient effort, but also slowness, heaviness, passivity" (Bally, 1940: 196). What Bally describes here reminds one of what a cognitive linguist would call the ox scheme, that is, one of those conceptual models which play a strategic role in our shared categorization of experience and provide cognitive criteria for the correct use of words in actual texts and discourses. In spite of their relevance on cognitive grounds, however, it is a fact that only a part of Bally's associations are true lexical structures, accessible to a commutative criterion — namely, the oppositions between "boeuf", "taureau", "vache" and "veau", and the lexical solidarity with "beugler". Other cognitively relevant associations — for instance, the association with "labour" and "charrue", not to speak of the ideas of "lenteur" or "lourdeur" — have no effect upon the immanent lexical value of "boeuf".[197]

The case of lexical solidarities highlights the reasons for and limits of a formal analysis of immanent lexical structures. On the one hand, a lexical analysis is not formal if it does not rigorously distinguish language-specific lexical structures from general cognitive and conceptual structures. On the other hand, it is precisely this kind of methodological coherence that betrays the inherent limits of a purely formal approach to lexical analysis, which by definition is blind to any functional reason. Once its limits are clear, a coherent formal description overtly pleads for a complementary functional description, that is, for a description focusing on the positive conceptual content carried by words.[198]

A clear awareness of the specific properties and limits of formal lexical structures in general, and lexical solidarities in particular, is all the more strategic within our project, for lexical solidarities show a striking structural resemblance with both complex cognitive structures and consistency criteria. As lexical solidarities, complex cognitive structures and consistency criteria look like restrictions imposed on the range of arguments admitted by relational terms. As we shall see in the next chapter, it is owing to this surface resemblance that consistency criteria can easily be identified with both lexical solidarities and cognitive models.

2. Formal and functional relevance criteria on the content plane

The fact that lexical structures contain relations and correlations between content units suggests that these content units, which are relevant to the formal articulation of lexical structures, can also be considered the building blocks — the atoms, or the components — of a functionally relevant definition of lexical contents. Such a suggestion directly transfers onto the content plane a general methodological conclusion authorised in the expression plane by the results of phonological analysis — namely, the perfect coincidence between formally and functionally oriented relevance criteria.

In the expression plane, formal and functional relevance coincide because the differential content of phonemes, which defines their value from a formal and immanent point of view, is also relevant in functional terms. In order to define the formal identity of phonemes, phonological analysis regards as relevant — as "pertinent" — a small set of features among the many to be found in the phonic purport, that is, distinctive features. Insofar as the relevant linguistic function of phonemes is the distinctive function, however, the bundle of phonic features which defines the formal identity of a phoneme coincides exactly with the set of phonic features that are relevant to its function — that language users rely upon for distinguishing significant words.

Accordingly, in order to justify the function of phonemes in linguistic use, one has only to take into account their differential structure. The inclusion within the definition of a phoneme of any aspect of the phonic purport devoid of distinctive power would not only be redundant, but also misleading, for the identification of phonemes and words within the speech chain is essentially differential. The irrelevant features of the phonic purport do not contribute in any way to the distinctive function; on the contrary, open as they are to any kind of variation, they represent as such a potential source of disturbance. If it were not kept under control by a network of shared distinctive features,[199] the intricate patchwork of individual, social and geographic variations which characterise the non-distinctive features would create chaos.

If we compare the form-function balance holding in the expression plane with the content plane, two intertwined questions are at issue. The first question is an empirical one: can the differential structure that is at the basis of the formal and differential characterisation of lexical values provide an adequate lexical definition of them? The second question is a theoretical one, focusing on the general ideas about linguistic structure and function that underlie semantic enquiry: do formal and functional relevance criteria coincide in the content plane as they do in the expression plane?

2.1 The identification between formal and functional relevance criteria: componential analysis

> The *genus* ought to separate the subject from all other things, and the *differentia* from something in the same *genus* (Aristotle)

The identification between formally and functionally-based relevance criteria is the leading idea of the componential analysis of lexical units.

Within a componential framework, the formal relevance criterion is at work insofar as the atomic components isolated by semantic analysis are meant to be differential in nature — they differentiate the sense of a word from the sense of other words, or the coexisting senses of a polysemous word, from one another. Katz & Fodor (1963: 185–186) define meaning components as "the means by which we can decompose the meaning of one sense of a lexical item into atomic concepts, and thus exhibit the semantic structure IN a dictionary entry and the semantic relations BETWEEN dictionary entries. That is, the semantic relations among various senses of a lexical item and among the various senses of different lexical items".[200]

In spite of its focusing on lexical oppositions and relations, however, the overt aim of the componential project is not the description of immanent, language-specific lexical structures, but a functionally adequate explanation of linguistic use: "semantics takes over the explanation of the speaker's ability to produce and understand new sentences at the point where grammar leaves off" (172–173).

Componential analysis is based on formal criteria, but its aim is openly oriented towards function. As a consequence, either form and function are solidary in the content plane as they are in the expression plane, or the componential project is destined to collapse, torn as it is between the criteria it is based upon and the objectives it aims at. This is the reason why a critical examination of both theoretical assumptions and empirical issues of the componential programme against lexical data is the most straightforward way of examining the relationship between form and function in the content plane.

2.2 Beyond the form of content

The main theoretical presupposition of componential analysis — the identification between formal and functional criteria for meaning analysis — has some corollaries which can be checked against empirical evidence. According to the first corollary, the possibility of analyzing the meaning of lexemes into such simpler conceptual factors — or components — as semantic radicals and oppositive dimensions is taken for granted for all lexical fields. According to the second, an exhaustive lexical definition of a given lexeme contains no more than the bundle of differential features which distinguishes its meaning from the competing meanings. Both the first and second corollary rest on the presupposition that any lexical definition necessarily takes the form of a differential definition, which is taken as a generally adequate model for lexical definition.[201] A careful evaluation of a significant sample of empirical data shows that all these assumptions are untenable.

2.2.1 *Lack of lexical components*

The project of componential analysis assumes the general validity of a sort of ideal type of lexical paradigm, circumscribed by a root meaning identified on differential grounds and organised by clear oppositive dimensions. Such an assumption is encouraged by the observation of some very simple paradigms such as those analysed by Hjelmslev — for instance, the paradigm which organises the root meaning "sheep" along the dimension of sex into the opposite values "ram" and "ewe". If this model were of general application, the lexical structure would look like a perfect pyramid. Within this pyramid each field, circumscribed by a superordinate hyperonym, would include a set of distinct units, each of which would dominate, in turn, a subordinate field, down to the most specific values. This ideal type of lexical paradigm, however, cannot be assumed as a general model for lexical structures. Most lexical fields do not match it, because they lack either a differentiated root meaning or definite oppositive dimensions.

With some lexical fields, the identification of a root meaning is in itself very difficult. Lyons (1963: 80) remarks, for instance, that "the common factor, y, of *good* and *bad* is no more easily described in terms of reference than is the meaning of *good* and *bad* themselves".

In some cases, a root concept is not difficult to define in itself. The paradigm formed by such verbs as *breathe*, *eat* and *drink*, for instance, could be described as organising, along an oppositive dimension identified by the nature of the appropriate object, the absorption of substances by a living body in order to keep alive. This is certainly a consistent concept, easily identifiable on cognitive grounds. Yet, it cannot be considered as a language-specific root meaning, for it does not correspond to the meaning of a hyperonym lexeme.

In other cases, a lexeme denoting the root meaning of a field is easy to identify, but its content cannot be analysed as a bundle of differential features. For instance, the content of the lexeme "kill", which is the root meaning of a field including, among others, the values "assassinate", "murder", "slaughter", is analysed by Lehrer (1974: 113) into the components "CAUSE TO BECOME DEAD". Independently of their being adequate on conceptual grounds,[202] however, such components cannot be considered as true oppositive features, for they are independent of the network of lexical relations, and not differential in nature. Though highly schematic, such a definition is not differential, but is clearly oriented towards an analytical description of the substantive content of the verb.

The absence of a clear differential characterisation of the root meaning is not incompatible with a sharp inner organisation of the field, but deprives it of the complementary property which defines, according to Trier, the ideal type of lexical field, that is, its forming part of a higher level paradigmatic structure. The paradigms of this kind look like well-managed estates devoid of definite outer borders and surrounded by wilderness.

In some cases, a well-defined root meaning circumscribes a paradigm whose values, though kept distinct as meanings of different lexemes, cannot be differentiated on the basis of well-defined oppositive dimensions. When a field lacks clear oppositive dimensions, it is its inner structure that is defective, whereas its links with the lexical structures of higher level are strong. Instead of resembling well-managed estates surrounded by wilderness, such paradigms look like patches of loosely organised terrain delimited by clear borders.

The field of flowers, for instance, is well circumscribed by a root meaning — the content of the hyperonym "flower". Its inner organisation, however, cannot rely on language-specific oppositive dimensions. As a consequence, the differentiation of the competing values of the field cannot be anchored to sharp differential features of their content. Of course, an indefinite set of differences can be imagined between, say, a hyacinth and a rose on empirical and cognitive grounds. Yet, none can be seen as diagnostic on language-specific grounds — that is, as far as the relationship with distinct expressions is concerned.[203] Any could be sufficient; yet, none can be held as necessary. A tentative analysis of the meaning of the different lexemes into differential features is bound to fail on both formal and functional grounds. On formal grounds, because no such feature would be clearly connected with the relevant distinctions among expressions; on functional grounds, because a list of differential features would be both potentially endless and incapable of justifying the use of distinct concepts for identifying different kinds of flowers.[204]

When no relevant oppositive dimension can be identified in order to differentiate the competing meanings of a field, the consequence is that the value of each lexeme depends more on the relation with the denoted objects than on the network of correlations with the competing lexemes. The value of the lexeme "hyacinth", for instance, relies more on the stability of its relation with the natural kind of flowers we call hyacinths, than on the structural stability of the field of flowers. As a matter of fact, the structure of the field recalls more an open series — a nomenclature — than a true paradigm. In the presence of an open series, the main principle of differential analysis of meaning — "The value of a word is only recognised when it is set off against the value of neighbouring and opposing words. It has meaning only as part of a whole; meaning only exists in a field" (Trier, 1931(1973: 45)) — does not really hold.

What is challenged by the observation of real lexical fields is the general idea that the lexicon is a rigid formal system of differential values. The lexicon certainly displays a systematic and differential structure insofar as its values are identified as members of relations and correlations. In spite of this, the lexicon cannot be considered as the manifestation of an abstract model of formal system governed by a strictly differential principle, but is to be seen as a sort of confederation of conceptual territories whose interconnections and inner structures receive a specific shape in each case. The map traced by lexical structures within the territory of concepts and experience recalls more the unforeseeable, contingent outcome of a disordered occupation by heterogeneous and conflicting waves of pioneers than the result of a planned activity of *centuriatio*.

If we look at lexical structures through an ideal abstract model, we cannot help seeing in it all kinds of gaps, redundancies and asymmetries, and interpreting them as a strong argument against the idea that the lexicon has an immanent formal structure. If lexical structure is taken as it really is, however, its formal imperfections are the best argument in favour of this idea. If lexical structures were the faithful expression of an independent, maybe universal abstract structural principle, they would not be true lexical structures — they would be, just as scientific nomenclatures are, a passive mapping onto sets of words of independent cognitive structures. The lexicon is neither a pure form, nor does it simply express an independent form — it has a form of its own to the extent that it shapes the heterogeneous areas open to experience, and not beyond. The function of lexical structures is not to display a form, but to provide the formal conditions for the linguistic elaboration and expression of concepts. The effectual formal conditions under which such a function is performed are the result of a complex and variable negotiation with the peculiar and differentiated characteristics of the shaped conceptual purport. The accurate networks of distinctive criteria which are indispensable for organising socially and culturally specific constructed fields would be redundant if applied to concrete beings open to direct experience, which lexical values are called upon to express rather than to construct. The form of content has to be looked for where and to the extent that it is actually at work, and not beyond.

2.2.2 *Formal differentiation, differential definitions, substantive definitions*

> Vanity and pride are different things,
> though the words are often used synonymously.
> A person may be proud without being vain.
> Pride relates more to our opinion of ourselves,
> vanity to what we would have others think of us (Austen)

The second assumption of componential analysis is the identification of formal differentiation and lexical definition: according to the componential hypothesis, the definition of a lexeme contains no more than the set of distinctive features which keep apart the meaning of a lexeme from the meanings of the competing lexemes. As Nida (1975: 32) points out, "In order to analyze any referential meaning [...] one must identify those 'necessary and sufficient' features that distinguish the meaning of any one form from every other form which might compete for a place within the same semantic territory [...] The related meanings of *walk*, *run*, *hop*, *skip* and *crawl* — for instance — constitute such a cluster of contiguous meanings. They all share the feature of movement by an animate being, using the limbs; but the number of limbs, the order of movement, and the relation of the limbs to the supporting surface involve clearly definable contrasts".

As this assumption rests on the previous condition that any lexical definition is necessarily differential,[205] the most straightforward way of falsifying it is simply to identify some conceptual areas which, requiring substantive definitions, would necessarily reject the differential model and, *a fortiori*, the distinctive model. Such a step, however, would have the disadvantage of leaving aside the complex and revealing links between different kinds of concepts and different models of definitions, and between the formal differentiation of lexical values and a positive description based on the shared experience of things. This is the reason why the whole question will be examined in some detail.

The core of a given concept may be provided either by a language-specific bundle of distinctive features or by a point of reference directly located outside lexical structures, in the field of shared experience. The concept may be defined as endocentric in the former case, as exocentric in the latter. According to the kind of concepts it is applied to, a definition aims either at differentiating a concept from a set of competing values, or at describing its content in a positive way. The definition is differential in the former case, substantive in the latter. While exocentric concepts sometimes require a differential definition and sometimes a substantive one, endocentric concepts are only compatible with differential definitions, which implies that substantive definitions are restricted to exocentric concepts. The application of different models of definition to different kinds of concepts thus gives rise to three ideal types of definitions: differential definitions of endocentric concepts, differential definitions of exocentric concepts and substantive definitions of exocentric concepts.

2.2.2.1 *Differential definitions of endocentric concepts.* The differential definition of an endocentric concept is the kind of definition that is closest to the componential model. Even in these highly favourable cases, however, a functionally adequate definition of a lexeme cannot be reduced to a bundle of distinctive features. In order to examine this point, let us consider Lehrer's description of the field dominated by the root meaning "kill", and including the values "murder", "assassinate", "slaughter", "exterminate", "execute", "slay", "butcher", and "massacre".

As the lexemes of the field are supposed to provide the root meaning "kill" each with a peculiar modification, their definition takes the general form "kill so and so". In particular, "murder" adds to the root meaning "kill" such features as "WITH MALICIOUS INTENTIONS, ILLEGAL or IMMORAL ACT, etc. on the part of the agent of the verb [...];'assassinate' adds the restriction that the object must be a person in a position of political importance and that the agent has a political motive for killing. 'Slaughter' and 'butcher' seem to be terms used primarily for the killing of animals for food [...] 'Slay' is applied to humans or higher animals, overlapping somewhat with 'slaughter', but it has an archaic, especially biblical, connotation. 'Exterminate' is usually used for intentionally killing in order to get rid of fairly low forms of animal life, e. g. insects, or animals that are considered pests, e. g. rats [...] 'Massacre' adds the feature that the object consists of a group of people [...] 'Execute' is like 'kill', and adds the qualification that the act is a punishment for a crime and is carried out according to the laws or mores of a social group"[206] (Lehrer, 1974: 123–124).

Lehrer's analysis is both a good model of differential definition and a good illustration of the difficulties one is bound to meet when trying to reduce a differential definition to a bundle of differential features. Even in the most favourable cases, when the differentiation among the contents of a set of competing lexemes depends on a definite set of modifications applied to a root meaning, it is one thing simply to assume this circumstance, another to make explicit exactly what modifications are at work as distinctive features, and yet another to range these putative differential features along systematic oppositive dimensions.

It is certainly highly plausible that the co-hyponyms of "kill" are differentiated from each other by different modifications and restrictions applied to a common root meaning. In spite of this, the observation of the proposed definitions shows that the formulation of such features looks like an analytical and informal description, which cannot easily be reduced to a matrix of oppositive values distributed according to clear dimensions. Moreover, even if these difficulties were overcome, this would leave the major problem that most differential definitions of the kind proposed by Lehrer look redundant if aimed at a purely formal differentiation among competing lexical values. For instance, the characterisation of "assassinate" in terms of both solidary object — "a person in a position of political importance" — and attitude on the part of the agent — who "has a political motive for killing" — though fully justified on functional grounds, is redundant in terms of formal differentiation. The reason is that it takes into account more features than are required to justify the differences.

Such a circumstance, moreover, is not at all exceptional. A satisfactory differential definition is almost bound to go far beyond the scope of a purely formal differentiation. In order to provide a formal differentiation with a conceptual body, a small difference in content is a sufficient condition. But if a definition has to account for the real uses of a word, a single conceptual difference with the competing values is not necessarily sufficient.

As a rule, there are more functionally relevant properties to be taken into account in a differential definition than are required for a formal differentiation. When analysing the field of cooking, Lehrer (1974: 72) observes that "one could specify components minimally — that is, put in just enough features to separate the cooking items from one another — or one could specify components maximally — that is, fill in as many other components as possible. The first alternative is appealing because it results in a simpler or at least shorter characterisation of lexical items. The second alternative, however, results in a more complete description". But the alternative is not merely, as Lehrer seems to maintain, a matter of economy. What is at issue, in fact, is the choice between two competing relevance criteria. The first alternative is formally oriented towards a pure differentiation; the second is functionally oriented towards an exhaustive definition.

While a differential analysis specifies only those "' necessary and sufficient' features that distinguish the meaning of any one form from every other form which might compete for a place within the same semantic territory" (Nida, 1975: 32), a differential definition aims at specifying *any* possibly differential feature: "the right definition of a lexical term is the one which makes explicit all the distinctive features differentiating it from all other lexical terms within the same system" (Alinei, 1974: 22). If a differential definition does not coincide in principle with a bundle of purely differential features, it is because the relevance criterion at work is not the same. Accordingly, even the differential definition of an endocentric concept makes visible the tension between a form-oriented differential analysis and an exhaustive descriptive definition.

Once this point has been made clear, the fact remains that the definition of an endocentric concept is necessarily differential, or at least constructed around a differential core. Though richer than a bundle of purely distinctive features, and even ready to make room for substantive components, an endocentric concept has to be considered an expansion of it. An interesting example is provided by kinship terms.

A kinship term could hardly be defined without taking into account its position within the network of correlations organising the relevant field. If the meanings of "primary kinship terms, identifying so-called 'blood-relations' are compared [...], the resulting relations constitute a systematic cluster, in which the three sets of components — sex, generation and lineality — serve to define the basic distinctions" (Nida, 1975: 34). A concept like "father", for instance, has at its core the bundle of differential features which "serve to distinguish this meaning from others in the same domain", that is, "male sex, one ascending generation above ego, and direct line of descent" (Nida, 1975: 33). As Nida himself remarks, the presence of a language-specific differential core is perfectly compatible with substantive implications: "In a simile such as *he was like a father to the boy* — for instance — the diagnostic components of the central meaning of *father* become secondary, and other components become diagnostic,[207] e.g. (1) watchful care for and (2) companionship. In the use of *father* as a name for God, e.g. our *Father in Heaven*, the principal component meanings are (1) watchful care (on the part of God) and (2) appropriate respect (on the part of the worshipper)" (Nida, 1975: 35). If we consider the concept in its whole structure, however, these implications are supposed to cluster, along with any other non-distinctive shared ideas about fatherhood, around the restricted set of diagnostic components, just as planets revolve around the sun.

2.2.2.2 *Differential definitions of exocentric concepts*

> STRANGER: But it would be unreasonable not to divide hunting into two parts.
> THEAETETUS: Say how it can be done.
> STRANGER: By dividing it into the hunting of the lifeless and of the living (Plato)

Endocentric concepts necessarily require differential definitions, because they are rooted in the differential structure of lexical values. Differential definitions, on the other hand, are not limited to endocentric concepts. If this were the case, we would be forced to conclude that the only differences to be found among concepts are the differences imposed on experience by language-specific lexical structures. In fact, it is not difficult to admit such differentiated experiences of different things as to provide an independent ground for differential definitions.

The common experience of rocks, stones and pebbles, for instance, is an experience of differences, and in the first place of differences among what one can do with each kind of thing. One can climb rocks but not stones or pebbles, throw stones and pebbles but not rocks; "*pebbles*, on the other hand, differ from *stones* in being small enough to be picked up with a finger and a thumb" (Wierzbicka, 1988: 510). Being hit by a stone and being hit by a pebble is not the same. Differences in behaviour and perception of this kind are salient enough to provide a differential definition of such lexemes as *rock*, *stone* (as a count noun) and *pebble* with relatively firm "cognitive anchors" (Wierzbicka, 1996: 318) or even "centers of perception" (Cassirer, 1944: 134).

A differential definition of an exocentric concept is like a differential definition of an endocentric concept, in that it takes into account the whole paradigm of competing values. It differs from it in that the criteria for differentiation are not rooted in a bundle of distinctive features organising the paradigm and systematically correlated with differences in expression, but are found outside the lexical structure, directly in the structure of a shared experience of things. Owing to their dependence on a whole paradigm, differential exocentric concepts are open towards language-specific shaping. Owing to their roots in a common experience, they are sensitive to the pressure of things. The possible issues of this tension between language-specific shaping and outer pressures ideally form a *continuum*, along which each paradigm finds its peculiar point of equilibrium. While the paradigm containing *rock*, *stone* and *pebble* seems significantly moulded by salient differences in experience, the system of colour concepts encapsulates fragments of independently shaped experience in highly language-specific shells.[208]

Colour concepts are at one and the same time language-specific, even highly idiosyncratic for their form, and exocentric, that is, identified and differentiated thanks to external cognitive anchors. Colour lexemes do not form an open series but a true paradigm, or hierarchy of paradigms. Accordingly, the value of a colour lexeme can only be defined with reference to the complex structure of the whole field. Before describing a colour category in terms of shared experience of typical phenomena, one has to circumscribe the area it covers in differential terms. At the same time, the differentiation of colour concepts does not rely on definite differential dimensions internal to lexical paradigms, but rests on the identification of salient chromatic differences within a largely shared, if not universal experience — the experience of seeing things against familiar backgrounds: for instance, "the sky (often blue), the ground (often brown), the grass (typically green), the sun (often yellow and brilliant), the sea (often dark blue), the broad expanse of snow (normally white)" (Wierzbicka, 1996: 289).

Differential definitions of exocentric concepts remind us that we can see substantive differences between things named by different lexemes even if these differences are not rooted in the differential content of linguistic paradigms. This in turn implies that the experience of things has to a certain extent a structure of its own, independent of the form imposed on it by lexical structures.

2.2.2.3 *Substantive definitions of exocentric concepts*

> What's in a name? That which we call a rose
> By any other word would smell as sweet (Shakespeare)

Though raising more problems than a strict componential hypothesis would admit, endocentric differential definitions do not radically challenge the idea that the functional aspect of word meaning is rooted in formal differentiation. The idea becomes untenable in the case of exocentric differential definitions, and above all when dealing with substantive definitions of exocentric concepts.

A substantive definition of an exocentric concept is like its differential counterpart in two respects: it is typical of those paradigms of lexemes which lack any clear oppositive dimension, and the core of the concept is located outside the language-specific lexical patterns.[209] It differs from its differential counterpart in that each *definiendum* is immediately and independently anchored in a fragment of experience, without taking into account the whole paradigm of competing values. As a consequence, the paradigm itself does not behave as a closed structure formed by interdependent values but as an open series of independent labels. It is this circumstance that deprives a differential definition of its structural basis.[210]

The most typical examples of open series are provided by the fields giving expression to natural kinds. If we consider the field of flowers, for instance, the natural starting point for a definition is the root meaning of the field — the meaning "flower". A definition of "rose", for instance, takes the form "A rose is a flower that…". At the moment of explicating the specific properties of this particular kind of flower called *rose*, however, a differential characterisation would strike us as unnatural.

A differential definition of a given lexeme is supposed to take into account the whole set of competing meaning units. Now, such a condition contradicts our real experience of natural kinds. Unlike what happens in true paradigms, the gain or loss of a term in the series of flowers would not radically affect the definition of each individual lexeme. If a new name of flower entered the language, or a flower lost its name, sinking among the hundreds and hundreds whose smell or beauty defies anonymity, such a circumstance would not affect the actual content of the word *rose*. As it is not taken into a network of interdependent values, the content of each lexeme critically depends on its vertical relationship with things. Speakers' natural attitude is consistent with this premise. In order to answer the question "What kind of flower is a rose?", one is unlikely to take as a starting point what kind of flower a rose *is not*, and in what respects. Instead, one would probably try to make out what a rose can positively be said to be. One would probably show a good instance, or describe a schematic model of rose. If any difference with other familiar flowers were taken into account, it would be only for illustration's sake, and at random.

A differential definition is based on the assumption that any relevant property of a given item is *ipso facto* a differential one. Now, a rigid application of the differential criterion to such fields as natural kinds inevitably ends in absurdity. If one had to define the meaning of *carrot* according to a componential criterion, for instance, one would have to face the following embarrassing dilemma: on the one hand, "the tapered shape of a carrot seems to be a criterial condition in the definition of English CARROT"; on the other hand, "there appears to be no English word designating a vegetable similar to a carrot in all ways except that it is spherical in shape" (Weinreich, 1975: 34), the only circumstance which would give the criterial feature the dignity of a differential one.[211] Instead of dreaming of a world of vegetables created to match differential definitions by filling imaginary lexical gaps, it is wiser to admit that a positive property of a thing can be critical for a definition without being differential.

Even if a differential characterisation of natural kind lexemes were feasible, moreover, it would not have at its core a formal differentiation, for the differential structure of the lexical field is empty of any conceptual purport. One could know the exact position of the meaning unit "rose" among the lexical structures of English, not only without being able to identify a single distinctive property of it, but also without knowing anything about roses. One could even translate a book about flowers without actually being able to identify any of them. As Lyons (1977: 293) points out, "it is important to note that one can learn, in this way, that one lexeme is a hyponym of another or that two lexemes are co-hyponyms without in principle knowing anything more of their meaning [...] We might know, for example, that 'banyan' is a hyponym of 'tree' or 'osprey' of 'bird' and yet be unable to say how banyans differ from other trees or ospreys from other birds".

In the field of exocentric concepts, the organisation of lexical fields in distinct values presupposes a parallel differentiation between the corresponding concepts without providing it with a body. The differentiation is not rooted in differential lexical structures but in the structures of experience. Unlike exocentric differential concepts, on the other hand, exocentric substantive concepts do not rely on differences directly offered by experience in order to identify different kinds of things, but attain differentiation thanks to the positive identification of a clear-cut model for each different kind of thing. In the case of the differential definition of exocentric concepts, we immediately see significant differences among kinds of things. Positive identity is grounded on sharp differentiation. In the case of the substantive definition of exocentric concepts, we see different kinds of things because each kind of thing offers itself to experience with a strong identity. Differentiation is grounded in positive identity.

For all these reasons, the dictionary definitions of such exocentric concepts as "rose" look more like a tentative description of good samples of the denoted thing than like an exploration of lexical structures. It is no wonder, then, that the lexical fields connected with such natural kinds of beings as flowers or creatures are the elective domain of prototype semantics and, more generally, of cognitively and perceptually based descriptive criteria.

2.2.3 *The structure of concepts: Arbitrariness and motivation*

The fact that the form of exocentric concepts rests more on the independent structure of experience than on the differential lexical structures calls into question the arbitrariness of word meanings. Insofar as the structure of a concept critically depends on the form of shared experience, the way concepts are cut out is motivated to a given extent from outside lexical structures. Saussure's well-known remarks, however, could lead us to think that if the structure of concepts is motivated from outside, the idea that concepts are arbitrary can no longer be maintained. Now, an inference of this kind would only be justified if the concepts of "arbitrariness" and "motivation" formed an exclusive opposition. This assumption, however, is not confirmed by the logical behaviour of our couple of concepts.

When two correlative concepts form an exclusive opposition, to state one concept amounts to negating the opposite. If one says that a person is dead, for instance, one necessarily negates that this same person is alive. This does not hold when a couple of concepts form a paradigm of gradable antonyms — for instance "good" and "bad" or "warm" and "cold". Whereas exclusive opposites cut up the conceptual area into two incompatible halves, antonyms define the opposite end points of a graded scale. This implies that the ranges of application of polar concepts are not reciprocally exclusive, but overlapping and therefore in competition. To say that a stone is warm, for instance, does not exclude coldness from its determination and vice-versa, because what we call warm or cold are in fact different degrees of heat and thus different points of equilibrium between the opposite poles of warm and cold.

The logical behaviour of the concepts "arbitrariness" and "motivation" is exactly the same. Arbitrariness does not exclude motivation because arbitrariness and motivation are the opposite poles of a graded scale. Absolute arbitrariness and absolute motivation are ideal points of reference, which are not instantiated in facts. As far as real conceptualisation is concerned, there is no such thing as absolute arbitrariness or absolute motivation. Absolute arbitrariness and absolute motivation are equally incompatible with the life of language, just as absolute warmth and absolute cold are equally incompatible with life on earth. In the same way as we call warm and cold different degrees of heat, we call arbitrariness and motivation different points of equilibrium between an immanent form stemming from lexical structures and the independent structure of experience. Arbitrariness and motivation, in other words, are opposite outcomes of one and the same conflict between two antagonistic forces: the impulse of linguistic structures to impose their form on cognitive structures, and the impulse of cognitive structures to project their form onto their means of expression. If arbitrariness does not exclude motivation, it is because a language-specific organisation of lexical fields cannot avoid interacting with an independent experience of things. Arbitrariness, thus, does not mean that a linguistic sign cannot be motivated at all. It simply means that a sign holds as a sign irrespective of any motivation.

If these remarks are true, the only consistent way of speaking of arbitrariness in relation to concepts is to consider the concept of arbitrariness as a sort of unmarked term — as a term which refers to the conceptual space circumscribed by the opposition instead of simply denoting one of its poles. In this sense, to say that concepts are arbitrary amounts to saying that there is a question about arbitrariness to be asked about concepts. Starting from this premise, however, the appropriate question about arbitrariness is not the polar yes/no question asked once and for all, but a graded question to be asked for each concept. It is not so much whether concepts are arbitrary or motivated, as to what extent each of them is motivated. The general polar question about arbitrariness is senseless on two accounts. First, it is senseless as a polar question, because it rests on the false presupposition that concepts are either arbitrary or motivated. Second, it is senseless as a general question, because the struggle for form between cognitive purport and linguistic modelling is open to many different outcomes. Asking to what extent concepts are motivated makes sense because its presupposition — for each concept, it is possible to identify a specific balance between arbitrariness and motivation — indicates the path towards an empirical enquiry about arbitrariness. As a matter of fact, which kind of balance between arbitrariness and motivation is attained by each particular concept is an empirical question.[212]

Looked at from this standpoint, the case of natural kinds is a good example of the complex interaction between the structure of experience and the shaping power of lexical structures. On the one hand, the living language of a community cannot possibly avoid putting a label on salient and familiar objects of shared experience. The outcome is the presence, among lexical structures, of open series of labels whose composition is essentially motivated by the impulse of salient things towards expression. In these cases, the structure of experience overcomes the immanent lexical organization in the struggle for form. On the other hand, nothing prevents lexical structures from imposing on experience an independent organization grounded in autonomous lexical structures, and many significant examples of arbitrary divisions are to be found precisely among natural kinds.[213] It depends on the specific lexical structure, in particular, which natural kinds are focused on and which are not — how many kinds of flowers have a name, for instance — and what degree of accuracy is attained in differentiation — for example, how many ways of categorising a horse are to be found.[214] In these cases, the struggle for form has an opposite outcome.

In fact, there is no contradiction between the idea that lexical fields receive an arbitrary articulation in each language and the idea that some areas of the real experience of things can be largely shared — if not, in some cases, universal. The language-specific organisation of the content plane is certainly arbitrary, in the sense that the structure of semantic fields across languages cannot be fully predicted from within the structure of experience. This, however, is only one side of arbitrariness — the side one sees from within linguistic structures. The other side of arbitrariness — the side one sees from the standpoint of experience — implies that the specific shape of linguistic fields does not prevent a shared experience from taking place and projecting a form of its own onto lexical structures. Taken as a whole, arbitrariness means that both linguistic structures and experience have a specific and autonomous shape. After all, if experience is not a prison for linguistic structures, why should linguistic structures be a prison for the structure of experience?

2.3 The conflict between form and function on the content plane

> Words, as is well known,
> are the great foes of reality (Conrad)

The tendency to identify a formal, differential description of lexical relations with a functionally oriented semantic analysis is not justified by the empirical reality of lexical data, but is the outcome of a deeply rooted set of assumptions about linguistic form and functions whose basis lies in the conception of language as a closed semiotic system. This idea of language, which dates back to an intuition of Aristotle,[215] has imposed itself among linguists as the leading idea of Prague School phonology, and is explicitly formulated by Hjelmslev (1943(1961)).

Looked at from a semiotic point of view, a language is defined as a relationship of bilateral implication between two planes, expression and content: "The sign function is itself a solidarity. Expression and content are solidary — they necessarily presuppose each other. An expression is expression only by virtue of its being an expression of a content, and a content is a content only by virtue of its being a content of an expression" (Hjelmslev, 1943(1961)). Postulating a complete reversibility of the relation between expression and content, such a formulation clearly displays the limits of the semiotic idea of language. If anybody is ready to admit that an expression is an expression only insofar as it is the counterpart of a content, the idea that a content is just the counterpart of a linguistic expression severely narrows the scope of semantic research.

The relationship between expression and content — or semiotic function — is perfectly reversible as far as linguistic form is concerned. The expression plane becomes a linguistic reality — it receives a language-specific form — insofar as it is connected to the content plane. The content plane, in turn, becomes a linguistic reality — it receives a language-specific form — insofar as it is related to expression. If we take into account linguistic function, however, this perfect symmetry between expression and content plane no longer holds.

The function of the expression plane can be defined within the boundaries of a closed semiotic structure, on the basis of its relation with its counterpart within the semiotic system — with the content. Starting from this premise, the Prague School phonologists succeed in defining the relevant formal units and relations of the expression plane — the phonemes, their paradigmatic structures, syntagmatic dispositions and inner composition in distinctive features — by grounding the formal analysis in a commutation test. This criterion is both immanent, that is, defined within the limits of the semiotic relation, and functional, that is, able to account for the linguistic function of sounds. A phonic unit is considered as a linguistically relevant form — it is a phoneme, or a distinctive feature — if and only if it performs a function in the content plane — if it contributes to the discrimination of distinct words, bearing distinct meanings. The expression plane both receives its linguistic shape and performs its linguistic function owing to its relationship with the solidary plane inside the semiotic structure — namely, the content plane. As both the form and function of sounds are grounded in the semiotic relation, the formal analysis of the expression plane can be based on functional criteria, and its formal units are at the same time functionally relevant units. Form and function run, so to speak, in the same direction.

The form-function *ratio* to be observed in the expression plane no longer holds in the content plane. In the content plane, the form of meaning — the structure of lexical fields — depends on the specific supply of distinct expressions a given language possesses. Therefore, it can be defined within the limits of the semiotic relation between content and expression. What is relevant on functional grounds, on the other hand, is no longer the immanent semiotic relationship between linguistic meanings and the expression plane, but the external, extrasemiotic relationship between linguistic meanings and the world of cognition and emotionality. The function of the distinct meaning units provided by a language is not, of course, to draw distinctions between forms of expression, but to categorize and describe the whole universe of inner and outer experience.[216]

This plain fact has huge theoretical and empirical implications. The formal analysis of the content plane cannot be based on a functional relevance criterion, for the relevance criterion is directed outside the semiotic structure, while the form of meaning is an intrasemiotic datum. Reciprocally, a purely formal analysis of the content plane cannot be taken as relevant on functional grounds, for it leaves aside the relevant extrasemiotic relation between lexical values and categorisation of things. In other words, the analysis of the content plane cannot be both formally and functionally relevant. It cannot at the same time, and on the basis of a single relevance criterion, both characterise the language-specific formal organisation of a given lexical structure and provide an adequate account of the way words are used when engaged in the manipulation of complex conceptual realities.

As far as linguistic expressions are concerned, form and function are parallel vectors, both running from expression to content. When the content of linguistic expressions is involved, form and function run in opposite directions. While the formal vector runs from linguistic content to linguistic expression, the functional vector runs from linguistic content to the world of experience. While the trajectory of the formal vector is internal to the semiotic system, the goal of the functional vector is located outside it. This is the reason why the idea of language as a closed semiotic system becomes inadequate as the guiding idea for a functional analysis of linguistic contents. A semantic analysis of the content plane cannot be both immanent to the linguistic system and functionally relevant.

Though based on a theoretical reflection upon the semiotic idea of language and its implications for form and function, the cleavage between form and function on the content plane is supported by the findings of cognitive semantics (see § 3.4). If it can ignore relevant, basic aspects of human experience, the arbitrary linguistic shaping of the content plane can hinder neither independent access to functionally relevant empirical data nor the construction of shared cognitive models, which in turn can have access to linguistic expression independently of the peculiar lexical structures of a given language. This means that the different conceptual areas open to experience display an independent structure, whose configuration and interaction with immanent lexical structures can be made the object of empirical investigation.

In conclusion, there are many good reasons, both empirical and theoretical, for sharply distinguishing the formal organization of lexical forms from the positive content of concepts. If lexicon is considered as a language-specific reality, it is no more than a purely formal structure. If it has to be substantial, it can no longer be a purely linguistic reality. The only consistent path open to semantic description is to take into account this plain fact, and to describe the formal and functional side of lexical contents on the basis of distinct relevance criteria. A sharp differentiation of relevance criteria secures both the structural autonomy of lexical forms and the autonomous accessibility of substantive contents.

2.4 Having a form and imposing a form

If we maintain that our experience has a structure of its own, and that this structure is to a variable extent independent of the specific lexical form of a given language, we can better grasp the real function of linguistic forms in the active processing of inner and outer experience.

As well as having a form, language is traditionally considered to be a powerful tool — the most powerful, indeed — for imposing a form on our experience, a point which has been made popular by Humboldt's distinction between a static conception of form — *ergon* — and a dynamic and active one — *energeia.* The extent to which linguistic structures can be said to have a form, and the extent to which they can be said to have shaping power, however, are not the same. Any level of linguistic structure — phonology, morphology, lexicon, syntax — displays a specific form in the static sense, or *ergon*, which is the object of linguistic description. But not all these levels are actively involved in shaping experience. The function of phonology, of course, is not immediately connected with shaping experience, and the function of morphology is probably marginal. The question becomes of interest when we take into account lexical and syntactic structures.

The lexicon certainly has a form in the static sense; within the same limits, it can be said to impose a form on the conceptual purport, in that the latter, once worked out by lexical structures, displays a static form — the form of a hierarchy of fields. If, however, we consider form as *energeia* in an active sense, as effectually involved in shaping inner and outer experience, its field of action is certainly not to be found within the borders of lexical structures but outside them, in the active construction of complex meanings by means of syntactic structures.

It is in this sense that syntactic structures are really creative. Formal syntactic structures do not find their function in themselves, but in the ideation of complex meanings. Accordingly, the import of syntactic creativity does not lie so much in the productivity of the mechanism itself — in the possibility of making "infinite use of finite means" (Chomsky, 1965: Chapter 1) — as in the occasion it offers of combining atomic meanings in a virtually unlimited and unforeseeable way — of manipulating concepts in a potentially endless way. If the linguistic shaping of concepts were limited to the organisation of lexical structures, the construction of complex meanings would be no more than a manifestation, in Hjelmslev's sense, of a static form, that is, of a hierarchical system of concepts already moulded once and for all by lexical paradigms. Lexical structure would not be a useful tool at the service of conceptual creativity, but an inescapable conceptual prison. But our experience of texts and discourses tells us all the time that this is not the way things go. In texts and discourses, concepts are called upon to meet a potentially endless demand for categorisation, which endlessly enriches their content, displaces their borders, stresses their very core, and slowly but inevitably affects the configuration of lexical structures.

3. The functional lexicon: A repository of concepts

If considered from a functional point of view, the lexicon can be roughly conceived as a repository of definitions, whose ideal task is to make explicit the tacit criteria governing the use of words. Instead of being seen as a language-specific network of relations and correlations between negative values internal to language-specific structures, the lexicon is taken in its instrumental function, as a system of labels connected to contents of experience which are located outside the linguistic system. Accordingly, the relevance criterion for functionally adequate definitions of lexical contents is not based on a network of semantic contrasts connected with differences in expression, but is directed outside the linguistic system, towards the nebula of contents of experiences which undergo linguistic coding and expression.

Against this background, a first tentative answer to the question of what definitions are about could be the following. Lexemes are used for constructing complex expressions, and the function of complex expressions is to identify complex situations open to real or imaginative experience. Accordingly, the positive content of lexemes can be defined on the basis of their contribution to the identification of complex situations in terms of real or imaginative experience. The idea that to describe a lexical meaning is to make explicit its contribution to the identification of complex situations is explicitly formulated by Fillmore: "the meaning of individual lexical items can best be understood in terms of their contribution to the process of interpreting a text", which in turn amounts to reconstructing coherent scenes activated by (coherent chains of) linguistic expressions: "A word or phrase or sentence or text identifies a scene, and it foregrounds, or highlights, some portion of it" (Fillmore, 1977: 86).

According to Fillmore, a scene is a psychological kind of entity — a picture of a familiar situation, built up out of a mix of actual experiences, memories and imaginings: "I use the word *scene* in a maximally general sense, including not only visual scenes but also familiar kinds of interpersonal transactions, institutional structures, enactive experiences, body images, and, in general, any kind of coherent segment of human beliefs, actions, experiences or imaginings"[217] (Fillmore, 1975: 124). The actual activation of a scene is obviously independent of the presence of any linguistic input, but it is a common experience that linguistic expressions activate scenes.

Texts certainly activate scenes, and in most cases very complex and coherent networks of interconnected scenes, and so do utterances. But even single lexemes are ready to activate scenes, and it is precisely this fact that opens a path towards definitions. The connection with scenes is not at all surprising when the definition of relational lexemes is at issue. It is not surprising, for instance, that in order to define the meaning of *alimony* Fillmore tells a little story: "If A pays alimony to B, we know that at one time A and B were married, we know that roughly at the time of the divorce an agreement was made between the two participants to the effect that one of them would pay money to the other" (Fillmore, 1977: 114). But even the definition of non-relational nouns of individuals is intrinsically relational. One can hardly describe what a bird is, for instance, without any reference to nest making, egg laying and flying, while the most natural starting point for defining a chair is to see it as an artefact for people to sit on (see § 3.5).

The idea that complex scenes are the relevant units for the functional definition of words is a tempting fruit, but a fruit which can be picked only at the end of a difficult path, and maybe a fruit which looks more attractive than it really is. On the one hand, the idea provides lexical description with a relational framework of reference — in other words, scenes are to functional analysis of positive lexical contents what lexical fields and lexical solidarities are to formal analysis of negative lexical values. On the other hand, the contribution to scenes cannot really hold as a relevance criterion for lexical definitions unless one makes clear what kind of complex structure a scene is — namely, whether it is a contingent configuration of empirical data or a shared conceptual structure, a psychological content or a scheme holding *a priori*.

3.1 Scenes and meanings

> Language gives a fuller image [than painting],
> which is all the better for being vague (G. Eliot)

Narrating his first meeting with Friday, Robinson Crusoe expresses himself in the following way: *I beckoned him again to come to me, and gave him all the signs of encouragement that I could think of.* If we try to translate this description into a visual image, we meet some significant difficulties, whose elucidation gives us some hints about the nature of scenes and their relationship with linguistic meanings.

The first difficulty we meet is the fact that the content of the expression, if looked at from the standpoint of a scene, is hopelessly poor. If we were to draw a picture of the described event, for instance, we could not remain as vague as Robinson as to the exact nature of the "signs of encouragement" he sent. If compared with the content of a scene, the meaning of a complex expression easily looks defective, and the meaning of our example certainly is. Yet, the compound sentence is a meaningful one, and its meaning is in no way ambiguous or defective. All the relevant formal connections among its constituents are clearly identified, and so is the role played by each of them. A complex meaning which lacks relevant information in order to be processed into a cognitive scene is not *ipso facto* a defective meaning. If a well-constructed complex meaning does not necessarily provide the entire cognitive purport relevant to building a scene, it is because a well-constructed linguistic meaning and a well-constructed cognitive scene are two different kinds of object, carved out of different raw materials.

A complex meaning — a process — is a conceptual structure drawn in symbolic language, that is, a network of relations among roles provided with a conceptual content, such as agent, patient or instrument, and taken on by entities which are no more than instances of abstract and stylised kinds. A scene is a picture of a concrete situation packed with individual persons and things, drawn in empirical and imaginative language. Accordingly, the processing of a cognitive scene out of a complex meaning is a creative process in two respects: because it supplements the input meanings with specific data and relations which are not specified by the linguistic expression; and above all because it translates the symbolic structure of the complex meaning into a non-isomorphous kind of language, that is, into empirical and imaginative language. Complex meanings are made of concepts. Scenes are made of perceived or imagined things and relations.

Owing to this cleavage, cognitive scenes bear no systematic one-to-one relationship with linguistic meanings. On the one hand, the same scene may be described by different linguistic expressions, each of which, however accurate, inevitably stylises it to a given degree. A fly, for instance, can be said to *cling to a wall* or simply to *be on a wall*. If measured against a scene, the latter expression is decidedly less accurate than the former. As a consequence, its cognitive processing demands a substantial imaginative and empirical complement.

Owing to the degree of stylisation they introduce into the description, on the other hand, complex meanings which construct the same kind of symbolic relationship are in principle open to different forms of cognitive processing[218] according to the relevant positive information about things which is taken as relevant in each case. The expressions *The cat is on the wall* and *The fly is on the wall*, for instance, construct exactly the same kind of abstract, symbolic relationship: in both cases, what is said is that there is a contact between the denoted animal and a wall. This of course does not hold for the corresponding scenes. However simplified, the two scenes cannot help characterising the relationship between the animal and the surface in a more accurate way, which leads to a significant difference in empirical content. Thanks to general perceptual data about flies, cats and walls, one can easily imagine the fly clinging to a vertical surface, while the cat can be consistently imagined only on a wall provided with an (unnamed) top. If the relevance criterion for lexical meanings is their contribution to the processing of scenes, such items of information about flies, cats and walls have to be in some way included in the definition of the lexemes. More generally, if the relevance criterion for lexical definition is the contribution of words to the identification of scenes, there seems to be no clear limit to the amount of empirical or imaginative information which may be relevant, for there is no clear limit to the amount of data one has to master in order to process scenes.

The last obstacle towards the use of scenes as relational backgrounds for definitions is their contingent dimension. Scenes are open to contingency on two sides, as empirical structures and as cognitive counterparts of meaningful linguistic expressions.

On the one hand, if scenes are made up of empirical and imaginative materials, their structure depends to a given extent on contingent experiences of contingent things. In particular, there is no clear limit imposed on the characterisation of things and situations involved in them. How far can one go, for instance, in depicting the actual cat and the actual wall within a cat-on-the-wall scene?

On the other hand, the activation of a scene out of a meaningful expression takes place when the expression is actually used in a text or in an act of communication. This implies that the activation of a scene is, just like any part of an interpretative process, a contingent act, which gathers into a coherent interpretative field a great amount of encyclopaedic and contingent information. The following verses, for instance, can be coherently interpreted only against a field that contains a certain amount of encyclopaedic knowledge about Greek mythology:

> The river is fateful
> Like the last one. But there is no ferryman.
> He could not bend against its propelling force
> (W. Stevens)

Moreover, the amount of knowledge which is normally required in order to interpret a contingent act of communication spreads far beyond any imaginable corpus of encyclopaedic information, and necessarily includes data which are as ephemeral as the act they are involved in.

Insofar as scenes are contingent outcomes of contingent acts, made of empirical substance which in turn is open to contingency, the relevant information required for processing scenes out of linguistic expression is, at least to some extent, situational and contingent. At this point, if the relevance criterion for lexical meanings is their contribution to the processing of scenes, is a lexical definition assumed to contain any piece of information, even contingent, which proves to be relevant to the processing of a scene? If this is so, how can a lexical definition be exhaustive without exploding into a nebulous mass of random data? If this is not so, under which supplementary conditions can the idea that "meanings are relativized to scenes" (Fillmore, 1977: 84) be consistently maintained?

The sense of the above remarks and questions is not that the idea of anchoring definitions in relational structures located in experience has to be given up. In fact, semantic description cannot help facing the relationship between meanings and scenes because it cannot help facing the complex relationship between linguistic meanings, concepts and experience, whose construction and description is in any case the end point of the use of words. Certainly the fruit has to be picked. But if one decides to pick it, one ought to be aware of the traps laid along the path.

3.2 Lexical meanings and encyclopaedic information

It is widely held that the content of a lexical definition should be a concept, that is, a long-lasting model of a kind of thing, quality or process systematically connected with a lexeme. It is in this sense that a dictionary, even if its content is not limited to purely formal, immanent meaning relations, is held to deal primarily with words — with word meanings — rather than with things. Following this idea, a dictionary is distinguished from an encyclopaedia, which is considered as a repository of positive information, both long-lasting and contingent, about the things we speak of.

If the distinction between dictionaries and encyclopaedias is to be something more than a theoretical *desideratum*, it has to be based on a sharp relevance criterion, capable of keeping apart systematic definitions of word meanings, or concepts, from random data about things. However, a dividing line of this kind can be drawn neither by commutation towards the expression plane nor by reference to scenes. If the relevance criterion is commutation, the distinction between lexical and encyclopaedic information is certainly sharp, but it is as certainly devoid of functional import. If the relevance criterion is the contribution of lexical contents to the construction of cognitive scenes, on the other hand, the idea itself of concept dissolves into a psychologically and textually variable and contingent conglomerate of encyclopaedic data.

The commutative criterion draws a sharp distinction between language-specific formal data about lexical structures and any kind of datum located outside the linguistic system. Though relevant on formal grounds, this dividing line is devoid of functional value, because it leaves any kind of substantive data, both essential and contingent, on the same side. According to a commutative criterion, for instance, the relationship between "blond" and "hair" is an immanent lexical fact — a lexical solidarity — while that between "blue" and "sky" is not (cf. Coseriu, 1970: 107; 1967: 294). In order to define the content of the word *blue*, however, the cognitive datum that blue is the colour of the sky, which holds as a cognitive reference point for the concept "blue", is no less relevant than the fact that blondness is a property of hair for defining *blond*.

If the functional relevance criterion is identified with the contribution of word contents to the processing of scenes, the distinction between lexical definitions and encyclopaedic information fades away. When a complex meaning has to be processed into a cognitive scene, the most idiosyncratic piece of knowledge may become as relevant as any essential property of concepts. What one has to know about both typical and individual walls, cats and flies in order to extract coherent pictures out of such sentences as *The cat is on the wall* or *The fly is on the wall* is more than one would expect to find in a dictionary. This point is stressed by Haiman (1980: 329): "One does not expect to find in a dictionary a compendium of everything that is known about horses: if one did, the entry for 'horse' alone would be considerably longer than an entire dictionary. But where exactly does one stop? And, more important, *why* does one stop?".

Once concepts are reduced to open stocks of empirical information devoid of inner form, it is really impossible to draw a sharp line between putative lexical meanings and positive knowledge about things, because it is impossible to state once and for all what kind of information is possibly relevant to the coherent understanding of individual utterances.[219] While a sharp dividing line can be drawn between formal lexical structures and cognitive information located outside the linguistic system, no clear boundary exists between the different strata forming the realm of cognition, where a continuous transition leads gradually from the most generally shared concepts and cognitive structures down to the most idiosyncratic and occasional pieces of contingent information about individual beings mobilised by the unforeseeable uses of words. If the rule of formal lexicon is sharp differentiation, the rule of functional lexicon seems to be continuity. If "meanings are relativized to scenes", one can no longer deny that "dictionaries *are* encyclopaedias" (Haiman, 1980: 331).

3.3 The nature of concepts

> One person's idea is a utopia; a shared idea is a fact
> (A parson to his flock)

If concepts are defined against scenes, functional adequacy inevitably conflicts with systematicity and *a priori* validity. On the one hand, a purely formal characterisation, if it holds *a priori* as a systematic structure, is far from being exhaustive from a functional point of view. A functional definition, on the other hand, cannot even aim at exhaustiveness without opening up to all kinds of random data about things — without losing the systematicity and relative stability which characterises structures that hold a *priori.* If functional adequacy is taken into account, lexical definitions undergo a drift towards encyclopaedic data which threatens the very idea of a general concept. If its formal roots are not strong enough to delimit its content, while its functional profile is threatened by a virtually endless drift, what exactly is a concept?

The first point to be stressed is that concepts are thought of and relied upon as a specific kind of abstract tool designed to perform a social function, that is, to provide a community with a system of shared models of things and situations anchored in distinct words. If the social function of concepts is of this sort, concepts either do not exist at all or have to be something other than constituents of scenes. Scenes are contingent configurations of empirical and psychological data about things and situations located in the minds of individuals. In order to be relied upon by a community, shared models of things and situations cannot be reduced to more or less contingent collections of, or at best selections among, empirical and psychological data. Concepts cannot be formed out of the same purport as actual experience, memory and imaginings. Before being empirically true or false, the idea that concepts are entities of the empirical and psychological order is inconsistent. The only conceivable consistent picture of concepts is the picture of an ideal, social, non-empirical and long-lasting kind of entity. On such a premise, if there is a path leading to concepts, this path has to be looked for elsewhere than in the territory occupied by scenes. If concepts have a relational background, this cannot be formed by empirical or imaginative pictures of things and situations.

Like any other object of investigation in the field of human sciences, concepts are not independent empirical data which happen to be shared by a group of people, but structures which are real only insofar as they are shared and relied upon by a group of people. In the field of human sciences, sharing is not an empirical property of independent objects of experience, but the constitutive property of objects. For an object of human sciences, to be is to be shared. The reality of concepts, accordingly, is not a reality of the empirical order, but a reality of the ideal order.

What is relevant to concepts is not so much what contents of experience people really (happen to) share, but what kinds of content people assume they share and rely upon as if they were shared in their practical behaviour.[220] Empirically speaking, the continuity between word contents and encyclopaedic information is a plain fact, which cannot be falsified. Empirically speaking, there are not two uses of a word which actually mobilise the same amount of data and impose exactly the same inner perspective on the mobilised data. Empirically speaking, nobody knows what kind of information about things is actually shared by his addressee, let alone the members of a large community. What kind of experience about things is shared by whom is a contingent fact, culturally and individually variable, and it is highly probable that "there is no unquestioned stock of shared experience" (Haiman, 1980: 335). While this is unquestionable, it is equally unquestionable that people trustfully rely on concepts and behave as if concepts were as firm as the ground they walk upon. Is this no more than a delusion?

People do not behave as if there were no shared concepts — they behave as if shared concepts really did exist. Between the empirical evidence which dissolves systematic concepts into a nebula of idiosyncratic data and the shared idea that we think and communicate with each other by relying on concepts there seems to be an absolute contradiction. In fact, there is no contradiction but conflict, or, to put it in Kant's terms (1763(1992)), real opposition.

The idea that concepts exist is not the picture of a fact, but the constitutive criterion for symbolic action. It is not the proof that people are given concepts, but the proof that people give themselves the task of differentiating and identifying them — that people struggle for concepts, so to speak. Concepts are not given as a direct consequence of the mere fact that distinct words exist. Rather, the simple fact that words exist proves that people are really interested in concepts and engaged in constructing them and protecting their "intersubjective stability" (Kleiber, 1990: 13). What is shared in connection with a word is not necessarily a set of previously given conceptual contents, but the idea that if experience has to be shared, a system of distinct concepts must be within our reach. Insofar as it is shared, the idea that shared concepts exist is not just an empty claim, for it has the result of making them effectively exist. Insofar as it effectually directs intersubjective action towards the practical realisation of it, the idea that shared concepts exist is a true fact — a social fact.[221]

3.4 Categorisation and differentiation

What shapes shared and solid concepts out of the dense nebula of raw empirical data is an ideal impulse towards foregrounding and differentiation which directs symbolisation — "the human tendency once a contrast exists to define attributes for contrasting categories so that the categories will be maximally distinctive" (Rosch, 1978: 37). Two powerful tools, structurally independent but functionally allied, are at the service of differentiation: the differential nature of lexical structures, and the construction of shared cognitive models of things and facts within the borders of experience itself.

Since it is organised as a network of differences, lexical structure naturally pushes towards the imposition of sharp differential grids on the dense complexity of things. This point is stressed by Baldinger (1980: 30–31): "Where, in reality, is the border between 'cold' and 'hot'? In these scales, reality knows no borders [...] And nevertheless, we know well how to distinguish between 'cold' and 'hot'. Yet the 'clarity' is not in the borders, but in the oppositions".

Baldinger's remark grasps a significant portion of the truth, but only a portion. The differential linguistic mould is a necessary condition for a differential categorisation of experience, but is not as such sufficient. Although it encourages a clear-cut differentiation of concepts, the differential structure of lexical fields does not necessarily provide each paradigm with a substantive content. The structure of exocentric concepts, in particular, clearly shows that lexical differentiation is not necessarily grounded in clear oppositive dimensions internal to lexical structures. In such cases, the mould for concepts has to be found in experience itself — in its autonomous form.

The autonomy of cognitive criteria in shaping concepts is stressed mainly within the framework of prototype semantics. As Rosch (1978: 28) points out, it is thanks to prototypical models and categories that "the perceived world comes as structured information rather than as arbitrary or unpredictable attributes". Experience does not offer itself as a shapeless nebula, but is organised in a complex network of cognitive structures and models. This network provides a supplementary mould for concepts, which is at once located outside differential lexical structures and complementary to them. If lexical structures ground identity in negativity and difference, prototypical concepts attain differentiation thanks to the stability of substantive cognitive anchors.

A prototype is neither an image of a paradigmatic instance[222] — because its range of application is extended to instances which do not match a given image — nor a simple collection of empirical data — because it has a hierarchical structure which imposes a strong perspective on experience data. A prototype is not part of actual experience, but a model filtering our access to experience.[223] The prototype of bird, for instance, is neither the image of a given bird nor a collection of random data about birds, but a hierarchy of shared ideas about what a bird should ideally be and what a bird is empirically allowed to be — a filter organising the experience of real birds. This means that some properties of birds are constitutive of the category without being either necessarily shared or shared to the same degree by all the instances which are subsumed under the category. The ability to fly, for instance, is an essential property of the prototypical category of bird but is not shared by all kinds of bird. Conversely, instances which do not share the typical properties are admitted within the category with a peripheral status, which do not affect the content of the category. Birds which cannot fly, for instance, do not contribute to the prototype.

Thanks to the cleavage between the ideal properties of the model and the empirical properties of the subsumed individuals, prototypical categories attain differentiation, stability and intersubjective sharing while making room to the complexity of real experience. They are at once sensitive to unforeseeable experience in their use and protected from its centrifugal drifts in their content.

The availability of prototypical categories shows that the perception and categorisation of experience has a structure of its own, which cannot be reduced to language-specific lexical structures. And it is precisely in the form of an organised system of categories and models, and not in the form of a collection of random data, that the contents of experience meet language-specific formal moulds to build up lexical meanings.

Lexical meanings are a peculiar kind of conceptual structures, which can be reduced neither to formal linguistic organisation nor to cognitive modelling of experience, but are rooted in both. The structure of lexical meanings is the outcome of a complex and manifold interplay of language-specific lexical structures and general cognitive criteria of categorisation. On this assumption, one can reasonably expect lexical structures to shape some conceptual categories in a specific way while simply expressing others, or to express concepts up to a given point while shaping them in a specific way from this point onwards. When analysing lexical meanings, therefore, one cannot simply and exclusively look for the mark of either a linguistic or a cognitive mould; instead, one has to make room for the idea that each concept displays a peculiar balance of linguistic and cognitive shaping.

3.5 The relevance criterion for definitions: The faithful description of natural concepts

Nur beschreiben kann man hier (Wittgenstein)

The availability of distinct and shared concepts — of concepts which are taken as if they were distinct and shared — is thus a social fact, that is, a fact born out of a shared idea. As ideal facts, concepts are no less real than empirical facts, and have to be described accordingly.

A natural concept is neither a linguistic nor a cognitive structure, but has a structure of its own, which attains a specific point of equilibrium between linguistic and cognitive modelling. A natural concept is neither a bundle of distinctive features, nor a cognitive prototype — it is a higher kind of structure, which can incorporate, at a variable degree, parts of both models. Accordingly, the description of concepts cannot be reduced to an abstract external model. Any model may have something to say, but the final aim of description is to grasp the changing profile of each real concept as it offers itself.

The golden rule of conceptual analysis is the criterion of faithful description as it is explicitly formulated by Husserl (1913(1931: 92)): "*whatever presents itself in 'intuition' in primordial form* (as it were in its bodily reality), *is simply to be accepted as it gives itself out to be*, though *only within the limits in which it then presents itself*". The "principle of all principles" of phenomenological description is transferred into the field of lexical analysis by Apresjan (1992: 33): "The task of a lexicographer (unless he wants to go beyond his discipline and turn into an encyclopaedist) consists of discovering the naive picture of the world hidden in lexical meanings and presenting it in a system of definitions". The naive picture of the world entrusted to words has simply to be taken as it offers itself and within its limits. It is in this sense that lexical definitions can be considered tautological — in the sense that they make explicit something which is, so to speak, already there. To define words is not to increase our body of positive knowledge about things — it is to increase our degree of awareness about a body of ideas and assumptions we tacitly rely upon when we use words.

One direct way of exploring the use of words and digging out their conceptual background is to make explicit their distribution in selected types of sentences depicting consistent models of typical situations.[224] As they are constrained by conceptual criteria, such maps of consistent and appropriate[225] distributions of words send back precisely "the naive picture of the world hidden in lexical meanings".

A distributional approach is rather obvious for relational, unsaturated concepts. One can hardly describe the meaning of a relational term without identifying its consistent and appropriate arguments. Such a verb as *hit*, for instance, is consistent with any concrete object, while *sleep* is restricted to human and animal subjects and *speak* to humans. Within the borders of consistency, *fly* is appropriate to birds — typical birds can fly — to some kinds of insects and to a class of human artefacts designed for flying; *read* is appropriate to any text or writing support, *bark* to dogs and *darn* to socks. As the examples show, to make explicit the appropriate use of relational terms requires building up fine-grained and even idiosyncratic classes of arguments, which are called "object classes" ("*classes d'objets*") by Gross (1994).

In a less obvious way, the meaning of classifying words expressing punctual, saturated concepts receives in turn a relational background when it is described in terms of consistent and appropriate predicative frames. In order to analyse the different senses of the word *book*, for instance, one has to make explicit what it makes sense to say about books.

A book is in the first place a concrete object. Just like any concrete object, it has a shape, a weight and a colour, can be bought or sold, lost or found, and so on. More specifically, a book is a writing support, which can be printed, published and read. By metonymy, the noun *book* refers to its content, and thus to a kind of text which can be written, read,[226] understood, summarised or corrected. Insofar as it metonymically stands for its author, a book can speak of a subject or support a theory, criticise a hypothesis or make popular a system of ideas.[227]

Once such a complex network of co-occurrences is drawn, one may have the feeling that very little has been said about the real content of words. Yet, almost everything one can say about the content of words ideally presupposes such a preliminary work.

As each sense of a polysemous word has a specific distribution, drawing a complete map of the different environments open to a polysemous word amounts to isolating its different senses (see Clas & Gross, 1997). To the extent that most words of natural languages are polysemous, the relevant units of lexical description are the different senses of each lexeme.[228] A careful identification of distributional patterns is thus a preliminary condition for both formal-lexical and conceptual analysis.

Such relations as lexical solidarity, synonymy and antonymy, which are relevant to the form of the lexicon, are relations between distinct senses of words. For instance, when applied to a concrete object or material, *hard* is a synonym of *rigid* or *stiff* and an antonym of *soft*. When said of a task, it is a synonym of *difficult* and an antonym of *easy*. If applied to a person and his behaviour, it is a synonym of *harsh* or *severe* and an antonym of *good-hearted* or *sympathetic*. When said of the climate, it is a synonym of *bleak* and an antonym of *mild*, and so on.

Models of consistent and complex situations, which are relevant to lexical content, take distinct senses as their constituents. According to whether it is considered as a writing support, a text or a metonymy for its author, for instance, a book, enters into different complex conceptual models — into different scripts and schemata.

3.6 Dictionaries are not encyclopaedias

> Sia colore di fuoco il rosso,
> dell'aere il cilestrino, dell'acqua il verde
> et la terra bigia e cinericcia (L. B. Alberti)

Drawing exhaustive distributional maps is essential for the description of endocentric concepts, for it makes it possible to identify complex networks of sense relations. But it is above all in the field of exocentric concepts that distribution is strategic. Giving direct access to the whole set of complex conceptual models a linguistic community relies upon when using words, a careful distributional study clearly shows that concepts, even when they are not provided with a core strongly anchored in linguistic structures, cannot be reduced to more or less arbitrary selections of encyclopaedic data, but have a specific structure of their own. In this way, a faithful description of the use of words provides lexical contents, and first of all exocentric concepts, with a solid anchor against an encyclopaedic drift.

Colour concepts are a good illustration of this point. Colour has a well-known physical reality, and its perception is constrained by specific neurophysiological channels, which are probably the same for all human beings, and the structure and function of which have been widely explored by the neurosciences. If semantics were, according to an idea which dates back at least to Bloomfield (1933: § 9.1), a matter of encyclopaedic knowledge bearing a purely extrinsic link with linguistic forms, nothing would be easier than to find a distinct set of physical or neurophysiological correlates for each colour lexeme, and attain in this way a system of sharp differential definitions of colour categories. Such definitions, however, would not be a faithful picture of the peculiar "social fact" of colour categorisation and use of colour terms.

Colour terms are used to qualify the objects of our experience, and can be understood and described only on the basis of this shared social function. As Casati (1990: 113) points out, "colour terms are taught so as to distinguish and classify substances, tangible as opposed to intangible objects, and colours are taken by common sense to be properties qualifying substances". Accordingly, to draw a lexical definition of colour categories does not amount to improving our body of positive knowledge, but to becoming aware of our shared use of colour terms. The only way to attain this goal, in turn, is to identify for each term the set of objects to which it can be applied in a consistent and appropriate way.

The difference between a lexical definition and an encyclopaedic description is not simply a matter of quantity of information — "where exactly does one stop?", as Haiman puts it — but of relevance. The best way to illustrate this point is to observe the kinds of concepts that seem to defy the very basis of the distinction, that is, the concepts subsuming such concrete objects as natural kinds or artefacts. The relevant point is not so much the fact that an encyclopaedic description of a concrete object is expected to contain a great amount of data which it would be senseless to include in a lexical definition. What is more important is that an encyclopaedic description and a lexical definition look at things from opposite perspectives.

An encyclopaedic description ideally contains what people are assumed not to know and would like to know about the objects denoted by words, and takes for granted what can be assumed as shared by everybody. An encyclopaedic description of a car, for instance, is not expected to explain at length its socially assumed function, whereas one would be surprised not to find in it a considerable amount of technical and historical data, and an accurate description of many types and famous models of cars. All this forms a considerable amount of empirical data about cars, likely to enrich one's empirical knowledge. The definition of a concept, on the other hand, tries to make explicit the tacit assumptions that are ideally shared by everybody, that is, everything everybody takes for granted and relies upon when using a word. As the nature of these tacit assumptions is not empirical, their explication does not expand our body of positive knowledge. That is why a concept, even if it necessarily contains some positive information about things, is not simply a selection of encyclopaedic data.

3.7 Concepts are designed for human beings

> – [...] mais ceci est-il une véritable bataille?
> – Un peu (Stendhal)
>
> Elizabeth, agitated and confused,
> rather *knew* that she was happy,
> than *felt* herself to be so (Austen)

Concepts are not contingent configurations of empirical data; yet they are used to describe real or imaginary empirical facts. Concepts are not psychological contents belonging to individual human beings; yet they are used by individual human beings on contingent occasions and for contingent purposes. It is against such a set of assumptions that the relationship between lexical contents, encyclopaedic information and contingent data must be clarified.

When words are actually used, any piece of information, whether long-lasting or contingent, is likely to become relevant when interpreting the content of a given text or act of communication. However, this does not imply that any piece of information that is possibly relevant when interpreting a text or an act of communication is intrinsically relevant to a lexical definition. What is relevant when identifying a lexical meaning is not the amount of encyclopaedic data possibly mobilized by the unforeseeable use of a word, but an intersubjective agreement about some strategic anchor — a set of critical differential properties, a "cognitive reference point" (Rosch, 1975), or a "center of perception" (Cassirer, 1944: 134) — which makes it possible to share a stylised model.[229]

Once such a reference point has been identified and a stylised model is shared, the user must be ready on any occasion to take into account any piece of positive information which proves to be relevant. To account for this, however, is not the task of lexical definitions. Let us suppose that in order to understand a given message one has to realise that red is the colour of the Communist flag, or even the colour of Ann's shirt. Many pieces of information of precisely this kind have to be part of the stock of data available to the interpreter when contingent interpretative acts are performed within the borders of an occasional interpretative field. But it is obvious that neither the piece of encyclopaedic knowledge about Communist flags nor the piece of occasional information about Ann's shirt has to be located in the lexical content of the word *red*. The activation of such kinds of information is not a condition for the speaker's understanding of the meaning of the word *red*, but presupposes it. In other words, it is not the definition of lexical meanings that depends on the ability to interpret texts and activate scenes. It is the ability to interpret texts and activate scenes that depends, among other things, on the previous sharing of lexical meanings.

It is a fatal error to seek in lexical meanings what can be found only in the minds of individual human beings exchanging messages within the borders of contingent fields.[230] When describing lexical meanings, one does not forget that they are used by individual human persons in contingent occasions for performing contingent acts. If the role of individuals is not taken into account and distinguished from the role of concepts, one ends up both locating concepts in the minds of people and attributing to concepts what is located there. In this way, lexical meanings are reduced to mental contents of individual persons, while the mental contents activated in persons when concepts are used are attributed to lexical meanings. Now, lexical meanings are not more or less contingent psychological contents, that is, (part of) what is located in the mind of persons, but long-lasting concepts, that is, socially shared models of things and situations. When concepts are used, it is up to the individual to activate any kind of data relevant to the things being spoken about, and to make appropriate assumptions. When concepts are used, they are taken into a contingent game, and exposed to the risk of contingency, but do not become contingent on this account.

Concepts are as they are and work as they do because they are designed to be used by human beings, and this is an essential property of natural concepts, which accounts for their peculiar structure. The description of concepts has to be made accordingly, that is, on the presupposition that their structure is such as to make possible their real use.

The most straightforward way of using a concept is to apply it to a given instance in a predicative form: for instance, *This is a bird*; *This is a speech-act*;

This is a battle. The application of a concept to a given instance, on the other hand, is not simply a matter of checking the correspondence between the properties of the latter and the diagnostic criteria provided by the former. An act of predication made by a human being cannot be reduced to the passive task of subsuming given tokens under rigid categories — a task a programmed machine could perform equally well. Predication is a permanent, endless endeavour to describe complex and surprising objects and situations on the basis of concepts which need to be at one and the same time shared, reliable and long-lasting in terms of their essential properties, and flexible in making room for marginal instances.

Predication is not a passive process of inclusion but an act of judgement,[231] a creative device that cannot be reduced to a rigid procedure of automatic matching of types and tokens. Concepts are not applied by stupid machines following blind rules, but used by clever human beings, who are held to be capable of evaluating in each case how far, within which limits and under what conditions a concept can be applied. If we observe the active use of concepts in an unprejudiced way, we realise that the application of concepts to instances is a matter of decision. A person has to decide whether or not, within which limits and under what conditions he is entitled to subsume an instance under a given category.[232]

If predication is an act of judgement, it is not consistent to imagine natural concepts as if they were rigid structures leaving no room for human judgement. This holds in particular for the idea that concepts are closed sets of necessary and sufficient conditions for category membership. This idea certainly provides specialised scientific languages with a good normative model, for the ideal type of artificial category is a category whose application to instances is not negotiable but governed by rigid conditions. If it is applied to natural concepts, however, this idea is misleading in two ways. It is misleading *a parte obiecti*, so to speak, because it makes no room for the complexity of human experience. As Black points out, «Absence of a necessary and sufficient criterion is not a symptom of inadequacy of the language, but accurately reflects the complexity and continuous variability of the subject matter to which language refers» (Black, 1952(1954: 28)). And it is misleading *a parte subiecti* because it makes no room for human judgement, which is an essential constitutive factor of real categorisation. Besides being factually out of reach, a rigid kind of category would not be a faithful model of the structure of natural concepts and of the way they are actually used by human beings in dealing with things.[233]

People who handle concepts are fully aware that their use is inseparable from judgement, evaluation and decision, and many signs of this awareness emerge from both linguistic coding and use.

On the one hand, many lexical hedges such as *real* or *a sort of*, are meta-conceptual devices, so to speak, grading the commitment on the part of the speaker to a given act of categorisation. A *real brother*, for instance, is a person who fully meets all the relevant criteria for brotherhood, whilst *a sort of jacket* is meant to be a jacket in a loose sense only.

The dynamic of concepts in texts and discourses, on the other hand, can be justified only on the assumption that the application of concepts to instances is naturally considered by the speaker himself as a matter of judgement. A tautology — *This woman is a woman*, for instance — can be used to suggest that an instance is taken as a good example of a type. And the exceptionality of the tool clearly shows that this circumstance is not at all considered self-evident. For the same reasons, contradiction is the best tool to stress that a concept does not exhaust the essential properties of a thing, or that the thing is not worthy of the word: *This woman is not a woman.*[234]

Texts and living discourses offer many examples of how the application of categories to things can be made the object of negotiation, argumentation and even disputation.

The experience of things which are not readily subsumed under the proper concept is by no means unusual, as Jane Austen remarks with telling irony:

> As a house, Barton Cottage, though small, was comfortable and compact; but as a cottage it was defective, for the building was regular, the roof was tiled, the window shutters were not painted green, nor were the walls covered with honey-suckles.

On the other hand, it is by virtue of their open margins that concepts can easily be adapted to new, unforeseen objects. This is the way the hero of *Treasure Island* describes an unknown sort of tree:

> I had crossed a marshy tract full of willows, bulrushes, and odd, outlandish, swampy trees [...] and a great number of contorted trees, not unlike the oak in growth, but pale in the foliage, like willows [...] — live, or evergreen, oaks, I heard afterwards they should be called — which grew low along the sand like brambles, the boughs curiously twisted, the foliage compact, like thatch.

What is at issue in relation to concepts is not always, as in the quoted examples, just the proper classification of borderline cases: is this a real cottage? is this a sort of oak? The definition of the conceptual core itself — what is a real cottage?

what is a real oak? — may well bring about disagreement. Whereas disagreement about borderline cases is a natural condition of the life of concepts, the lack of agreement about the conceptual core itself seriously affects their function as shared structures. Discrepancies about essential, core properties are rather usual with such abstract concepts as "good", "happiness", "justice" or "love", which are at one and the same time complex, fleeting and pregnant with practical issues. It is a sure sign of crisis when the content of a word, instead of being silently taken for granted and trustfully relied upon,[235] is made the object of competing and conflicting definitions. This circumstance is not only a matter of theoretical import — the most typical occasion for analytical elucidation. It also has far-reaching consequences for practical life, and may be exploited for practical purposes. For these reasons, pieces of spontaneous conceptual analysis are often found in arguments:

> "Will you never learn a proper use of words?" answered the aunt. "[...] It is impossible you should hate a man from whom you have received no injury. By hatred, therefore, you mean no more than dislike, which is no sufficient objection against your marrying him [...]"(Fielding).

The close connection between tendentious definitions of concepts and practical purposes is made particularly clear by political discussion. What kind of freedom is to be considered, for instance, as true liberty — political freedom, freedom from evil or from economic need? For instance, the communist habit of discrediting such respectable liberal concepts as "liberty" under the pretext that their shared definition allegedly leaves aside what really defines "true liberty" is well known. At the other end of the political spectrum, Conrad gives a telling description of an Englishman's reaction to the use of such terms as *liberal* or *democracy* made by Sulaco's military men:

> Liberals! The words one knows so well have a nightmarish meaning in this country. Liberty, democracy, patriotism, government — all of them have a flavour of folly and murder. Haven't they, doctor?

Chapter 7

Lexical structures, lexical information and consistency criteria

When the combinatory constraints known as selection restrictions were first made an object of inquiry by linguists, it was in order to prevent — or detect — inconsistency in complex meanings. This holds beyond any doubt for Harris (1946) and Chomsky (1957; 1965). The essential link between selection restrictions and consistency, however, has now generally been lost. In current linguistic literature the category of selection restriction is normally used in so broad a sense as to include either lexical solidarities or cognitive structures or both. Fillmore (1975: 129; 1977: 130) and Haiman (1980: 345), among others, explicitly reduce selection restrictions to cognitive structures and even to cognitive data. The identity of selection restrictions and lexical solidarities is implicitly assumed by Dik (1989(1997: 91)) and Wierzbicka (1980: 87), who apply the label of selection restrictions to clear cases of lexical solidarities, and explicitly stated by Geeraerts (1991: 38), according to whom "syntagmatic semantic relations, known in transformational grammar as selection restrictions [...] had actually been discussed earlier by Porzig (1934)".

The tendency to merge different kinds of combinatory restrictions into an undifferentiated *continuum* is psychologically justified from the layman's point of view. What an average language user is inclined to consider a typical complex meaning is a consistent meaning depicting a familiar cognitive scene, framed by a well-formed syntactic structure and free of lexical mistakes.[236] Accordingly, it is not surprising that any kind of deviation from this prototype, at whatever level, is equally taken as an instance of oddity. Looked at from the user's point of view, such conflicting sentences as *Sunrise kissed my Chrysalis* (Dickinson), *John is riding a bough* and *The whole hill-back was one billowy, white ocean* (E. Brontë) have in common the property of framing cognitive scenes which are contrary to average expectations.

As far as linguistic research is concerned, the tendency to superimpose different kinds of combinatory restrictions is the outcome of the tendency to treat consistency criteria as a matter of lexical import, without at the same time clarifying the nature of lexical structures and contents, and the complex relationship between them. Now that the concept of lexicon has been analysed in its different aspects, we are ready to go back to consistency criteria — to differentiate them from both lexical and cognitive combinatory restrictions, and to characterise their nature and functions.

As formal lexicon and functional lexicon are different kinds of object, grounded in autonomous relevance criteria, the relationship between consistency criteria and the lexicon has to be examined with regard to both lexical structures and lexical information. If the place of consistency criteria is among lexical structures, they form a kind of lexical solidarity. If their place is among lexical information, they are a kind of cognitive content or cognitive structure.

In the following pages, we shall put forward some arguments in support of the hypothesis that consistency criteria are neither a kind of lexical solidarity nor a kind of cognitive data or structure, but autonomous conceptual structures which delimit from outside the conceptual territory shaped by both lexical and cognitive structures. The most interesting among these arguments are based on careful observation of the conflictual complex meanings issuing from the transgression of each kind of constraint. The idea is that there are different kinds of conflict, displaying different qualifying properties, which in turn implies that different layers of constraints are involved in each case, as shown by the quoted examples.

An expression like *John is riding a bough* is a lexical mistake, which violates a specific lexical solidarity of the English language. Like any true lexical mistake, it lends a conflicting expression to a consistent kind of process.

The description of a stretch of hills covered with snow as if it were the surface of the ocean runs against a shared stock of cognitive models which govern our shared expectations about the structure of the empirical world. The contrast between typical states of affairs and odd ones, however, is internal to a consistent world.

A sentence like *Sunrise kissed my Chrysalis* is a truly inconsistent expression, which violates a basic ontological restriction. As both lexical mistakes and cognitively odd situations presuppose consistency, the range of action of consistency criteria has to be logically preliminary to both lexical and cognitive modelling.

1. Lexical solidarities and consistency criteria

According to Dik (1989(1997: 91)), the sentence *John was eating a glass of beer* sounds odd because it violates a selection restriction. This does not simply imply that the sentence depicts an odd kind of situation. According to Dik, its "strangeness is a function of the linguistic properties of *eat* and *a glass of beer*, and [...] these properties must somehow be coded in the linguistic description".[237] The main argument put forward by Dik in support of his hypothesis is the language-specific nature of selection restrictions, which "are determined by semantic factors, and this is a fact about the predicate rather than about the 'world' to which we apply the predicate" (76).

In order to illustrate this last point, Dik considers the coding of the act of blowing one's nose in English and Dutch. Both languages frame the act with a verb taking the nose as direct object — which, by the way, is not a trivial fact; French, for instance, has a single specialised pronominal verb: *se moucher*. But while English uses a verb — *blow* — which accepts a wide range of objects, Dutch has a specialised verb, "*snuiten*, which is practically restricted to 'noses'. On the other hand, Dutch *blazen*, which is the closest equivalent to English *blow*, cannot be said of noses" (92). As a consequence, the sentence *Jan blies zijn neus*, which is the word by word translation of *John blew his nose*, is not correct in Dutch.

Dik's discussion is a good argument for an indisputable fact — namely, that a certain number of combinatory restrictions between predicates and arguments are coded in a specific way within the lexical structure of language as lexical solidarities. Such a premise, however, does not entail the consequence expected by Dik — namely, that selection restrictions, that is, consistency criteria, are encoded among lexical structures in a language-specific way. Dik's example — the solidarity between «snuiten» and the nose — is a good instance of lexical solidarity, but is not an instance of consistency criterion.

Consistency criteria and lexical solidarities display some surface analogies, which may, at a first glance, encourage their identification. However, if we compare a paradigmatic case of lexical solidarity — for instance, the solidarity between "snuiten" and the nose, or between "bark" and dogs — with a paradigmatic instance of consistency criterion — for instance, the fact that moral responsibility is restricted to human beings, or sleeping to animate beings — it is not difficult to realise that consistency criteria and lexical solidarities are very different structures, performing very different functions.

Consistency criteria are largely shared conceptual structures securing the consistency — the conceptual lawfulness, so to speak — of complex meanings. Lexical solidarities are language-specific lexical structures, which contribute to the inner organisation of lexical paradigms.

Consistency criteria involve a conceptual categorisation of beings — a natural ontology. This ontology is not as such relevant to the lexical structure of a given language, but is essential when characterising the life form of a cultural community reaching far beyond the borders of a given linguistic community. True lexical solidarities are essential for defining the specific lexical structures of a given language, but are of no consequence for the conceptual categorisation of beings, which is presupposed as a firm ground.

The fact that only human beings are responsible moral subjects gives us a deep insight into our shared way of conceiving of both human beings and responsible action. The fact that an Englishman *blows* his nose, while a Dutchman *snuits* it and a Frenchman simply *se mouche*, gives us a lot of useful information about the lexical structures of these languages but is of no consequence with regard to conceptual matters. The fact that a German is allowed to *reiten* — that is, to ride — a bough but not a bicycle, while the reverse holds for an English speaker, while a Dutchman can *rijden* any vehicle, does not imply an essential difference in the way the three communities see the conceptual profile of horses, boughs and vehicles. These schematic insights, suggested by the simple observation of some typical examples, can be supported by several arguments, which we shall now examine more closely.[238]

1.1 Lexical mistakes and inconsistency

A lexical solidarity can be violated just as a conceptual restriction can, and in certain cases the result seems identical. An utterance like *John barks*, for instance, seems no less anomalous than *The moon smiles.* In both cases, a tension is felt between the connected terms. In both cases, moreover, the presence of a conflicting argument does not irreversibly saturate the involved valency. If a person is said to bark, the identity of the actual subject — the man — is challenged by the virtual presence of the solidary one — the dog. In the same way, if a non-human being is said to smile, the human being consistent with the verb is virtually present on stage. In both cases, the most typical issue is a relational metaphor. Such analogies, however, easily lead to essential differences being overlooked.

Whereas the violation of a consistency criterion necessarily produces a conflictual meaning, the link between breaking lexical solidarities and conceptual conflict is neither systematic nor essential.

Many true lexical solidarities are devoid of any conceptual relevance. As a consequence, their transgression, if it results in a lexical mistake, does not imply any conceptual conflict whatsoever. Such complex meanings as *Jan blies zijn neus* or *Jean a soufflé le nez* are lexically ill-formed — because they violate a language-specific lexical solidarity — but absolutely not conflictual. When a conceptual conflict arises, on the other hand, the reason for this conflict is not that a lexical solidarity has been violated, but that this particular lexical solidarity happens to mobilise a relevant conceptual opposition. The German sentence *Hans frißt*, for instance, is conflictual because a verb designed to denote the process of eating by animals is constructed with a human being, a category which requires the correlative verb *essen*. As a lexical solidarity, the link between "snuiten" and the nose is no less relevant than the link between "essen" and the ontological category of human beings. Lexical solidarities as such are indifferent towards conceptual lawfulness; their conceptual relevance, if any, is no more than an accident.

The least we can say on the basis of such observations is that lexical anomaly is not a sufficient condition for conceptual conflict. Two hypotheses may be put forward at this point: either lexical solidarities and consistency criteria are independent phenomena, whose conceptual purport may coincide at random, or the former include the latter. Our line of argument pushes towards the first hypothesis.

1.2 Reversible and irreversible conflicts

Even when it leads to conceptual conflict, the transgression of a lexical solidarity cannot be considered as a true instance of inconsistency.

The German utterance *Hans frißt*, for instance, is conflictual but not inconsistent. It is conflictual because it superimposes a specific deformation, made possible by a language-specific lexical constraint, on a process which is as such consistent on ontological grounds. The action of eating is consistent with a human being. The anomaly is due to the fact that German lexical structures restrict the use of the verb *fressen* to animals. The barrier between the man and the act of *fressen* is not conceptual, but formal-lexical.

The violation of a consistency criterion, on the contrary, builds up a process which is essentially and irreversibly inconsistent and does not admit a consistent ideation. The utterance depicting a smiling moon, for instance, ascribes to the heavenly body an action which is inconsistent with its essential properties as an inanimate being. What is wrong is not the choice of the word but the action itself. The barrier between the moon and the smile is not just lexical — it is ontological. This is a case of true inconsistency.

As they are a question of correct use of words, that is, of lexical lawfulness, the conflicts due to lexical mistakes can be effaced by substitution. Given an anomalous utterance, the relational term determined by the violated lexical solidarity — typically, the verb — can be replaced by another, which is solidary with the textually relevant argument. If a true lexical solidarity has been broken, the substitution test[239] gives a positive answer, for it is always possible to find a more or less direct path through lexical structures, leading to at least one alternative solidary lexeme on the basis of a common root meaning.

The simplest cases of substitution can be observed when a common root meaning is attained by simply dropping the broken lexical solidarity. At this point, the substitute will be either the generic expression of the root meaning itself, or a specific co-hyponym of the replaced term, which is solidary with the relevant argument.

The first alternative is illustrated by such examples as *John murdered a spider*, which can be replaced by *John killed a spider*. The use of *kill*, the generic hyperonym of the field containing *murder*, is not affected by the specific lexical solidarity applied to the latter. On the other hand, no specialised term, directly competing with "murder" and compatible with spiders, is available in English.

The second alternative is illustrated by the utterance *John murdered a calf*, which can be replaced by *John slaughtered a calf*. In this case, the substitute belongs to the same elementary field as the replaced term, and applies to the common root meaning "kill" a correlative lexical solidarity. It is worth pointing out, however, that the expression of the general root meaning "kill" would do as well as a substitute, for the purpose of the test is to verify whether or not the conflictual process is open to a non-conflictual linguistic framing, and no more. The latter option is not open, of course, if the general root meaning has no direct linguistic expression. In German, for instance, no generic hyperonym of *essen* and *fressen* is available. Accordingly, the sentence *Hans frißt* can only be reformulated as *Hans ißt*.

In some cases, a common root meaning does not immediately coincide with the root meaning of the field containing the non-solidary term. In order to attain it, one has to dig more deeply into the intricate network of lexical structures. In these cases, the path is less straightforward, but clearly traced. As barking is a dog's cry, for instance, the sentence *John barks* can be corrected by any verb fit to express a human cry — for instance, *John shouts*. The greater complexity of the lexical path and the availability of many solidary alternatives is due, in this case, to the fact that the cries of human beings, unlike animal cries, form a complex hierarchical network including different paradigms of lexemes which are finely differentiated along such inherent dimensions as presence or absence of articulation, intensity or affective tenor.

Other complex cases involve relational terms constrained by more than one lexical solidarity. The sentence *O western orb sailing the heaven* (Whitman), for instance, contains a verb which requires that the motion take place on water, and the subject be a ship. As the correlative verb framing the motion in air — that is, *fly* — does not seem appropriate for a heavenly body, which is neither a bird nor a flying craft, the lexical anomaly can be corrected by dropping from the content of the main verb not only the solidarity with a specific location, but also that with a specific subject — that is, by looking for a more general root meaning: *The sun crosses the heaven*, for instance. Though the substitution is not so immediate, it is none the less clear that the described process — a motion in the heavens — is as such consistent, and therefore can be consistently framed with appropriate words.

As it is a question of conceptual lawfulness, inconsistency cannot be effaced by lexical substitution. If a poet depicts the moon as a smiling creature, no consistent alternative formulation can be attained by lexical substitution:[240]

> The moon, like a flower,
> In heaven's high bower,
> With silent delight
> Sits and smiles on the night (Blake)

There is no English verb that is at the same time correlative or structurally connected to "smile" and fit for inanimate beings. What is barred to the moon is not a given lexeme, but the whole conceptual area of human expression, no matter what lexeme is used.

1.3 Translation

A further argument in favour of a structural cleavage between consistency criteria and lexical structures is offered by translation. Lexical structures are by definition language-specific, and so are lexical mistakes. The French lexicon, for instance, distinguishes two kinds of rivers: a "fleuve" is a river which flows into the sea, and a "rivière" is a river which flows into another river. To call a "fleuve" "rivière" is of course a lexical mistake in French. In an English translation, the mistake disappears, because English has only one noun for the two types of river. In the same way, the violation of a lexical solidarity is bound to disappear in the case of translation, unless the target language happens to share the same solidarity as the source language. If we translate the German sentence *Hans frißt* into English, for instance, the lexical mistake disappears. If the anomaly of the English utterance *The horse is mewing* does not disappear in French (*Le cheval miaule*) or in Italian (*Il cavallo miagola*) it is only because the solidarity is shared by all three languages.[241] On the other hand, if the anomaly of the Dutch sentence *Jan blies zijn neus* does not disappear in the French translation *Jean a soufflé le nez*, it is because French has a specialized verb: *se moucher*. The anomaly of both the Dutch and the French sentence, however, disappears in English and Italian: *John blew his nose*; *Giovanni ha soffiato il naso.*

Unlike a lexical mistake, a true instance of inconsistency is not due to the violation of a language-specific lexical structure but to the violation of a conceptual restriction shared by a larger cultural community. In such a case, the translation has no effect on the conceptual conflict. In one of his sonnets, the French poet Charles Baudelaire attributes to the moon the inconsistent attitude of dreaming:

> Ce soir la lune rêve avec plus de paresse

Whatever language belonging to the same ontological community the utterance is translated into, be it English, German, Italian, Spanish or Polish, for instance, the inconsistency does not disappear. For the utterance to lose its inconsistency, it is not enough to imagine another lexical structure; one has to imagine another conceptual landscape — an ontology which, unlike ours, would allow heavenly bodies to dream. For a person brought up within such an ontology, on the other hand, our utterance would in any case be taken as consistent, no matter what language expressed it.

1.4 The nature of determinant classes

Conceptual structures that hold as consistency criteria presuppose a rigorous classification of beings into general classes which are both ontologically relevant and not language-specific. Examples are classes such as concrete and abstract entities, animate and inanimate beings, human and non-human creatures. All these conditions either do not hold, or hold at random, for the classes which determine lexical solidarities.

As we have already observed, some lexical classes determining lexical solidarities coincide with ontologically relevant classes. For instance, the lexical classes determining the German verbs *essen* and *fressen* are human and non-human creatures respectively. This, however, cannot be generalized. The most characteristic lexical classes are language-specific; most are highly idiosyncratic and conceptually immaterial; some are non-homogeneous, odd or even inconsistent.

According to Coseriu (1952), Tamanaco, a Brasilian language, has three verbs which translate English *eat*: "*jucurú*, *jemerí*, *janerí*, which mean, respectively, 'eat bread', 'eat fruits or honey', 'eat meat'". The composition of the second class — the association of fruits and honey — is overtly non-homogeneous.[242] Zgusta (1971: 43) quotes an interesting example from Georgian: "the Georgian verb *makvs* 'to have' is applied in reference to things: *cigni makver* 'I have a book'. *Mqavs* 'to have' is applied in reference to persons and animals: *dedmama mqavs* 'I have parents', *mona mqavs* 'I have a slave', *cxeny mqavs* 'I have a horse': but motorcars are treated not as things but as animals, because one says *mankana mqavs* 'I have a motor-car'".

Like the class determining the English verb *ride*, the class determining the Georgian verb *mqavs* is not only non-homogeneous — it is also inconsistent, for it includes an inanimate kind of being among animate creatures.[243] Insofar as it is seen as a language-specific fact, however, the inconsistency of lexical classes is devoid of any ontological import. The fact that the possession of a car is expressed by the same lexeme as the possession of a horse or a friend, for instance, has no effect on the speaker's ontological attitude towards these distinct kinds of being. This is a further, strong argument for an essential distinction between lexical classes and ontological classes.

Finally, the determinant term in a lexical solidarity often coincides with a single lexeme — that is, the solidarity ranges over a single kind of being or, in extreme cases, a single individual. In such cases, the lexical solidarity is a purely idiosyncratic relationship involving no classification at all. We have already considered the solidarity between the Dutch verb *snuiten* and the nose. The French adjective *alezan* and Italian *baio* are restricted to horses. The English verb *darn*, like French *ravauder*, takes as direct objects only socks and stockings. According to Zgusta (1971: 43), "Arabic *razaqa* 'to present a person with something' [...] is used only when the donor is Allah".

The presence of idiosyncratic, non-homogeneous, odd and even inconsistent lexical classes is maybe marginal in literate languages. But it is probable that a systematic enquiry into so-called primitive languages and dialects would yield valuable results. In my native Gallo-Italian dialect, for instance, the phrasal verb *fa 'dʒu* ("make down") is used with two heterogeneous direct objects: the nose, in the sense of blowing, and the unproductive buttons of the vine, which are torn off in spring. *tra 'fø* ("throw out") is used with grass, hay and dung in the sense of spreading, and with clothing in the sense of taking off.

If lexical solidarities are distinguished from selection restrictions by an essential borderline, so are the classes that determine them. Lexical classes, which determine lexical solidarities, are as such devoid of ontological import. When they come across an independent conceptual categorisation, they may as well assume it as disregard its most basic borders. In any case, the structure of lexical classes has no effect on the shared ontological attitude of the speakers. Under such conditions, it would be absurd to maintain that ontological classes underlying selection restrictions — such categories as concrete and abstract entities, animate and inanimate beings, human and non-human creatures — coincide with language-specific lexical data.

1.5 Lexical organisation presupposes consistency

Uccidiamo il chiaro di luna! (Marinetti)

The arguments we have discussed support the conclusion that lexical well-formedness and consistency are mutually independent properties of complex meanings, which implies that consistency criteria and lexical solidarities are independent kinds of structures.

Consistency is the outcome of the use of words according to general ontological restrictions which are neither language-specific nor encoded as such in lexical structures, and is independent of lexical well-formedness. An inconsistent complex meaning, therefore, is neither necessarily nor typically a lexical mistake. When a lexical mistake leads to conceptual conflict, a lexical substitution is enough to restore the essential consistency of the process.

Lexical well-formedness is the result of the use of words according to language-specific lexical restrictions, and is independent of consistency. A lexical mistake, therefore, is not necessarily conflictual, and never inconsistent.

If lexical solidarities and consistency criteria are mutually independent structures, it is because they perform complementary functions, as can be seen in some clear cases. Let us consider, for instance, the lexical articulation of the concept of dying in English.

As Cruse (1986: 278–279) points out, the use of the verb *die* is constrained by a "selectional restriction" which is "logically inescapable" — ontologically inescapable in our terms. "The only things that can without oddness be said to die are those which are (a) organic, (b) alive (and possibly also (c) mortal [...])". This of course holds for the conceptual area of dying in general, irrespective of its language-specific lexical articulation. Once the contours of the consistent concept of dying have been traced, the language-specific lexical structures are allowed to shape it into a paradigm of interconnected lexemes, and to impose further restrictions on the use of each.[244] The colloquial English phrasal verb *kick the bucket*, for instance, "imposes further semantic requirements on the subject [...] Unlike *die*, *kick the bucket* (in its idiomatic sense) is fully normal only with a human subject".

This further restriction is not motivated by a requirement of consistency — it is "semantically arbitrary", in Cruse's own terms — and therefore does not affect the conditions imposed on the consistency of the conceptual area of dying. More generally, the language-specific lexical organisation of a consistent conceptual area does not affect the conditions of its consistency.

On the one hand, the restrictions on consistency, which hold for a whole conceptual area, are automatically extended to any further language-specific organisation of it. If *kill* is consistent with animate objects, for instance, so are its hyponyms. Any living being which can consistently be killed can consistently be executed, or assassinated, or murdered. To execute, or assassinate or murder a spider is as consistent a process as to kill it, in spite of the fact that the corresponding expressions count as lexical mistakes.

Conversely, the inconsistent process of killing an inanimate being is just as inconsistent if it is framed by one of its more specialised hyponyms: to assassinate, murder, slaughter or execute the moonlight, for instance, is neither more nor less inconsistent than Marinetti's project of simply killing it.

The division of labour between consistency criteria and lexical solidarities made visible by the previous examples can easily be generalised. The function of consistency criteria is to circumscribe from outside the area of consistent concepts. It is within this area, and only within this area, that lexical structures, and in particular lexical solidarities, draw further language-specific boundaries and impose language-specific constraints. A conceptual area organised into a lexical field is by definition consistent. Lexical articulation presupposes consistency.

The fact that lexical articulation is by definition internal to consistency implies some non-trivial corollaries.

First, no lexical veto bars the construction of inconsistent utterances. Inconsistent utterances are not lexical mistakes, but a form of exploration of conceptual territories made possible by the syntactic structure of complex linguistic expressions. Looked at from the standpoint of lexical structures, inconsistency is a sort of no man's land. If a word is used outside the borders of consistency, it does not occupy the territory of a competing lexeme — it behaves, so to speak, like a pioneer crossing uncharted terrain. Being inconsistent, the conceptual area it occupies avoids the alternative between lexical well-formedness and lexical ill-formedness, which only makes sense within the borders of consistency.

Second, as lexical articulation is confined to the territory of consistency, no specialised lexeme is ever available for expressing inconsistent concepts. For instance, no specialised lexeme is designed to express the smiling of the moon or the sleeping of the mountains. It is for this reason that inconsistent concepts, unlike lexical mistakes, cannot be corrected by lexical substitution.

Finally, the fact that an extended and potentially conflictual use of a lexeme is accepted as a shared lexical value by definition implies that this use has been annexed to the territory of consistency. Once feelings are accepted as objects for a verb like *cultivate*, for instance, *to cultivate a feeling* becomes by definition a lexically correct expression of a consistent concept. The feeling one cultivates is not changed into a piece of land. Instead, it is the meaning of the verb that drops any inherent and relational feature which would be inconsistent with the new kind of argument.

2. Lexical information and consistency criteria

On the assumption that consistency criteria are part of lexical data, if they are not a kind of lexical structure, they are to be considered a kind of lexical information. In the current literature, in particular, consistency criteria are identified either with beliefs about the world (as in Haiman, 1980) or with shared cognitive models (as in Fillmore, 1977). On the following pages, we shall discuss these two points.

2.1 Consistency criteria and beliefs about the world

According to Haiman (1980: 345), consistency criteria are no more than "beliefs about the world", which are not, as such, generally shared: "semantic constraints and beliefs about the world are not to be distinguished. Thus, selection restrictions: the sentence 'the rock is pregnant' violates a selection restriction. But the categorization of rocks as inanimate and hence, *a fortiori*, barren, is a belief about the world, and one which is not necessarily shared by everyone".

Consistency criteria and beliefs about the world have in common one qualifying property, that is, their non-empirical character. Unlike an occasional piece of knowledge, and like a selection restriction, a true belief — for instance, a religious or metaphysical belief — is not justified by our experience of the empirical world. Unlike a cognitive model, moreover, a true belief is even insensitive to experience — it can be neither confirmed nor falsified by experience. What sharply distinguishes beliefs about the world and consistency criteria beyond such analogies is their different nature as social facts, that is, the different way in which the two kinds of structures are shared within a given community.

As Haiman correctly remarks, a belief is neither necessarily nor normally shared by all the members of a community: this is the case, for instance, with religious or metaphysical beliefs. Sharing a belief within a given community is no more than an empirical fact. Sharing may be, depending on circumstances, total or partial, to a large or to a small extent. This is not true for consistency criteria. Of course, it may happen that some people, within a given community, do not share some consistency criteria. It may happen, for instance, that someone normally addresses questions to the moon expecting an answer, and thus behaving as if heavenly bodies had their own psychological life. The lack of sharing, however, is not the same kind of fact in the two cases.

The sharing of beliefs about the world cannot be considered constitutive of a cultural community. The lack of sharing and its corollaries — namely, doubt, changing one's mind, the presence of many competing beliefs, arguments or the quest for evidence — are even familiar features of the cultural landscape of a community which do not challenge, under normal circumstances, its status as a community. In this sense, a cultural community may be defined, among others things, as a discussing community. On the contrary, there is no discussion or argument about consistency criteria. The sharing of consistency criteria is an essential, constitutive fact for a given community. A systematic lack of sharing of consistency criteria would undermine its being a cultural community.[245]

2.2 Consistency criteria and cognitive models

Consistency criteria are likened to cognitive models by Fillmore (1977: 130), who considers them as restrictions imposed on linguistic frames by prototypical models of processes, or schemata:

> The concept of *selection restriction* or *co-occurrence constraints* can be spoken of in terms of the linguistic frames that are associated with given schemata. Some words are limited to the kinds of schemata they activate and are constrained, therefore, to appear with the other words that belong to the frames matching such schemata.

> The notion of selection restriction can thus be formulated in terms of the properties of schemata and frames, and not in the usual way, i. e., in terms of the pairing of inherent features on lexical items.[246]

The verb *smile*, for instance, forms a frame with a human subject because the cognitive schema it activates identifies a human attitude. If it is assigned a different kind of subject, the resulting complex meaning is conflicting with the underlying schema, and therefore inconsistent.

Unlike the contents of positive knowledge, cognitive models of things and processes are not empirical facts belonging to actual experience but schematic structures which filter and shape our access to experience. On this premise, the idea that consistency criteria are a kind of cognitive model is not immediately incompatible with their non-empirical, essential character. In spite of this, our hypothesis is that consistency criteria cannot be reduced to a kind of cognitive model.

Cognitive models aim at truth. According to our cognitive models, for instance, it is true that birds fly in the air and fish swim under the surface of water, whereas the reverse is false. Of course, the truth of cognitive models is a general rather than occasional kind of truth. Cognitive models do not predict how individual beings occasionally look, but how general kinds of beings are generally expected to look. Accordingly, the truth of cognitive models is not tested punctually against actual experience, but is taken for granted and relied upon until proof of the contrary. So is, for instance, the fact that fish swim and birds fly.

The fact that cognitive models aim at general truth has three relevant implications, which will be discussed in the following paragraphs.

First, general truth, like the alternative between truth and falsity in general, is located within the borders of consistency. This implies that the question about consistency is logically prior to the question about truth and cannot be confused with it.

Moreover, general truth by definition admits of occasional falsification by non-typical things and situations documented in real experience. The idea that birds fly, for instance, is falsified by the actual existence of species which, though classified as birds, do not fly. This of course does not hold for consistency criteria. As they draw the outer boundaries of both typical and untypical consistent experience, consistency criteria cannot be falsified by actual experience. Experience is by definition, and therefore tautologically, consistent.

Finally, whereas cognitive models are shared to a variable and negotiable extent within a given community, the sharing of consistency criteria is the necessary condition for conceptual lawfulness within a cultural community.

2.2.1 *General truth and consistency*

Cognitive models predict the range of properties generally and typically displayed by different kinds of beings, that is, which definite properties of beings one can rely upon in the first instance and until proof of the contrary. A model of the sun, for instance, tells us that its typical colour is yellow and not, for instance, green; on a sunny day, the sky is blue and not green or black. The question about the colour of a given being, however, presupposes that this being has a colour, that is, it makes sense if and only if the being in question is included in the category of things to which the property of being coloured applies.

The task of consistency criteria is precisely to specify what kinds of entities are admitted within the range of application, both occasional and general, of the different properties. What is relevant from an ontological point of view, for instance, is the fact that both the sun and the sky are allowed to have a colour, while an idea is not. The scope of natural ontology is not reality *de facto*, however typical and schematic, but essential possibility *de iure*, that is, what can consistently be, and how it can consistently look.

Existing beings are not taken into account by natural ontology as kinds of individuals displaying typical or occasional properties, but as members of distinct categories whose relevance is defined in connection with the admissibility of essential properties. A tree is always a tree. But if the focus is on colour, a tree is conceived of as a physical body offering an extended surface to the sight, like a wall, or a piece of fabric, or a living body. If sensorial life is at issue, a tree is conceived of as an inanimate being, like a stone, a stream, or a car. If responsible action is concerned, the same tree is seen as a non-human entity, like a heavenly body or a beast.

As Sommers (1963(1967: 160)) sums up, "The *ontologist* is interested in categories; he is, *qua* ontologist, not interested in whether a thing is red or whether it is green but in whether it is coloured. Even this is not altogether accurate: he is interested in its character of being coloured or colourless", that is, in its aptitude to receive a colour. The immediate consequence of ontological categorisation is that the distinction between true and false predicates, which is relevant not only to cognitive contents but also to cognitive modelling, is of absolutely no importance, because it is located inside the border that consistency criteria draw from outside: "whenever a predicate P is significantly applicable to a thing, then is its complement non-P [...] Thus, any predicate P can be constructed as |P| or 'the absolute value of P', by which we mean that P spans the things which are either P or non-P but does not span things which are neither P nor non-P. For example, if P = philosopher, then |P| defines the class of things that are either philosophers or non-philosophers", that is, human beings. "In the class of things that are |P| are Bertrand Russell and Cleopatra, but not the Empire State Building" (159).[247]

The circumstance that Bertrand Russell is a philosopher and Cleopatra is not is a matter of fact. The circumstance that birds fly and fish swim is a matter of conceptual modelling. Both facts and conceptual models are devoid of ontological import. Consistency is neither a matter of fact nor of conceptual modelling, but a matter of conceptual lawfulness. Conversely, both questions of fact and conceptual models only make sense once their ontological presuppositions are satisfied, that is, once the domain of consistent predicability has been delimited by consistency criteria. Applied to the sky, for instance, the question about colour makes sense. Applied to an idea, the same question is groundless and senseless.[248]

2.2.2 *Consistency criteria and cognitive models: two ways of simplifying the empirical world*

Unlike positive knowledge, both cognitive models and consistency criteria do not draw a picture of the world as it actually appears, but a picture of some possible world. The two kinds of picture, however, are drawn according to different relevance criteria, and therefore each bears a peculiar relation to the world of real experience.

The rule of cognitive simplification is typicality. Accordingly, cognitive models draw a simplified picture of what our shared world would look like if it were inhabited only by typical beings behaving in a typical way. The typical world is simply a poorer copy of ours, containing no more and much less. The typical world, for instance, does not contain a single bird unable to fly.

The rule of consistency is substantive possibility, and therefore ontological lawfulness. Accordingly, consistency criteria disclose an indefinite set of worlds, including any possible world that combines in any imaginable way any kind of beings and properties compatible with conceptual lawfulness. From a strictly ontological point of view, the inverted world of baroque poetry is as admissible as its real counterpart. Strolling among consistent worlds, one could meet feathered fish — *De l'océan de l'air les poissons emplumés* (Chevreau) — flying under a black sun:[249]

> Le feu brûle dedans la glace
> le soleil est devenu noir (Théophile)

Though independent of actual experience insofar as they are held to be *a priori* generally true, cognitive models are sensitive to it. Cognitive models not only admit the possibility of being falsified by experience, but actually entail it, for the question about typicality arises only insofar as experience makes room for non-typical instances. In most cases, the falsification of expectations raised by cognitive models is taken as a normal fact: this is the case, for instance, of birds which cannot fly. In some others, it is seen as somehow odd, but in any case conceivable. In spite of the expectations aroused by the restaurant script shared in our culture, for instance, we can easily imagine a customer trying to pay his bill by offering a goat for barter. The customer's behaviour would look very strange, but fully conceivable, because it would not cross the borders of consistency.

An inconsistent fact is not just a kind of non-prototypical fact. A non-prototypical fact is a consistent fact that does not match shared expectations. An inconsistent fact is a fact that has no room either in actual or possible experience. Should we ever encounter a restaurant customer trying to barter a goat, we would certainly be taken by surprise, but no more than that. Should a tree ever address us, or the moon answer one of our poetic questions, we would not just be taken by surprise. The pillars of our form of life would be profoundly shaken. The alternative between protypicality and non-prototypicality only makes sense within the borders of consistency. Before being judged as a non-prototypical instance of restaurant customer, a goat barterer is to be identified as a consistent instance of restaurant customer. A tree or a heavenly body could be neither.

Typicality entails non-typicality in a syntagmatic way, in the sense that the two kinds of facts by definition coexist in our real, non-simplified world. Consistency contrasts with inconsistency in a paradigmatic way — in the sense that the former cannot by definition coexist with the latter in our shared world. There is no room, within real experience, for such inconsistent beings as pregnant rocks or such inconsistent processes as the smiling of the moon. Inconsistent beings and processes are conceivable only as complex meanings of significant expressions, that is, as semantic structures of the symbolic order. Consistency criteria draw the borders of possible experience from outside. As they impose a form on actual experience, cognitive models are necessarily located within these borders.

2.2.3 *Sharing*

Owing to their different relations with experience, consistency criteria and cognitive structures are not shared under the same conditions.

As they are the result of a complex negotiation with actual experience and its variable contents, cultural models are not necessarily shared by everybody in the same way. The degree to which a given cultural model is shared by the members of a community is an empirical fact, which has to be ascertained case by case.

If cognitive models were actually shared in the same way by any member of a given community, the borders between concepts — models of possible things and situations — and general information about actual things and situations — broad encyclopaedic information — would not be so difficult to draw. In fact, the general intersubjective sharing of cognitive models is not an empirical fact, but an assumed idea. It is in this sense that Apel (1976: 58) considers the sharing of word meanings as an aim which could only be attained under ideal conditions:

> A solution of this problem [of word meaning] — and thereby a dissolution of the syndrome of problems characterised by the philosophical terms 'essence', 'definition', 'idea', 'concept', and 'meaning' — might [...] be reached if one would not expect to get an immediate answer to the platonic questions about the 'essence' of things by description of the actual use of the corresponding words, but rather by postulating a consensus about an adequate use of the words which *would* be reached by all participants of a language game if they would discuss the problem long enough under the conditions of an ideal communication-community.

As they are designed to draw the outer border of any possible experience, consistency criteria cannot be shared to a variable extent by the members of a cultural community. For a common experience to be simply conceivable, they are to be assumed and shared just as they are.

Natural ontology can be considered as a sort of silent *magna charta*, whose sharing is a diagnostic criterion for identifying a community, its possible common experience and its members. People who do not share exactly the same conceptual models remain members of the community in a full sense; people who do not share the common ontology, on the contrary, are taken either as fools or as aliens, that is, as members of another community, ruled by a different ontology. Consistency is not a matter of discussion or negotiation on the part of the members of a community. Its ruling criteria are to be taken or rejected simply as they are.[250] This confirms the idea that sharing of consistency criteria is not an empirical fact about communities, but a constitutive fact, or, in Kantian terms, a fact of the transcendental order, that is, a non-empirical fact which is constitutive of the empirical order itself.[251]

2.2.4 *Processing consistent states of affairs out of inconsistent meanings: the role of cognitive models*

A further argument supporting the idea that cognitive models are by definition consistent, and therefore rely on an underlying system of consistency criteria, is the role they play in interpreting inconsistent complex meanings as expressions of consistent states of affairs.

As metaphors based on the transgression of lexical solidarities, metaphors which introduce an alien concept into a familiar cognitive scene are open to non-conflictual reformulation. While lexical substitution is based on the structure of lexical paradigms structuring consistent conceptual areas, a cognitive reformulation is backed by the activation of a consistent cognitive model.

An inconsistent meaning can be interpreted in two ways: either it is designed to construct an inconceivable state of affairs, or it is intended to depict in conflictual words a non-conflictual state of affairs. Such an utterance as *Prata rident*, for instance, attributes a human behaviour to an inanimate being, building up an inconsistent meaning. In spite of this, it can easily be interpreted as depicting such a consistent state of affairs as the visual impact of a meadow covered with flowers. This kind of reduction is rather trivial, and certainly amounts to killing the metaphor. Looked at from our point of view, however, it is of some interest, because it provides a good vantage point for looking at the relationship between cognitive modelling and consistency.

The simplest case of reduction takes place when a conflicting referential expression is introduced into a familiar cognitive scene. In such a case, the consistent paraphrase is attained by a punctual substitution. Once the intended referent has been identified, a consistent substitute of the referring noun is by definition available. Conrad, for instance, describes *a ship coming in from sea and* folding her white wings *for a rest.* A ship can be said to have wings for two purposes: either the ship has changed into a bird, or the wings are meant to refer to a consistent part of the ship. In the latter case, if we superpose the consistent ship scheme on the conflictual description, the inconsistent concept of wing is picked out as a jarring note in a familiar score, and a consistent alternative is immediately provided: a ship's wings are its sails.

When the inconsistent concept is a relational one, consistency is not attained through a punctual substitution of the conflicting term within the framework of the given process, as in the case of lexical substitution, but through a global reformulation of the whole process against the background of a consistent cognitive model. The smile of the moon described by Blake — *The moon [...] Sits and smiles on the night* — is a good example of this. The verb *smile*, conflicting with the moon, does not admit a punctual lexical substitution because there is no English lexeme capable of expressing the smile of the moon in a non-conflicting way. This in turn points back to the fact that the conflict is not due to the lexical choice but to a real ontological obstacle: the moon is not allowed to smile. The only way of restoring consistency is to interpret the concept of smiling as referring to a completely different kind of process, consistent with the moon — for instance, as referring to its glittering light. Any time one takes an inconsistent meaning as a conflictual way of drawing a consistent state of affairs, the metaphor is reduced thanks to the identification of an alternative model of process which is by definition consistent.[252]

2.3 Cognitive modelling presupposes consistency

All the arguments we have examined lead to one and the same conclusion: consistency criteria are not cognitive models, but draw the outer borders of possible, conceivable experience, and therefore provide cognitive modelling with its raw material. It is within these borders that beliefs about the world, cognitive data and cognitive models receive their form and content.

Thanks to consistency criteria, inconsistent beings and processes are *a priori* filtered out of the domain of possible experience and confined to the realm of constructed linguistic meanings. Within the range of ontological possibilities disclosed by consistency criteria, empirical control tries to tell the difference between what actually is the case and what is not, that is, between true and false contents of knowledge, while rational argument questions the beliefs about the world. Within the territory of (consistent) truth, in turn, a selective criterion of typicality constructs cognitive models of things and processes, that is, positive contents of concepts. Just like the whole enterprise of cognition of which it forms the most systematic part, cognitive modelling presupposes consistency.

3. Inside the borders of consistency: Lexical structures and cognitive models

The distinction between lexical substitution and cognitive paraphrase is well illustrated by a great number of clear instances. *John murdered a spider* or *John barks*, for instance, are clear cases of lexical mistakes, which can be corrected by lexical substitution. *The moon smiles* or *The flowers in this old garden awake*

(E. Brontë), on the other hand, are irreversible conflicts which can be paraphrased into consistent cognitive scenes. In some cases, however, the consistent reformulation is attained through such a long and complex lexical path as to resemble more a cognitive paraphrase than a true lexical substitution. The latter, so to speak, merges into the former. Let us consider an example.

Like many other languages, English has a rich paradigm of specialised verbs for the expression of both specific animal cries and human articulated and non-articulated sounds, while it is very imprecise in depicting the rich and picturesque range of sounds of the inanimate world. Given such a lack of balance, it is no wonder that a faithful picture of inanimate sounds is often compelled to borrow lexical means from the fields of animate or even human sounds: *The wind sang in a strenuous note* (Conrad); *The stream sings merrily* (E. Brontë); *The sea speaks in a kingly voice* (D. Thomas); *The wind I hear is sighing / With Autumn's saddest sound* (E. Brontë).

These transfers are rather difficult to characterise. On the one hand, one cannot really say that the distinction between noises, cries of animate creatures and human articulated sounds, which is clear enough on cognitive grounds, matches true lexical borders. On the other hand, the inanimate beings which are made to cry, bark, sigh, whistle or whisper are in any case allowed to emit some kind of sound, a circumstance which provides a common ground for a consistent reformulation through lexical substitution. Consistency can be attained at a very low level indeed, but it can at last be attained

The question about the overlapping of lexical structures and cognitive models is certainly relevant to linguistic description, first of all because it is connected with the question of the degree of conceptual motivation of lexical solidarities. As far as our present topic is concerned, however, the relevant point is that both lexical substitution and cognitive paraphrase share one and the same essential condition, that is, the condition that a consistent state-of-affairs can be identified. Both lexical structures and cognitive models are consistent concepts; the only difference is that the latter are very largely shared while the former are language-specific. Being under the jurisdiction of lexical structures and being under the jurisdiction of cognitive structures, thus, both equally presuppose being inside the territory of consistency.

The relative position of consistency criteria, lexical structures and lexical information now becomes clear. Consistency criteria delimit from outside a consistent conceptual territory. It is within the borders of consistency, and only within these borders, that language-specific lexical structures and shared cognitive models take shape and interact to shape concepts. Consistency criteria are not caught within this complex interplay — they delimit the playing field from outside.

The fact that concepts are cut out from among consistent cognitive material is the reason why descriptive lexicography does not explicitly state consistency criteria: cultural models of things and events either shaped or expressed by lexical structures and dealt with by descriptive lexicography are previously assumed as consistent.[253] Their consistency is not called into question but presupposed in lexical definitions.

Black (1952(1954: 32)) compares the presuppositions taken for granted in lexical definitions to the felicity conditions of speech acts: "It has long been recognized that bets, promises, commands, and other such linguistic acts may depend upon suppositions, in the sense that they become 'null and void' if those suppositions prove false. It has not been so clearly recognised that definitions also may become null and void for precisely similar reasons". The definition of a bicycle, for instance, is only conceivable if a given set of shared presuppositions is taken for granted. A bicycle, for instance, is not a living being which was born, grows old and is bound to die. If these presuppositions were not previously shared, it would be pointless even to try to define a bicycle.

Consistency criteria are a qualified part of the set of presuppositions underlying lexical definitions. As they delimit from outside the conceptual territory where the *definiendum* is located, these presuppositions generally remain "outside the jurisdiction of the definition" (32): "Normally, the 'suppositions' involved in a range definition are not explicitly stated". Insofar as they are assumed to be necessarily shared, "it is unnecessary to allude to them" (34).

Once this point is made clear, however, it should be stressed that providing a ground for consistent concepts is not the most crucial property of consistency criteria. As we shall see in the next chapter, consistency criteria hold as presuppositions for both lexical structures and lexical definitions only insofar as they hold as presuppositions of our consistent practical behaviour. If our lexical structures do not articulate a field of emotions for inanimate beings and our definitions take for granted that the question of feelings is not relevant to them, it is for the same reasons that ordinary people do not give orders to inanimate beings or ask them questions.

Chapter 8

Consistency criteria as presuppositions of natural attitude

> If we had a keen vision and feeling
> of all ordinary human life,
> it would be like hearing the grass grow
> and the squirrel's heart beat,
> and we should die of that roar
> which lies on the other side of silence.
> (G. Eliot)

In the popular Italian novel *Pinocchio*, the shift from our common world towards a world of fiction is marked by an extraordinary event. While being shaped by a carpenter, a piece of wood expresses its pain in words:

> As soon as Mr. Cherry saw this piece of wood, he was very pleased [...] Without losing a moment he took his sharp hatchet, and was going to strip off the bark and trim it into shape. But just as he raised the hatchet to strike the first blow, he paused with his hand in the air, for he heard a tiny, tiny voice which said warningly:
> "Don't strike me too hard!"
> Imagine Mr. Cherry's surprise![254]

The carpenter's astonishment is readily understood. Of course, a piece of wood can neither suffer nor fear suffering, let alone express its pain or fear in words. Our behaviour towards pieces of wood is consistent with these assumptions: one cuts, saws, planes or burns them without caring whether they may suffer. Their silence, on the other hand, is not interpreted as a proof of endurance — of a successful struggle against expression of pain — but as proof of lack of life, and therefore lack of pain.

Just like a layer of solid rock hidden beneath a sandy plain, a system of firm certainties grounds the consistency of our natural attitude towards the world (Husserl, 1913: §§27–30). Under normal circumstances, consistency criteria are not explicitly stated in linguistic expressions. At the same time they cannot be negated, or even simply questioned, without tearing down the whole scaffolding of our spontaneous behaviour. Consistency criteria do not form part of what is normally said, but of what is generally assumed, or, in a broad sense, presupposed, not only by our verbal, but above all by our general behaviour. This is the reason why the most direct access to the function of consistency criteria in our form of life is to consider them as silent presuppositions underlying our spontaneous behaviour.

1. Below the threshold of expression: Consistency criteria as general presuppositions

1.1 From discourse presuppositions to general presuppositions

The most typical and best studied opportunity for observing presuppositions is consistent speech. Within the borders of a given speech act, a presupposition can be defined as a non-expressed felicity condition[255] for the consistent use of an utterance. If someone says "I'll lend you my bike", for instance, he does not say that he actually owns a bike, but this fact is an essential condition for the consistency of the act. It cannot be called into question without depriving the act of its ground. A person who does not own a bike cannot possibly lend it. Under such circumstances, it makes no sense either to state or to negate that the bike will be lent, nor to wonder whether it will or will not be lent.

To make a presupposition is not to believe that something is the case, but to behave as if something were the case. As Stalnaker (1973: 447) points out, presupposition is a notion of the practical order, and presupposing is an act made by a person:[256] "the basic presupposition relation is not between propositions or sentences, but between a person and a proposition. A person's presuppositions are the propositions whose truth he takes for granted, often unconsciously, in a conversation, an inquiry, or a deliberation. They are the background assumptions that may be used without being spoken — sometimes without being noticed". A speaker who makes an act of presupposition "does *act as if* he takes the truth of the proposition for granted, and as if he assumes that his audience recognizes that he is doing so" (451).

As underlined by the last quotation, a presupposition is not simply taken for granted by the speaker. In order to perform its function, it has also to be accepted by the addressee. Insofar as they are shared by the actors of a speech act, presuppositions mould, so to speak, the river-bed of coherent and consistent speech: "To presuppose a certain content is to assume its acceptance as the condition to which further dialogue is subject" (Ducrot, 1972(1980: 91)).

Presuppositions frame a sort of legal setting for "the game of speech", which binds both the speaker and his addressee: for instance, "the only answers a question allows are those which maintain its presuppositions" (90). As far as they are not constituents of the ongoing discourse but of its river-bed, presuppositions are not called into question, but relied upon "as self-evident truths"[257] (94).

A practical definition of discourse presuppositions as felicity conditions of the corresponding acts sheds light on two points which are relevant to our topic.

On the one hand, those presuppositions which are immediately bound to the content of the expression form only one layer — and the most shallow and volatile layer — of what is practically presupposed during a speech act. If I promise a friend to lend him my bike, for instance, I certainly presuppose that I own a bike, but I also presuppose that my addressee is a human being like myself, ready to interact with me. My promise fails if I do not own a bike, of course, but also if I address my promise to a stone. A speech act rests on a layered hierarchy of presuppositions, ranging along a scale from the most contingent and idiosyncratic to the most general and systematic. The most idiosyncratic layer is specific to speech acts, for it has to do with a given linguistic content. The presuppositions of this kind affect the consistency of the act indirectly, by affecting the coherence of its content. The most general presuppositions, for their part, are not specific to speech acts, for they are not connected with a linguistic content and, above all, do not require the presence of any. A general presupposition affects the consistency of a speech act not in that it is a *speech* act, but in that it is an act — a piece of human behaviour.[258]

If the relation of presupposing is dissociated from the content of linguistic expressions, on the other hand, it turns out that any kind of human practice, from strolling around to solving complex theoretical problems, necessarily rests on a hierarchy of presuppositions, which in turn cannot be negated, or simply questioned, without depriving the practice concerned of its very basis. Such a remark naturally leads to a generalised concept of presupposition, which includes discourse presuppositions as a particular case within a wider category. The consistent act of cutting a piece of wood, for instance, presupposes that the piece of wood exists and that it is an inanimate kind of being which does not feel pain.

Generally speaking, a presupposition can be defined in terms of consistency, that is, as a condition imposed on the consistency of a given practice. If a presupposition belonging to any layer of the hierarchy is not satisfied, the practice which presupposes it is inconsistent. My promise to lend my bike, for instance, is equally inconsistent if a discourse presupposition is not satisfied — if I do not own a bike — and if a general presupposition is not satisfied — for instance, if I address my promise to a stone. The difference is that my act is inconsistent for contingent reasons and as a speech act in the former case and for more general reasons and simply as an act in the latter. The difference between discourse presuppositions and general presuppositions does not lie in the structure of presupposing, which is exactly the same, but in the nature of the presupposed content. What is presupposed in the former case is a contingent, empirical datum; what is presupposed in the latter is a systematic ontological categorisation of beings.

On these premises, consistency criteria can naturally be defined as a kind of general presuppositions which occupy the very bottom rank of the hierarchy.[259] This means that their content is bound neither to the specific content nor to the general properties of this or that occasional act, but is taken for granted as a shared background for any kind of human practice. Once this point is made clear, discourse presuppositions can be used as a model for describing consistency criteria, on the sole condition that the same properties that apply occasionally to the former are systematically applied to the latter.

Discourse presuppositions are by definition contingent conditions for contingent acts. Consistency criteria hold as conditions for consistent behaviour, and hence consistent discourse, in general. Discourse presuppositions are shared within the limits of an utterance act and by its occasional actors. Consistency criteria are shared by the members of a whole community irrespective of given, contingent speech acts and acts of behaviour. If discourse presuppositions define the legal setting of contingent utterance acts, consistency criteria define the legal setting of our form of life. If the former are challenged, the concerned speech act becomes senseless; if the latter were called into question, the very pillars of our spontaneous attitude towards the world would collapse.

Expression is the threshold of questioning and doubt. Accordingly, there is an obvious correlation between the function of presuppositions in securing consistency, their being taken for granted and their lack of explicit formulation in linguistic utterances. In order to protect them from questioning and doubt, discourse presuppositions are not stated during utterance acts. For the same reasons, consistency criteria are systematically kept below the threshold of expression. If consistency criteria are ever stated, this means that the subject has momentarily taken leave of the game of spontaneous life. He has given up his role as a consistently behaving human being in order to take over a role of a higher order: for instance, he is a philosopher interested in analysis, or a teacher engaged in answering the questions of a naive pupil.

The circle which keeps essential conceptual structures below the threshold of expression, and protects their obviousness from explicit articulation and questioning is a virtuous circle from the point of view of the layman engaged in the game of life. The living being cannot at one and the same time live and challenge the background assumptions on which life itself rests, just as it would not be wise for a wood-cutter to saw off the bough he is sitting on. Insofar as he shares the common ontology, the analyst himself cannot push his enquiry to the point of challenging its presuppositions, which would amount to sawing off the bough he is sitting on. All he can do is to make explicit and describe the presuppositions of natural ontology as they actually are, and analyse their manifold connections with the different aspects of the game of life.

1.2 Natural ontology and consistency criteria

I am the poet of commonsense (Whitman)

An explicit formulation of natural ontology tries to answer three interconnected questions: what exists? Which formal kinds of beings exist? Which substantial kinds of entities can be conceived of, and what relations can they enter into?

The first question defines ontology in a narrow sense. Its object is the kinds of beings which are actually assumed to exist or to have existed in our shared world. Wolves, for instance, are generally assumed to exist, whereas unicorns are not. It is within these limits that Quine (1953: 1) defines ontology: "A curious thing about the ontological problem is its simplicity. It can be put in three Anglo-Saxon monosyllables: 'What is there?'".

The second question does not look at the actual existence of beings but at their formal possibility. It governs the distribution of possible entities among such formal kinds as particular individuals, classes, masses and instances of masses, properties, and processes. Unicorns, for instance, do not exist in the real world; if they existed, they would be individuals belonging to a class. The smile of the moon does not occur; if it occurred, it would be a process.

The third question has also to do with possibility. This possibility, however, is not formal but substantial. The substantial side of natural ontology classifies different substantial kinds of beings and governs their access to different substantial kinds of properties and processes. If unicorns existed, they would be animate non-human beings, like horses or lions. They would be allowed to sleep and eat, suffer and die, but not to speak an articulated language.

Natural ontology is interested in all these questions, each of which seeks to understand some of our natural presuppositions. Consistency criteria form the subset of natural presuppositions that is included within the scope of the third question.

As far as I know, consistency criteria have never been explicitly described as natural presuppositions. At the same time, the characteristics of the natural standpoint and some of its presuppositions have been analyzed as *a priori* conditions for our spontaneous behaviour by such philosophers as Husserl (1913(1931)), Moore (1925(1959); 1939(1959)), Wittgenstein (1969), Strawson (1959; 1992) and Searle (1983). If consistency criteria are included among the conditions governing our spontaneous behaviour, our tentative definition of their form and function may take as its starting point the results attained by philosophical analysis in the more general field of natural presuppositions.

In a well-known paper which seeks to dig out the very roots of "the inexpugnable strength of common sense",[260] Moore (1925(1959: 33)) describes a corpus of propositions which express, in his view, a shared system of indisputable pieces of knowledge.[261] In fact, these propositions can be considered as expressing a set of shared presuppositions underlying our immediate contact with the world:

> There exists at present a living human body, which is my body [...] there have also existed many other things, having shape and size in three dimensions [...]. Among the things which have, in this sense, formed part of its environment [...] there have, at every moment since its birth, been large numbers of other living human bodies [...] But the earth had existed also for many years before my body was born; and for many of these years, also large numbers of human bodies had, at every moment, been alive upon it [...]. Finally [...] I am a human being, and I have, at different times since my body was born, had many different experiences, of each of many different kinds.

A supplementary assumption is that other human beings rely on a similar set of propositions: "each of us [...] has frequently *known*, with regard to himself or his body and the time at which he knew it, everything which [...] I was claiming to know" (34).

Moore's commonplaces belong to an eccentric territory with regard to consistency criteria. Their content, though very heterogeneous, has essentially to do with the first question of natural ontology, that is, with the immediate givenness of the objects of direct experience. If Moore's commonplaces have to do with consistency, it is not on the basis of their specific content, but in the way any presupposition has, that is, in the sense that it would be inconsistent with our overall behaviour either to negate them or to cast doubt upon them.[262] Accordingly, the analogy between Moore's truisms and consistency criteria lies in their common function of general practical presuppositions, and it is within these limits that a discussion of Moore's truisms casts light on consistency criteria.

1.3 Presupposition beneath cognition

The most disputable point of Moore's analysis is that it rests on a false assumption — namely, on the assumption that natural presuppositions are to be considered as part of our common knowledge. This identification between natural presuppositions and contents of knowledge — and, more generally, between presupposing and knowing — can be criticised from the standpoint of both knowledge and natural presuppositions. On the one hand, the nature and function of knowledge, which is formed by a set of consistent synthetic propositions backed by empirical evidence or rational argument, is misunderstood if it is seen as a set of indisputable truisms.[263] On the other hand, the nature and function of natural presuppositions cannot be grasped if they are treated as contents of knowledge. Natural presuppositions are both devoid of any cognitive value and practically more effective than any piece of knowledge would be.

A significant property of natural presuppositions is their indisputable firmness — their being located outside the scope of doubt. This kind of absolute certainty which eludes the struggle with doubt is not to be confused with the sort of relative firmness we are ready to grant the contents of knowledge. Whereas a piece of knowledge is a proposition which has, until proof of the contrary, overcome doubt, the certainty of natural presuppositions is no more than absence of doubt.

Doubt is indissociable from knowledge insofar as it makes people look for evidence or arguments for securing the truth of hypotheses. Whether it is the issue of empirical evidence or of persuasive argument, truth is built against, and thus intrinsically threatened by falsity.

Natural presuppositions undergo neither empirical control nor persuasive argument. They are neither built up against falsity nor threatened by the prospect of it, because truth and falsity, empirical control and persuasive argument can only be conceived against their background. As Wittgenstein

(1969: prop. 88) points out, "all enquiry on our part is set so as to exempt certain propositions from doubt, if they are ever formulated. They lie apart from the route travelled by enquiry".

Of course, natural presuppositions are held as if they were true. But it is senseless to consider as strictly true a set of propositions which are not threatened by falsity because they elude doubt and even expression. As Wittgenstein (1969: prop. 94) points out, our natural ontology is not a system of propositions which have turned out to be true. Natural ontology is simply relied upon as "the inherited background against which I distinguish between true and false".[264] "If the true is what is grounded, then the ground is not *true*, nor yet false" (prop. 205).

Under such premises, Moore's idea that natural presuppositions are *known* by everybody is criticised by Wittgenstein (1969). According to Wittgenstein, natural presuppositions are not known,[265] but shared and relied upon as a layer of indisputable certainties. A man who is reading a book does not know that the book exists; he simply makes visible by his behaviour that he relies on its existence. "Does a child believe that milk exists? Or does it know that milk exists?", Wittgenstein asks (prop. 478). The child simply behaves as if the existence of the milk he is drinking were not disputable. When "used as a foundation", a given set of propositions "simply gets assumed as a truism, never called into question, perhaps not even formulated" (prop. 87).

As a subset of natural presuppositions, consistency criteria share all these qualifying properties, and in particular the property of being silently relied upon as a firm background barred to question and doubt. Doubt does not threaten consistency criteria because doubt itself and its issues, empirical control and persuasive argument, truth and falsity, can only be conceived within the borders of consistency. Within the borders of consistency, no question is meaningless; outside these borders, any is. If doubt is cast on the grounds of consistency, the quest for truth becomes senseless.[266] In order to be checked against empirical evidence, or to be argued for, propositions have to be consistent. It makes sense, for instance, to ask whether a stream is or is not frozen, and collect evidence for it, because it is consistent, for a stream, to be either frozen or not. It makes sense to wonder whether a man is responsible for a murder, and argue for or against it, because moral responsibility can be consistently attributed to a human being. But it makes no sense to wonder whether a stream is responsible for a man's drowning in it.

Before forming "the river-bed of thoughts"[267] (Wittgenstein, 1969: 97), natural presuppositions, and among them consistency criteria, form the river-bed of the whole game of life. Accordingly, the categorisation of beings which is assumed by natural ontology is not a theoretical or cognitive kind of categorisation but a practical categorisation, that is, a categorisation which is not framed in propositions but tacitly presupposed by actions. A man using a stone to drive in a nail practically categorises the stone as an instrument. He does not explicitly define the stone as an instrument, but simply uses it as if it were one. An individual who argues with another practically categorises the addressee "as a person, a rational agent" (Dennett, 1969: 177), who can evaluate different options and make a rational choice. If trees are classified as non-human beings within our shared ontology, it is insofar as people do not behave towards them as they behave towards human beings.[268] The practical relevance of a presupposed layer of complex conceptual structures shows that shared concepts do not reduce themselves to either cognitive contents or cognitive structures. Beyond their different categorial contents, it is a different attitude on the part of the subjects that draws a sharp line between presupposition and cognition.

The qualifying properties of natural presuppositions refer us back to Husserl's remarks about natural attitude and its assumptions. A typical characteristic of natural attitude towards the world is the fact that existing things and beings and their salient properties are not called into question, but simply taken as they offer themselves to direct experience: "Through sight, touch, hearing, etc., in the different ways of sensory perception, corporeal things somehow spatially distributed are *for me simply there*, in verbal or figurative sense 'present' [...] Animal beings also, perhaps men, are immediately there for me; I look up, I see them, I hear them coming towards me, I grasp them by the hand; speaking with them, I understand immediately what they are sensing and thinking, the feelings that stir them, what they wish or will" (Husserl, 1913(1931: 101)). Natural presuppositions are both insensitive to the changing flow of knowledge and irrelevant to its positive content. They tell us nothing about how things run. But they tell us much about our shared attitude towards things: "This 'fact world', as the word already tells us, I find to *be out there*, and also *take it just as it gives itself to me as something that exists out there.* All doubting and rejecting of the data of the natural world leaves standing the *general thesis of the natural standpoint*" (106).

2. Consistency criteria as a priori conceptual structures

Consistency criteria are not a set of empirical contents of knowledge but a system of conceptual structures ruling *a priori* the possible contents of practical behaviour, empirical knowledge and consistent discourse.

When we think of *a priori* structures, independent of actual experience, we are naturally inclined to take into account such kinds of structures as are simultaneously formal, necessary, and analytical:[269] for instance, mathematical rules, geometric postulates or logical principles. Now, consistency criteria certainly do not resemble formal and necessary structures, because they have a substantive content and are culturally specific, and therefore contingent. If they have an analytical character, on the other hand, it is not immediately visible. Our hypothesis, however, is that the substantial and contingent nature of consistency criteria is not an obstacle to their holding as *a priori* structures, while their content is ultimately tautological.

The starting point of our line of argument is provided by two distinctions. The first distinction is a matter of viewpoint. A given practice — be it the game of chess, the game of speaking or the game of life — can be analysed either from the inside or the outside. The second distinction is a matter of definition. One can say either that a given structure *is a priori* or that it *holds as* (if it were) *a priori.* The two distinctions are clearly intertwined, for the choice of the definition entails the choice of the viewpoint. If we ask the absolute and essential question "What *is a priori?*", we place ourselves, or pretend to, outside the game. If we ask the functional and relational question "*What holds as a priori and within which limits?*", we place ourselves within a given and well-defined game.

2.1 Consistency criteria as necessary conceptual structures

> Est-ce que tu ferais des objections
> aux règles du whist? (Stendhal)

If we place ourselves within the horizon of natural attitude, the first obstacle towards considering consistency criteria *a priori* structures simply dissolves. If consistency criteria have a substantive conceptual purport, and it is precisely this conceptual purport that is relevant as a basis for our natural standpoint, this simply proves that a structure has not necessarily to be formal in order to hold as *a priori.* Insofar as consistency is a matter of substantial compatibility between concepts, the criteria which govern consistency either have to be substantial, or not to be at all.

Unlike formality, necessity is a necessary condition for something to be *a priori.* The concept of necessity, however, cannot be defined absolutely — it can be defined only from within a given practice. What is contingent if looked at from an external point of view may turn out to hold as necessary if looked at from inside.

The best examples of empirical, historically and socially variable structures which nevertheless hold *a priori* are the structures of language. Looked at from an historical or social point of view, the phonological, grammatical and lexical structures of a given natural language are as contingent as any historical or social fact. If a given language has the sounds, the meaningful words and grammatical forms and rules it has, it is only because the interplay of largely unforeseeable events through which its history has passed has shaped it in this way — in a way which can be described only *a posteriori*. In spite of this, if we look at a given natural language from a synchronic, internal point of view as a condition for speech, its structures, contingent as they are as historical products, prove to be necessary structures holding *a priori*. "It is perfectly conceivable — Ayer (1936(1990: 81)) observes — that we should have employed different linguistic conventions from those which we actually do employ. But whatever these conventions might be, the tautologies in which we recorded them would always be necessary. For any denial of them would be self-stultifying".[270]

In a similar way, consistency criteria may look like historical or anthropological data about a culture from an external point of view. In this sense, they are no more than contingent facts — it is a contingent fact that in our culture we share precisely these consistency criteria. One could easily imagine a change within our culture, or a culture that does not share our consistency criteria, or even come across one during field work. What gets lost in such an external perspective, however, is precisely the role played by consistency criteria in shaping the river-bed of our form of life. If we look at consistency criteria from within the borders of the contingent form of life we happen to share, they do not look like contingent facts, but like conditions holding *a priori* for consistent behaviour, including the construction and processing of empirical knowledge and the contents of linguistic expressions. If we call them into question, we pull down the whole edifice of our form of life.

2.2 Consistency criteria as tautological conceptual structures

The identification of *a priori*, analyticity and tautology is made explicit by Ayer (1936(1990: 83)):

> Having thus shown that [...] the truths of logic and mathematics are all of them analytic, we may safely adopt it as the only satisfactory explanation of their *a priori* necessity. And in adopting it we vindicate the empiricist claim that there can be no *a priori* knowledge of reality.[271] For we show that the truths of pure reason, the

> propositions which we know to be valid independently of all experience, are so only in virtue of their lack of factual content. To say that a proposition is true *a priori* is to say that it is a tautology.

The idea of analyticity moulded on mathematics and logic can be extended to natural languages as far as the formal scaffolding of expressions is concerned, as in the case of linking words and expressions. As Ayer (1936(1990: 73)) points out,

> a proposition is analytic when its validity depends solely on the definitions of the symbols it contains, and synthetic when its validity is determined by the facts of experience [...] The proposition 'There are ants which have established a system of slavery' is a synthetic proposition. For we cannot tell whether it is true or false merely by considering the definitions of the symbols which constitute it [...] On the other hand, the proposition 'Either some ants are parasitic or none are' is an analytic proposition [...] If one knows what is the function of the words 'either', 'or' and 'not', then one can see that any proposition of the form 'Either p is true or p is not true' is valid, independently of experience. Accordingly, all such propositions are analytic.

Tautologies in language, however, are not confined to the meaning of linking words and expressions. Unlike positive lexical information, which is sensitive to experience, the description of formal lexical structures is entirely analytical — it forms a set of tautological equivalencies. To state that *bark* denotes the cry made by dogs in English, or that *essen* denotes eating as performed by people and *fressen* eating as performed by animals in German, or that in French a *fleuve* flows into the sea while a *rivière* flows into another river, amounts to stating tautologies, that is, propositions which are true exclusively in virtue of the lexical structures of English, German and French. In order to state these equivalencies, one does not have to look for evidence or arguments — one just has to take linguistic structures as they are.

Though filled with a substantive purport, language has a formal structure, and it is this formal structure that holds *a priori* and is analysed in tautologies. In the field of natural ontology, on the contrary, it is substantial conceptual structures that hold *a priori*. The linguistic expression of consistency criteria ends in a set of propositions — for instance, "A piece of wood is an inanimate being which cannot feel pain" — which do not look, at first glance, like tautologies. If we consider them from inside our form of life, however, we realise that such propositions are "valid independently of all experience". If they are held as true, it is exclusively by virtue of the structure of our shared ontology. Since they are true by internal necessity, the presuppositions of natural attitude are analytic and tautological, "entirely devoid of factual content" to the point that "no experience can confute them" (Ayer, 1936(1990: 73)).

The analytical elucidation of natural presuppositions inevitably takes the form of "a whole long list of propositions, which may seem, at first sight, such obvious truisms as not to be worth stating" (Moore, 1925(1959: 32)). Truisms are in the field of substantial *a priori* what tautologies are in the field of formal *a priori*. Like the analysis of lexical and mathematical structures, the analytical description of natural ontology is no more than a system of equivalencies. To say that a human being can make responsible decisions is just as tautological as to say that 2 + 2 makes 4 or that dogs bark. To say that a non-human being is not morally responsible of its behaviour is as tautological as to say that 2 + 2 does not make 5 or that cats do not bark. One does not have to look for evidence in order to state these equivalencies.

The fact that the analysis of *a priori* structures ends in truisms and commonplaces does not mean that it is totally devoid of interest. In fact, it is not the bare content of consistency criteria that justifies the analysis, but their functional relationship to our form of life, which they provide with its solid ground. It is a fact that the ground supporting our form of life, once carved out, generally looks less attractive than the manifold and surprising universe of phenomena resting on it. In spite of the trivial contents it uncovers, however, the analysis of *a priori* structures is a subtle and non-trivial task, as Husserl (1901(1984: 345)) underlines: "The *a priori* [...] is, at least in its primitive forms, obvious, even trivial, but its systematic demonstration, theoretical pursuit and phenomenological clarification remains of supreme scientific and philosophical interest, and by no means easy". The analytical exploration of the layer of tautologies located on "the other side of silence" is one of the tasks of philosophy, or, to confine ourselves to our own field, of the philosophical component of a philosophical grammar: "He [the philosopher] must surely also know that it is precisely behind the obvious that the hardest problems lie hidden, that this is so much so, in fact, that philosophy may be paradoxically, but not unprofoundly, called the science of the trivial. In the present case at least what seems at first quite trivial, reveals itself, on closer examination, as the source of deep-lying, widely ramifying problems".

2.3 Cognitive models: *A priori* structures *sub condicione*

The tautological character of both lexical structures and consistency criteria makes a real difference with regard to propositions conveying contents of knowledge, but raises an intriguing question about cognitive models.

Propositions conveying cognitive contents of any kind, from very general models such as *Birds can fly*, to occasional pieces of information about particular beings such as *John is running*, are true synthetic propositions, which ultimately deal with, and are sensitive to, empirical data. In spite of this, typical models and schemata underlying categorisation are not taken as if they were descriptions of actual experience, but as if they were a preliminary condition of its structure and content. Cognitive models are not propositions which prove themselves empirically true on particular occasions, but propositions which are relied upon as generally true irrespective of actual experience, and even against it. Empirical propositions are tested against experience. If it is not the case that John is running, for instance, the utterance *John is running* is taken as false. Cognitive models, for their part, are kept apart from empirical control. If some birds prove unable to fly, this does not falsify the cognitive model of birds as flying animals.

According to Kleiber (1990: 73–74), this is an argument for considering typical properties incorporated into lexical models as a kind of *a priori* truths:

> they [typical properties] cannot be necessary conditions, since all members do not need to share them, but they can equally not be considered as contingent, since they would otherwise not be distinguishable from mere encyclopaedic data. There is actually a fundamental difference *vis-à-vis* the latter: they do not need prior verification, which allows a possible solution — considering them as *a priori* truths.

Cognitive models based on typical properties have in common with *a priori* truths the function of "transcendental" conditions of actual experience. The prototypical model of the bird, for instance, is not the outcome of an actual act of experience — it is what justifies the categorisation of certain empirical data as (more or less typical) instances of birds. At the same time, it is a fact that true analytical properties holding *a priori* admit no empirical falsification, whereas typical models coexist by definition with data from experience which do not satisfy them. Prototypical properties, therefore, can be considered as *a priori* structures, so to speak, only in a non-prototypical way — they instantiate a kind of *a priori* which holds only *sub condicione*. More precisely, they tend to be taken as *a priori* structures until proof of the contrary and are ready, if necessary, to yield to conflicting empirical data.

The relationship between true *a priori* structures and prototypical models can be better understood if it is considered as a case of a more general semantic opposition — the opposition between conventional implicatures (Grice, 1975) and invited inferences (Geis & Zwicky, 1971).

A conventional implicature is an item of non-asserted information bound *a priori* to the use of a given linguistic expression; as such, it cannot be effaced by conflicting occasional information. Whenever I use the verb *bark*, for instance, I cannot help associating a dog with it. In a similar way, any use of the verb *speak* evokes a human being. If *bark* is constructed with a non-canine subject, or *speak* with a non-human subject, the solidary subject — the dog, the human being — conflicts with the actual subject, giving rise to a peculiar kind of relational metaphor.[272] As they are indissociable from the use of a given word, both lexical solidarities and consistency criteria are real *a priori* structures, insensitive to occasional data to the point of surviving conflict.

An invited inference, on the other hand, is a piece of non-asserted information which is tendentially associated with the use of a given expression but can be dropped in the case of conflict with co-occurring data. The concept of "bird", for instance, is associated in this way with the property "able to fly". The use of the concept for denoting a given instance invites the inference that the intended individual is able to fly. If a given instance proves to be unable to fly, the application of the inference is blocked for this instance.

For their part, non-typical properties which are not invited by the cognitive model can be considered as a sort of admitted inference. One would not consider them as a first step, because they conflict with shared cognitive models; nevertheless, one is ready to make room for them when positive experience fails to meet the expectations raised by the model. The behaviour of invited inferences shows not only that there is a conflict between ideal models and empirical data of actual experience, but also that the model is sensitive to experience without yielding to it. The non-typical, admitted properties have no effect on the structure of the model. Instead of falsifying the model, their activation is taken as proof that the involved instances have a non-prototypical status. The fact that some birds cannot fly does not threaten the cognitive model of bird, but confines these instances to a peripheral status.

Thanks to the peculiar properties of invited inferences, cognitive models practically share the qualifying functional properties of true *a priori* structures without sharing either the analytical character or the internal necessity of the latter.

2.4 Language as a model for *a priori*

> Le schéma de notre langue peut être contingent
> mais il est sans doute inexpugnable (Ricoeur)

The whole of the above discussion was intended to support the hypothesis that consistency criteria are neither linguistic nor cognitive structures. Yet, consistency criteria are generally placed by both linguists and philosophers either among linguistic structures or among cognitive models. Taking consistency criteria as cognitive models simply makes one underestimate their function as *a priori* conditions of consistent behaviour and thought. Their inclusion among linguistic structures, on the contrary, is the wrong way of expressing a sound insight, that is, the idea that consistency criteria are not empirical facts but "essential" (Husserl), "analytical" (Ayer) or "transcendental" (Kant, Wittgenstein) structures, which hold as *a priori* conditions for the processing of experience without forming part of it.

Language is undoubtedly the most typical, familiar and pervasive example of a system of shared structures constraining *a priori* the form of our experience. In order to extend this property to consistency criteria, however, it is not necessary to consider them linguistic structures — it is sufficient to think that their function is similar to the function of linguistic structures. The inclusion of consistency criteria among linguistic structures required a supplementary assumption, which can be traced back to the empiricist tradition and lies at the roots of the linguistic turn in philosophy — namely, the assumption that any *datum* involved in the processing of knowledge is either an empirical fact or a linguistic structure.

A good example of this attitude is provided once more by Ayer (1936(1990: 44)), who sets up an opposition between factual propositions, dealt with by empirical knowledge, and linguistic propositions, the object of philosophical analysis: "the philosopher, as an analyst, is not directly concerned with the physical properties of things. He is concerned only with the way in which we speak about them. In other words, the propositions of philosophy are not factual, but linguistic in character — that is, they do not describe the behaviour of physical, or even mental, objects; they express definitions, or the formal consequences of definitions". Wittgenstein (1953(1968: 371)) is more straightforward, but the overall sense is the same: "*Essence* is expressed by grammar",[273] that is, anything which is not factual is grammatical. On such an assumption, "linguistic" and "grammatical" become synonymous with "*a priori*", and the inclusion of consistency criteria among linguistic structures obviously looks like the only way of securing their essential, non-empirical character against an empirical and psychological drift.

In the light of our analysis, Ayer's and Wittgenstein's statements should not be taken as meaning that any kind of *a priori* structure actually belongs to language, but that these structures belong to an order of lawfulness whose most clear, familiar and widespread example is language. Language and grammar, in other words, are seen as the model of *a priori* lawfulness. If it is taken within these limits, the idea that ontological lawfulness is a kind of grammar is certainly true. An inconsistent conceptual link — the idea of a smiling moon, for instance — is not just felt as something odd and unusual in our everyday cultural landscape, but rather as something absolutely excluded on conceptual grounds, exactly as a grammatical mistake is seen as something absolutely excluded on grammatical grounds. Consistency criteria, in this sense, form a true grammar of concepts.

3. The groundless ground of our form of life

If the concept of *a priori* is defined through the concept of presupposition, the functional and relational structure of the latter is extended to the former. While an absolute and essential definition states that a given structure or content *is* in itself *a priori*, a functional-relational definition states that a given structure or content *holds as a priori* when it is taken as the ground for a given practice. The relevant question about *a priori* is no longer: what is *a priori* — for instance, are the phonemes of English, or our shared consistency criteria, kinds of *a priori* structures? — but: what holds *a priori* with regard to what — for instance, do the phonemes of English hold as *a priori* structures if looked at from within English language? Do our shared consistency criteria hold as *a priori* structures if looked at from within our form of life?

The functional-relational definition has two advantages over its essential counterpart: it dissolves the dichotomy between contingent and *a priori*, and is ready to make room, if necessary, for an essential kind of *a priori*.

The alternative between contingent and *a priori* does not reflect the way human beings deal with things, but is a spurious consequence of the essential definition. If a given structure or content is considered as *being a priori* in essential terms, it cannot at the same time be seen as contingent. But if a given structure or content is considered as *holding a priori* with regard to a given practice, nothing prevents it to be a contingent datum outside this practice. My owning a bike is a necessary condition holding *a priori* for my consistent promise to lend it. Outside this act, however, it is no more than a contingent datum.

The question may look immaterial as far as discourse presuppositions are concerned, for their holding as *a priori* conditions is too ephemerous a phenomenon to deserve notice. It becomes of some interest, however, when the object of social sciences is at issue. Dissolving the spurious alternative between contingent and *a priori*, a functional-relational definition opens up linguistic, cognitive and ontological structures to empirical analysis without losing sight of their essential function as conditions *a priori* of experience.

The clearest example of this is provided once more by human languages. From an absolute and essential standpoint, it would be difficult to reconcile the typological, historical and social variability of natural languages with their function as *a priori* structures.[274] If *a priori* is seen as a functional relation, the contradiction disappears. A phonological system, for instance, is no more than a contingent historical fact in its actual configuration. But as far as it is relied upon as a ground for the differentiation of meaningful words within a given language, this same phonological system has to be taken as a structure holding *a priori*. In the light of distinctive function, what is contingent as a historical fact becomes necessary as a systematic fact. More generally, the object of synchronic linguistic description — Saussure's *langue* — is not a sort of theoretical fiction based on a rough simplification of the rich phenomenology of historical and sociological data, but a real object of the eidetic order, that is, a shared system of formal presuppositions. This system is real insofar as it is practically relied upon by users and makes speaking possible.

The second advantage of the functional-relational definition is that it is ready to make room for *a priori* structures of the essential kind, if ever there are any. Looked at from a functional-relational point of view, the essential definition of *a priori* structures may simply be considered as the limit of a relational and functional definition. When saying that some structure *is a priori*, in other words, one imagines a sort of ultimate, absolute *a priori* which is necessary in itself, with regard to any conceivable practice.

The condition for an absolute *a priori* is that internal and external viewpoints are made to coincide. Now, it is not certain that such an absolute viewpoint can be positively attained. In order to attain it, we would have to quit our essentially contingent condition as finite human beings — just as we would have to quit the geometry of our shared space in order to touch the point where two parallel lines meet. What we can easily conceive of, however, is a progressive approximation to such a limit.

The presuppositions of an act of utterance, for instance, are located very far from the essential limit, for they are in themselves absolutely contingent facts. Insofar as they are independent of actual experience, mathematical, geometric and logical structures are very close to it — for practical purposes, they can be relied upon as if they actually were absolute *a priori* structures. Though contingent in themselves, linguistic structures are closer to mathematical rules than to contingent discursive presuppositions. Insofar as they delimit a form of life which encompasses many different linguistic communities over a very long period whose origins are located beyond any recorded memory, consistency criteria are even closer to the limit of absolute *a priori* than linguistic structures. This is the reason why, when describing basic ontological presuppositions, one has the feeling of dealing with a sort of ultimate ground, which it is almost impossible to envisage from an external point of view — a sort of groundless ground.[275]

The fact that a ground may be in itself groundless is of some philosophical relevance. Since its origins, philosophy has always been supposed to deal with the ground of things and questions. The philosophical attitude towards knowledge, for instance, consists in looking for its ground — in making explicit the conditions under which and the limits within which knowledge may be provided a ground. Philosophy is, in a sense, the art of asking questions about any kind of presupposed assumption. To accept the idea that a ground is groundless seems, in a way, to put an end to philosophical enquiry. In fact, a groundless ground is not an end to philosophical enquiry — it is just another beginning.

When philosophy stops excavating the ground of things and questions, it begins describing the shape and functions of the ground itself: "At some point — Wittgenstein (1969: 189) suggests — one has to pass from explanation to mere description". To put it in Strawson's words, the project of describing the system of consistency criteria can be considered a province of descriptive metaphysics, engaged in explicating the silent presuppositions which are hidden beneath the flat soil of natural attitude and which justify its consistency.

"Descriptive metaphysics — Strawson (1959(1964: 9)) points out — is content to describe the actual structure of our thought about the world". Descriptive metaphysics aims at uncovering hidden conceptual structures which are so basic as to defy history:

> there is a massive central core of human thinking which has no history — or none recorded in histories of thought; there are categories and concepts which, in their most fundamental character, change not at all. Obviously these are not the specialities of the most refined thinking.[276] They are the commonplaces of the least

> refined thinking; and are yet the indispensable core of the conceptual equipment of the most sophisticated human beings[277] (10).

When engaged in descriptive metaphysics, a philosopher has nothing to construct or to reconstruct or to criticise, let alone to ground or justify. The shared natural ontology, to put it in Reid's terms, "declines the tribunal of reason [...] To reason against [its principles] is absurd; nay, to reason for them is absurd. They are first principles".[278] It would be only too easy to dissolve the whole system of natural ontology, for its most basic assumptions would not pass the simplest empirical or dialectic test. But equally it would be perfectly pointless, for the result of the most severe examination would not change our natural attitude towards the world by so much as an inch.

Part III: The ideation of complex meanings

Simple sentence, interclausal links, conflictual complex meanings

Introduction

In this final section we shall examine in some detail the interaction between formal and conceptual structures, coding and inferencing, relational coding and punctual coding, in the ideation of consistent and inconsistent complex meanings.

The first topic to be examined is the ideation of the simple process through a nuclear simple sentence (Chapter 9). Our aim is to draw a plan of a typical process, considered in its twofold nature of constructed linguistic meaning and expressed independent conceptual structure.

According to our hypothesis, the process contains a core whose construction is supported by a network of grammatical relations, or functional categories. This core, which coincides with the territory of relational coding, can be described by means of formal criteria, based on the formal properties of the coding expressions.

Outside the network of grammatical relations, a punctual form of coding interacts with inferencing. The structure of this area, therefore, can be described only by means of conceptual criteria, referring back both to the content of linking words, relevant to linguistic coding, and to the conceptual structure of the expressed processes, relevant to inferencing.

The functional core, governed by a relational form of coding, does not coincide with the core of the process, formed by the verb and its controlled arguments. In particular, such roles as Location and Goal, which are arguments of state and motion verbs, are coded punctually, in the same way as margins. As a consequence, the analysis of the simple process deals with two relevant boundaries, which must be defined independently, and by means of independent criteria, that is, the borderline between the area of relational coding and the area of punctual coding, and the borderline between the core of the process and its margins. The first boundary is drawn by means of the observation of prepositions, which behave as formal words when engaged in coding grammatical relations and as lexical words, provided with a positive content, when engaged in a punctual form of coding. The borderline between the core of the process and its margins can be defined exactly according to textual criteria: any marginal role can be expressed outside the sentence which ideates the core of the process, and readmitted into it by means of cohesive devices of the textual order. No argument of the verb can be specified in this way. This foreshadows a significant division of labour between grammar and text: whereas the core of the process can only be ideated within the sentence structure, marginal roles can be specified outside it thanks to cohesive devices. Outside the core of the process, in other words, grammar is itself an option. Between sentence and text there is both a sharp grammatical border and a smooth functional transition.

Once the arguments of the verb are kept away from any kind of margin, the second step consists in defining the exact position of the different marginal roles with regard to the process and its main constituents. Syntactically, each expression of marginal roles can be considered as an expansion either of the predicator, or of the predicate, or of the whole process. To focus on the position of marginal roles amounts to taking into account a second parameter besides verbal control, which governs the linguistic ideation of processes. This parameter is the degree of closeness of both controlled arguments and margins to the ideal centre of the process — to the predicator.

Our discussion of the ideation of interclausal linkage (Chapter 10) will first call into question its traditional identification with the structure of complex sentence.

Whilst the ideation of inherently complex processes is significantly connected, at least in the mainstream European languages, to the form of complex sentences and governed by a relational form of coding, interclausal linkage can use a wide range of grammatical and textual devices, based on a variable balance between grammatical connection and textual coherence and cohesion, punctual coding and inferencing. At one end of this *continuum* is a complex sentence which codes both the link and its content; at the opposite end is a mere juxtaposition which, in the total absence of coding, leaves the ideation of both the link and its content to inferencing. The space in-between is accounted for by a manifold interaction between coding and inferencing, grammatical connection and textual cohesion. The wealth of means — grammatical, textual and lexical — open to interclausal connection will be examined in greater detail against a restricted but significant constellation of links, including cause, motives and purpose.

So far, the interaction between formal and conceptual lawfulness has been considered in its co-operative outcome. But of course whenever an interaction takes place between two independent structural orders, conflict is one of the admitted outcomes. This is the reason why the semantic study of conflictual complex meanings is one of the defining components of a philosophical grammar — of a grammar which focuses on the manifold bases of significance in complex expressions.

Conflict is neither more marginal nor less interesting than co-operation. Besides their epistemological privilege, conflictual complex meanings provide the most celebrated figures of content with their raw material (Chapter 11). In our culture, the experience of conceptual conflicts is inextricably intertwined with the reception of a highly valued and prestigious form of linguistic creation, that is, the construction and interpretation of figures of meaning — oxymoron, synecdoche, metonymy and metaphor — in both literary texts and everyday discourse. The main figures of the conceptual conflict will be examined primarily as linguistic structures, which best highlight the shaping power of syntactic structures.

The book is closed by some concluding remarks (Chapter 12). After a short overview of the main topics, purposes and results of the monograph, we shall briefly examine some implications and perspectives in the field of both general theoretical reflection and empirical investigation.

Chapter 9

The ideation of the simple process

The nuclear sentence is the elective tool for the ideation of simple processes, and the only one for their construction. The simple process, therefore, can be defined as the meaning of a simple nuclear sentence.

A process can be reduced neither to a language-specific formal structure nor to the structure of an independent complex concept. As we have argued in Chapter 3, a process is a layered structure, whose ideation depends on the structure of the sentence up to a given point, and on the structure of an independent complex concept from that point onwards. A process is constructed to the extent that its organisation rests on the formal properties of the sentence, and expressed to the extent that its structure mirrors the form of an independent state of affairs. In particular, a process is constructed in the area of relational coding, in the presence of a network of grammatical relations, and essentially expressed in the area of punctual coding, outside the network of grammatical relations. Accordingly, the subject of this chapter is neither the formal structure of the nuclear sentence, whose configuration is independent of the structure of a complex concept only to a certain extent, nor the structure of an independent complex concept, whose formal possibility is governed, up to a given point, by the form of the sentence, but the specific and subtle interaction between these two autonomous structures.

Our study of the structure of the process is subject to a double limitation. First, it is restricted to the simple extended process formed by the predicator, its arguments and the inner and outer margins,[279] with exclusion of "extra-clausal constituents" (Dik, 1989(1997: 49–50)). Moreover, our analysis is visibly inspired by the observation of English structures, and occasionally takes into account other languages belonging to the European mainstream. In spite of this, the general problems it focuses on, that is, the interaction between relational and punctual coding, punctual coding and inferencing, formal and conceptual lawfulness, are assumed to be relevant for language in general. If their solutions are by definition language-specific, it is difficult to imagine a human verbal language that does not have to face them in some way.

Within these borders, our project pursues two interconnected aims. First, it aims at drawing a distinction between the core of the process, formed by the predicator and its required arguments, and the heterogeneous constellation of non-controlled roles, or margins. Second, it aims at identifying the exact position of marginal roles and the relation each bears to the whole process or some part of it.

At first sight, one could be inclined to think that the discrimination between arguments and margins is independent of, and logically prior to, the differentiation of margins. In fact, one of the leading ideas of this chapter is that the two dimensions of the study of the process are closely intertwined. Owing to the conditions under which the core of the process is coded, the diagnostic criteria that draw a borderline between arguments and margins overlap the criteria that make possible an accurate definition and layering of marginal roles.

The core of the process coincides neither with the syntactic core, formed by the cluster of obligatory constituents whose specification is essential to the well-formedness of actual utterances, nor with the functional core, characterised by the presence of a network of grammatical relations.

Owing to the presence of facultative arguments, the core of the process spreads beyond the syntactic core. This implies that the discrimination between arguments of the verb and marginal roles cannot be directly based on the syntactic well-formedness of actual utterances, but requires more complex and indirect criteria.

Owing to the presence of arguments located outside the functional core, and therefore coded in a punctual way, the discrimination between arguments and margins cannot completely rely on formal criteria, but partly depends on conceptual criteria. While the arguments entrusted to grammatical relations can be identified thanks to the formal properties of their expression, the identification of the arguments located outside the functional core is based on the structure of consistent and typical states of affairs mirrored by the expression. In this way, the discrimination between arguments and margins depends on the same criteria that make visible the exact position of margins with regard to the core of the process.

These criteria are at one and the same time conceptual and textual. They are conceptual because they are sensitive to consistency, and textual because they explicitly take into account the role of textual coherence and cohesion in the ideation of consistent extended processes.

Whereas the arguments of the verb can only be specified inside the sentence that contains the main predicator, marginal roles can be specified either inside the same sentence or outside it, in a textual dimension. This already provides a reliable criterion for a sharp differentiation between arguments and margins outside the network of grammatical relations. Moreover, when marginal roles are specified outside the sentence structure, the ideation of an extended process is entrusted to a chain of grammatically independent sentences, so that the consistency of the process as a whole coincides with the coherence of a fragment of text supported by appropriate cohesive devices. This implies that hypotheses about the position of marginal roles within the extended process can be checked by analysing the properties of the cohesive devices involved in their coherent textual expression. In this way, thanks to the same conceptual and textual criteria that draw a sharp line between arguments and margins, marginal roles can be distributed in different positions, both outside and inside the process, according to a parameter of closeness.

In the following paragraphs, we shall first analyse the structure of the functional core of the sentence as a mould for processes ruled by a relational form of coding. The functional core certainly contains the subject and the direct object, both accessible through formal criteria (§1). However, the boundary of the functional core, that is, the borderline between the area of relational coding and the area of punctual coding, cuts across the territory of prepositional phrases. As a consequence, the critical threshold between the realm of formal criteria and the realm of conceptual criteria is made visible by the observation of prepositions. According to which side of the borderline they occupy, prepositions behave either as formal words or as lexical words, bearing a relevant conceptual content (§2).

Outside the functional core, both the identification and layering of marginal roles and the characterisation of the punctually coded arguments relies on textual and conceptual criteria (§3). The position of verb modifiers, for its part, escapes both kinds of criteria and is only accessible if one ideally tracks the building up of a consistent process step by step. Along with the layering of marginal roles, this last procedure makes visible a second structural parameter that defines the structure of a process besides verbal control, that is, closeness (§4).

1. The functional core of the sentence: Formal criteria

1.1 Reduction

If sentence nuclei of natural languages were built in the same way as the strings of artificial languages, that is, if the core of a well-formed sentence exactly mirrored the core of a state of affairs, the specification of the arguments of the predicator would be obligatory, while the specification of the margins would be optional. Under such circumstances, a reduction test — a test checking which expressions can be dropped from a sentence and which cannot — would identify at the same time the syntactic core of a well-formed sentence and the core of the process. In fact, the structure of natural languages is such that the expression of all the arguments of the verb is not necessarily required for the syntactic well-formedness of the sentence.

The expression of such roles as goal and location is optional in most contexts, and so is, almost systematically, the expression of indirect object. Many transitive verbs do not require the specification of the direct object, while the expression of the subject itself is optional in many languages. As a consequence of this fact, reduction "is no criterion for distinguishing between actants and free margins, but between obligatory actants on the one hand and optional actants and free margins on the other" (Helbig, 1982: 33).

The fact that such an immediate criterion as reduction is not reliable induces one to take into account more indirect formal criteria, which are both language-specific and specific for each involved functional category. An example is provided by the formal properties which characterise the grammatical relations of subject and object in English and similar languages.

In connection with this point, it has to be stressed that our line of argument requires neither that such functional categories as subject or object be universal nor that, within a single language, each instance of each grammatical relation be univocally detectable in isolation through a consistent set of criteria. It simply requires that firm networks of grammatical relations, not affected by the connected conceptual contents, be accessible by purely formal criteria. These are the conditions of relational coding, which make possible the construction of conflictual processes and, more generally, allow us to speak of construction, rather than expression, of processes. On the one hand, it is sufficient that the available formal criteria for the identification of a given functional category — just as the category itself — be language-specific. Our line of argument, for instance, does not require that the subject be a universal category, and even less that the formal criteria for subjecthood be universal. It simply demands that some kind of formal grammatical relations, or functional categories, may be defined on the basis of independent formal criteria within the sentence structures of a given language. On the other hand, local problems of definition within a single language, such as the conflict of criteria for the direct object in English (see Croft, 1999: 71), are easily overcome if whole networks of relations are taken into account instead of isolated categories. This idea is consistent with our definition of relational coding, which implies that sentence nuclei provide formal moulds for processes as integrated wholes.

1.2 The subject

In English, the subject of a simple nuclear sentence is marked by a cluster of formal properties, involving both its coding and behaviour (on the distinction between coding and behavioural properties, see Keenan, 1976: 324; Cole, Harbert, Hermon & Sridhar, 1980). As will become apparent, most of these properties not only qualify the subject as a purely grammatical relation, but also highlight it as an immediate constituent of the sentence structure, the counterpart of the predicate.

An inherent coding property of subjects is their exclusive form. While the structure of any other argument belonging to the network of grammatical relations is controlled by the main predicator, the subject has a form of its own — it belongs to the distributional class of noun phrases *qua* subject. In such languages as German or Latin, which have a case system, the subject is characterised by a special case — Nominative — a trace of which survives in English pronominal subjects: *He / *him loves her.* A coding property which involves the immediate relationship between subject and predicate is agreement with the finite verbal form of the predicate: *He loves her*; *They love her.*

In some languages, including English, the expression of the subject is required for the syntactic well-formedness of the simple nuclear sentence. In other languages, the expression of the subject is optional — that is, it is not dictated by grammatical lawfulness but is an option ruled by textual and discursive criteria. Whether obligatory or optional, however, the subject is systematically such *qua* subject, irrespective of the identity of the predicator and even of the nature — nominal, adjectival or verbal — of the predicate. As well as agreement, both obligatoriness and optionality characterise the subject as an immediate constituent of a nuclear sentence, and not as the simple expression of a role of the process.

Behavioural properties can be observed when simple sentence structures are either transformed or included in more complex constructions.

When a simple nuclear sentence is made passive, the subject is marginalised:[280] *John has broken the Chinese vase*; *The Chinese vase has been broken* (*by John*). In imperatives, the subject is deleted, unlike any other argument: *John sent the book to Mary*; *John, send the book to Mary.* Unlike other arguments, the subject controls a reflexive pronoun (Dik, 1989(1997)): *The man looked at himself*; **The man reconciled the boy$_i$ with himself$_i$.*

In complex sentences, the subject manifests some typical «pivotal» properties (Foley & Van Valin, 1984: 108ff.). It controls the unexpressed subject of non-finite embedded clauses[281] — *John$_i$ tries ø$_i$ to finish his paper* — and is the only argument of a participial clause to admit control: *$Ø_i$ seeing nobody, $John_i$ left the hotel*; **Nobody seeing $Ø_{i,}$ $John_i$ left the hotel* (Dik, 1989(1997: 261)). An embedded subject can be raised to occupy both the subject and object position of the main clause (Foley & Van Valin, 1984: 109): *It seems that Paul has caught the wombat*; *Paul seems to have caught the wombat*; *John expects that Paul will catch the wombat*; *John expects Paul to catch the wombat.*[282] Finally, when two predicates are co-ordinated, the shared subject is dropped: *John buys cars and repairs them.* In English, this is not allowed for a direct object — **John buys cars and repairs* (Dik, 1989(1997a: 204)) — a behaviour which highlights the subject as the structural counterpart of the predicate in simple nuclear sentences.

1.3 The direct object

The direct object is a noun phrase which holds as direct complement of a two- or three-place verb. This implies that it makes sense to define the formal profile of the direct object within a whole network of grammatical relations including the subject and, in presence of ditransitive verbs, the indirect object.

The only diagnostic, though marginal coding property of direct objects in English is accusative case marking. Given a two-place verb saturated by a nominative and an accusative pronominal form, the accusative one is certainly the direct object, and so are all the noun phrases that can substitute it: *John loves Ann*; *He loves her / *she.*

To pass to behavioural properties, the direct object is pronominalised by an accusative form in the case of dislocation: *This book, I've read it twice.* Just like a subject, it is allowed to control the unexpressed subject of an embedded clause: *John persuaded $Mary_i$ $ø_i$ to leave.* Finally, if the active sentence is turned into the passive, the direct object becomes the subject, and is led to share its formal properties: *Ann is loved by John.*

As Croft[283] (1999: 71–72) points out, the results of usual criteria for objecthood do not match perfectly, so that their joint application can end in conflict. The presence of a prepositionless noun phrase in post-verbal position is not a sufficient condition for objecthood, as shown by such sentences as *John slept the whole afternoon* or *The apples weigh four pounds.* Moreover, promotion to passive subject is open to indirect object, while accusative case marking is extended even to a beneficiary in post-verbal position: *John gave a book to Mary*; *John gave Mary / her a book*; *Mary was given a book by John*; *John bought a book for Mary*; *John bought Mary / her a book.* Before jumping to hasty conclusions about the formal identity of direct objects, however, two circumstances should be considered.

First, the undesired outcomes of one test can well be corrected by another. The tests of case-marking and passivization, for instance, unmask such pseudo-objects as expressions of duration or quantity. In *John slept the whole afternoon*, the noun phrase *the whole afternoon* can neither be pronominalised nor dislocated nor become a passive subject: **John slept it* (= *the whole afternoon*); **The whole afternoon, John slept it*; **The whole afternoon was slept by John*. The same holds for the intransitive use of *weigh*: *The man weighed the apples / them*; *The apples, the man weighed them*; *The apples were weighed by the man*; *The apples weighed four pounds*; * *The apples weighed them*; **Four pounds, the apples weighed them*; **Four pounds were weighed by the apples*.

Second, coding and behavioural overlapping of direct object, indirect object and beneficiary is easily overcome if one observes whole constructions instead of single categories, as is required in the area of relational coding. Both indirect objects[284] and post-verbal beneficiaries by definition co-occur with direct objects: **John gave to Mary*; **John gave Mary*; *John bought Mary* *(*a book*). Now, if each construction is described as a whole, accusative case marking and promotion to a passive subject cannot really conflict, for they apply under different conditions to each category.[285] More generally, the observation of different grammatical relations within a complex construction shows some differences in behaviour which strengthen the formal identity of each. In this paragraph, we shall discuss the co-occurrence of direct and post-verbal indirect object. The opposition between indirect object and beneficiary as alternative partners of a direct object will be discussed later (§2.5).

If the indirect object becomes a passive subject, the direct object is also specified: *John was given a book by Mary*; **John was given by Mary*. If the direct object becomes a passive subject, the indirect object cannot be specified as a noun phrase: *A book was given to Mary by John*; **A book was given Mary by John*. Just like a direct object, an indirect object can be pronominalised by an accusative form: *John, I gave him a letter*. However, when both direct and indirect object are expressed by pronouns, the prepositionless form is exclusive of the direct object: *John, I gave it to him*; **John, I gave him it*.

Unlike a prepositionless indirect object, a direct object can control the object of an infinitival completive: *He gave her* it_i *to eat* $ø_i$; **He gave* her_i *it* $ø_i$ *to cheer up*. A predicative adjective is accepted by a direct object even in the presence of an indirect object, which for its part is reluctant to take it: *I ate the meat raw*; *John gave Mary the meat raw*; **The nurse gave John the medicine sick*. The behaviour of verbal particles is also different in the presence of direct and indirect objects (Anderson, 1984: 42): *John gave back the money* (*to the girl*);

John gave the money back (to the girl); **John gave back the girl the money*; *John gave the girl the money back.* A prepositionless indirect object cannot naturally be questioned with a *wh*- form: *What did Mary give to John?*; *Who did Mary give a book to?*; ?*Who did Mary give a book?* Finally, an indirect object cannot occur as the genitive complement of a gerundive nominalisation (Blake, 1982: 75): *The giving of a book to the little girl* * *The giving of the little girl (a book)*.

Our sketch of the distinctive formal properties of subject and object is sufficient to conclude that these functional categories, expressed by simple noun phrases, are very likely to be identified on formal grounds, irrespective of both the content of the noun phrases and the role they are called upon to play within the framework of different processes. If, instead of single categories in isolation we consider whole networks of grammatical relations, their aptitude to shape formal moulds for concepts is unquestioned.

2. The behaviour of prepositions

Beyond the subject and direct object, we enter the territory of prepositional phrases, which is occupied by a very heterogeneous set of expressions. The realm of prepositional phrases contains both essential roles of the process — namely, prepositional object, indirect object, goal, location, — and such marginal, non-essential roles as instrument, cause, or spatial circumstances. It contains both expressions belonging to the functional core — namely, prepositional object and indirect object — and expressions located outside it, which in turn may express either essential roles — goal and location — or margins: for instance, instrument and cause. Though possessing very different formal and functional properties, all the considered expressions share the presence of a preposition. What one can reasonably expect at this point is that the key for analysing this picturesque constellation of roles is provided by the behaviour of prepositions.

Even at a superficial glance, it is clear that a preposition may behave in two different ways, that is, either as a formal word, devoid of autonomous content, or as a full lexical word, possessing an independent, positive content.

In the former case, the preposition is required and controlled by the verb and has a purely formal function — namely, it encodes an empty grammatical relation between the verb and the prepositional complement. When performing this kind of function, a preposition behaves as if it were devoid of any positive content. Its content, in any case, does not take part in coding the content of the role associated with the prepositional phrase, whose profile is controlled by the content of the main predicator. Normally, the preposition cannot be chosen; if it can, the choice is connected with a change in the valency-scheme and meaning of the verb.

In the latter case, the preposition is chosen independently of the main verb; it does not encode a purely grammatical relation behaving as an empty formal word, but directly contributes with its positive content to the definition of the conceptual profile of a given role; accordingly, it belongs to a paradigm of alternative options.

At first glance, the relevant criterion for the behaviour of prepositions seems to lie in verbal control. According to this hypothesis, a preposition should behave like a formal word when coding an argument of the verb, and like a lexical word when coding a marginal role. In fact, this prediction is only partially borne out by linguistic data. While it is confirmed by the observation of marginal roles, it is not accurate enough as far as the complements of the verb are concerned. If prepositions behave as true formal words when coding the prepositional object, in the case of the indirect object many diachronic as well as synchronic arguments suggest that the choice of the preposition is somehow justified on the basis of its positive lexical content. Finally, and above all, when coding such roles as location with verbs of state and goal with verbs of motion, prepositions behave as full lexical words, belonging to a paradigm of options, whose content actively takes part in defining the content of the role. As far as the behaviour of prepositions is concerned, location and goal behave in the same way as the expression of spatial circumstances, and cannot be distinguished from them.

While the behaviour of the indirect object can somehow be justified (see §2.5), the case of location and goal clearly falsifies the prevision. If we maintain that location and goal are not spatial circumstances framing a process from the outside, but essential roles required by verbs of state and motion, we are forced to admit that the critical factor governing the behaviour of prepositions is not the position of the prepositional phrase with regard to the structure of the process — namely, its holding either as the expression of an argument or of a margin — but the form of coding it is engaged in. The behaviour of prepositions, in other words, does not mark the borderline between the core of the process and its periphery, but the borderline, internal to the core of the process, between a relational and a punctual form of coding. A preposition behaves as a purely formal word when it is engaged in a relational form of coding, and its content is not relevant to the definition of the role.[286] It behaves as a full lexical word when it is engaged in a punctual form of coding, and its content contributes critically to the definition of the role.

The last remark implies that the roles of the process entrusted to full prepositions are submitted to a punctual form of coding. Owing to this, the behaviour of prepositions is no criterion for discriminating between arguments and margins outside the functional core of the sentence. The exact position of the roles located in this grey area can only be defined through different criteria, based on the structure and expression of consistent states of affairs.

2.1 The relational coding of a prepositional argument: The prepositional object

A prepositional object (Steinitz, 1969; Kirkwood, 1969; Faarland, 1998) is a direct complement of a two-place verb, which has the form of a prepositional phrase: for instance, *New cars must comply* with *high standards.* Owing to its immediate link with the verb, a prepositional object can be considered as a formal variant of the direct object.[287]

The preposition that introduces a prepositional object clearly behaves as a formal relational word, whose function is similar to the function of a morphological case.[288] This is clearly to be seen in languages with case systems, where prepositions alternate with cases in connecting verbs with their second arguments: see, for instance, German *Jemanden lieben* (Acc.); *Jemandem helfen* (Dat.); *Auf jemanden warten* (*auf* + Acc.).

In the same way as case, the preposition is not chosen, but imposed by the main verb. As Steinitz (1969: 41) points out, "For every verb that requires a prepositional object only some prepositions are available. In most cases there is precisely one preposition which is fixed for one verb: *glauben : an, taugen : zu, achten : auf* [*believe in, be of use to; pay attention to*]". Under such conditions, a substitution of the preposition ends in agrammaticality, as does a change in case (Andresen, 1973: 59): *Rely on something*; **Rely over something*; *Auf jemanden warten*; **An jemanden warten*; *Jemandem helfen*; **Jemanden helfen*; *Jemanden lieben*; **Jemandem lieben.*

When it encodes a prepositional object, the preposition loses its semantic relevance (Steinitz, 1969), as becomes apparent if we compare the following pairs of expressions:

(1) Hans wartet *auf* einen Freund
(2) Hans traf Sophie *auf* einem Berg

(3) You must comply *with* these conditions
(4) John cut the bread *with* his pocket knife

The preposition that occurs in the first expression of each pair is not the same as that which occurs in the second. In sentences (2) and (4), the preposition has a full lexical content, which directly takes part in defining the conceptual profile of a role — of spatial circumstances and instrument, respectively. In sentences (1) and (3), the preposition is a "colourless" relational term, which simply encodes the void grammatical relation of prepositional object. Once the grammatical relation has been encoded, the task of the preposition is completed. The content of the preposition — or, more exactly, the content it is ready to take on when used outside the network of grammatical relations — does not take part in defining the content of the role entrusted to the prepositional object, which is directly imposed on it by the content of the main verb.[289] The way it is assigned a content of role not only suggests that the prepositional object is an argument of the verb. It also shows that, in spite of the presence of a preposition, it is a purely grammatical relation belonging to the functional core of the sentence.[290]

2.2 The punctual coding of margins: Spatial circumstances and instrument

In the presence of punctual coding, as we have seen, the behaviour of prepositions undergoes a radical change. As the observation of such marginal roles as spatial circumstances or instrument clearly shows, the preposition no longer behaves as a purely formal word, but fully recovers its semantic relevance, and takes a direct and active part in coding the content of the role.

The coding of spatial circumstances, for instance, is entrusted to a wide range of prepositions, each of which is chosen, irrespective of the main verb, for its content, in order to define a given spatial relation:

(5) I met Elizabeth in Warsaw (near the castle, in front of the University).

To say that the content of a preposition is actively engaged in defining the profile of a role does not imply that this content is always adequate to the task.[291] A preposition like *with*, for instance, has a very light content, which is not up to the task of coding a definite role. But this is beside the point. What is relevant is not whether the preposition is adequate for coding a definite role, but the fact that, in the absence of grammatical relations, this role is encoded to the extent, and only to the extent, to which the content of the preposition is capable of encoding it. If this content is not rich enough to encode the role, its function is relayed by inferential enrichment, motivated under the pressure of the conceptual environment. A prepositional phrase of the form *with + SN*, for instance, is interpreted as expressing the role of instrument if, and only if, it is connected with an action and the noun phrase refers to an object which can be seen as a consistent and adequate instrument for this action.

2.3 The choice of prepositions in the area of punctual coding: The conceptual motivation

A preposition with a light content in the area of punctual coding is not the same thing as a colourless preposition in the area of relational coding. When it encodes a grammatical relation like a prepositional object, a preposition puts aside its content, changing itself into a purely relational word. When a preposition is directly engaged in the expression of a role, what happens is exactly the opposite. The encoded content of the preposition, however weak, is highlighted by its interaction with the conceptual environment it enters into. It not only provides the starting point for one or more paths of inferential enrichment, but is also open, just like any other conceptual content, to any kind of metaphorical and metonymical shift.[292] If the choice of a preposition appears unmotivated by its basic meaning, this simply means that the motivation has to be sought in some metaphorical or metonymical extension of it. A significant illustration of this point is provided by Dirven's analysis of the expression of emotional causality.

According to Dirven (1997: 67), the field of emotional causality is formed by a constellation of different though connected notions, each expressed by a specialized prepositional phrase. Contrary to all appearances, the choice of the prepositions engaged in the expression of emotional causality in English is not random, but rigorously motivated by a chain of interconnected extensions of the basic meaning of each preposition to fit the salient conceptual properties of each notion.

A sentence like *Bill bridled* with *anger at Hillary's remark*, for instance, expresses "an uncontrollable link between the emotional cause and the physiological effect". The preposition *with* is obviously too weak to encode a causal relation, which is attained by inference, but is definite enough to encode a qualifying property of this peculiar kind of cause, that is, the fact that cause and effect co-occur during a given span of time: "the physiological reactions and their emotional causes are by necessity contiguous" (59). This circumstance "excludes the use of non-events or hypothetical events [...] since metonymy presupposes the simultaneous presence" of the involved events. The preposition *for* "is indispensable in such contexts: *He can't speak for excitement*" (60). The prepositions *by* and *with* are both "used metonymically to denote two different phases in the chain of emotional causality. Whereas *with* is used in the context of a physiological reaction to an emotion, *by* denotes the state of emotional arousal": for instance, *I was struck by a sense of the injustice of life.*

"Whereas the prepositions *with* and *for* imply processes and are not compatible with actions", Dirven goes on, "*out of* can only be used in the expression of emotional causality when it is combined with actions as in [...] *I concealed my feeling out of pity for him* [...] We can also see that these actions are deliberate and intentional ones, and that the *out of*-phrase denotes the rational motivation for the action" (61). This last aspect points to the metaphorical source of this use: the idea of a "'free' movement out of a container" (62). This idea contrasts with the idea of "an exit from a confined or closed container" to be found, for instance, in the sentence *John escaped from prison*, which is at the basis of the metaphorical uses of *from*: *His face was aglow with terror from what had happened to them all.* The cognitive differences among the source-domains, in particular, justify the fact that "*from* can denote the outer cause of an event", while *out of* is confined to inner, emotional causation of an action. To complete this sketch, "*in* denotes emotions as static containers which may merely evoke a circumstantial situation" — *They were holding hands in dumb misery* — but can easily be enriched by inference to attain "a weaker type of uncontrollable, circumstantial cause" (64): *They hopped around in joy.*

2.4 The punctual coding of prepositional arguments: Location and goal

If the core of the process coincided with the functional core, as the examined paradigmatic cases seem to suggest, all the prepositional arguments of the verb should behave like the prepositional object, and all the expressions behaving like spatial circumstances or instrument should be considered margins. In fact, there are at least two roles expressed by prepositional phrases which, though belonging to the core of the process, behave exactly like margins, and more exactly like spatial circumstances, as far as the properties of prepositions are concerned. These roles are location and goal: for instance, *Elizabeth lives in Warsaw*; *Elizabeth went to Warsaw.*

If we look at the conceptual structure of the process, location and goal can easily be distinguished from spatial circumstances. While the latter locate a complete process against a spatial background, location and goal are essential constituents of peculiar kinds of processes — namely, processes of state and directed motion — which are hardly conceivable without taking into account locative relations.[293] This intuition is confirmed by the fact that if location and goal are not specified, a form of latency is felt, as in the absence of any argument of the verb.

In spite of these essential differences, however, location and goal are "dressed up to look like circumstantial elements" (Halliday, 1976: 160) as far as their coding is concerned. The expressions of both location and goal and spatial circumstances exploit exactly the same prepositions, whose content takes an active part in defining the content of each role, that is, a given spatial relation. Unlike the more central arguments of the verb and like circumstantial elements, moreover, location and goal are open to recursive specification.[294] This means that the common function of drawing a given spatial relation overcomes the difference between arguments of the verb and outer circumstances. The prepositional phrases incorporated within the following sentences, for instance, though expressing spatial circumstances in (6), location in (7), and goal in (8), behave in the same way:[295]

(6) Elizabeth met Ralph *in* Warsaw (*near* the castle, *in front of* the University)
(7) Elizabeth lives *in* Warsaw (*near* the castle, *in front of* the University)
(8) Elizabeth went *to* Warsaw (*near* the castle, *in front of* the University)

The behaviour of location and goal appears consistent if we realise that these roles belong to the core of the process but lie outside the functional core, which implies that their content is built up with the essential contribution of the preposition. As their names suggest, location and goal are not grammatical relations possessing exclusive formal properties, but roles defined by a substantive conceptual content and coded in a punctual way. Location and goal can be considered as arguments of the verb insofar as their presence is required for framing a consistent process of state and motion. However, no trace of verbal control is to be found in their form. A verb of state or motion certainly qualifies its locative argument as an instance of location or goal respectively, but it controls neither its final content, which has to be determined in each case, nor the form of its expression, which remains open to choice. On this premise, the behaviour of prepositions is simply consistent with their function, and perfectly matches the expected properties of a punctual form of coding. The choice of the preposition is not governed by the formal properties of the main verb, but is justified by the suitability of its content to characterise the particular spatial relationship that is called upon to specify the general content of the role in each particular case. These are the reasons why the preposition fully recovers its semantic relevance, the same it displays when engaged in defining the profile of a local circumstance. The function of the preposition — to draw an exact spatial relation — is the same in both cases.

Our conclusions rest on the assumption that location and goal are arguments of verbs of state and motion respectively. While this may be a correct intuition, a strong argument supporting it has yet to be found. A definitive answer to the question can be obtained by using conceptual and textual criteria, that is, criteria assessing the expression of the different roles of a consistent process outside the borders of the sentence which forms its core (§3).

2.5 A debatable case of relational coding: Indirect object

In English, the indirect object is typically expressed by a prepositional phrase of the form *to* + *NP*. Unlike a prepositional object, it is not an alternative to the direct object as a second argument of a two-places verb, but co-occurs with the direct object to express the third argument of a three-place verb: for instance, *I gave a copy of my book to Mary.*

Intuitively, the location of the indirect object within the core of the process is unquestionable. It is quite impossible to describe the indirect object without making reference to the valency-scheme of a definite class of verbs. Conversely, it is impossible to define such verbs as *give* without referring to the indirect object. If an indirect object is dropped for textual reasons, it remains latent: *I have already given*; *The bad weather counselled prudence.* What is not so clear is whether the indirect object belongs to the functional core — whether or not it can be considered a true grammatical relation encoded independently of its conceptual content.

The verbs requiring an indirect object — or ditransitive verbs — belong essentially to two classes, which possess the same valency-scheme — namely verbs of giving and verbs of saying: *I gave a copy of my book to Mary*; *I told the whole story to Ann.* If one takes into account only verbs of giving and saying, the indirect object looks more like a conceptual category than a grammatical relation. Unlike subject and direct object, the indirect object identifies a definite role of the process — the typically human end point of a transaction. The preposition that marks it does not vary depending on the main verb, as in the case of a prepositional object, but is shared by all the verbs of the class. This would be of no consequence if the preposition were a formal word devoid of positive content. But this is not so certain, for the preposition *to* clearly retains its allative meaning, a fact which can easily be justified if the processes of giving and saying are seen as metaphorical kinds of movement of a thing or a message from a source to a goal, expressed by the indirect object.[296]

So far, there seems to be no particular reason for not considering the indirect object of the verbs of giving and saying as a conceptual rather than a functional category, that is, the expression of recipient as a metaphorical goal, punctually encoded thanks to the allative content of the preposition *to.* However, there are also arguments for considering that the indirect object is a grammatical relation.

The indirect object is not limited to verbs of giving and saying. Though sharing the same ditransitive valency scheme as the verbs of giving and saying, such verbs as *envy* or *deny* shape processes which cannot be reduced, even metaphorically, to the model of an allative transaction. Accordingly, they assign to the indirect object a role that has nothing allative about it. The form of the indirect object, in such cases, is absolutely unmotivated with regard to the content of the role. In Italian, such verbs as *rubare* (*steal*) or *togliere* (*take away*) confer on their indirect objects the role of source, whose orientation is ablative.[297] In French, the converse verbs *prêter* (*lend*) and *emprunter* (*borrow*) have exactly the same valency scheme — *Jean a prêté mille francs à Luc*; *Luc a emprunté mille francs à Jean.* As they impose two opposite ideational perspectives on the same transaction, they confer two opposite roles on the indirect object, that is, the role of goal and source respectively: *Jean lent a thousand francs to Luc*; *Luc borrowed a thousand francs from Jean.*

When the content of the indirect object is not allative — for instance, in the presence of such verbs as *deny, emprunter* or *rubare* — we indisputably find the typical form of role assignment holding within the functional core. The referent of a given phrase is assigned a role controlled by the conceptual content of the verb on the basis of an independent grammatical relation, that is, the relation of indirect object. What is encoded by the expression is not immediately, and thus more or less iconically, the role itself, but an empty grammatical relation. It is only if we look at the expression from the viewpoint of the substantive content of the corresponding role that the question of motivation arises. In such cases, the same form looks motivated in some instances — in the presence of verbs of giving and saying — and unmotivated in others — namely, with such verbs as *deny, emprunter* or *rubare.*

The idea here is that, contrary to all appearances, coding is relational in both cases. When the indirect object expresses an allative role, the preposition looks motivated, as if it actively contributed to defining the content of the role. However, such a contribution is not required, for the definition of a role demands no more than the coding of a grammatical relation and a predicator controlling its content. This is clear when the content of the indirect object is not allative, or even ablative — when the content of the preposition, if it were relevant, would be inconsistent with the content of the role. In these cases, the indirect object clearly behaves like an empty grammatical relation.

The behaviour of the indirect object shows that arbitrary relational coding, that is, the coding of grammatical relations logically prior to their conceptual filling by the main predicator, is consistent with both conceptual motivation and its absence. The traditional opposition between arbitrariness and motivation can thus be challenged not only in the field of atomic concepts, but also in the field of complex significant structures.

Starting from Saussure (1916(1974)), arbitrariness and motivation tend to be seen as incompatible properties. Accordingly, the presence of aspects of motivation in linguistic signs is either simply negated, or over-estimated as an argument against "the Saussurian dogma of arbitrariness" (Jakobson, 1966: 36). Now, if arbitrary relational coding is compatible with both conceptual motivation and its absence, the very basis of this dispute — the idea that arbitrariness, as a property of symbolic structures in their synchronic functioning, is incompatible with any kind of motivation — must be challenged. Arbitrariness does not mean that a given coding device is devoid of any kind of motivation. It simply means that motivation is not required for a coding device to perform its task.[298]

The concept of motivation has two interconnected but independent sides. On the one hand, a given form is historically motivated if its content has played a role in its formation and evolution. On the other hand, a given form is synchronically transparent if this motivation is accessible to the consciousness of the speakers. What is normally called motivation from a synchronic point of view is in fact a form of transparency, that is, a window open on the historical origin and development of the expression, which are almost inevitably motivated in some way. If this premise is true, the opposite of transparency is not arbitrariness, which is an essential property of linguistic symbols in general, and in particular of any expression coding an empty grammatical relation, but opacity, which means that the window on history is closed. Opacity, of course, does not exclude motivation. It simply means that no shared motivation is accessible to the synchronic consciousness of speakers. If so, the supposed incompatibility between arbitrariness and motivation is simply the effect of a double confusion, between historical evolution and synchronic functioning on the one hand, and between arbitrariness and opacity, motivation and transparency on the other. Once it is recognised that the outcome of historical motivation can be either transparency or opacity, which are both compatible with both historical motivation and synchronic arbitrary coding, the whole question simply dissolves.

In the area of punctual coding, an expression is by definition iconic in the diagrammatic sense, insofar as the structural skeleton of the expression mirrors the configuration of the state of affairs expressed. This, however, does not prevent the punctual coding expressions from having a language-specific, and therefore arbitrary form of their own, which in turn is sometimes transparent and sometimes opaque.

At the level of sentence nuclei, expressions engaged in a relational form of coding are by definition arbitrary in a synchronic perspective. What is encoded is a grammatical relation that is absolutely devoid of conceptual content, and therefore not affected in its formal properties by the content of the roles it may receive in each particular case. This, however, implies neither that the inner form of the expression — particularly the preposition — is unmotivated in its historical evolution, nor that it is necessarily opaque to the speaker's consciousness.[299] The behaviour of the indirect object is a particularly good example of this.

Historically, the coding of the indirect object through the preposition *to* is the consequence of a metaphorical extension of the most typical coding form for goal, which is both punctual and motivated owing to the allative content of the preposition *to*. Once the receiver of an act of giving and the addressee of an act of communication are seen as metaphorical kinds of goal, the expression which punctually codes the most paradigmatic instances of the latter role is ready to be extended to the former. In the following passage, for instance, we observe the transition from the classical way of coding the indirect object of the *verbum dicendi* in Latin — the dative case — towards the vulgar and innovative form *ad* + accusative:

> 9. Ait autem *ad illos* Iesus: Interrogo vos si licet sabbatis benefacere, an male: animam salvam facere, an perdere? Et circumspectis omnibus *dixit homini*: Extende manum tuam (Luke, 6, 9–10)

The form *ad* + accusative, which foreshadows the Romance outcome, clearly takes as its model the punctual coding of the goal of transitive verbs of movement, which may coincide either with a place — *Caesar* ad flumen *exercitum duxit* — or with a person metonymically connected with it:[300] *Magister pueros* ad Camillum *perduxit* (Livy).

Of course, the fact that such allative prepositions as *ad* and *to* have been used to code the indirect object of the verbs of giving and saying potentially starts a drift towards a punctual form of coding. In other words, a sort of short-circuit has taken place between the prepositional phrase and the conceptual content of the role, as if the preposition were able to encode the content of the role immediately, bypassing the level of grammatical relations. Once a motivated and transparent form of coding of the indirect object — *ad illos, to them* — has taken place, two questions become relevant: do such prepositional phrases as *ad illos* or *to them* directly encode a sample of allative roles, or do they encode the void grammatical relation of indirect object, which for its part is ready to receive any content of role according to the content of the predicator? And, in the latter case, how can a historical conceptual motivation, which is consistent with a drift towards a punctual form of coding, be compatible with the presence of a relational form of coding in synchrony?

The first question is an empirical question, whose answer depends on whether or not the roles entrusted to the prepositional phrase belong to a consistent conceptual domain — whether or not they share an allative content. If they do, the drift is bound to end in punctual coding. If they do not, the drift is blocked and coding remains relational. Now, as far as English and the most common European languages are concerned, it is clear that the set of roles entrusted to the indirect object does not form a consistent domain.[301]

Under such conditions, the second question simply dissolves. In spite of the prototypical character of the allative content, which justifies the transparency of the form in synchrony,[302] the drift towards punctual coding and iconicity is blocked. Insofar as it spreads beyond the areas of giving and saying, a form whose origin was motivated by a punctual coding device for a given content of role is irreversibly grammaticalised as a relational coding device for an empty grammatical relation. Accordingly, the indirect object has to be considered an empty grammatical relation encoded as such by the prepositional phrase, and therefore ready to receive any role imposed on it by the content of the main predicator.

Once a form is grammaticalised and engaged in the coding of a grammatical relation, the alternative between presence and absence of motivation has no effect on coding, for the simple reason that a grammatical relation is by definition devoid of content. The two Latin forms of our example, which identify the opposite outposts of opacity and transparency, perform exactly the same function, and the same can be observed in most common European languages. German, for instance, has a dative form (*Sie teilten* den Schülern *die Ergebnisse mit*; *Er sagte* mir, *daß er bald abfahren würde*), while Italian accomplishes the drift towards a prepositional form borrowed from the punctual expression of goal: *Disse* all'uomo: *Stendi la mano*. English occupies an intermediate position, for the expression of indirect object possesses some interesting coding and behavioural properties which are typical of an opaque grammatical relation.

The most significant coding property of the indirect object in English is its occurring as a noun phrase before the direct object: *John gave Mary a book*. Unlike the marking by preposition, this marking by relative position looks distinctly relational. The disadvantage of this property from our point of view is that it is shared by the beneficiary, which is neither an argument of the verb nor *a fortiori* a grammatical relation (see below, §3.2): *Mary bought a book for John*, for instance, is allowed to become *Mary bought John a book*. The beneficiary, however, does not share two revealing behavioural properties of the indirect object. First, the indirect object, unlike the beneficiary, is admitted to the position of passive subject, a property which «establishes the need to recognize the Dative as a grammatical relation» (Palmer, 1994: 34). If *John gave Mary a book* is allowed to become *Mary was given a book*, *John bought Mary a book* cannot so easily be changed in ?*Mary was bought a book*. In any case the beneficiary enjoys a less easy access to passivisation than location — *This chair has been sat on by Washington* — goal — *Chicago has been driven to in an hour and a half* — instrument — *This spoon has been eaten with* — and even some instances of time expression: *This experience can be lived through* (see Davison, 1980). Secondly, the indirect object is allowed to control the subject of a completive clause, like a subject or a direct object: *John*$_i$ *tried* $ø_i$ *to climb the wall*; *Ann forced Peter*$_i$ $ø_i$ *to resign from his job*; *The sergeant ordered the soldiers*$_i$ $ø_i$ *to clean the room*; *My mother told me*$_i$ $ø_i$ *not to go out*.

3. From the outer margins inwards: Textual criteria

Formal and conceptual criteria run, so to speak, in opposite directions. While a formal analysis moves from the "centre of gravity" of the process outwards, an analysis grounded on conceptual criteria moves from the extreme periphery inwards — from the outer and inner margins of the process towards its core. The two kinds of criteria are bound to meet and to shed light on one another precisely in the grey zone where the distinction between arguments and margins blurs, that is, in the presence of roles which cannot be clearly identified on the basis of the formal properties of their expression.

The most interesting property of the marginal roles is that they can be specified outside the sentence structure which constructs the core of the process, and subsequently incorporated into the process through cohesive means at the textual level:

(1) A falling tree hit my car yesterday
a. A falling tree hit my car. *It happened* yesterday
(2) John cut the firewood with an axe.
a. John cut the firewood. *He did it* with an axe.

The behaviour of marginal roles is a most interesting example of a functional overlap between the domain of grammar and the domain of textual cohesion.[303] In general terms, the distinction between grammatical connection and textual coherence and cohesion is clear enough both on formal and functional grounds. The structural skeleton of the sentence is essentially a grammatical network whose elective function is the construction of a process. The structure of a text, on the other hand, is a coherent network of relations among consistent contents of independent utterances, that is, among independent processes, which is typically underlined and supported by a set of cohesive means. Yet, an extended process does not necessarily coincide with the content of a single sentence, nor does a textual link necessarily connect different processes. As our examples show, the ideation of some extended processes stretches beyond the borders of a single sentence to spread along a textual chain, exploiting cohesive relations to perform a task which is shared by grammatical connection. While the core of the process can only be constructed by grammatical structures within the framework of a simple sentence, any marginal role can be incorporated into the simple sentence as well as specified outside it, in a textual dimension.

This area of overlap between grammatical connection and textual cohesion could easily be seen as a supplementary obstacle towards a proper analysis of the margins of the process. In fact, the behaviour of marginal roles outside the sentence structure highlights the relational properties of each, which are kept in the shade when the same roles are specified within the sentence structure. If we think of the nature of marginal roles, this is not at all surprising. A marginal role is not associated with the process because of the formal grammatical properties of its expression, but according to the suitability of its content to fit a consistent conceptual model, that is, according to the same substantive criteria which underlie textual coherence.

If the study of marginal roles is displaced outside the borders of sentence structure, the question about the consistency of an extended process becomes the question about the contribution of specialised cohesive means to the coherence of a fragment of text. Whereas grammar says nothing about consistency, cohesion is revealing. When the consistency of a process is entrusted to cohesive means, the conditions under which different kinds of margin are consistently connected to different kinds of process are overtly questioned and checked. As a consequence, an accurate analysis of the formal and conceptual properties of the anaphoric substitutes and general verbs engaged in the textual expression of processes sheds light on their structure.

The study of marginal roles in a textual dimension is revealing in two ways. The fact that only marginal roles can be specified outside the sentence provides a sharp criterion for drawing a clear line between the core of the process — the cluster of arguments required by the main predicator — and its margins. As far as the specification of arguments is concerned, the sentence structure has no alternative.

As the most qualifying property of margins is that they can be specified outside the sentence structure, it is thanks to textual criteria that marginal roles can be carefully described. The different conditions under which the detached margins can be reinserted into the process when specified in a textual dimension make visible the peculiar relationship each of them bears with the core of the process.

3.1 Outer circumstances: Place, time, cause, concession

Such marginal roles as spatial and temporal circumstances, cause and concession can be specified outside the structure of the sentence which ideates the core of the process and reinserted as complements of a verb like *happen* (Arbeitsgruppe Marburg, 1973):

(3) A falling tree hit my car. *It happened* last night (in front of my house, because of the wind, in spite of a high wall).

What makes it possible to associate with a process one or more marginal roles specified outside the sentence which frames it is an anaphoric relationship across the two juxtaposed utterances — namely, the fact that the subject of *happen* is an anaphoric substitute for the core of the process:

(4) A falling tree hit my car. It (that is, the fact that a falling tree hit my car) happened yesterday

As it is replaced by a saturated anaphoric expression like *it* or *this*, the antecedent process is also treated as a saturated kind of structure — that is, not only as a process whose essential roles have already been specified,[304] but also as a process whose internal structure is irreversibly closed. If this is true, the paraphrase containing *happen* is ready to enrich a process with any role which is located outside it, but cannot be applied to internal roles. In particular, it is not consistent to specify a role belonging to the inner structure of a process through an anaphoric substitute that behaves as if this same role were already incorporated into the antecedent process.

The first prediction is supported by the behaviour of such roles as spatial and temporal circumstances, cause and concession. As they frame a closed process from the outside, these roles can be consistently associated with the process as complements of *happen.*[305]

According to the second, no complement of the verb can consistently be incorporated into the structure of the process as a complement of *happen.* This point is illustrated by the behaviour of such arguments as prepositional object and indirect object:

(5) John relied. *It happened on your aid.
(6) John gave a book. *It happened to Mary.[306]

The test of anaphoric substitution is particularly valuable for the correct description of such roles as location and goal, which are characterised as arguments neither by the formal properties of the expression nor by the behaviour of prepositions. The test of anaphoric substitution clearly shows that location and goal, though having the same form as local circumstances, do not bear the same relationship to the process. Local circumstances can be specified outside the sentence structure because they provide a saturated process with an outer frame; location and goal cannot because they are arguments of the verb, which take part in its saturation:[307]

(7) John met Mary in London. John met Mary. It happened in London.
(8) John lives in London. John lives. *It happens in London.
(9) John sent Mary to London. John sent Mary. *It happened to London.

3.2 Margins of the predicate: Instrument, purpose, beneficiary and co-performer

The complements of the verb are not the only roles that refuse to be incorporated into the process as complements of *happen*. This behaviour, in particular, is shared by such roles as instrument, purpose, beneficiary and co-performer:

(10) John cut the firewood. It happened *with an axe, *for John, *for cooking the meat, *with William.

This behaviour is not difficult to justify on intuitive grounds.

Though non-essential for shaping the core of the process, instrument, purpose, beneficiary and co-performer cannot be seen as kinds of outer circumstances. Once they are specified, they do not provide the process with an outer background, but are located inside the process, and make a peculiar contribution to its profile. Accordingly, they cannot consistently occur as complements of *happen*, whose subject refers back to an irreversibly closed process, barred to any further inner contribution.

As they are located inside the process, instrument, beneficiary, co-performer and purpose are by definition sensitive to its essential conceptual properties. These roles, in particular, are not consistent with any kind of process whatsoever, but only with intentional actions made by responsible agents. This shows a further correlation between the relational properties of the different marginal roles and the conditions under which they can consistently occur with anaphoric substitutes. Such a verb as *happen* treats its subject, and through it the antecedent process, as an unspecified kind of event. As subjects of *happen*, an intentional action and an impersonal event are put on one and the same level. This does not affect the behaviour of outer circumstances, which are in principle compatible with any kind of actualised process:

(11) An old man murdered his wife. It happened last night.
(12) It rained heavily. It happened last night.

But if a role is sensitive to the conceptual profile of the process it is part of, it is obviously incompatible with an anaphoric substitute which neutralises the essential conceptual properties of the antecedent process.

The fact that instrument, purpose, beneficiary and co-performer behave as roles belonging to the inner structure of the process, however, is not sufficient reason to consider them as arguments of the verb. To consider them as such would amount to confusing two logically distinct questions: on the one hand, which roles are essential to the process and which are not; on the other hand, which roles form part of the inner structure of the process and which provide it with an outer background. Now, if it is logically necessary that what is essential to a given structure should form part of its inner configuration, the idea that a role is both non-essential and located inside the process is not in itself contradictory. Whether a process has internal margins or not is an empirical question, open to empirical investigation. Indeed, actions are a kind of process which allow for internal margins.

The textual behaviour of such roles as instrument, beneficiary, purpose and co-performer is consistent with the hypothesis that these roles are both non-essential and located inside the structure of consistent actions.[308]

Intuitively, such roles as instrument, purpose, beneficiary and co-performer cannot be considered arguments of the verb. They are both compatible with any kind of action — any action, be it cutting wood or peeling potatoes, may be performed with an instrument, for someone, with someone or with some purpose in mind — and yet essential for none. They are not included in the valency of any verb of action, and no latency is felt when they are not specified. Once one of these roles is specified, on the other hand, it deeply affects the conceptual profile of the process, which can be consistently received only as an intentional action performed by a responsible agent. All this makes sense, in turn, only if instrument, purpose, beneficiary and co-performer are considered as inner constituents of an action.

If these insights are correct, the fact that such roles as instrument, purpose, beneficiary and co-performer do not consistently occur as complements of *happen* does not imply that they are arguments of the verb. It simply implies that they share with the complements the property that is relevant in this connection, that is, the property of being located inside the process as constituents of an extended predicate: instrument, purpose, beneficiary and co-performer, in particular, are inner margins, that is, margins of the predicate.

As non-essential, marginal roles, instrument, purpose, beneficiary and co-performer can be specified outside the main predication.[309] Unlike outer margins, however, they can be incorporated into the process only through an anaphoric substitute which safeguards the essential conceptual property of the antecedent process — it being an action — and its main articulation into a subject and a predicate ready to be extended. Examples of such a substitute are the forms *do it*, or *do so*:

(13) John cut the firewood. He did it with an axe (for John, for cooking the meat, with William).

The anaphoric substitute at work here is neither the verb *do* nor its complement (*it*) or modifier (*so*) but the whole predicate formed by the verb *do* and its complement (*do it*) or modifier (*do so*). The predicates *do it* and *do so* are unsaturated substitutes whose antecedent is not the whole action, which is a saturated structure, but its predicate.[310] The pro-predicate either inherits as its subject the subject of the antecedent predicate, or takes a coreferential substitute of it, which implies that the subject is left aside by the substitution:

(14) John *cut the firewood.* He (=John) *did it* with an axe.

The structural and conceptual properties of the anaphoric substitution are consistent with the structural and conceptual properties of the margins of the predicate. On the one hand, if a saturated pro-sentence treats the antecedent process as if it were irreversibly closed, a pro-predicate leaves its structure open and therefore ready to make room for any kind of inner margin. On the other hand, the generic predicates *do it* and *do so* are predicates of action, and therefore as ready as any more specific predicate of action to incorporate any marginal role compatible with an action, in particular instrument, beneficiary, purpose and co-performer.

If a pro-sentence treats the antecedent process as if the predicator were saturated by all its arguments, a pro-predicate treats the antecedent predicate as if all the complements of the verb were already specified, and neutralises its inner structure. Accordingly, it cannot reinsert into the process any complement of the verb:

(15) You can rely. You can do it *on me.
(16) John lives. *He does it in Florence.

The combined observation of both kinds of textual device makes it possible to draw a sharp line between essential roles and margins on the one hand, and between inner and outer margins on the other. The essential roles of the process, which are by definition internal to it, cannot be specified outside the main predication, while any kind of margin can. Outer margins can occur as complements of *happen*,[311] while inner margins are compatible only with a pro-predicate like *do it* or *do so*.

3.3 Verb modifiers

A typical non-essential constituent of a process is the expression of manner. An example is the adverb *aloud* in *John read aloud* or the prepositional phrase *with care* in *John approached the task with care.*

Manner does not introduce a role into the process — it simply qualifies the process, making explicit a feature about which the verb content remains vague. For instance, there are many ways of speaking, which are all compatible with the content of the verb *to speak* and can be specified, if required, by an appropriate verb modifier: one can *speak aloud* or *softly*, *formally* or *inaccurately*, *fluently* or *frankly*.

As manner directly modifies the content of the verb, its expression cannot be considered a margin of the whole predicate, and even less an outer margin of the whole process — it is an expansion of the verb. According to such a premise, one would expect that verb modifiers could not be detached from the modified verb. As a matter of fact, many modifiers can be detached, and some can even occur with *happen*:

(17) The tower suddenly fell down.
  a. The tower fell down. It happened suddenly.
(18) The river suddenly overflowed.
  a. The river overflowed. It happened suddenly.
(19) John washed the car carefully.
  a. John washed the car. *It happened carefully.
  b. John washed the car. He did it carefully.
(20) Isabel shook her head with a touch of melancholy.
  a. Isabel shook her head [...] she did it with a touch of melancholy (H. James).
(21) John spoke aloud.
  a. John spoke. *It happened aloud.
  b. John spoke. ?He did so aloud.

Before jumping to hasty conclusions, however, rough distributional data should be carefully evaluated. Besides bearing an anaphoric relation to an antecedent process or predicate, each anaphoric substitute either is associated with or contains a verbal form — *happen* or *do* — which is ready to take a modifier. Now, the criterion which governs the co-occurrence of verb modifiers and anaphoric substitutes is not the relationship between the modifier and the antecedent process or predicate — whether it is an outer margin, a margin of the predicate or an expansion of the verb — but its compatibility as a modifier with the verb associated to the substitute (*happen*) or engaged in it (*do*).

Some modifiers are general enough to be consistent with any kind of event. Such modifiers naturally occur with a verb like *happen*, whose subject is a generic event. Anything that may happen, for instance, may happen suddenly or slowly. Some modifiers are less general, and consistent with a specific subclass of processes, that is, with actions. Accordingly, they can occur with a verb like *do*, which is a verb of action in its more typical uses. Anything that can be done can be done carefully, or with care. Some modifiers, on the other hand, are so specific as to require a specific kind of process. They co-occur with a restricted kind of process, belonging to a given conceptual area, and therefore cannot be easily associated even with a verb like *do*, whose content is too general for them.

The obvious conclusion to be drawn from these remarks is that anaphoric substitution is not a criterion for defining the exact position of verb modifiers within the structure of the process; in some cases, it is not even a criterion for locating the modifier inside the process. At this point, if we want to find a reliable criterion, the only way to do so is to directly question the conditions under which the consistency of a process is constructed.

The construction of a process can be seen as a succession of steps which defines for each constituent of the process — whether it be essential or optional — a peculiar degree of closeness to the verb. Intuitively, for instance, a direct object is closer to the verb than an indirect object, while a subject is closer than a local circumstance.

As we have already noted, the consistency of a process is at issue at any stage of its construction. In other words, consistency is sensitive to closeness, so that hypotheses about closeness can be checked against consistency. In particular, every time the integration of a constituent into the process imposes a specific restriction on the selection of another constituent, we may say that the former is closer to the centre than the latter. This provides an immediate criterion for defining the position of verb modifiers. If a verb modifier imposes supplementary conditions on the selection of the direct object, we may conclude that its position on the scale of closeness is between the verb and its direct complement. A verb like *hit*, for instance, is ready to take as its consistent direct object any concrete entity. If such a modifier as *mortally* is associated with it, however, the set of consistent objects is narrowed down to animate beings — to the kind of beings of whom death can be consistently predicated. More generally, if the sentence contains a verb modifier, the consistency conditions of the object may be stated only after the modifier has been associated with the verb. The verb and its modifier face the object, so to speak, as a unitary, integrated concept.[312]

4. Control and closeness: The relevance of subject and predicate

The behaviour of verb modifiers makes visible a more general property of the expression of processes, that is, the relevance of closeness[313] as an autonomous structural parameter. If a verb modifier can be closer to the verb than any controlled argument, it is because the degree of closeness of a given determination is not simply a function of the presence or absence of verbal control, but is independent of it. On this premise, the hierarchical network of connections underlying a process cannot be accounted for by focusing exclusively on the parameter of verbal control. This parameter sets up an opposition between a controlled core, formed by the verb and its arguments, and an undifferentiated set of non-controlled constituents such as time, place, cause, instrument or manner. In order to grasp the complexity of processes, the structural information about verbal control has to be completed by structural information about closeness.

The different behaviour of inner and outer margins with regard to anaphoric substitutes is revealing about closeness. If a predicate contains such a margin as an instrument, for instance, the consistency of the subject is submitted to more severe conditions. Any concrete object, for instance, may consistently hit a person. But only a human being can do it with an instrument:

(22) John hit William with a stick
(23) A falling tree hit William *with a stick

This implies that the expression of instrument is closer to the verb than the subject. Accordingly, instrument forms part of the predicate, and that is the reason why it is ready to be associated with such a pro-predicate as *do it*. The same holds for such roles as beneficiary, purpose and co-performer:

(24) John hit Mark for Mary (for stealing his money, with Simon)
(25) A falling tree hit John *for Mary (*for stealing his money, *with Simon)

The predicate is the unsaturated immediate constituent of the process. Once the predicate has received the subject, the predication is ideally closed, and behaves like a saturated expression, which can be replaced by an anaphoric noun phrase or pronoun. A complete process is also ready to receive any kind of outer circumstance, which are compatible with a saturated anaphoric substitute, and whose consistency is checked against the whole process.

In general terms, only an actual event may consistently be located at a point in space and time:

(26) John told the story to Paul in the garden, at twelve o'clock
(27) John has a good command of German *in the garden *at twelve o' clock

Within these limits, some circumstances are fit for some processes and not for others.[314] A person's soul and head, for instance, are only metaphorical locations in the following examples:

(28) It is a damp, drizzly November in my soul (Melville)
(29) A thousand smiths' hammers are beating in my head (E. Brontë).

The stress on closeness forms the most relevant difference between the model of the process presented here and Dik's model of predication as a layered structure (Dik, 1989(1997: Chapter 9); Dik, Hengeveld, Vester & Vet, 1990; Hengeveld, 1990). In Dik's model, two layers of satellites are relevant for the description of "extended predications", that is, "predicate satellites" and "predication satellites". Predicate satellites, to be interpreted as predicator satellites in Lyon's (1977: 434) terms, include source, path and goal, manner, and such "additional participants" as instrument, beneficiary and coperformer. Predication satellites include spatial and temporal setting, cause, condition, concession, result, reason (our motive, see Chapter 10, §3.2) and purpose.

According to our criteria, based on anaphoric substitution and consistency, the layer of "predication satellites" is split between true external margins — spatial and temporal setting, cause — and internal ones: motive and purpose. Result, condition and concession can be considered either external or internal according to their connection with cause or motive respectively. The layer of "predicate satellites" not only includes some roles which behave as arguments — in particular, goal — but above all gives the same status to manner, which is a verb modifier, and to such margins of the whole predicate as instrument, purpose, beneficiary and coperformer. This point is particularly relevant because the distinction between verb modifiers and margins of the predicate, and more generally the hierarchy based on closeness, presupposes the relevance of the category of predicate as distinct from the predicator, which is generally denied within the functional framework.

While verbal control is a digital parameter, the nature of closeness is scalar. A given role of the process is either controlled or not. Of course, verbal control is exerted to different degrees. Roughly, a verb fully controls its direct complements, whose form and content are both defined by its valency. Control over the subject is limited to role assignment, while the form is a function of the sentence structure. At the other end of the scale, such arguments as goal and location are controlled by the verb for their general content, while their specific profile is due to the presence of a preposition, which is chosen in each particular case in order to draw a given spatial relationship. In spite of this, the transition between presence and absence of control — between the essential core of the process and the margins — is in principle clear, as the test of detachment and reinsertion clearly shows. Closeness, on the contrary, forms a *continuum*, which puts both controlled and non-controlled roles along a scale. Closeness is a path running from the "centre of gravity" of the process to the outer circumstances which form its background, gradually passing through verb modifiers, complements, margins of the predicate, and subject.[315]

An exclusive focus on verbal control favours a monocentric model of the structure of the process — namely, the Copernican model of a core, formed by the verb, surrounded by its controlled arguments and foregrounded against an outer space occupied by any kind of non-controlled constituent. If taken at its face value, the metaphor of the core encourages the implication that the core of the process and its periphery are kept apart by a real border. But the distinction between arguments and margins, however sharp, is not marked by a real borderline, because the inner structure of the process contains marginal constituents as well as arguments of the verb. If we imagine drawing a map of the process on a surface, what is marked on the ground is not the border between the core of the process and its periphery, but the border which separates the inner constituents — including arguments, verb modifiers and inner margins — from the outer margins. This border is marked by the subject, which is by definition the least close among the arguments of the process and, more generally, among its inner constituents.

While the study of control pushes towards a monocentric predicator-arguments model, the study of closeness highlights the image of sentence as an exocentric structure, and therefore underlines the relevance of such functional categories as subject and predicate.

The predicate is the variable part of the process. Its structural framework is controlled by the valency scheme of the verb, while its marginal constituents, if they are ever specified, are anchored each to an essential constituent of the core: the verb modifiers can be considered expansions of the main verb, and the inner margins expansions of the verb phrase. It is in this way that the essential constituent structure of the verb phrase, formed by the verb and its complements, provides the whole predicate with its structural skeleton.

When the construction of the predicate is completed, in its essential as well as marginal parts, the subject irreversibly closes the process. The subject is thus the very seal of the process, whose incorporation makes room for any kind of external role.

The essential structure of the process, consisting of controlled and uncontrolled elements each characterised by a given degree of closeness, cannot be captured in a single structural parameter, that is, verbal control, but requires at least two, that is, control and closeness. The meaning of a sentence can be considered neither as a simple monocentric structure connecting a predicator with its arguments, nor simply as a path gradually leading along a decreasing scale of closeness from the centre to the outer margins. Control and closeness form two independent but interconnected parameters. Like two Cartesian coordinates, they imply each other, and it is only against the two of them that a first step can be made towards grasping both the general structure of the process and the exact position of each nuclear and marginal role.

Chapter 10

The ideation of interclausal links

Interclausal linkage can be defined as the relation which occurs when two or more virtually independent simple processes are brought together to form a complex process. The complex sentence *The fields are green because it rained heavily*, for instance, expresses a complex process whose constituents — the process expressed by the sentence *The fields are green* and the process expressed by the sentence *It rained heavily* — are both simple processes.

The complexity that results from an interclausal link has to be carefully distinguished from the inherent complexity which characterizes the inner structure of some kinds of processes. Though containing two predicators, such a complex sentence as *I hope that it will rain* cannot be considered as an instance of interclausal linkage, because one of the intertwined processes which form it is not a simple process. Unlike the embedded process *It will rain*, the main process — the concept of hope — is inherently complex, and contains the embedded simple process as one of its arguments: what one hopes is an essential constituent of the process of hoping. This implies that the whole plan of the complex process is controlled by the main predicator, while its expression is contained within the core of a sentence structure.

Inherently complex processes and interclausal links bear a different relationship to the structure of a complex sentence. In the languages belonging to the European mainstream (Kortmann, 1997), the relationship between inherently complex processes and the structure of complex sentence is direct and almost exclusive.[316] Though traditionally associated with the complex sentence, the ideation of such interclausal relations as cause, concession or purpose is neither necessarily nor typically dependent on it. Insofar as they are wholly saturated processes, the constituents of an interclausal linkage can be expressed in independent sentences. Once two independent processes are identified, in turn, all that is needed to ideate an interclausal link is to build up a given conceptual bridge between them. This means that the expression of interclausal links has at its disposal an impressive amount of heterogeneous linguistic means, and the complex sentence is simply one of them.

The most relevant consequence of this wealth of interchangeable means of expression is that neither the interclausal link nor its content are necessarily encoded. In fact, the domain of interclausal linkage displays the full range of modes of interaction between punctual coding and inferencing, which are the indissociable factors of expression outside the network of grammatical relations.

The first point in this chapter is the distinction between the ideation of true interclausal links and of inherently complex processes (§1). Then we shall examine the qualifying properties of the various means used to express interclausal links, spanning between grammatical connection and textual coherence, punctual coding and inference (§2).

Once the logical space open to the ideation of interclausal links has been explored in its full breadth, the relevant question is to define which section of this space is electively occupied by each kind of link. This point will be examined with reference to a restricted but significant constellation of interclausal links, including cause, motives and purpose (§3).

1. Inherently complex processes and linkage of simple processes

If we define a complex sentence as a sentence frame containing two or more predicators belonging to different hierarchical layers, there are at least two kinds,[317] as in (1) and (2):

(1) I hope that it will rain
(2) The fields are green because it rained heavily

The complex sentence (1) is an instance of a completive embedding, whereas (2) is an instance of a non-completive subordinative link, which in turn is a kind of interclausal linking device. While the distinction itself is well known, its conceptual, syntactic and coding implications are not always made explicit.

According to a widespread tendency, the two kinds of structure are seen as different outcomes of one and the same process of ideation: in both cases, some position available in a matrix sentence model is occupied by clauses instead of noun and prepositional phrases. This attitude is not confined to strictly formalist approaches, but is widely shared among functional frameworks. Dik (1989(1997a: Chapter 6)), for instance, extends to interclausal links the layered model fit for the simple sentence, drawing a distinction between "embedded constructions as complements" and "embedded constructions as satellites".[318] This move, which presupposes that the structure of the complex sentence is logically prior to its variable functions, is justified to the extent that this structure is the only means, or at least the elective one, to secure one function.

Now, this can reasonably be assumed in the presence of completive embedding, but not in the case of an interclausal linkage. A complex sentence of type (2), for instance, is only one among many options for building a causal bridge between two independent processes. It is only against the whole constellation of alternative means of expression that it makes sense to study, as a particular case, the structure of the complex sentence.[319] To study interclausal links as kinds of complex sentences amounts to taking the structure of one solution as if it were the structure of the problem.

In order to support this idea, we shall first argue (§1) that sentences of type (1) and (2) are incommensurable kinds of complex sentences for at least three reasons. First, they ideate different kinds of conceptual structure: (1) constructs an inherently complex process; (2) draws a link between two simple processes. Second, they instantiate different kinds of syntactic structure, that is, exocentric structure (1) and endocentric subordinative structure (2). Finally, the coding of (1) is relational, while the coding of (2) is punctual, and therefore graded and open to inferential enrichment. All these structural differences, in turn, are grounded in an underlying difference in terms of form — function *ratio*. A structure of type (1) is in the first place a self-contained formal architecture designed to build up a sentence. A structure of type (2) is in no way to be considered a self-contained formal architecture, but can only be justified by its function. Considered from the standpoint of its function, however, the complex sentence is not in the first place a kind of embedding, but one option among many for expressing a conceptual link between two independent processes (§2).

1.1 Kinds of complex concept

1.1.1 *Inherently complex processes*

The most revealing instances of inherently complex processes are framed by the predicators of psychological attitudes. Such concepts as "wonder", "doubt", "believe", or "regret", for instance, are hardly conceivable as simple processes. On purely conceptual grounds, one cannot simply wonder, doubt, believe or regret. One has to wonder, doubt, believe or regret about something else, and in the most typical cases the object of such psychological attitudes is in turn a whole process.[320] This is precisely the kind of complexity displayed by a process like (1): *I hope that it will rain.* Example (1) cannot be described as a link between two simple processes, but as a single complex process which contains a process as one of its arguments.

The relationship between such an embedding concept as hope and the embedded concept is an instance of intentional relation — namely, the relationship between an intentional attitude felt by a subject and an intentional object.[321] An intentional relationship is dyadic and asymmetric in two senses.

If we look at the two processes in isolation, independently of the structure of the complex sentence, we are faced with an overt asymmetry. An intentional attitude cannot be conceived in the absence of an intentional content: "every Intentional state consists of a representative content in a certain psychological mode" (Searle, 1983). The content, for its part, can be conceived of independently of a given intentional attitude, and is compatible with any. An individual's hope, for instance, is consistent only in the presence of an object of hope, be it specified or latent, determinate or indeterminate. Such a process as rain, on the contrary, can be conceived of independently of it being the content of any intentional attitude: for the consistent process of raining to be conceived of, it being an object of hope, or fear, or doubt is irrelevant.

Once the intentional content is embedded within the matrix process thanks to a complex sentence, however, the asymmetry is overturned. The predicator of intentional attitude frames the main process, and the embedded one is taken into its perspective. In the example (1), the main process is an instance of hope, and the rain is categorised as an object of hope. Looked at from this perspective, the rain becomes a dependent part of a complex conceptual structure.

In the conceptual structure of an inherently complex process, the whole — the intentional relation — is logically prior to the constituent parts, and confers its value on each part. The structure descends, so to speak, from the whole to its parts.

1.1.2 *The linkage of simple processes*

When it is not justified by an inherent conceptual complexity, the complexity of a process is the outcome of the linkage of two or more simple and independent processes. In a complex process like *The fields are green because it rained heavily*, for instance, the rain and the fact that the fields are green are connected through a causal relation.

Outside the interclausal link, the connected processes are at once completely saturated and independent both of one another and of the relationship superimposed on them. In our example, both the rain and the fact that the fields are green are simple and independent processes. Once the relation is superimposed, on the other hand, it dominates two processes of equal rank. In purely conceptual terms, interclausal links do not have a dyadic and asymmetric structure, in which a main process governs and takes into its perspective a subordinate one, but a triadic, symmetric structure: a superordinate conceptual relationship — cause, for instance — bridges two simple processes located at the same hierarchical level.

The asymmetry in complex sentences does not mirror the inner hierarchy of the interclausal link, but is imposed on it by the syntactic properties of the expression, which subordinates one process to the other. In the complex sentence *The fields are green because it rained heavily*, for instance, the cause is subordinate to the effect because of the structure of the complex sentence, which is formed by an independent main clause and a margin.

When two simple processes are linked together to form a complex unit, there is no whole which is prior to the parts. Each part — that is, each simple process — is logically prior to the structure of the whole, that is, to the relationship that is imposed on them from outside. The structure is ascending, from the parts to the whole: two independent processes are connected through a conceptual bridge.

1.2 Kinds of syntactic structures: Exocentric end endocentric subordinative

The generic concept of subordination masks an essential difference in syntactic complexity between sentences of kind (1) — *I hope that it will rain* — and sentences of kind (2): *The fields are green because it rained heavily.* Sentence (1) is an instance of exocentric structure, while (2) is an instance of endocentric subordinative structure.

An exocentric structure is a structure which puts together two constituents, each belonging to a given distributional class, in order to form a structure which can be reduced to neither of its immediate constituents. In our example, a verb and an objective clause are put together in order to form a verb phrase — a predicate. An exocentric connection really constructs a structure, which both depends for its integrity on its parts and confers a specific value on each. The embedded clause *that it will rain* is an essential constituent of the predicate of the matrix (*I*) *hope*, whose structure requires it, and receives its value from it. Within the syntactic structure too, the whole construction — a unitary network of grammatical relations — is logically prior to the constituent parts, one of which is the embedded clause.

An endocentric subordinative structure is a structure which combines a core and a periphery to obtain a structure which belongs to the same syntactic category as the core. In our example, an independent sentence — *The fields are green* — and a margin — *because it rained heavily* — are put together to obtain a sentence. An endocentric subordinative connection does not construct a structure: it simply expands a structure which is already there — a sentence, in the present case — into a more complex instance of the same syntactic type. Within the syntactic structure too, the whole construction does not pre-exist as a mould to the connection of the parts but result from a combination of autonomous parts.

Strictly speaking, the concept of subordination can only be applied to the endocentric type of structure. Like coordination, subordination presupposes an endocentric relation: both require the presence of at least one core. Once one core is given, it can be either expanded by a periphery or associated to another core. In the former case, the resulting structure is subordinative; in the latter, coordinative. In the absence of any core, that is, in the presence of an exocentric structure, it is senseless to speak of subordination

The skeleton of a sentence nucleus, which is a network of purely exocentric relations, defines a construction in the strong sense, that is, a configuration that cannot be reduced to a combination of simpler constituents. Within this threshold, the complex construction holds as a whole that is logically prior to its parts and confers a specific value on each of them. Beyond this threshold, each nuclear structure can be expanded into more and more complex configurations by simply adding parts or wholes thanks to independent conceptual bridges. Completive relations are located within the critical threshold: they are essential parts of the construction. Even when they are incorporated within complex sentence structures, interclausal links are located beyond the critical threshold: they expand the nuclear structure without affecting its construction.[322]

1.3 Relational coding and punctual coding in complex sentences

When an inherently complex process is constructed, the relational scaffolding of the whole complex process is contained within the core of a nuclear sentence, and its relational content stems from the conceptual structure of the main predicator. The embedded clause is designed to occupy a definite position within the structural skeleton of the main process, and forms part of the main clause both as one of the predicator's arguments and as the term of a grammatical relation. Unlike an interclausal link, which is identified by its content, a completive relation does not directly encode a relational content, but a grammatical relation, that is, a relation of subject — as in *It's a pity it's raining* — or object — as in *I hope it will rain.* This relation is devoid of any content and open to receive many. The coding of completive relations, in other words, is clearly relational.[323]

The grammatical relation is generally encoded through a linking word or complementizer, that is a conjunction — *I hope that it will rain* — or a preposition — *I promise to leave at nine*. In English, a linking word is not required by all predicators in all their uses:[324] *Perry knows Hug is vulnerable*; *Olaf thinks the Mets will win; Leonid helped Boris see the error* (Noonan, 1985). The presence or absence of a complementiser, however, does not affect the building up of the relevant grammatical relation. There is no difference in grammatical structure between *Perry knows that Hug is vulnerable* and *Perry knows Hug is vulnerable.* The embedded clause holds as direct object in both cases.

As a true grammatical relation, that between subject and predicate or between verb and object is neutral with regard to the semantic content of either, which is controlled by the main predicator. Though opposite in intentional content, for instance, the object of hope and the object of fear are encoded in the same way: both are expressed by an objective clause. In *Paul says that John is silly* the object clause expresses the content of an act of assertion made by Paul; in *Paul regrets that John is silly*, the object clause expresses the content of an act of presupposition; in *Paul thinks that John is silly*, it expresses the content of a belief. In spite of these differences, the form of the expression is the same. Once an embedded clause is identified as the term of a grammatical relation belonging to the matrix process, its relational content is tautologically predetermined by the content of the main predicator via the grammatical relation. The content of the objective clause controlled by the verb *hope*, for instance, can only be defined, tautologically, as the object of the subject's hope. This is the reason why to describe the semantic properties of the different kinds of completive link amounts to classifying the matrix predicators (see for instance Noonan, 1985: §3.2; Dik 1989(1997a: Chapter 5)). An inventory of the contents of margins, instead, would require a classification of the linking words and expressions — a move that, while not sufficient (see §2), is certainly necessary.

An apparent objection to this claim is the fact that in some cases the choice of the complementiser seems to be somehow connected with the value of the embedded clause as a speech act. In particular, a reported belief or statement requires *that*, a reported order *to*, and a reported question *whether* or *if*:[325]

(3) John believes that the moon is a living being
(4) John ordered Peter to leave
(5) John asked whether / if Mary had left

In spite of appearances, there are at least three arguments for concluding that the content of the embedded clause is not punctually encoded by the complementiser.

In the first place, there is no one-to-one correspondence between complementisers and speech acts. While *whether*-clauses are really specialized for questions, *if*-clauses acquire this value when controlled by verbs of question or uncertainty, and both *that*- and *to*-clauses are ready to express a very large sample of very different speech acts and intentional attitudes. What is certain in all of these cases is that the content of the embedded clause is by definition coherent with the content of the matrix verb. The object of a constative verb is the content of a statement or belief, the object of a directive verb is the content of a directive, and the object of a verb of question or uncertainty is the content of a question.

Owing to this premise, typologies of speech acts are traditionally based on a classification of matrix verbs (see Austin, 1962(1975: Chapter 12)), whereas a classification of complementisers would be pointless. Conversely, it would be senseless to restrict the variety of speech acts and intentional attitudes to the availability of complementisers. A commissive verb like *promise*, for instance, takes the same complementiser as *order*. In spite of this, its object expresses the content an absolutely different speech act, engaging the speaker:

(6) John ordered Peter to leave
(7) John promised Peter to leave

The alternation of complementisers looks relevant in the presence of such verbs as *persuade* or *ask*. But these verbs are clearly polysemous: *persuade* between a constative and a directive sense, and *ask* between an interrogative and a directive sense:

(8) John persuaded Peter that turtles give milk
(9) John persuaded Peter to open the safe
(10) John asked Bill whether Mary had left
(11) John asked Bill to leave

If the variety of speech acts is grounded in the semantic variety of matrix verbs, the conditions for relational coding are fully restored: the complementiser encodes a grammatical relation controlled by a given verb, and the value of the embedded clause as the content of a speech act stems from the main predicator via the relevant grammatical relation.

Finally, the distribution of *that* and *to* is also influenced by the form — either finite or non-finite — of the embedded sentence and therefore by the status — either expressed and non-controlled or unexpressed and controlled — of the embedded subject. When the embedded subject is controlled from within the matrix clause, the subjectless non-finite form with *to* is used, as in (13), (16), (19), (20), (22), (23) and (25). When the embedded subject is expressed, and therefore not controlled, the finite form with *that* is preferred, as in (12), (15) and (21), and *to* is admitted in some cases, as in (14), (17), (18) and (24). As the examples show, this implies that *to* is used with many predicates which have nothing directive or manipulative about them:

(12) It is impossible that he is in Holland
(13) It is impossible to write a book in a week
(14) It is impossible for you to write a book in a week
(15) I hope that he will be here tomorrow
(16) I hope to be here tomorrow
(17) ?I hope you to be here tomorrow
(18) I'm longing for John to arrive on time
(19) I'm longing to arrive on time
(20) John forgot to close the door
(21) John forgot that Mary had closed the door
(22) John managed to open the door
(23) John began to eat[326]
(24) He wanted himself to be rich
(25) He wanted to be rich

The status of the embedded subject and the content of the matrix verb interact in a very intricate way. In (26) the embedded subject is both controlled by the addressee of a directive verb and engaged in action. In (27), it is engaged in action but expressed, because it does not coincide with the addressee of the directive verb. In (28), the embedded subject is both controlled by the subject of a commissive verb and engaged in action. In (29), the embedded subject is engaged in action but not controlled by the main subject, for *tell*, in its directive use, engages in action the addressee, as in (30):

(26) The general ordered the troops to march towards the river
(27) The general ordered that the troops march towards the river
(28) John promised Mary to leave
(29) John told Mary that he would leave
(30) John told Mary to leave.

All the above remarks support the idea that the content of completive relations is not encoded thanks to the inherent properties of the complementiser but stems from the content of the matrix predicator through a grammatical relation. This is precisely what is expected in the area of relational coding.[327]

Things look different in the area of interclausal linkage. When a complex sentence expresses an interclausal link, neither the relation nor its content stem from one of the connected processes, but are both imposed from outside on a pair of simple processes which are each independent of this relation. As the subordinate clause is located outside the network of grammatical relations of the main clause, the coding of the link is punctual, and critically depends on the content of a linking word or expression. As the linking word in turn may be more or less accurate in imposing a substantive conceptual content on the relation, punctual coding gradually shades into inferencing. In (2), the conjunction encodes a relationship of cause; in (31), it encodes a relationship of temporal succession, and cause is attained trough inferential enrichment:

(2) The fields are green because it rained heavily
(31) After it rained heavily the fields are green

In the domain of interclausal linkage, as in the domain of punctual coding in general, inferencing is a constitutive, essential factor of expression.

1.4 Types of conceptual structures and types of expressions

Although it contains two sentence structures, the exocentric relation of embedding is internal to a single sentence nucleus. Embedding, which incorporates a clause into the structure of a superordinate matrix sentence, is the elective, almost exclusive form of expression for the conceptual structure of an inherently complex process, which incorporates a process into the structure of a superordinate process. Embedding entrusts a unitary and hierarchical complex conceptual structure to a unifying and hierarchical syntactic structure.

The endocentric subordinative complex sentence, for its part, does not mirror the conceptual structure of a true interclausal link, because it turns a triadic and symmetric conceptual structure into a dyadic and asymmetric semantic structure. A faithful expression of a causal relationship, for instance, would have a syntactic form such as *The fact that p causes the fact that q*. A complex sentence like *The fields are green because it rained for a week* subordinates the expression of the cause to the expression of the effect. Its asymmetric structure can hardly be justified on conceptual grounds, and its functional motivation is actually to be sought in terms of perspective, both ideational and communicative, as we shall see later on.[328]

Given the triadic and symmetric structure of the interclausal linkage, the complex sentence is neither the exclusive nor the most typical form of expression. In principle, any means is admitted for the expression of a given interclausal link, on the sole condition that two independent processes can be independently ideated and a relationship between them can somehow be made known. Interclausal links are not contents of complex sentences, but conceptual structures ready to be expressed, among others, by complex sentences. As consistent complex conceptual structures, interclausal links are relations of the textual order which can be lent, so to speak, to grammar. Starting from this premise, it is no wonder that interclausal linkage exploits textual coherence and cohesion as well as grammatical connection.

All the arguments examined in the last paragraphs, regarding conceptual structures, syntactic structures and forms of coding, suggest that a sharp line should be drawn between exocentric structures framing inherently complex processes and endocentric subordinative structures expressing relations among simple processes. Complex sentences of the exocentric type will be considered as instances of *embedding* (Lehmann, 1988; Matthiessen & Thompson, 1988). Relations between clauses of the endocentric subordinative type will be considered as instances of *hypotaxis* (Lehmann, 1988; Matthiessen & Thompson, 1988). In the case of embedding, "we do not have a clause combination [...] but simply a case of one clause functioning as a constituent, a complement, within another clause" (Matthiessen & Thompson, 1988: 279). In the case of interclausal linkage, or hypotaxis, the complex sentence is formed by an independent main clause "with structural units called *sentence margins*[329] draped around the edges" (Thompson & Longacre, 1985: 206). The term *subordination* can be maintained as a useful generic term for any kind of relationship involving more than one predicator,[330] on condition that its implications are not pushed too far: it is "extremely important [...] not to group embedding and hypotaxis together as 'subordination'" (Matthiessen & Thompson, 1988: 311–312).

1.5 The expression of interclausal links: A set of options

The traditional image of a complex sentence is the image of a sentence frame, which fills with clauses the same positions open to noun phrases and prepositional phrases in simple sentences. According to Lehmann (1988: 216), for instance, any kind of dependent clause is an "elaboration of a phrase into a more fully developed construction which contains its own predication with all the accessories. Methodologically, this implies starting from the simple independent clause and gradually elaborating it into a complex sentence by expanding its constituents into clauses".

This image is certainly adequate for complex sentences of the exocentric type, encharged with the expression of intrinsically complex processes, but is misleading in the presence of complex sentences of the endocentric subordinative type, encharged with the expression of interclausal links. First, the simple sentence model contains no purely structural position, independent of both a given conceptual content and a given option made by the speaker, ready to be occupied by a marginal clause. Second, if function is taken into account, a complex sentence of the endocentric subordinative kind forms part of a larger paradigm of interchangeable means.

The elective function of a simple sentence is to construct a process. In view of this function, the simple sentence has no structural alternatives. One cannot speak by simply juxtaposing words and phrases. Words have to be connected in sentence structures.

The elective function of a complex sentence of the exocentric type is the construction of an intrinsically complex process. In view of this function, the complex sentence is correctly described as a simple sentence expanding some constituents into clauses.

The elective function of a complex sentence of the endocentric subordinative type is to link two or more independent processes into a higher unit. In view of this function, however, the complex sentence is no more than one option among several. Insofar as each simple process can be constructed by an autonomous sentence structure, an interclausal link can be drawn by any means capable of imposing a given conceptual bridge on two syntactically independent sentences. Accordingly, the ideation of interclausal links can be attained within a complex sentence as well as transferred outside the boundary of the sentence structure. In the former case, it is entrusted to a unitary grammatical frame; in the latter, to a coherent fragment of text.

Each of the following examples, for instance, makes accessible a causal relation between two simple processes in a specific way:

(2) The fields are green because it rained heavily
(31) After it rained heavily the fields are green
(32) It rained heavily and the fields are green

(33) The fields are green. It rained heavily
(34) It rained heavily. For this reason, the fields are green

Complex sentences (2) and (31) and compound sentence (32) are unitary and unifying grammatical structures, while (33) and (34) are juxtapositions of independent grammatical structures. If they form a unitary structure, it is only because they are interpreted as coherent textual units. Examples (33) and (34) show that whilst we cannot speak by simply juxtaposing words, we can speak, and normally do so, by juxtaposing independent utterances. Example (34) also shows that a sequence of juxtaposed utterances can be reinforced by more or less specialised cohesive devices, which work as useful signposts on the path towards textual coherence.

Each of these options involves a specific point of equilibrium between punctual coding and inferencing. Example (2) is the only structure that encodes both the link and its causal content. Example (31) expresses a link which reaches far beyond the encoded content: the encoded relationship of temporal sequence is promoted to cause through inferential enrichment. Example (32) encodes an almost empty connection whose content is inferred. Example (33) encodes neither the link nor its content, which is inferred on the assumption that the juxtaposed utterances form a unitary message. Example (34) encodes the content but not the link, which rests on the previous identification of a coherent antecedent of the anaphoric adverbial *for this reason*. In (31), (32) and (34), coding and inferencing take turns; in (33), inferencing replaces coding.

So far, our discussion has shown that it is not inconsistent to think of interclausal linkage as a functional task open to a wide and heterogeneous set of means of expression, ranging from complex sentence structures to textual configurations bridging simple independent sentence structures. It has also shown that there are enough different kinds of grammatical and textual devices to suggest that in the field of interclausal linkage the function — the imposition of a conceptual link on two or more independent processes — is prior and constant, whereas the structures are secondary and variable. Once a conceptual structure is explicitly defined, any form belonging to the set of available options can be considered as a functional equivalent of any other, and as such is open to analysis.

At the same time, these conclusions simply open up a space of logical possibility whose real import for linguistic description can be delimited for each kind of link only through empirical investigation. In particular, for each kind of interclausal link it has to be ascertained to what extent its expression in a given language really exploits the heterogeneous set of grammatical and textual devices open to interclausal linkage, all of them or only some and, if so, which.

On the following pages, we shall first explore the logical space of options in its full breadth (§2). The second point will be treated with reference to a restricted but paradigmatic domain of interclausal links, that is, the constellation formed by cause, motive and purpose (§3).

2. The expression of interclausal links: Coding and inferencing

In the case of embedding, both the link and its content stem from a unitary sentence structure: the link is drawn by a grammatical relation, and its content is predetermined by the content of the main predicator. In the case of interclausal linkage, both the relationship and its content are imposed from outside on two independent simple processes, neither of which contains them. At this point, two questions become relevant: first, how can two or more simple processes be connected to form a unified structure? Second, how can the conceptual profile of the link be identified?

These two questions are intertwined but independent, as we can easily see by looking at two extreme but significant cases.

At one end of the scale, we can imagine a grammatical link void of conceptual content. Unlike a simple juxtaposition like *It rained for a week. The fields are green*, for instance, a compound sentence like *It rained for a week and the fields are green* connects two simple processes into a unified grammatical framework. In spite of this, the compound sentence is just as vague as the bare juxtaposition about the content of the relation, which has to be inferred in both cases.

At the other end of the scale, a juxtaposition which contains adequate cohesive means can fully encode the profile of an interclausal link in the absence of any kind of formal connection of the involved processes: *It rained for a week. In spite of this, the fields are dry.*

2.1 The unification of the processes: Syntactic connection, coherence and cohesion

When a complex sentence or a compound sentence are constructed, the processes involved are integrated as constituents into a unified syntactic structure.

When two independent sentences are juxtaposed, no grammatical link is engaged in the unification of the processes. If a form of unification is eventually achieved, it is thanks to an act of interpretation on the part of the addressee. A co-operative addressee faced with a set of independent utterances which simply happen to be there together has no structural reason for taking them as if they were intended to form a unitary message. If he actually does so, it is because he assumes that the speaker is not presenting him with a random set of utterances but with a unitary message.

This co-operative behaviour on the part of the addressee seems a matter of course, because we are accustomed to it and rely on it when communicating.[331] But if we question it, we soon realise that the assumption made by the addressee about the intention of the speaker plays the same role as the unifying grammatical frame within a complex sentence: it is the only thread that keeps together the *disiecta membra* of the message.[332] This assumption is logically prior to the definition of the content, for it is in order to be consistent with it that the addressee tries to make a coherent message out of the unconnected expressions entrusted to him.

Coherence, the constitutive property of texts, may be defined as a link between the contents of two or more grammatically unconnected expressions, on the preliminary assumption that they form part of a unitary message. When such a link is encouraged and confirmed by the presence of specialised linguistic cues, we speak of cohesion, which can thus be defined as a set of linguistic devices at the service of coherence.

Coherence is in itself a somehow elusive, volatile property. Cohesion represents, so to speak, its visible linguistic body. According to Halliday & Hasan (1976: vii), "Cohesive relations are relations between two or more elements in a text that are independent of the structure; for example between a personal pronoun and an antecedent proper name, such as *John … he*". Cohesive relations "may be set up either within a sentence or between sentences". When a cohesive relation "crosses a sentence boundary, it has the effect of making the two sentences cohere with one another" (Halliday & Hasan, 1976: 11). In this way, the means of textual cohesion, above all anaphoric relations, are put at the service of interclausal linkage. Thanks to anaphoric expressions, "the sentences are hooked to one another, so to speak" (Lehmann, 1988: 211).

The link created by anaphora is not to be confused with a grammatical link. In a pair of juxtaposed utterances like

(1) It rained heavily. In spite of *this* the road is dry

the phrasal adverb *in spite of this* does not grammatically connect the contiguous utterances. As it contains an anaphoric expression, which can be used coherently only if it refers back to an antecedent within the co-text,[333] the adverb invites the interpreter to look for some antecedent outside the utterance which contains it. In our case, this antecedent is naturally identified with the first utterance of the juxtaposition, whose content is thus involved in the concessive relationship imposed on the content of the anaphoric substitute *this* by the phrasal preposition *in spite of*. Once more, what makes the link is not grammar but the addressee's previous assumption about coherence.

It is in this sense and within these limits that a cohesive expression holds as "an invitation to a text" (Halliday & Hasan, 1976: 28). Whether or not to accept the invitation and look for an actual antecedent somewhere in the immediate co-text is left up to the addressee. However effective in underlining and confirming coherence, cohesion presupposes it.[334] A cohesive expression is, to take up one of Bühler's suggestive metaphors, a sort of signpost — *Wegweise* — on the path towards coherence. Signposts are useful in finding out the path and confirming that it is the right one; but they do not bring the path into existence.

2.2 The conceptual profile of interclausal links

The content of an interclausal linkage results from a variable balance between grammatical connection and textual coherence, and between coding and inferencing.

Looked at from a functional point of view, the wide range of means designed for the expression of interclausal links forms a *continuum*. This, however, does not imply that the different formal and conceptual devices involved in it merge into one another. On the contrary, each of them — and in particular hypotaxis, coordination and juxtaposition as formal configurations; inferential bridging, inferential enrichment and anaphora as conceptual links — can be rigorously, or at least reasonably defined with regard to each other in differential terms. Once this differentiation has been made, it is clear that devices belonging to different levels interact to variable degrees.

Complex and compound sentences, for instance, imply some degree of coding, ranging from undercoding to overcoding. In the case of undercoding, a given amount of inferential enrichment is required, which is inversely proportional to the degree of coding. Juxtaposition, for its part, ranges from a total absence of coding to full coding in the presence of specialized cohesive means

— *therefore, nevertheless, in spite of this*, for instance — and even to overcoding. This happens, in particular, when anaphoric adverbials incorporate a relational encapsulating noun, such as *with this purpose, aim, desire, dream* (§3.5).

2.2.1 *Complex sentence*

2.2.1.1 *Full coding.* In the presence of full coding, the linking word performs its task as a serviceable tool is expected to do, neither more nor less. In other words, it brings to expression an interclausal link which has a conceptual structure of its own, independent of the formal properties of a specific linguistic expression. For instance, in a complex sentence like *Though it rained heavily, the fields are dry*, the subordinative conjunction encodes neither more nor less than a concessive relationship.

Full punctual coding, that is, the perfect match between the content of a given expression and an independent relational concept, is traditionally considered the prevailing, or at least the most paradigmatic case of expression. In fact, it is the least revealing case, for it is undercoding and overcoding that under the best conditions make visible the complex interplay of linguistic and conceptual structuring. By combining linguistic coding with inferential enrichment, undercoding highlights the role played by conceptual and cognitive structures in the ideation of complex meanings in the area of punctual coding. By grafting a linguistic-specific layer of concepts on a largely shared basis, overcoding shows that even in the area of punctual coding language is not merely a passive instrument of expression.

2.2.1.2 *Undercoding and inferential enrichment.* If expression is reduced to coding, the system of conceptual structures involved in interclausal linkage is identified with the meaning of a set of adverbial clauses, if not directly of subordinators. Inferential enrichment shows that both assumptions are false.

Inferential enrichment presupposes both some degree of coding and an evaluation of the connected contents against the background of shared cognitive models or data. When the encoded link does not fill a coherent conceptual model, the gap is filled by inferential enrichment.

Such an expression as (2), for instance, encodes a relation of temporal sequence, but is immediately taken as expressing a concessive relation:

(2) The president approved selling military arms to Iran and trading them for hostages after proclaiming publicly that he would do neither (Kortmann, 1997)

Against the background of shared assumptions about consistency standards in public behaviour, the content of the complex sentence is enriched by the non-asserted implication that the president's declaration should have held as a strong argument against selling arms to Iran. The same non-asserted component of the content, which is essential for the ideation of a concessive relation, is encoded as a conventional implicature if the conjunction *although* is used:

(2) a. The president approved selling military arms to Iran and trading them for hostages although he had proclaimed publicly that he would do neither.

The interclausal links involved in inferential enrichment form a system of interconnected conceptual structures of increasing complexity.[335] The more complex structures imply the simpler ones, which in turn may be developed into the more complex ones by inference. Both cause and concession, in particular, encapsulate a more basic relationship of temporal sequence. Owing to this, the content of a complex sentence that encodes a relationship of temporal sequence is open towards two alternative lines of inferential enrichment, one ending in cause, the other in concession. When cause or concession is inferred, the upper limit of inferential enrichment is reached. When cause or concession is fully encoded, therefore, there is no room left for inference.[336] As it is a far more complex conceptual structure than cause, however, it is concession that can be considered the real outpost of inferencing.[337]

2.2.1.3 *Overcoding: Conceptual structures and semantic structures.* While cause is a good example of an independent conceptual relation which can be inferred irrespective of the degree of coding, and even in the total absence of coding, the connected relationship of result[338] is a good instance of a purely semantic structure bound to overcoding.

Besides a core causal relationship, result contains two non-asserted components: the idea that the effect takes place when the intensity of the cause reaches a critical degree, and the idea that, once this threshold has been crossed, the effect is not just a matter of fact, but a sort of necessity. Compare the following examples:

(3) The snow melted because it rained heavily
a. It rained so heavily that the snow melted.

The implicit components of result cannot be inferred. They can only be activated as conventional implicatures of a grading intensifier like *so*, and are thus indissociable from the presence of one of such terms in the expression. This does not imply that the expression of result requires a complex sentence, for the intensifier is also compatible with juxtaposition:

(4) Our various tasks forward occupied us for hours, the two men with us moved so slowly and had to rest so often (Conrad).

Insofar as its ideation depends on the availability of linguistic-specific coding devices, result cannot be considered as an independent conceptual structure open to linguistic expression, but rather as a constructed semantic structure.

If the relationship between conceptual structures and expression is called into question, and the full range of means of expression is taken into account, a cleavage becomes visible between a *conceptual* space of autonomous interclausal relations and a *semantic* space depending on the availability and structural properties of specific coding devices.[339] The first domain contains a system of purely conceptual structures, which can be fully defined irrespective of linguistic coding and are likely to be shared far beyond the borders of a single speech community. The second contains a system of semantic structures, which can be conceived of only as contents of specific linguistic structures and are not necessarily shared among languages. The discriminating criterion is accessibility by inference. Autonomous conceptual structures can be inferred on conceptual grounds when linguistic coding is either absent or too weak. Semantic structures require language-specific coding. When linguistic forms bring independent conceptual structures to expression, the form of the expression is essentially at the service of the content. When linguistic expressions construct semantic structures, a specific content is grafted on shared concepts.

2.2.2 *Juxtaposition: Inferential bridging*

Our experience as language users tells us that conceptually autonomous interclausal relations — for instance, cause — can easily be expressed by a bare juxtaposition of independent utterances. In such cases, inference builds up a conceptual bridge between two independent processes in the absence of any formal frame. In the following juxtaposition, for instance, a co-operative addressee easily infers the relevant causal relation:

(5) The fields are green. It rained heavily

Unlike cause, concession seems to be almost incompatible with simple juxtaposition and to require some degree of coding, however low. In the area of concession, in other words, inference practically means inferential enrichment.

According to Kortmann (1997: 208), the reason for such behaviour is that concession, unlike cause, is too complex a structure to be simply inferred: "a concessive interpretation can hardly be inferred. This is exactly the reason why Concession typically requires some sort of lexical or morphological marking [...] The knowledge of the world, of compatibilities and, above all, incompatibilities of states of affairs it requires is too complex to be simply inferrable".

Kortmann is right when he argues that concession is a very complex cognitive structure.[340] But if the reason for the behaviour of concession were cognitive complexity, inferential enrichment would be as difficult to justify as inferential bridging. Now, concession is typically inferred not only from an encoded temporal sequence, as in the example quoted above, but also from such a void structure as coordination with *and*:

(6) As to the kind of trade she [the ship] was engaged in and the character of my shipmates, I could not have been happier if I had had the life and the men made to my order by a benevolent Enchanter. And suddenly I left all this (Conrad)

As the example shows, the relation of incompatibility is easy to see independently of any linguistic marking. In spite of this, a simple juxtaposition would not be as natural:

(6) a. As to the kind of trade she [the ship] was engaged in and the character of my shipmates, I could not have been happier if I had had the life and the men made to my order by a benevolent Enchanter. Suddenly I left all this

What concession actually requires is not so much a full coding of its substantive content, but a unitary syntactic frame, as if only a formal bridge, however empty, were able to counterbalance the incompatibility of the linked processes.[341]

While inferential enrichment presupposes some degree of coding and takes over its function at a given point, inferential bridging is a substitute of coding. In the presence of inferential bridging, interclausal linkage completely leaves the domain of grammatical connection for the domain of textual coherence.

The balance of coding and inferencing is a matter of division of labour between speaker and addressee. Responsibility for coding lies with the speaker; responsibility for inferencing lies with the addressee. Both speaker and addressee rely on shared structures: coding relies on shared grammatical and lexical means; inferencing relies either on shared systematic conceptual structures and cognitive models, or on occasional data shared within the boundaries of a contingent speech situation.

The work performed by a co-operative addressee engaged in bridging inferencing is well illustrated by the metaphor of *bricolage* (Lévi-Strauss, 1962). The interpreter of a unitary message entrusted to a juxtaposition cannot rely on specialised means expressly conceived for the relevant relation. All he can do is to use the means he occasionally has at his disposal, on the assumption that the speaker is sending him a coherent message.

Juxtaposed utterances have a certain content, which one has to evaluate against shared long-lasting conceptual structures and shared occasional data. The utterances follow each other in a given linear order which, under some conditions, can offer significant clues. Finally, it is possible that the juxtaposed utterances display a unitary intonation profile, which suggests that they are designed to form together a unitary message. Of all these resources, the most reliable are shared conceptual structures and shared information.

The value of linear order is not independent of the content of the juxtaposed processes, but is subject to strong conceptual restrictions. It is certainly true, as Jakobson (1966: 27) points out, that "If the sequence of verbs *veni, vidi, vici* indicates to us the order in which Caesar's actions occurred, it is first and foremost because the sequence of coordinated perfect forms is used to reproduce the order of events". The diagrammatic effect, however, is not an outcome of the pure succession.

First and foremost, its activation is subject to the condition that the temporal order is relevant to the content of the juxtaposed processes. In this case, and only in this case, the linear order of the expressions is taken as an index of the temporal order of the corresponding processes.[342] The chain *Veni, vidi, vici* is interpreted as a temporal sequence because the expressed processes can be seen as following each other in time. The chain *The sun was shining and a sweet breeze was blowing* is not, because the expressed processes can only be interpreted as simultaneous.

Moreover, if the conceptual link between the juxtaposed processes is more complex than temporal order, the involved inferences grow in complexity. In the presence of a causal relationship, in particular, the linear order of the expressions cannot be simply taken at face value. The following juxtapositions, for instance, are both interpreted as expressing the same causal relationship:

(7) It rained heavily. The fields are green
(8) The fields are green. It rained heavily

In order to do so, both juxtapositions are interpreted as expressing a temporal sequence. But if the temporal sequence has to be consistent in both cases, it cannot involve the same terms. In (7), the linear order reflects the objective order of facts, from cause to effect. In (8), it reflects a subjective order, from the perception of the effect to the tentative identification of the cause by the speaker (see §3.2.2). In the case of result, the subjective order is even the only one compatible with juxtaposition:

(4) Our various tasks forward occupied us for hours, the two men with us moved so slowly and had to rest so often (Conrad).

The presence of an intonation profile belongs to oral communication, and is only roughly mirrored in written texts. As written texts are as open to inferential bridging as oral messages, the role of intonation cannot be considered essential. Moreover, even in oral texts, it is not certain that the intonation profile has to be considered a systematic coding device rather than an index, and therefore an occasional cue whose relevance and content can be decided only within an interpretation field, and therefore in each individual case.[343]

2.2.3 *Anaphora and encapsulation*

The most typical cohesive expressions engaged in interclausal links are adverbs or adverbials, which from within the second term of a juxtaposition refer back anaphorically to the first.

An adverb or adverbial can be anaphoric in a loose or in a strict sense. A strict anaphora is an expression that contains a substitute for the antecedent process. In such expressions as *because of this* and *in spite of this*, for instance, the pronoun *this* is an anaphoric substitute:

(9) It rained heavily. *In spite of this*, the fields are dry

A weak anaphora refers back to an antecedent process without containing a substitute for it. This holds for such expressions as *therefore*, *nevertheless*, *all the same*:

(10) It rained heavily. *Nevertheless*, the fields are dry

Anaphoric expressions, both in the loose and in the strict sense, owe their linking power to a characteristic sort of non-saturation, which reminds one of conjunctions. In spite of this, anaphoric linking expressions cannot be considered as a kind of coordinative conjunction

In the presence of a conjunction, the first term of the relation is required for the syntactic well-formedness of a complex or compound sentence. In the presence of an anaphoric expression, the first term of the relation is required for the coherence of the message. As their functions are different, a conjunction and an adverb can co-occur, as Dik (1968: 34) points out:

> Given a particle which might tentatively be regarded as a coordinator (in a structure like M1 co? M2), consider the possibility of adding a further particle, the coordinator-status of which has already been established. If this is possible (i. e., if there is a structure like M1 co co? M2), then co? is not itself a coordinator. If this is impossible (and there are no further counter-arguments), then co? is itself a coordinator. This test is based, of course, on the premise that two members can never be coordinated by more than one coordinator.

To go back to our topic, such anaphoric forms as *nevertheless* or *in spite of this* are not coordinative conjunctions but adverbs or adverbials, because they can co-occur with both a juxtaposition and a true coordinative conjunction,[344] as shown by (13) and (14):

(11) The vase fell off the table. *In spite of this*, it didn't break
(12) The vase fell off the table. *Nevertheless*, it didn't break
(13) The vase fell off the table *and in spite of this* it didn't break
(14) The vase fell off the table *and nevertheless* it didn't break

Syntactically, adverbs and adverbials belong entirely to the second utterance of the juxtaposition. It is only on the content plane that they take the first utterance as a coherent antecedent, constructing an anaphoric bridge over a formal border.

A special case of anaphoric substitution is anaphoric encapsulation.[345] In the case of encapsulation, the anaphoric substitute does not reduce itself to an empty pronoun, but contains a noun that categorises the antecedent.

Some encapsulating nouns simply classify the antecedent inherently as a kind of process, for example as an instance of "accident" or "wedding". Such nouns can be found in anaphoric linking expressions, but do not take part in the interclausal linkage:

(15) The vase fell off the table. *In spite of this accident*, it didn't break.

Some encapsulating nouns, however, categorise the antecedent process relationally, that is, as the term of a relationship involving the consequent. The antecedent, for instance, is defined as a *purpose*:

(16) She wanted to examine a picture. *For this purpose*, she stopped in front of it

Beside working as anaphoric substitutes in the presence of juxtaposition, relational encapsulating nouns can be incorporated into subordinative linking expressions within the framework of complex sentences. In this case, they are oriented cataphorically:

(18) She stopped in front of a small picture [...] for the purpose of examining it (James).

Relational encapsulation is not simply a way of encoding independent conceptual relations. By virtue of the specific content of each available encapsulating noun, a differentiated surplus of fine-grained categorisation can be attained, which is a form of overcoding. Purpose is certainly the best example of this, for a rich and heterogeneous set of such nouns as *aim*, *plan*, *desire*, *dream*, *illusion* can be used for a fine-grained modulation of the purposive link (see §3.5).

2.2.4 *Coordination*

Coordinative conjunctions formally link constituent clauses into a unified grammatical structure designed to form a unitary message. As far as the content of the link is concerned, two points are relevant: the content of the conjunction itself, and the presence of anaphoric adverbs and relational encapsulators.

2.2.4.1 *The content of the conjunction.* The conjunction *and* is almost devoid of content. In any case, its content remains far below the set of contents actually open to compound sentences. What is encoded when two processes are coordinated by *and* is simply their co-occurrence, without any further restriction independent of the coordinated contents. Any positive content a coordinated sequence is ready to receive is the outcome of inferential enrichment.

Such a sentence as *The sun was shining and a sweet breeze was blowing* expresses no more than what is coded by *and*, that is, the pure co-occurrence of two independent processes in some point of time. From this very low starting point, a coordinate sequence containing *and* is open to any path of inferential enrichment, from temporal sequence[346] — *The sun set and the moon rose* — to the opposite end points of inference, that is cause — *The moon rose and the river became visible* — and concession: *I sent you three letters and I got no answer.*

At the opposite end of the scale, the conjunction *but* has a very strong semantic profile, characterised in particular by the implicit content that "a contrast exists between the conjuncts, or between the implications of the conjuncts"[347] (Payne, 1985: 6). Owing to its syntactic and semantic properties, *but* can be considered as a sort of *Idealtypus*[348] of conjunction engaged in interclausal linkage, for it imposes both a relationship and its content on two processes of equal syntactic rank, a formal configuration which exactly mirrors the structure of the expressed complex concept.

Along the path towards expression, inferential enrichment takes over coding at a variable point: the greater distance has been covered by coding, the less is left to inferencing. As their contents are located at the opposite ends of the scale, *and* and *but* mark the extremes of inferential enrichment.

The coordinative conjunction *and* combines the lowest degree of coding with the widest range of options and the longest path open to inferential enrichment. *But* allows a single path of inferential enrichment, and a very short one — namely, the path leading from the encoded adversative relation to the concessive relation.

The encoded content of *but* is very close to concession, to the point that it is difficult to keep the two conceptual structures apart if we take borderline cases into account. If we focus on the most typical instances, concession appears as a particular case of adversative relationship — namely, the case where the contrast depends on the frustration of an expected causal relationship. In other words, a typical concessive relation takes place when a process *p*, which is expected to cause a process *q* in normal circumstances, ends in a process of the non-q kind. If the contents of the coordinated sentences fit this conceptual mould, the adversative relationship is improved to receive a concessive interpretation: for instance, *It has been raining for a week but the corn isn't growing.*

2.2.4.2 *The synergy of conjunction and anaphora.* Coordinative conjunctions, and in particular *and*, typically co-occur with anaphoric adverbials and encapsulating predicative nouns:

(19) It has been raining for a week *but in spite of this* the corn is not growing
(20) It has been raining for a week *and in spite of this* the corn is not growing
(21) It has been raining for a week, *and as a consequence* the corn is growing
(22) She wanted to examine a small picture *and for this purpose* she stopped in front of it.

In the presence of the conjunction *but*, the anaphoric adverbial either is redundant or simply fills the short gap between adversative and concessive relation. In the presence of the conjunction *and*, the synergy of coordination and anaphora shows perfect complementarity. Through coordination, two processes of equal rank are formally linked; through the anaphoric adverbial, the content of the relationship that dominates both is fully and independently encoded.

2.3 A grammar of options

According to Halliday (1978: 4), two models of grammar are in competition in linguistic research: a "grammar of rules" and a "grammar of options". This, however, should not to be taken as implying that the two models are alternative, but rather as implying that they are complementary. Each model is fit for a specific set of facts, depending on the conditions under which syntactic structures are constructed, complex contents are ideated, and inner and outer functions are fulfilled.

The model of grammar as a set of rules is relevant to the description of the functional core of nuclear simple and complex sentences, that is, in the area of relational coding and strict grammatical lawfulness. The construction of the functional core complies with rigid and immanent formal standards, which are not really open to choice.

Outside this core, when function is logically prior, what a grammar is called upon to do is to provide paradigms of alternative options in order to match independent relevant functions, at the ideational, textual or interpersonal level. The most typical domains of a grammar of options are the expression of marginal roles and of communicative perspective at the level of the simple sentence, and the ideation and perspective of interclausal links.

When the content of grammar is a set of options, no grammatical structure is absolutely indispensable for securing the function at issue, and therefore virtually any structure can be replaced by alternative means. In the field of interclausal links, in particular, the relevant question is not: What is the form of expression of a given interclausal linkage?, but: What is the set of available means to express a given interclausal linkage and what are the reasons which induce a speaker to choose one form instead of another?

In the field of interclausal links, the reasons for the choice can hardly be located at the ideational level, for the complex sentence enjoys no particular privilege over its alternative options. Functionally speaking, provided that the relevant conceptual link can be identified, the formal properties of the expression are of little import. What is really affected by the form of expression are the textual and interpersonal functions.

At the textual level, the complex sentence enables the user to impose on the connected processes a complex communicative perspective, distributed over two layers, which is highlighted above all in narrative texts. Such a complex sentence as *John left his native hamlet in order to look for a job*, for instance, reproduces at the level of the complex sentence a bas-relief perspective, that is, the linear progression from theme to focus which is typical of simple sentences. But an expression like the following shows that the complex sentence can also impose on the complex process a high-relief perspective: *As she drove through the Blackmore Vale, and the landscape of her youth began to open around her, Tess aroused herself from her stupor* (Hardy). While the main clause displays an independent communicative perspective of its own, a linear progression from theme to focus, the subordinate clause forms a sort of background to it. This is obviously connected to the fact that the subordinate clause occupies the initial position, which is characterised by the lowest degree of communicative dynamism, and is cut off from the main clause by a pause, so as to form a distinct communicative unit (Halliday, 1968). The combination of initial position, communicative independence, a low degree of communicative dynamism and syntactic subordination produces a supplementary dimension of communicative perspective, that is, an opposition between foreground and background.[349]

Remaining within the borders of the textual function, in such a complex sentence as

(23) John fell ill *only* because he had walked in the rain

the focusing particle *only* is directly applied to the causal link, an option which is barred in case of juxtaposition. In *John fell ill. He had only walked in the rain*, the focus does not coincide with the causal relationship, but with the predicate of the antecedent process.

Equally, at the level of interpersonal function, complex sentences make it possible to modalise the relation, grading the commitment of the speaker to it:

(24) John fell ill, *probably* because he walked in the rain.

In this case, juxtaposition makes it possible to modulate the speaker's commitment to the truth of either simple process but not to the relevance of the causal relation: *John fell ill. He had probably walked in the rain*; *John probably fell ill. He had walked in the rain.*

The last two functions, however, are not exclusive of the complex sentence, but can also be performed in the presence of anaphoric encapsulators:

(25) John walked in the rain. *This is the only reason* why he fell ill
(26) John walked in the rain. *This is the probable reason* why he fell ill
(27) John walked in the rain. *This is probably the reason* why he fell ill

All considered, it seems thus natural to conclude that the building up of a multi-layered communicative perspective, and in particular of the opposition between foregrounded and backgrounded information, is the only exclusive function of a complex sentence. Once this choice has been made by the speaker, the complex sentence is not just an option among others — it becomes absolutely irreplaceable.[350]

3. Conceptual structures, coding and expression: The case of cause, motives and purpose

In the area of interclausal relations, and more generally in the elective territory of a grammar of options, function is prior and constant, whereas expression is instrumental and variable. This implies that the expressed concepts form a compact network of interconnected relations, whereas the available means of expression look like a heterogeneous set of devices belonging to different domains. If interclausal links are often dealt with not as a highly structured conceptual space (one exception is Kortmann, 1997) but as a shapeless list of subordinate clauses (see for instance Dik, 1989(1997a); Cristofaro, 2003), it is precisely because they form a system only as concepts. Their means of expression — grammatical connection and textual coherence and cohesion, coding devices and inference — do not form as such a coherent set. The only reason that justifies their unitary treatment is their common function.

Given such a premise, the first step to be made in the study of interclausal links is to draw an exact map of the relevant conceptual space. Once the relevant concepts are identified, defined and connected to one another within this map, it makes sense to ask what kinds of means are available for the expression of each. In order to illustrate this point, we shall first define the consistent constellation of concepts including cause, motives and purpose. Then, we shall consider in greater detail the means of expression available for cause, motive and, above all, purpose, paying particular attention to the specific balance of full coding, overcoding, undercoding and inferencing documented by the different forms.

The distinction between causes and motives is deeply rooted in the most basic categories of our natural ontology. Cause is relevant to the description and explication of complex chains of phenomena in the natural world, whereas motive is relevant to the description and explication of free and responsible human action. As it is rooted in a presupposed rather than in an overt layer of conceptual structures, the distinction between causes and motives sinks into the underground of our cognitive landscape, among the categories which are both relied upon in practical behaviour and sheltered from direct questioning. The analytical clarification of this conceptual underground is the specific task of the philosophical component of grammar.

Looked at in purely conceptual terms, purpose is no more than a kind of motive underlying human behaviour. What qualifies purpose is not a distinct conceptual structure but a specific semantic perspective, whose ideation is subject to the availability of language-specific coding devices.

If we consider the entire set of available means of expression, which has full coding at its centre, halfway between lack of coding and overcoding, the expressions of cause and purpose tend to occupy opposite ends of the spectrum.

Cause is the most typical example of a conceptual category which is both basic and natural, and its expression spans from lack of coding to full coding. Depending on language-specific coding devices, the purposive perspective is barred to inferencing, and spans from full coding to overcoding.

The difference between cause and purpose is highlighted if we compare the provision of encapsulating nouns in the two areas. In the area of cause, encapsulation is practically negligible as a means of expression, and above all conceptually unreliable. In the area of purpose, it provides both an impressively fine-grained network of concepts organising the fields of human intentions and feelings, and the richest and most heterogeneous paradigm of encapsulating nouns engaged in interclausal connection.

3.1 Cause

The description of the natural concept of cause as it is revealed by consistent linguistic use requires a preliminary step, that is, enclosing within brackets the whole system of concepts of the nomothetic paradigm.[351]

According to the nomothetic paradigm, a given causal relation between a fact *p* and a fact *q* is seen as a particular case subsumed under a law, that is, as an instance of a regular relationship between a (sufficient or both necessary and sufficient) condition and its consequences. As a matter of fact, neither the reference to a rule nor the reduction of cause to condition, which form the core of traditional philosophical analysis,[352] are immediately relevant for the natural linguistic use of causal constructions.

Let us examine an example. A complex sentence like (1):

(1) The house caught fire because there was a short-circuit

is normally understood as if it expressed the following facts:

a. There was a short-circuit
b. The house caught fire
c. The short-circuit made the house catch fire.

Of these facts, (c) is explicitly stated, while (a) and (b) are entailed. Entailment is not an empirical relation of factual truth, but a condition imposed on the consistency of the whole structure: a consistent causal relationship can only take place if both cause and effect really take place.

To say that cause is a relationship between two real facts, however, confines the relevance of the category to a contingent dimension: the aim of a natural causal judgement is not to make predictions but to connect real facts. In this case, it is neither pragmatically relevant nor logically necessary to consider a causal relationship as an instance of a general rule of the kind "Any time *p* takes place (for instance, there is short circuit in a house), it makes *q* take place (the house catches fire)". Natural causal reasoning is naturally idiographic rather than nomothetic, a circumstance which shelters it from the typical difficulties met by explicit definitions of causes as instances of rules.

The previous remarks do not imply that natural reasoning never takes into account either the regularity of causal relations or the links between causes and conditions. It simply implies that natural reasoning faces such questions only when it is pragmatically relevant to do so, that is, when the truth of the premise is suspended, as in conditional reasoning, or when an expected causal relationship fails to take place, as in concession.

Conditional reasoning makes it necessary to take into account the relationship between cause and condition, while concessive structures betray the subject's expectations about the regularity of causal relations. This is the reason why a conceptual analysis of the natural category of cause can be fulfilled only if the structure of conditional and concessive relations is taken into account.

3.1.1 *Conditional reasoning: Cause and condition*

In natural causal reasoning, cause is seen as a condition which is *de facto* sufficient, and no more. The question whether this condition is also necessary does not even arise: insofar as the fact holding as cause actually took place, it makes no sense to ask whether or not another cause could have produced the same effect. The same question becomes relevant in the case of conditional reasoning.

Natural conditional reasoning can be defined as the position of a non-factual causal relation, for which the truth of the cause is not entailed. Once the truth of the premise is suspended, it makes sense to ask not only what one has to expect in case *p* takes place, but also what one has to expect in case *p* does not take place. Given a conditional structure like (2), for instance it is relevant to ask whether the taking place of *q* is excluded or admitted as the effect of another cause, which amounts to asking whether *p* holds as a necessary and sufficient condition or simply as a sufficient condition of *q*:

(2) If it hails, the harvest will be lost

A conditional structure can be used consistently only if the question is answered in one way or the other. It is clear that it cannot be both at the same time without ending in contradiction.

As we observed in Chapter 2, however, the layman practically avoids the logical difficulty because he stops before the fork. For him, cause is not defined *a priori* in terms of either sufficient or necessary and sufficient conditions. When facing a given use, he is ready to make a decision after evaluating the relevant circumstances. In particular, he takes the premise as a necessary and sufficient condition in the first instance, but is ready to admit that it is a merely sufficient condition if the invited inference of biconditionality conflicts with contextual information.

3.1.2 *Concession: Cause and regularity*

Concession is an antiphrastic conceptual structure. The most typical kind of concessive relationship can be defined, roughly, as the relation between a premise *p* and a consequence –*q* which frustrates an expected consequence *q*. The utterance (3), for instance, can be interpreted consistently only if it carries the implicit assumption that the expected causal relationship between rain and growth has failed.

(3) Though it has been raining for a week, the corn isn't growing

The analysis of concessive relations is relevant to the definition of cause on two grounds.

If concession can be defined as the frustration of an expected causal relationship, this implies that typical causal relations are considered instances of rules. Concession, thus, betrays a nomothetic component of the natural concept of cause that remains hidden in the direct expression of causal links.

At the same time, the layman is ready to drop this expectation if the regularity of a causal relationship is falsified in given circumstances — he is ready to rely on the rule though admitting exceptions. Once more, the logical *impasse* is avoided thanks to the flexible logical and cognitive tool of invited inference. In the presence of a premise *p*, the layman is oriented towards the consequence *q*, which implies that he relies on a rule. If *q* does not take place, however, he is ready to admit the exception without calling the rule into question. Concession shows that cause is considered as a sufficient condition under standard circumstances, without excluding failures under non-typical circumstances.

Summing up this last conclusion and the reflections prompted by conditional reasoning, cause can be defined as a condition which is expected to be necessary and sufficient; in some cases, it is admitted to be only sufficient, and in some non-typical circumstances it can even prove to be non-sufficient. This means that the concept of cause has a flexible and layered structure, open to a hierarchical set of relatively favoured and admitted options. This hierarchy of expectations is consistent with the fact that the category of cause is adapted to the way of thinking of its user — the intelligent human being endowed with the faculty of judgement and capable of selecting in each case the ideal match between a long-lasting value of the category and the variable circumstances of use.[353] This shows that the subject of causal reasoning, and more generally the subject who applies consistent concepts to facts in his cognitive behaviour, is the same who makes decisions and acts in his practical behaviour.

3.2 Motives

At the root of the distinction between cause and motives lies the action of free and responsible subjects capable of decision. The subject is a spectator — not altogether passive, but essentially a spectator — when facing the causal chains of the phenomenal world, but he becomes an actor in the field of motivation.

Pushed by independent events, either observed in the past or foreseen, or pulled by his own plans, the subject makes his decisions and takes responsibility for them (§3.2.1). Among motivated human actions, a peculiar place is occupied by speech acts and acts of thinking. As we shall see, thinking and speaking are not simply actions like any other, because they are spoken of in a way that cannot be used to talk of any other action (§3.2.2).

3.2.1 *Motives for action*

The basic distinction between causes and motives is not necessarily connected with overt distinctions on the expression plane. Though they share the same subordinator *because*, the following examples express very different conceptual structures:

(1) The house caught fire because there was a short-circuit
(4) Mark punished his son because he came home late

(1) expresses a relation of phenomenal cause between two events, while (4) expresses the relation between a human action and a motive. This conceptual difference, which does not escape the intuition of the average language user, is ignored by the subordinator *because*. If an interclausal link were no more than the content of a set of complex sentences, or directly of subordinators, one would not even be able to keep apart causes and motives.[354] To put it in Danto's (1968: 43) words, the standard linguistic expression "allows us to ignore differences between men and stones".

The difference between causes and motives becomes clearly visible, on the other hand, if we consider the content of the connected expressions. A cause makes something happen. A motive pushes a free and responsible subject to make a decision and to do an action. Given a structure like *q because p*, if *p* is a motive, *q* is necessarily an action, and vice versa. Moreover, a cause is something that has happened before its effect, whereas a motive can be as much a real fact preceding the action (4) as the content, located in the future, of a prediction (5) or intention (6):

(5) I took the umbrella because it is going to rain
(6) I took the umbrella because I wanted to go out in the rain

The relationship with the actions and intentions of a subject and the structure of temporal relations provide the conceptual key towards the explication of the "logical barrier" (Taylor, 1964: 55) between causes and motives.

3.2.1.1 *Motive, decision and action.* The difference between cause and motives, which is hardly visible within the grammatical framework of the complex sentence, can easily be observed if the subordinate clause is taken apart and the process put back together again using consistent vicarious forms.

The expression of cause can be readmitted into the process by using an anaphoric substitute and a form of the verb *happen*:

(1) The house caught fire because there was a short-circuit
a. The house caught fire. *It happened* because there was a short-circuit

Such a reformulation is interpretable, but not consistent, in the presence of motives:

(4) Mark bought a new car because the old one was damaged in an accident

a. *Mark bought a new car. It happened because the old one was damaged in an accident

(5) I took the umbrella because it is going to rain

a. *I took the umbrella. It happened because it is going to rain

(6) I took the umbrella because I wanted to go out in the rain

a. *I took the umbrella. It happened because I wanted to go out in the rain

(7) I dug a channel because I wanted the water to flow out of the meadow

a. *I dug a channel. It happened because I wanted the water to flow out of the meadow

The expression of motives, on the other hand, is consistent with the use of the pro-predicates *do it* or *do so*:

(4) Mark bought a new car because the old one was damaged in an accident

b. Mark bought a new car. He did so because the old one was damaged in an accident

(5) I took the umbrella because it is going to rain

b. I took the umbrella. I did so because it is going to rain

(6) I took the umbrella because I wanted to go out in the rain

b. I took the umbrella. I did it because I wanted to go out in the rain

(7) I dug a channel because I wanted the water to flow out of the meadow

b. I dug a channel. I did it because I wanted the water to flow out of the meadow

The behaviour with the vicarious forms shows that cause is an outer margin of the main process, that is, a circumstantial, whereas motive is an internal margin of the main action, that is, a marginal constituent of the predicate. This difference of position, in turn, is conceptually motivated by the different relationship between a cause and an event on the one hand, and a motive and an action on the other.

The reformulation with *happen* categorizes the antecedent as a general event: an event is something that happens. At the same time, the subject of *happen*, which is an anaphoric substitute of the main process, neutralises its internal structure, not relevant to the consistency of a causal relationship, but relevant for motives.

The reformulation with the pro-predicate *do it* not only categorises the main process as an action (an action is something one does), but also leaves the predicate open to further inner determination and maintains its agent. Without the presence of a responsible agent, there cannot be a consistent relationship of motive.

Between a cause and its effect there exists an impersonal and blind law. Between a motive and an action, there exists a subject that makes a decision. Unlike a cause, a motive implies a subject's decision: neither a past event nor a foreseen, planned or desired action or event is in itself a motive, irrespective of the subject's decision. A past event, a foreseen, planned or desired fact becomes a motive only when a subject's decision turns it into a ground for action. There is no motive without a subject's decision, which in turn is the outcome of an inner "deliberation", as Aristotle calls it with a telling metaphor taken from the life of the *polis* (*Nicomachean Ethics, Book III*). It is with reference to the subject and his decision-making process, therefore, that the structure of motivation and action can be consistently described.

3.2.1.2 *The consistent action and the consistent agent*

Man is the ground for actions (Aristotle)

Against this background, the whole arsenal of concepts built up to describe cause entirely loses its meaning in the field of motives. In the presence of a motivated action, in particular, it is inconsistent to speak of conditions, whether sufficient or necessary and sufficient. There is no sufficient, let alone necessary and sufficient condition for action. It is impossible to describe the structure of a motivated action without referring to such concepts as "intention", "desire", "decision", "freedom", "responsibility" and "conscience", whose relevance is presupposed by our consistent behaviour.

A syntax of action — its formal configuration — as well as its semantics — its shared content — cannot be dissociated from the presence of an agent who has intentions and makes decisions. A very simple action such as saying goodbye, for instance, requires some bodily movement such as raising one's arm. However, it cannot be reduced to the external description of these movements, for the chain of bodily movements makes no unitary sense outside any reference to a subject and his intentions. The raising of one's arm in a given way is the action of saying goodbye if — and only if — the agent is assumed to raise his arm precisely with this intention, which is designed to be intersubjectively interpreted as such.

To describe an action amounts to attributing an inner unifying sense to a visible chain of events, that is, to interpret it as the realisation of an intention (Searle, 1983: Chapter 3). If we ask a subject about one of his actions, "we want to be provided with an interpretation" (Davidson, 1963(1968: 85)). This in turn amounts to saying that a consistent action necessarily contains an inner purpose: "our ordinary action concepts generally pick out the behaviour they are used to describe not just by its form or overt characteristics or by what it actually brings about, but also by the form or goal-result which it was the agent's purpose or intention to bring about" (Taylor, 1964: 27). A cause can determine a bodily movement but no action: "a movement which brought about a given result is not the same thing as an action which was directed towards this result"[355] (Taylor, 1964: 55). The inner purpose is the essential constitutive property of an action in the same way as significance is the essential constitutive property of an expression:[356] "Intentional behaviour, one could say, resembles the use of language. It is a gesture whereby I mean something" (Von Wright, 1971: 115).

In paradigmatic cases, the interpretation of an action identifies the agent's intention, which is expected to contain the sense of the action. Of course, this does not imply that an empirical agent is fully aware of the content of his intentions. It simply implies that one cannot consistently describe the structure of an action without assuming an intention on the part of the agent: "When we speak of action we are accounting for the behaviour in terms of the man's desires, intentions and purposes. And this is why we hold him responsible" (Taylor, 1964: 35). As we have already observed, the explanation of the presuppositions, that is, of the consistency conditions of a complex conceptual structure, ends in a set of tautologies. To say that the sense of an action coincides with the agent's intention, in particular, does not tell us how much a given empirical agent controls his intentions and purposes. It simply tells us that the question of intentions, purposes and awareness is relevant to a consistent description of action (see §3.6).

3.2.2 *Motive for thinking and speaking*

A very peculiar kind of motive is connected with two very peculiar kinds of action, that is, the actions of thinking and speaking. Given such an expression as

(8) John has returned home, because the windows are open

the circumstance that the windows are open is not the motive of John's described action, but the motive which pushes the speaker to think and say that John performed it.

The existence of complex sentences expressing motives for thinking and speaking was first pointed out by the Groupe λ-l (1975) and Daneš (1985). On closer examination (see Sweetster, 1990: Chapter 4; Dik, Hengeveld, Vester & Vet, 1990: 37–39), the category is split between two different types, characterised by distinct linguistic properties, carefully described by Verstraete (1998; 1999). Besides such examples as (8), in particular, there are instances like (9):

(9) John has arrived, because I know you need to see him urgently (Verstraete 1998)

Forms of type (8) describe an act of inference (or abduction, in Peirce's 1932 terms), whereby the fact described by the subordinate clause — the windows are open — is interpreted as an index of the fact described by the independent clause: John has returned home. Forms of type (9) express the motive leading the subject to perform the speech act. In (8), the subordinate clause expresses "a fact which supports the fact designated by the propositional content of the speech act" (Dik, Hengeveld, Vester & Vet, 1990: 37–39), and therefore is considered a "proposition satellite", active "on the argumentative level" (Verstraete, 1999: 120–123). The structure (9) is considered a "speech act satellite", which "provides a motivation for why the speech act is carried out"[357] (Dik, Hengeveld, Vester & Vet, 1990: 39).

What is relevant for our topic is a property shared by both kinds of construction, that is, the presence of a structural cleavage between the two associated clauses, which is signalled by a pause in intonation[358] (Sweetster, 1990: §4.1.2; Verstraete, 2002). In both cases, the motive is connected with a main action, that is, the speaker's action of thinking or speaking, which however is not described by the expression, but is directly shown by the utterance act itself. The presence on the stage of the main action shifts from the realm of symbolisation to the realm of indexical ostension, a circumstance which breaks the structural connection between either the speech act or the content of an act of thinking, both unexpressed, and their expressed motive.[359] In the absence of the main predicator, the expression of the motive (for instance, *The windows are open*) bears no structural relation to what looks like the main clause (for instance, *John has returned home*), which expresses the content of an unexpressed action.

The absence of a structural relationship between the two associated clauses, which is the most revealing property of the discussed form, is made visible by the impossibility of both connecting the motive to the pro-predicate *do it* and focusing on it through a cleft sentence:[360]

(8) a. *John has returned home. He did it because the windows are open
b. *It is because the windows are open that John has returned home

(9) a. *John has arrived. He did it because I know you need to see him urgently
b. *It is because I know you need to see him urgently that John has arrived

Structures (8a) and (9a) break down because both the pro-predicate *do it* and its subject are devoid of a textual antecedent, due to the fact that both the relevant action and its agent — the speech act or act of thinking and the speaker — are not expressed in words but directly exhibited.

The breakdown of structures (8b) and (9b) is even more revealing. A cleft sentence focuses on the relationship between the cleft constituent and the backgrounded part, which in turn presupposes that some kind of relation holds between them. In such an expression as *It's John that paid for the drinks*, for instance, John is focused on as the agent of the action of paying. If no relation is actually drawn, as in our example, clefting cannot apply — or, if it applies, it creates a spurious relation between the clefted motive and the backgrounded process.

The purely indexical relation between the main action of thinking or speaking and its motive can be readmitted into the symbolic order if this action is in turn overtly expressed. In this case, a complete network of relations is restored around the main predicator. The content of the act of thinking or speaking is the direct object of the main predicator, while the motive takes its natural place at the margins of the predicate:

(8) c. I think that John has returned home because the windows are open
(9) c. I say that John has arrived, because I know you need to see him urgently

What distinguishes speaking and thinking from normal actions is not a conceptual specificity, but a privilege in expression. Whereas a normal action necessarily has to be expressed in order to be connected to a motive, the action of thinking and speaking can be connected to a motive even if it is not actually framed in words but offered by direct ostension. This is one of the best examples of the intertwining of symbolic and indexical dimension in real communication focused on in Chapter 1.

Once they are overtly expressed, on the other hand, thinking and speaking behave as normal actions. Both the reformulation with *do it* and the clefting of the motive are accessible and consistent, though not so elegant:

(8) d. I say (I think) that John has returned home. I do so because the windows are open
e. It is because the windows are open that I say (I think) that John has returned home.

(9) d. I tell you that John has arrived. I do so because I know you need to see him urgently
e. It is because I know you need to see him urgently that I tell you that John has arrived

3.2.3 *The temporal structure of cause and motives*

The temporal structure of cause is simple and rigid: in the outer world, a consistent effect (t_0) necessarily follows its cause (t_{-1}).

The temporal structure of motive is complex and two-layered. A first temporal line reproduces the temporal structure of cause but is internal to the subject, and goes from decision to action: a consistent action necessarily follows the subject's decision. A second line, whose structure is specific to motivation, connects the subject's action and the inner or outer trigger that pushes the agent to make his decision. Though belonging to the phenomenal world, this temporal line is not submitted to the rigid temporal sequence of phenomenal causes, but points towards the future as well as towards the past. This means that the trigger of a decision may chronologically precede or follow the main action:

(4) Mark bought a new car because the old one was damaged in an accident
(5) I took the umbrella because it's going to rain
(6) I took the umbrella because I wanted to go out in the rain

A motive springing from a past event as in (4) can be defined as a "backward-looking motive" (Anscombe, 1957: 20; 1968: 149); a motive inspired by a future event can be defined as a "forward-looking motive"[361] (Anscombe, 1957: 21; 1968: 150). A forward-looking motive, in turn, may coincide with the content of either a prediction, as in (5), or an intention, as in (6).

The past event and its perception by the subject precede the decision and, *a fortiori*, the main action; the foreseen or planned future event follows the main action and thus the decision. The subject's formulation of both a prediction and a plan precedes the decision. As a consequence, four points in time are relevant to the description of the whole set of motives, instead of the two required by cause: the time when a past event is perceived, or a future event is foreseen or planned (t_{-2}); the time of decision, which corresponds to the time of cause (t_{-1}); the time of action, which corresponds to the time of effect (t_0); the time occupied by the foreseen or planned event, which by definition follows the main action (t_{+1}).

In the presence of forward-looking motives all these points are relevant: the time of either the prediction or the plan, the time of decision, the time of action, and the time of the foreseen or planned event. In the presence of backward-looking motives, only three points are relevant: the time of the past event's perception, the time of decision, and the time of action.

3.3 From forward-looking motives to purpose: Prediction and intention

According to some philosophers, the borderline between intention and prediction is not so easy to draw.[362] If we observe the natural use of concepts, however, some clear discriminating criteria are available.

A foreseen event is independent of the subject's intentions or desires, as is an event located in the past. A planned event is the content of an intention or desire. Accordingly, its expression through a causal form typically requires, and is in any case compatible with, the presence of a predicator expressing will, intention or desire:

(6) I took the umbrella because I wanted to go out in the rain
(7) I dug a channel because I wanted the water to flow away

Unlike both backward-looking motives and predictions, moreover, the expression of intentions in complex sentences is not restricted to the causal form exemplified by (4), (5) (6) and (7), but is open to a specific purposive form, exemplified by (10) and (11):

(4) Mark bought a new car because the old one was damaged in an accident
a. *Mark bought a new car so that the old one be damaged in an accident

(5) I took the umbrella because it is going to rain
c. *I took the umbrella so that it should rain

(6) I took the umbrella because I wanted to go out in the rain
(10) I took the umbrella to go out in the rain
(7) I dug a channel because I wanted the water to flow away
(11) I dug a channel so that the water would flow away

Like the causal form, the purposive form of expression is located within the action, at the margins of the predicate, as is shown by the reformulation with *do it*:

(6) a. *I took the umbrella. It happened because I wanted to go out in the rain
b. I took the umbrella. I did it because I wanted to go out in the rain

(10) a. *I took the umbrella. It happened to go out in the rain
b. I took the umbrella. I did it to go out in the rain

(11) a. *I dug a channel. It happened so that the water would flow away
b. I dug a channel. I did it so that the water would flow away

A complex sentence of purposive form like (10) or (11) and a complex sentence of causal form like (6) and (7) express one and the same conceptual structure. Conceptually speaking, the path toward purpose is at its end: purpose is no more than a kind of forward-looking motive, that is, the content of an agent's intention. As far as linguistic description is concerned, however, this is more of a starting point, for the purposive form of expression shapes this shared conceptual substrate in many specific ways.

On the one hand, the purposive form of expression imposes a peculiar perspective on the conceptual structure of the intention.

On the other hand, the expression of purpose relies on a rich and heterogeneous supply of encapsulating nouns, each of which depicts the purposive relationship in a specific light.

In the following paragraphs, we shall examine both the purposive perspective built up by the complex sentence (§3.4) and the modulation of purpose achieved by using encapsulating predicative terms (§3.5).

3.4 The purposive perspective

The difference between a purposive and a causal complex sentence is a difference of ideational perspective, and above all of temporal orientation and equilibrium between what is said and what remains unsaid.

A causal form like (6) — *I took the umbrella because I wanted to go out in the rain* — takes the causal relationship as a model, treating the intention as a sort of cause.[363] It thus faithfully expresses the full conceptual structure of the motive, from intention and decision to action.

A purposive form like (10) — *I took the umbrella to go out in the rain* — immediately connects the main action to its future outcome. As a consequence, it removes from the expression any reference to the agent's intention and decision.

The causal form does not impose on the structure of the forward-looking motive a peculiar ideational perspective of its own, distinct from the inner articulation of the complex concept. The proof is that the same content that is encoded by a causal form like (6) can be inferred out of a simple juxtaposition like (12):

(6) I took the umbrella because I wanted to go out in the rain
(12) I took the umbrella. I wanted to go out in the rain

Upon the same conceptual basis, the purposive form (10) grafts a specific perspective, which highlights the future outcome of the action at the expense of the subject's decision and intention. This peculiar perspective is inseparable from the specific form of expression:

(10) I took the umbrella to go out in the rain

While the shared conceptual content can be inferred as well as encoded, one cannot infer the language-specific perspective imposed on it by the purposive form of expression.

3.5 Encapsulators of purpose

Within the realm of motivated human action, the English language owns a dense network of fine-grained semantic distinctions, which both organise the lexical field of purpose, intentions and prospective emotions, and provide the expression of forward-looking motives with a broad set of means.

On the critical border between phenomenal cause and motivated and purposeful action, on the contrary, we find very few words — *cause*, *motive* and *reason* — whose use is absolutely unreliable in conceptual terms. In the following example the three words co-occur, which suggests that their use does not answer rigid consistency criteria:

(13) The reason for this is that the circumstances of the situation are just as much a cause of behaviour as the underlying motive (British National Corpus, hence BNC).

Reason is used as a synonym of both cause (14) and motive (15), while *cause* happens to be used in an absolutely non-conflicting way in the area of human action, as in (16):

(14) She told me that she was relieved to know that there was a reason for it, even if the root cause had occurred so long ago (BNC)

(15) Although this may be a powerful motive, it is not the best reason (BNC)

(16) Neither I, nor my friends who borrow them, have any cause for complaint (BNC)

The distribution of these words looks rather surprising. In fact, it simply shows that neither linguistic coding nor consistent use are called upon to draw the conceptual boundary between cause and motives. This, in turn, is consistent with the idea that linguistic coding shapes its specific conceptual distinctions on the presupposition that the line is already drawn, and consistent use relies on that presupposition as on a solid ground.

Both the structure of lexical fields and the speakers' behaviour can be considered consistent only on condition that the boundary between cause and motives is sufficiently clear in conceptual terms to exempt language from overtly coding it and speakers from overtly marking it in use. Language draws its more or less subtle distinctions within conceptual areas whose consistency is not overtly encoded but presupposed, and therefore unchallenged. If we speak of purposes, desires, intentions and hopes, plans and illusions, the form of the expression is not required to remind us that we are in the field of human action rather than in the realm of phenomenal cause — that we speak of men and not of stones. This is also proof that the most basic conceptual structures underlying consistent human action, thought and expression are not the product of language-specific categorisation, but are presupposed by linguistic categorisation, consistent thought and expression, and practical behaviour.

3.5.1 *Distribution*

The encapsulating nouns engaged in the expression of purpose can be incorporated into both phrasal prepositions and adverbials.

Phrasal prepositions have the same function as simple prepositions engaged in the expression of a purposive complex sentence. In this case, the specific perspective imposed on the motive of action by the purposive form of the complex sentence undergoes further semantic modulation according to the specific content of the predicative noun:[364]

(17) John left his country *to* learn foreign languages
(18) John left his country *for the purpose of* learning foreign languages
(19) John left his country *with the intention* of learning foreign languages
(20) John left his country *with the desire to* learn foreign languages

Adverbials, for their part, anaphorically qualify the relation between two juxtaposed or coordinated utterances:

(21) John wanted to learn foreign languages. *To this end* he left his country
(22) John wanted to learn foreign languages and *to this end* he left his country

When the expression of forward-looking motives is entrusted to either juxtaposition or coordination, the peculiar perspective imposed on it by the complex sentence of purposive form gets entirely lost. Both juxtaposition and coordination explicitly bring to the forefront the intention, desire or decision of the agent, that is, the same subjective side of motivation which is highlighted by the causal complex sentence and left aside by the purposive complex sentence. This circumstance entails two consequences.

In the first place, the juxtaposition receives a purposive interpretation only if the adverbial occurring in it contains such a predicative noun as *purpose*, *end*, *goal*, *aim*, *objective*, *view* or *prospect*, as in (21) and (22). In the presence of such nouns as *intention* or *desire*, denoting a subject's attitude, there is nothing in the expression that goes beyond the coding of a motive coinciding with an intention:

(23) She would do it! She would get away from here as soon as the snow began to melt. *With this intention* firmly planted in her mind, she headed for the back stairs leading down into the kitchens (BNC)

Furthermore, even if a specific encapsulator is used, what is categorised by it as *purpose*, *end*, *goal*, *aim*, *objective*, *view* or *prospect* is the relation between the main action and the subject's attitude or decision, and not directly the relation between the main action and its future outcome.

3.5.2 *Typology*

Among encapsulating nouns, the concept of *purpose* can be considered the neutral option, that is, the option that merely expresses a purposive relation without adding any further determination to its content:

(24) More disturbing are reports that the extremist Khordad Foundation is planning to stage a meeting in Tehran to mark the fourth anniversary of

the fatwa on 14th February, "*for the purpose of* reviving the world Muslims' zeal and ardour" (BNC)

All the remaining nouns modulate the content of the intention, each in a specific way. According to G. Gross[365] (1998), they can be grouped into three main semantic classes: locative metaphors, like *goal* and *aim*; intellectual predicators, like *intention* and *will*; and emotional predicators, like *longing* and *desire*.

3.5.2.1 *Locative metaphors.* The most typical locative metaphors, that is, *end*, *goal*, *aim* and *objective*, see a purpose as if it were the end point of a trajectory whose source coincides with the main action:

(25) Various changes to the technical procedures were also introduced *with the aim of* making the system more effective and rapid (BNC)

(26) Producing quality products is important if the company is to continue to compete in the international marketplace. *To this end,* the analytical department is designing on-line analysers, e.g. on-line gas chromatography, which can analyse products and intermediates in 'real time' (BNC)

(27) Both linguists wish to produce accurate descriptions of the particular language studied. *In pursuit of this goal,* the grammarian will concentrate on a particular body of data and attempt to produce an exhaustive but economical set of rules which will account for all and only the acceptable sentences in his data (BNC)

The noun *view*[366] metonymically evokes the metaphorical trajectory towards the aim:

Typesize and layout have been chosen *with a view to* maintaining the flow of reading (BNC)

In spite of their metaphorical content, locative encapsulators categorise purpose in a way which is consistent with the perspective imposed on the forward-looking motive by a complex sentence of the purposive form. If a locative metaphor is incorporated into the phrasal preposition, the purpose remains the future end point of a trajectory:

(29) Various changes to the technical procedures were also introduced *to* make the system more effective and rapid.

(30) Various changes to the technical procedures were also introduced *with the aim of* making the system more effective and rapid (BNC)

Both intellectual and emotive predicators, for their part, foreground the roots of the main action in the subject's intention and decision. Accordingly, when they are incorporated into a complex sentence of causal form, any trace of purposive perspective disappears:

(31) He sold everything he owned *because he had the intention of* leaving the country

(32) He had bought land *because he felt the desire to* build a house

When intellectual and emotive predicators are incorporated into a complex sentence of purposive form, the orientation of the main action towards its future outcome, as in (33), is combined with the stress on the subject's attitude and decision which characterises complex causal sentences like (31) or (32):

(33) Jens Jorgen Thorsen came to Britain *to* make a film.

(34) In 1976, a Danish film-maker called Jens Jorgen Thorsen came to Britain *with the intention of* making a film, provisionally entitled *The Many Faces of Jesus* (BNC)

(35) Many little girls attend a dancing school *with the wish to* become a famous dancer (BNC))

3.5.2.2 *Intellectual predicators. Thought* — or, more exactly, its metonymically denoted content — is a general concept, which can be considered a hyperonym of such more specific predicative nouns of intellectual attitude as *intention, intent,*[367] *will* and *willingness.* The content of an intention is a thought which, instead of depicting a fact, is designed to become a fact through action. In Kant's terms, a thought destined to give birth to a fact is an *idea*:

(36) If she could think of a good reason to ask questions about the missing don among his colleagues, she might well come up with some interesting answers. *With this thought in mind*, Loretta set off for Paddington (BNC)

(37) In La Rochelle we never start a game *with the intention of* doing harm (BNC)

(38) He who wounds *with intent to kill* [...] shall be as if he had succeeded (BNC)

(39) We approached it *with a will to* get things done with socialist thinking (BNC)

(40) Sefa-Dedeh is looking at the hydration properties of legumes *with the idea* of developing a variety that takes less time (BNC)

Any kind of motive can lead a subject to make a *decision*. Its content, however, is an action to be performed by the subject itself. The same can be said of *deliberation*, *determination*, *resolution* and *resolve*:[368]

(41) *With the decision to* scrape multilateral preliminary talks, the USA decided to send Assistant Secretary of State Adolf Berle [...] to Canada and Britain for bilateral talks (BNC)

Such encapsulating nouns as *endeavour*, *effort* or *attempt* suggest that the path leading from the main action to its goal is a difficult one:[369]

(42) In all humanities disciplines the computer is used *in an endeavour to* replace intuition with quantification (BNC)

(43) The Community yesterday promised 44,000 tonnes of new food aid for Ethiopia *in an effort to* save millions of people threatened by starvation (BNC)

(44) Ivan Foster, *in an attempt to* show that Knox and Calvin were democrats, pointed out that they sought such popular mandates as were available in their societies (BNC)

Expectation seems more consistent with prediction (45) than with intention, though such an interpretation is admitted (46) or even invited (47) when the main process is an action:

(45) The black cloud was right above them now and some of the congregation had begun to stir uneasily *in expectation of* the downpour (BNC)

(46) We both made new wills last week, *in expectation of* marriage (BNC)

(47) Turkey has committed itself to its friends, *in the expectation that* its commitment will be rewarded

Such concepts as *plan*, *project*, *design*, *object* or *objective* imply a certain control over the purpose on the part of the agent.[370] Electively, the purpose coincides with an action performed by the subject himself:

(48) Patients were admitted the evening before the procedure *with the plan of* discharging the patient on the second or third day after the procedure (BNC)

(49) As expected, the conference carried the policy review statement on multilateral nuclear disarmament — *with the objective of* achieving a nuclear-free world by the end of the century (BNC)

(50) In the same century universal history also flourished, mainly *with the object of* determining the end of the world, after the year 1000 had passed without any sign of its impending occurrence (BNC)

3.5.2.3 *Emotional predicators.* Such concepts as *hope, dream, illusion, pretence* and *pretension* form the transition between the sphere of plans and the sphere of emotions. The common core of all these concepts is a plan, enveloped by a variable mix of emotional and axiological attitude on the part of the speaker. Owing to the axiological component, the consistent application of some of these concepts to the speaker himself is subject to significant restrictions.

Hope is midway between project and expectation, more passive than the former and more active than the latter, with an added emotional component: to hope is to expect a plan's fulfilment with emotional involvement. A *dream* is a plan which is not supported by an adequate share of faith, but is not necessarily given up by the speaker. Implying or at least admitting a sympathetic attitude on the part of the speaker, both *hope* and *dream* can be consistently applied to the speaker himself as well as to a third person. An *illusion* is a condemned project, one in which the subject has no faith at all. Though not implying moral blame, what can consistently be called an illusion is necessarily a third person's project, or a project entertained by the speaker himself but now dead and buried. If predicated of the subject's present attitude, it is self-defeating, or self-ironical. A *pretence* or *pretension* is a project marked by moral blame on the part of the speaker. Accordingly, it cannot be consistently predicated to the speaker himself, except in the case of a self-critical attitude toward past experience:[371]

(51) Very few men took clerical orders *in the hope of* devoting themselves to pastoral work at parish or diocesan level (BNC)

a. I fished on, more as an act of defiance than *in the hope of* catching anything (BNC)

(52) A couple have been murdered after emigrating from Britain to Jamaica *with the dream of* starting a new life (BNC)

a. "I started out *with a dream* [...] *to* be a musician [...]" Starr said (BNC)

Desire is the hyperonym of the whole paradigm of emotional nouns. It provides a general root meaning which is open to different modulations by its hyponyms.

Wish is an intense sort of desire. *Longing* adds to desire the melancholy of uncertain issue, *yearning* is particularly intense, *eagerness* is impatient, while *anxiety* is a mixture of impatience and fear that the desired objective might not be attained.[372] *Ambition* is qualified by its aim: it is a desire connected with personal achievement, "the desire to be successful, powerful, rich or famous" (Collins Cobuild). The speaker's attitude is neutral between praise and blame, so that a moral evaluation is generally expressed by a modifying adjective:

(53) He was quite prepared to crush her *in his desire to* force her into seeing what she did not wish to see (BNC)

(54) *Out of a desire to* protest against the 'oppression and exploitation' he saw around him, he began to write short stories (BNC)

(55) Many little girls attend a dancing school *with the wish to* become a famous dancer (BNC)

(56) Robert actually trembled *in his longing to* protect and to keep all trouble from her (BNC)

(57) *In his eagerness to* depict the cloudy psychology of an adolescent, Motion has forgotten to give the boy a personality (BNC)

(58) I fear, however, that *in my anxiety to* win the support of Mrs Clements and the girls, I did not perhaps assess quite as stringently my own limitations (BNC)

(59) She [...] returned home in 1928 *with the ambition* of developing ballet in her native land (BNC)

Such predicators as *fear* and *dread* — an intense kind of fear — denote a negative sort of purpose. The phrasal prepositions they are incorporated into are equivalent to the simple preposition *lest*: the agent's purposeful action is not intended to promote the taking place of a positive fact, but to avoid the taking place of a negative one. Forms like (60) and (61) are halfway between purpose forms like (60a) and (61a) and causal forms like (60b) and (61b):

(60) Several employers hereabouts had begun to promise higher payments *under the dread* of seeing the population armed against them (BNC)

a. Neither Andy Saunders nor Peter Dimond shy away from the fact that a broader, more general aviation history needs also to be presented, *lest* "Joe Public" be made to feel alienated (BNC)

b. "Some people now fear living more than dying *because they dread* becoming passive prisoners of technology," said Prof Jennett (BNC)

(61) At one point when my mother was ill, the district nurse refused to enter her home and treat her, *for fear that* she would be contami-

nated and consequently place her other patients in danger (BNC)

a. Tertullian [...] was the first Church Father to declare that Christians ought to abstain on Sunday from secular duties or occupations, *lest* these should give pleasure to the Devil (BNC)

b. Too often in communication we try to teach the other person our language and concepts and then communicate in this language.We do this *because we fear that* the other language may not contain the sophisticated concepts we may need in the communication (BNC)

3.6 Desire, consciousness and freedom

While the predicators of the area of intention and decision spotlight the rational and active side of the subject's motivation and action, emotional predicators connect the subject's decision to its passive and unconscious roots. The concept of desire, the most typical of the whole family, is the best illustration of the tension between action and affection which characterises the field of emotions.

As far as temporal orientation is concerned, both desire and intention contrast with the whole family of backward-looking emotions. Like intentions, and unlike backward-looking emotions, a consistent desire has an intentional content located in the future. By virtue of its forward-looking orientation, desire is ready to put its energy not only at the service of action, but also of purpose and its expression. A backward-looking emotion, on the contrary, is ready to motivate an action (62) but is incompatible with purpose and, *a fortiori*, with its expression (63):

(62) John returned home because he felt a strong regret for the way he had left his parents

(63) *John returned home with the regret of seeing his parents again

At the level of rational control, however, desire and the whole area of emotions jointly contrast with the area of intention. Intention belongs to the conscious side of human action, and is supposed to provide the decision with an overt ground. Desire resembles a blind force springing out of a dark underground, which can lead to decision and action independently of — and even in opposition to — the subject's awareness. Unlike intention, desire confines the subject to a passive role: "Between desiring and doing, there is the difference between passivity and activity" (Ricoeur, 1977: 88). This calls into question not so much the relationship between desire and action, as the relationship between desire, purpose and awareness.

The relationship between desire, decision and action is less immediate than that between intention, decision and action. Intention implies, if not action, a decision to act, while action implies intention. An intention is not consistent if it is not designed to produce action, and therefore accompanied by an act of decision, nor can an instance of behaviour be considered an action unless some intention is attributed to it. As Searle (1983: 82) stresses, "There are many states of affairs without corresponding beliefs and many states of affairs without corresponding desires, but there are in general no actions without corresponding intentions". A desire neither implies purposeful action nor is implied by it. A passive desire is a consistent concept. It is not inconsistent to desire something without deciding, still less without doing anything to attain the object of that desire. Conversely, the consistent aim of an intentional action is not necessarily an object of desire. For instance, if the doorbell rings and I go to open the door, my action necessarily implies the intention and decision of doing so but not the corresponding desire. In spite of this, desire is not only compatible with action, but is also beyond any doubt one of the most powerful springs of human action.

Once it has been admitted that desires motivate actions, the relevant question is whether, or to what extent, the content of a desire may be considered a purpose, which amounts to calling into question the relationship between purpose and awareness.

Intention can be defined as a conscious kind of intentional attitude. When we speak of an intention, it is assumed that the content of which the subject is aware coincides with its real content. When we speak of a desire, it is assumed that a significant part of the intentional content remains below the threshold of awareness: intentionality — a subject's orientation towards an outer object — does not necessarily entail consciousness (Merleau-Ponty, 1945: Part I). Accordingly, if it is contradictory to speak of unconscious intentions, it is absolutely consistent, and on many occasions empirically adequate, to speak of unconscious desires:

(64) *He went home after so many years *with the unconscious intention of* seeing her again

(65) He went home after so many years in the unconscious desire to see her again

To admit a blind desire, unaware of its roots and contents is to admit that the agent who acts spurred by desire is not necessarily and not fully master of his decisions, which are pushed by uncontrolled forces. In other words, if one admits desire as grounds for purposeful action, one also admits that decision and action are not altogether free and responsible.

In a sense, it is a truism that a human being engaged in action is never absolutely free and master of his decisions. His behaviour is constrained both from outside and inside, and above all he is neither necessarily nor fully aware of these constraints. In another sense, a human being engaged in action is necessarily free, for if he were not so it would be senseless to speak of decision, responsibility and action. When we say that acting human beings are not free and when we say that they are free, however, we are not in contradiction, because we use the concept of freedom in two different ways: in an empirical sense, and in an essential (Husserl), or ideal (Kant), or ontological sense.

When used as an empirical concept, freedom is the positive pole of a *continuum* whose negative pole is its deprivation. Absolute empirical freedom is obviously beyond the reach of human beings living inside their own bodies and inside a social group, which implies that the behaviour of any empirical agent locates itself somewhere between freedom and its opposite. More generally, to locate oneself in some satisfying point within this space — to struggle for freedom against inner and outer constraints — is the moral task of any human being. But the struggle for (some degree of) freedom only makes sense if human beings are considered free in the essential sense,[373] that is, if they have access to the logical space of freedom. Taking into account desire simply highlights the intrinsically polyphonic character of the subject's deliberation, torn between reason and desire, described by Aristotle in the *Nicomachean Ethics.*

When used as an essential concept, freedom no longer identifies the positive value of an opposition, but delimits the whole conceptual space of consistent predicability ranging from absolute freedom to its deprivation by some antagonistic force.[374] To state that human beings are free and responsible in an essential sense does not imply that human behaviour is not subject to any kind of inner and outer constraint. It simply amounts to saying, tautologically, that human behaviour can only be conceived of consistently within the horizon of freedom — that freedom and its antagonist forces compete to define human behaviour. Accordingly, the question about freedom and responsibility is relevant even to a consistent description of those instances that might prove to be totally devoid of freedom. Freedom in an essential sense is compatible even with its total deprivation in an empirical sense.

When speaking of freedom in an essential, ontological sense, one is not describing the actual state of some empirical human being — some contingent and frail point of equilibrium between freedom and determinism, self-aware intentions and blind desires — but defining from outside the consistent conceptual space of human behaviour. Once the logical space of freedom is open to human beings, ascertaining what kind of balance between freedom and inner and outer constraints is attained by a given human act of behaviour becomes an empirical question. In particular, it is only when a subject has free access to the space of freedom, responsibility and conscience that it makes sense to ask to what extent he is free, responsible and aware of his decisions and to what extent he is affected by his desires and instincts.[375] Within the bounds of consistency, the question of freedom, responsibility and conscience allows the whole range of answers from one extreme to the other. For an inanimate being the question makes no sense, while it makes sense only in an analogical way for animals.

3.7 At the edges of purpose

When the canonical structure of a purposeful action is constructed through a complex sentence of purposive form, a specialised form of expression is combined with a given conceptual structure — the purpose is the content of an intention — and with a given relational configuration of the complex process — the purpose is a margin of the main predicate. Now, the structures we shall examine in the following paragraphs have in common the fact that one or more of the previous conditions are not satisfied.

The structures described in §3.7.1 display a canonical form of expression but share neither the content nor the structural position of a true purpose clause: a purposive form of expression contains a restructured purposive relation or no purpose at all.

The purpose clauses described in §3.7.2 share the form and the content of a true purpose clause but not its position with regard to the main action, for the purpose is connected with a non-expressed action — the speech act itself.

The structures analysed in §3.7.3, finally, describe true purposeful actions. The expression of purpose, however, is not a margin of the predicate, but an argument of an inherently complex process. As a consequence, the purpose clause is embedded in the syntactic structure of the main action, and its form is controlled by the main verb.

3.7.1 *Coding and consistency: The inferential deconstruction of purpose*

Unlike a complex sentence of causal form like (6), a complex sentence of purposive form like (10) presents "in perspective", to put it in Fillmore's terms, only a section of the complex process framed by a purposeful action:

(6) I took the umbrella *because I wanted* to go out in the rain
(10) I took the umbrella to go out in the rain

When it is expressed by a causal form, the whole conceptual structure of the forward-looking motive is overtly expressed. All its constituents are equally exposed to the light, so to speak, as in a surreal world devoid of shadows. In a complex sentence of purposive form, only part of the conceptual structure is fully exposed to the light, whereas the rest remains in the shadows, like the figures in some paintings by Caravaggio. In particular, the purposive form highlights the part of the stage connecting the action to its future outcome, while leaving in the shade the part occupied by the subject's intention and deliberation.

When looking at one of Caravaggio's paintings, of course, one easily imagines the half figures kept in the shadows thanks to shared models of beings. In the same way, a complex sentence of purposive form can be consistently interpreted as the expression of a purposeful action if one has some access to the conceptual components kept in the shade, that is, if the subject's intention and decision are somehow reintegrated into the content of the expression. This, however, does not necessarily imply that the subjective side of purpose is encoded by the purposive form of expression. When facing a purposive complex sentence, the relevant question is thus the following: how is the hidden section of a purposeful action brought to expression?

The question does not even arise in the presence of such encapsulating nouns as *intention*, *desire*, or *will*, which combine the purposive form of expression and perspective with a direct encoding of the subjective side of the purposeful action. But when such reticent linking words or expressions as *to*, *in order to* or *so that* are used, no explicit reference is made to intention and decision. In this case, it becomes relevant to ask whether the restoration of the subject's intention and decision is due to the coding potential of the linking word or to inferencing, that is, to an evaluation of the ontological properties of the involved processes and entities, and their consistency with the conceptual structure of the purposeful action.

This simple but essential question cannot be answered, it should be noted, as long as consistent instances of complex sentences are focused on. Given such examples as the following:

(10) I took the umbrella to go out in the rain
a. I took the umbrella in order to go out in the rain

one cannot tell to what extent each linking expression has the power to encode the subject's intention and decision. As the main clause actually ideates a consistent action performed by a human being, the presence of intention and decision can easily be inferred independently of the coding potential of each form of expression.

On the contrary, the alternative hypotheses can be directly tested if we observe the behaviour of conflictual complex sentences, that is, sentences combining the formal grammatical structure of a purposive expression with a content which fails to match the conceptual standards of purposeful action. In the case of conflict, if the conceptual structure of the purposeful action is really encoded by the expression form, it cannot be undone under the pressure of conflicting contents. Conversely, if the purposive structure collapses under the pressure of conflicting contents, the obvious conclusion is that the attribution of intention and decision to the subject is not a conventional implicature independent of the connected contents, but a kind of inference, and in particular, as we shall see, an invited inference.

Consider the following pairs of consistent and inconsistent examples:

(66) John took the umbrella in order to go out in the rain
a. The river cuts across the plain in order to flow into the sea

(67) John took the umbrella with the aim of going out in the rain
a. The river cuts across the plain with the aim of flowing into the sea

(68) John took the umbrella to go out in the rain
a. The river cuts across the plain to flow into the sea

Forms (66) and (67) really encode the whole conceptual structure of a purposeful action, including the subject's intention and deliberation, which are activated as conventional implicatures. The proof is that in (66a) and (67a), in spite of the presence of inconsistent contents, the implicature that there is an intention and deliberation on the part of the subject is not dismantled, so that the non-human subject is humanised. In the form (68), on the contrary, the presence of an intentional subject is only inferred, because it does not survive in the presence of an ontological obstacle, as shown by (68a). In (68a), the presence of an inanimate subject in the main action obstructs the inference about intention and decision, and the whole structure of the purposeful action is dismantled. This means that the form *to + infinitive* does not encode a purposive relation.

When the conceptual standards of a purposeful action are not satisfied, a set of conceptually simpler options is available, each of which deconstructs the structure of purposeful action to a certain extent.

The least radical case of inferential deconstruction is illustrated by such expressions as the following:

(69) Plants have roots to feed themselves (with)

(70) The microtubules condense in the cell cortex around the cell equator to form a band, which becomes more and more compressed during prophase (BNC)

In both cases, the connected contents do not match the conceptual model of a purposeful action. In spite of the conflict between form and content, however, purpose is not dismantled but redefined, for the co-occurring concepts are compatible with an objective kind of purpose. Purpose is dissociated from human intention, deliberation and action, and projected onto the phenomenal order. The idea of a teleological organisation is in fact our shared way of categorising the relationship of adequacy perceived by human beings between the structure of living beings and their function: the function of roots, for instance, is really to feed plants.[376]

The most immediate interpretation of such expressions as (71) and (72) implies that the content of the subordinate clause does not describe the subject's intention, but an event which frustrates it, as shown by a comparison with (71a) and (72a):

(71) He went to bed early only to lie awake all night

a. He went to bed early only because he wanted to lie awake all night

(72) She began to turn into the hotel park, only to find her way blocked by the Mercedes (BNC)

a. She began to turn into the hotel park, only because she wanted to find her way blocked by the Mercedes

This antiphrastic component of the consistent complex process can be made explicit, without loss of ideational content, by an adversative paraphrase:

(71) b. He went to bed early but lay awake all night

(72) b. She began to turn into the hotel park but found her way blocked by the Mercedes

When the main process is not an action performed with a view to a purpose, any link between purposive form and purposive content is severed. Such examples as:

(68) a. The river cuts across the plain to flow into the sea
(73) Many a flower is born to blush unseen (BNC)
(74) We are [...] flowers pent in vases with our roots sliced off, to shine a day and perish (BNC)

are normally taken as expressing relations of temporal sequence or at best cause, which are made explicit by such paraphrases as

(68) b. After crossing the plain, the river flows into the sea
(73) a. Many a flower is born and then blushes unseen
(74) a. Being flowers pent in vases with our roots sliced off, we shall shine a day and perish

Of course, an inconsistent and metaphorical purposive interpretation is one of the admitted options, and can be activated in the presence of a favouring context:

(75) The wind blows southward to hinder us from landing on the island

The activation of a purposive interpretation of the forms *to + infinitive* follows the typical path of invited inference. An invited inference is an inference that is encouraged until there is proof of the contrary when a given expression is used. If some obstacle arises either from the connected contents or from the data of the interpretation field, the invited inference is ready to make room for an alternative admitted option. Whereas an ordinary inference is actually drawn under the positive pressure of a consistent conceptual background, an invited inference is dismantled under the negative pressure of a conflicting conceptual background. This is precisely what happens when a purposive form *to + infinitive* is used.

If all the conceptual and contextual conditions for a consistent purposeful action are given, intention and decision are attributed to the subject, and the structure of a purposeful action is fully activated. If some of these conditions are lacking, the invited inference about the subject's intention and decision is deconstructed down to the point of consistency. In (68a), (73) and (74), the invited purposive interpretation is blocked by an ontological obstacle: neither a river nor a flower can perform an action. In (71) and (72), the obstacle is cognitive: to remain awake is not seen as the true intention which prompts one to go to bed. Likewise, having one's way blocked is not the reason for turning into a park. Deprived of its purposive content as a void shell, the formal scaffolding of the purposive form is reduced to its perspectival function: the purposive form imposes on the temporal sequence of events its characteristic unifying perspective, which depicts the main action as an arrow flying towards its final destination.

In the light of the last few remarks, purpose can certainly be seen as the specific semantic content of a specific form of expression. At the same time, the purposive form does not necessarily encode the essential conceptual constituent of purpose, that is, the subject's intention. When it does not, the result is an apparently paradoxical mix of overcoded perspective and undercoded conceptual structure. This mix, however, has nothing surprising about it, for either layer of the complex purposive content — that is, temporal perspective and conceptual content — can be entrusted to different means of expression.

3.7.2 *The purpose of the speech act*

Some complex sentences contain subordinate clauses which, though sharing the typical form of a non-finite purpose clause and expressing a purposive content, do not take part in ideating the content of what is said but directly motivate the performance of the speech act:

(76) To sum up, then, English has a very definite and complex grammar with some variation (Quirk).
(77) To be sincere, I would rather sleep instead of eating something
(78) To tell the truth, Kate was anxious to change her job (Swan 1980)
(79) To be frank I was a bit upset with the way it finished (BNC)
(80) I'm sure, sir, but to speak frankly, the Great Army prefers to rely upon its own enquiries into such matters (BNC)

Such constructions as these share some features with the expression of motive for thinking and speaking, but are different for two reasons. First, purpose clauses can affect only the speech act. Owing to their forward-looking perspective, they could hardly apply to an act of inference whose premise is located in the past. Second, they occupy the initial position, like a subset of adverbs affecting the speech act:

(81) Sincerely, I would rather sleep instead of eating something
(82) Frankly, the Great Army prefers to rely upon its own enquiries into such matters

The complex configuration contains a purpose clause (*To tell the truth*) and an independent clause (*Kate was anxious to change her job*), hence *p*, which however does not express the main action connected with the purpose. Again, as in the case of motive for thinking and speaking, there is no structural relationship between the two clauses, for each of them bears an independent relationship with a speech act which has no linguistic expression but is directly exhibited by the speaker's behaviour. Again, the lack of any direct structural relationship between the two clauses is confirmed by the behaviour of the complex sentence.

The subject of a non-finite purpose clause is controlled by the agent of the main process. In the previous examples, this agent does not coincide with the subject of the independent clause, which does not express the main action, but with the agent of the speech act, and therefore with the speaker himself.

As the independent clause does not express the relevant action, the purpose clause can neither be connected to an anaphoric substitute of *p*'s predicate, nor can it be cleft:

(78) a. *Kate was anxious to change her job. She did it to tell the truth
b. *It is to tell the truth that Kate was anxious to change her job

As in the case of the motive for speaking, the first structure breaks down because neither the pro-predicate *do it* nor its subject find within the expression their antecedent, that is, the unexpressed speech act and speaker. The second structure fails because clefting presupposes a given relationship between the cleft constituent — the purpose clause — and *p*. But there is no such a relationship here.

The purpose clause and the independent clause are no more than two floating fragments of a submerged complex process that includes both. Both the purpose clause and the independent clause are constituents of the speech act, which takes *p* as its content and the subordinate clause as its purpose. Outside the speech act, no relationship holds between its content and its purpose.

For the same reason, if the action of speaking is expressed, the complex process recovers its unitary structure: *p* expresses the object of the verb of saying, and the purpose clause its aim:

(83) To tell the truth, I tell you that Kate was anxious to change her job

Under such conditions, the purpose clause recovers its canonical position at the margins of the main predicate. As such, it can both be connected with an anaphoric substitute of the predicate and undergo clefting:

(83) a. I tell you that Kate was anxious to change her job. I do it to tell the truth
b. It is to tell the truth that I tell you that Kate was anxious to change her job

The previous remarks are true insofar as the structural scaffolding of the complex process is concerned. If communicative function is taken into account, however, things become rather paradoxical. The expression of the speech act certainly restores the structural unity of the complex process, but at the price of undermining its function. If purpose is directly connected with the expression of the speech act, as in (83), its content, that is, the subject's intention to tell the truth, is explicitly treated as the main purpose of the speech act itself. Now, this corresponds neither to the content of (78) nor to what a speaker is normally expected to do. In the following examples, such a perspectival deformation of the communicative structure of the speech act displays a *crescendo* from (78) to (83b):

(78) To tell the truth, Kate was anxious to change her job

(83) To tell the truth, I tell you that Kate was anxious to change her job

b. It is to tell the truth that I tell you that Kate was anxious to change her job

In (78), the speaker's assumed purpose is to communicate a given message, whereas his intention to tell the truth remains in the background. In (83), and above all in (83b), this intention is explicitly offered as the main purpose of the speech act.

When a speaker wants to make his attitude known to the addressee, a structurally floating expression, functionally connected to the direct ostension of the speech act, performs this duty better than an expression perfectly integrated into a well-constructed grammatical structure. If one ever sees a paradox in this, it is only because one is victim of the prejudice that sees explicit coding as functionally preferable to any indirect form of communication. Now, when a speaker's attitude has to be made known, the opposite is true: a floating expression immediately anchored in the speech act itself upstages the speaker's attitude, avoiding any interference with the internal equilibrium of what is said.

3.7.3 *Purpose as argument*

Purpose is not a margin of the predicate but an argument of the predicator when the main verb denotes an intrinsically purposive action. This happens, in particular, in the presence of verbs of motion, verbs of trying and directive[377] verbs.

Intransitive and transitive motion verbs are ready to receive two different kinds of goal, that is, a prepositional phrase expressing the goal of the movement and an embedded clause expressing a purpose intrinsically connected with the main action. This behaviour is consistent with the prevailing categorisation of purpose as a metaphorical kind of goal:

(84) I went to the baker's
(85) I went to get some bread
(86) Ann sent George to the baker's
(87) Ann sent George to buy some bread

Intransitive verbs of trying denote actions whose intrinsic purpose is an action to be performed by the main agent itself:

(88) I tried to track down an ancient vase.

Transitive directive verbs denote actions whose intrinsic purpose is an action to be performed by the addressee of the speech act:

(89) I persuaded Jessica to read the letter
(90) I convinced George to leave.
(91) I begged Steve to help me.

The content of the quoted embedded clauses is certainly a purpose. This however does not mean that an independent purpose is connected to an independent action, but rather that the main action, be it a movement in space, an attempt or a directive, is an intentional act intrinsically oriented towards a purpose. One cannot simply go or send someone — one has to go or send someone somewhere or to do something. One cannot simply try or persuade someone — one has to try, or persuade someone, to do something. This intuition is confirmed by some behavioural properties of embedded purpose clauses.

As true arguments, embedded purpose clauses cannot be detached even through the pro-predicate *do it*:

(85) I went to get some bread
a. *I went. I did it to get some bread

(87) Ann sent George to buy some bread
a. *Ann sent George. She did it to buy some bread

(88) I tried to track down an ancient vase.
a. *I tried. I did it to track down an ancient vase.

(89) I persuaded Jessica to read the letter.
a. *I persuaded Jessica. I did it to read the letter.

The incompatibility between the pro-predicate *do it* and the purpose embedded clause is not simply a matter of inconsistency, but of grammatical ill-formedness. The anaphoric substitution cuts out a true grammatical relation, which cannot be displaced outside the sentence structure, that is, the relation between the main predicator and its object.

In examples (87a) and (89a), moreover, the anaphoric substitution cuts out the elliptical subject of the non-finite purpose clause from the coreferential argument that controls it from within the main action.

When a purpose clause is a margin of the predicate, its elliptical subject coincides in any case with the main action's agent, irrespective of its specific content. As it takes over the main action's subject, the substitute *do it* does not disrupt the relationship of control:

(10) I took the umbrella to go out in the rain
b. I took the umbrella. I did it to go out in the rain

In the presence of completive relations, on the contrary, it is the main predicator that determines which among its arguments controls the elliptical subject of the embedded clause. With verbs of motion, the subject of the completive clause coincides with the entity that undergoes motion, that is, with the subject in the case of intransitive verbs and with the direct object in the case of transitive verbs:

(85) I_i went $ø_i$ to get some bread
(87) Ann sent $George_i$ $ø_i$ to buy some bread

With verbs of trying, the subject of the completive clause coincides with the main action's subject:

(88) I_i tried $ø_i$ to track down an ancient vase.

With directive verbs, the subject of the completive clause coincides with the addressee of the directive:

(89) I persuaded $Jessica_i$ $ø_i$ to read the letter

If the embedded subject is controlled by the subject of the main clause, the relationship is not broken, because it is taken over by the substitute *do it*, as in (85a) and (88a). If the embedded subject is controlled by another argument, the relationship is broken, because the pro-predicate *do it* neutralises the argument structure of the main predicate, as in (87a) and (88a). In both cases, in the absence of the main predicator that controls it, the relationship loses its transparency.

As it is controlled by the main verb, the expression of purpose as an argument is severely constrained, and therefore barred to the range of forms that are open to the expression of purpose as a margin. Examples (b–d), below, show that any form other than *to + infinitive* blocks the control of the embedded clause's subject by the main predicator:

(85) I went to get some bread
b. *I went in order to get some bread
c. *I went with the aim of getting some bread
d. *I went with the desire of getting some bread

(87) Ann sent George to buy some bread
b. *Ann sent George in order to buy some bread
c. *Ann sent George with the aim of buying some bread
d. *Ann sent George with the desire of buying some bread

(88) I tried to track down an ancient vase
b. *I tried in order to track down an ancient vase
c. *I tried with the aim of tracking down an ancient vase
d. *I tried with the desire of tracking down an ancient vase

(89) I persuaded Jessica to read the letter
b. *I persuaded Jessica in order to read the letter
c. *I persuaded Jessica with the aim of reading the letter
d. *I persuaded Jessica with the desire of reading the letter

Unlike a non-expressed margin, a non-expressed argument remains latent. This makes it possible to interpret some of the last examples as expressing canonical purpose clauses on the assumption that the main clause contains a non-expressed inner purpose:

(89) e. I persuaded Jessica [to ø]. I did it in order to read the letter
f. I persuaded Jessica [to ø]. I did it with the aim of reading the letter
g. I persuaded Jessica [to ø]. I did it with the desire of reading the letter

With verbs of motion, the latency is less perceptible, for once the goal is specified the process looks complete, and therefore ready to receive a purpose in the position of margin:

(92) I went to the baker's to get some bread
(93) I went to the baker's with the aim of getting some bread
(94) I went to the baker's. I did it with the aim of getting some bread

Finally, the main verb controls the ontological status of the embedded process.

The content of a marginal purpose clause can coincide with any kind of process, on condition that the main agent can exert some control over it. The content of a completive purpose clause, on the contrary, is by definition an action, as in (95), or a state of affairs resulting from action, as in (96):

(95) I persuaded George to leave before half past eight
(96) I persuaded Ann to slim before she goes to the seaside

The properties examined show that the expression of purpose as an argument is a normal completive clause, and thus the term of a grammatical relation that is as such devoid of content. If the clause receives a purposive content, it is not because of the intrinsic properties of a linking word, as in the area of punctual coding, but because of the control exerted on it by the main predicator through the grammatical relation direct or indirect object.[378]

Chapter 11

Conflictual complex meanings

A philosophical grammar of tropes

The object of this chapter is a linguistic description of the main figures of the content plane, or tropes, that is, oxymoron, metonymy, synecdoche and metaphor.

Looked at from the standpoint of a philosophical grammar, tropes can be defined as figures of conceptual conflict, which valorise the creative power of linguistic structures in constructing complex concepts. A conflictual complex meaning is a meaning which, besides containing a supplement of structure due to the presence of a conflict, shares all the qualifying properties of complex linguistic meanings in general. On this assumption, nothing prevents us from describing oxymoron, metonymy, synecdoche and metaphor as if they were in the first instance linguistic expressions, which possess both a grammatical structure and a semantic content, and are normally used to convey messages in communication.

The reader of this book will perhaps not be too surprised that a study about complex meanings ends with an analysis of conceptual conflicts. Yet, the study of tropes is traditionally kept apart from the mainstream of linguistic research. Tropes are sometimes located below the proper object of linguistic enquiry; sometimes, they are located above it; very seldom are they considered an essential part of it.

An epistemological prejudice shared by most philosophers of language and linguists is made explicit by Carnap's idea that inconsistent sentences are *Scheinsätze*, that is, deceitful arrays of words which have only the outer appearance of true sentences. According to Chomsky, conflictual sentences are deviant (Chomsky, 1957), or even ungrammatical (Chomsky, 1965). At best, they can be considered "semi-sentences" (Katz, 1964), which only possess a low "degree of grammaticalness" (Chomsky, 1964).

The structural prejudice towards conflictual meanings is paralleled by a sort of pragmatic censure. If conflictual expressions are ultimately interpreted in actual discourse, it is not because they are true sentences articulating true meanings which can be used as indexes of coherent messages, but owing to special interpretative strategies which are not required when consistent expressions are used: "Indirectness and figurativeness are in some ways parasitic on canonical situations, where language use is direct and conventional (though perhaps less than fully explicit) and where the aims of communication are the cooperative exchange of information"[379] (Chierchia & McConnel-Ginet, 1990: 202).

Whilst most linguists and philosophers locate conflictual meanings below language, literary rhetoric seems to assume that tropes are above language. Tropes are not seen as linguistic expressions which have a specific grammatical structure and semantic content, but are viewed as if they were made out of a separate essence of their own. The ideation of tropes is more or less explicitly attributed to a kind of deviation — or *écart* — from plain linguistic expression, incommensurable with it. This idea, which confuses creation and transgression,[380] is a sort of native theory that transfers into the field of artistic creation the naive attitude of the average reader of literary texts.

The average reader meets conceptual conflicts within the same texts which push to interpret them as tropes. Under such circumstances, one is obviously inclined to bypass the structural reality of the conflict and jump immediately to its contingent textual solution. As a consequence, inconsistent sentences are not taken as if they directly meant inconsistent concepts, but as if they indirectly meant consistent concepts that were in some way accessible.[381] For instance, by way of analogy, as Fielding humorously underlines:

> At least the Ocean, that hospitable friend to the wretched, opened her capacious arms to receive him [Tom Jones]; and he instantly resolved to accept her kind invitation. To express myself less figuratively, he determined to go to sea.

Likewise, the speaking flowers depicted in the following passage are not taken by the average reader as if they were actually said to speak, but simply as if their imposing beauty intensely invited the observer to pick them:

> The flowers [...] whispered, as she passed, "Adorn thyself with me, thou beautiful child, adorn thyself with me!" — and, to please them, Pearl gathered the violets, and anemones, and columbines, and some twigs of the freshest green, which the old trees held down before her eyes (Hawthorne).

If our spontaneous attitude is directly transferred into the domain of analysis, describing a trope does not amount to analysing the grammatical structure and meaning of a linguistic expression, but to apprehending a contingent textual value. The complex and multi-layered structure of a trope is reduced to one of its contingent interpretations, which hides the structure of the conflict just as a building hides its foundations. Now, a linguist should not forget that the figurative elaboration of a complex meaning, far from effacing the grammatical and semantic properties of the linguistic expression, and in particular the conceptual conflict, presupposes them.

A peculiar position within this landscape is occupied by cognitive metaphorology (see, for instance, Lakoff & Johnson, 1981 and Lakoff & Turner, 1989). Cognitive metaphorology does not share the assumption that metaphors, and in general tropes, are deviant kinds of expression. On the contrary, they are considered expressions of the most typical kind, that is, expressions which guarantee the elaboration and social circulation of shared concepts, from the most down-to-earth to the most sophisticated. In this way, cognitive metaphorology readmits metaphors into the mainstream of linguistic expression and categorisation, but it does so at the price of reducing linguistic expression to a mere instrument at the service of the social circulation of independent conceptual structures. Metaphors are admitted into the domain of linguistics only insofar as they are consistent conceptual structures independent of their specific linguistic articulation. Accordingly, the role of linguistic expression in shaping concepts, which is highlighted by the construction of conflictual complex meaning, is seriously underestimated.

The common denominator of all the perspectives so far examined is a negative attitude towards conceptual conflict. Whether it is confined to the pathology of language, bypassed to focus on its contingent textual solution, or simply left aside and negated, the conceptual conflict is never acknowledged as a true semantic structure. In the following paragraphs, tropes in general and metaphor in particular will not be immediately described as cognitive strategies for solving conceptual problems, but as linguistic expressions ideating conflictual complex meanings. The reason for this choice is that the structure of the conceptual conflict, that is, the conditions under which a conceptual conflict roots itself in the structure of a linguistic expression, is the only conceivable object of a linguistic description of tropes. If conceptual conflict is not taken into account, the ground itself for such a study disappears. Conversely, a linguistic description of tropes can take as its only starting point the inner structure and typology of conceptual conflicts.

The meaning of a metaphorical expression is not any solution the conflict is open towards, but the conceptual conflict itself.[382] Any solution of a conceptual conflict is by definition a contingent and reversible option, belonging to the indexical dimension. It is contingent because its relevance can only be assessed on the background of a given text or communicative situation. It is reversible because any contingent solution for a conceptual conflict can both lose its relevance in another use of the expression and be challenged by competing options within the same text or situation. And it is indexical because its content is the outcome of an act of inferential interpretation in a given field. A conflictual complex meaning, for its part, is a long-lasting semantic structure of the symbolic order, whose formal and conceptual constituents can be exactly described as any complex semantic structure can.

In order to illustrate this point, let us consider Alcman's famous *Nocturne*,[383] and in particular the conflictual expression in the first two lines:

> They sleep, the mountain peaks,
> the clefts, ridges, and gullies
> and all the creatures that the dark earth feeds,
> the animals of the glen, the tribe of bees,
> the monsters of the salt purple deeps.
> They sleep, the tribes
> of winging birds.

The meaning of the expression is absolutely clear: it attributes the conflictual state of sleeping to mountains and other inanimate beings. Due to the conflict, the complex meaning acquires a surplus of structure, that is, supplementary concepts and relations: the mountains are opposed to the consistent subjects of sleeping, that is, to animate beings, while a virtual double of the verb, consistent with the actual subject — with the mountains — is ready to be called on stage. But what about the solution?

The first point to be stressed is that a metaphorical interpretation, however natural it seems, is a contingent textual option for a conflictual meaning. As we have already observed, our expression could be meant to describe an alien world, crowded with animate mountains: in this case it would not be taken as conflictual, and even less as metaphorical.

Within the limits of our shared world, the conceptual conflict can be interpreted either as a metonymy, if the subject is focused on, or as a metaphor, if the verb is. In the former case, it is not the mountains that sleep, but the living beings that inhabit them, consistent with the predicate. The paradigm opposing the mountains to the living beings triggers a shift in reference.

If a metonymy is activated, the conflict simply disappears. If the metaphorical option is chosen, as the co-text seems to encourage, the conflict is not avoided but has to be passed through, so to speak. At this point, one is tempted to think that the metaphorical solution coincides with the identification of some analogy, but this is of no use, for analogy is not necessarily a definite and substantive kind of relation. Nobody can say once and for all, for instance, in what sense mountains are said to sleep.

In the presence of metaphorical verbs, and more generally of relational metaphors, the unpredictability of analogy acquires a supplementary dimension. The conceptual interaction is allowed to take two different formal frames and to follow two different paths, which are not alternative but ready to overlap to some extent. To say that mountains sleep, for instance, is either a way of projecting the model of sleeping upon a consistent state of the mountains, or a way of projecting on the mountains the model of animate beings, which can sleep. In the former case, the paradigm opposing a consistent state of mountains to sleeping is taken as substitutive: sleeping stands for something else. In the latter, the paradigm opposing the mountains to living beings is not taken as substitutive, but as purely interactive, and there is no shift in reference: mountains do not stand for something else, but are seen as if they were something else. In either case, the set of options open to interpretation spans from some trivial and ready-made analogy — for instance, the peaceful immobility of the mountains reminds one of a sleeping creature — to the most unpredictable and unexplored issues.

At the source of such a complex constellation of configurations and interactions of concepts there is one single expression, which has both a canonical syntactic structure and a conflictual meaning. While any solution is a contingent and reversible outcome of an occasional interpretative act, the conflictual meaning is an endlessly renewable source of conceptual energy, whose potential spans far beyond any imaginable solution it may receive on given occasions.

A conflictual meaningful expression is not different in structure from any complex meaningful expression, and is open to analysis as any complex meaningful expression is. What forms its specificity, is a surplus of structure, which coincides with the inner formal configuration of the conflict. The conflicting focal concept can occupy different positions within the structure of the sentence: it can coincide with a noun, referential or predicative, or with a verb, an adjective or an adverb. In each case, the conflict is constrained by a specific formal frame, which circumscribes a specific set of interpretative paths.

The first step of our study of conflictual complex meanings is a typology of conflicts. In particular, a distinction between contradiction (§1) and inconsistency[384] (§2) provides the semantic ground for the distinction between oxymoron (§3) and the most typical instances of metonymy, synecdoche and metaphor.

A careful analysis of the distribution of tropes within the sentence structure provides at one and the same time a typology of the inner forms open to conceptual conflicts and a first ground for the distinction between synecdoche, metonymy and metaphor (§4). The traditional distinction between synecdoche, metonymy and metaphor assumes that any trope is a kind of transfer and is therefore based on the nature of the transfer, that is part-whole relation, contiguity and analogy, respectively. In fact, both assumptions are false. Metaphor is the only trope that transfers concepts in stranger domains, while metonymy and synecdoche connect concepts within consistent domains. Metonymy and synecdoche are punctual tropes confined to saturated concepts, and in the first place to referential nouns; metaphors are punctual or relational transfers which are accessible to all the categorematic classes of words in all their uses. Accordingly, the alternative between metaphor, metonymy and synecdoche is restricted to the nominal domain. Even within the borders of the nominal domain, finally, analogy cannot be reduced to a definite track guiding the transfer, but coincides with the absence of any definite track.

The final section of this chapter deals with the inexhaustible realm of metaphor (§5). A metaphor can be consistent as well as inconsistent, simply expressed as well as constructed by a specific linguistic expression, based on a substantive analogy or projected towards an unknown end point. Once one realises the full complexity of the domain, the reply to the Socratic question — What is metaphor? — can define a common essence shared by all metaphors only at the price of leaving out of its scope the most interesting instances of metaphors. If a general definition of metaphor can be framed, therefore, it is only to provide grounds for a differential typology of the heterogeneous family of metaphorical transfers. At this point, what remains to be done is to isolate, using a set of structural parameters, the most typical kind of metaphor, which best illustrates the potential of conceptual creation open to the figure.

1. The structure of contradiction

Contradiction takes place when two opposite terms are syntactically connected within a single expression uttered by a single speaker and without temporal cleavage. This means that the analysis of contradiction includes a description of both the kinds of underlying opposition and the forms of syntactic connection between the opposite terms.

1.1 Kinds of opposition

> [He] now wandered in a kind of limbo,
> because he wasn't good or bad enough [...]
> Life didn't exist any more (Greene)

The most immediate, direct kind of opposition is the relation between a term and its negation, for instance "good" vs "not good", or "to be a woman" vs "not to be a woman". The opposition is a case of paradigmatic correlation, defined by Hjelmslev (1943(1961)) as the 'either-or' function. The opposite terms can consistently substitute for each other as determinations of a given subject but cannot jointly apply to it, that is, they are incompatible with the 'both-and' function. A human being, for instance, can be consistently said to be either good or not good, but not to be both good and not good.[385]

If negation creates opposition, the domain of opposition is not confined to negation, but includes lexical contrasts. Such pairs as "good" vs "bad", or such series as "hot" vs "warm" vs "cool" vs "cold" are instances of opposition (Lyons, 1977: 275). A human being, for instance, can be consistently said to be either good or bad, but cannot be said to be both good and bad. A stone can be consistently said to be either hot, or warm, or cool, or cold, but not to be at the same time warm and cold, or cool and hot, or hot and warm, or cool and cold.

In a syntactically built paradigm, two terms form an exclusive opposition, which divides the universe of discourse into two complementary subsets (Lyons, 1977: 271). Between "good" and "not good", for instance, *tertium non datur*. If it is false that a person is good, it is automatically true that he is not good. In lexical paradigms, on the contrary, exclusivity coexists with grading. A correlation like "alive" vs "dead", for instance, forms an exclusive paradigm: a creature that is not alive can only be dead. In other cases, however, the opposition is graded, and a neutral territory can be found between two polar terms. In presence of such series as "hot" vs "warm" vs "lukewarm" vs "cool" vs "cold", this is obviously shown by the availability of intermediate concepts between the polar values. In other cases, as with "good" vs "bad", this neutral territory is not expressed in words but is nevertheless conceptually accessible. If a man is not good, for instance, he is not necessarily bad — he can also be neither good nor bad.[386]

Lexical oppositions define a homogeneous conceptual space. Death, for instance, is as positive a reality as life itself. The correlative concepts of life and death, for instance, define the whole destiny of living creatures, and their consistent predicability keeps them apart from the realm of non-living beings.

The correlations between a term and its negation, on the contrary, are typically asymmetric. While "living" defines a positive and homogeneous concept, for instance, the notion of "non-living" defines a negative and non-homogeneous area, which includes the deprivation of life through an antagonistic force as well as the pure lack of life. In the former case, the concept can only be applied consistently to living creatures; in the latter, it can also be applied to inanimate beings: to a stone or to a heavenly body.[387]

If two terms of a paradigm are connected within a syntagmatic relation, the result is in any case a contradiction, no matter if the paradigm is syntactic or lexical, exclusive or gradable: *Peter is alive and non-alive*; *Peter is alive and dead*; *Peter is good and bad*; *This coffee is hot and lukewarm.*

1.2 The syntactic configuration of contradiction

There are three main ways of syntactically connecting opposite terms in a relationship of contradiction: predicative relation, modification and coordination.

The predicative relation — a typical exocentric construction connecting two complementary constituents into a higher order structure — is preferred when the correlative terms are nouns — *This stone is not a stone* — and also possible when an adjective is the predicate of a noun: *Jugum meum suave est, et onus meum leve* (Matthew).

The relation of modification connects terms belonging to different ranks into an endocentric subordinative structure — typically a head-noun and a modifying adjective, or a verb and a modifying adverb: *Cette obscure clarté qui tombe des étoiles* (Corneille); *It always seemed to me a sort of clever stupidity only to have one sort of talent* (G. Eliot); *Les legislateurs des pays membres se hâtent lentement d'harmoniser leurs législations* (Journal de Genève); *'Twas not my blame — who sped too slow* (Dickinson).

The coordination of the opposite terms, jointly applied to a given subject, is the more open form, ready to receive any term of equal rank: *Odi et amo*[388] (Catullus: *I hate and love); Ann is a woman and is not a woman*; *I lived six years in this happy but unhappy condition* (Defoe).

More elaborate forms, distributing the correlative concepts among less predictable positions or within more complex relationships, can be found in texts: *A deep, autumnal tone, / Sweet though in sadness* (Shelley); *Nella mia infedeltà sono sempre stata fedelissima* (L'Espresso); *Occidis nos, ne moriamur abs te* (St. Augustine); *You cause him to die daily a living death* (Hawthorne). In any case, for a contradiction to occur, it is essential that an underlying correlation between opposite concepts be detectable.

The resources of the different forms of expression are unequal. The head-modifier structure is the most highly praised in literary texts, and therefore the most typical form taken by oxymoron, the figure of contradiction par excellence.[389] The coordinative form, which simultaneously attributes to a subject two opposite predicates, and the predicative form, identifying a term with its opposite, offer the epistemological advantage of directly displaying the essential logical property of contradiction — its being the simultaneous attribution of two opposite properties to a single subject.

2. The structure of inconsistency

2.1 Inconsistency as a kind of synthetic predication

> Lorsqu'une proposition n'est pas identique,
> c'est à dire lorsque le prédicat
> n'est pas compris expressément dans le sujet,
> il faut qu'il y soit compris virtuellement (Leibniz)

Inconsistency can affect any node of a sentence structure.[390] We can find or imagine as many kinds of inconsistent links as functional or conceptual links:

a. between a subject and a predicate: *My heart was a habitation* (Hawthorne); *The little stream [...] still kept telling its unintelligible secret* (Hawthorne);
b. between a verb and a direct object: *This City now doth, like a garment, wear / The beauty of the morning* (Wordsworth) — or another kind of complement: *She had wandered, without rule or guidance, in a moral wilderness* (Hawthorne);
c. between a verb and a modifier: *I tried to burst open the door, but it stubbornly resisted* (Melville);
d. between the core of a predicate and an instrument: *I miei buoni parenti ricamavano con seta e oro mille e mille progetti sul mio avvenire* (Dossi); *The flower of beauty [...] / Never fleets more, fastened with tenderest truth / To its own best being and its loveliness of youth* (Hopkins);
e. between a complete predication and its circumstances: *A thousand smiths' hammers are beating in my head* (E. Brontë);
f. On the scale of noun phrase, between a noun and a complement — *A fountain of friendship* (G. Eliot) — or between a noun and a modifier: *Un canuto pomeriggio* (Fenoglio: *A bald afternoon*).

In order to define the specific properties of inconsistency, we do not have to range over the whole set of relevant connections. In fact, it will be enough to focus on one of these relationships — namely, that between a subject and a predicate. Apart from being the most basic functional connection to be found within sentence structure, the subject-predicate link offers the additional advantage of making possible a direct comparison between inconsistency — *This stone is sleeping*, for instance — and the two most direct forms of contradiction, namely the identifying form — *This stone is not a stone* — and the coordinative form: *This stone is cold and warm.*

Let us begin by comparing an inconsistent instance of predication — *This stone is sleeping* — with an instance of contradiction of the coordinative form — *This stone is warm and cold.*

The contradiction — *This stone is warm and cold* — does not involve the relation between the subject and the predicate, but is confined to the predicate. The coordinated constituents of the predicate enter into contradiction because they are opposite terms, but either of them is perfectly compatible with the subject: a warm stone is as consistent an object as a cold stone. This means that a contradiction of the coordinative form is grafted onto a consistent predicative structure.

Unlike contradiction, inconsistency directly affects the relation between subject and predicate. In the sentence *This stone is sleeping*, for instance, the predicate is conceptually incompatible with the subject. When involving the immediate constituent structure of a predication, inconsistency and contradiction are, so to speak, perpendicular structures. Whereas inconsistency links a subject with a conflicting predicate, contradiction connects a subject with two consistent predicates conflicting with each other. Since they are not coextensive, the two structures can be superimposed within a single sentence, cumulating an inconsistent predicative link and a contradictory compound predicate. Within such a sentence as *This stone is sleeping and awake*, for instance, two coordinate predicates, both inconsistent with the subject, contradict each other.

When it takes the identifying form, as in *This stone is not a stone*, the contradiction directly affects the relationship between subject and predicate. In this case, however, the contradictory identification of two opposite terms is no more than the negative counterpart of a tautology. A contradiction like *This stone is not a stone*, for instance, simply negates the tautological identification *This stone is a stone.*

An inconsistent predication like *This stone is sleeping*, of course, cannot be reduced to the negative counterpart of a bare tautology. As it applies to the subject an informative, though inconsistent predicate, an inconsistent predication is a kind of synthetic predication, the inconsistent counterpart of a consistent synthetic predication like *This stone is warm.* Unlike the terms of a tautology, the main constituents of a synthetic predication cannot be reduced to a pair of identical terms. Unlike the terms of a contradiction, the main constituents of an inconsistent synthetic predication cannot be reduced to a couple of opposite terms. An inconsistent synthetic predication shares with its consistent counterpart the inclination towards a determination of the subject; it simply pushes this determination beyond the borders of consistency.

The direct comparison of contradiction and inconsistency makes visible their structural differences. If it co-ordinates two opposite predicates, a contradiction coexists with a structurally independent synthetic and consistent predicative link. If it directly affects the predicative structure, a contradiction is no more than the negation of a tautological identification of the subject with itself. Either because it is not involved in it, or because it fails to satisfy its requirements, a contradiction, unlike inconsistency, cannot be considered as a true form of predicative connection.

Though not reducing itself to a kind of contradiction, an inconsistent sentence encapsulates a contradiction of the identifying form at the level of its presuppositions — it is built up, so to speak, on contradictory foundations. When Blake writes that *The moon smiles*, for instance, he applies to a heavenly body, which is inanimate — and thus non-human — a predicate whose consistent use presupposes a human subject. Thus, the identity of the subject with itself is negated at the level of presuppositions. When it is said to smile, the moon is no longer the moon. With the help of a rather cumbersome but useful device, we can easily bring the hidden contradiction to the surface of the expression: *The moon, which is* a non-human being, *smiles, which presupposes that it* is a human being. A building does not reduce itself to its foundations — once the foundations have been laid, the building has yet to be constructed. So inconsistency does not reduce itself to contradiction. Nevertheless, the foundations are an essential part of the building and essentially affect its shape and functions.

If the inconsistent predication encapsulates a contradiction, its consistent counterpart can reasonably be expected to encapsulate a tautology. A consistent predication cannot directly state the identity of the subject without falling into mere tautology, but is bound to safeguard it in order to avoid inconsistency. The presence of an encapsulated tautology succeeds in performing both tasks. Such a synthetic sentence as *The moon shines*, for instance, applies to the subject a predicate which confirms its identity with itself: *The moon, which is* an inanimate being, is *shining, a process which applies to* an inanimate being. When it is said to shine, the moon remains the moon.

The coordinative form of contradiction, as we have seen, is grafted on a consistent predicative link. Accordingly, it is reasonable to expect that a contradictory predication of this form is built, like a consistent predication and unlike an inconsistent one, upon an encapsulated tautology. The sentence *This stone is warm and cold*, for instance, can be developed into the form *This stone, which is* an inanimate being, is *warm, a property which applies to* an inanimate being, *and cold, a property which applies to* an inanimate being. Unlike inconsistency, contradiction does not affect the conceptual identity of the subject, which is confirmed twice. While a sleeping stone is no longer a stone, a stone said to be both cold and warm remains a stone. In spite of its being theatrically displayed, contradiction is a form of conceptual conflict that is both external to the structure of a synthetic predication, internal to a given conceptual area, and circumscribed by the same correlative terms which compete for a consistent determination of the subject. As it defies the lexical articulation in oppositive paradigms, which is internal to the area of consistency, contradiction has no ontological relevance. Ontology is not interested in the actual properties of things, which form the content of lexical paradigms, but in their aptness to receive whole paradigms of properties.

2.2 Formal lawfulness and conceptual lawfulness

Like tautology, contradiction is a logical and formal structure. Even if it cannot always be detected on purely formal syntactic grounds, contradiction rests on a formal order of lawfulness. This makes a further essential difference between contradiction and inconsistency, which involves a substantive conceptual order of lawfulness.

The syntactically based contradiction — *Peter is good and non-good* — is a formal logical structure in the strong sense. Besides behaving as a logical structure, it can be detected on purely formal syntactic grounds, for the syntactic form makes immediately visible its logical structure, irrespective of its conceptual contents. If we extract from the last example a skeleton of empty symbols — *x is P and non-P* — the logical structure of contradiction remains perfectly transparent.[391] The lexical contradiction — *This stone is warm and cold* — is a logical structure in a weaker sense, which is kept hidden by the syntactic form. If we extract from such a contradictory sentence as *Peter is good and bad* a skeleton of empty symbols — *x is P and Q* — the contradiction disappears with the content of the symbols. The opposition and the consequent contradiction have to be carved, so to speak, out of the content of the terms involved. Consequently, the description of a lexical contradiction goes beyond the scope of a purely formal grammar — a grammar which studies the formal configurations of expressions irrespective of their conceptual contents — but not beyond the scope of a formal analysis of language. In fact, even when it is embodied in conceptual substance, a lexical opposition remains a formal kind of structure. In order to unmask the contradiction, one does not have to know the actual content of the opposite terms; one only has to know that they form an opposition. While syntactic contradiction rests on the formal configuration of syntactic structures, lexical contradiction rests on the formal articulation of lexical structures.

The restrictions which govern consistency bear neither on syntactic forms nor on formal lexical structures, but depend on the conceptual substance of a shared natural ontology. It is true that any consistent predication encapsulates a tautology and any inconsistent predication encapsulates a contradiction. These logical structures, however, cannot be brought to the surface by a purely formal analysis.[392] As they are embodied in the conceptual substance itself, the contradictions and tautologies which lie at the foundation of inconsistent and consistent predications can only be detected through an analytical explanation of the system of compatibilities and incompatibilities contained in natural ontology. This is the reason why inconsistency can be mastered only within the framework of a philosophical grammar, which implements the formal syntactic and lexical structures of language through an analysis of the essential conceptual structures of natural ontology.[393]

3. The textual life of contradiction

3.1 Logical properties and discourse values

> La divina scienza, che piena è di pace
> […] non soffera lite alcuna (Dante)
> Die Wahrheit der Tautologie ist gewiß,
> des Satzes möglich,
> der Kontradiktion unmöglich (Wittgenstein)

The most famous anathema thrown against contradiction is also the first known to us. At the very dawn of Western philosophy, Parmenides curses "mortals knowing nothing / Wander, two-headed; for helplessness in their /

Breasts guides their distracted mind; and they are carried / Deaf and blind alike, dazed, uncritical tribes, / By whom being and not-being have been thought both the same / And not the same".[394] In order to prevent the discursive expression of thought from falling into contradiction, Aristotle formulates the "most certain" of all principles of thought: the identity principle, in its positive (A is A) or negative form (A is not non-A). According to this principle, "it is impossible for the same attribute at once to belong and not to belong to the same thing and in the same respect".[395]

In spite of the hasty inferences they might encourage at first sight, neither Parmenides' anathema nor Aristotle's identity principle entail that contradictory sentences should actually be banished from communicative discourse, or that they cannot possibly carry a true message. The presence of contradictory utterances in texts and discourses, and their aptness to carry true messages is too widespread a fact to escape notice. This, at any rate, did not escape the sensitive eye of the father of the identity principle. Speaking of Heracleitus' bent on contradictory statements, Aristotle points out that a contradictory statement can well express a consistent thought, for "what a man says does not necessarily represent what he believes".[396] When Heracleitus writes, for instance, that "Into the same rivers we step and do not step; we are and we are not",[397] the message is not so difficult to grasp — it refers to the changeability of things and experiences through irreversible time.

If we are really allowed to speak of a veto on contradiction, it is not with regard to discourse as such, but to one of its most specialised and peculiar uses — namely, the use of linguistic utterances for shaping and conveying philosophic and scientific propositions aiming at truth. If taken within its limits, Parmenide's attitude towards contradiction is seen in a new light.

A contradictory utterance is certainly capable of carrying a true message. Nevertheless, such a truth does not appear in the form of a complex meaning built up by a linguistic expression on the basis of its systematic properties; on the contrary, it shows itself as the volatile issue of a contingent act of interpretation performed by a co-operative addressee ready to embark on a hazardous enterprise. If we go back to Heracleitus' statement *Into the same rivers we step and do not step; we are and we are not*, it is easy to realise that the message it actually conveys is totally devoid of this structural guarantee grounded on linguistic form which philosophers have traditionally looked for. Instead, its truth shares the human frailty of a contingent act freely performed by a free subject. In short, the expression of a true content through a contradictory utterance is not incompatible with discourse as such. It is incompatible with a philosophic and epistemological ideal — the ideal of a discourse exclusively designed for the expression of truth by its structural properties, and of a truth-content integrally resting on an intersubjective, autonomous vehicle, sheltered from individual power of decision. Before protecting the expression of truth from contradiction, philosophers are engaged in protecting it from the risk of arbitrary interpretation.[398]

The linguistic meaning of a contradiction cannot be immediately taken as a true message, without a specific act of interpretation performed by the addressee. Such a cleavage between meanings and messages, however, is a general property of communication. What is specific to contradiction are the conditions under which the cleavage takes place. While the utterance of a consistent expression is in any case liable to perform a consistent speech act, the utterance of a contradictory expression immediately appears as the performance of a contradictory speech act. When uttering a contradiction, a speaker commits himself to communicating a message while using an expression that is by itself unable to perform the task. As Strawson (1952: 2–3) points out, "a man who contradicts himself may have succeeded in exercising his vocal chords. But from the point of view of imparting information [...] it is as if he had never opened his mouth. He utters words, but does not say anything [...] The point is that the standard purpose of speech, the intention to communicate something, is frustrated by self-contradiction".

The fact that the utterance of a contradiction turns out to be a contradictory speech act can easily be misunderstood. Namely, we can easily be led to infer from it that the pragmatic properties of a speech act — its being a consistent or contradictory act — depend on the logical properties of the sentence involved — on its being respectively consistent or contradictory. This conclusion however is false.

Looked at from a logical point of view, tautology is the opposite of contradiction — it is by definition a consistent sentence and lies at the foundation of any consistent predication. Taken as such, it is necessarily true, while a contradiction is necessarily false. In spite of this, uttering a tautology is as contradictory a speech act as uttering a contradiction. As Hegel (1812–13(1969: 415)) points out, when uttering a tautology, the speaker does not fulfil his communicative commitment — after promising to say something, he says nothing: "If, for example, to the question 'What is a plant' the answer is given 'A plant is — a plant', the truth of such a statement is at once admitted by the entire company on whom it is tested, and at the same time it is equally unanimously declared that the statement says *nothing* [...] we see that the beginning, 'The plant is -', sets out to say *something*, to bring forward a further determination. But since only the same thing is repeated, the opposite has happened, *nothing* has emerged. Such *identical* talk therefore *contradicts itself*".[399]

As contradictions, tautologies are easy to find in texts and discourses: *Poison is poison. Tropical fever is tropical fever* (Conrad); *A river's a river, and if you've got a mill, you must have water to turn it* (G. Eliot); *Wickedness is always wickedness, but folly is not always folly* (Austen). As with the utterance of a contradiction, the blockage is overcome in actual communication by the active contribution of the addressee. Faced with such a tautology as *Home is home*, an addressee would normally gather enough hints from the speech situation to infer, for instance, that the speaker in unwilling to sell his home, or that he does not like to travel.

A lame horse is still a horse, but is not very good at ploughing. So, a contradictory or tautological complex meaning is still a complex meaning, but is not as such good for speaking about things. Significance is an essential property of linguistic expressions as such; making sense within a coherent speech act is a functional property of utterances when used as signals of contingent messages. Though presupposing significance, making sense goes beyond it. As Wittgenstein (1922 (1961: 4.461; 4.462; 4.4611)) points out, tautology and contradiction are significant expressions whose utterance in actual speech does not immediately make sense. "Tautology and contradiction lack sense; tautologies and contradictions cannot be immediately taken as pictures of reality. They do not represent any possible situations. In spite of this, tautologies and contradictions are not nonsensical. They are part of the symbolism, just as '0' is part of the symbolism of arithmetic".[400]

If tautology and contradiction succeed in filling the gap between significance and consistent speech in practical terms, it is thanks to the co-operation of the addressee, who infers an informative message from tautology and a consistent message from contradiction, overturning the essential logical property of each.[401] In this way, paradoxically, the interpretation of tautologies and contradictions makes visible the relevance of consistency and informativeness as complementary criteria of meaningful speech. Turning a contradictory meaning into a consistent message, the interpretation of contradiction highlights the normative value of the identity principle as a regulating criterion of informative speech, whose maxim should be: "Once a topic is uttered, the comment cannot negate its identity". Turning an empty meaning into an informative message, the interpretation of tautology highlights the normative value of the informativeness principle as a regulating criterion of consistent speech, whose maxim should be: "Once a topic is uttered, the comment cannot reduce itself to it".[402] Tautology and contradiction, in a sense, delineate the borders of sensed speech from the outside.

A predication that is at one and the same time informative and consistent is both significant and able to carry a message on the grounds of its autonomous, structural strengths. Such a predication is of course a consistent synthetic predication — a predication which can be freely uttered without betraying the communicative commitment. A synthetic predication can in turn undergo creative interpretation in speech — it can be taken by an addressee as conveying a message reaching far beyond its linguistic meaning. However, this point is not relevant to our discussion. First, a creative interpretation of a consistent synthetic predication is a possible, but not a necessary move in order to get a message from it. Second, and above all, no interpretative development would be such as to overturn the essential logical properties of a synthetic predication, for any message drawn from a consistent and synthetic predication would in turn be expressed by a consistent and synthetic predication.

3.2 The figure of contradiction: Oxymoron

3.2.1 *The contradiction is dissolved*

> Proinde saepe ac multum cogitavi
> si quis inveniri posset incantus
> qui me absentem tibi praesentem et longinquum propinquum
> et tacentem loquentem faceret (Guarino to Leonello d'Este)

> Vos cogitastis de me malum
> et Deus vertit illud in bonum (Genesis)

When used in actual speech, contradiction is essentially subjected to two complementary interpretative strategies: a strategy grounded in the dynamics of utterance acts, and a strategy grounded in the dynamics of the involved concepts.

A speaker can dissociate his responsibility from the content of what he says, or from a part of it. On these grounds, the most immediate way of defusing a contradiction is to ascribe the opposite concepts to different responsible subjects, as if the utterer preferred not to acknowledge the relevance of one of them to the topic. In this case, the contradiction between concepts turns into a conflict between different subjects and different points of view. In Sophocles' tragedy, Antigones says to Ismenes: *I shall have accomplished a blessed crime.* Her deed, which is a crime according to the tyrant's law, appears blessed in the light of common moral sense. What seems a burden to human judgement is seen as light by the eyes of the soul: *Jugum meum suave est, et onus meum leve* (Matthew). A person may well consider stupid what ordinary people see as clever: *It always seemed to me a sort of clever stupidity only to have one sort of talent* (G. Eliot).[403] If the conflict between the different points of view is explicitly described, the contradiction disappears: *If their praise is censure, your censure may be praise* (Austen).

The dissociation of speakers is, in a sense, a way of dissolving a contradiction, rather than a way of solving it. If we turn to conceptual devices, we also find some cases when contradiction is only apparent. The most typical instances, however, require a true interpretation of contradiction — namely, an accurate and consistent delimitation of the relevant textual value of the competing concepts on the assumption that a contradiction really takes place.

The most obvious way of dissolving a contradiction on conceptual grounds is to introduce a temporal gap between the application of the correlative concepts to the topic. If a given subject cannot simultaneously instantiate two correlative concepts, it is allowed to run from one conceptual pole to the other, either both ways for reversible processes like the maze of feelings, or one way for irreversible processes, like life. Heracleitus plainly says that *Cold things become warm, warmth cools, moisture dries, the parched gets wet*, and Defoe seems to echo him when he writes that *To day we love what to morrow we hate; to day we seek what to morrow we shun; to day we desire what to morrow we fear* [...] *Such is the uneven state of human life.* On these grounds, if the presence of a temporal gap can be inferred, an utterance sharing the structure of a contradiction can easily be interpreted as if it were a consistent description of a change in time. An utterance such as *Odi et amo*, for instance, is ready to be interpreted, out of its context, as a consistent description of a cyclic change of attitude on the part of the subject, and more so would be its expression in the past: *I hated and loved.* Many literary examples seem purposefully to exploit the virtual indeterimination between the contradictory expression of a conflict and the consistent expression of a change: *Direis que me he perdido / que andando enamorada, / me hice perdidiza, y fui ganada* (S. Juan de la Cruz).

A subtler instance of apparent contradiction exploits the polysemy of the involved lexemes. Owing to polysemy, the meanings of two linked terms can escape correlation, and hence contradiction. A telling example is Hegel's shocking statement that *Das Böse* [...] *ist die positive Negativität* (*Evil is positive negativity*). The claimed contradiction dissolves entirely if one realises that the connected concepts are not members of the same paradigm. The term *negativity* refers to the fact that evil is the negative pole of the correlation whose positive term is *good*. The term *positive* means that evil is not just the absence of good but its antagonist force, which shares with it the positive reality of possessing an active strength.[404]

3.2.2 *The contradiction is interpreted*

> Lis est in vocibus ipsis;
> Sed litem totam sedat sententia vocum
> (G. de Vinsauf)

The interpretation of contradiction as an expression of a consistent message is encouraged from within the structure itself. Contradiction, as we have seen, is grafted onto a consistent predication, and rests on tautological foundations. This means that it gives expression to a potentially consistent state-of-affairs, which as such admits a consistent expression.

The most compelling reason why a speaker utters a contradiction is its ability to give an overall picture of complex and conflictual processes.

When facing a complex situation, the speaker has the feeling that it cannot be exhaustively rendered by selecting just one single term out of a conceptual correlation. Ann, for instance, is physically, but not yet psychologically, a woman. Thus, Ann is a woman from a certain point of view but not from another — in short, she is and is not a woman. Complexity — the simultaneous instantiation of opposite concepts — is the familiar way things offer themselves. A concept rarely goes without its correlative within complex phenomena. Beauty is never without shade, nor happiness without some bitter drops of sorrow; as Defoe's hero reminds himself and all of us, *All evils are to be considered with the good that is in them*. Complexity easily turns into conflict, as when a human soul is torn between incompatible attitudes: *Odi et amo* (Catulle); *Ardo et son di ghiaccio* (Petrarch); *I both wished and feared to see Mr Rochester* (Ch. Brontë); *Vorrei e non vorrei* (Da Ponte).

If it is typical, for things and creatures, to remain far below the perfect instantiation of a single concept, God is generally thought to be absolutely above any attempt to conceptual determination. According to Heracleitus, *God is day and night, winter and summer, war and peace, surfeit and hunger*. If God is, to put it in Cusanus' words, "*coincidentia oppositorum*", theology can only be conceived of as "*docta ignorantia*". The first oxymoron theatrically suggests that God escapes any finite conceptual determination; the second, that it is impossible to speak of him consistently.

The interpretation of contradictions makes visible a textual phenomenon which generally remains hidden in consistent speech: the conceptual content carried by different occurrences of a single lexeme is ready to undergo significant modulations[405] in different texts and speech situations. As a consequence, the different uses of a word make up a complex constellation of distinct and potentially conflictual values. When interpreting such a contradiction as *Ann is and is not a woman*, for instance, one takes the two occurrences of the noun *woman* as if they brought into the discourse two distinct conceptual perspectives upon the woman — two different focalisations of textually relevant features of the concept: for instance, the woman in a physical and in a moral sense.

This behaviour of concepts is far from being confined to oxymoron. The use of a given concept in connection with a given entity neither requires the full applicability of the concept nor does it imply the full application of it. The fact that the entity shares one constitutive property of a concept is considered by the language user as a sufficient condition for applying the concept to it. As a consequence, the different textual occurrences of a word do not necessarily convey isomorphic instances of the same general concept. If the utterance *Ann is a woman* is used to suggest that Ann has reached physical maturity, for instance, the speaker does not necessarily commit himself to the whole set of properties which qualify the prototypical concept of womanhood — for instance, to psychological maturity. Accordingly, the sequence *Ann is a woman, but you wouldn't entrust her with a child* is not contradictory. In other conditions, a speaker can use the same utterance in order to focus on psychological maturity, without committing himself to the question of physical maturity. Accordingly, a sequence like *Ann looks rather childish but is a woman* is not contradictory.

Concepts are not used in discourse to classify objects along rigid categories but to describe beings in their changing complexity according to partial perspectives which are relevant to given discourse situations. When speaking about a subject, we do not just "judge that some general concept has application in some particular case" (Strawson, 1992); more or less unconsciously, we tend to adapt the concepts we are using to our occasional expressive and communicative ends. In spite of their being taken by speakers as solid units of measure, concepts in use do not share the most relevant property of the latter — namely, their being fixed and defined independently of occasional uses.[406] On these grounds, it is easy to understand how contradictions are ready to become consistent and tautologies informative. A woman who is said not to be a woman is, roughly, a woman to whom not all the properties implied by the prototypical concept can be applied. A woman who is said to be a woman is a woman in the full sense, to whom all the properties implied by the prototypical concept can be applied.

As far as ephemeral, everyday acts of communication are concerned, heterogeneous and potentially conflictual uses of words see the light and die without even being noticed. But if we consider the endless shaping and reshaping of concepts in written texts, with its interplay of tradition and innovation, the accumulation of different perspectives upon concepts inevitably ends in conflict.[407] Within the texts of the *New Testaments*, for instance, the concepts of life and death receive the indelible mark of faith in the afterlife. Within the framework of generative transformational grammar, to pass to a completely different field, the concept of knowledge, when applied to language, is meant to refer to a kind of practical and implicit command of the rules constraining the use of linguistic signs. When a new concept is shaped, however, it does not substitute the old ones, but coexists with them. The Christian concepts of heavenly life and death do not wipe out the more immediate, worldly ones. The idea of knowledge made popular by generative grammar does not cancel the traditional idea of knowledge as theoretical and explicit — rather than practical and implicit — command of necessary and sufficient conditions of phenomena. Such a virtual conflict between incompatible coexisting concepts referred to by different uses of the same word inevitably attracts contradictory expression: *Occidis nos, ne moriamur abs te* (St. Augustin); *Mas, ¿cómo perseveras, / oh vida, no viviendo donde vives?* (S. Juan de la Cruz). The Renaissance philosopher Campanella addresses his body as *Morte viva* (*Living death*), while Tasso's baroque sensibility overtly delights in piling up paradoxes:

> Talché morendo morte, alfin in morte
> La vita si converte, e morte in vita

3.2.3 *Contradiction, analytical description and conceptual analysis*

> Thus we never see the true state of our condition
> till it is illustrated to us by its contraries,
> nor know how to value what we enjoy,
> but by the want of it (Defoe)
> Great minds against themselves conspire
> And shun the cure they most desire (Nahum Tate)

The fact that oxymoron is a favourite linguistic tool for expressing complex and conflictual situations does not imply that there is a necessary connection between complexity or conflict and contradiction. As Kant (1763(1992: 211)) points out, a contradiction is located in linguistic expression, whereas a conflict involves things.

A logical contradiction "consists in the fact that something is simultaneously affirmed and denied of the very same thing. The consequence of the logical conjunction is *nothing at all* (*nihil negativum irrepraesentabile*), as the law of contradiction asserts. A body which is in motion is something; a body which is not in motion is also something (*cogitabile*); but a body which is both in motion and also, in the very same sense, not in motion, is nothing at all".

A conflict in reality — a "real opposition" in Kant's terminology — "is that where two predicates of a thing are opposed to each other, but not through the law of contradiction. Here, too, one thing cancels that which is posited by the other; but the consequence is something (*cogitabile*). The motive force of a body in one direction and an equal tendency of the same body in the opposite direction do not contradict each other; as predicates, they are simultaneously possible in one body. The consequence of such an opposition is rest, which is something (*repraesentabile*)".[408] Complexity and conflict are constitutive properties of the finite existence of things and creatures; as a consequence, they can naturally be framed in consistent expressions. But if complexity and conflict are not in themselves contradictory states of affairs, why is contradiction one of their favourite expressions?

What makes a contradictory utterance an attractive expression of complexity and conflict is not so much the contradiction itself, but the simultaneous presence within a simple expression of the correlative terms involved in the conflictual or complex situation. This condition, however, can equally be fulfilled by a consistent expression. In order to prevent the simultaneous use of two opposite terms from falling into contradiction, it is enough to articulate their relation with appropriate linguistic devices:

> That sentence was true — because I had really said that I could not speak about that book — and false, because it indirectly but vigorously put about a supposed opinion of mine which actually did not exist (Magris).

> Joy and sadness / are merged / in this spring air (A. M. Bacher).

If we take away the two parallel explanations from the first utterance, or link with a copula the two opposite terms occurring in the second, the result is an oxymoron: *That sentence was true and false*; *Joy is sorrow*. As a linguistic picture of complexity and conflict, oxymoron can be considered an alternative to analytical description — to a description capable of distributing the characterisation of a topic among correlative terms without contradiction.

Complexity and conflict can occur, as we have seen, at two distinct levels — namely, at the level of the described reality, and at the level of the describing concepts. Accordingly, the analysis can take the form either of an analytical description of complex and conflictual situations, or of an analytical elucidation of complex and potentially conflicting uses of concepts.

Many instances of analytical description can be found in narrative texts:

> Tess had never before known a time in which the thread of her life was so distinctly twisted of two strands, positive pleasure and positive pain (Hardy)

> [...] and the respect he felt for her high rank, and his veneration for her as his patroness, mingling with a very good opinion of himself, of his authority as a clergyman, and his rights as a rector, made him altogether a mixture of pride and obsequiousness, self-importance and humility (Austen)

> He was standing two yards from her with his mind full of contradictory desires and resolves — desiring some unmistakable proof that she loved him, and yet dreading the position into which such a proof might bring him (G. Eliot)

With its consistent elaboration of the opposite predicates, the last passage avoids both contradiction — *I both wished and feared to see Mr Rochester* (Ch. Brontë) — and tautology: *Catherine sometimes [...] hoped or feared that she had gone too far* (Austen).

The two ways of expressing a conflict — the analytical description and the oxymoron — typically coexist in texts. Sometimes, a description holds as an explanation of a previous oxymoron:

> I wished, yet feared, to find him. I felt the terrible news must be told, and I longed to get it over; but how to do it, I did not know (E. Brontë)

Sometimes an oxymoron holds as a sort of recapitulation of a previous description:

> He had uttered precisely what her soul yearned for, but which her reason dreaded [...] and she was both frightened and made happy thereby (Tolstoy).

On the other hand, philosophical elucidation of concepts in use, the paradigmatic instance of analysis, becomes necessary precisely when the uses of concepts are complex if not confused, and thus potentially conflictual or even contradictory. Describing two different and potentially conflictual uses of the verb *know*, Strawson (1992: 7) openly defies the contradiction on its own field: "We have mastered a practice, but can't state the theory of our practice. We know the rules because we observe them and yet we don't know them because we can't say what they are".

Oxymoron, the figure of logical contradiction, is thus a functional counterpart of analysis, the paradigm of consistent philosophical discourse. Philosophical analysis and oxymoron stem from the same roots, that is, the complexity of things and the drift of concepts in texts.[409] If this is true, the difference between oxymoron and analysis has not so much to do with the conceptual purport, which is the same and equally consistent in both cases. Instead, it has to do with a different division of labour between linguistic expression and interpretation on the one hand, and speaker's and addressee's responsibility on the other. Analysis wagers on the articulating power of language, and rests on the assumption that everything can and must be said consistently. Its regulating criterion, thus, is a combination of the principles of expressability[410] and non-contradiction. Oxymoron bets on the addressee — on his willingness to come to an understanding by any means. At first sight, it looks as if the maxim of oxymoron were that expressability and non-contradiction are two incompatible ends — that not everything can be said consistently. In fact, the best proof of the regulatory value of the criterion of consistent expressability is precisely the role it plays in interpreting contradictions. The textual life of an oxymoron ends in any case in analysis. If the speaker does not directly perform it, the addressee is asked to take turns.

4. The figures of inconsistency: Synecdoche, metonymy and metaphor

4.1 Ways of interpreting inconsistency

When we think of inconsistent meanings, metaphor is the most immediate, almost obvious association. In fact, between metaphor and inconsistency, there is not the same direct association which holds between contradiction and oxymoron. On the one hand, the inconsistent sentence is not the only form of metaphorical expression; on the other hand, not any inconsistent sentence is actually interpreted as a metaphor in speech.

A living metaphor can be defined, roughly but adequately, as a linguistic device for promoting an interaction (Richards, 1936; Black, 1954(1962); 1979) between conflicting concepts.[411] Richards (1936) defines metaphor as the expression of a given "idea" — its tenor — by means of a term — its vehicle — which independently carries another idea. If a girl is said to be a nightingale, for instance, the girl referred to is the tenor, the concept of nightingale is the vehicle; if a speaking girl is said to be singing, similarly, the process of speaking is the tenor, the singing is the vehicle. The two conflicting concepts — the concept of nightingale and the concept of girl; the concept of singing and the concept of speaking — "interact" in such a way as to encourage the addressee to "find connections" (Richards, 1936: 89) between them. As a result, the vehicle is applied to the tenor as a model.

If we define metaphors in terms of conceptual conflicts and interactions, inconsistency is merely one way, though a privileged one, of promoting them. Besides ontological categorisation, general knowledge and even direct acquaintance with given individual referents are open to conflict. The identification of a landscape of snow-white hills with the ocean — *The whole hill-back was one billow white ocean* (E. Brontë) — is conflictual, and metaphorical, without being ontologically inconsistent. It is metaphorical because the hills are described through an alien model, the ocean, but is not inconsistent because both hills and ocean fall into the same basic category of inanimate realities, which implies that the conflict is internal to our consistent cognitive space. Similarly, if a girl who is actually speaking is said to be singing, the concepts of speaking and singing conflict with each other and interact: the girl's speaking is seen as a kind of singing. Nevertheless, the expression is perfectly consistent, and the conflict is simply a matter of fact.

If inconsistency is not the only way of framing metaphors, metaphorical interaction is equally not the only way of interpreting an inconsistent expression.

As we have already observed,[412] an inconsistent utterance allows itself to be interpreted as a consistent description of an alien world, governed by a peculiar ontology, rather than as an inconsistent description of ours.

Moreover, inconsistent utterances describing our shared world escape conceptual interaction and metaphorical interpretation if a positive relation between the conflicting concepts opens a path towards a consistent interpretation. This provides a key for metonymy — *In a few days they* [the birds] *would devour all my hopes* (Defoe) and synecdoche — *Had anybody asked her of what she was thinking, […] her frankness would have had to avoid the question*[413] (Conrad). The quoted utterances are inconsistent in an obvious way: hope, an abstract entity, cannot be devoured as something concrete; frankness, an abstract, non-human entity, can neither answer a question nor avoid it. However, if a substantive relation is activated between vehicle and tenor, consistency is restored and conceptual interaction is prevented. If what is actually devoured by the birds is not hope but some corn that feeds Robinson's hope, consistency is restored. At the same time, if corn is taken as a motive for hope, hope cannot possibly interact with corn — hope cannot be seen as a model for corn. Similarly, if it is a frank person that is meant to answer the question, frankness is reduced to a consistent property of the person, and cannot be seen as a model for that person.

Though not exclusive, the link between inconsistency and metaphor is none the less significant — it is a deep link of elective affinity. Inconsistency is the paradigmatic kind of conceptual conflict open to a metaphorical interaction, and metaphor is the most valorising outcome of conceptual inconsistency.

The traditional distinction between metaphor, metonymy and synecdoche is based on the notion of transfer, which traces back to Aristotle. According to Aristotle,[414] "Metaphor is the application of a strange term (*onomatos allotriou epiphora*) either transferred from the genus and applied to the species, or from the species and applied to the genus, or from one species to another or else by analogy". The transfer of a word into an alien conceptual area — or trope — is traditionally taken as the primitive notion — a sort of *genus proximum*. What distinguishes and characterises metaphor, metonymy and synecdoche — the *differentia specifica* — is the different kind of relationship which is supposed to hold in each case between the two ideas involved in the transfer: a whole-part relationship for synecdoche; some kind of contiguity, ranging from spatial proximity to causal relationship for metonymy; analogy for metaphor. The subject of the utterance "*Va bene*", *rispose il naso sonnacchioso* (Fogazzaro) — the nose — refers to the person of whom it is a part; it is an instance of synecdoche. The noun phrase *Red coats* in the following example refers to a group of officers who are wearing red coats: *Elizabeth* [...] *looked in vain for Mr Wickham among the cluster of red coats there assembled* (Austen); it is an instance of metonymy. The noun phrase *These pure fountains of pure colour* (G. Eliot) refers to a handful of jewels, whose brilliant glare is supposed to recall the effect of water gushing out of a fountain; it is an instance of metaphor.

The traditional frame of analysis, with its classifications and leading criteria, has aroused an ever deeper sense of dissatisfaction among scholars; yet it contains a core of truth whose intuitive strength has remained indisputable across the centuries. The authors who try to give it up are more likely to avoid essential problems than to face them with clearer formulations and stronger criteria.[415] In fact, what deserves critical analysis is not so much the explicit contents of traditional definitions as their underlying silent assumptions. What is openly asserted can always be corrected and improved if the underlying assumptions are correct. What is tacitly presupposed, on the contrary, easily escapes critical analysis.

Among the presuppositions of traditional classifications, we shall examine three, which are inextricably intertwined: the idea that both metaphor, metonymy and synecdoche are forms of transfer; the idea that their range of action is essentially the same; and the idea that whole-part relation, contiguity and analogy are three different ways of performing a similar task — that is, providing a conceptual transfer with a definite conceptual track. All these ideas are false, or, at best, inaccurate, and assuming them to be true forms the most serious obstacle towards a satisfactory structural description of metaphor, metonymy and synecdoche.

The first step towards dismantling these assumptions is to call into question the notion of transfer as a primitive category of analysis. The idea of transfer cannot be applied to all kinds of tropes. Even when it can be applied, moreover, it implies other, more basic notions. First and foremost, a transfer is the transfer of something. Before asking if the transfer is guided along some kind of track — part-whole relation, or contiguity, or analogy — one should ask whether something is transferred or not, what can be transferred and under what grammatical conditions. One can transfer either punctual concepts or relations. In the former case, the transfer focuses on a saturated concept — a thing or a process; in the latter, it focuses on an unsaturated term — typically, on a verb, an adjective, or a relational noun. In other words, the first question to be asked about tropes does not concern the issue of the conceptual conflict, the leading criteria of its interpretation as a definite instance of figure, but the grammatical conditions for its taking shape within linguistic expressions.[416]

Examining the distribution of the different tropes among the main grammatical and functional positions of the sentence structure, we shall first challenge the assumption that the range of action of metaphor, metonymy and synecdoche is essentially the same. The main figures of conceptual conflict are allowed different locations within the sentence structure, which entails deep structural differences (§4.2). As a consequence, they cannot be seen as directly competing.

These differences in distribution and structure, in turn, bring us back to a deeper conceptual difference: metaphors really transfer punctual and relational concepts in stranger domains, whereas metonymies and synecdoches do not transfer concepts, but simply connect consistent saturate concepts within consistent domains (§4.3).

The third assumption of traditional analysis — the idea that whole-part relation, contiguity and analogy provide conceptual transfers with definite conceptual tracks — will be raised later, once the structural and functional domain where the different figures are really competing has been isolated (§4.4).

4.2 Synecdoche, metonymy and metaphor: Grammatical distribution and inner forms

Metonymy and synecdoche have free access to noun phrases only,[417] both in referential and predicative position: *He saw, more than a mile away, the ugly enormity of the Custom House* (Conrad); *Passe un manteau de velours* (Butor); *I was all flour* (E. Brontë); *Soon he found out that war was a Mickey Mouse gas mask* (Lodge). Metaphor, on the contrary, can occupy any available structural position. Metaphorical nouns can be both referential and predicative: *These pure fountains of pure colour* (G. Eliot); *Her sin, her ignominy, were the roots which she had struck into the soil* (Hawthorne); *Thy words are swords* (Marlowe). There are also metaphorical verbs, as in *This City now doth, like a garment, wear / The beauty of the morning* (Wordsworth), adjectives, as in *Twenty centuries of stony sleep* (Yeats), and adverbs, as in *I tried to burst open the door, but it stubbornly resisted* (Melville); *The turbid waters mixed with those of the lake, but mixed with them unwillingly* (Shelley).

The conceptual conflict adds a supplement of structure to the complex meaning of the expression, introducing into it a surplus of concepts and relations. The conflict, so to speak, has its specific inner form, which depends on distributional factors. Occupying different grammatical and functional positions implies, for the different kinds of tropes, exhibiting different inner forms. In particular, metonymy and synecdoche are confined to the paradigmatic correlation *in absentia* (B replaces A) and to the syntagmatic relation *in praesentia* (A is B) whereas metaphor opens to more complex forms combining a syntagmatic relation with one or two paradigmatic correlations.

Richard's model of interaction is fit for two structural configurations, open to both metaphor and metonymy and synecdoche, that is, for the paradigmatic correlation *in absentia* — a vehicle B stands for a tenor A — and for the syntagmatic relation *in praesentia* — A (the tenor) is B (the vehicle). In other words, the model is fit for metaphors which take an individual, process or property (the vehicle) as a model for a different kind of individual, process or property (the tenor), which can be independently identified. Now, the access of metaphors to such relational concepts as verbs, adjectives and adverbs multiplies the available structures underlying conceptual interaction, and demands a sharpening of descriptive tools. For this purpose, the first step is to distinguish, along with Black (1954(1962)), the structural configuration of the metaphorical utterance from the structure of the conceptual interaction.

From the standpoint of its structural configuration, a metaphorical utterance can be considered as the connection *in praesentia* between a frame and a conflicting focus. The frame is identified on the basis of its coherence with the text or the ongoing discourse. The focus is defined against the frame as the expression that introduces an alien, incoherent and conflicting topic. If a text about human beings contains the metaphorical utterance *This girl is a nightingale*, for instance, the noun phrase *This girl*, coherent with the textual topic, identifies the frame, while the noun phrase *a nightingale* identifies the focus, that is, the incoherent and conflicting part.[418]

The conceptual interaction, for its part, involves two subjects of discourse — namely, a principal subject, which is talked about, and a subsidiary subject, which is applied to the principal subject as a conceptual model.

If two pairs of terms are needed, that is *frame* vs *focus*; *principal subject* vs *subsidiary subject*, instead of one, that is *tenor* vs *vehicle*, it is because there is no one-to-one correlation between the terms of the interaction — principal subject and subsidiary subject — and the constituents of the metaphorical utterance — frame and focus.

In the example analysed above — *This girl is a nightingale* — the principal subject — *the girl* — coincides with the frame, and the subsidiary subject — *the nightingale* — with the focus. If this coincidence were regular, one pair of terms would suffice. In fact, the coincidence is a specific property of one structural kind of metaphor — namely, the metaphorical definition of a subject, whose focus is a noun in predicative position. Under such conditions, the interacting concepts — the girl and the nightingale — are linked by a syntagmatic relation *in praesentia*: the principal and the subsidiary subject are both expressed and coincide with the immediate constituents of the sentence.

When a metaphorical noun is used in referential position, the subsidiary subject coincides with the focus, but the principal subject does not coincide with the frame: it coincides with the unnamed referent of the focus — in traditional terms, with a virtual substitute for the focus. If the utterance *I saw a nightingale* is meant to refer to a girl, the principal subject does not coincide with the frame *I saw*, but with the unexpressed girl. When principal subject and frame are dissociated, the interaction is framed by a paradigmatic correlation *in absentia*: the subsidiary subject, that is, the focus (the nightingale), is expressed, while the principal subject (the girl) is not.

As a saturated noun denotes a classifying concept, a metaphorical noun can be defined as a conflictual classifier. The classification is explicit when the noun occupies the predicative position — *This girl is a nightingale* — and implicit when the noun occupies the referential position: *I saw a nightingale.*

A relational term — typically, a verb — associates two functions: it classifies processes — singing or smiling, for instance — and relates referents: for instance, it attributes to a human being the process of smiling or singing. Accordingly, a verb can be used metaphorically in two ways: either it achieves a conflictual categorisation of a process — an instance of speaking, for example, is described as a kind of singing — or it involves conflictual beings in a process: such an inanimate being as the moon, for instance, is said to smile. The most typical and specific metaphorical uses of a verb are connected with the relational dimension. As the examples will make clear, however, verbal metaphors mix the two functions in different proportions. For simplicity's sake, we shall examine this point with reference to one kind of argument only, that is, the grammatical subject of an intransitive verb coinciding with the predicate. But our remarks can easily be generalised to include any other argument.

If a verb is constructed with a non-conflicting subject, it gives rise to a metaphor if — and only if — it is meant to produce a conflictual categorisation of a different kind of process. As in the case of referential nouns, the conceptual interaction is framed by a paradigmatic correlation *in absentia*: the verbal focus identifies the subsidiary subject, while the virtual consistent substitute coincides with the principal subject. If the utterance *Ann is singing* is meant to describe Ann's speaking, for instance, the focus — the concept of singing — holds as the subsidiary subject, while speaking is the non-expressed principal subject. Since singing is as consistent with the human subject as speaking, the verbal content is transferred as if it were a punctual concept, while its relational dimension — its aptitude to characterise its arguments — is not highlighted at all. As it takes the place of a consistent verb, the metaphorical focus is by definition replaceable.

The syntagmatic relation *in praesentia* and the paradigmatic correlation *in absentia* can be considered as the elementary forms of interaction. When a relational term — and in particular a verb — is constructed with conflicting arguments, the structural skeleton of the interaction combines the two elementary forms into more complex structures. The syntagmatic relation between the principal subject and the verbal focus is enriched by a paradigm grafted onto the principal subject and, in some cases, by a paradigm grafted onto the verbal focus.

A metaphorical verb which conflicts *in praesentia* with one of its arguments — the subject, in our examples — either is inconsistent — *The moon smiles* — or breaks a lexical solidarity: "*You have a good name out here, though*", *he growled savagely without looking at me* (Conrad).

In the case of inconsistency, the consistent subject of the metaphorical verb is projected onto the principal subject as a subsidiary subject. In our example, the moon is seen through a human model. In the case of a lexical mistake, it is the solidary subject that is projected onto the principal subject as a subsidiary subject: the man is seen as a lion.

In both cases, the principal and subsidiary subject form a paradigmatic structure *in absentia*, perpendicular to the syntagmatic link *in praesentia* between principal subject and focus. This paradigm, it should be stressed, is not potentially substitutive but purely interactive. It is not substitutive because it is not grafted onto the incoherent focus but onto the coherent principal subject: the metaphors are respectively about the moon and about a man. If the moon were replaced by a human being, or the man by a lion, the relevant textual referent would be lost. The only function of this paradigm is thus to make possible an interaction between the principal subject — the moon, the man — and a subsidiary subject — the human being, the lion.[419]

If the verbal focus — *smile* or *growl* — is interpreted as a substitute for a non-conflictual process, a second paradigm sets up an opposition between the focus and its intended substitute. In this case, the metaphorical focus — the verb — acquires the function of a subsidiary subject, which is applied to its virtual substitute as a model.

In the case of a lexical mistake, the availability of a non-conflictual substitute of the focus is immediate, for the conflicting verb describes a consistent process, which can be framed in proper words. The man's growling is in fact a kind of shouting, and it is on this shouting that the metaphor imposes a lion's growling as a model.

In the case of inconsistency, the double of the focus is a radical reformulation of the process against the background of an independent and consistent cognitive structure.[420] If the moon's smile is interpreted as denoting its brilliant glittering, for instance, the human smile is imposed on the moon's glittering as a model.

Owing to its complex structure, the conflictual verbal metaphor admits two parallel interpretative developments: an interaction between the principal subject and its double — between the man and the lion; between the moon and the human being — and an interaction between the metaphorical process and its non-conflictual substitute — between growling and shouting; between smiling and glittering. The two potential developments are tendentially complementary: insofar as the metaphorical process is seen as a substitute for a consistent double, the interaction between the principal subject and the virtual double projected on it by the conflicting verb is weakened, and vice-versa. In the examples quoted, for instance, the more the growling of the man is interpreted as a substitute for the process of shouting, solidary with the human subject, the less the lion is projected on the human subject, and vice-versa. The more the smile of the moon is interpreted as a substitute for the process of glittering, consistent with the moon, the less the moon is humanised, and vice-versa.[421]

When an inconsistent metaphorical verb is not immediately taken as a substitute for a consistent process, the structure of the verb metaphor is simpler. As no virtual substitute is opposed to it, the verbal focus cannot be taken as a subsidiary subject, which implies that the metaphorical interaction no longer takes the focus as its active centre. The only subsidiary subject involved in conceptual interaction is in this case the paradigmatic counterpart of the principal subject, consistent with the verb. In the example *The moon smiles*, for instance, the process of smiling is literally predicated of the moon. Owing to this, the concept of human being is projected onto it as a model.

A similar distribution of constituents is found with any relational concept, and in particular with metaphorical adjectives. When an adjective conflicts with the modified noun, for instance, an interactive paradigm opposes the modified noun to a double which is consistent with the adjective, while a substitutive paradigm opposes the focus to a double consistent with the modified noun. When Pliny calls the new moon *Silens luna*, silence is naturally intended as a model for the absent concept of obscurity. When G. de Vinsauf speaks of a man *Nudus amicis*, on the contrary, friends are seen as a sort of protective cloth, as Brooke-Rose (1958: 241) points out. When Dante writes *Io venni in loco d'ogni luce muto*, a reductive paraphrase is immediately to hand — *I came to a dark place* — but the complementary interpretative move — the identification between word and light — is encouraged by the cultural background of the work.

4.3 The grammatical and conceptual conditions for a transfer of concepts

4.3.1 *Relations without transfer: Synecdoche and metonymy*

The difference in distribution between metaphor and non-analogical figures can easily be justified on the basis of a different attitude towards relational concepts.

Metaphors include as vehicles the full range of relational terms, and in particular finite verbal forms, adjectives, relational nouns and even adverbs, because they are able to transfer unsaturated relations into stranger domains.

Synecdoches and metonymies include a restricted range of forms of relational terms among their vehicles because they do not mobilise relational terms to transfer relations but simply to place them within consistent relationships.

The most typical vehicles of synecdoches are nouns of parts, whose content encapsulates the connection with the whole structure they belong to. The concept of eye, for instance, encapsulates its relation with the hierarchical structure of the living body. Nouns of parts can be considered relational nouns in a weak sense only. Being open to processes, metonymies include true relational nouns and non-finite, noun-like forms of verbs — infinitives and gerunds — not only among their vehicles — *In a few days they* [the birds] *would devour all my hopes* (Defoe) — but also among their tenors: *Pleasure is to hear iwis the birdès sing* (Cornish); *Morning is milking.* In spite of the involvement of relational terms, synecdoche and metonymy do not transfer unsaturated relations from one domain to another, but simply activate consistent relations between saturated terms within a single domain. The most direct way of checking such a statement is the observation of the borderline lexical category of relational nouns.

Relational nouns lend the distributional properties of nouns to relational concepts, whose canonical expression would be a verb or an adjective. A relational noun has, so to speak, the body of a noun and the soul of a verb or adjective. Like verbs and adjectives, relational nouns are unsaturated terms. Instead of classifying entities, as saturated nouns do, they enter into relation with entities, or relate entities to each other. An instance of death, for instance, is not an individual but a process involving an individual. An instance of sadness, similarly, is the sadness felt by a person. Once they have received their arguments, relational terms denote processes, which are saturated concepts of the second order.

Sharing the distribution of nouns, relational nouns have access to both the referential and the predicative position, and in either position they can be used as vehicles of metaphors — *The voice of the shuttle* (Sophocles) — or metonymies:[422] *In a few days they would devour all my hopes.* This common distribution, however, highlights a number of differences.

When used as a vehicle of metaphor, the relational noun fully preserves its relational structure: the metaphorical noun is transferred as an unsaturated relation, ready to be saturated by inconsistent arguments belonging to the target domain. The metaphor *The voice of the shuttle* transfers the unsaturated concept of human voice into the inanimate domain of artefacts, and saturates it within this inconsistent domain: the shuttle speaks. Relational terms are involved in metaphors as "centres of gravity" of processes and qualities. They therefore perform a task that is open to nouns but is typical of finite forms of verbs and adjectives, and this justifies the access of these categories of words to metaphor.

When used as a vehicle of metonymy, the relational noun entirely loses its relational structure. Instead of entering into a relationship with a conflicting referent belonging to a stranger domain, the noun exploits a substantive relationship as a traced path for attaining a consistent target. It stops working as a relational term to behave as an oblique classificatory term.

When the vehicle of a metonymy is a relational concept like *hope*, its final target can be either a thing or a process. Both, however, are saturated and consistent concepts.

Within the utterance *The birds would devour all my hopes*, the conflicting relational noun *hopes* actually refers to a connected and consistent thing — namely to a stretch of growing corn in which poor Robinson's hopes are placed.

In such examples as *Pleasure is to hear iwis the birdès sing* or *Morning is milking*, the final target is in turn a process, that is, a saturated structure of the second order. This means that relational nouns and non-finite forms of verbs are admitted within metonymies on condition that they are saturated by consistent arguments: *pleasure* means "pleasure felt by human beings"; *milking* means "milking of animals by human beings". Even when it connects relational terms, therefore, metonymy never transfers an unsaturated relation — *pleasure, milking* — in an alien domain, but activates a substantive and consistent relation between two saturated processes: *To hear the birds sing gives pleasure*; *"Morning" — means "Milking" — to the Farmer* (Dickinson) within a consistent domain.

Relational terms are involved in metonymies and synecdoches as terms of relations, and therefore as classifiers of things, processes or qualities. This task is open to non-finite, noun-like forms of verbs but is typical of nouns, and this justifies their distributional limitations.

4.3.2 *Punctual and relational metaphors*

When we speak of punctual and relational metaphors, we have to take into account two interconnected but independent questions. The first is a purely structural question, which has to do with the kind of concept — punctual or relational — involved in the transfer. The second is a functional question, and concerns the kind of conceptual mapping activated by the metaphorical transfer. In traditional terms, it is the distinction between punctual and proportional analogy. The first question can be answered within the borders of the metaphorical sentence; the second can only be faced when the metaphor is actually interpreted in a given text or discourse situation.

4.3.2.1 *Punctual and Relational Transfers.* The structural distinction between punctual and relational transfers is connected with the distinction between saturated concepts, which classify entities, and unsaturated concepts, capable of either entering into relation with entities or putting entities into relation with each other. This distinction is purely conceptual, and is independent both of lexical categorisation — because of the presence of relational terms among nouns — and of the functional distinction between reference and predication, because both kinds of concepts — classificatory and relational — can occupy either position.

Even when it occupies the predicative position, a classificatory noun does not put the subject into a relation, but simply classifies it. This holds for consistent predications — *This man is an engineer* — as well as for metaphorical ones: *My heart was a habitation large enough for many guests* (Hawthorne).

A referential position, for its part, becomes the core of a connection if it is occupied by a relational noun, be it consistent — *I like the colour of these flowers* — or metaphorical — *I've dreamt in my life dreams that have altered the colour of my mind* (E. Brontë).

The distinction between classificatory and relational concepts is closely connected to the two complementary dimensions of natural ontology — the consistent categorisation of different kinds of beings, and the connection of beings within consistent processes. It is at this point that the question about relational transfers meets the question about the inconsistency of expressions.

A punctual transfer, that is, an inconsistent categorisation, is as such compatible with the consistency of the utterance that contains it. The classification of a girl as a nightingale — as a non-human creature — is as such inconsistent. An instance of it, however, can be found within a perfectly consistent sentence: for example, *I saw a nightingale.* When its vehicle occupies the referential position, the inconsistent classification has a non-relational structure — it does not involve the predicative link. If the predicate is compatible with the vehicle as well as with the intended referent, as is the case with our example, the sentence is consistent. We fall into inconsistency if a predicate consistent with the intended referent, the girl, is not consistent with the metaphorical noun: *A nightingale told me this story.* But in this case the inconsistency of the whole sentence is external to the link between the predicate and the intended referent — the girl — which remains consistent. The sentence is systematically inconsistent, on the other hand, if the inconsistent classifier occupies the predicative position and the expression of the intended referent is entrusted to the subject: *This girl is a nightingale.* In this case, however, the inconsistent sentence does not shape an inconsistent connection; it simply gives explicit expression to an inconsistent act of classification.

While the relationship between inconsistent expression and inconsistent classification is unsystematic and non-essential, the link between inconsistent connection and inconsistent expression is systematic and essential. Unlike inconsistent classification, inconsistent connection is inseparable from the construction of inconsistent expressions. For this reason, the paradigmatic instances of inconsistent sentences are certainly not those which contain an inconsistent classification of some referent, but those which give expression to an inconsistent connection. As only metaphor can transfer relational concepts, metaphorical connection is thus to be considered as the paradigmatic type of inconsistent expression.

If metaphor is the paradigmatic outcome of inconsistent connection, inconsistent connection in sentence structures is the privileged linguistic support of relational metaphors. The most typical metaphorical verb or adjective is not a verb or adjective that is meant to express a different process or property, but a verb or adjective constructed with inconsistent arguments: *The little stream* [...] *still kept telling its unintelligible secret* (Hawthorne); *The summer day / Had died in smiling light away* (E. Brontë);

The most striking illustration of the essential link between relational metaphor and inconsistent connection is provided, in an apparent paradox, by the metaphorical use of impersonal verbs.

An English impersonal verb frames a process devoid of participant roles. For this reason, one would not expect impersonal verbs to be used metaphorically as the source of inconsistent connections.[423] In fact, the construction of inconsistent metaphorical links is one of the reasons that lead to the construction of impersonal verbs with one or two arguments.

When constructed with a single argument, as in *It rains cold water*, the impersonal verb receives a subject that gives an independent nominal expression to the substance typically encapsulated within the process — to an internal subject,[424] so to speak. When the verb is used with two arguments, as in *The heavy clouds rain cold water*, the expression of the involved substance shifts to the direct object, while the grammatical subject refers to an external agent.[425] The inconsistency of either or both these arguments is a sufficient condition for relational metaphor: *Des pétales neigent sur le tapis* (Gide: *Petals snow on the carpet*); *The free heaven* [...] *rains fresh light and dew / on the wide earth* (Shelley); *If heaven would rain on me / That future storm of care* (E. Brontë).

4.3.2.2 *Punctual and proportional analogy*

> But the old architect was sure of readers.
> He knew [...] that they would rejoice in possessing
> the vaulted leaves of his stone manuscript (Ruskin)

We can speak of punctual analogy when the inherent properties of one thing located in the source domain are projected onto one thing located in the target domain. We can speak of proportional analogy when a network of relations is projected onto the target domain.[426] At first sight, one is tempted to anchor either kind of analogy in the corresponding kind of transfer, that is, punctual analogy in punctual transfer and proportional analogy in relational transfer. Things, however, are more complex, for a relational transfer can easily end in a punctual projection, whereas most punctual transfers are ready to become the irradiation point of networks of relations. This means that the two kinds of analogy are deeply intertwined in real metaphors.

As observed in a previous section (§4.2), when a metaphorical verb is not taken as the substitute for a consistent process, a paradigm opposes the inconsistent argument to a consistent double. Now, this paradigm frames an interaction between punctual concepts, which is therefore open to a punctual kind of analogy. In the metaphor *Des pétales neigent sur le tapis*, petals are probably said to snow in order to be seen as flakes.

The concept of an object can be applied to an alien target as a punctual model if no more than its inherent properties is taken into account. If a girl's hair is said to be a sheaf of corn, for instance, it is probably because of its colour. But an object can also be projected as a knot belonging to a network of relations within a complex conceptual model.[427] In Ruskin's *The Stones of Venice*, for instance, *churches, temples, public edifices* are *treated as books of history*. The masonry of the Ducal Palace is *one document*, whereas *the whole wall of the palace was considered as the page of a book to be illuminated*. The punctual transfers activate the whole relational background of the shared concept of book, as material object as well as writing support. If a monument is a book, one can unfold it and read the injuries of nature and time on its pages. If one is able to decipher the characters of its writing and masters its language, *the idea of reading a building* and drawing messages from its walls becomes conceivable.[428]

What can be projected when a metaphor is interpreted, thus, is the whole network formed by the vehicle and its consistent and appropriate conceptual environment. If the vehicle is a punctual term, its environment is formed by the set of relations it can enter into. If the vehicle is a relational concept, its environment is formed by a constellation of punctual concepts capable of saturating its empty places. This shows once more that metaphorical creativity does not threaten our shared concepts and networks. Thanks to the formal strength of linguistic expressions, our shared concepts and networks are transferred in stranger domains just as they are provided by our shared ontology and consistent cognitive modelling.

4.4 The nominal domain: Metaphor, metonymy and synecdoche as competing figures

An overview of distributional data and structural configurations argues strongly against the idea that the three main tropes are directly in competition, and highlights metaphor as a privileged figure. Before taking into account the specific relations involved in tropes and opening a way out of them, metaphor can be distinguished from metonymy and synecdoche as the figure that is allowed to transfer both punctual and relational concepts, and therefore to occupy any position and to take any structural configuration. The complex structures displayed by transferred verbs and other relational terms are exclusive to metaphor, while the elementary syntagmatic and paradigmatic forms involved in nominal tropes are shared by metonymy and synecdoche. In this latter case, what is exclusive to metaphor is not the formal mould of the trope but its conceptual structure and content.

It is within these limits, and only within them, that the traditional differential definition of the main tropes regains its meaning. On the one hand, the question about whole-part relations, contiguity and analogy is relevant only within the nominal sphere, where the three figures really compete. On the other hand, if the interpretative strategies that distinguish metaphor, metonymy and synecdoche are carefully analysed within the borders of their common grounds, the assumption that whole-part relations, contiguity and analogy are simply three different ways of working out a transfer completely dissolves. Whole-part relations and contiguity are consistent conceptual bridges whose activation blocks any conceptual transfer. Analogy is neither necessarily nor typically an underlying track provided with a substantive content, but rather a name for the absence of any definite track and any independent content.

4.4.1 *Nominal tropes in reference and predication*

The primary function that justifies the use of a referential noun phrase is the occasional identification of a given intended referent, real or textual.[429] Beside its instrumental function, however, an identifying noun phrase displays a specific conceptual content, and thus a potential power of characterisation of the intended referent. In normal conditions, the identifying function and the conceptual qualification support each other. Whenever a given noun phrase is used to make reference, it works as a sort of downgraded predication implicitly applied to the referent. If a given weapon is referred to as *a sword*, for instance, the addressee is normally allowed to infer that it really is a sword. When the referring noun phrase is not consistent with the intended referent, on the contrary, its two functions — identification and qualification — conflict with each other.

The conflicting functions, of course, are not put on one and the same level. The conceptual qualification of the referent necessarily requires its previous identification, but the latter does not entail the former. Once the intended referent is identified, it is an open question whether the conceptual content of the inconsistent referring expression applies to it or not, and under which conditions. It is at this point that the path taken by metaphor diverges from the path taken by both metonymy and synecdoche.

A metaphorical noun phrase, though conflicting with the assumed identity of the referent, does not give up its conceptual commitment towards it. In a sense, we can even assert that an inconsistent noun phrase is to be considered metaphorical if — and only if — its conceptual content is taken as relevant to the qualification of the referent. If a piece of jewellery is metaphorically said to be a fountain of colour, for instance, the addressee is called upon to apply to the jewel the concepts of fountain and colour — to ask himself in what sense the concepts of fountain and colour are possibly relevant to its definition. The content of a referring noun is really transferred into a stranger domain and is applied as a conflictual classifier to the intended referent.

By virtue of conceptual interaction, metaphorical referring expressions share with consistent ones free access to the predicative position. From the use of the noun phrase *A fountain of colour* to identify a piece of jewellery we can pass to the predication *This piece of jewellery is a fountain of colour* as freely as from the use of the noun phrase *a sword* to refer to a weapon to the predication *This weapon is a sword.* Metaphor is the only figure that turns inconsistent predication into a form of conceptual categorisation.

If the inconsistent referential expression is interpreted as a metonymy or a synecdoche, the conceptual qualification of the referent is suspended. We can even say that an inconsistent noun phrase is interpreted as an instance of metonymy or synecdoche if — and only if — its content, instead of applying to the referent and interacting with it, enters into a positive and consistent relationship with it. If a man is referred to by the noun phrase *A hat*, for instance, the addressee cannot at the same time interpret it as a metonymy, that is, as referring to a man *wearing* a hat, and infer that the man *is*, in any sense of the term, a hat. If the latter inference were made, the utterance would be interpreted as a metaphor. The independent, positive relations exploited, and thus presupposed, by metonymy and synecdoche prevent the application of the content of the referential noun to the referred entity — of the concept of hat to the person. In the presence of metonymies and synecdoches, in other words, there is no transfer of concepts from one domain into another, and therefore no conflictual classification of the intended referent.

For the same reason, it is easy to predict that metonymies and synecdoches are not really fit for the predicative position — a position that explicitly applies concepts to referents. If synecdoches and metonymies are actually allowed to occupy the predicative position, it is on condition they drop their predicative commitment. When a metonymy or a synecdoche is found in the predicative position, the independent relation holding between the subject and the predicate tends to dissolve the direct predicative link expressed by the copula and to take its place. The expression *I was all flour* (E. Brontë), for instance, can be interpreted as a metonymy only on the assumption that the subject was in fact all *covered with* flour. Otherwise, the figure would be interpreted as a metaphor, that is, the concept of flour would be projected upon the subject.[430]

Synecdoche and metonymy contrast jointly with metaphors as nominal tropes which, instead of transferring concepts, exploit independent links between the involved concepts. They stand in opposition to each other only because of the nature of the assumed relation. Synecdoche focuses on complex objects taken in isolation, and exploits the relations holding among complex *Gestalten* and their constituent parts.[431] Metonymy focuses on complex networks of roles involved in typical processes, and is interested in objects only insofar as they take a role within a process. Therefore, metonymy can be founded upon any relation between roles, or between a given role and a whole process, or between saturated processes. The set of relevant relations ranges from very simple ones — like the location of objects in space and time — to more complex ones — like the relation between an instrument and the action it serves to accomplish, or between a cause and its effect.[432]

4.4.2 *The textual work of synecdoche and metonymy*

> We no longer buy oranges,
> we buy vitality (Huxley)

The absence of a true conceptual interaction, due to the presence of a substantive and consistent relation between tenor and vehicle, does not prevent metonymies and synecdoches from performing specific and highly praiseworthy textual functions. If metonymies and synecdoches do not affect the conceptual identity of objects and processes, they can impose a marked perspective on the perception and presentation of objects and processes whose conceptual integrity is assumed.

By naming a complex object with the name of one of its parts, synecdoche naturally tends to distort the perception of it. The synecdoche *Une main frappe sur le carreau* (Butor) presents the person as a sort of background to his hand. A woman has a huge nose; we can see her as a mere appendix of her nose — she is her nose:

> "Avrà avuto bisogno di prender aria" osservò la *marchesa nel suo naso imperturbabile* [...].
> "Don Franco viene adesso, signora marchesa", disse la nipote del fattore dopo aver dato un'occhiata al lago.
> "Va bene" rispose *il naso sonnacchioso* (Fogazzaro).

Highlighting the peculiar features of a given entity while backgrounding the shared ones, synecdoche is a most powerful instrument of caricature,[433] as the last example shows.

There is a threshold beyond which a description, isolating the parts as if they were autonomous from the whole, goes on to threaten the integrity of the object: *Freddy Malins' left hand accepted the glass mechanically, his right hand being engaged in the mechanical readjustment of his dress* (Joyce); *If he stretched his hand out to get a piece of bread, his fingers clenched before they reached it, and remained on the table, forgetful of their aim* (E. Brontë). If this threshold were really crossed — if the hands were no longer seen as parts of a person, but as personified autonomous entities — synecdoche would turn into metaphor.

When focusing on a property instead of the object, the figure that is traditionally called abstraction synecdoche turns our canonical perception schemata upside down. Instead of seeing the property as an attribute of the object, we see the object as if it were an accident of an independent property. The effect is a sort of abstractive estrangement:

> I could see nothing except a faint phosphorescent flash revealing the glassy smoothness of the sleeping surface (Conrad).

> Nam saepe in colli tondentes pabula laeta
> lanigerae reptant pecudes, quo quamque vocantes
> invitant herbae gemmantes rore recenti,
> et satiati agni ludunt blandeque coruscant;
> omnia quae nobis longe confusa videntur,
> et velut in viridi candor consistere colli[434] (Lucretius)

> A patch of white, which I first took to be a cat, moved stealthily along the house-front (G. Greene).

Within narrative texts, synecdoche easily shades into the expression of a partial perception from a partial point of view or of a tentative construction of the object out of a partial perception:

> [Don Rodrigo] guarda all'uscio, lo vede aprirsi, vede presentarsi e venire avanti due logori e sudici vestiti rossi, due facce scomunicate, due monatti, in una parola[435] (Manzoni).

> He had perceived in the very act of turning away that he was exchanging glances with a pair of eyes in the heap of mats. He saw a shifting gleam of whites. "Come out!" he cried in a fury, a little doubtful, and a dark-faced head, a head without a body, shaped itself in the rubbish, a strangely detached head, that looked at him with a steady scowl (Conrad).

The most striking property of metonymies is their aptitude to compress into simple frames complex networks of actantial relations, whose explicit statement would result in long-winded pedantry.[436] One can be said to hold in one's arm hope instead of its designed instrument, which happens to be a lamp:

> So [...] after many failures Starbuck contrived to ignite the lamp in the lantern; then stretching it on a waif pole, handed it to Queequeg as the standard-bearer of this forlorn hope [...] There, then, he sat, the sign and symbol of a man without faith, hopelessly holding up hope in the midst of despair (Melville).

The descriptive or argumentative strength of a metonymical short-cut ranges from the pure laziness of the stereotype — *a glass of Burgundy* instead of *a glass of wine produced in Burgundy* — to the brutal revelation of a truth which a canonical expression would keep hidden: *Il épouserait une grosse dot* (Zola: *He would marry a huge dowry*); *The tocsin rings the scare* (Huizinga). As the examples show, the typical paraphrase of a metonymy is not a simple substitution of the vehicle by the tenor, but an analytical explication of their consistent relationship within a given process.[437]

4.4.3 *Metaphor as an open conceptual conflict*

As even the most impressive examples suggest, the textual work performed by metonymies and synecdoches, however rich and deep, rests on the previous identification of a positive, independent link between tenor and vehicle within the structure of a consistent object or process. The focusing of the hand as a performing entity can easily upset our perception of the person as a whole; however, it can do so only against a previous assumption of the canonical relation between a hand and the person. One cannot appreciate the polemic potential of a dowry being described as the partner in a wedding without having in mind the canonical relationship between a bride and a dowry. These relations, far from being created by metonymies and synecdoches, are presupposed by them. They form part of our basic categorisation of things and processes, and would outlive the complete disappearance of metonymies and synecdoches from discourse. This point is relevant to a correct understanding of the peculiar nature of analogy and the peculiar link between analogy and metaphor.

As we have seen, a deeply rooted, widespread assumption takes for granted that metaphor is grounded on analogy, and analogy, just as part-whole relation or contiguity, is a substantive relation holding among things and processes, independent of the construction of metaphors and providing metaphorical transfers with a track. If we look at the effective structure of conceptual interaction free from prejudice, however, we realise that metaphor is characterised precisely by the absence of any independent relation holding between its terms. Metaphor is in fact an open conceptual conflict, whose terms are not necessarily linked by a previous, substantive relation, and whose issue is the result of a free interaction between its terms. If this is true, the relationship between the traditional underlying tracks and conceptual transfer is overturn. What makes a conceptual transfer possible is not the presence of a substantive relation between vehicle and tenor but its absence. If a positive relation is activated, there is no room left for transfer, and therefore no metaphor. If there is a transfer, and therefore a metaphor, it is because an open interaction takes the place of a positive track. Analogy is not a positive relation, but one issue of this open interaction.

This characteristic of the metaphorical way of working out a conceptual conflict is highlighted by the observation of ambivalent structures, admitting both a metaphorical and a non-metaphorical issue. The noun phrase *Our dear samovar* (Tolstoy), for instance, inconsistently referring to a woman, potentially admits interpretation, out of context, either as a metonymy or as a metaphor. The utterance would be interpreted as a metonymy if and only if an independent relation between the woman and the samovar were textually relevant — if the woman were the person who typically used it, for instance. It would be interpreted as a metaphor if no independent relation between the woman and the samovar were taken as relevant. In the first case, the positive relation between the two concepts would keep the samovar within the same conceptual domain of the woman, preventing it from being transferred and projected onto the woman. In the second case, the samovar would be transferred and projected upon the woman as a stranger concept, and no obstacle would prevent the conflicting concepts from interacting with each other. Knowing that a conceptual interaction takes place, however, is not the same as knowing what its outcome is likely to be — it is only stepping into an open space (see §5.3.3).

5. Metaphor

> For we all of us, grave or light,
> get our thoughts entangled in metaphors,
> and act fatally on the strength of them (G. Eliot)

Following our path of analysis — the study of complex meanings at the crossroads of linguistic forms and conceptual structures, between co-operation and conflict — has afforded us a new point of observation upon the complex and picturesque world of tropes. Placing ourselves at this vantage point, we are now ready to rise the Socratic question about metaphor: what is metaphor?

In its most direct form, the question is decidedly too ambitious. Metaphor is too complex a phenomenon to admit a simple definition of the form *Metaphor is such and such.* A first tentative reformulation of the essential question should be framed in the following terms: is metaphor an independent conceptual structure brought to expression by linguistic tools, or is it a semantic structure imposed on reluctant concepts by autonomous linguistic forms?

Asked in this way, the question has the advantage of locating the answer within an enclosed space delimited by two options. For precisely this reason, however, the polar form of the question is inevitably self-defeating. As a polar question, it presupposes that one — and only one — of the two answers is true, whereas the other is false. However, both alternatives are actually supported by empirical evidence, for there are plenty of metaphors of either kind. There are plenty of independent metaphorical concepts brought to expression by a wide set of linguistic expressions, and there are plenty of metaphorical semantic structures, which can only be conceived of as meanings of linguistic expressions provided with specific forms.

This implies that the very form of the question is wrong, which leads us to approach metaphor from the opposite perspective. Instead of looking for an illusory all-purpose definition, we shall look for a minimalist definition that identifies in the first instance the largest common denominator shared by any kind of metaphor. A minimalist definition, of course, can be justified only if it provides the basis for an exhaustive typology of the heterogeneous realm of metaphor. At this point, the Socratic question will no longer focus on metaphor in general, but on typicality: what kind of metaphor can be considered the *Idealtypus* of the figure?

5.1 Metaphors, expression and construction: Conceptual structures and semantic structures

The idea that metaphor is essentially a kind of conceptual structure has been coherently worked out within the framework of cognitive semantics. From a cognitive point of view, metaphor is not to be seen as a figure which violates shared conceptual structures and cognitive models, but is itself one of the most powerful, widespread and pervading sources of shared conceptual structures and cognitive models: "General conceptual metaphors are thus not the unique creations of individual poets but are rather part of the way members of a culture have of conceptualizing their experience" (Lakoff & Turner, 1989: 9). Metaphorical concepts form a constitutive part of "conceptual schemas" which "organize our knowledge. They constitute cognitive models of some aspect of the world, models that we use in comprehending our experience and reasoning about it" (65). This holds above all for very rich conceptual realities, whose complexity we could not grasp through simple categories.[438] In such cases, metaphors are not the dispensable, purely decorative devices classified by traditional literary rhetoric. Instead, they are to be seen as indispensable tools for grasping and describing our experience: "The basicness of a metaphor is its conceptual indispensability" (56).

Along this line of argument, cognitive analysis meets some classic European studies, which draw attention to the existence of basic, non-dispensable and inherently metaphoric conceptual structures, and to the role they play in the construction of everyday experience and even philosophic arguments and scientific knowledge: for instance, Blumenberg's monograph about "absolute metaphors" (Blumenberg, 1960), or Weinrich's works about such "metaphorical fields" as "words as coins", or "memory as wax writing tablets or files" (Weinrich, 1958; 1964a).

The main idea underlying cognitive metaphorology is certainly beyond dispute, and has the indisputable merit of reinserting metaphor into the mainstream of symbolisation, rescuing it from its peripheral position as deviant structure. Intrinsically metaphorical topics like "argument as war", "people as plants", "lifetime as a day or as a journey", are coherently worked out to their last implications in poetic texts as well as in ordinary speech. The cognitive conception of metaphor, however, takes for granted that the question about metaphor is polar, and should receive one exclusive right answer: metaphors are not an outcome of the use of words, but basic conceptual structures involved in the categorisation of experience. As Lakoff & Turner (1989: 2) put it, "metaphor resides in thought, not just in words". If this statement amounts to saying that metaphors are not simple ways of speaking but above all ways of thinking, there is nothing to be added. But if it implies that the whole cycle of metaphor, from creation to textual interpretation, is confined within the realm of concepts and owes nothing to the specific formal properties of linguistic expressions for its ideation, something more needs to be said. The plain fact that inconsistent meanings are found in texts suggests that some metaphors at least, and maybe not the least significant ones, owe very much to words.[439]

Similar to Blumenberg's absolute metaphors and Weinrich's metaphorical fields, the metaphorical conceptual structures analysed by Lakoff are independent of linguistic expression because they are consistent. Like the activation of consistent concepts in general, their activation does not depend on the formal properties of a specific linguistic structure, but is compatible with many distinct and interchangeable forms of expression. These metaphors are rooted in consolidated analogical relations, largely shared and taken for granted as such, whose role and behaviour remind us of the role and behaviour of the constitutive relations of metonymy and synecdoche. Unlike metonymy and synecdoche, however, metaphor is capable not only of bringing to expression independent and consistent conceptual structures; it is also capable of constructing conflictual complex meanings which impose on concepts unexpected relations. As they can hardly be justified from within the realm of concepts, which are by definition consistent, inconsistent conceptual relations depend, for their very taking shape, on the specific grammatical structure of specific linguistic expressions.

If these remarks are true, the consequence is that the concept of metaphor circumscribes so complex and heterogeneous a field as to admit two competing and potentially conflicting definitions. There are metaphors that can be defined as consistent conceptual structures and are simply brought to expression by a set of linguistic forms. And there are metaphors that must be defined as conflicting semantic structures and can only be constructed owing to the specific formal properties of a given linguistic expression. Either competing definition is supported by a corpus of revealing, non-trivial data, and falsified by a corpus of equally revealing, non-trivial data. Neither definition is altogether false and neither is altogether true. Neither definition can be generalised at the expense of the other; yet, they cannot simply be summed up. One cannot without contradiction say at one and the same time that metaphors are consistent concepts and conflicting concepts. At this point, either one gives up the idea itself of a general definition of metaphor, or the quest for it has to stop before the path forks — before the alternative between consistency and conflict presents itself.

A definition which is compatible with both conflict and its absence is a definition which contents itself with identifying the largest common denominator shared by any kind of metaphor. As a starting point, we can take a revised version of Aristotle's definition of "*metaphora*": a metaphor is the transfer of a punctual or relational concept into an alien conceptual domain.[440]

The advantage of such a general definition is that it is really compatible with any kind of metaphor. But this advantage also represents the limit of the definition: it says almost nothing about metaphor. To take G. de Vinsauf's suggestive metaphor, a metaphor is a sheep feeding in a foreign meadow — "*Et proprias cognoscis oves in rure alieno*". But once the sheep has jumped across the fence, the adventure is not at its end — it is merely at its beginning. Whether the sheep comes into conflict with the natives or not, chases them, is chased or reaches an accommodation, yields or imposes its rule — all this cannot be known in advance. In plain terms, the structural and discursive properties that most clearly define metaphors can be identified only on the condition of systematically exploring all the paths open to conceptual interaction once a concept has been transferred into an alien territory. The identification of a largest common denominator, in other words, only makes sense if it is taken as the common ground for a differential typology.

5.2 A typology of metaphorical transfers

The first and most relevant parameter to be taken into account when drawing up a typology of metaphorical mappings is the alternative between consistency and conflict.

Consistent metaphors include two different kinds of conceptual structure, that is, lexical catachreses — for instance, the *wing* of a building — and metaphorical concepts. Among metaphorical concepts, some are spontaneous and anonymous, while others are creations of individuals. An example of the first kind is the metaphor of "life as journey"; an instance of the second is Kuhn's (1962) metaphorical concept of "scientific revolution". Though belonging both to consistent concepts, lexical catachreses and metaphorical concepts are in contrast in terms of their specific ways of attaining consistency.

Catachresis is simply a way of expressing an obvious concept using an alien word. It attains consistency by dropping any feature of the source concept that is not compatible with the target — it is a regressive kind of consistent transfer. When the side annex of a building is christened *wing*, for instance, a bird's body is taken as a metaphorical model for the structure of the building. At the same time, any attribute of a bird's wing that is in conflict with the assumed conceptual profile of buildings — for instance, its being an instrument of flight — is left aside.[441]

When a metaphor is created by an individual in order to shape a new concept, it attains consistency in a progressive and projective way. The qualifying properties of the source are projected upon the target concept in order to threaten its assumed conceptual identity and to reshape it under the active influence of the source.[442] The metaphor of scientific revolution, for instance, leads one to scan the assumed properties of political revolutions in order to apply the most relevant of them to the history of science. Instead of adapting the concept of revolution to the inherited idea of scientific discovery, the concept of scientific revolution radically challenges the traditional idea that the history of science is a sort of linear progress. The conceptual conflict is not avoided but actively provoked. At the same time, it is provoked only to disappear when an autonomous consistent concept is created.

Shared metaphorical concepts are located half-way between catachreses and individual creations. Unlike individual creations, shared metaphorical concepts are regressive kinds of metaphorical mappings. Unlike catachreses, shared metaphorical concepts cannot be reduced to dead metaphors, but are grounded in living and productive metaphorical schemes of thought, which proves that "what is conventional and fixed need not be dead" (Gibbs, 1994: 277). Shared metaphorical concepts are not consistent because they simply adapt the vehicle to the tenor, as catachreses do, but because the underlying metaphorical mappings are fully integrated in our ordinary way of thinking as already acquired, and yet alive, conceptual mappings.

Among conflicting metaphors, we may draw two perpendicular distinctions. Along the first dimension, punctual metaphorical transfers contrast with relational transfers in terms of both grammatical distribution and inner structure of the conceptual interaction. Along the second, we have to distinguish lexical conflicts, systematic and contingent cognitive conflicts, and ontological conflicts. Lexical and cognitive conflicts, both systematic and contingent, only affect the surface of concepts — their linguistic-specific organisation, their cognitive content, or even their application to particulars — without challenging their consistency. Ontological conflicts defy the essential properties of beings, which lie at the basis of consistency.

As we remarked in a previous chapter,[443] any kind of punctual conflict by definition allows consistent expression. In the field of relational transfers, lexical and cognitive conflicts, both systematic and occasional, can easily be reduced to consistent expression, whereas ontological conflicts are intrinsically irreversible, and cannot so easily be considered mere substitutes of consistent states of affairs.

A transversal opposition, which crosses the whole territory of metaphor with the only exception of lexical catachresis, is the alternative between regressive and projective analogy. Both consistent concepts and irreversible ontological metaphors, punctual and relational metaphors, referential and predicative, are liable to be located at some point on the scale ranging from purely regressive analogy to endlessly projective analogy.

5.3 The question about typicality

Once a typology of metaphorical transfers has been drawn up, the relevant question focuses on typicality: what kind of metaphor best instantiates the exclusive structural properties and the semantic and textual potential of the figure?

The question about typicality is relevant to all those multi-layered concepts that cannot be univocally delimited by a set of necessary and sufficient conditions. Metaphor is certainly one of these concepts. The only set of necessary and sufficient conditions which can reasonably be attributed to the whole set of metaphors simply draws the outer border of the category, and says almost nothing about its content, that is, about the qualifying properties of actual metaphors. In order to find out these properties, one has to reverse the direction of the search. This means approaching the question not from the bottom — from the common ground shared by all metaphors — but from the top — from the properties displayed by the richest and most complex instances of metaphor. In this way, the different kinds of instances are distributed within a hierarchic, multi-layered category according to their distance from the selected model. It is at this point that the question about metaphors meets the idea of typicality and thus the question of prototype.

A multi-layered category specifies at its core the necessary and sufficient conditions, or, at least, the qualifying properties, for a restricted but representative subset of items — the prototypical instances. At the same time, it opens its peripheral layers to a heterogeneous set of instances, which neither necessarily nor to the same extent share the nuclear properties. A variable category is at once generous in admitting instances and extremely selective in characterisation. It elegantly solves the conflict between inclusivity and characterisation without paying for broad inclusivity with trivial characterisation. Now, the structure of a category like "metaphor" is exactly as multi-layered and hierarchic as, say, the structure of the category "bird", and this holds for a significant number of descriptive and theoretical categories to be found in human sciences. These are the reasons why the prototype model of description is extended from natural categories to constructed theoretical categories, first of all to linguistic categories. According to Lakoff (1987: 67), "Linguistic categories, like conceptual categories, show prototype effects. Such effects occur at every level of language, from phonology to morphology to syntax to the lexicon. I take the existence of such effects as *prima facie* evidence that linguistic categories have the same character as other conceptual categories".

The extension of the prototypical model from the domain of natural categories to such descriptive and theoretical categories as metaphor is at once necessary and problematic. It is necessary because categories of the same structure can be found in both domains; it is problematic because the criteria for typicality cannot be the same.

In spite of the unquestionable structural analogies, categories like "metaphor", "word" or "sentence" do not belong to the same level as categories like "bird". The former are second-level categories, that is, categories which do not immediately deal with things, as first-level categories do, but with first-level categorisations of things. The difference of level obviously changes the conditions under which the most typical instances are identified and the criteria according to which the qualifying properties of the prototype are defined.

As far as first-level categories are concerned, the relevant criteria for identifying the prototypical instances and properties rest on the naive attitude shown by average people who use these categories. On these grounds, criteria based on psychological and statistical salience are adequate and revealing. For an average European, for instance, a prototypical bird is capable of flying, and therefore is more easily identified with a blackbird than with a chicken or an ostrich. This is the kind of bird an average person would imagine when asked about birds — the one a child would draw if asked to do so. As far as natural first-level categories are concerned, a faithful description of the way people spontaneously deal with a given category immediately leads to an optimised focalisation of the category core.

Second-level categories, however, are not natural categories but artificial constructions. If natural categories must just be taken and described as they offer themselves to observation, second-level categories must be evaluated, discussed and tried against critical data. They are constructed and reconstructed, accepted, rejected or adapted in order to attain descriptive and explicative adequacy, and their multi-layered structure must be justified with reference to this function. As a rigorous definition of the qualifying properties of the core forms an essential part of the structural description of a second-level category, the criteria for typicality must in turn be justified with reference to the descriptive and explicative function of the category. Therefore, they must be structural criteria, based on an explicit evaluation of the critical structural properties that differentiate the competing instances.

If the structure of artificial second-level categories were simply based on psychological and statistical data, the criterion for typicality would be circular and deeply misleading — it would either reflect the peculiar attitude of a given scientific community, or simply assume common sense views about the objects of enquiry. In the specific case of metaphor, an immediate transplantation of the idea of prototype would probably lead to identifying the most typical instances of the category with the "metaphors we live by" (Lakoff & Johnson, 1981), that is, with the set of metaphorical and consistent concepts which are familiar landmarks of our symbolic landscape just as blackbirds are familiar guests in our gardens. If our interest lies in finding out how far metaphor can push the limits of linguistic creation in shaping concepts, however, a typical instance of metaphor is not so much a familiar instance as an instance which best valorises the ontological, cognitive, lexical, grammatical and textual resources involved in its creation and interpretation.[444] It is on such a premise that we shall examine three structural parameters of typicality for metaphors.

5.3.1 *Consistent and inconsistent metaphors*

> This was a Poet — It is That
> Distils amazing sense
> From ordinary Meanings
> (E. Dickinson)

Consistent metaphors are one kind of conceptual structure among others. They form a continuum with any other kind of consistent conceptual structure, and share the essential properties of them. Similarly to any other consistent concept, in particular, consistent metaphors can be conceived of independently from a specific linguistic expression and its specific structure.[445]

The content of an inconsistent metaphor, on the other hand, cannot be reduced to an independent conceptual structure, but is a purely semantic structure, the exclusive outcome of the shaping power of a specific linguistic form upon concepts. Inconsistent metaphors are probes launched beyond the borders of consistent thought, to explore a conceptual territory that is the exclusive domain of both metaphor and linguistic structuring. As it makes maximum use of the resources of linguistic creation, it is the inconsistent rather than the consistent transfer of concepts that can be considered as the most typical sort of metaphorical transfer.

5.3.2 *What is seen as what?*

> Do you think we have the same pair of eyes,
> only different spectacles? (Woolf)

Like traditional conceptions of metaphors, and competing with them, cognitive semantics identifies a general formula for metaphor, which is in fact inherited from the interactive conception. This formula takes neither the form "B replaces A", typical of the substitutive conceptions, nor the form "A is like B", the comparative paraphrase which, as a metonymy or a synecdoche would do, weakens the identifying power of the copula. The form it takes is that of a direct identification: "A is B".

The formula admittedly coincides with one of the grammatical forms open to metaphors — namely, the predicative use of a metaphorical noun: *Thy words are swords* (Marlowe). However, it is meant to convey a general, independent conceptual structure holding for any kind of metaphorical interaction. This structure is in fact a kind of definition, and in particular a kind of classification, which applies an inconsistent *definiens* to the *definiendum*.[446]

A grammatical analysis of metaphorical expressions calls into question precisely the universality of the identifying formula and of the underlying model of metaphor as a kind of definition and classification of a given principal subject. If metaphors can take many different forms, in turn, it makes sense to ask which can be considered the most typical.

Though directly displayed by the application *in praesentia* of a metaphorical predicative noun to a subject, the identifying formula can be extended to other grammatical and functional types of metaphor. The relevant question at this point is whether the generalised model captures the qualifying properties of the different kinds of metaphor.

The formula is certainly open to the referential use of metaphorical nouns. For instance, insofar as the sun can be identified by the noun phrase *nature's eye*, as in:

> Fair nature's eye, rise, rise again, and make
> Perpetual day (Marlowe)

the same noun phrase can be predicated of the sun: *The sun is nature's eye.*

Owing to the general accessibility of any sort of concept to the nominal category, the identifying formula is accessible to relational terms, but on one strict condition: the metaphorical process or quality must allow an alternative consistent formulation, capable of saturating the subject position of the formula. A metaphorical process such as *The brook sings*, for instance, can be transposed into such an identifying formula as *The sound of the brook is a kind of singing*, whereby a process is subsumed under an inconsistent category.

The validity of such a manipulation is uneven, and its limits are the limits of classifying concepts.

The textual value of a metaphorical act of reference cannot be reduced to a sort of predication. In spite of this, the predicative reformulation does not radically betray the conceptual work performed by the referential metaphor, that is, a conflictual classification of the referent. Things grow more difficult with relational concepts, and in particular with processes.

If the focus admits a consistent substitute, the application of the formula is immediate. Such a metaphor as *The brook is singing*, for instance, can easily be reduced to *The sound of the brook is a kind of singing.*

If no consistent double of the metaphorical process can be identified within the target conceptual area, the subject position of the formula cannot be saturated. If we try to reduce a verbal metaphor like *The moon smiles* to the identifying formula, the subject's place is condemned to remain empty: *The moon's Ø is a kind of smile.*[447] Such behaviour is consistent with the structure of the relational metaphor, whose primary function is not to give indirect expression to a consistent process but to put one or more arguments into an inconsistent relation. Of course, this side of the interaction can in turn be expressed by an identifying formula, say *The moon is a human being.* But this equation grasps only a part of the message, for it leaves aside the metaphorical focus itself. If the moon is said to smile, it is certainly not simply in order to identify it with a human being.

Within the borders of a definite text, we can certainly imagine an occasional consistent paraphrase of the metaphorical process itself: the smile of the moon could denote, for instance, no more than its brightness. It is only on these conditions — if the metaphorical verb is taken as a substitute for a consistent process — that the metaphor can be reduced to the identifying formula: *Moon's brightness is a kind of smile.*

The consequences of such a move, however, are far-reaching. The supposed universality of the identifying formula rests on the supposed universality of classification, and therefore of substitution. If metaphor is reduced to the conflictual classification of a clearly identifiable principal subject, a consistent expression of this principal subject, alternative to the metaphor, is by definition accessible. Insofar as they are confined to the identifying formula, then, both interactive and cognitive conceptions ultimately share no less than the main assumption of substitutive theories: for any metaphorical focus, a consistent alternative principal subject can and must be found.

If we admit that the focus of relational metaphors does not necessarily hold as both a substitute and a subsidiary subject, the natural conclusion is that we must give up the idea of a general structural framework for metaphorical interaction, and analyse the different specific formal moulds shaped by the different grammatical and functional configurations of metaphorical sentences. Among the different sorts of expression which can promote a metaphorical interaction, the most typical is certainly the most specific and exclusive — that is, the inconsistent and non-substitutive metaphorical relation, which is the least ready to give up its peculiar formal properties in order to be reduced to a general classifying formula independent of the form of the expression.

5.3.3 *Substantive and projective analogy*

> It was doubtless an ingenious idea
> to call the camel the ship of the desert,
> but it would hardly lead one far
> in training that useful beast (G. Eliot)

It is a commonplace that metaphor has to do with analogy. But what kind of relationship is analogy? If we look at some sorts of metaphor, we are inclined to think that analogy is a ready-made relationship — the traditional *tertium comparationis* — provided by shared conceptual models, like a part-whole relation or contiguity, different from them in content but not in function. When faced with a metaphor like *The vindictive fire was still burning in him* (G. Eliot), for instance, we immediately see an obvious, independent relation of analogy between fire and passion: both burn. Independent relations among things of this kind, based on the activation of a definite *tertium comparationis*, are instances of a regressive, and therefore substantive, kind of analogy.

If we look at some other sorts of metaphor, we enjoy a very different insight. Instead of being offered the expression of a pre-existing and independent analogy, we are faced with a complex meaning mixing different concepts from different areas, which invites us to look for some non-trivial analogy in order to give it a textually coherent interpretation. In this case, analogy is not an underlying relation but an invited issue of the metaphor — it is a projective, and therefore empty, kind of relationship. A projective metaphor does not depend on the previous identification of a substantive analogy, but calls for the production of one. In this case analogy, if there is any at all, is but the guiding maxim of a creative conceptual task yet to be carried out.

Projective analogy provides conceptual creation with one of its most powerful tools. Most contemporary definitions of metaphor are in fact definitions of projective metaphors, which are therefore considered as the only true metaphors, or at least as the most typical ones. In the presence of a projective metaphor — Weinrich (1963: 338) points out — "we can be certain that our metaphors do not, as traditional metaphorologies have it, represent real or previously thought-out shared qualities, but produce analogies, create correspondences, as demiurgic tools". Richards (1936: 117) is more categorical: "A metaphor may work admirably without our being able with any confidence to say how it works or what is the ground of the shift [...] one of the worst snares of the study [is] the assumption that if we cannot see how a metaphor works, it does not work". "It would be more illuminating in some of these cases — Black

(1954(1962: 37)) echoes him — to say that the metaphor creates the similarity than to say that it formulates some similarity antecedently existing".[448]

When it creates new concepts out of conceptual conflicts, projection results in consistent categorisation, and therefore in a kind of analogy which is in turn substantive, designed to join the rich family of available regressive analogies. Such metaphorical concepts as "Scientific revolution" or "Snake" are consistent because they rest on a network of analogies which, though being the result of a creative projection, are now definitely identified and relied upon.

In the presence of the most creative instances of poetic metaphor, on the other hand, the metaphorical projection is not expected to result once and for all in a definite analogy, but remains potentially open to an indefinite set of possible outcomes:

> When the green woods laugh with the voice of joy,
> And the dimpling stream runs laughing by:
> When the air does laugh with our merry wit,
> And the green hill laughs with the noise of it (Blake)

In such cases, the incompatibilities between the involved concepts are not irreversibly suppressed, and are as essential as analogies in shaping the metaphorical message. The tension between the conflicting concepts is not bound to disappear, but to form a qualifying part of the metaphorical content. As Richards (1936: 127) points out, "When Hamlet uses the word *crawling* its force comes not only from whatever resemblances to vermin it brings in but at least equally from the differences that resist and control the influence of their resemblances. The implication there is that men should not crawl".[449] Nothing of this sort is felt with metaphorical consistent concepts. If life is metaphorically seen as a journey, there is no implication that it should not be so. In the presence of endless projections, we may go on speaking of analogy; but analogy is no more than the name we give to the absence of any previous substantive relation between the conflicting concepts.

Regressive and progressive analogy are not exclusive options, but the extreme poles of a wide and heterogeneous range of virtual options, within which each textual occurrence of each metaphor is ready to find out its peculiar path. One and the same conflictual expression is virtually open either to the identification of a ready-made regressive analogy or to the most unpredictable projective developments. In spite of this, however, regressive and projective analogy cannot be put on a level. A drift towards projection is latent in any conceptual conflict, and no regressive analogy proves solid enough to block it once and for all. When one is told that truth is light, for instance, it is only too easy to evoke one of the building conceptual metaphors of Western thought.[450] In spite of this, when Tocqueville writes that *La vérité est […] une lumière que je crains d'éteindre en l'agitant* (*Truth is light for me, for I fear to put it out by shaking it*), truth is light because both of them are frail, and one must take care of both in the same way.

Such drifts suggest that projection is always within the horizon of metaphor, so that it can be considered the most typical kind of analogy, which instantiates the peculiar characteristics of metaphor at their best.

The identification of a substantive analogy is not a necessary condition for metaphor. All that is required for a metaphor to take place is a conceptual interaction free from independent, positive tracks — that is, an open conceptual conflict. Of course, if a salient substantive analogy is at hand, and is coherent with the context, it has some chance of being preferred. Even in such cases, however, a given substantive analogy is nothing more than a contingent option, virtually competing with both alternative substantive analogies and the activation of projective kinds of analogy. If this is true, even substantive analogy is not on a level with the relations underlying synecdoche and metonymy. As it is never a necessary condition for metaphor, substantive analogy is in any case built on sliding ground. This insight is confirmed by a careful observation of stereotyped metaphors and even of so-called dead metaphors.

In the presence of stereotyped metaphors, the activation of a substantive analogy provides a ready-made way of restoring consistency, as in the case of part-whole relation or contiguity. If the categorisation of passion as fire — *The vindictive fire was still burning in him* — is merely a way of implying that passion burns, the conflict disappears. The projective character, on the contrary, is a specific property of analogy — it does not hold for such substantive links as part-whole relation or contiguity.

A stereotyped metaphor is not irreversibly bound to one and the same substantive analogy. It is sufficient that it brings to expression at any occurrence some kind of substantive analogy. A metaphor like *John is a lion* can be considered as the paradigm of the stereotyped metaphor. Yet, all we can predict for its interpretation being stereotyped is that some evident substantive analogy between the identified subjects can be found at any textual occurrence. What analogy exactly, it is hard to say out of context — maybe John is brave and strong, but why not red-haired, or accustomed to leaving to his female partner the task of providing food?

Even for the most stereotyped metaphor, a standard interpretation is not an irreversible destiny. A favourable context is a sufficient condition for encouraging a projective interpretation. Let us consider the metaphor of man as wolf. Given that a social image of the wolf is deeply rooted in our culture as a source of substantive analogies with men, a simple activation of the shared commonplaces about wolves is more likely to take place than a creative projection. As Black (1954(1962: 41) points out, "If the man is a wolf, he preys upon other animals, is fierce, hungry, engaged in constant struggle, a scavenger, and so on".[451] Yet a metaphor is never the prisoner of commonplaces. In a chapter of St. Francis' *Fioretti,* a wolf which terrorises the town of Gubbio perfectly sticking to our most familiar stereotypes is persuaded by the saint to give up its way of life. In exchange, Gubbio's citizens agree to provide it with food during its life. By yielding to persuasion, the wolf becomes a living allegory of the dawning bourgeois public ethic, replacing violence with peaceful and rational transaction,[452] and thus a model for Gubbio's citizens.

Substantive analogy can be justified as a particular case of projective analogy. The most stereotyped metaphors are not different in structure from projective metaphors, and can be found in exactly the same grammatical positions. Just as a girl said to be a nightingale in everyday conversation is immediately taken to be a girl with a beautiful voice, a smiling meadow is a meadow covered with flowers in a given literary tradition. Stereotyped metaphors are virtually projective metaphors that for contingent reasons — the weight of shared commonplaces, the influence of a literary tradition, the inherited laziness of generations of interpreters — do not exploit their whole potential. If this is true, however, the concept of dead metaphor is almost an oxymoron. Indeed, what is commonly called the death of a metaphor lacks the irreversibility of real death — like the sleeping girl of the fairy tale, a dead metaphor can be raised to new life at any moment. The identification of a substantive analogy is no more than an accident for metaphor. Its immortal soul is conflict, which is an everlasting source of conceptual energy.

A conceptual conflict does not have to be founded on an independent substantive relation in order to be seen as a metaphor, and this radically distinguishes metaphor from metonymy and synecdoche. Projective analogy contains no more than an empty presumption of analogy, which suggests a task to be performed. Analogy in itself has no limits. Potentially, it is everywhere — and nowhere: "everything is like everything and in endless ways" (Davidson, 1978(1984: 254)); "Similarity is a vacuous predicate: any two things are similar in some respect or other" (Searle, 1979: 95). Taken in this sense, analogy is just a useful word — it is a lazy name for the unknown ending point of virtually endless work.[453]

Summing up, we may conclude that the most typical metaphors — those which best instantiate the potential resources of the figure — are projective, inconsistent, relational and non-substitutive, that is, relational metaphors which take the form of inconsistent connections open towards virtually endless projections.

5.4 Last but not least: The place of metaphor in a philosophical grammar

Our definition of the most typical kinds of metaphor is consistent with the inclusion of a metaphorology in a philosophical grammar.

Metaphor is the most direct and creative textual valorisation of inconsistent complex meanings. The formal possibility of inconsistency, in turn, makes visible the constitutive factors involved in the construction of complex meanings, that is, the formal grammatical lawfulness and the substantive conceptual lawfulness, whose interaction is the focus of a philosophical grammar.

The treatment of metaphors within a philosophical grammar dissociates creation from transgression. Metaphors transgress neither linguistic nor conceptual lawfulness. Instead, they valorise both. For making room to conceptual conflicts, one has simply to take language and concepts as they are. For a conflict to take place, language must be provided with a system of formal structures whose articulation is independent of the organised concepts, and concepts must have a structure of their own, which is no less constraining than the formal grammatical mould. The formal patterns of language are valorised if instead of holding as passive means of expression they impose a mould on concepts, and the shared conceptual structures are valorised if instead of being tautologically assumed by linguistic expressions are projected into stranger domains. If this is true, metaphor resides neither in words nor in thought. It resides in the free and open interaction of the two orders of structures, each of which is equally active, and it is this interaction, rather than one of its terms taken in isolation, that forms the most basic datum of our symbolic experience, consistent as well as inconsistent.

The grammar and semantics of conflictual complex meanings, and in particular of metaphors, occupy the last chapter of this monograph. However, they do not form the least relevant topic within a philosophical grammar. A philosophical grammar is not simply a grammar that makes room for the study of conceptual conflicts. Instead, it locates conceptual conflict at its very core, for conceptual conflict is at one and the same time the outpost and the overt manifestation of the shaping power of linguistic structures.

Chapter 12

Concluding remarks

These concluding remarks first outline the main points that emerged from the previous chapters, and then suggest further perspectives in the field of both general theoretical reflection and empirical investigation.

1. Looking back

Part I deals with the semiotic background of a philosophical approach to grammar, focusing in particular on the question of the significance of complex linguistic expressions. Two important points in this respect are delimitation of the research field and definition of its contents.

The first aim is pursued in Chapter 1, which focuses on the distinction between the meaning of complex expressions and the messages they can convey when actually used in communication. Meanings belong to the symbolic order, and are in the first place long-lasting structural properties of expressions, shared by the members of a linguistic community. Messages belong to an indexical dimension, and are in the first place contingent aims of individual persons. Thanks to this distinction, communication is not seen as a mere outcome of the meaningfulness of expressions, but as an independent form of purposeful human action, involving ethical responsibility. The aim of Chapter 1, however, is not to outline a theory of human communication, but to justify independent description of complex meanings and delimit its terrain. If communication is grounded on autonomous practical principles, a complex meaning can be studied irrespective of its changing communicative functions, as a long-lasting kind of structure essentially resting on a set of factors, both formal and conceptual, that are in turn long-lasting.

Chapters 2 and 3 focus on the formal and conceptual roots of significance, and in particular on the interaction between coding and inferencing in the ideation of complex linguistic meanings. The exploration of the conceptual and grammatical roots of significance, at the crossroads of formal and conceptual lawfulness, coding and inferencing, is the elective task of a philosophical grammar.

Coding is traditionally depicted as a one-way relationship. According to a formal paradigm, coding projects independent forms onto shapeless concepts; according to a functional paradigm, it maps independent concepts onto instrumental forms. According to both, inferencing is opposed to coding as a pragmatic device resting on ephemeral, occasional data.

The idea put forth in this book is that coding is not a one-way relationship between forms and concepts, but a two-way relationship. In each complex expression, coding is ready to shape concepts thanks to autonomous forms up to a certain point, and to map concepts onto instrumental forms from this point onward. In the former case, we speak of relational coding; in the latter, of punctual coding.

Relational coding operates in sentence nuclei. In the presence of relational coding, a sentence core codes the roles of the process as a whole — as a network of grammatical relations. The whole is logically prior to its constituent parts, and the inner architecture of the expression prevails over its instrumental functions. A good example of relational coding is the coding of the agent as subject of a sentence depicting an action.

Punctual coding operates in the peripheral strata of sentence structures and at the level of interclausal connections. In the presence of punctual coding, a sentence core is expanded by adjunction: a given expression is connected to a sentence core or to one of its constituents insofar as it expresses a given conceptual content connected to a consistent state of affairs. Punctual coding is not supported by a network of grammatical relations, but is grounded in the inner properties of the phrase engaged in it, that is, on the coding potential of a linking word improved, when required, by inferencing. In purely grammatical terms, the parts, that is, a sentence nucleus and a marginal role, are logically prior to the resulting whole, and instrumental functions prevail on inner structures. A good illustration of punctual coding is instrument: a prepositional phrase is connected to a sentence structure insofar as the latter depicts an action, and the former is decoded or interpreted as expressing a consistent and appropriate instrument.

Inferencing is traditionally opposed to coding as a pragmatic device resting on occasional data. This attitude is justified as far as external inferencing is concerned, the function in this case being to draw contingent messages out of meaningful expressions within the limits of a contingent field. It is misleading when applied to internal inferencing, which is called upon to improve the coded meaning of a complex expression. While external inferencing is a true pragmatic device, based on contingent data and pursuing contingent aims, internal inferencing is essentially based on long-lasting conceptual structures and takes part in the ideation of a complex meaning, which is a kind of structure.

The competition between language-specific coding devices and consistent conceptual structures characterises any complex meaning, but is made best visible by observation of conflictual complex meanings. Like the stability of a building, the structural firmness of a complex meaning is not due to the absence of tension, but is the outcome of a dynamic equilibrium between competing forces. While some styles of building hide the struggle for equilibrium under a smooth outer structure, others make it fully visible as a significant component of their form. A French Gothic cathedral, for instance, highlights the tension between competing forces by dramatically displaying the opposite thrusts of vaults and flying buttresses. In a similar way, conflictual meanings unveil the impressive dynamism hidden in structural architectures that look absolutely static at a superficial glance.

Part II aims at digging out the conceptual roots of meaning, that is, the complex conceptual structures which feed internal inferencing. Among these structures, a central place is occupied by consistency criteria, traditionally known in linguistics as selection restrictions. Consistency is presented in this monograph as the counterpart of grammatical well-formedness in the field of conceptual structures. Just like grammatical well-formedness, conceptual consistency rests on a system of restrictions, that is, on a grammar of concepts, which is just as open to description as a grammar of forms.

After an intuitive presentation of the place of consistency and consistency criteria in our everyday experience, Chapter 4 examines this topic within philosophical and linguistic research. Consistency criteria tend to be considered by both philosophers and linguists as either a kind of linguistic structure or a kind of cognitive models or data. The hypothesis defended here is that they belong neither to language nor to cognition, but form the core of a shared natural ontology which lies at the ground of our spontaneous attitude towards the world. In particular, consistency criteria are not contents of knowledge but presuppositions relied upon in practical behaviour, which implies that the realm of shared conceptual structures spreads far beyond the realm of shared cognitive structures.

The following chapters support this view. Chapter 5 explores the formal framework of our shared natural ontology and its intricate connections with a set of basic linguistic structures. At a general level, it makes explicit the correlation between punctual concepts and saturated expressions, and between relational concepts and unsaturated expressions. More specifically, it explores the deep links between the structure of the noun phrase and the classification of beings, and between the structure of the sentence, the ideation of processes involving beings, and the attribution of qualities to beings. The conclusion of the chapter is that the formal framework of natural ontology is conceptually neutral, whereas consistency is rooted in substantive conceptual contents.

When dealing with conceptual contents, it is natural to think of the lexicon as a proper home for them. Chapters 6 and 7 are designed to challenge this assumption. The lexicon of a language is a complex structure, organising into a language-specific network of lexical relations and correlations a more widely shared stock of cognitive models and data. In other words, the same tension between language-specific formal shaping and independent conceptual categorisation that characterises the active construction of complex meanings is also at the basis of the static structure of lexical contents (Chapter 6). Against this background, if consistency criteria belong to the lexicon, they have to be either a kind of lexical structure, that is, lexical solidarities, or a kind of cognitive model. Chapter 7 provides arguments against both ideas, and concludes that consistency criteria are neither lexical structures nor cognitive models. Both formal lexical structuring and cognitive modelling of experience are located within the borders of consistency. The function of consistency criteria is to draw these outer borders.

If consistency criteria are presupposed by both lexical structures and cognitive modelling, it is because they provide our form of life with its solid conceptual grounds. This is the reason why consistency criteria are not overtly known but silently assumed. Chapter 8 develops a general idea of presupposition as a kind of *a priori* structure, relied upon in practical behaviour and set apart from both explicit expression and questioning. Consistency criteria form the deepest layer of general presuppositions shared and relied upon in our practical behaviour, and hence in our consistent thought and speech. Looked at from a functional point of view, consistency criteria behave exactly as *a priori* structures are expected to do. To consider them as such, however, entails re-examination of the very idea of *a priori*, which receives a functional definition relative to a practice instead of an essential and absolute one. For consistency criteria, the relevant practice is the most long-lasting we can imagine: it coincides with our form of life.

Part III illustrates how the conceptual equipment of philosophical grammar can offer a contribution to the analysis of complex meaningful expressions, both consistent and conflictual. The examination of simple processes and interclausal links is mainly focused on the interplay of relational and punctual coding on the one hand, punctual coding and inferencing on the other.

Chapter 9 describes the simple nuclear sentence as the only tool for the construction of simple processes. A simple nuclear sentence is supposed to contain in its core a network of grammatical relations, which forms the territory of a relational kind of coding. This core is surrounded by a layered periphery whose general form is governed by the conceptual structure of consistent states of affairs, and whose organisation is shared between a punctual form of coding and internal inferencing. The analysis of the functional core is essentially accessible to formal criteria, based on the grammatical properties of expression. The peripheral strata can be described only through textual and conceptual criteria, based on the consistency of complex concepts checked against the coherence of simple textual chains. As the core of the process does not coincide with the realm of relational coding, but is also accessible to punctual coding, the use of textual conceptual criteria is the only means to distinguish arguments and marginal roles. Moreover, thanks to conceptual criteria sensitive to consistency, a fine layering of both arguments and margins can be attained according to the parameter of closeness.

The subject of Chapter 10 is interclausal linkage. True interclausal linkage, involving two (or more) simple processes, is first distinguished from the expression of inherently complex processes, containing an embedded process in their core, thanks to arguments pertaining to conceptual structure, grammatical structure and form of coding. Interclausal linkage is the most significant example of the priority of function over structure beyond the functional core. Interclausal links are not grammatical structures, but conceptual structures, which can be both expressed and semantically modulated by textual as well as grammatical means. In order to draw interclausal links, the sentence structure is far from being the only tool, but is simply one of several options. The same function can be performed either within the border of a complex sentence or outside it, in a textual dimension, and therefore thanks to textual coherence, typically supported by cohesive devices. Under such conditions, there is more room left for inferencing, and the typology of its interaction with coding is broadened. Beside enriching undercoded grammatical connections within the borders of complex sentence structures, inference is ready to bridge independent utterances. Conversely, thanks to anaphoric relations, the coding of interclausal links is allowed to cross sentence boundaries.

The idea of a logical priority of conceptual structures over linguistic expression in the area of interclausal linkage is tested against a constellation of significant links, including cause, motives and purpose. In this conceptual space, the relationship between conceptual structures and expression is very intricate and ranges from lack of coding to overcoding. The essential conceptual distinction between phenomenal cause and motives for action is neutralised by linguistic coding, and only accessible through textual criteria based on consistency. Cause is a natural concept, easy to infer even in a total void of coding. At the opposite end of the scale, purpose imposes on its conceptual content — the forward-looking motive coinciding with an agent's intention — a specific perspective bound to a specific form of coding. First, the underlying conceptual structure can be seen under different perspectives, owing to the availability of a cause-like and a purposive form of expression. Moreover, it can be indefinitely modulated thanks to the availability of a wealth of encapsulating nouns belonging to the areas of metaphorical goal, intentions and emotions.

Chapter 11 is about conflictual complex meanings, and therefore about tropes, which are the instances of conceptual conflict actually documented in real texts. If looked at as instances of conceptual conflict, tropes are not seen as somehow deviant expressions requiring special interpretative devices, but as meaningful expressions provided with both a grammatical framework and a unitary meaning.

The tropes focused on are oxymoron, metaphor, metonymy and synecdoche. The differentiation and positive characterisation of tropes is not immediately grounded on interpretative strategies, but is seen in relationship with significant differential properties of linguistic expressions and their conflictual contents. This is certainly a partial point of view, though justified insofar as it counterbalances the prevailing attention traditionally paid to textual interpretation strategies at the expense of grammatical and semantic patterns.

The distinction between oxymoron and the constellation formed by metaphor, metonymy and synecdoche is drawn against the distinction between contradiction and inconsistency. Within the field of inconsistency, the distinction between metaphor and the couple formed by metonymy and synecdoche is connected with the distinction between non-saturated and saturated expressions, their different distribution in sentence structure, and their aptitude to transfer concepts in stranger domains. Metaphor is the only figure that transfers both punctual concepts and relational networks from one conceptual territory into another, highlighting conceptual conflicts as instruments of conceptual creation. Metonymy and synecdoche do not transfer concepts, let alone relations, but simply exploit independent relations among consistent saturated concepts. In this way, they affect the perspective from which objects and processes are looked at without challenging their conceptual identity.

The variety of metaphorical transfers defies any conceivable definition of the figure: a metaphor can be punctual as well as relational, consistent as well as conflictual, regressive as well as projective, conventional as well as creative. The only reasonable definition of metaphor is a minimalist definition, leaving room for both the richest and the poorest examples. This, however, implies that a general definition is almost devoid of content. It has therefore to be completed by a typology broad enough to distinguish the different kinds, highlighting the distinctive properties of each. As metaphor forms a complex and layered category, its description requires the identification of the most typical kind, which is supposed to push the creative potential of the figure farthest. According to our analysis, the most typical metaphors are inconsistent, relational, non-substitutive and projective, that is relational metaphors which take the form of inconsistent connections open towards virtually endless projections. As they highlight the ability of linguistic forms to impose an independent mould on concepts, the most typical metaphors occupy a central place in a philosophical grammar.

2. Looking forward

The aim of this monograph is not so much to do empirical work as to clarify underlying assumptions, carefully exploring the conditions, both formal and conceptual, which support the significance of complex linguistic expressions. Theoretical reflection, however, almost inevitably opens empirical paths. In these final pages, I will try to put forward some suggestion about possible empirical work inspired by a philosophical style of approaching grammar.

Chapter 1 examines, and tries to justify on theoretical grounds, the manifold relationship between meaningful expressions and occasional messages. It is a primitive fact belonging to our everyday experience as language users that very similar messages can be entrusted to very different kinds of expression, while one and the same expression is ready to be put at the service of very different communicative aims. As an empirical fact, this can become the subject of empirical investigation, be measured and quantified. Something of this sort has been done, for instance, by Gile (1995). His data, which are not at all trivial, highlight the psychological reality of the instrumental role acquired by expressions during communication: "given exactly the same Message presented under exactly identical conditions at the same point in time, individuals sharing the same mother tongue tend to write different sentences to express it" (Gile, 1995: 52).

According to our hypothesis, expression is a complex phenomenon, which involves different forms of coding and different kinds and degrees of internal inferencing. The content of the expression, in turn, does not coincide with the message, but simply points to it, requiring a variable amount of external inferencing. This implies that the reception of a message by an addressee, which is perceived as an easy path by the actors in communication, actually hides under a smooth surface a very intricate mix of very different linguistic, semiotic and cognitive strategies and abilities. This suggests some developments in the field of psycholinguistic and typological research.

In the field of psycholinguistics, it would be interesting to test whether and to what extent the different forms of coding and inferencing have different costs in terms of elaboration effort and time. The question has been widely and deeply explored as far as the link between meanings and messages is concerned, that is, at the level of external inferencing. As Gibbs (1994: 110) points out, empirical data support the idea that literal interpretation enjoys no particular advantage over non-literal strategies in terms of cognitive effort: "What is extraordinary in the psycholinguistic literature is that the difficulty participants have in recovering speakers' intended meanings — as measured by reading and paraphrase times — is relatively invariant across manipulations of pragmatic complexity".[454] It is reasonable to think that this style of empirical work could be extended to the ideation of complex meanings, and provide a model for a comparative analysis of different proportions of decoding and internal inferencing in terms of psychological effort.

In the field of linguistic typology, it would be interesting to test a rich and diversified sample of languages for the peculiar equilibrium between relational coding and punctual coding, and between punctual coding and inferencing, as found in the languages of Europe.

The interaction between punctual and relational coding can be ideally studied at the level of the simple nuclear sentence, focusing on the formal conditions under which the core of the process is constructed.

All languages are bound to express processes, and therefore to organize and give grammatical expression to networks of roles in sentences. In this sense, Palmer's (1994: 22) question — "Are there languages [...] that do not grammaticalise basic notional roles such as agent and patient?" — is certainly rhetorical. The availability of some kind of long-lasting coding device is inseparable from the very idea of human language. In order to qualify human languages, however, this is not enough. A further question has to be asked about coding, namely, whether coding is simply a way of bringing independent conceptual structures to expression, or contains the formal means for imposing a shape on concepts.

This is, roughly, the question that lies at the basis of a "philosophy of symbolic forms" as outlined by Cassirer (1923(1953)). According to Cassirer, what qualifies a human language as a symbolic form is not simply its aptitude to mark independent concepts, but its aptitude to build up expressions whose inner formal architecture is not shaped by the structure of independent contents, and is therefore ready to impose an independent mould on complex concepts. If coherently explored, this idea has far-reaching implications, both theoretical and empirical.

Theoretically speaking, the relationship between form and function is seen under a new perspective. Instead of opposing the autonomy of forms and their functional motivations, as if autonomy absolutely excluded functional motivation and functional motivation absolutely excluded autonomy, one can imagine not only a dynamic competition between inner form and instrumental motivations, but also a functional motivation for the very idea of formal autonomy.

Self-contained form is neither a flight into a functional void nor simply a fortuitous and somehow undesired outcome of competing functional motivations, but a true counterpart of instrumental functions. Languages tend to answer ever-changing functional pressures developing relatively long-lasting, and therefore relatively arbitrary and autonomous, grammatical forms. The networks of grammatical relations that organize sentence nuclei, not bound to a single specific conceptual content and ready to receive many, are the best example of this. Starting from this premise, we can imagine competition not only between different kinds of motivations interacting in shaping forms, but also between the tendency of means of expression to form long-lasting, autonomous formal patterns and the tendency of functions to shape serviceable coding instruments.[455]

At first sight, the hypothesis of competition between an inner tendency of forms towards self-containedness and the pressure of instrumental motivations seems to introduce a disturbing factor of entropy into the form-function *ratio*. Looked at from a strictly functional point of view, formal self-containedness seems to imply absolute self-reference. Of course, the availability of self-contained forms can be justified in retrospective terms, particularly in terms of competing motivations, but seems absolutely devoid of prospective motivation, and therefore of function: What is the use of it? — one is inclined to ask. This question, however, remains open to a consistent answer.

Formal autonomy implies lack of immediate instrumental motivation, which however does not imply lack of function. Insofar as one can imagine higher-level functions, not immediately bound up with instrumentality, the incompatibility disappears. Shaping concepts in a creative way is certainly one such function. Shaping concepts in a creative way, however, is not only compatible with, but actually requires structural autonomy, as is shown by the formal possibility of conflictual complex meanings. A language is able to shape concepts only insofar as its grammatical structures have withdrawn, so to speak, from both immediate experience and acquired conceptual categorisations, and are therefore ready to challenge both. Absolute dependence on instrumental functions would make languages run this course backwards. If it is relative distance and autonomy that make conceptual creativity possible, however, some degree of freedom from conceptual and pragmatic motivation is the price to be paid for a higher-order function. Formal autonomy of sentence nuclei and relational coding, which cannot be justified as instruments at the service of independent concepts, recover a functional justification as instruments of conceptual creativity, a function that is highlighted by the formal accessibility of conflictual complex meanings.

The ability of sentence structures to shape complex concepts in a creative way cannot be simply assumed as an absolute property for any conceivable language, but has to be seen as a grading property, whose relevance and weight can be investigated for all human languages. For each of them, it makes sense to ask whether and to what extent its coding devices are ready to impose a formal mould on concepts, or simply provide independent concepts with serviceable means of expression. However, once the aptitude of a language to shape concepts is connected to relational coding, which in turn depends on the presence of grammatical relations in the core of sentence structures, the main question of a philosophy of symbolic forms becomes an empirical question.

Centuries of grammatical research based on European languages have made us familiar with the presence of solid networks of purely grammatical relations, ready to frame sentence nuclei irrespective of both conceptual contents and outer functions. In the languages of Europe, as Lazard (1998: 118) points out, "the structuring of the sentence [...] is subject to grammatical rules which are, to a greater extent than in other languages, independent of both the conceptual content and the communicative purposes. In other words, the languages of Europe, above all those of western Europe, are characterised by the relative autonomy of their morphology and syntax in relation to semantics and pragmatics". Unlike the presence of punctual coding devices, which is inseparable from the very idea of human language, the presence and the extent of a relational form of coding based on pure grammatical relations cannot be simply presupposed as a sort of analytical property of language in general. While "the existence of roles is inevitable", as Blake (1982: 90) points out, "grammatical relations are not, and one can easily imagine a language without them". Since it is consistent to imagine a language devoid of pure grammatical relations, however, their presence in the languages of the world and the extent of their autonomy from organised concepts become consistent factual hypotheses to be tested against empirical data. For any natural language, it makes sense to ask whether and to what extent it has an independent network of grammatical relations insensitive to the pressure of concepts, and therefore endowed with a relational form of coding. Against this background, a philosophical enquiry concerning significance focusing on the interplay of grammatical forms and conceptual structures can open a new frontier to typological investigation.

Before being a matter of typological differences, the changing equilibrium of punctual coding and inferencing is a systematic resource of human languages, which documents how deeply coding systems are rooted in consistent thought. Starting from this premise, it is reasonable to expect that recurrent patterns of equilibrium can be documented cross-linguistically.

The competition between coding and inferencing, which takes place outside the network of grammatical relations, can be observed in the marginal strata of sentence structures, and above all in interclausal connection.

Within the peripheral strata of the simple sentence, inference is a constitutive factor of expression, systematically improving punctual coding. A useful empirical question in this connection is whether the changing equilibrium of coding and inferencing is unpredictable and random, or tends to form significant and recurrent patterns, both intra- and interlinguistically.

A good example of such a pattern is the combination of undercoding and inferential enrichment that leads the preposition *with* to express such a heterogeneous constellation of roles as instrument, coperformer and manner in English and other languages of Europe. At first sight, this pattern looks like a rather idiosyncratic feature restricted to some historically related languages. According to Croft (1990: 9–10), however, things are quite different: "Intuitively, there seems to be little if any semantic correlation between these three distinct uses of the same preposition, but a typological study of the distribution of adposition/case uses reveals that the subsumption of these and certain other uses under the same adposition or case marker is actually quite common". If the interaction of punctual coding and inferencing is explicitly focused on as a systematic resource for expression, it is reasonable to expect that many other forms of equilibrium will prove to be quite widespread among the languages of the world.

At the level of interclausal connection, coding has been long overestimated at the expense of inferencing, which is traditionally considered an occasional improvement of coded meaning rather than a systematic resource for expression. If the roles and responsibilities of both strategies are restored, some traditional questions can be approached in a new light. A good example is the connection between coding devices in a given language and certain basic concepts in the conceptual equipment of its speakers, a question which periodically emerges in the discussions about so-called primitive languages.

As Goddard (1991, quoted by Wierzbicka, 1996: 186) points out, "it was a commonplace of an older generation of ethnographic commentary, still sometimes encountered, e.g. Sayers and Bain (1989), that Australian Aboriginal languages and cultures are less explicit than Indo-European languages about the expression of causality, or even that they are positively indifferent to it". A traditional argument supporting this claim is that these languages lack such overt coding devices as English *because*, so that the expression of cause and other relational concepts is at best the outcome of occasional interpretations of forms designed for coding the simpler concept of temporal sequence.[456] This idea can be argued against in two ways: either by showing that so-called primitive languages contain more coding than appears at first glance, or by showing that the expression of such concepts in Standard Average European is less explicit than one is inclined to think, or perhaps would wish. The first line of argument depends on the assumption that the availability of a concept depends on its coding. The latter rests on the assumption that our shared conceptual equipment is not bound up with coding, but has a structure of its own. A basic system of concepts is shared by speakers of different languages, and can be either coded to a variable extent, ranging from undercoding to overcoding, or simply presupposed, both by linguistic structures and in linguistic use.

A good example of the first line of argument is provided by Wierzbicka (1996: Chapter 6), who argues that the Australian Aboriginal forms traditionally described as expressing temporal sequence and occasionally developed into cause are in fact polysemous between temporal sequence and cause. The proof is that there are contexts in which the temporal interpretation would not be coherent: "If we find [...] that in some contexts the 'after' interpretation doesn't make sense whereas a 'because' interpretation does, then we have to postulate polysemy" (1996: 186). The conclusion is that Australian Aboriginal languages achieve by other means a level of coding comparable to English and other European languages.

Wierzbicka's argument is convincing, but it would be even more so if it were also allowed to run the other way around. The fact that so-called primitive languages have more coding than is traditionally assumed does not hinder English and other familiar European languages from having and using less. This of course has important implications on the relationships between concepts and coding. Three remarks can be made on this point.

As a premise for her discussion, Wierzbicka (1996: 186) subscribes the traditional claim that "in English, the idea of causality is expressed in an absolutely unambiguous way in the simple everyday word *because*". As we have seen in Chapter 10, this statement is false. Like its equivalents in other European languages, *because* neutralises the distinction between cause and motives, which is essential in conceptual terms, and as such is systematically recovered thanks to inferencing. What looks at first sight like the paradigm of full coding is in fact an instance of undercoding, systematically requiring inference. When interpreting the expression *John sold his house because he was going to move to another country* as describing the link between an action and its forward-looking motive, an English speaker behaves like an Australian Aborigine inferring cause from the expression of temporal sequence.

One of the most impressive results of Kortmann's (1997) fine-grained examination of the languages of Europe is to have brought to light the enormous role of inferential enrichment, both in improving the synchronic use of subordinators and in motivating their diachronic shifts. Kortmann's extensive enquiry demonstrates once and for all that differential full coding of such key concepts as cause is far from being the rule, even for the languages belonging to the European mainstream. Far from being a feature of primitive languages, the synergy of undercoding and inferential enrichment in expressing essential conceptual structures is a common strategy in any language.

While correctly arguing that many apparent cases of undercoding and inferential enrichment are in fact cases of polysemy, and therefore of differential coding, Wierzbicka puts inferencing and polysemy into spurious opposition. In fact, the polysemy of linking words typically entails a previous stage of inferential enrichment, and is ready to hold as an intermediate stage on the path towards full differential coding. If we imagine a drift from temporal relationships towards more sophisticated concepts, we are made aware that different forms belonging to different stages perfectly coexist in the synchronic supply of coding devices of a given language. In contemporary Italian, for instance, the form *dopo che* ("after that") codes temporal sequence, but is normally used to express cause or motive through inferential enrichment. At the other end of the spectrum, *poiché*, though betraying its origin as an expression of temporal sequence ("after that"), univocally encodes cause or motive,[457] having come to incorporate systematic inferential enrichment. The subordinator *mentre* ("while") is polysemous and occupies an intermediate position. Having originated as an expression of temporal simultaneity, it has incorporated an adversative inferential enrichment ("whilst") without losing its original sense.[458]

The idea that independent long-lasting concepts accessible by way of inference systematically interact with linguistic coding shows the grammaticalisation of inferential enrichment in a new light.

As we have observed, enriching inferences are generally considered a pragmatic kind of inference (see for instance Hopper & Traugott, 1993: 72–77). This implies that grammaticalising them amounts to "conventionalizing conversational implicature" (König & Traugott, 1988): owing to grammaticalisation, the contingent content of repeated occasional inferences becomes the long-lasting conventional meaning of an expression. Seen in this way, grammaticalisation entails a logical leap from the realm of occasional events, belonging to the indexical order, to the realm of long-lasting structures, belonging to the symbolic order and holding a *priori*.

According to our hypothesis, enriching inferences are not conversational implicatures resting on contingent data, but systematic inferences backed by long-lasting conceptual structures. As Hopper & Traugott correctly point out, "one would not expect grammaticalization of such strictly local and idiosyncratic, highly contextualized, inferences as are exemplified by:

(9) a. What on earth has happened to the roast beef?
The dog is looking very happy

(understood to implicate that perhaps the dog has eaten the roast beef) (Levinson, 1983: 126)". The kinds of inference one expects to grammaticalize are indeed systematic inferences, based on long-lasting conceptual structures:[459] for instance, "inferences of causality from temporal sequence" (Hopper & Traugott, 1993: 75).

Looked at from this standpoint, grammaticalisation shows a different profile. What a linguistic expression takes as its long-lasting meaning is no longer the occasional content of a conversational implicature, but the content of a systematic inference, that is, a long-lasting conceptual structure. When an independent concept becomes a coded meaning, there is no logical leap from the area of contingency to the area of long-lasting *a priori*, but simply a shift from one realm of long lasting structures holding *a priori* to another. The conventionalisation of enriching inferences is not a special fact, requiring a special explanation, but a special outcome of a more general transaction between different kinds of grammar — between a grammar of forms and a grammar of concepts.

The dissociation between systematic inferencing and contingent, pragmatic inferencing is not simply a point of detail in semantic study, but the theoretical move which opens the conceptual space of a philosophical grammar to both theoretical reflection and empirical enquiry. If systematic inferencing is kept apart from pragmatic inferencing, a whole system of ideas about coding, inferencing and their interaction is called into question.

The ideation of complex meanings is not the work of coding, occasionally improved by pragmatic strategies, but the outcome of a true competition between coding and inferencing, and therefore between a formal and a conceptual kind of lawfulness. The outcome of this competition is a rich typology of forms of expression, which can be described in empirical terms.

What is in competition with coding is not essentially a pragmatic, external kind of inferencing, but an internal kind. The occasional bases of external inferencing cannot be systematically described, but at best illustrated through significant examples. The systematic bases of internal inferences, on the contrary, can be systematically analysed, as they are within the framework of descriptive metaphysic. In this way, a careful and empirically adequate analysis of shared long-lasting concepts and conceptual structures can be annexed to the realm of linguistic semantics as one of its sources, along with grammatical, lexical and cognitive structures.

What is in competition with inferencing is not coding in general, but a punctual form of coding, which is at the service of independent concepts. Insofar as both presuppose the independent availability of shared conceptual structures, punctual coding and inferencing are only two different ways of performing the same task — of making complex concepts accessible through complex expressions. Just as punctual coding is rooted in long-lasting grammatical and lexical structures, inferencing is grounded to a significant extent in a system of shared conceptual structures that are in turn long-lasting.

The interaction between formal and conceptual structures can be both co-operative and conflictual. In this perspective, conflictual complex meanings are not seen as somehow deviant kinds of structures, but as the very outpost of conceptual creativity, made possible by the same formal and conceptual resources that make human language a symbolic form. This not only throws a new light on conceptual creativity, but also opens the broad territory of figures based on conceptual conflicts to a rigorous grammatical and semantic description.

Notes

1. The terms *construction* and *expression* (of complex meanings) will be used in a technical sense, the former to denote the active shaping of complex meanings by linguistic forms thanks to autonomous formal relational properties, the latter to refer to the instrumental use of expressions at the service of independently accessible complex concepts (see Chapter 3, §2). The term *ideation*, inspired by Halliday (1970: 148), will be used as a generic hyperonym of both: "The linguistic expression of processes [...] comes under what we have called the 'ideational' function of language".

2. The concept of paradigm is borrowed from Kuhn (1962): a paradigm is a system of basic assumptions shared within a scientific community at a given moment, "from which spring particular coherent traditions of scientific research" (Kuhn, 1962: 10). A distinction between "the formal and functional paradigm" is drawn by Dik (1978: 1–5; 1989(1997: 2)), who also illustrates the main «beliefs and assumptions» shared within the functional paradigm (Dik 1989(1997: 4–8); see also Langacker, 1999). The reference to a common paradigm is perfectly compatible with significant differences in the explicit formulation of its content and in the degree of commitment to its tenets (see Newmeyer, 1998: Chapter 1, §§4, 5 for a survey of the different versions of functionalism). Accordingly, to oppose the formal and the functional paradigm does not imply that there is only one way of being formalist or functionalist — it simply means that internal differences are ideally backgrounded by a common polarisation. As Kuhn puts it, "Scientists can agree [...] in their *identification* of a paradigm without agreeing on, or even attempting to produce, a full *interpretation* or *rationalization* of it" (Kuhn, 1962: 44). "One cannot really make explicit a 'manual of theoretical style'" echoes Croft, 1999: 61).

3. The concept of autonomy is a complex, layered and graded one: see in particular Croft (1995), Newmeyer (1998: Chapter 2), Harder (1999). We shall consider the implications for significance of the different conceptions of autonomy in Chapter 3, §4.2.

4. The constraints we call *consistency criteria* are traditionally referred to as *selection restrictions* (Harris, 1946; Chomsky, 1965). The arguments for considering selection restrictions neither linguistic nor cognitive structures but consistency criteria grounded in a natural ontology will be examined in Chapter 4, 7 and 8.

5. On the relevance of the different non-linguistic factors to the message, see Goodwin (1981) and Oreström (1983). O'Connor (1973: 268, quoted by Whitman-Linsen, 1992: 44-45) speaks of "attitude markers": "in one sense [...] they are of greater importance than the actual words we use, because if there is any conflict between words and attitude markers, the latter invariably prevail".

6. Fuchs (1982: 177) speaks of "the necessary illusion of the transparency of signs".

7. It is essential to the nature of an instrument that it is taken by its user as something "at hand" (Husserl 1913: §27). A good instrument is simply relied upon.

8. This is the reason why functional theories tend to rely on natural attitude as a faithful picture of linguistic facts, while structural theories are generally grounded on a severe criticism of natural attitude's main presuppositions — sometimes so severe, in fact, as to challenge the most deeply rooted of speakers' insights. Functionally oriented theories, which are careful in accounting for the communicative purpose of linguistic structures, share with the natural attitude the idea of an essentially instrumental nature of language. See, for instance, Dik (1989(1997: 5)): "A natural language is an instrument of social interaction. That it is an instrument means that it does not exist in and by itself as an arbitrary structure of some kind, but that it exists by virtue of being used for certain purposes. These purposes concern the social interaction between human beings". Structurally oriented theories, which are inspired by a genuine interest in the internal structure of language *in se*, apart from the contingencies of communicative events, reduce communication to a mere manifestation of systematic patterns, devoid as such of any structural autonomy. Hjelmslev (1961: 39), for instance, writes that "the existence of a system [i.e. a language] is a necessary premise for the existence of a process [i.e. a text or discourse]"; "A process is unimaginable — because it would be in an absolute and irrevocable sense inexplicable — without a system lying behind it".

9. The contingent character of the link between language structures and communication is strongly underlined by Sperber & Wilson (1986: 173): "Now the fact that humans have developed languages which can be used in communication is interesting, but it tells us nothing about the essential nature of language". According to Sperber & Wilson, the fact that linguistic structures and contingent communicative events are put together in verbal communication does not imply that language is by essence communicative and communication by essence linguistic. However contingent it may appear if considered from God's point of view, however, the functional vocation of language to communication is, in our form of life, a true cultural *a priori*.

10. This definition sends back to Aristotle. According to him, an index (*semeion*) is either a state of affairs or a proposition that holds as a premise for inferencing: "A sign (*semeion*), however, means a demonstrative premise which is necessary or generally accepted. That which coexists with something else, or before or after whose happening something else has happened, is a sign of that something's having happened or being" (*Prior Analytics*, II, 70a. Engl. transl. by H. Tredennick: *Prior Analytics*, The Loeb Classical Library, London-Cambridge/Mass. 1962). On Aristotle's semiotics, see Manetti (1987: Chapter 5).

11. The fact that both states of affairs and symbolic descriptions can be interpreted as indexes (*semeia*) is not explicitly stated by Aristotle, but he makes reference to both indifferently, as Manetti (1987: 116) remarks.

12. Cf. Peirce (1932). Peirce's notion of symbol dates back to Aristotle, according to whom a *symbolon* is "a sound having a meaning established by convention [...] No sound is by nature a noun: it becomes one, becoming a symbol" (*De interpretatione*, II, 16a. Engl. transl. by H. P. Cook: *The Categories; On Interpretation*, The Loeb Classical Library, London-Cambridge/Mass. 1962). As a non-natural kind of sign, Peirce's symbol also resembles

Saussure's *signe* (Saussure, 1916). Saussure's *symbole*, on the other hand, shares some essential properties with Peirce's icon. Unlike contemporary semiotic theories issued from Saussure (see for instance Eco, 1975), Aristotle does not conceive of a generic concept of sign including both *symbolon* and *semeion*.

13. The indexical nature of linguistic expressions exchanged in communication is independently stressed by Malinowski (1923(1952: 307)): "each verbal statement by a human being has the aim and function of expressing some thought or feeling actual at that moment and in that situation, and necessary for some reason or other to be made known to another person or persons".

14. If a message is structurally autonomous from the meaning that occasionally carries it, a meaning is equally independent of the occasional messages it may carry. If this is true, a semantic structure cannot be defined on the basis of a prior notion of "utterer's meaning", as Grice (1957(1971: 55)) suggests: "the meaning (in general) of a sign needs to be explained in terms of what the users of the sign do (or should) mean on particular occasions".

15. If the expression *literal meaning* is used as synonym of *sentence meaning* (see for instance Dascal, 1987), "the expression 'literal' in the phrase 'literal meaning of the sentence' is pleonastic", as Searle (1978(1979: 118)) point out, "since all these other sorts of meaning — ironical meaning, metaphorical meaning, indirect speech acts and conversation implications — are not properties of sentences at all, but rather of speakers, utterances of sentences".

16. Given this premise, it is neither necessary to argue for literal meaning in order to secure the meaning of the expressions from the drift of interpretations (for an example, see Eco, 1990: §1), nor sufficient to destroy the idea of literal meaning — all too easy a task, indeed — in order to destroy the concept of meaning (as Derrida, 1967 and Fish, 1980, among others, assume). The idea of literal meaning is a theoretical monster, the deconstruction of which is a preliminary move towards understanding both the structure of complex meanings and the availability of open interpretations. The virtual plurality of interpretations does not challenge the structural reality of meaning, but takes it for granted, just as the plurality of visions does not dissolve the reality of the object, but is the best proof that the object is not reduced to any contingent vision. The point of view is constitutive of the vision it opens, not of the object itself.

17. The primacy of contextual coherence over literality is supported by psycholinguistic research. See for instance Gibbs (1994: 110): "as long as the contexts are equally explicit the same utterance can be used in any one of a variety of pragmatic roles (e.g., literally, metaphorically, sarcastically, as an indirect request) without significantly affecting the manifest difficulty of processing".

18. The assumption about literal interpretation can be considered a generalised kind of invited inference (Geis & Zwicky, 1971). An invited inference is systematically activated by the use of some expressions, on condition that it is coherent with contextual data; in the event of conflict, the expression admits an alternative option (see Chapter 2, §2.2.1). The assumption about literal interpretation is a generalised kind of invited inference because it is not activated by the use of a given expression, but by the use of any expression for communicative purposes.

19. The structure and interpretation of contradictory and inconsistent utterances are described in Chapter 11.

20. Given this premise, the theory of metaphor as a device for creating possible worlds (cf. for instance Levin, 1977) is clearly untenable, for metaphoric interpretation requires that the inconsistent utterance be applied to our shared world, whereas an inconsistent utterance receives a literal interpretation when referring to an alien world. The alleged connection between metaphor and possible worlds is criticised by Ricoeur (1975: *7e étude*, §5) and Eco (1990: 149).

21. The illusion that the interpretation of a metaphor depends on some systematic properties of the underlying conceptual conflict is at the basis of the concept of "metaphorical span", or "angle of an image" (*Bildspanne*), criticized by Weinrich (1963). In fact, the most common metaphors may be called to a new life thanks to a new context (cf. Chapter 11, §5.3.3), while the most surprising ones may receive, in a given context, a trivial value. For a good example of the latter case, see Genette (1966: 205): "In his sonnet commemorating the duke of Osuna, Quevedo writes:

Su tumba son de Flandes las Campañas
Y su Epitaphio la sangrienta Luna.

[...] Borges considers it better to ignore that this is a reference to the Turkish Crescent, bloodstained by the victories of the fearsome duke. The poetic vision would be swept away before an allegory devoid of mystery".

22. See Chapter 11, §1.

23. About hyperbole, see Perrin (1996). Hyperbole is so familiar a figure of speech that the plain expression of huge things may easily be taken as the hyperbolic expression of small things. In this passage from Hawthorne's novel *The Scarlet Letter*, Pastor Dimmesdale's somewhat reticent admissions of guilt are taken by his flock as if they were a hyperbolic expression of humility: "He had told his hearers that he was altogether vile, a viler companion of the vilest, the worst of sinners, an abomination, a thing of unimaginable iniquity; and that the only wonder was, that they did not see his wretched body shrivelled up before their eyes, by the burning wrath of the Almighty! Could there be plainer speech than this? Would not the people start up in their seats, by a simultaneous impulse, and tear him down out of the pulpit which he defiled? Not so, indeed! They heard it all, and did but reverence him the more. They little guessed what deadly purport lurked in those self-condemning words. "The godly youth" said they among themselves. [...] He had spoken the very truth, and transformed it into the veriest falsehood."

24. Textual coherence is not a relation among meanings but a relation among interpreted messages. The essential link between inferencing and coherence is underlined, among others, by Van de Velde (1984: 3): "the inference-making process and the construction of coherence constitute the most fundamental ingredients of discourse interpretation".

25. An interesting question at this point is whether the cleavage between meaning and truth conditions is restricted to some peculiar kinds of expression or is, along with the cleavage between meaning and messages, a generalised, essential property of linguistic images of facts. The traditional identification of meaning and truth conditions (or, more generally,

"conditions of satisfaction" (Searle, 1983)), which leads some scholars to define the former in terms of the latter (see, for instance, Davidson, 1967; 1970; Kempson, 1977) is challenged by Austin, who insists on the relevance of occasional, non-systematic factors for the determination of truth conditions: "The truth or falsity of a statement depends not merely on the meaning of words but on what act you were performing in what circumstances" (Austin, 1962(1975: 145)). According to Searle, a sentence "may determine a set of truth conditions relative to one set of assumptions and another set relative to another set of assumptions even though the sentence is not ambiguous and the variation is not a matter of indexical dependence [...] and without some set of background assumptions the sentence does not determine a definite set of truth conditions at all" (Searle, 1978(1979: 133); see also Searle, 1995: 130-131). If it is rigorously defined as a structural object, a meaning is too abstract to provide definite truth conditions, which are displayed, in principle, only by context-bound interpretations. In favour of this idea a Kantian argument may be put forward. The process of verification connects two heterogeneous domains: the symbolic realm of complex meanings and the empirical order of the perceptual world. For a verification to take place, the two domains have to be rendered commensurable by contextually translating the symbolic meanings into schemes made up of empirical data. In other words, one has to imagine some models of empirical states of affairs compatible with linguistic meanings — something like Kant's schemes — and see whether any of them is compatible with empirical data: see Chapter 6, §3.1.

26. The historical model of structure as a hierarchical configuration *in praesentia* of constituent parts unified by a hierarchy of functions is the biological organism, and above all the human body. The parts of the human body are connected into a specific configuration, which gives each a peculiar value connected with a specific function. When a part of the body is defined, it is the relation with the whole disposition that is crucial. Before being characterised by its outer shape, for instance, a hand is defined by its position and function relative to the structure and functions of the human body. For the role played by the living organism as a formal model for the concepts of *Gestalt* and structure, see Cassirer (1946).

27. Bühler (1934(1982: Chapter 2)). Our extension of the concept of field is implicitly backed by Bühler himself (Bühler 1934(1982: 84)): "Once inserted into the field of a speech situation in an everyday exchange, linguistic signs acquire a given field value".

28. As Hanks (1992: 50) points out, the meaning of deictic expressions does not lack a descriptive dimension. What is peculiar is the fact that "they describe not the referent itself, but the relation between the utterance framework and the referent". Bühler's indexical field is called by Hanks "indexical ground of reference".

29. See Chapter 5, §1.3 for the distinction between saturated and unsaturated expressions

30. When an utterance is actually used in discourse, the saturated noun phrases it contains become referential indexes at the very moment the sentence as a whole is taken as an index of a given message. At this very moment, "a text represents a breeding-ground of indexes", as Cornish (1990) remarks.

31. This holds for anaphoras *stricto sensu*. For an accurate analysis of the various forms of indexical reference within texts, see Conte (1988: §§1.5); for an analysis of non-typical cases of anaphora, see Conte (1990).

32. As Karttunen (1969) points out, a referent is given in a text or discourse when anaphoric substitution is allowed. On these grounds, reference is dissociated from the physical existence of individual referents. Existence is only a particular case of the givenness of referents. These topics are fully examined by Bonomi (1987: 137 ff).

33. Lyons (1963: 84) criticises the identification of the context with "the non-verbal matrix of the 'speech event'" and underlines the constructional character of the interpretative background: "Context is to be regarded as constantly 'building up' from the universe of discourse, taking into itself all that is relevant (we cannot escape in general theoretic discussion from the crucial term 'relevant') from what is said and what is happening". The link between relevance, ongoing construction of a relevant context and interpretation of a message out of the meaning of an utterance is analysed by Sperber & Wilson (1986: 132 ff).

34. The field assumes as its core, in other words, the "context of situation" as defined by Malinowski (1923(1957: 306)) and Firth (1950(1957: 182)): "A context of situation for linguistic work brings into relation the following categories:

A. The relevant features of participants: persons, personalities.
   (i) The verbal action of the participants.
   (ii) The non-verbal action of the participants

B. The relevant objects.

C. The effects of the verbal action".

35. The most significant case is the use of sounds and sound arrangements for phonosymbolic purposes, beyond their semiotic, distinctive function. Whilst the occurrence of expressive sounds is not generally taken as relevant for an occasional message in living discourse, it is highly praised, and expected, in poetic texts. The text-dependence of phonic symbolism is a particular case of a more general phenomenon, that is, of the possibility that extrasemiotic features of the expression be taken as relevant for the construction of the communicative signal.

36. The field seems a more adequate model for a text than the idea of system put forward within the semiotic tradition: see, for instance, Segre (1969: 31): "The stylistic system of a work of art is a closed system".

37. T. Tasso, *Gerusalemme liberata*, Einaudi, Turin, 1971. The complex phenomena of textual memory, allusion, explicit or implicit quotation which bind a text to other texts are collectively referred to as intertextuality: see Segre (1985: 85-90).

38. Freud (1920 (1940)).

39. More than a discovery of deconstructionalism, the endless interpretability of literary texts is a plain fact in everyday experience. The fact that many different, and even incompatible interpretations may be justified, however, does not mean that interpretations cannot be evaluated, compared or preferred. If an interpretation cannot be directly evaluated, the data of the field are open to monitoring — empirical evidence supporting them can be found, or they can be subjected to rational examination. The question at this point is to what extent the data drawn into interpretation fields are made explicit, and to what extent they are silently taken for granted as obvious data. On this point, see Fish (1980).

40. Within our framework, the essential question — how is communication possible? — has the typical flavour of a transcendental question in Kant's sense — that is, a question which tries to justify the possibility of an indisputable *datum* against a theoretical difficulty.

41. Between the two extreme typical cases — face-to-face conversation and the delayed reception of a written text — we find many types of complex interactions, which share some essential features with both. One of the most interesting examples is psychotherapeutic talk. Such talk resembles, *prima facie*, a face-to-face conversation, but shares with the reception of a written text the asymmetry of roles, which entails lack of reciprocity and reversibility. Like the interpreter of a written text, the therapist aims at a radical kind of interpretation. This is not bound to the alleged intentions of the speaker, and justifies inclusion within the interpretation field of relevant data which escape his control. Unlike the interpreter of a written text, however, the therapist cannot avoid interacting with the patient, who has to be brought somehow to share the proposed interpretations and to give his assent. To make things more complicated, I imagine that even assent could partially elude the patient's conscious control, a circumstance which once more puts the final decision and responsibility back in the hands of the therapist. The asymmetry of the speech situation seems to leave the therapist with a responsibility comparable to that of the interpreter of a written text. The difference is that the therapist's interpretations are not designed to influence the reception of a text, but to pierce to the quick a fellow human being.

42. "We might then formulate a rough general principle which participants will be expected (ceteris paribus) to observe, namely: Make your conversational contribution such as it is required, at the stage at which it occurs, by the accepted purpose or direction of the talk exchange in which you are engaged. One may label this the Co-operative Principle" (Grice, 1975: 45). Unlike conventional implicatures, conversational implicatures are inferences motivated within the borders of a given speech situation: "I wish to represent a certain subclass of non-conventional implicatures, which I shall call Conversational Implicatures, as being essentially connected with certain general features of discourse", that is, the Co-operative Principle and its maxims.

43. Cf. Sperber & Wilson (1986: 156-157): "The relevance of a stimulus is determined by two factors: the effort needed to process it optimally, and the cognitive effects this optimal processing achieves".

44. See Hume, A *Treatise of Human Nature* (1739-40; Repr.: Penguin Books, Harmondsworth, 1984: 521): "In every system of morality, which I have hitherto met with, I have always remark'd, that the author proceeds for some time in the ordinary way of reasoning, and establishes the being of a God, or makes observations concerning human affairs; when of a sudden I am surpris'd to find that instead of the usual copulation of propositions, *is*, and *is not*, I meet with no proposition that is not connected with an *ought*, or *ought not*. This change is imperceptible; but is, however, of the last consequence. For as this *ought*, or *ought not*, expresses some new relation of affirmation [...] a reason should be given, for what seems altogether inconceivable, how this new relation can be a deduction from the others, which are entirely different from it". See also Kant (1787(1963: 259)): "As far as nature is concerned, experience provides us with the rule, and is the source of truth. In the field of moral laws, on the contrary, experience is (alas!) the mother of illusion. It is highly

blameworthy to infer the laws concerning what I must do, or set a limit upon them, on the grounds of what is actually done".

45. See Norman (1989: 325): "In trying to define 'respect for persons' we could start by drawing a contrast with sympathy; whereas 'sympathy' is a capacity to *identify* with others, 'respect' involves a sense of separateness from others. This initial contrast will do as a starting point, but is too simple. 'Respect' too involves a measure of identification with others, recognising that they too, like oneself, have their own desires and projects, loves and hates, fears and hopes, and being affected by these. But whereas 'sympathy' consists essentially in a spontaneous inclination to adopt other people's needs and interests as one's own and thus seek to help them, 'respect' is a reaction of distancing oneself, recognising that the other person's projects are his, not mine".

46. On the basis of such remarks, scholars such as Apel (1987) and Habermas (1986) have put forward the idea that an ethic of communication may provide a sort of foundation of ethics: "In communicative development processes the identity of the individual and of the collective are formed and maintained *out of the same origin*. With the system of personal pronouns a forceful drive towards individualisation is built within the interactive use of language, which is oriented towards mutual understanding. But socialising intersubjectivity comes out through the same very medium of everyday language" (Habermas 1986: 20). It is a fact that symmetric communication, implying a full reversibility of roles, is a good opportunity for displaying a pure form of respect, free of any hierarchical implication that might turn respect into paternalism or servilism. But however good examples may be, they are not rules. Many forms of communication are essentially asymmetric, not conceivable as symmetric even in a community of the ideal type: for instance, communication between a teacher and a pupil or between a doctor and a patient. In such cases, far from providing the general ethical behaviour with a model, the ethical quality of communication depends in turn on general moral values.

47. See, for instance, Prandi (1991). The evaluation of the extrasemantic features of an utterance in living dialogue places a high degree of responsibility on the interpreter. In interpreting written texts, on the contrary, extrasemantic features (for instance, the iconic appeal of sound configurations) are systematically taken into account.

48. Black (1962a: 17). Designed as it is for describing an external act of interpretation, Black's formula does not hold as a definition of the lexical content of linguistic signs independently of occasional use: "a dictionary entry such as "Loch' means a narrow lake' will not be a meaning formula, since it does not refer to a particular speaker and a particular occasion" (Black, 1962a: 17).

49. See below, §2.

50. As Dascal (1987: 264) points out, sentence meaning "need not be retained as *a part of* speaker's meaning. All that is required is that it *play a role* in the determination of that meaning". According to Sperber & Wilson (1986: 228-229), on the contrary, the content of a linguistic utterance may represent a thought thanks to a relation of resemblance: "Any representation with propositional form, and in particular any utterance [...] can represent some other representation which also has a propositional form — a thought, for instance — in virtue of a resemblance between the two propositional forms; in this case, we will say that

the first representation is an interpretation of the second one". What leads Sperber & Wilson to give resemblance a central place in communication is the privilege accorded to the interpretation of "rough" utterances and metaphors as paradigmatic cases. This, however, does not imply that the relation between meaning and message is an iconic one. On the one hand, the similarity between a meaning and a message is not a necessary condition for the institution of the communicative link, which is an indexical link motivated by a contingent field. On the other hand, even when it plays an essential role, as in the case of rough utterances or metaphors, resemblance is itself a context-bound relation, as Sperber & Wilson (1986: 229) remark. Insofar as it is context-bound, resemblance is no more than a special case of an indexical relation.

51. To take an example from a contiguous field, distinctive and expressive sound features are not phenomenologically separable in actual phonic chains. In the most interesting cases, the same phonic purport is called upon to discharge both functions. In spite of this, the phonic structures taken into account and their functions are different in each case, and can be distinguished on the basis of distinct relevance criteria.

52. See Chapter 1, §3.1.2.

53. Dik (1989(1997: 10)), for his part, gathers under the umbrella term of "pragmatic information" practically anything that is not language-specific: "By pragmatic information I mean the full body of knowledge, beliefs, assumptions, opinions, and feelings available to an individual at any point in the interaction".

54. I use the generic term *consequence* because the conjunction *because* is indeterminate between cause and motives: see Chapter 10, §3.2.

55. Lyons (1977: 29). The distinction between sentence and utterance traces back to Praguean structuralism: "Mathesius distinguishes between the sentence as a pattern belonging to the language system and the sentence as a part of the context i.e. an utterance (a component of the discourse)" (Firbas, 1974: 15).

56. The actual form of text-sentences is the outcome of a dynamic "conflict between the functional and the formal patterning" (Mathesius, 1975: 85), that is, of a tension between the requirements of grammatical models and the communicative dynamism of the ongoing text or discourse. The notion of communicative dynamism is defined by Firbas (1964). See also Daneš (1974) and Givón (1983).

57. The role played by systematic patterns in interpreting fragmentary utterances is an argument for their reality as objects of enquiry. Even if it is not necessarily actualized in speech, the structure of the system sentence works as a shared model against which actual utterances are interpreted. On such a premise, the opposition between utterance and sentence cannot be reduced to the opposition between concrete, empirical data and abstract idealisations. Though not belonging to the empirical order but to the order of *a priori* structures or, in Kant's terms, of structures of the transcendental order, system-sentences are none the less real data for linguistic research. This, on the other hand, is a general property of perceptive and cognitive objects. A well-known topic of phenomenology, for instance, is the fact "that in visual perception of a thing only certain 'sides' or 'aspects' are really seen, whereas other sides of the same object remain outside the field of vision (e.g. the rear side, the underside, a hidden side, etc.). And yet in the simple act of perceiving a thing,

we understand that we see *the* thing, not just its front side; and yet the side we actually see necessarily focuses out thought on the sides we cannot actually see, in other words on the entire structure of the thing as a whole" (Bernet, Kern & Marbach, 1989: 109).

58. Reference to coding makes it possible to draw a line between constructional ambiguity and vagueness: see Chapter 5, §4.1.1.3.

59. See also Martin (1976: 84, note 4): "Situational paraphrases are nothing more than the ambiguity of a sentence out of context".

60. Invited inferences are a special case of "default assumptions". See, for instance, Kittay (1987: 55): "By default assumptions I mean those assumptions upon which speakers rely, in both verbal and non-verbal behaviour, in the absence of any contextual evidence cancelling or questioning such assumptions". See also Reiter (1980).

61. The invited inference is even stronger if the condition does not concern the phenomenal world or the behaviour of a third person but a decision by the speaker. If a father says to his son *If you do your homework you can play with your friends*, for instance, the invited inference — *If you don't do your homework you won't be able to play with your friends* — is even less easy to cancel.

62. In fact, the paradigm formed by an invited option and an admitted alternative is one of the most pervasive structures one comes across in linguistic analysis, from communicative interaction (see note 18) to lexical definitions (see Chapter 8, §2.3). What is peculiar to conditionals is the fact that what is reduced to an admitted option is the encoded meaning of the expression itself.

63. See Kortmann (1997: 91): "The question concerning the two *after*-clauses in (31) is whether, in addition to Anteriority, Cause and Concession should be added to the range of meanings which *after* may express:

(31) a. After we read your novel we felt greatly inspired. (Anteriority amounting to Cause) (Hopper & Traugott, 1993: 74).
b. The president approved selling military arms to Iran and trading them for hostages after proclaiming publicly that he would do neither. (Anteriority amounting to 'although, despite the fact that') (Kortmann, 1991: 131).

The answer in both cases is 'no', as the causal and the concessive readings are both heavily *context-dependent*" (my emphasis).

64. See Hopper & Traugott (1993: 74): "We turn now to the question whether there are pragmatic as well as semantic polysemies. Consider for instance *after* in (8a):

(8) a. After we read your novel we felt greatly inspired.

This may be interpreted as a literal statement of temporal sequence, or it may implicate:

b. Because we read your novel we felt greatly inspired.

[...] example (8a) suggests that there can be pragmatic ambiguities/polysemies as well as semantic ambiguities/polysemies".

65. Following Tesnière, the term *process* is used here in a technical sense to denote in a generic way the meaning of a nuclear sentence. This use is shared by Halliday (1970: 146),

who explicitly uses *process* as hyperonym for "actions, events, states and relations"; see also Halliday (1967: 38). As it does not take into account *Aktionsart*, this use is more general than Langacker's (1991: 5), who opposes processes to atemporal relations: "A process is characterized as a relationship followed sequentially in its evolution through conceived time, whereas an atemporal relation [...] views a scene holistically".

66. The term *predicator* is used by Lyons (1977: 434) in order to distinguish the main predicative term of a predication from the functional category of predicate, coinciding with the verb phrase of a nuclear sentence: "We can say that 'play' in 'Caroline plays guitar' is a two-places predicator independently of whether we also say that 'play the guitar' is a predicate".

67. According to Chomsky's intuition (1957).

68. On functional sentence perspective, see Mathesius (1928), Halliday (1968; 1970), Daneš (1974), Firbas (1974) and Firbas (1992). The categories of "theme" and "rheme", typical of the Prague School, are often replaced by "topic" and "comment" (Hockett, 1958: 191). Dik (1989(1997: Chapter 13)) uses both "theme" and "topic": the theme is an extra-clausal kind of "pragmatic function", while the topic is intra-clausal. The notion of communicative dynamism is first defined by Firbas (1964: 270): "by a degree of C[ommunicative] D[ynamism] I understand the relative extent to which a linguistic element contributes towards the development of communication". See also Firbas (1992: 7) and Svoboda (1974). Being unmarked, the perspective of a nuclear sentence is also natural — that is, characterised by a perfect balance of topic, comment and focus, and by a continuum progression from theme to focus. For this reason, it is within the limits of the simple nuclear sentence that the main categories of the perspective can be observed and defined under ideal conditions. When specialised syntactic means are involved, the communicative balance is more or less upset. First, when a category is marked, its function is to some extent emphasised. A marked topic, for instance, cannot be pronominalised — or dropped, in languages which allow for it — even if it is already known, and can be used contrastively (see Bernini, 1992: §3). Second, the more a category is marked, the more the communicative balance of the utterance is affected. The most interesting example is the cleft sentence, the focus of which is no longer the end point of a gradual progression, but a peak against communicative flatness.

69. The distinction between nuclear and derived sentence types is based on the form-function relationship, and does not require a transformational justification. The presence of specific structures designed for imposing a given perspective on a process presupposes the presence of structures designed for its ideation, while the reverse does not hold. This justifies the idea of a paradigm that associates a given nuclear sentence structure with a set of derived structures, each of which imposes a different perspective on the same process. Moreover, one can use phonological rather that syntactic means for imposing a marked perspective on a message, but cannot construct a complex meaning by simply juxtaposing isolated words. On the interplay of syntactic and phonological means in communicative perspective, see Firbas (1970). For a comparative analysis of German, which extensively exploits word order changes, and English, which combines rigid word order with mobile stress, see Kirkwood (1969: 93 ff.).

70. The term *grammatical relations* has been made popular by relational grammars (see Perlmutter, 1980; Perlmutter (ed.), 1983; Perlmutter & Rosen, 1984; Johnson, 1977 and Blake, 1990 for an overview), but has spread among scholars of different tendences to become synonymous of *functional categories* (see for instance, Cole & Sadock (eds.), 1977; Fillmore, 1977a; Comrie, 1982: 96; Palmer, 1994). From the standpoint of our project, the term *grammatical relations* has over the alternative label of *functional categories* the advantage of explicitly underlining both their relational character and their purely grammatical nature. Thanks to the latter property, "pure" grammatical relations, which are ready to receive a role within a given predicative frame but are in themselves devoid of inherent content, can directly be opposed to roles, which are substantial conceptual relations ready to be expressed by grammatical means (see Chapter 3, §2.1 on the distinction between inherent and relational content of expressions). Perlmutter calls "impure" — as opposed to "pure" grammatical relations — such relations as instrument or locative, which are inseparable from an inherent conceptual content.

71. This is particularly clear when a given expression can be assigned different roles, bearing different relations with the process, on the base of different inferential enrichments. A prepositional phrase of the form *with NP*, for instance, can be interpreted as expressing the instrument, the co-performer of the action, the manner, or some kind of circumstance (see Chapter 2, §2.5.3.2). Before being assigned a role, it bears no definite relation with the structure of the sentence. Once it is assigned a role, it takes the position of this role: instrument and co-performer are margins of the predicate, manner is a verb modifier, circumstances are outer margins of the whole process (see Chapter 9, §§3–4).

72. The structural parameter of closeness will be defined in Chapter 9, §4.

73. The idea that grammatical relations are as such void of inherent content is perfectly compatible with the idea that whole networks of grammatical relations tend to carry a typical content, due to the fact that roles are entrusted to available grammatical relations according to their position within a hierarchy (see for instance Anderson, 1984: 45). The idea that grammatical constructions organise typical configurations of roles is at the basis of construction grammar: see for instance Fillmore, 1985; 1988; Goldberg, 1995; Croft, 1999; 2001.

74. The terms *conceptual* and *semantic* cannot be used as synonyms. Conceptual structures are structures which can be conceived of independently of their expression, and therefore inferred. A semantic structure, for its part, is the content of a linguistic form, which is not accessible irrespective of it.

75. It is worth remarking in this respect that the content of simple prepositions — the linking words *par excellence* within simple sentences — is typically unspecialised, and systematically requires inferential enrichment. What is said about prepositions can be extended to cases operating outside the network of grammatical relations. A good example is provided by Dik (1989(1997: 371)): in the following expression by Caesar, three different functions — temporal circumstances, manner and duration in time — are entrusted to the same ablative case: *Incredibili celeritate magno spatio paucis diebus confecto.*

76. This provides a general criterion for distinguishing construction and expression: the content of a role is expressed insofar as its final profile can be attained by both coding and inferencing. The content of a role is constructed insofar as its final profile is accessible only by coding.

77. Peirce's concept of diagram is applied to linguistic description by Jakobson (1966: 28): "in the diagram, the resemblance between the '*signifiant*' and the '*signifié*' is confined to the relationship between their parts". This is also the sense of Wittgenstein's 1922(1961) remarks: "The fact that the elements of a picture are related to one another in a determinate way represents that things are related to one another in the same way" (2.15); "What a picture must have in common with reality, in order to be able to depict it — correctly or incorrectly — in the way it does is the pictorial form" (2.17). The diagrammatic view of sentence structure is assumed without discussion by most linguists. See for instance Lazard (1998: 12): "*Actants* are the elements or groups of elements giving morphosyntactic representation to the participants involved in the process which the sentence expresses".

78. See Bloomfield (1933: 12.10): "the English actor-action construction is *exocentric*: the resultant phrase belongs to the form-class of no immediate constituent". See also Hockett (1958: 21.2).

79. The point at issue here is whether the subject simply expresses an argument of the verb among others or enjoys a structural privilege. The tradition which goes back to Tesnière (1959(1966: §49)) claims that the subject is no more than one argument among others, while the asymmetric subject-predicate structure is a passive heritage of a logical point of view on linguistic structures. Rather paradoxically, Tesnière comes to this conclusion just after logic has finally rejected the basic Aristotelian subject-predicate structure, inspired by a constituent analysis of the nuclear Greek sentence, and replaced it with a monocentric structure of the predicate-arguments form. Unlike the sentence structures of natural languages, this form of expression exactly mirrors the conceptual structure of a state of affairs. Halliday (1967: 39) is less extreme on this point: "The primary elements S[ubject] and P[redicate] are inserted in the clause as realizations of features outside the transitivity network". Martinet (ed., 1979: 59) restricts the relevance of valency to the inner structure of the predicate, that is, to the number and structure of the complements.

80. On this point, see Daneš (1964: 227): "the grammatical categories such as subject, object, etc. are not based on the semantic content, but on the syntactic form only; they are bearers of linguistic function in the given system".

81. This "logical fallacy" of classic distributionalism is considered by Croft a powerful argument for a "radical construction grammar". The conflict, Croft argues, should be resolved in favour of distribution, and therefore of constructions: "The distributional method is perfectly valid: it accurately and completely describes the grammatical patterns of language. There is no proper alternative to distributional analysis. Instead, we should abandon the assumption that syntactic structures are made up of primitive categories and relations" (Croft, 1999: 73-74; see also Croft, 2001: §1.5).

82. This is visible mainly in interclausal linkage: the contents of two independent sentences are connected thanks to a conceptual bridge, which in turn is not necessarily coded through a grammatical link, but can be either coded or inferred to a given degree in the presence of either a grammatical link or a textual device (see Chapter 10, §2).

83. For a typology of non-agentive subjects in English, see Hawkins (1986: 58-59).

84. What has just been said is absolutely true for relational coding. Punctual coding is sensitive to conceptual contents to the extent that it is open to inferencing.

85. An exclusive focus on consistent processes encourages the assumption that understanding complex meanings is no more than recovering independent conceptual structures, and coding a simple cue for it. See for instance Croft (2001: 235): "There is no need for overt relational coding with prototypical role-fillers, because their role can be reconstructed from the semantics of the state of affairs denoted by the verb and the semantic type of the participants denoted by the argument phrases". The empirical reality of conceptual conflicts challenges this assumption.

86. One consequence of explicitly calling consistency into question is that metaphor is dissociated from the idea of transgression and readmitted within the mainstream of linguistic symbolisation and description. Moreover, this holds not only for the consistent metaphorical concepts studied by cognitive semantics (see, for instance, Lakoff & Johnson, 1981), but also — and chiefly — for the most creative poetic metaphors, which are in fact significant and inconsistent utterances. Owing to the fact that conceptual conflicts illustrate the shaping power of linguistic structures, a philosophical grammar makes room for a semantic description of metaphor at its very core (see Chapter 11).

87. See Givón (1984: 143): "It is thus not the physical role of the instrument which makes it an instrument, but rather its use by the agent". According to Wierzbicka (1985: §4.3), instrument is a "purely functional concept".

88. Conversely, the presence of an instrumental role may select an agentive reading in indeterminate cases — for instance, in the presence of passive perception verbs. Thus, a sentence like *John saw the comet with the binoculars* would be interpreted as meaning *John succeeded in seeing the comet using the binoculars.*

89. According to White (1968: 5), "Nor does the ascription of responsibility serve to distinguish human action from the action of a physical object, for we can as properly say, without any trace of animism, that the wind is responsible for the damage to the window as that a person is responsible for it". But the ascription of responsibility is not a linguistic device based on syntactic well-formedness — it is a conceptual device based on consistency. Accordingly, the use of such an expression as *The wind is responsible for the damage to the window* does not imply that we attribute responsibility to it more than metaphorically. Conceptual analysis is not simply the analysis of linguistic expressions — it is an analysis of the content of linguistic expressions against consistency criteria.

90. When the subject position is occupied neither by an intentional agent nor by a force, it may be occupied by an instrument on condition that an intentional agent is latent: *This key opens the front door* is normally interpreted as "It is possible (for a person) to open the front door using this key". On this point, it is significant that the role of *The hammer* in the expression *The hammer broke the window* is indeterminate: the noun phrase can be taken as expressing either an instrument, if the agent is latent, or a force. As Fillmore (1968: 22) points out, agent and instrument cannot be coordinated in subject position: *John broke the window*; *A hammer broke the window*; **John and a hammer broke the window.*

91. See Chapter 9: §3. The conceptual structures involved in defining the profile of an instrument belong to different layers. The general conceptual framework of the instrumental relation is provided by consistency criteria, thanks to a system of restrictions circumscribed by such basic ontological categories as concreteness, animacy and humanity. The

fact that the use of an instrument is restricted to human beings, while human beings and abstract concepts are not conceivable as instruments, is a matter of consistency. The appropriateness of a given instrument with regard to a given action, on the other hand, is evaluated against general cognitive models of intentional actions. If a knife is seen as an appropriate instrument for cutting bread but not for strolling around, it is certainly a matter of general cognitive models about knives, cutting and strolling.

92. If ambiguity is the occasional collapse of a construction in the area of coding, indeterminacy and vagueness are typically correlated to systematic undercoding (see Chapter 5, §4.1.3.3, in particular about the structures N + complement).

93. Owing to their twofold profile, spatial relations are built out of a mix of expression and construction: a language-specific semantic building is constructed on more general conceptual foundations, which go back to a primary and largely shared categorization of space.

94. Bühler (1934(1982: Chapter 2, §7)) defines the *origo* as "the here- now-I system of subjective orientation".

95. The alternative option of locating Surana with reference to the speaker's real position — *gɔ ˈnbryːʎu ˋdʒa syˈraːnə.* ("I've got an orchard *down* at Surana") — is not considered correct by the eldest inhabitants, who are less exposed to interference from Italian. When the goal of an ongoing motion is pointed at by a speaker located above it, however, the ground-oriented *origo* is dismissed to the advantage of the subjective one: *ˋvagi ˋdʒa sy'ra:nə.* ("I'm going down to Surana). In this case the location of the goal in the objective field would contradict the actual orientation of the speaker's motion.

96. This raises the question of ecological motivation. It is obvious that ecological motivation is absolutely transparent and natural if considered *a posteriori*, but it is equally evident that the physical structure of the landscape is capable of justifying *a priori* neither the relevance of peculiar dimensions nor the availability of a given set of expressions, which are language-specific. On this point, see Levinson (1997: 37).

97. It is worth remarking that though the lateral valleys are very steep, the vertical dimension is not relevant when the path leading to the goal or location goes upstream. Accordingly, a place located at the head of a lateral valley has to be referred to as being *inside* rather than *up*.

98. The presence of both speaker-oriented and ground-oriented dimensions in deictic systems is confirmed by Krier's description of the adverbs expressing spatial relations in some Alemannic dialects spoken in the Valais Alps in Switzerland. Krier (1986) identifies a dozen relevant dimensions, distributed among three subsystems. One of these systems (B) is subjective, that is, speaker-oriented, while the others (A and C) relate to the configuration of a typical Alpine landscape: the elevation of the mountainside, the direction of the main river (A) and the presence of lateral valleys (C). The speaker-oriented subsystem contains an opposition between "distance", "proximity with a natural obstacle" and "proximity without a natural obstacle". The ground-oriented subsystems contain such oppositions as "altitude" vs "plain" and "up-river" vs "down-river" with reference to the main valley (A), and "on the inside" vs "on the outside" with reference to lateral valleys (C).

99. This is, for instance, Krier's opinion: "The purpose of the study is to analyse the pragmatic significance of those elements which indicate spatial dimensions" (Krier, 1986: 44).

100. See Quirk, Greenbaum, Leech, Svartvik (1984: 678): "The main difference is that *over* and *under* tend to indicate a direct vertical relationship or spatial proximity, while *above* and *below* may indicate simply 'on a higher/ lower level than': *The castle stands on a hill above (?over) the valley*; *Keep this blanket over (*above) you*; *The doctor and the policeman were leaning over (*above) the body when we arrived*".

101. As Levinson (1997: 21) points out, "speaking requires a regimentation of thoughts, a 'thinking for speaking' as Slobin (1996) has put it". Some interesting remarks on this point are made in Ramat's (1998) review of Nuyts & Pedersen (1997). About the discrepancies between cognitive and linguistic categorization of space, see Mühlhäusler (2001).

102. The well-known distinctions between "actants" and "circonstants" (Tesnière, 1959), "Ergänzungen" and "freie Angaben" (Helbig, 1971), "arguments" and "satellites" (Dik, 1978; 1989(1997: 86)) are made according to this criterion.

103. As its delimitation is based on an independent criterion, the functional core of the sentence does not necessarily coincide with the core of the process. As we shall see below (Chapter 9, §2.4), such roles as location and goal, however essential for the structure of the process, are not included within the functional core of the sentence because they are not coded through grammatical relations.

104. To put it in Halliday's terms (Halliday, 1970), this kind of perspective is not connected with textual function, but with ideational function.

105. The high frequency of passive sentences in English texts, first underlined by Mathesius (1928), is only a case of a more general tendency to identify grammatical subject and topic, and hence to attain marked communicative perspective through ideational perspective. Synchronically, this requires the accessibility of a great variety of roles to the position of subject through flexible valency schemata and easy passivization (see Davison, 1980; for a significant comparison with German, see Hawkins, 1986: 58-59). Diachronically, the tendency to identify topic and grammatical subject is responsible for significant drifts of valency schemata: see Cole, Harbert, Hermon & Sridhar (1980) and Kirkwood (1969; 1978) about the verb *like*.

106. The communicative perspective of an utterance can be functionally justified only on the basis of its coherence with a contingent communicative background — a co-text or a context — but it is shaped by systematic means belonging to the structure of the expression. For this reason, communicative perspective belongs, as a distinct layer, to the semantic structure of the sentence, and its inclusion within pragmatics is not justified.

107. The distinction between the two kinds of perspective is made by Daneš (1968: 68): "The hierarchy of syntactic meanings [...] should not be identified with the so-called 'functional perspective of utterance', i. e. with the Theme-Rheme (or Topic-Comment) bipartition of utterance". "Two sentences as *John likes music* and *Music pleases John* display opposite hierarchies, and therefore different communicative perspectives, while *The boy is hitting the balls* and *The balls, the boy is hitting them* impose different communicative perspectives on the same hierarchy". Dik (1989(1997: 26) distinguishes "the informational status of a constituent within the wider communicative setting in which it occurs" and "the perspective from which a State of Affairs is presented in a linguistic expression". The distribution of roles in subject and object position is relevant in relation to this second point.

108. Fillmore himself (1977a: 79) remarks that "some verbs allow a choice of perspective [...] Others, as we are reminded in Mellema (1974), have fixed perspectives", and in this cases the choice of the verb implies a peculiar perspective: "any verb identifying any particular aspect of the [...] event requires us to choose one particular perspective on the event" (72).

109. This conception is coherently elaborated by Fillmore (1977a: 74): "whenever we understand a linguistic expression of whatever sort, we have simultaneously a background scene and a perspective on that scene. Thus, in our examples about buying and selling, the choice of any particular expression from the repertory of expressions that activate the commercial event scene brings to mind the whole scene — the whole commercial event situation — but presents in the foreground — in perspective — only a particular aspect or section of that scene".

110. This is the reason why passives, which attain a marked communicative perspective through ideational perspective, are the less marked kinds of non-nuclear sentences. In a passive sentence, just as in a nuclear one, the relation between functional categories and categories of the communicative perspective — subject and topic, predicate and comment — is rigid. In both cases, the communicative perspective is simply a by-product of the construction of the process.

111. Ramat (1984: 73) defines the argument structure of the process as "The lowest common denominator allowing us to compare differences between languages (from, among others, a typological viewpoint)". Even if the provision of predicators and the formal side of their valency-schemata are language-specific data, the kinds of processes they frame (for instance, actions, affections, states) and the conceptual roles involved (for instance, agent, patient, experiencer) may be defined in general conceptual terms. The idea that interlinguistic comparison is bound to rely on "largely syntax-free" conceptual categories (Keenan & Comrie, 1977: 63; see also Greenberg, 1966; Croft, 1990; Wierzbicka, 1995) is challenged by Newmeyer (1998: 342ff), according to whom such grammatical relations as subject admit definitions which are both cross-linguistic and structural. The same methodological question is relevant for diachronic comparison and for the study of language acquisition. See, for instance, Meisel (1987: 206).

112. See Comrie (1981: 100).

113. This statement is not always literally true but is reasonable: see Chapter 9, §1 for more detail.

114. See Comrie (1981: 114): "humans have a strong tendency to select more agentive entities as topics of discussion, which means that there is a natural correlation between agent and topic: other things being equal, one would expect agent and topic to coincide".

115. As Keenan (1976: 312) points out, a general definition of the subject cut off from its language-specific formal properties is "a multi-factor concept" — he would have said "a prototypical concept", if he had had the term — so that an expression may be a subject "in different ways and to different degrees. And being a subject is, we claim, more like being intelligent than, for instance, being a prime number".

116. Of course, general definitions based on conceptual and discursive properties like Comrie's are no criteria for identifying subjects, but for qualifying the preferred functional

properties of subjects once they have been independently identified: see Comrie (1981: 100).

117. See Comrie (1981: 101): "there are two important characteristics of this definition: first, it is multi-factor; second, it is stated in terms of prototypes, rather than in terms of necessary and sufficient criteria for the identification of subjects. The second point is particularly important, given that many subjects in many constructions in many languages are not topics, or are not agents, or are neither".

118. As far as sentence meaning is concerned, the constellation of contingent data that take part in defining utterance meanings is not taken into account. This implies, of course, that a sentence is by definition significant even when its meaning is not fully determinate, i.e. when it is ambiguous or vague.

119. The term *distillation*, which refers to the empirical origin of cognitive structures, is used by Fillmore (1977: 126) and Langacker (1993: 466). On "simplified models of the world", see Holland & Quinn (eds. 1987).

120. It is possible that a sharp line between consistency criteria and consistent cognitive models is not always easy to draw. But the very question — what makes cognitive models consistent — seems to me unavoidable and deserving analysis.

121. The concepts of consistency and coherence are not kept distinct in all languages, as they are in English. In Italian, for instance, a single word — *coerenza* — encompasses both concepts (see Conte, 1988, Chapter 2).

122. The immanent nature of coherence does not imply that it has to be taken as a sort of objective property of a text. If some texts seem to display their coherence, essentially thanks to the presence of a compact network of cohesive devices, in other cases a given array of utterances is interpreted in such a way as to make it coherent thanks to a positive effort by a co-operative addressee. This point is stressed, among others, by Coates (1994: 40): "The analysis of naturally-occurring conversation is a challenge to the analyst because spontaneous speech often appears *incoherent*. Yet, inasfar as the internal evidence of these texts is that they were successful [...] we have to treat such texts as *coherent*". According to Conte (1988: Chapter 2) textual coherence stretches between two poles, that is coherence *a parte objecti* and coherence *a parte subjecti*.

123. This point is stressed by Reichling (1961: 1), quoted by Daneš (1968: 55): "the function of syntactic grouping is not to establish the relations between the forms as such, but with the aid of formal relations, to effect a semantic connection, i. e. a connection of meanings".

124. Like functional and cognitive grammars, generative semantics challenges formal syntax on the point of arbitrariness of syntactic structures: see Graffi (1975).

125. Harder (1999: 200) argues for a "partial autonomy" of syntactic structures as a particular case of subsystems functionally integrated within larger systems: "we need to understand simultaneously the ways in which subsystems obey special laws of their own and the ways in which they depend on the larger systems of which they form part".

126. According to Givón (1995: 11-12), to deny the formal nature of grammar would amount to empty the functional programme itself: "the assertion that function correlates with structure is an empty tautology unless both function *and* structure are defined inde-

pendently of each other. But the only meaningful definition of 'structure' is formal". See also Givón (1997: §1).

127. Humboldt (1836(1963: 418)).

128. The same holds if the question is displaced from synchrony to diachrony: Grammar can be at one and the same time autonomous in that it is characterised in terms of an immanent "algebra", and yet motivated to the extent that this algebra has been shaped in time by functional pressures: "There is no reason that such an algebra could not have been shaped — and continue to be shaped — in part by forces external to it" (Newmeyer, 1998: 366-367).

129. We shall consider this point later on: Chapter 11.

130. Consistency as a prerequisite for verifiability cannot be interpreted as a purely internal property, or self-consistency, which holds for purely formal systems devoid of empirical import. Consistency is a prerequisite for verifiability in the sense that the object itself of verifiability, that is, the alternative between true and false, is located within the realm of consistency. An inconsistent proposition can be neither true nor false in the empirical sense (on the relationship between consistency and empirical knowledge, see Chapter 7, §2; Chapter 8, §1.3).

131. It is worth remarking that Carnap's thesis is more radical than it may appear from the English translation. Unlike the English word *statement*, the German word *Satz* does not denote one specialised use of a sentence, but the expression itself. What Carnap denies is not just the aptness of a given string of words to state something, but its being a complex linguistic expression — a sentence. Significantly, Carnap uses as a weapon against metaphysics one of its most glorious tools: the opposition between appearance and essence.

132. The relationship between terminology and referred categories in Husserl and Carnap forms a singular sort of semiotic chiasm. Husserl's "meaning categories" are in fact formal distributional classes, whereas Carnap's "grammatical subcategories" are in fact conceptual categories.

133. I use the term "conceptual", which recalls Jespersen's (1924: Chapter 3)) "notional", instead of the more widespread "semantic", in order to stress the reciprocal autonomy of general conceptual and semantic structures: see note 74.

134. The attribution of such features as "animate" or "human" to a lexical item like a noun is, indeed, in itself a "category mistake". This paradox emphasises the difficulty of considering consistency criteria as syntactic rules.

135. The negated metaphor is a complex figure of meaning, which shares some features with metaphor, tautology and litotes: see Prandi (1992: Sect. II, Chapter 1, §1.2).

136. *If I were fire, I would burn the world; if I were wind, I would storm on it; if I were water, I would drown it; if I were God, I would sink it.*

137. *If someone wanted to blame me for the fact that even trees speak, not only beasts, it would be good to remind him that we only take pleasure from telling stories.*

138. On this point, which makes visible a scalar parameter of closeness in the structure of complex meanings, see Chapter 9, §4.

139. See Chapter 7, §2.2.

140. About orders of entities, see Lyons (1977: 442 ff.). The concept of process is used here in a purely structural sense to denote the content of a sentence structure (see note 65), and is thus a hyperonym of such functional concepts as *action* or *event* on the one hand, and *proposition* on the other (see Vendler, 1967; 1970). As Lyons (1977: §11.3) points out, these differences are of ontological import: such processes as actions and events can be called second-order entities, while propositions are third-order entities: "By second-order entities we shall mean events, processes, states of affairs, etc., which are located in time and which, in English, are said to occur or to take place, rather than to exist; and by third-order entities we shall mean such abstract entities as propositions, which are outside space and time" (Lyons 1977: 443). The distinction between second-order entities and third-order entities, however, is not relevant to the present discussion. On the one hand, the formal possibility and articulation of either kind of process is secured by the formal structure of the sentence. On the other hand, the distinction between second- and third-order entities cannot be drawn within the borders of the simple sentence, for it becomes visible only when processes occur as arguments of predicators within the framework of a complex sentence (see Chapter 10, §1.1.1). Events are processes which can be said to happen; actions are processes which are performed by agents; both kinds of process can be observed in contingent spatial and temporal conditions. Propositions "are entities of the kind that may function as the objects of such so-called propositional attitudes as belief, expectation and judgement: they are what logicians often call intensional objects" (Lyons, 1977: 445).

141. See §5.1 for some general suggestions.

142. In some European languages (e. g. Italian, French, Catalan and modern Greek) the diminutive form of certain mass nouns can be used as a strategy of mass instantiation. In Italian, for instance, *zuccherino* (diminutive of *zucchero*, "sugar"), means "piece of sugar": see Grandi (2002: 107 and Chapter 3, §1.3.1). This documents the variety of possible instantiation strategies.

143 On the features "shape" and "homogeneity", see Rijkhoff (2002: 50-51).

144. See Aristotle, *Categories*, 5, 2a. Engl. transl. by H. P. Cook: *The Categories; On Interpretation*, The Loeb Classical Library, London/Cambridge/Mass. 1962: "suppose we take 'white' as an instance. Now, 'white' is, no doubt, in a body and thus is affirmed of a body, for a body, of course, is called 'white'. The definition, however, of 'white' — of the colour, that is, we call 'white' — can never be predicated of any such body whatever".

145. Owing to their nominal morphology, relational nouns need a support verb in order to be used as predicators: see §4.1.1.2.

146. Colour, for instance, is open to nominal, verbal, and even adverbial categorization: *The tops of the trees shone rosily in the sun* (Stevenson); *A grove of crosses stood up blackly against the sky* (Greene). The specific expression deeply affects the perception of a quality. According to Waisman (1945(1968: 55)), "The sky which blues is seen as something that continually brings forth blueness — it radiates blueness, so to speak; blue does not inhere in it as a mere quality, rather it is felt as the vital pulse of the sky". According to Wierzbicka (1988: 487), if we compare two utterances as *Rosa rubra est* and *Rosa rubet*, "the adjective *rubra* suggests a permanent property of the rose, whereas the verb *rubet* suggests a momentary feature of a scenery".

147. Cf. Lyons (1966; 1977: 440-442).

148. Cf Quirk, Greenbaum, Leech, Svartvik (1984: 246): "If we disregard special grammatical environments like *the Sid I mean is tall* [...], proper nouns have no article contrast (*Sid* / **the Sid*), and will therefore be said to have 'no article'". Many forms marked by an asterisk are not really ill-formed, but torn between the form of instantiation imposed by the noun phrase and the formal ontological characterisation of the referent: see note 151.

149. Whereas common nouns identify individuals as members of classes, proper nouns identify, so to speak, absolute individuals, individuals *per se*. For an analysis of this notion within the framework of descriptive metaphysics, see Strawson (1959: Chapter 3).

150. A fourth class includes nouns with dual class membership, which can be instantiated either as count nouns or as mass nouns (cf. Quirk, Greenbaum, Leech, Svartvik 1984: 247). *Lamb*, for instance, behaves as a count noun when denoting the individual animals — *a lamb*, *some lambs* — and as a mass noun when denoting the meat from the animal — *lamb*, *some lamb*. Some objects of experience, on the other hand, are consistent with both forms of instantiation and formal categorisation. The most typical case in English is the couple *oats* / *wheat*: see Wierzbicka (1988).

151. The correlation between the form of instantiation and the formal ontological categorization is underlined *ex negativo* by the examples of conflicting instantiation which occur in real texts. In an expression like *Maria is no longer the Maria you remember*, the temporal path of individual life is treated as if it were a sequence of distinct spatio-temporal individuals. In such expressions as *John is not a Shakespeare* or *Einsteins and Bohrs*, the names of paradigmatic members denote by *antonomasia* the class they belong to, that is, poets and scientists: cf. Jespersen (1924: 81). In a similar way, an exchange of models of instantiation masses individuals, depriving them of shape and individuation, and individualises instances of masses: *The priest said, 'We don't need that any more', standing up with his hands full of wet shirt* (G. Greene); *There was a huge Buick there, just acres of car* (an overheard piece of conversation, quoted by Croft 2001); *L'autobus, de section en section, dégorgeant du lycéen et de la dactylo, atteignait les confins de Neuilly-Plaisance* (H. Bazin, quoted by Wilmet 1986); *And then he drank a Dew* (E. Dickinson); *A thousand weaknesses both of body and mind* (Sterne). In such forms of *as if* instantiation, the conflict between the denotation of a lexeme and the formal ontological implications of the form of instantiation highlights the strength of the latter — its capacity to impose a formal ontological categorization even on reluctant concepts.

152. Or, rather, to a paradigmatic subclass, representative of the whole class — typical cats.

153. See Jespersen (1933: 21.1.): "'mass words' [...] stand for something that cannot be counted; such 'uncountables' are either material [...] — or else immaterial". Quoting Frege and Spinoza, Wierzbicka (1988: 512-513) underlines the essential link between classification and counting: "the idea of counting implies not just the presence of separate objects, but the presence of separate objects OF THE SAME KIND". This is the reason why such nouns as *furniture* or *cutlery* do not admit count instantiation; though denoting sets of distinct objects, they do not subsume them under a class: "supercategories such as *bird* or *tree* are 'taxonomic', i.e. they belong to hierarchies of kinds (where each 'kind' is identified on the basis of similarity between its members); supercategories such as *crockery*, *cutlery*, *furniture*

or *kitchenware* are not taxonomic — they include things of different kinds, grouped on the basis of contiguity and/or function, not on the basis of similarity". See also Wierzbicka (1996: 155-156).

154. Jespersen (1909(1954: §5.225)) criticises Sweet (1891-1898) on this point: "The division here made [between count and mass nouns] seems to me logically more consistent and at the same time better suited to account for the grammatical facts than the one found in Sweet's NEGr §150 ff. According to him, the chief division is into substance-nouns or concrete nouns and abstract nouns". Abstract entities are not only instantiated, but also described in the same way as concrete ones. The symbolic manipulation of the abstract world does not rely on a specialized set of predicators, but is entrusted to a subclass of the predicators which apply to concrete entities: "Take *belief*. It is like a child: it is conceived, adopted, or embraced; it is nurtured, held, cherished and entertained; finally, if it appears misbegotten, it is abandoned or given up. The same is true, with lesser variety, of thoughts, suspicions, intentions and the like" (Vendler, 1970: 91). That's why it is so difficult to construct creative metaphors across the boundary between concrete and abstract entities. As Weinrich (1963: 330) points out, "Metaphors of precisely this kind, which connect the material and the non-material, are so common that when we speak we need to make an (often unsuccessful) effort if we want to avoid them. Avoiding such metaphors is almost a bolder move than using them".

155. The metaphor of the strong and weak mould is taken from Blinkenberg (1960: 276).

156. Criticising Lees (1963), Allen (1978: 91) calls this open relationship "Variable R": "the relationship between the two nominal elements is not, as Lees assumes, a constant [...] but a variable".

157. A compound noun like *windmill* relates two things in the same way as a complemented noun would do. Coseriu (1982) points out that the denotation range of such lexicalised compound nouns as *windmill* is actually restricted by linguistic norms, but stresses at the same time the fact that a linguistic norm selects from among many virtually open options. If we had good contextual reasons for conceiving of a "huge machine used to create powerful drafts in wind-tunnels for aerodynamic research [which] operates by means of rotating blades" (Lees, 1963: 17), no formal obstacle would hinder such an interpretation of *windmill*, which, however untypical, is consistent.

158. For a noun phrase, this behaviour is not at all surprising. Systematically designed for inclusion in the larger grammatical structure of the sentence, the meaning of a complex noun phrase has both the lowest degree of structural autonomy and the highest degree of contextual dependency.

159. The same holds when two sentences are juxtaposed and the relevant interclausal link has to be inferred: see Chapter 10, §2.2.2. As in the case of complex sentences, this does not hold when the head noun is a relational noun that requires a process as its argument. In this case, the content of the relation stems from the main predicative term: *The desire for revenge.*

160. The grammar of support verbs ("verbes support") is studied by Daladier, 1978; Gross, 1987; 1993, and Giry-Schneider, 1987. Vendler (1970: 91) calls them *light verbs*: "There is a common device of reverbalizing a nominalized verb by using an *ad hoc* auxiliary. Instead of saying *I kicked*, I can say *I gave a kick*; instead of *I looked*, *I took a look*, and so on".

161. Even as a support verb, *give* thus determines the formal régime of the predication and, hence, of the nominal form. This proves that support verbs, while not contributing to the content of the process, are nevertheless allowed to govern its formal framing.

162. The proposed analysis "makes it possible to account naturally for the choice of preposition in the noun group. This is made up starting from the sentence with a support verb, through deletion of this verb within the framework of relativisation" (Gross, 1992: 256). The model is based on Harris (1970; 1976), whose transformations can be defined as regular paradigmatic correlations among types of syntactic structures. Gross' analysis holds for the complements introduced by such prepositions as *pour*, *à*, *de la part de* (*for*, *to*, *by*) and cannot be extended to the preposition *de* (of), which introduces a true complement of the head noun. Whereas the complements inherited from the sentence structure are typically specialised, the structures "N de N" "can represent dozens, even hundreds of different structures" (257). Incidentally, the proposed analysis brilliantly puts an end to disputes about nominalisation by connecting the nominal form not with a sentence containing a predicative verb, but with a sentence containing the same predicative noun and a support verb. This move forestalls the criticism expressed by Chomsky (1970), whose significance is stressed by Gross (1987: 112): "As there are more 'isolated' predicative nouns than predicative nouns connected to a verb, and all predicative nouns behave in the same way with support verbs, there is no reason for treating the latter apart from the former".

163. See, for instance, Lees (1963).

164. The term *indetermination* is used by Matthews (1981).

165. Landheer (2002) considers this difference internal to ambiguity, and distinguishes a selective and a cumulative kind of ambiguity.

166. See, for instance, Empson 1930(1953). Most cases of what Empson calls "ambiguity" are in fact cases of indetermination or vagueness. This certainly holds for what he writes about Shakespeare's verse *The untented woundings of a father's curse*: "The *wounds* may be cause or effect of the *curse* uttered by a *father*; independently of this, they may reside in the father or his child" (89).

167. In poetic texts, vagueness often borders on ineffability — the risk of utter nonsense seems constitutive of the special semantic intensity we are accustomed to feel with poetry. This is certainly part of the charm of fragments, and our first example — *The voice of the shuttle* — is a perfect fragment. As we know the whole plot of Sophocles' lost drama, we understand its sense: a raped girl, whose tongue has been cut off to prevent her talking, makes her story known by weaving it into a sheet — the shuttle being part of the loom. Taken out of context, this expression could mean anything — or nothing. As Hartman (1970: 347) remarks, "Poetry will always live under a cloud of suspicion which it discharges by such lightnings". The last example is the most radical, for the co-text, though entirely at our disposal, is of no use: *Der Tisch, aus Stundenholz, mit / dem Reisgericht und dem Wein. / Es wird / geschwiegen, gegessen, getrunken.*

168. This is actually the title of a collection of poetic translations by René and Tina Char (Paris 1981).

169. This is also a title: C. Leotta, *L'acqua dei sogni*, Genoa 1994.

170. Our tentative paraphrases may give the impression that the linkage of a nominal process to a noun covers exactly the same range of conceptual relations which could be framed by such specialised syntactic forms as relative clauses: for instance, *The water which makes us dream*, *The water I dreamt of*, and so on. If the paraphrase with a relative clause is illuminating, however, it is chiefly because of its limitations. The relative clause is bound to make one and only one pivotal term of the connection explicit — for instance, the fact that water is the cause of dreams, or their content, or their spatial setting. But a noun phrase is compatible with an open, indefinite set of connections, some of which remain non-determinable. Because of its conceptual latitude and indetermination, the noun phrase linking a process to a thing is highly praised in poetry. Here are some examples taken from Emily Brontë's poems: *Above that spirit flows / The waveless ocean of repose*; *Across the waters of despair*; *Go! we must break affection's chains*; *No moon of hope for me will shine.*

171. An interesting case is the anaphoric re-identification of a process already framed by a sentence. In Coleridge's poem *Frost at Midnight*, a personification of the frost is first framed by a sentence — *The Frost performs its secret ministry* — and then referred back to with a noun phrase: *The secret ministry of frost* (capital dropped). This functional alternation fits well Langacker's telling metaphor of scaffolding: "once the complex structure is in place (established as a unit), the scaffolding is no longer essential and is eventually discarded" (Langacker 1987: 461, quoted by Croft, 2001: 238).

172 On the metaphorical primary categorisation of basic experience data, see Weinrich (1958), Lakoff & Johnson (1981), Lakoff & Turner (1989), Gibbs (1994).

173 Catherine Linton, the heroine of E. Brontë's novel *Wuthering Heights*, speaks of her death, which is to deliver her from suffering and conflict: *I'm tired, tired of being enclosed here. I'm wearying to escape into that glorious world, and to be always there: not seeing it dimly through tears, and yearning for it through the walls of an aching heart.*

174. Such shifts in modification provide the linguistic basis for the traditional figure of hypallage: see Prandi (1992: 96-102).

175. In the last example, the oblique attribution in predicative position points back to a previous attributive link. A detailed analysis of a rich corpus — the work of the Italian writer B. Fenoglio, who makes intense use of oblique modification (Prandi, 1988) — confirms this intuition. When something like a shift in modification takes place within a sentence, it is generally because of a metonymical shift of reference. The sentence *Il villaggio era [...] assolutamente sordo e muto* (*The village was absolutely deaf and dumb*) can be interpreted as if muteness and deafness were metonymically ascribed to the inhabitants of the village. The difference between a metonymical shift and an oblique modification should not be undervalued. In the case of metonymy, the reintegration of the consistent term — the inhabitants of the village, who are mute and deaf — also brings the relevant discourse topic into expression. In the case of oblique modification, on the other hand, the substitution of the inconsistent noun by the final objective of modification takes away the relevant discourse topic. In the sentence *Ettore [...] se ne andò con* passo sorridente (*Hector went away with* a smiling step), Ettore is the final objective of the modification. In spite of this, we cannot substitute Ettore for the step, which is the relevant topic in this position: *Hector went away with a smiling Hector.* Unlike metonymical substitution, the shift in modification safeguards both consistency and the relevant textual referent.

176. *On interpretation*, 11, 21a. Engl. transl. by P. Cook: *The Categories — On Interpretation*, The Loeb Classical Library, London/Cambridge/Mass. 1962. On this point, see Benveniste (1969(1974)).

177. Bally (1932(1944: 97)) describes the most relevant properties of relational adjectives in French. If we leave aside position, his remarks also hold for English: "Thus in *chaleur solaire*, *solaire* cannot come before the noun (*solaire chaleur* being impossible); it cannot be modified by adverbs normally used with adjectives, so that *chaleur très solaire* cannot be said; last but not least, it cannot be a predicate, so that *Cette chaleur est solaire* would be unintelligible". It is mainly owing to the presence of relational adjectives that a consistent definition of the category adjective must address the question of typicality: cf. Dixon (1977; 1994); Bhat (1994).

178. Relational adjectives are functionally interchangeable with nominal links: compare for instance Engl. *railway station* and It. *stazione ferroviaria*. Relational adjectives sometimes admit a qualificative use, but this use is clearly derivative, generally by analogy, as Coseriu (1982: 7) points out: "the relational adjective [it.] *invernale* means either 'belonging to the winter' or 'similar to something belonging to the winter' (cf. giornata invernale)". In this case, intensification and comparison are possible: *Una giornata molto invernale*; *Questa giornata è più invernale che estiva.*

179. An example of an almost grammaticalized use of adjectives for expressing roles is provided by such expressions as *Medical care*, *Soins médicaux*. In German and Hungarian, this is the standard grammatical form for expressing such links: *Ärztliche Pflege*; *Orvosi kezelés*: see Fónagy (1975: 49). The use of qualifying adjectives with this peculiar function is rare but not excluded. Shakespeare's *I have* / Immortal *longings in me*, for instance, is translated into French as *J'ai des désirs* d'immortalité *en moi* — as if the adjective expressed the object of the desire (cf. G. Hartman, "La voix de la navette", in Todorov, Empson, Cohen, Hartman & Rigolot, 1979: 141).

180. According to Bolinger (1967: 15), it is even ungrammatical: "The ungrammaticality of **The policeman is rural* illustrates the divergent restrictions that apply to the two uses of the noun, as subject of a predication and as part of a noun phrase". When predicative use is allowed, on the other hand, the adjective is interpreted as qualifying, in general by analogy: *Questa giornata è invernale.*

181. In fact, there is a conflict between the typical profile of adjectives as a distinct word class and their most typical function of ascribing properties. Whereas the qualifying function is highlighted by the predicative position, the identity of adjectives as a distinct word class is connected to the attributive position. See, for instance, Bhat (1994: 47): "Adjectives show the maximum number of differences from verbs only in the former [attributive] usage. They are more similar to verbs in the latter [predicative usage]" and Wetzer (1996: 70): "To the extent that adjectivals display distinctive syntactic properties not shared by nouns and verbs, they typically do so in attributive constructions, not predicative constructions". It is probably owing to this conflict that the category adjective is cross-linguistically unstable.

182. On this point see Dixon (1977; 1994), and Rijkhoff (2002: §4.3.3) for an overview. The question about the universality of adjectives presupposes that such a category can be ultimately identified. This point, however, is controversial in literature: whereas Dixon

(1994) and Bhat (1994: 258) consider adjective an independent major word class, Wetzer (1996: 3) claims that the class of adjectives "will virtually never have an independent status comparable to that of major word classes Noun and Verb".

183. Wetzer (1996) puts forwards a possible counterexample: "Some languages [...] have (a subclass of) prototypical adjectivals which can *only* function as noun modifiers. For these adjectivals the functional equivalent of, say, *the man is tall* must be expressed by means of a predicate noun phrase, the head of which is modified by the adjectival in question, i.e. *he/this man is a tall man*". Wetzer himself remarks that "the phenomenon of 'noun modifier only' adjectivals is generally restricted to a small set of lexical items and must be considered rather marginal in the languages in which it is found to occur". Besides, the described behaviour does not hinder the expression of modification in sentence structures.

184. Among functional and cognitive linguists, an opposite view is held for instance by Nuyts (1990) and Nuyts & Pederson (eds., 1997), who distinguish two layers of categorisation: an independent conceptual layer and a language-specific one. See also Croft (2001: 93): "there are some good reasons to differentiate between a language-universal conceptual structure and a language-specific semantic structure".

185. This Saussurean idea is challenged by Trier (1931(1973)) and the linguists of Prague school: see for instance Jakobson (1976(1988: 349)).

186. A coin, for instance, "can be exchanged for a given quantity of a different thing, e. g. bread" and "can be compared with other values of the same system [...] or with coins of another system" (116).

187. The iconic value of sounds in isolated words, and *a fortiori* in complex textual dispositions of words, for instance in poetry, is no objection, because it is a phenomenon of the textual order which lacks the systematicity of coding. See Samuels (1972: 46): "the validity of a phonaestheme is, in the first instance, contextual only; if it 'fits' the meaning of the word in which it occurs, it reinforces the meaning, and, conversely, the more words in which this occurs, the more its own meaning is strengthened; but if the phoneme or phonemes in question do not fit the meaning, then their occurrence in that context is of the common arbitrary type, and no question of correlation arises. Furthermore, just as a phonaestheme may or may not be significant, depending on its context, so it may have two or more separate values which are again contextually determined". While phonic symbolism seems to suggest that sounds are motivated, the correlative figure of paronomasia highlights arbitrariness, associating similar sounds with opposite meanings. A telling example can be found in a duet between Æneas and Dido in Purcell's opera:

> ÆNEAS: Let Jove say what he will: I'll stay!
> DIDO: Away, away! No, no, away!
> ÆNEAS: No, no, I'll stay, and Love obey! (N. Tate).

188. These lexical relations are defined by Lyons (1963: Chapter 4; 1977: Chapter 9).

189. See, for instance, Sebeok (ed., 1986: 1036): "Two words, phrases, in general expressions, or, still more generally, signs are regarded as synonymous if and only if they have the same meaning, e. g., *aim* and *purpose*". See also Asher (ed., 1994: 4455): "'Synonymy' is a relationship of semantic identity between words".

190. For lexical solidarities, see below, §1.3.

191. Statements of this kind would be unsatisfactory if their aim were functional exhaustivity, but are correct if their aim is to make explicit purely formal equivalences. See also Jakobson (1953(1971: 566)): "one of the most illuminating of Peirce's theses propounds that the meaning of a sign is the sign it can be translated into"; such a "semantic equation" as "cent = hundredth of dollars" "is not a matching of a linguistic sign with something outside language; it is a correspondence between two linguistic expressions" (Leech, 1974: 5).

192. The distinction between root meaning and oppositive dimension is made by Lounsbury (1964: 1073-1074): "We shall regard as a paradigm any set of linguistic forms wherein: (a) the meaning of every form has a feature in common with the meanings of all other forms of the set, and (b) the meaning of every form differs from that of every other form of the set by one or more additional feature. The common feature will be said to be the ROOT MEANING of the paradigm. It defines the semantic field which the forms of the paradigm partition. The variable features define the OPPOSITIVE DIMENSIONS of the paradigm". See also Goodenough (1951: 107): "We can say that a series of symbolic behavior patterns belong to the same semantic system if (1) their significata include one characteristic in common, (2) the differences between their significata are functions of one (simple system) or more (complex system) variable characteristics, and (3) their significata are mutually contrasting and complement each other".

193. For a historical sketch of the idea of phoneme, see Jakobson & Waugh 1979(1988: Chapter 1, §8).

194. The commutative criterion is at the basis of Troubetzkoy's (1939) definition of phonological opposition, and hence of phonological unit, or phoneme. According to Jakobson, the commutative criterion can be extended from the identification of overt phonemes in a chain to the identification of covert distinctive features hidden in a single phoneme, which are at the basis of the distinctive power of phonemes: "all phonemes of any language can be fully disintegrated into further indivisible distinctive features [...] When ascertaining thus the intrinsic composition of a phoneme, we apply strictly semiotic criteria, the same as for the higher units: *signans* is envisaged in relation to *signatum*" (Jakobson, 1949: 8-9).

195. See Hjelmslev, 1943(1961: 38): "We shall thus understand by correlation the either-or function, and by relation the both-and function". The distinction goes back to Saussure's distinction between "rapports associatifs" and "rapports syntagmatiques" (Saussure, 1916: Part II, Chapter 5).

196. Beside verbs and adjectives, nouns of processes and qualities, together with nouns referring to objects involved in such cognitive patterns as part-whole relations, can be determined by lexical solidarities. The Italian noun *rancio*, for instance, refers to a meal eaten by soldiers. As for part-whole relations, some parts of the body have different nouns for animals and humans: in English, for instance, we have such couples as *udder* vs *breast*, *paw* vs *leg*, *rump* vs *bottom*.

197. Coseriu (1967: 293-294; 1970: 107) criticizes Porzig himself for confusing true lexical solidarities with cognitive associations.

198. Looked at from a functional point of view, lexical solidarities and more generally sense relations, seem of no use, as Haiman (1980: 336) points out: "Relations of sense are useless unless the words are at some point anchored in reality". For similar reasons Fillmore (1977: 76) criticises the attempts at defining lexical structures from a language-specific, immanent point of view: "Some linguists — Coseriu, for example — have gone to great pains to ensure that they are limiting themselves to what is exclusively and purely linguistic, free of contamination from knowledge about cultures, belief systems, or facts about the world". The criticism loses its force if the formal description of lexical structures is rigorously kept within its limits and complemented by a functional counterpart.

199. As a matter of fact, the full sharing of a phonological system in empirical terms is not a necessary condition for a linguistic community. For there to be a linguistic community, it is enough for the speakers to share the idea that everybody relies on the same structures, and this idea is perfectly compatible with local discrepancies. In Italian, some phonic oppositions with a low functional charge are taken as distinctive in some areas and not in others. Such discrepancies are accepted as an obvious fact devoid of functional import, and their perception, if it provides material for jokes, does not threaten the idea that the same language is spoken: see Lepschy & Lepschy (1977: Chapter 4). Such observations confirm the primacy of shared attitudes over rough empirical facts as objects of social sciences.

200. Katz & Fodor distinguish two kinds of semantic components, that is, markers and distinguishers: "The distinction between markers and distinguishers is meant to coincide with the distinction between that part of the meaning of a lexical item which is systematic for the language and that part which is not" (188). "Semantic markers are the elements in terms of which semantic relations are expressed in a theory"; "the distinguishers assigned to a lexical item are intended to reflect what is idiosyncratic about its meaning" (Katz & Fodor, 1963: 187).

201. See Nida (1975: 203): "referential meaning [of a unit] consists of a bundle of conceptual features which set off the referential potential of such a unit from all other units in the language. This definition of meaning [...] consists of the listing of those features of the tokens which are regarded (usually unconsciously) by the users of the language as being the basis for contrasts between designations". See also Goodenough (1956: 208): "The components of signification, then, are the formal criteria by which we differentiate one thing from another".

202. For a discussion of this point, see Wierzbicka (1980: Chapter 5; 1996: 211-213). The lack of a true hyperonym holding as root meaning for a given field often encourages componential semanticists to include in lexical analysis such spurious values as "bovine" or "mammal" (for a criticism, see Wierzbicka (1972: 37) and Lyons (1977: 293)).

203. This difficulty is stressed by Nida (1975: 94).

204. These paradigms offer cognitive semantics the best grounds for criticising the model of categorisation based on necessary and sufficient conditions for category membership: see Taylor (1989: Chapter 2).

205. A differential definition, which is first exemplified in Plato's *Sophist*, is based on the identification of *genus proximum* and *differentia specifica*. See Aristotle: "he who defines

must put the subject into its genus and then add the *differentiae*": *Topica* (139a (§1)). Engl. transl. by E.S. Forster: *Topica*, The Loeb Classical Library, London/Cambridge/Mass. 1960.

206. As Lehrer points out, these restrictions are highlighted by metaphorical uses: *slaughter* and *butcher*, for instance "are used for killing human beings in a violent manner where the victims are treated as animals". In a similar way, *exterminate* "can be used with human victims — the Nazis' systematic killing of Jews has been described as *extermination* — and the description is effective because it emphasises the dehumanisation of the victims". On metaphorical uses of verbs see Chapter 11, §4.2).

207. As the example shows, the inner perspective of a concept is ready to undergo significant modulation when used in real texts and situations (see Chapter 11, §3.2.2), so that even essential differential properties of the concepts can be occasionally dropped. An adoptive father, for instance, does not share the component "direct line of descent".

208. This anchorage in experience justifies the relative stability of colour foci across languages and cultures, underlined by Berlin & Kay (1969(1991:10)) against the structuralist claim (see for instance Hjelmslev, 1943(1961: 52); Nida, 1959: 13; Gleason, 1961: 4) that the experience of colour is in itself shapeless outside arbitrary linguistic forms.

209. Bolinger (1965: 568) suggests that two different kinds of definitions, resting on different criteria and fit for different kinds of lexical meanings, compete in the analysis of lexical items: "A CONSTRUCTIVE definition applies to a social construct, with markers defined *a priori*. A SUBSTANTIVE definition applies to the hard objects of natural world", which are to be described just as they offer themselves to our shared experience.

210. Labov's tentative differential definition of a typical cup (Labov, 1973) is criticised by Wierzbicka (1985: 37): "For example, Labov says nothing about the shape of the bottom of a cup or about the size or shape of the handle. The reason for this omission seems clear: what Labov was really trying to do was not so much to *describe* fully the 'denotation conditions' of the word *cup* (much less to portray fully the concept of cup) as to *distinguish* these conditions from those of words referring to other objects made for drinking from, such as mug or glass". See also Wierzbicka (1972: 41): "the purpose of semantic description is the modelling of meanings, and not of minimal semantic antitheses (distinctions)".

211. Componential analysis is torn by an inner tension: it imposes a purely differential model on an analysis which is meant to grasp, beyond a network of meaning relations, the "referential meaning of words".

212. In a sense, the question of arbitrariness with regard to concepts is reminiscent of the question of freedom with regard to human beings. The question is either pointless, if it presupposes that the presence of outer constraints in human behaviour excludes freedom, or simply means that the question about freedom is relevant when consistently defining the behaviour of human beings. On this point, see Chapter 10, §§3.2; 3.6.

213. See, for instance, the classic examples of Boas (1911: §2.3.2) about the different ways of denoting seals and snow in Eskimo.

214. When a natural kind undergoes a finer analysis according to non-natural, language-specific criteria, the hyponym lexemes are open to differential definitions: see Wierzbicka (1985: 229-231). In the historical lexicon of Italian, for instance, the natural kind "cavallo" ("horse") is further divided up into artificial kinds distinguished on the basis of the function of the beast and the social rank of its users. A "destriero", for instance, is roughly a horse used in fights and tournaments by nobles; a "palafreno" is a parade horse, mainly used by noble ladies; a "ronzino" is a horse used by humble people for humble tasks.

215. *Poetics*, §20. Engl. transl. by W. Hamilton Fyfe: *The Poetics*, The Loeb Classical Library, London/Cambridge/Mass. 1973: "A letter [*stoicheion*] is an indivisible sound, not every such sound, but one of which an intelligible sound can be formed" (1456b). An example of "intelligible sound" is the noun: "a noun is a composite sound with a meaning [*phone sunthete semantike*]" (1457a).

216. This is why stress on the purely differential, negative character of meanings seems quite unnatural. See, for instance, Nida (1975: 60-61): "Meaning must be regarded as serving primarily a negative role in setting boundaries to semantic territories".

217. The concept of scene forms part of a paradigm, as Fillmore (1977: 127) points out: "We can use *scene* to refer to real world experiences, actions, objects, perceptions, and personal memories of these. We can use *schema* to refer to one of the conceptual schemata or frameworks that are linked together in the categorisation of actions, institutions and objects [...] as well as any of the various repertories of categories found in contrast sets, prototype objects, and so on. We can use *frame* to refer to the specific lexico-grammatical provisions in a given language for naming and describing the categories and relations found in schemata [...] The integration of these concepts can be talked about in this way: from experiences with real-world scenes people acquire conceptual schemata [via "memories and distillations of real world scenes in people's mind"]; in the acquisition of schemata, sometimes items from language frames are learned for labelling these and their parts; words from a language frame activate in the mind of the user the whole frame and the associated schema; the schemata can be used as tools or building blocks for assembling, on the basis of the words in a text, a text model — i.e., a model of the world that is compatible with the text. We can think of a schema, as here defined, as a standard set of conditions, or as a conceptual framework, that characterizes ideal or prototypic instances of some category".

218. See Fillmore (1977: 133).

219. This point is stressed mainly within cognitive grammar. See, for instance, Langacker (1993: 468): "A basic tenet of cognitive grammar is that lexical meanings cannot be sharply distinguished from general knowledge of the entities referred to".

220. See Wierzbicka (1985: 115): "Linguistic concepts reflect [...] assumptions about shared ideas"; "What matters is not so much the shared knowledge as the shared stereotype: people's ideas of what people in general ('anybody') could say" about something. While the extent to which knowledge about something is actually shared is an empirical fact, the connected stereotype is a model.

221. It is in this sense that Matoré (1953), inspired by the French sociological school, defines a word as a social fact: "The word has a social existence, being first and foremost a social fact". According to Searle (1995: 26), a social fact is "any fact involving collective intentionality".

222. As Taylor (1989: 59) points out, "There are two ways in which to understand the term 'prototype'. We can apply the term to the central member, or maybe to the cluster of central members, of a category. Thus, one could refer to a particular artefact as the prototype of

CUP. Alternatively, the prototype can be understood as a schematic representation of the conceptual core of a category. On this approach, we would say not that a particular entity *is* the prototype, but that it *instantiates* the prototype". The second alternative has an undisputable Kantian flavour: "Indeed it is schemata, not images of objects, which underlie our pure sensible concepts. No image could ever be adequate to the concept of a triangle in general. It would never attain that universality of the concept which renders it valid of all triangles, whether right-angled, obtuse-angled or acute-angled; it would always be limited to a part only of this sphere [...] Still less is an object of experience or its image ever adequate to the empirical concept [...] The concept 'dog' signifies a rule according to which my imagination can delineate the figure of a four-footed animal in a general manner, without limitation to any single determinate figure such as experience, or any possible image that I can represent *in concreto*, actually presents" (Kant, 1781(1963: 182-183)). Kleiber (1990) discusses a connected point, that is, the relationship between prototype and Wittgenstein's idea of family resemblances: "La différence décisive avec la théorie du prototype standard est que la théorie de la ressemblance de famille de Wittgenstein n'implique pas l'existence d'une entité centrale, qui 'représente' la catégorie, soit comme meilleur exemplaire, soit comme combinaison de propriétés typiques, et par rapport à laquelle sont évalués les membres de la catégorie" (Kleiber, 1990: 158). On the difference between monocentric and polycentric categories, see also Geeraerts (1988).

223. The layered internal structure of natural categories was first stressed by Black (1952(1954: 28)): "If we examine instances of the application of any biological term, we shall find ranges, not classes — specimens arranged according to the degree of their variation from certain typical or 'clear' cases". According to D'Andrade (1987: 112), "A cultural model is a cognitive schema that is intersubjectively shared by a social group". Insofar as it holds as a schema, a model is not part of actual experience, for "experience does not direct us to derive anything from experience" (Wittgenstein 1969: prop. 130); insofar as it is intersubjectively shared, it is not a psychological content.

224. The relational background of a concept is in turn a concept: a complex conceptual structure which sets up relations between models of individuals, properties and processes. Such complex conceptual configurations are referred to as *scripts* by some authors (Schank, 1975; Schank & Abelson, 1977) and *schemata* by others (Fillmore, 1977; Rumelhart, 1980). According to Schank & Abelson (1977: 41), "A script is a structure that describes appropriate sequences of events in a particular context. A script is made up of slots and requirements about what can fill those slots. The structure is an interconnected whole, and what is in one slot affects what can be in another. Scripts handle stylised everyday situations [...] Thus a script is a predetermined, stereotyped sequence of actions that defines a well-known situation». According to Rumelhart (1980: 34), «A schema, then, is a data structure for representing the generic concepts stored in memory. There are schemata representing our knowledge about all concepts: those underlying objects, situations, events, sequences of events, actions and sequences of actions. A schema contains, as part of its specification, the network of interrelations that is believed to normally hold among the constituents of the concept in question». As Fillmore (1977: 127) points out, «As human beings, we can interpret an experience if we can succeed in assigning some sort of conceptual schema to it, that is, if we can locate the experience as an instance of the schema».

225. The term *appropriate* (*approprié*) is used by Gross (1994) to qualify predicates which match given classes of arguments and arguments which match given predicates at a more specific level than the level of selectional restrictions. Cruse (2000: 222) uses the term *inappropriateness* in a similar way. As shown by the examples below, appropriateness and consistency cannot be put on a level, because appropriateness presupposes consistency. Moreover, appropriateness has a double root, either formal-lexical, and thus language-specific, or cognitive. The fact that typical birds fly, for instance, is a general cognitive datum. The fact that the verb *darn* is restricted to socks is a language-specific lexical solidarity. This point will be treated in Chapter 7.

226. There is an interesting difference between *write* and *read*: one can read both a text and a writing support — for instance, a poem and a parchment — but write only a text: *John wrote a poem on a parchment*: see Le Pesant (1994).

227. The construction of systematic distributional maps of both relational and punctual terms against consistent and appropriate sentence models is the aim of a project for a complete electronic description of French lexicon, which is being carried out by the *Laboratoire de Linguistique Informatique* at the University of Paris 13. It is within this framework that such concepts as "classe d'objet" have been set up: see for instance Gross (1992a), (1994); Le Pesant & Mathieu-Colas (eds.,1998).

228. According to Gross (Forthcoming), the French Dictionary *Le Petit Robert* contains 60,000 entries and 300,000 meanings, which implies an average of five meanings for each word. The relevance of distribution to the analysis of polysemy is also stressed by Croft (2001: Chapter 2).

229. This point is stressed by Cassirer (1944: 134): "the function of a name is always limited to emphasising a particular aspect of a thing, and it is precisely this restriction and limitation upon which the value of the name depends. It is not the function of a name to refer exhaustively to a concrete situation, but merely to single out and dwell upon a certain aspect. The isolation of this aspect is not a negative but a positive act. For in the act of denomination we select, out of the multiplicity and diffusion of our sense data, certain fixed centers of perception".

230. The actual experience of some objects is socially variable owing to a "social division of work" (Putnam, 1973). A cow, for instance, is not the same kind of being for a townsman, a countryman or a biologist. Our experience of asses is almost completely drawn from books. This fact, however, does not hinder the social circulation of concepts.

231. See Kant (1781(1913: 138-139)): "If understanding in general is to be viewed as the faculty of rules, judgement will be the faculty of subsuming under rules; that is, of distinguishing whether something does or does not stand under a given rule (*casus datae legis*)". But the subsuming of instances under a rule cannot in turn be governed by a rule: "If it [general logic] sought to give general instructions how we are to subsume under these rules, that is, to distinguish whether something does or does not come under them, that could only be by means of another rule", whose application would be a question of judgement, and so on *ad infinitum*. While it cannot rely on rules, the faculty of judgement is trained by the observation of good examples: "Such sharpening of the judgement is indeed the one good benefit of examples" (Kant, 1771(1963: 177-178)).

232. If the use of words is a matter of judgement, it is also a matter of responsibility, which in turn implies that there is an ethics involved in the use of words. In Italian press reports, for instance, the verb *giustiziare* (*execute*) is frequently used in describing Mafia killings. Like English *execute*, the verb *giustiziare* implies that the killing is an act of justice against a person who has broken a law and has consequently been declared guilty by a recognised authority (see §2.2.2.1). Now, the idea that the killing of an enemy is an act of justice is precisely what Mafia pretend and try to impose on people, so that the use of the verb ends by giving undue support to the Mafia's point of view.

233. See Black (1952(1954: 25)): "The kind of definition that consists in giving the connotation of a term in the form of a necessary and sufficient condition determining a class, far from being normal or customary, is something exceptional and remarkable". The most adequate definitions for natural concepts are of the kind called by Black *range definitions*. A "'*range definition*' requires the *exhibition* or *delineation* of one or more *typical*, or 'clear' cases" (29). "It is customary to represent the relation of a class of things to the rest of the universe by a circle or some other closed curve [...] For a spatial representation of the mutual relations of the things referred to by a word [...] we may think of the way in which a mountain range gradually merges into the plains to which it descends" (7)). Langacker (1987: 86) underlines the gap between the geometrical concept of circle — which is defined in terms of necessary and sufficient conditions as "the set of points in a plane which lie at a specific distance from a reference point" — and the natural concept, which "is probably first learned as a shape *Gestalt*", that is, "the simplest or minimal closed curve, lacking any dimensional asymmetries or any departures from a smooth trajectory as one traces along its perimeter".

234. For the textual interpretation of tautologies and contradictions, see Chapter 11, §3. In Italian, reduplication, which is similar to tautology, is sometimes used with this value: a *caffè caffè* ("coffee coffee") is a kind of coffee which "instantiates the typical qualities [...] of real coffee" (Grandi, 2002: 256).

235. See D'Andrade (1987: 113): "One result of intersubjective sharing is that interpretations made about the world on the basis of the folk model are treated as if they were obvious facts about the world".

236. The term *lexical mistake* is used in a technical, non-evaluative sense to denote the transgression of a language-specific lexical solidarity as distinct from both inconsistency and cognitive oddity.

237. The whole passage is worth quoting: "The role of selection restrictions has been controversial ever since they were first proposed. Two positions on this matter can be distinguished, and these can be illustrated by the following example: (32) *John was eating a glass of beer*. Both positions recognize that there is something strange about (32), but they differ on how this strangeness could be accounted for. Position I holds that the strangeness is a function of the linguistic properties of *eat* and *a glass of beer*, and that these properties must somehow be coded in the linguistic description. Position II says that the strangeness can be attributed to our knowledge of the world: we know that people do not normally eat beer, and that is why (32) is strange. Linguistically speaking, there is nothing wrong with (32). I take position I" (Dik, 1989(1997: 91)).

238. In fact, neither of Dik's examples is an instance of selection restriction in the narrow sense. The link between "snuiten" and "nose" in Dutch is clearly a lexical solidarity. The link between a drinkable liquid such as beer and "drink" is a more complex case, involving a cognitively self-evident distinction, which roughly coincides with a lexical solidarity. An argument in favour of there being a lexical solidarity is that the very distinction between eating and drinking, though widely widespread, is after all a linguistic fact. On the one hand, there are languages — German, for instance — which make finer distinctions. On the other hand, we may easily imagine languages which would not mark this opposition: "Consider for instance the case of Persian 'khordan', which translates two Spanish verbs, *comer*, 'eat', and *beber*, 'drink'" (Coseriu, 1952: V, 6.2).

239. The substitution test is a diagnostic test, which authorises no assumption concerning the interpretation of metaphors, although the fact that a metaphor is open to lexical substitution is relevant to its interpretation (on this point, see Chapter 11, §§4.2; 5.3.2).

240. A consistent alternative can of course be produced through cognitive paraphrase, that is, by taking the inconsistent meaning as the indirect expression of a consistent cognitive scene independently of any lexical path: see below, §2.2.4.

241. The paradigm of animal cries is an interesting example of how the language-specific organisation of a lexical area may interact with a cognitively salient, independent categorisation: the oppositive dimension for the paradigm of cries is essentially based on a culturally motivated choice among natural kinds of animals, while the cries themselves can be easily differentiated thanks to salient inherent differences. The degree to which lexical solidarities are typical as language-specific structures is inversely proportional to their degree of motivation.

242. The label does not imply that no justification can possibly be found *post festum*. After all, it can be argued that honey "grows" on trees. But there is nothing in the natural experience of honey that justifies *a priori* its classification among fruits.

243. This implies that a class is not necessarily "determined by a classeme", that is, by such a general conceptual feature as "human" or "living being" (Coseriu, 1968: 11). This circumstance is not at all surprising. The criterion of lexical classes is not conceptual but formal: a class is defined as a set of lexemes holding as the determinant term of a lexical solidarity; conceptual consistency may follow, but is not required.

244. An example of a very fine language-specific articulation of the concept of dying along very peculiar oppositive dimensions is to be found in Chinese (cf. Zgusta, 1971: 40).

245. On this point, see below, §2.2.3. According to Haiman (1980: 345-346), the fact that consistency criteria can be transgressed in discourse proves that they are not shared by everybody: "I happen to know at least one myth, the Hittite story of the monster Uli Kummi, in which a rock does get pregnant". Haiman's example, however, is no argument. First, Hittites are not immediately felt as belonging to the same cultural community as ourselves. Moreover, a myth is not necessarily a belief, and even less an essential conceptual structure. But above all transgression is not an argument against sharing. In fact, a complex meaning is taken as conflictual — typically, as metaphoric, or as depicting an alien world — if and only if the consistency criteria it violates are actually shared.

246. See also Fillmore (1975: 129): "Other areas in which scene-and-frame approach could give sensible alternatives to traditional accounts are: selection restrictions [...]. Briefly, the standard theory of selection restrictions recognizes as a relation between elements in a frame [i. e. verbs and nouns] something that should be recognized as the relationship between a frame and a scene".

247. The denotation range of the negative predicate is intended as being internal to the relevant conceptual area: "non-philosopher", for instance, may mean "scientist" or "carpenter" but not "car" or "star"; "non-living" means "dead creature", and not "inanimate being". A stone and a corpse, for instance, can both be defined as non-living entities. The two statements, however, do not have the same content. When a corpse is defined as non-living, it is understood that it has been the body of a living person. When a stone is defined as a non-living being, what is meant is that the stone is outside the consistent predication range of life, and hence of death. Whereas the corpse is a body deprived of life, the stone simply lacks it. The distinction between the pure lack of a property on the part of a given kind of being and its deprivation by an antagonistic force is drawn by Kant (1763(1992: 217)): "A negation, insofar as it is the consequence of a real opposition [i.e. of a conflict between opposite determinations], will be designated a deprivation (*privatio*). But any negation, in so far as it does not arise from this type of repugnancy, will be called a lack (*defectus*, *absentia*) [...] In a body, rest is either merely a lack, that is to say, a negation of motion, in so far as no motive force is present, or alternatively, such rest is a deprivation, in so far as there is, indeed, a motive force present, though its consequence, namely the motion, is cancelled by an opposite force".

248. If the essential properties of beings are not kept apart from the empirical ones, the question about consistency and the question about truth merge into one another, and any reasonable ontological characterisation of beings becomes impossible — beings explode into a shapeless and uncontrolled nebula of properties. See, for instance, Todorov (1966: 115): "To draw up a classificatory system predicting all the referential anomalies, we would have to class the whole of our world knowledge [...]. If the semantic theory were to register *The blue sun* as an anomaly, it would have to specify for *sun* the semantic category *yellow* (or *red*). But once one does this, there is no longer any limit to the list of the sun's properties".

249. The examples are quoted after Genette (1966: §1).

250. A closely connected point, which will be treated in Chapter 8, is the fact that consistency criteria are not shared in the form of explicit statements of theoretical import, but as tacit assumptions of practical import.

251. The comparison with beliefs is revealing on this point. The exclusion from a cultural community of people who do not share a given set of beliefs is a true act of violence. The exclusion of people who do not share the common natural ontology, on the other hand, may well end in violence (as the putting away of lunatics shows) but is not, as such, a violent act. In fact, it is not even an act, but the unavoidable outcome of the impossibility to take part in a common experience. A person who does not share the common ontology does not take part in the cultural life of a community just as a person who does not speak a language cannot take part in a conversation held in that language.

252. A cognitive paraphrase is a contingent act of interpretation, which relates a process to a state of affairs belonging to a lexically and conceptually unrelated area. The fact that the consistent concept of the moonlight is metaphorically categorised as an act of human expression in a given text implies neither that glittering is a non-human correlate of smiling in the lexical structure of English nor that glittering is conceptually a kind of smiling. The relationship between the input and the output of a cognitive paraphrase — in our case, between the smile of a person and the glittering of moonlight — can be justified only on the basis of its coherence with a given text or discourse. The proof of this is the fact that as a rule many alternative consistent reformulations, backed by different cognitive models, are admitted for a given expression. The reader who runs across such an utterance as *The flowers in this old garden awake* (Ch. Brontë) would probably imagine at least two alternatives: the disclosing of the corollas at dawn, or the full restoration of their colour by the morning light. It is a fact that the metaphor *Prata rident* is routinely interpreted as meaning "The meadows are blooming", but why impose such severe limits on imagination?

253. It is significant that the most complex tentative definitions of concepts — the descriptive analyses proposed by Wierzbicka (1972; 1980; 1985; 1996) — make no room for consistency criteria. The analysis of consistency criteria, on the other hand, is an essential component of a philosophical grammar which aims at elucidating the systematic conceptual factors involved in significance. As far as it is meant to contain an explicit formulation of selection restrictions, therefore, a generative grammar can be considered a kind of philosophical grammar. The limitation of the generative programme is that selection restrictions are exclusively focused on in their negative function of detecting inconsistent meanings, while their positive function in ideating complex meanings — their holding as a true syntax of concepts — is not taken into account.

254. C. Collodi, *Pinocchio*, Fontana Paperbacks, London 1977.

255. See Austin (1962(1975: Chapter 2); for the relationship between presuppositions and felicity of acts, see Chapter 4.

256. Stalnaker's definition explicitly rejects the traditional view of presuppositions as semantic relations between sentences (see for instance Strawson, 1952): "My notion will thus contrast with the standard account of presupposition which has been given by philosophers and linguists. According to this standard account, one sentence presupposes another just in case the latter must be true in order that the former have a truth value at all" (Stalnaker, 1973: 447). Dissociating presuppositions from truth values and, more generally, linguistic contents, Stalnaker opens the path towards a general definition of presupposing as a kind of practical attitude.

257. See Ducrot (1972(1980: 94)): "The presupposition, placed beyond the discourse sequence, may appear to be beyond question — because it is, indeed, what we refuse to question".

258. Garcia-Murga (1999: 107) distinguishes "*linguistic or immediate presuppositions*" from "*general or underlying presuppositions*", which form "a set of background assumptions held by every person within the same cultural background".

259. According to Strawson (1992: 21-22), the relationship between "the theoretical concepts of the special disciplines" and "the pre-theoretical concepts of ordinary life" is a case of presupposition: "the ability to operate with one set of concepts may presuppose the ability to

operate with another set, and not vice versa. In this case we may say that the presupposed concepts are conceptually prior to the presupposing concepts; which suggests, according to what I have just said, that it is among the concepts employed in ordinary non-technical discourse and not among those employed only in specialised technical discourse that the philosophically basic concepts — if indeed there really are such things — are to be found".

260. This expression is used by Conrad, *The Shadow-Line*, Chapter 4.

261. See Moore (1925(1959: 33)): "They are, in fact, a set of propositions, every one of which (in my own opinion) I *know*, with certainty, to be true".

262. On these grounds, Moore extends to the sceptical philosopher as a philosopher the inconsistency which would affect the layman (or the philosopher as a common man) if he negated natural presuppositions: "The strange thing is that philosophers should have been able to hold sincerely, as part of their philosophical creed, propositions inconsistent with what they themselves *knew* to be true" (41). As Ayer (1966(1969)) points out, however, a philosopher, even if he relies, as a human being, on natural presuppositions, cannot take them as if they were an object of knowledge. A philosopher can include in his corpus of knowledge only what his theoretical concepts are able to justify. Zeno, for instance, cannot accept as a piece of knowledge the plain fact that Achilles outstrips the tortoise insofar as his mathematical language cannot consistently describe it. Of course, this is not a way of negating the fact; it is a way of negating that one knows it in the narrow, specialised sense of the scientist or the philosopher.

263. This point is stressed by Ayer (1966(1969: 71)). Natural presuppositions are solid if they are taken within their own limits: "When the ordinary man speaks of a chair or a clock or a piece of paper, he plainly does so with the implication that these things exist unperceived. Perhaps he ought not to, but that is another question. There is no doubt that he does". This, however, is a relevant fact about natural attitude, not about the external world. The fact that natural attitude assumes the existence of an external world cannot be taken as a "Proof of an external world" (the very title of Moore, 1939).

264. Cf. Wittgenstein (1969: prop. 162): "I have a world picture. Is it true or false? Above all it is the substratum of all my enquiring and asserting".

265. Cf. Wittgenstein (1969: prop. 151): "I should like to say: Moore does not *know* what he asserts he knows, but it stands fast for him, as also for me; regarding it as absolutely solid is part of our method of doubt and inquiry". The sharing of natural presuppositions is a constitutive condition for a cultural community: "If Moore were to pronounce the opposite of those propositions which he declares certain, we should not just not share his opinion: we should regard him as demented" (prop. 155).

266. Cf. Wittgenstein (1969: prop. 450): "A doubt that doubted everything would not be a doubt"; "A doubt without an end is not even a doubt" (prop. 625); "If you tried to doubt everything you would not get as far as doubting anything. The game of doubting itself presupposes certainty" (prop. 115). The scientist who makes experiments, for instance, cannot cast doubt on his own existence, on his being an intelligent human creature, on the fact that his instruments are inanimate things there to serve him rather than evil spirits ready to deceive him: "If I make an experiment, I do not doubt the existence of the apparatus before my eyes. I have plenty of doubts, but not *that*" (Wittgenstein, 1969: prop.

337). An endless doubt reminds one of Descartes' "hyperbolic doubt": cf. Descartes, *Discours de la méthode, Quatrième partie.*

267. Or "the *scaffolding* of our thought" (Wittgenstein 1969: prop. 211).

268. According to Searle (1983: 158-159), it is in this sense that realism is "part of the Background": "My commitment to 'realism' is exhibited by the fact that I live the way I do, I drive my car, drink my beer, write my articles, give my lectures and ski my mountains [...] My commitment to the existence of real world is manifested whenever I do pretty anything [...] This is not to say that realism is a true hypothesis, rather it is to say that it is not an hypothesis at all, but the precondition of having hypotheses".

269. The peculiar value of *a priori* structures is stressed by Wittgenstein (1922(1961: prop. 3. 0321)) with an evocative image: "Though a state of affairs which would contravene the laws of physics can be represented by us spatially, one that would contradict the laws of geometry cannot".

270. This remark sheds light upon a difficult point connected with Saussure's insight about the arbitrariness of linguistic signs. If the link between a given *signifiant* and a given *signifié* is defined as being arbitrary, what is implied is that this relation is both unmotivated by external reasons and necessary from within the system. Internal necessity and external arbitrariness do in fact coincide — and this seems the right interpretation of a remark by Benveniste (1939(1966: 51)): "between the *signifiant* and the *signifié*, the link is not arbitrary but necessary. The concept (*signifié*) 'boeuf' is necessarily identical in my awareness to the sound sequence (*signifiant*) *böf*'.

271. On the position of cognitive models with regard to *a priori*, see below, §2.3.

272. See, on this point, Chapter 11, §4.3.2. It is this systematic property, shared by both lexical solidarities and consistency criteria, that justifies the idea of "transfer features" (Weinreich: 1966: 430): "The meaning of *to sail* may be said to differ from that of *to operate* by the presence of a transfer feature (say, 'water vehicle'), which, when transferred to a neutral term like *craft*, specializes it as a water craft. When the feature is transferred to *ship*, it adds no new information; when transferred to *car*, it adds contradictory information, which requires further interpretation".

273. According to Apel (1976: 32), this is the sense of the linguistic turn in philosophy: "One could — and, as I think, one should — wonder whether in our day philosophy of language has in fact taken over the role of a *First Philosophy* which was ascribed (attributed) to *Ontology* by Aristotle and later claimed for *Epistemology* or *Transcendental Philosophy* in the sense of Kant". Apel quotes, among other examples, "Wittgenstein's claim that philosophy is 'Critique of language', that 'the limits of my language are the limits of my world' or, in his later work, that the essence of things lies in grammar".

274. Innatism seems to me a way of securing the *a priori* character of language — of its deep essence if not of its actual configuration — against its contingent historical and typological drifts, on the (false) assumption that *a priori* structures are necessarily non-contingent.

275. Cf. Wittgenstein (1969: prop. 253): "At the foundation of well-founded belief lies belief that is not founded"; "The difficulty is to realise the groundlessness of our believing" (prop. 166).

276. For instance, of metaphysics in a traditional sense. Metaphysics in its traditional sense deals with topics and questions — for instance, is there a world, God, an individual soul? — that are inevitably subject, unlike essential presuppositions, to endless discussion and argument: see Van Inwagen (1993).

277. Descriptive metaphysics is not simply a form of linguistic analysis, for it analyses basic conceptual structures which hold as preliminary conditions of the language-game itself: "when we ask how we use this or that expression, our answers, however revealing at a certain level, are apt to assume, and not to expose, those general elements of structure which the metaphysician wants revealed. The structure he seeks does not readily display itself on the surface of language, but lies submerged. He must abandon his only sure guide when the guide cannot take him as far as he wishes to go" (Strawson, 1959(1964: 10)).

278. Th. Reid (1710-1796), *An Inquiry into the Human Mind on the Principles of Common Sense* (1764: 127-108), quoted by Skorupski (1993: 11).

279. In using the term *margin* to denote the non-controlled roles of a process, we extend to simple sentences the distinction made by Longacre (1985: §1.1) in the domain of complex sentences.

280. The agent not only becomes facultative, but is in fact ejected from the network of grammatical relations, as is revealed by the test of detachment and reinsertion: *The Chinese vase has been broken. This was done by John.*

281. This is a more general criterion for grammatical relations. As we shall see, it also holds for direct and indirect objects.

282. In fact, *Paul* could also be analyzed as the expressed subject of the non finite embedded clause.

283. See also Anderson (1984: 44): "there is not a list of properties, even within a single language, which selects a homogeneous set of arguments as objects".

284. Our discussion is consistent with the idea that the noun phrase *Mary* in *John gave Mary a book* is neither a promoted direct object (as argued for instance by Givón, 1984a) nor a true direct object, but an alternative way of coding the indirect object (see below, §2.5; see also Lazard, 1998: 57-58). This choice, based on the behaviour of indirect object in English, is perfectly compatible with the existence of more than one direct object in certain languages. According to Haiman & Duranti (1982: §2), for instance, verbs of giving have two direct objects in Bantu; Lichtenberk (1982: §3) describes sentence structures with three direct objects in Banam (New Guinea).

285. We are indebted to Hudson (1992: 263) for most arguments and examples.

286. This implies that the behaviour of prepositions can be used as a criterion for identifying the arguments of the verb only indirectly, insofar as the expressions belonging to the functional core are *a fortiori* arguments of the verb.

287. This is highlighted by interlinguistic comparison. The Italian transitive verb *aspettare*, for instance, is translated into German and English by intransitive verbs requiring prepositional objects: *warten* (*auf*) and *wait* (*for*).

288. De Boer (1926) speaks of "prépositions casuelles". Conversely, in addition to "grammatical cases", there are also "notional" or "concrete" cases, which are semantically as

characterised as full prepositions (Kuryłowicz, 1964: Chapter 8).

289. When the autonomous content of the preposition is consistent with the profile of the role it introduces, its content may be "revived". Such forms as *winken an* + acc. or *depend on* are easily interpreted as metaphorical extensions of more basic spatial relations. This also holds for cases. Some instances of dative — for instance, with Russian *pomogat* or German *helfen* — are easily interpreted as "a kind of recipient semantically (give help to someone)" (Newman, 1996: 83). In fact, such kinds of motivation (or re-motivation) have more to say about the natural attitude of human beings towards symbols — their bent towards motivation — than about the structure and functioning of linguistic expressions.

290. In the case of a prepositional object, it is not true that "Marking by preposition is an indication of merely peripheral roles" (Palmer, 1994: 10). See also Lazard (1998: 18): "Among arguments [*actants*] true and proper, terms taking an oblique case (i.e. not the zero or accusative cases) or an adposition are relatively peripheral".

291. De Boer (1926: 12-13) speaks of prepositions which code (*exprimer*) and prepositions which simply suggest (*suggérer*) the conceptual profile of the role they introduce: "In *Il fut jeté par la fenêtre par le peuple* the prepositions do not express the relations we understand in this sentence; they merely suggest these relations, or 'help express them', as it were, since the logic of thought is needed to understand them. The same is true of *mourir de froid*, *morire di freddo* and even *morire dal freddo* [...]. On the other hand, if we say *morire per causa di...*, the causal relation is expressed, since the preposition used in this case can mean nothing else".

292. On metonymical and metaphorical strategies for extending concepts, see, for instance, Taylor (1989: Chapter 7).

293. As Halliday (1970: 149-50) points out, "Within the function 'place', in

(9i) He was throwing stones at the bridge
(9ii) He was throwing stones on the bridge

at the bridge (the 'inner' type) seems more central to the process than *on the bridge*: we can say *what was he throwing stones at*? and not (in this sense) *what was he doing at the bridge?* (on the other hand, we can say *what was he doing on the bridge*? and not *What was he throwing stones on*?)".

294. If we maintain that location and goal are arguments, the constraint of non-recursive specification cannot be considered a necessary condition for arguments. On the other hand, the fact that such non-argumental roles as instrument, beneficiary and co-performer cannot be specified recursively shows that it is not a sufficient condition either: *Paul cut the wood *with an axe with a saw; *with John with Simon; *for his mother for his aunt.*

295. In a language like English, the expression of location, goal and spatial circumstances easily shade into one another. In languages with cases, like German, goal is formally marked by the accusative when the preposition allows for the choice of cases: *Hans fuhr in die Stadt, auf den Berg* (but *vor, hinter der Stadt, neben dem Berg, zwischen zwei Flüßen*). *Hans traf Marie in, vor, hinter der Stadt, neben, auf dem Berg, zwischen zwei Flüßen. Hans wohnt in, vor, hinter der Stadt, neben, auf dem Berg, zwischen zwei Flüßen.*

296. See what Newman (1996: 22) writes about giving: "There is inherent in the notion of giving a strong sense of directionality, with a THING proceeding from a person to another".

"A prototypical goal — Newman goes on — is to be understood here as the stationary entity located at the end of a well-defined path along which some other entity moves" (Newman, 1996: 88).

297. In Italian, the ablative role is coded as indirect object when it is seen as an individual, typically, a person, while it is punctually coded with a locative prepositional phrase when it is seen as a place. The case of *rubare* is particularly clear. The indirect object expresses the victim, while the locative prepositional phrase expresses the source (and it is interesting to note that some referents as banks, which are easily associated with persons, are consistent both as metaphorical victims and sources): *Hanno rubato il borsellino* a *Carlo*; *Hanno rubato il borsellino* dal *cassetto*; *Hanno rubato cento milioni* alla *banca; Hanno rubato cento milioni* dalla *banca*. The two roles can co-occur in consistent processes in two ways: *Hanno rubato centomila lire a Gianni dal borsellino*; *Hanno rubato centomila lire dal borsellino di Gianni.*

298. Since Aristotle (see note 12) it has been acknowledged that linguistic symbols (*semeia*) work insofar as they are shared as parts of a social institution, irrespective of any kind of external motivation. Paradoxically, however, the historical formation of symbols and linguistic structures is almost necessarily motivated in some way: "convention by definition plays no role in shaping grammatical structure, only in preserving structure that itself was shaped by (presumably) functional factors" (Newmeyer, 1998: 142).

299. As Alinei (1996: 9) points out, motivation — be it phonosymbolic, derivational (Saussure's relative arbitrariness), or cultural — is not a necessary condition for a sign to hold as a sign, but greatly facilitates its diffusion within the community: "Motivation is just one aspect of the sign's nature, but is an expedient allowing the arbitrary sign to be learnt immediately by everybody".

300. The metaphorical shift from movement to saying is clearly motivated by a real continuity in the field of experience. To tell someone something is a way of sending a message to someone, which in turn is close to sending an object somewhere. A strategic intermediate link in this chain is the application to the verb *scribere* of the valency scheme of *mittere*: *Litteras ad aliquem mittere. To write* a letter which contains *a message* and send it *to someone*, becomes, thanks to a metonymical contraction *To write a message to someone.* The two forms *scribere* + dat. and *scribere* + *ad* + acc. alternate in classical Latin, for instance in Cicero: *Nihil mihi scripsisti*; *Scis me solitum esse scribere ad te.* According to Newman (1996: 89), the distribution of allative cases or postpositions in Finnish follows a similar drift: "the allative case appears on the nouns indicating destinations in Finnish equivalents for 'put it on the table', 'go to the church', 'go to the market', etc. [...]. The recipient marking function of the allative in Finnish must be understood as an extension of the more basic function of marking the goal or destination".

301. On the other hand, some roles which could easily be entrusted to the indirect object as metaphorical goals are coded punctually by active prepositions. So is, for instance, the third argument of such verbs as *impose* and *confer*: *John imposes his style of life on the whole family*; *A castle confers status on its owner.*

302. It should be observed that transparency can only be partial, because the autonomous content of the preposition is taken into account when it is consistent with the content of the role, and simply dropped when it is conflictual.

303. On cohesion, see Halliday & Hasan (1976); de Beaugrande & Dressler (1981: Chapter 4). On the relation between coherence and cohesion, see Chapter 10, §2.1.

304. In real texts, the antecedent process may actually contain either more or less than the core — namely, it may contain some margins and lack some optional complements. What is relevant to our topic, however, is the fact that once the substitution is made nothing more can be reinserted into the core.

305. The reformulation with *happen* is sensitive to aspectual and *Aktionsart* properties of the antecedent process, which has to be actualized. In most cases, the restrictions involving *happen* coincide with those involving outer circumstances. Only an actualized process, for instance, can be situated in a spatial framework (see §4) and reformulated with *happen*: *John told the story to Paul in the garden, at twelve o'clock*; *It happened in the garden, at twelve o'clock*; *John has a good command of German *in the garden *at twelve o' clock*; **It happens in the garden, *at twelve o'clock.* When a circumstance is compatible with a process that is not consistent with *happen*, the detachment can be secured by alternative means: *The river is frozen because of the northern wind*; **It happens because of the northern wind*; *It is so because of the northern wind.*

306. The indirect object is in itself compatible with a form of the verb *happen*: *Did you ever lose all your money? It happened to me.* What is at issue here, however, is not the grammaticality of a single sentence but the coherence of the whole textual sequence. A form like *It happened to Mary* is not a coherent way of introducing the indirect object into a process.

307. See De Boer (1926: 48-49).

308. When the beneficiary is entrusted to a prepositionless post-verbal noun phrase, as in *John bought Mary a book*, the coding of the role becomes relational, in spite of the fact that it is not included in the valency scheme of the predicator. This treatment of the beneficiary is a particular case of a more general phenomenon, which has been studied within the framework of construction grammar (see in particular Goldberg, 1995: 141ff): a whole valency scheme is transferred, in a sort of grammatical metaphor, from a given class of verbs to a verb belonging to a different class. In *Sally baked her sister a cake*, for instance, *her sister*, which is the beneficiary, and therefore a marginal role in purely conceptual terms, is in fact coded as if it were the recipient, and therefore an argument, of a three-place process. This is possible thanks to the relational content that the ditransitive construction inherits from its prototypical use with verbs of giving, that is, a "transfer between a volitional agent and a willing recipient". Such transfers can be interpreted as arguments for the hypothesis that "the construction contributes semantics not attributable to lexical items involved". Metaphorical transfers of grammatical constructions are particularly productive in English, as shown by the high frequency of such examples as *They laughed the poor guy out of the room*, which transfers a "Caused-Motion construction", or the *River froze solid*, which borrows a "Resultative construction" (Goldberg, 1995). For a complete examination of "the English change network", see Broccias (2003).

309. This property is the critical argument for not considering it a complement of the verb in spite of many behavioural analogies. Like most complements (with the exception of goal and location), the instrument cannot be recursively specified. When a lexical solidarity

connected with a verb of action has a kind of instrument as its determinant term, the non-specified instrument is obviously latent. According to Halliday (1970: 150) the instrument is even latent in every clause of action: "Consider a pair of clauses such as (12):

(12i) Roderick pelted the crocodile with stones
(12ii) The crocodile got pelted

The verb *pelt*, as it happens, is always associated with three participant roles: a pelter, a pelted, and something to pelt with; and that holds for (ii) as well as for (i)".

310. According to De Beaugrande & Dressler (1981), *do* (or *faire, tun, fare*) is used as a pro-verb, that is, as a general substitute of a more specific verb. However, the use of *do* as a pro-verb is different from its use as a constituent of a pro-predicate, which is relevant for our test. When it holds as a pro-verb, "The general verb *do* [...] stands as a synonym for a set of more specific verbs, as in *do sums, do an essay, do the vegetables*" (Halliday & Hasan (1976: 126); see also Apothéloz (1995: 152)). The replaced verb is necessarily transitive, and the substitute *do* takes either the same direct object or an anaphoric substitute of it, which agrees with its antecedent — *Harris said he would* cook scrambled eggs. *It seemed, from his account, that he was very good at* doing them (Jerome) — or even an independent object if a simile is used: *Till Summer* folds her miracle — / *As Women* — do — their Gown (Dickinson). The pro-predicates *do it* and *do so*, on the contrary, are ready to replace any kind of antecedent predicate of action, irrespective of its internal structure. According to some scholars, it is the object pronoun of *do* that bears an anaphoric relationship with the antecedent action. According to Beccaria (ed., 1994: 577), for instance, the object pronoun *it* is a pro-predicate. If this were true, a saturated form would replace an unsaturated antecedent, which is inconsistent (such a saturated form as a pronoun is a consistent substitute of a saturated form, that is, either of a noun phrase or of a whole sentence). Dardano (1991: 36) argues that *it* is a substitute of the whole antecedent process. But this analysis is not correct either. It is true that the predicates *do so* and *do it* (which mean more or less «do this action») both refer back in some way to the action that has just been described. In spite of this, however, neither the pronoun *it* nor the noun phrase *this action* entertain a direct anaphoric relation, that is, a relation of substitution, with the antecedent process. If this were the case, it would be possible to replace the object pronoun of *do* by the direct expression of the antecedent process. For instance, it would be possible to construct an expression like *John did that he cut the firewood with an axe* just as we have *John said that he cut the firewood with an axe.* If the pronoun *it* were a true anaphoric substitute of the antecedent sentence, in other words, we would be faced with a true paradox. The substitute — *did it* — of a predicate which is a part of the antecedent process — *cut the firewood* — would contain as one of its parts — *it* — a substitute of the whole antecedent process — *John cut the firewood.* The fact is that *do* behaves as a predicative verb in such uses as *do dishes* or *do eggs* but behaves as a support verb (or "*verbe support*": see Chapter 5, §4.1.1.2) when its complement is either a noun of action — *to do a given activity* — or the gerund of a verb of action — *to do the cooking, the cleaning* — or a non-coreferential pronoun — *do it.* Now, the direct object of a support verb — the noun phrase or the pronoun — is in fact the main predicator. Even when it refers back in a general way to the action described in the preceding sentence, its function is to form a predicate with the support verb, and it is this predicate as a whole that can be considered a substitute for the antecedent predicate.

311. Of course, outer margins can co-occur with a pro-predicate like *do it* or *do so*, just as they can occur with any kind of predicate. What is relevant here, however, is not which roles can co-occur with a pro-predicate, but which roles can co-occur *only* with a pro-predicate.

312. A verb modifier adds to the content of a verb, from outside, the same kind of modification which can be incorporated into the content of a hyponym: "Hyponymy is a paradigmatic relation of sense which rests upon the encapsulation in the hyponym of some syntagmatic modification of the sense of the superordinate lexeme" (Lyons, 1977: 294).

313. While verbal control has been widely examined in all its facets, the study of closeness is rather neglected. The label "degree of closeness" is used by Kirkwood (1969: 86): "the place an element has in the 'hierarchy of elements' (cf. Fourquet, 1959: 134 ff) determined by the closeness of its relation to the verb". See also Bierwisch (1966: 35 ff), who suggests that the accusative object is more closely related to the verb than the dative object. Blinkenberg (1960) uses in this sense the term *cohésion*, as does Prandi (1987). The phrases "degree of cohesion" and "degree of grammatical cohesion" between the "constituent terms" of nominal compounds are used by Mithun (1984). However, the term *cohesion* is widely used in textlinguistics with a completely different meaning. On closeness, see also Jespersen (1924: 279) and Hudson (1992: 262).

314. An appropriate location of a process depends on an appropriate location of its actors, but the relations between the place where the process occurs and the place occupied by the actors is process-specific. For a more detailed discussion of this point, see Prandi (1987: 109).

315. The gradability of closeness cannot be interpreted as an argument against the presence of a clear border between arguments and margins, as Vater (1978) claims, for closeness and control are independent parameters: see Helbig (1982: 36).

316. This of course does not imply that the correlation between complementation and embedding is universal, both cross-linguistically and diachronically. On the one hand, "there are languages [a well known case is Lango, studied by Noonan 1992] where the dependent clause in a complement relation does not function as an argument of the main predicate, and is not embedded" (Cristofaro, 2003: 100). On the other hand, "In a number of languages, complementizers derive from relative pronouns occurring in correlative constructions [...] In these constructions (that are very frequent, for instance, in early stages of Indo-European languages), the main clause contains a pronominal element, and the dependent clause is adjoined as an afterthought conveying further specification about this pronominal element. Adjunction is obtained by means of a relative pronominal element [...] recalling the pronominal element in the main clause. It is the main clause pronoun, not the dependent clause, that functions as an argument of the main predicate" (101-102).

317. The present study does not take into account relative clauses.

318. Accordingly, Dik treats such questions as connectives, finite and non-finite forms, constituent order and mood irrespective of the distinction between completive and non-completive relations. As we shall see in detail, the choice of the mood (note 327), the function of the linking expression (§1.3) and the conditions under which the unexpressed subject is controlled (§3.7.3) are very different in completive and margins.

319. According to Kortmann (1997), the set of interclausal links coincides with the set of adverbial clauses, and therefore with the meaning of a set of adverbial subordinators. The title of a first draft of the work (Kortmann, 1991) was *Adverbial Subordinators in the Languages of Europe.*

320. As was pointed out in Chapter 3, §3.1, and note 140, the concept of "process" is used here in a purely structural sense to define the meaning of a clause. It is thus a hyperonym of such functional concepts as *action* or *event* on the one hand, and *proposition* on the other, which can be defined within a complex process according to the semantic properties of the main predicator (see Vendler, 1967; 1970; Lyons, 1977: §11.3).

321. Husserl's concept of intentionality (Husserl, 1901(1970: *Research V*)) is inspired by Brentano's analysis of psychological predicators, which are the best models of intrinsically complex processes.

322. In the area of interclausal linkage, in other words, the idea defended by construction grammars (see in particular Croft, 2001) that the whole construction is logically prior to the parts is not satisfied. More generally, the priority of construction is relevant in the area of relational coding but not in the area of punctual coding, when constructions actually result from the connection of logically independent parts.

323. In the structure of complex sentences, the coding of arguments is always relational. Unlike the corresponding complements, the completive clauses of verbs of motion are also included in the network of grammatical relations: the subordinator, in particular, is not subject to choice (see §3.7.3).

324. For similar cases in Italian — for instance, *Pareva dormisse profondamente* — Nillson-Ehle (1947) speaks of "juxtaposed completive clauses": in these cases, the relation of embedding is marked by the subjunctive, whose presence is a necessary condition for dropping the complementiser.

325. Most examples of this paragraph are taken from Dik, 1989(1997a: Chapter 5).

326. But *John stopped eating*: just like the presence or absence of a complementiser, the form of the non-finite clause shows some degree of arbitrariness.

327. This holds for most grammatical properties of the embedded clause. A significant case is the presence of the subjunctive, which plays a role in coding an empty grammatical relation and is therefore devoid of any autonomous content. Once this point is made clear, many puzzling paradoxes connected with the use of the subjunctive in Italian are dissolved (for a brilliant exposition from a British perspective, see Stewart (2002); for tentative solutions, see Giorgi & Pianesi (1997: Chapter 5) and Wandruszka (1991)). In Italian, for instance, such factive verbs as *dispiacere* (*regret*) require the subjunctive mood in the object clause — for instance, *Mi dispiace che tu ti* sia *ammalato* — in spite of the circumstance that the depicted state of affairs is presupposed as true. The presupposed truth of the object, however, has nothing to do with the subjunctive, which simply marks the relation of embedding. It entirely depends on the content of the main verb, which can be used consistently only if its object is a real fact: one cannot regret something which has not taken place.

328. See §2.3 for functional sentence perspective, and §3.4 for ideational perspective.

329. The label 'adverbial clause' is normally used for any kind of non-completive clause

(see for instance Kortmann, 1997) for the reason that "at least some of them [adverbial clauses] relate to main clause in the same way as adverbs do" (Chafe, 1984). Thompson & Longacre (1985: 178) call adverbial clauses only a subset of margins, that is, the clauses expressing time, location and manner, which "are substitutable for by a single word", and bear with the main clause the same "semantic relationships" which hold "between the adverbial word and the main clause". The concept of margin has the advantage of remaining vague as to the kind of structure it can be connected to as an expansion — namely, predicate, process (or predication in Dik's terms), proposition, speech act.

330. However inadequate, the use of the concept *subordination* to cover both embedding and hypotaxis is too common to be overtly challenged: see for instance Haspelmath (1995: 8): "the term *subordinate* is used here in the sense of 'embedded', or 'incorporated into the superordinate clause'". Cristofaro (2003: Chapter 2) argues for a conceptual definition of subordination in general, based on "the way in which the states of affairs expressed by the linked clauses are perceived and conceptualized, and the status they have in the discourse context" (26). However, there are some obstacles on this path. In purely conceptual terms, there is no trace of subordination in an interclausal relation, which by definition links two processes of equal rank (see §1.1.2); the background-foreground effect is thus bound to the imposition of a subordinative form of expression, and disappears when different means are used (see §2.3). For inherently complex processes, on the other hand, the hierarchical structure does not depend on "the way in which the states of affairs expressed by the linked clauses are perceived", but is an inescapable logical consequence of the structure of the complex concept, which survives even when the subordinate process is not directly embedded. In such expressions as *I fear it: The river is going to overflow*, or *I have a tremendous fear: The river is going to overflow*, for instance, the overflowing of the river is not directly embedded as object of the verb *fear*. In spite of this, it is taken in its perspective as the content of an attitude of fear thanks to a cataphorical relation triggered by the non-saturation of the concept "fear".

331. As Brown & Yule (1983: 65) point out, it is not coherence that needs marking in normal text or speech, but its absence: "When two sentences are placed together in sequence by a writer who does not want us to consider them as a continuous text, their separateness or disconnectedness must be positively indicated".

332. The peculiar conditions under which a bare juxtaposition is unified into a coherent whole makes the activation of bridging inferences a borderline case between internal and external inferencing. Like internal inferencing, it does not aim at connecting the content of an expression to an intended message, but at defining the structure of a complex content on the basis of conceptual structures and information. Like external interpretation, it makes assumptions about the communicative intentions of the speaker, and takes the co-occurring utterances as forming a field, that is, an occasional, non-coded, and yet relevant configuration of elements, located at the core of a larger interpretative field.

333. Or within the outer context, in the case of deictic use, as when one says: *That's why the road is wet*, pointing at the clouded sky. On anaphoric adverbs and adverbials, see §2.2.3.

334. See Halliday & Hasan (1976: 14); Brown & Yule (1983: §2.4). In fact, there is no formal rule for identifying the antecedent of an anaphoric expression. The only criterion is

coherence. The antecedent of *for this reason*, for instance, is different in (1) — *The glaciers are melting because of the rise in temperatures. The deserts are also advancing for this reason* — and (2): *The glaciers are melting because of the rise in temperatures. The inhabitants of the valley for this reason are worried.* Moreover, the presence of cohesive devices is neither a necessary nor a sufficient condition for textual coherence (see Conte 1977: 15-17). As a rule, a co-operative addressee is ready to assume coherence even when no explicit cohesive device is provided by the text itself. See Coates (1994: 42-43): "The evidence of real language data forces us to make the distinction between coherence and cohesion, since much real language data display coherence without cohesion [...] With or without the presence of formal textual markers, we will attempt to interpret what we hear: we *assume* text is coherent". See also Brown &Yule (1983: §2.4); Sanford & Moxey (1994); Cornish (1990).

335. See Kortman (1997: Chapter 7).

336. As we shall see later on, cause can be refined into result (§2.2.1.3), while the motive for action coinciding with an agent's intention may be looked at as purpose (§3.3). Result and purpose, however, are not independent conceptual structures, which can be inferred as well as encoded, but semantic structures, which cannot be dissociated from the peculiar properties of some specific linguistic expressions.

337. See König (1985: 2): concession is "a dead-end street for any kind of interpretative enrichment".

338. On result see Cuzzolin (1996).

339. Kortmann (1997: Chapter 7) identifies the two dimensions, and speaks of a "semantic space of adverbial relations". On the distinction between "semantic" and "conceptual", see Nuyts (1990) and Levinson (1997: 21): "the level of SR [semantic representation] cannot be the same as the level of CR [conceptual representation]. Why would we struggle to clothe our thoughts in words if skin and cloth were the very same layer?".

340. The fact that concession is both a basic and complex conceptual structure "shows very clearly that cognitive basicness, i.e. centrality for human reasoning, does not necessarily involve cognitive simplicity, and that these two parameters need to be kept separate" (Kortmann, 1997: 208).

341. In many cases, moreover, the shared background of incompatibilities required in order to attain a concessive interpretation can hardly be seen as cognitively complex, for it is formed by very trivial pieces of contingent information, popular beliefs and even base prejudices. Even in such cases, a bare juxtaposition seems inadequate. The compound sentences *It's Monday and John didn't call* and *Sam is English and doesn't like beer*, for instance, are readily given a concessive interpretation against the shared assumption that John normally calls on Monday and the sharing of some prejudices about Englishmen. Yet, the corresponding juxtapositions sound unnatural as expressions of a concessive link: *It's Monday. John didn't call*; *Sam is English. He doesn't like beer.*

342. This condition is the proof that the linear order of the expressions is not a coding device. While a coding device has in any case its own content, an indexical relation requires independent accessibility — the presence, in a sense — of what is indicated.

343. The idea that intonational profile belongs to a set of interacting coding devices is developed by Ferrari (1995).

344. For this reason, such labels as "conjunction adverbs" (Quirk, Greenbaum, Leech & J. Svartvik 1984: 927) are, if taken literally, misleading.

345. See D'Addio Colosimo (1988); Conte (1996).

346. Even if it shares with the complex sentence the presence of a formal unification, the coordination of processes by *and* is sensitive to the diagrammatic principle any time a temporal relationship is relevant, and even in a stronger way than juxtaposition. In particular, when a relationship of cause is involved it is impossible to invert the linear order of the expressions without affecting the content of the relationship. The compound sentence *It rained heavily and the fields are green*, for instance, is consistently interpreted as expressing a relationship of cause. If the order is inverted, the causal relationship disappears: *The fields are green and it rained heavily.*

347. The implicit component of contrast connected to the use of *but* is not an inference based on the coordinated contents, but a conventional implicature independent of them, for it is activated even if the overt contents of the coordinated sentences are not in themselves conflictual. The expression *It is Monday but John has not called*, for instance, conventionally implies that normally John calls on Monday, which means that even an addressee who is not acquainted with John's habits has to take note of it. At the same time, to say that a conventional implicature of contrast is activated does not necessarily mean that it receives a definite content. The expression *John is an architect but Peter is a lawyer*, for instance, conventionally implies that there is some contrast between the two contingent facts, and no more. One can imagine, for instance, that an invitation to the annual meeting of architects has been sent to both John and Peter on the false assumption, rectified by the speaker, that both are architects. If the addressee is not independently aware of the facts, he has no access to this content.

348. The question of the typicality of the categories dealt with by social sciences dates back at least to Weber's concept of *Idealtypus* (Weber, 1922).

349. The complex sentence has at its disposal a set of specific resources for marking the distinction between foreground and background, that is, the subordinative relationship itself and the aspectual implications of the interplaying verbal forms: see Weinrich (1964).

350. The asymmetry between foregounded and backgrounded information is extensively discussed within the functional literature, and in particular by Hopper, 1979, Hopper and Thompson, 1980, Reinhart, 1984, Thompson, 1987 and Tomlin, 1985. For the connected notions of figure and ground, inspired by the *Gestalt* psychology, see Talmy, 1978; 2000, and Croft (2001: Chapter 9). According to Cristofaro (2003: Chapter 2), the asymmetry between foregounded and backgrounded information and the connected asymmetry between assertional and non assertional component form the true conceptual basis of subordination.

351. On the distinction between a nomothetic and an idiographic paradigm, see Windelband (1894: 26): "In their search for a knowledge of reality, the empirical sciences either look for the general in the form of natural laws or for the individual in an historically determined form. [...] The former are sciences based on laws, the latter sciences based on

events; the former teach what always is the case; the latter what once was. Scientific thought is — if one can coin new artificial terms — in one case nomothetic (*nomothetisch*), in the other idiographic (*idiographisch*)".

352. See, for instance, Sosa (ed. 1975).

353. The structure of the concept of cause shares the layered and hierarchical structure of most natural concepts. But for this very reason any attempt to define the natural concept of cause in terms of necessary and sufficient conditions ends in contradiction: see Sosa (1975: 19). The fact that the concept of cause cannot be analysed outside use (see Anscombe, 1975) does not imply that one cannot describe the real use of the concept in discourse.

354. This is a further argument for considering conceptual relations, and not linking words and expressions, as primitives in the analysis of interclausal links.

355. See also Davidson (1963(1968: 90-91)).

356. This point is made visible under ideal conditions by very simple actions, or basic actions. See Danto (1968: 55): "In case of basic action, there is no action, distinct from the action itself, to be put into the *explanans.* This is due to what I am terming the givenness of basic actions". The basic action is an absolute beginning in the regressive chain from purposes of simpler actions towards an action which has its only purpose in itself: "In order to open a door — for instance — we must first do something else which will cause the door to open; but to move one's finger one simply moves it — no prior causal activity is required" (Feinberg, 1968: 107).

357. Dik (1989(1997: 304)) speaks of "illocutionary satellites", Thompson & Longacre (1985: §4) of "speech act adverbial clauses".

358. In this particular case, the connection between the discriminating power of split intonation and the indexical dimension which is called upon to fill the gap, so to speak, is very striking. It would be interesting to make a careful study of intonation focused on the question whether intonation is a true coding device or a kind of cue active within indexical fields.

359. Quoting Ross (1970), Hengeveld (1990: 6) writes that "One of the reasons to assume that every sentence is governed by an abstract performative predicate is that this predicate can be modified by adverbs". In fact, the ghost of an abstract predicate hides the reality of a concrete relation of the indexical order.

360. For an exhaustive discussion and evaluation of the shared as well as distinctive linguistic properties of motives connected to thinking and speaking, see Verstraete (1998). In some languages, the expression of speech act motives relies on specialised conjunctions. This is the case, for instance, of French *puisque* (see Groupe λ-l, 1975), English *since* and Latin *quoniam* (see Bolkenstein (1990: 78-79).

361. Unlike backward-looking motives, the truth of forward-looking motives is not entailed. Accordingly, a future action or event, foreseen or wanted, can consistently motivate an action even if it does not eventually take place. Even if it does not rain, the foreseen rain remains at the basis of the subject's decision to take the umbrella.

362. See, for instance, Ricoeur (1977: 65). Anscombe (1957 §2; 1956(1968: 150)) identifies "forward-looking motives" and "intentions".

363. This is perhaps the reason why some scholars describe motives as "mental causes" (see Anscombe, 1957: 22-23). However, even a backward-looking motive cannot be considered a mental cause for almost two reasons: the fact that a past event is not a mental entity and the presence of an act of deliberation.

364. It is worth pointing out in this connection that a phrasal preposition is neither necessarily nor typically an idiom, which implies that the noun incorporated in it maintains its whole content.

365. More generally, I am indebted to G. Gross' research for all the present section of this chapter.

366. Unlike *view*, *prospect* is more easily connected with prediction than with intention: *With the prospect of William and Harry joining them for a holiday afterwards, Diana was in good heart* (BNC).

367. "Intention simply indicates what one proposes to do or accomplish; intent may imply more deliberate and clear formulation" (Webster).

368. "*Determination* is the quality that you show when you have decided to do something and you will not let anything to stop you" (Collins Cobuild). *Resolve* suggests the irreversibility of decision. It "is absolute determination to do what you have decided to do" (Collins Cobuild).

369. "Attempt is an act of trying to do something especially when this is unsuccessful" (Collins Cobuild).

370. "Design may suggest careful ordering, calculating or scheming" (Webster). "A plan is a method of achieving something you have worked out in detail beforehand" (Collins Cobuild).

371. No example of phrasal preposition incorporating *illusion* has been found in BNC. *Pretence* and *pretention* are used with nominal complements: *with the pretence of friendship.*

372. "An anxiety to do something is a strong wish to do it, often mixed with a feeling of worry that you might not be able to" (Collins Cobuild).

373. The distinction between essential and empirical properties explains why the "deconstruction of the subject" traditionally attributed to such thinkers as Marx, Nietzsche and Freud has dismantled many illusions about human nature but not the meaning of such concepts as freedom, responsibility and decision for human action. If it is difficult to attain a satisfying degree of freedom against outer and inner constraints, human action still remains unthinkable outside the horizon of freedom. Empirical arguments can modify our perception of the content of a domain but not undermine the consistency of its outer borders.

374. For Kant's distinction between lack and deprivation of a property on the part of a kind of being, see note 247.

375. This point has a moral relevance. For a code of ethics to be consistently conceivable, it is not necessary that human beings be free in an empirical sense — it is sufficient that they are free in an essential sense, that is, that they are allowed to struggle for liberty.

376. The idea that the world of living beings is an ordered *cosmos* where structures match elective functions is rooted in a conceptual terrain which is affected neither by positive knowledge nor by religious or metaphysical beliefs. In fact, this idea is compatible as well with the Aristotelian teleological conception of the world as with the Darwinian evolution theory. As Dennett (1995) points out, intentionality provides a consistent model for describing the structure and behaviour of living beings. Darwin himself uses the lexicon of purpose to describe the reciprocal adaptation of animals' organs and functions: "Seeing this gradation and diversity of structure in one small, intimately related group of birds, one might really fancy that from an original paucity of birds in this archipelago [i.e. Galàpagos], one species had been taken and modified for different ends" (Charles Darwin, *The Voyage of the 'Beagle'*, Dent Dutton, London-New York, 1980, Chapter 17, "Galapagos Archipelago").

377. See Searle (1975). An interesting case is provided by communication verbs, which behave as constative when the object is a finite *that*-clause and as directive when the object is a non-finite *to*-clause: *I told* (*wrote, phoned*, etc.) *John that his mother is coming*; *I told John to come at once.*

378. Verbs of tendency (see Skytte, 1983) are a good illustration of this: they require the same syntactic pattern as verbs of trying, but their content is not a purpose. In such a structure as *George tends to neglect his friends*, for instance, the content of the embedded sentence neither necessarily nor typically coincides with the content of an intention.

379. The underlying assumption is that the quality of communication is directly proportional to the structural standard of the expression, an attitude which implies a hierarchy of values according to which explicit is better than implicit, coded better than inferred, plain better than figurative, consistent better than conflictual. But the quality of communication is a quality of the moral order, which has no direct link with the structural properties of the exchanged expressions.

380. The idea that creation is a form of transgression ending in deviant expression is explicitly formulated, in particular, in French *Néorhétorique*. In some cases, the deviation (*écart*) is defined with reference to a vague notion of average use: see for instance, Cohen (1966). In other cases, it is even defined with reference to linguistic coding: see, for instance, Groupe μ (1970(1982: 41)): "We perceive a rhetorical *écart* when the zero degree is altered". The zero degree, in turn, is "everything belonging to the *linguistic* code, [...]: spelling, grammar, word meaning" (38). One would say that Sapir had in mind precisely such kinds of excess when he wrote, fifty years before, that "The major characteristics of style [...] are given by the language itself, quite as inescapably, indeed, as the general acoustic effect of verse is given by the sounds and natural accents of the language [...] It is not in the least likely that a truly great style can seriously oppose itself to the basic form patterns of the language. It not only incorporates them, it builds on them" (Sapir, 1921: 242).

381. This attitude shows that the interpretation of tropes does not escape the tendency of the average addressee to jump to the contingent intended message bypassing the structural meaning of the expression. As Gibbs (1994: 119) points out: "psycholiguistic research indicates that people can understand many instances of figurative expression effortlessly, without the explicit recognition that such language is special or reflective of deviant thought". This circumstance, however, is a further argument for digging out the structure of

tropes as complex meanings, which escapes the speaker's notice. "The lack of difference in the moment-by-moment processing of figurative and of literal language — Gibbs goes on — should not automatically be taken as evidence against the legitimacy of some figurative meanings, such as those found in poetry, as special *products*" (118).

382. Davidson (1978(1984: 261)) criticises the common tendency to identify the meaning of the metaphor with "the *effects* metaphors have on us": "The common error is to fasten on the contents of the thoughts a metaphor provokes and to read these contents into the metaphor itself".

383. Engl. transl. in *Greek lyric poetry*, translation and notes by M.L. West, Oxford World's Classics, Oxford University Press, Oxford 1993: 35.

384. The two concepts are to be carefully distinguished, even if they are sometimes used as synonyms. Strawson (1952: 2), for instance, speaks of "inconsistency, or self-contradiction".

385. Of course, a man can be good and bad in reality, for the terms whose conjunction ends in contradiction denote properties which are in competition in real life, as pointed out by Kant (1763(1992: 217)): see §3.2.3.

386. The Aristotelian tradition uses the opposition between "contradictory" and "contrary" for distinguishing exclusive and non-exclusive oppositions. However, this use of the term *contradiction* has the disadvantage of identifying a virtual correlation and an actual relation in speech. In order to avoid confusion, we shall restrict the term *contradiction* to the relation, and speak of *opposition* — exclusive or non-exclusive — when referring to the correlation. The existence of a neutral conceptual area between the polar terms of grading paradigms suggests an interesting point. The same speakers who do not hesitate to use a contradiction in order to bring a complex situation to expression are reluctant to envisage the bare absence of determinations. As Sapir (1944: 101) points out, "To the naive, every person is either good or bad; if he cannot be easily placed, he is rather part good and part bad than just humanly normal or neither good nor bad". The absence of (positive or negative) qualities tends to be taken as a sign of mediocrity, both in everyday discourse — cf. the saying *To be neither fish, nor fowl, nor red herring* — and in narrative: *Within the coach was sitting a person who, though not being very handsome, looked not so bad, neither too fat not too slim; one could not tell that he was old, but he wasn't too young either* (Gogol).

387. The latitude of negative predicates is valorized by litotes. See, for instance, Fontanier (1968: 134): "When Chimène, weeping, tells Rodrigue:

... Va, je ne te hais point,

do we think she is content simply not to hate him, and should Rodrigue be less satisfied than if she had told him: *Va, sois sûr que je t'aime*?". Concerning the relationship between litotes, modulation and attenuation, see Caffi (1990).

388. Of course, the utterance is contradictory only if the identity of the direct obiects — here latent — is assumed; otherwise it is consistent: *Remember me, but ah! Forget my fate!* (Nahum Tate). More generally, when non-saturated terms are involved, contradiction depends on the identity of saturation. In such an expression as *Every limit is a beginning as well as an ending* (G. Eliot), contradiction is only apparent, for the complements of the

opposite terms — *beginning* and *end* — refer to different circumstances: the end of the novel is the beginning of a new life for its characters.

389. The different forms of contradictory utterance are seen as different kinds of figure by some scholars. Cellier (1965), for instance, uses the term *antithesis* to refer to the coordinative form — the type *Odi et amo* — and restricts the term *oxymore* to the subordinative form: see also Molinié (1992: 235). Morier (1961) distinguishes between *oxymore* — the direct contradiction, and in particular its subordinative form: for instance *symphonia discors* — and *paradoxisme*, which "avoids the abrupt confrontation of oxymoron" keeping a certain distance between the opposite terms: for instance, *Rétablit son honneur à force d'infamie* (Boileau). The term *paradoxisme* is Beauzée's translation of the Greek term *oxymoron*.

390. Contradiction and inconsistency, as we have seen, are not exclusive properties of linguistic expressions; we can also experience or imagine, and therefore consistently speak of, inconsistent or contradictory instances of human behaviour. There are two good reasons, however, for approaching inconsistency and contradiction from within linguistic expressions. The first reason is that, whereas inconsistency and contradiction in human behaviour are generally seen as pathological instances, the same structures are valorized in texts and discourses as specific forms of expression, conceptual elaboration and conceptual creation. This fact is certainly relevant to an exhaustive evaluation of inconsistency and contradiction, and human speech is the only field where it can be observed. The second reason is that contradiction and inconsistency in human behaviour are better understood on the basis of a previous understanding of linguistic instances than the other way round. The logical structure of inconsistency and contradiction can be defined with reference both to each other and to a couple of correlative concepts — namely, tautology and consistent synthetic proposition — which are documented in linguistic expressions.

391. See, on this point, Wittgenstein (1929: 162): "We get the picture of the pure form [of a proposition] if we abstract from the meaning of the single words [...] That is to say, if we substitute variables for the constants of the proposition".

392. Husserl (1901(1970): 4th *Inquiry*) distinguishes a formal, analytical sort of countersense, which violates the laws of logic, that is, contradiction, from a material, synthetic sort, involving the conceptual purport, that is, inconsistency.

393. Here we run across a dramatic problem of neopositivist epistemology. In order to be verifiable, a proposition has to be consistent — it has to encapsulate a tautology. But how is one to know that a tautology is actually encapsulated in a proposition? The problem of consistency essentially affects logic and epistemology; nevertheless, neither logic nor epistemology is able to solve it, for the key to consistency lies in a descriptive elucidation of the substantive content of our shared natural ontology.

394. Fr. 6. Engl. transl. by D. Gallop: Parmenides of Elea, *Fragments. A text and translation with an introduction by David Gallop,* University of Toronto Press, Toronto/Buffalo/London 1984.

395. *Metaphysics* 4, 1005b. Engl. transl. by H. Tredennik: *The Metaphysics*, I: Books I-9, The Loeb Classical Library, London/Cambridge/Mass. 1961.

396. *Ouk esti gar anankaion, a tis legei, tauta ka ypolambanein*: *Metaphysics* IV (1005b). Engl. transl. by H. Tredennik: *The Metaphysics*, I: Books I-9, The Loeb Classical Library, London/ Cambridge/Mass. 1961.

397. Fr. LXXXI. Engl. transl. by W. H. S Johnes: Heracleitus, *On the Universe*, The Loeb Classical Library, London/Cambridge/Mass. 1959.

398. This topic recalls Frege's programme for the "extrusion of thoughts from the mind" (Dummet, 1988: 17). As Dummet points out, "for Frege, thoughts — the contents of acts of thinking — are not constituents of the stream of consciousness" but shared, intersubjective realities "accessible to all" through symbolic expression. The idea of fully securing philosophical thoughts from their discursive drift is certainly a myth. Nevertheless, it belongs as a chief regulating idea to the mainstream of Western tradition — the ideal pursuit of an essential affinity, if not of an impossible identity, between the form of thoughts, their linguistic shaping, and their transmission through oral or written texts.

399. Hegel's remark is sound as far as the discursive use of tautology is concerned — but the same criticism holds, as we have seen, for his favourite logical structure, that is, contradiction. Hegel however, goes far beyond this point. The discursive value of tautologies is taken as proof against the identity principle as the leading principle of consistent discourse: "Identity is contradictory". When making this move, Hegel clearly shares the same presupposition he attributes to the tradition he claims to challenge — namely, an immediate identification between the logical properties of the utterance and its behaviour in speech.

400. The value of the last remark can be fully appreciated if we consider that a consistent proposition encapsulates a tautology, and an inconsistent one a contradiction. Wittgenstein (1961: 25.5.15) probably has this fact in his mind when he writes that "The tautology is asserted, the contradiction is denied, by *every* proposition".

401. See Grice (1975: 52), taken over by Levinson (1983: 111). About the argumentative implications of tautologies in discourse, see Schapira (2000: §§3.2.2; 3.2.3). Wierzbicka (1987: 96) argues that most tautologies both display characteristic and language-specific syntactic patterns and have highly conventional meanings: "The constructions in question have a language-specific meaning, and this meaning must be spelled out in appropriate semantic representations". This fact is interpreted by Wierzbicka as an argument against the Gricean idea that the interpretation of tautologies is a creative textual or conversational act (see Fraser's 1988 remarks and Wierzbicka's 1988a replay). In fact, both conventionality and creative interpretation are in the horizon of all kinds of figurative speech. There are conventional tautologies just as there are conventional metaphors, metonymies or hyperboles. A tautology is a whole utterance. When it is about a general topic, as Wierzbicka's examples are, its content is easily conventionalised to become a sort of proverb. Tautology, of course, is not the only form of proverb. The Italian translation of English *A promise is a promise*, for instance, is not tautological: *Ogni promessa è debito*. What seems indisputable is that the tendency of tautology towards conventionalisation is not shared by oxymoron, the figure of contradiction (see §3).

402. The behaviour of both tautology and contradiction in speech shows that consistency has no value as such; separated from informativeness, it shares the destiny of contradiction. The function of the identity principle is not immediately discursive; it is meta-discursive. It

does not encourage the actual utterance of tautologies as an ideal instance of consistent discourse, but provides a consistency criterion for constructing informative utterances and for interpreting contradictory and inconsistent utterances.

403. These are instances of polyphonic speaking, implying the reference to distinct responsible subjects: cf. Ducrot (1980); Mortara Garavelli (1985); Landheer (1996: §3).

404. Landheer (1996) defines paradox as the apparent contradiction which takes place when the connected terms "Are not [...] on the same level, so that making them equivalent [...] is by the same token not a real contradiction" (93). Owing to its aptitude to combine the consistency of thoughts and the appeal of contradiction, the apparent oxymoron is praised by Hegel, who throws it against the identity principle as a true war-machine. It is interesting to compare Hegel's way of forcing a conflict into logical contradiction to the analytical attitude displayed by Kant (1763(1992)) when facing a similar topic: "*Vice* (*demeritum*) is not merely a negation; it is a *negative virtue* (*meritum negativum*). For vice can only occur in so far as a being has within him an inner law [...] which is contravened by his actions. This inner law is a positive reason for a good action [...]. What we have here is, accordingly, a deprivation, a real opposition, and not merely a lack".

405. The concept of modulation is defined by Cruse (1986: 52): "a single sense can be modified in an unlimited number of ways by different contexts, each context emphasising certain semantic traits and obscuring or suppressing others". Modulation has nothing to do with polysemy: "the variation within a sense caused by modulation is largely continuous and fluid in nature", whereas the variation due to the selection of the contextually relevant sense of a polysemous word "proceeds in discrete jumps rather than continuously".

406. See on this point Chapter 6, §3.7.

407. When it is engaged in a fine-grained description of complex situations, the content of concepts moves into a drift which threatens the very condition of consistent use, that is, the identity of a concept with itself. In other words, the conflictual complexity of the described objects and situations tends to be transferred onto the structure of concepts, whose content becomes more and more complex and potentially conflictual. The linguistic meaning of a lexeme receives its value within a network of correlations and relations defined by the lexical structure of language. The concept entrusted to a lexeme in a given use receives its value from its position within a contingent configuration of concepts, that is, within a field formed by a text located in a network of relevant intertextual relations against the background of a given cultural tradition. The content of a concept in use is therefore a field value, and not simply the manifestation of a system value within a field. Accordingly, the object of philosophical analysis is not the definition of the lexical values of the system but the definition of concepts in use, as Ayer (1936: Chapter 3) points out.

408. It is clear that Hegel uses the term *contradiction* to denote complexity, that is, in Kant's terminology, real opposition: see, on this point, Poublanc (1991). Moreover, Hegel's use of the term *contradiction* is so generous as to include in its denotation field lexical correlations: "contradiction is [...] immediately represented in the *determinations of relationship*. The most trivial examples of above and below, right and left, father and son, and so on *ad infinitum*, all contain opposition in each term. That *is* above, which is *not* below; 'above' is specifically just this, not to be 'below', and only *is*, *in so far as* there is a 'below'; and conversely, each determination implies its opposite" (Hegel, 1812-13(1978: 441)).

409. Language could not guarantee the absolute stability of concepts without contradicting its nature as an instrument of active conceptualization in living texts. This is the reason why consistency has a value only insofar as it takes up the challenge of synthetic discourse.

410. As defined by Searle (1969: Chapter 1, §1.5).

411. The presence of both interaction and conflict separates living metaphors both from lexical catachreses, which imply neither conflict nor interaction, and from consistent metaphorical concepts, which imply interaction but not conflict. On this point, see §5.2.

412. See Chapter 1, §2.2.

413. If we agree with the classical tradition in considering abstraction — the focusing of the property to the detriment of its bearer — as a form of synecdoche. See, for instance, Fontanier (1968: 93): Abstracting synecdoche "consists of [...] taking a quality, considered in an abstract way and as something apart, for the subject supposed to have this quality". According to our criteria, abstraction should rather be considered a metonymy, for a quality is not so much a part of the object's *Gestalt* as something which can be predicated about it. But such classificatory questions should not be emphasised.

414. *Poetics*, (57b (21)). Engl. transl. by W. Hamilton Fyfe: *The Poetics*, The Loeb Classical Library, London-Cambridge/Mass. 1973.

415. The relative lack of interest in metonymy and synecdoche, compared with the deep interest in metaphor, is a remarkable feature of rhetoric studies in the last century. Among the exceptions, see Le Guern (1973), Bonhomme (1987), Taylor (1989), Gibbs (1994); Panther & Radden (eds., 1999), Barcelona (ed., 2000), Dirven & Pörings (eds., 2002). The study of metaphor outside the paradigm including metonymy and synecdoche leaves two alternative issues: either the adoption of a restricted definition of metaphor, which ignores metonymy and synecdoche (Cf. Black, 1954), or the adoption of a broad one, including any kind of figure of content (see, for instance, Richards, 1936, Brooke-Rose, 1958, Goodman, 1968, Davidson, 1978(1984), Wierzbicka, 1980: 160). Weinrich (1963: 334) considers oxymoron as a kind of metaphor: "an oxymoron is of course a metaphor". In the first case, the analysis tacitly shares the assumptions of traditional classifications without calling them into question; in the second case, either the description is as generic as to fit any instance of trope, or it is relevant and revealing for metaphor but inapplicable to metonymy and synecdoche.

416. Along a line of analysis which, through Brooke-Rose (1958), goes back to Geoffrey de Vinsauf (in Faral, 1924).

417. As we shall see later on (§4.3.1), in the case of metonymy the nominal positions are open to infinitives and gerunds, which are non-finite, and therefore noun-like verbal forms.

418. The presence of a conflict in the complex meaning is at the basis of the traditional distinction between such punctual tropes as metaphor, metonymy and synecdoche and such global tropes as allegory or irony or hyperbole, whose focus ranges over a whole utterance. While a metaphor opposes a conflictual focus to a coherent frame, an allegory is a whole sentence whose non-conflictual meaning taken as a whole enters into conflict with co-textual or contextual information, and therefore receives an analogical interpretation. In the following example, the first utterance is a metaphor, which applies to a coherent subject

— *the girls* — a conflictual focus — *are blooming*. The second is an allegory, ideating a consistent process which, because it does not cohere with the co-textual information, has to be adapted to the textually relevant topics — to the girls: *These girls are blooming. You better have your orchard well fenced or you'll be out of apples by October* (McGahern).

419. The existence of interactive paradigms, that is, of paradigms which do not include alternative terms but interacting terms, dissociates the idea of paradigm from the idea of substitution. The identification of paradigm and substitutive correlation is a favourite topic of structuralist rhetoric, inspired by Jakobson (1960). See, for instance, Genette (1968: 12): "We thus see that Fontanier states, in the clearest possible way, the substitutive essence of the figure", an attitude which displays "an acute, and most precious awareness of the *paradigmatic* dimension of the units of discourse (both large and small)".

420. See Chapter 7, §2.2.4.

421. The outcome of a metaphorical interaction is in any case a text or discourse value, which takes shape in a given field. In a passage of Verga's novel *I Malavoglia*, for instance, the "mooing" sea is explicitly connected to the canonical bovine subjects of the verb, a move which is coherent with a mythology of sea as a violent beast: *Il mare si udiva muggire attorno ai fariglioni che pareva ci fossero riuniti i buoi della fiera di S. Alfio.*

422. And synecdoches, if abstraction is to be considered so — *He saw, more than a mile away, the ugly enormity of the Custom House* (Conrad). But the behaviour of abstraction is an argument to consider it a kind of metonymy.

423. Our analysis focuses on English and similar languages, and implies neither that impersonal processes are necessarily devoid of participant roles nor that impersonal verbs cannot be used metaphorically: see Walsh, 1995.

424. The notion of internal subject is moulded on the notion of internal object. An internal object gives nominal expression to a concept encapsulated in the content of an intransitive verb — *He lived a marvellous life*. The presence of internal arguments is the consequence of a tension between the grammatical frame of a process and its conceptual structure. Raining, for instance, involves water, which however receives no expression in the canonical linguistic frame *It rains*.

425. The ex-capsulation of a consistent subject is typically motivated by the need to provide a nominal support for a modifying adjective: for instance, *It rains icy water*. The use of impersonal verbs with metaphorical arguments is typical of various idioms: *It rains cats and dogs*; *Il pleut des cordes*; *Fioccano multe*. Unlike internal subjects, external subjects admit a grammatically impeccable expression: *God makes it rain*.

426. The idea of proportional analogy goes back to Aristotle: "Metaphor by analogy means this: when B is to A as D is to C, then instead of B the poet will say D and B instead of C. For instance [...] old age is to life as evening is to day; so he will call the evening 'day's old age' or use Empedocles' phrase; and old age he will call 'the evening of life' or 'life's setting sun'" (*Poetics, 57b* (21). Engl. transl. by W. Hamilton Fyfe: *The Poetics*, The Loeb Classical Library, London/Cambridge/Mass. 1973).

427. This is consistent with the fact that the structure of a punctual concept depends as much on the network of consistent and appropriate relations it is involved in as on its inherent properties, as we have seen in Chapter 6, §3.5.

428. The metaphoric idea of the world as a book is analyzed in its manifold historical manifestations by Blumenberg (1981). The metaphorical topic of the monument as document is analysed by Le Goff (1978).

429. The traditional notion of a proper term rests on a confusion between the occasional identification of a referent and its conceptual categorisation as a given kind of being. If it makes sense to speak of a proper term for conceptual categorisation, it is doubly meaningless to speak of a proper term for identification. First, a given entity can be consistently identified by an open set of terms, for the identity of an individual is inexhaustible. Second, identification is an indexical relation, whose success is compatible with the use of conceptually defective or inconsistent terms, empty like a pronoun or an ellipsis, or even mistaken terms (see Donnellan, 1966).

430. The contrast between the activation of substantive relations between vehicle and tenor and the promotion of a conceptual interaction through conceptual transfer is a reliable criterion for differentiating metonymy and metaphor even in those complex cases which push Goossens (1990) to blend them into the hybrid figure called "metaphtonymy": see Riemer (2002).

431. The relevant structure of the complex object depends to a given extent on situationally relevant stereotypes. An engineer drawing a plan for a steamer, for instance, would not consider the smoke as an essential part of it. If he were asked by his child to draw a boat for him, the same engineer would probably draw an imposing plume of smoke. For Madame Butterfly, the plume of smoke — *Fil di fumo* — means the ship by synecdoche and her husband's return by metonymy.

432. Some scholars (see, for instance, Ruwet (1975) and Taylor (1989)) raise the question of possible cognitive restrictions on the transparency of metonymical relations, and therefore on the creation of metonymies. Taylor, for instance, claims that "not any product [...] can be referred to by the name of the person who created the product. I could hardly say *Mary was delicious,* meaning by *Mary* the cheesecake which Mary made, in spite of the analogy between Mary's mixing and processing of ingredients to produce her cake and Picasso's mixing and application of colours to produce his painting" (1989: 123). Of course, out of context the example of Picasso is more directly understood than the example referring to Mary, but no essential reason prevents one from imagining a context where such an act of reference would work. The essential point about metonymies and synecdoches (as well as about metaphorical nouns in their referential use) lies not so much in the transparency of the underlying relation as in the independent accessibility of the intended referent. Once the textual referent has been identified, it becomes relevant to ask whether the conflictual referential expression activates a given substantive and consistent relation with it or not. In the first case, we have a metonymy or synecdoche, in the second a metaphor.

433. On caricature, see Ross (1974: 286): "Caricature highlights selected aspects of a person's appearance by exaggerating faithful representations along certain parameters. Thus caricatured strong jaws are stronger and caricatured long noses are longer [...] exaggeration is selective. Some features are highlighted, others played down, others eliminated altogether".

434. *De rerum natura*, H, vv. 317-322.

435. Don Rodrigo, the plague-stricken negative hero of the novel *I promessi sposi*, realizes that his servant has called not the physician but the public attendants who are to take him to the hospital.

436. Compare, for instance, Zola's polemic metonymy *Des jupes avaient des rires languissants* with its consistent paraphrase *Des femmes qui portaient des jupes avaient des rires languissants.*

437. Commenting on the metonymy *La vengeance à la main, l'oeil ardent de colère* (Corneille), Fontanier (1968: 82) points out that "Vengeance in itself cannot be brandished [...]; what can be brandished is *any weapon to be used for vengeance*".

438. See Lakoff & Turner (1989: 52-53): "The reason why there are so many conventional metaphors for life, death, and time, is that these are very rich concepts for us. When we try to conceptualize the wealth of our experience of these domains, no single, consistent structuring of that experience is possible; instead we need to import structure from a wide variety of source domains if we are to characterize anything approaching the full richness of the target domain. Each metaphor provides structure for comprehending a different aspect of the target domain".

439. According to Lakoff & Turner (1989: 9), the poetic creation of metaphors is a creative elaboration and combination of shared metaphorical concepts rather than a creation of conceptual conflicts open to metaphorical interpretation: "Poets, as members of their cultures, naturally make use of these basic conceptual metaphors to communicate with other members, their audience"; "Poets must make the most of the linguistic and conceptual resources they are given. Basic metaphors are part of those resources, part of the way members of our culture make sense of the world. Poets may compose or elaborate or express them in new ways, but they still use the same basic conceptual resources available to us all. If they did not, we would not understand them" (26).

440. One is tempted to add a *caveat* like *on the supplementary condition that no previously identifiable track constrains the transfer and its discursive issues*. The *caveat* seems justified by Aristotle's definition of "*metaphora*", or transfer, quoted in §4.1, which includes, beside metaphor in the modern sense, metonymy and synecdoche. In fact, it is redundant because when a substantive track is activated, as in the case of metonymy and synecdoche, there is no transfer at all.

441. The conception of metaphor as an adaptation of the vehicle to the tenor by reduction of the incompatible "semantic features", made popular by the French structuralist *néorhétorique*, extends to creative metaphors this peculiar aspect of the more stereotyped kind of metaphors: see, for instance, Todorov (1970) and Groupe μ (1970).

442. The idea of conceptual creation through conflict is explicity excluded by Lakoff & Johnson (2003: 259): "Any would-be link that would lead to a contradiction with the inherent structure of the target domain will be inhibited". But this presupposes that the target domain already has an inherent structure, just as in the case of catachresis.

443. See Chapter 7, §§1.2 and 2.2.4.

444. In a similar way, a sociologist studying the role of cars in everyday life would not consider a Ferrari a prototypical car. A researcher in the field of mechanics, interested in finding out how far the construction and use of cars can go, certainly would.

445. As Lakoff & Turner (1989: 2) point out, for instance, there is a metaphorical conception of death as departure that can be expressed in many different ways, such as 'passing away', 'being gone', or 'departing'.

446. It is this form that makes metaphor a powerful instrument of categorisation, a circumstance which, in turn, justifies the privilege accorded to the identifying formula when metaphor is seen as an instrument of thought. The paragraph titles in Lakoff & Turner (1989), for example, are instances of the identifying fomula: *People are plants; A lifetime is a day; Life is a journey; Death is going to a final destination,* and so on. Ricoeur (1975: *Septième étude*) subtly analyses metaphor as a predication involving a self-contradictory copula: to say that a girl is a nightingale amounts to asserting that the girl both is and is not a nightingale. This analysis, though stimulating, has two major limits. First, the identification of two subjects of discourse is assumed to be a general formula for metaphor. Second, metaphorical predication itself cannot be reduced to a contradictory kind of predication. Unlike contradiction, metaphor does not put the predicative link expressed by the copula and its negation at the same level: while the predicative link is asserted, its negation is presupposed (see §2) against a non-asserted background of shared consistency criteria.

447. This point did not escape Aristotle (*Poetics*, 21, 57b. Engl. transl. by W. Hamilton Fyfe: *The Poetics*, The Loeb Classical Library, London/Cambridge/Mass. 1973): "Sometimes there is no word for some of the terms of the analogy, but the metaphor can be used all the same. For instance, to scatter seed is to sow, but there is no word for the action of the sun in scattering its fire. Yet this has to the sunshine the same relation as sowing has to the seed, and so you have the phrase 'sowing the god-created fire'". Aristotle's example is maybe not too well chosen, for it is not difficult to reformulate the intended process in a consistent way. The message, however, is clear: what Aristotle means is that the metaphorical focus cannot always be reformulated in consistent words.

448. For the role played by conceptual conflicts and metaphorical interaction in scientific discovery, see Hesse (1965); Boyd (1979); Kuhn (1979).

449. While Richards's remark is sound, his example is not very good, for a use of *crawl* with human subjects implying moral censure is lexicalised in English: «if you crawl to someone, you try to please them and to make them to like you in order to gain some advantage for yourself; used in informal English showing disapproval» (Collins Cobuild).

450. As Weinrich (1963: 338) points out, the analogies underlying shared metaphorical concepts are in turn metaphorical: "Between truth and light, there is no *tertium* which is not in itself metaphorical. A strange *tertium*, indeed, which is most difficult to find precisely where we use metaphors most frequently!".

451. See also p. 40: "Imagine some layman required to say, without taking special thought, those things he held to be true about wolves; the set of statements resulting would approximate to what I am here calling the system of commonplaces associated with the word "wolf" [...] From the expert's standpoint, the system of commonplaces may include half-truths or downright mistakes (as when a whale is classified as a fish); but the important thing for the metaphor's effectiveness is not that the commonplaces shall be true, but that they should be really and freely evoked". In fact, the existence of a system of commonplaces is not a necessary condition for metaphor — the existence of a conflictual utterance is a sufficient

one. It is a necessary condition for stereotyped metaphors. This remark does not affect the concept of projection, which, though defined by Black through the particular case of projected commonplaces, is independent of them.

452. As pointed out by Segre (1979: 14).

453. See Davidson (1978(1984: note 16)): "I hold that the endless character of what we call the paraphrase of a metaphor springs from the fact that it attempts to spell out what the metaphor makes us notice and to this there is no clear end".

454. This cleavage between structural complexity and subjects' effort is due to the fact that understanding messages is a form of "knowing how", whereas describing the structure of the involved strategies requires "knowing that", to put it in Searle's (1983: Chapter 5) terms. Performing a task does not amount to adapting one's behaviour to a set of explicit instructions, but relying upon a set of practical "background of abilities" (Searle, 1983). Though taken for granted as a matter of course during practical behaviour, these abilities prove to be very complex to analyze. This is the reason why psycholinguistic data on elaboration time and effort can not be used as an argument against the structural complexity of the input structures.

455. The competition between the changing pressures of socially and historically variable uses and the inertial force of long-lasting formal patterns is finely described by Sapir (1921: Chapter 7) as the factor that shapes linguistic drifts.

456. Incidentally, this would prove that native Australians *do* in fact master such concepts as cause with such assurance that they do not need to code it.

457. See Herman (1963) and Ehrliholzer (1965). The use of *poiché* as an expression of temporal sequence is confined to the early stages of Italian. In Dante, *poi che* expresses temporal sequence — *Poi che la voce fu restata e queta / vidi quattro grand'ombre a noi venire* (*Inferno* 4, 82) — and is open to enrichment towards cause or motive: *Quali fioretti dal notturno gelo / chinati e chiusi, poi che 'l sol li 'mbianca / si drizzan tutti aperti in loro stelo* (*Inferno* 2, 128). Thanks to its archaic and literary flavour, the temporal value occasionally surfaces in more recent texts: see for instance D'Annunzio: *Ella, poi che fu libera, adunò tutti i vasi sparsi per la casa.*

458. The polysemy of *mentre* is revealed by Wierzbicka's test: there are some contexts where temporal simultaneity, unlike contrast, would not make sense. While *Giorgio studia e lavora mentre suo fratello perde i suoi giorni* is compatible with a temporal interpretation improved through inferencing, *Giorgio è diventato musicista mentre Pietro studierà ingegneria* is not, because of the temporal gap between the two states of affairs.

459. "Strictly local and idiosyncratic, highly contextualized, inferences", that is, true conversational implicatures, which draw a message out of a meaningful expression, are open to lexicalization: an utterance as a whole can take a given message value as its coded meaning. In this way inference provides, along with metaphor, a major source of idioms (see Prandi, 1999). The idiom *To wash one's hands of something*, for instance, freezes the message of Pilatus's telling action. The psychological motivation of this drift towards conventionalization is documented in literary texts: for Proust's heroes Odette and Swann, for instance, *Faire cattleya* comes to mean "Make love"; In Mann's Buddenbrooks, for Tony and Morten *To sit on the rocks* comes to mean "Stay alone and to be bored".

References

Distrahit animum librorum multitudo
(Comenius)

Abraham, W., T. Givón & S. A. Thompson (eds.)
1995 *Discourse Grammar and Typology*. Amsterdam/Philadelphia: John Benjamins.

Alinei, M.
1974 *La struttura del lessico*. Bologna: Il Mulino.
1996 "Aspetti teorici della motivazione". *Quaderni di semantica* XVII, 7–17.

Allen, M.
1978 *Morphological Investigations*. PhD Dissertation. University of Connecticut.

Anderson, J. M.
1984 "Objecthood". In Plank (ed., 1984), 29–54.

Andresen, H.
1973 "Ein methodischer Vorschlag zur Unterscheidung von Ergänzung und Angabe im Rahmen der Valenztheorie". *Deutsche Sprache* 1, 49–63.

Anscombe, G. E. M.
1956(1968) "Intention". *Proceedings of the Aristotelian Society* 57, 321–332. Repr. in White (ed., 1968), 144–152.
1957 *Intention*. Oxford: Blackwell.
1975 "Causality and determination". In Sosa (ed., 1975), 88–104.

Apel, K. O.
1976 "The transcendental conception of language-communication and the idea of a first philosophy". In Parret, H. (ed.), *History of Linguistic Thought and Contemporary Linguistics*. Berlin/New York: de Gruyter, 32–61.
1987 "Grenzen der Diskursethik? Versuch einer Zwischenbilanz". *Zeitschrift für philosophische Forschung* 1, 3–31.

Apothéloz, D.
1995 *Rôle et fonctionnement de l'anaphore dans la dynamique textuelle*. Geneva: Droz.

Apresjan, Y. D.
1992 *Lexical Semantics*. Ann Arbor: Karoma Publishers.

Arbeitsgruppe Marburg
1973 "Aspekte der Valenztheorie". *Deutsche Sprache* 1, 3–48.

Asher, R. E. (ed.)
1994 *The Encyclopedia of Language and Linguistics*. Oxford/New York: Pergamon Press.

Auerbach, E.
1944 *Figura.* Bern: Francke.
Austin, J. L.
1962(1975) *How to do Things with Words.* Oxford: Clarendon Press. 2nd and revised edition. Oxford: Oxford University Press.
Ayer, A. J.
1936(1990) *Language, Truth and Logic.* London: Victor Gollancz. Repr.: Harmondsworth: Penguin Books.
1966(1969) "Metaphysics and common sense". In Kennick, W. E. & M. Lazerovitz (eds.), *Metaphysics.* Englewood Cliffs: Prentice-Hall. Repr. in Ayer, A. J., *Metaphysics and Common Sense.* London: Macmillan, 64–81.
Baldinger, K.
1980 *Semantic Theory.* New York: St. Martin's Press.
Bally, Ch.
1932(1944) *Linguistique générale et linguistique française.* 2nd edition. Bern: Francke.
1940 "L'arbitraire du signe. Valeur et signification". *Le français moderne* VIII, 193–206.
Barcelona, A. (ed.)
2000 Metaphor and Metonymy at the Crossroads. Cognitive Approaches. Berlin/New York: Mouton De Gruyter.
Beaugrande, R.-A. de & W. U. Dressler
1981 *Einführung in die Textlinguistik.* Tübingen: Max Niemeyer Verlag.
Beccaria, G. L. (ed.)
1994 *Dizionario di linguistica.* Turin: Einaudi.
Benveniste, E.
1939(1966) "Nature du signe linguistique". *Acta Linguistica* I. Repr. in Benveniste, E., *Problèmes de linguistique générale.* Paris: Gallimard, 49–55.
1969(1974) "Mécanismes de transposition". *Cahiers F. de Saussure* 25. Repr. in Benveniste, E., *Problèmes de linguistique générale II.* Paris: Gallimard, 113–125.
Berlin, B. & P. Kay
1969(1991) *Basic Color Terms.* Berkeley/Los Angeles: University of California Press.
Bernet, R., I. Kern & E. Marbach
1989 *Edmund Husserl. Darstellung seines Denkens.* Hamburg: Felix Meiner Verlag.
Bernini, G.
1992 *The Sentence Topic in the Languages of Europe.* Eurotyp Working Paper I-3. Strasbourg: European Science Foundation.
Bhat, D. N. S.
1994 *The adjectival Category.* Amsterdam/Philadelphia: John Benjamins.
Bickel, B.
1997 "Spatial operations in deixis, cognition and culture: where to orient oneself in Belhare". In Nuyts & Pederson (eds., 1997), 46–83.

Bierwisch, M.
1966 *Grammatik des deutschen Verbs. Studia Grammatica* 2. Berlin: Akademie Verlag.
Black, M.
1952(1954) "Definition, presupposition and assertion". *The Philosophical Review* 61. Repr. in Black, M., *Problems of Analysis. Philosophical Essays.* London: Routledge & Kegan Paul, 1954, 24–45.
1954(1962) "Metaphor". *Proceedings of the Aristotelian Society* 55, 273–294. Repr. in Black (1962), 25–47.
1962 *Models and Metaphors.* Ithaca/London: Cornell University Press.
1962a "Explanations of meaning". In Black (1962), 17–24.
1979 "More about metaphor", In Ortony (ed., 1979), 19–43.
Blake, B. J.
1982 "The absolutive: its scope in English and Kalkatungu". In Hopper & Thompson (eds., 1982), 71–94.
1990 *Relational Grammar.* London: Routledge.
Blinkenberg, A.
1960 *Le problème de la transitivité en français moderne.* Copenhagen.
Bloomfield, L.
1933 *Language.* New York: Holt, Reinehart & Winston.
Blumenberg, H.
1960 *Paradigmen zu einer Metaphorologie.* Bonn: Bouvier und Co.
1981 *Die Lesbarkeit der Welt.* Frankfurt am Main: Suhrkamp.
Boas, F.
1911 "Introduction". In *Handbook of American Indian Languages.* Washington: Smithsonian Institution.
Boer, Ch. de
1926 *Essai sur la syntaxe moderne des prépositions en français et en italien.* Paris.
Bolinger, D.
1965 "The atomization of meaning". *Language* 41, 555–573.
1967 "Adjectives in English: attribution and predication". *Lingua* 18, 1–34.
Bolkenstein, A. M.
1990 "Sentential complements in functional grammar: Embedded predications, propositions, utterances in Latin". In Nuyts, Bolkenstein & Vet (eds., 1990), 71–100.
Bonhomme, M.
1987 *Linguistique de la métonymie.* Bern: Peter Lang.
Bonomi, A.
1987 *Le immagini dei nomi.* Milan: Bompiani.
Boyd, R.
1979 "Metaphor and theory change: what is 'Metaphor' a metaphor for?". In Ortony (ed., 1979), 356–408.
Bracchi, R.
1994 "Profilo dei dialetti della Val Tartano". In Bianchini, G., *Vocabolario dei dialetti della Val Tartano.* Sondrio: Fondazione Pro Valtellina, XIII-LVII.

1995 "Profilo storico del dialetto di Grosio". In Antonioli, G. & R. Bracchi, *Dizionario etimologico grosino*. Grosio: Biblioteca Comunale, 51–159.

Broccias, C.
2003 *The English Change Network. Forcing Changes into Schemas*. Berlin/New York: Mouton de Gruyter.

Brooke-Rose, Ch.
1958 *A Grammar of Metaphor*. London: Secker & Warburg.

Brown, G. & G. Yule
1983 *Discourse Analysis*. Cambridge: Cambridge University Press.

Bühler, K.
1934 *Sprachtheorie*. Jena: Fischer.

Caffi, C.
1990 "Modulazione, mitigazione, litote". In Conte, Giacalone Ramat & Ramat (eds., 1990), 169–199.

Carnap, R.
1932(1959) "Überwindung der Metaphysik durch logische Analyse der Sprache". *Erkenntnis* II, 219–241. Engl. transl.: "The elimination of metaphysics through logical analysis of language". In Ayer, A. J. (ed.), *Logical Positivism*. New York: Macmillan, 60–81.

Casati, R.
1990 "Dizionari e termini di colore". *Lingua e stile* XXV, 103–118.

Cassirer, E.
1923(1953) *Philosophie der symbolischen Formen*. Oxford: Bruno Cassirer. Engl. transl.: *The Philosophy of Symbolic Forms*. New Haven: Yale University Press.
1944 *An Essay on Man. An Introduction to a Philosophy of Human Culture*. New Haven: Yale University Press.
1946 "Structuralism in modern linguistics". *Word* 1, 99–120.

Cellier, L.
1965 "D'une rhétorique profonde: Baudelaire et l'oxymoron". *Cahiers internationaux de symbolisme* 8, 3–14.

Chafe, W.
1984 "How people use adverbial clauses". In Brugman, C., M. Macaulay, A. Dahlstrom, M. Emanatian, B. Moonwoman & C. O'Connor (eds.), *Proceedings of the Tenth Annual Meeting of the Berkeley Linguistic Sociey*. Berkeley: Berkeley Linguistic Society, 437–449.

Chierchia, G. & S. McConnel-Ginet
1990 *Meaning and Grammar*. Cambridge/Mass./London: The MIT Press.

Chomsky, N.
1957 *Syntactic Structures*. The Hague/Paris: Mouton.
1964 "Degrees of grammaticalness". In Fodor & Katz (eds., 1964), 384–389.
1965 *Aspects of the Theory of Syntax*. Cambridge/Mass: The MIT Press.
1966 "Topics in the theory of generative grammar". In Sebeok (ed., 1966), 1–60.
1970 "Remarks on Nominalization". In Jakobs & Rosenbaum (eds., 1970). Repr. in Chomsky (1972), 11–61.

1972 *Studies on Semantics in Generative Grammar.* The Hague: Mouton.

Clas, A., & G. Gross

1997 "Synonymie, polysémie et classes d'objets". *Meta* 42: 147–155.

Coates, J.

1994 "The negotiation of coherence in face-to-face interaction: Some examples from the extreme bounds". In Gernsbacher & Givón (eds., 1994), 41–58.

Cohen, J.

1966 *Structure du langage poétique.* Paris: Flammarion.

Cole, P., W. Harbert, G. Hermon & S. N. Sridhar

1980 "The acquisistion of subjecthood". *Language* 56, 719–743.

Cole, P. & J. L. Morgan (eds.)

1975 *Sintax and Semantics. 3: Speech Acts.* New York/San Francisco/London: Academic Press.

Cole, P. & J. M. Sadock (eds.)

1977 *Syntax and Semantics. 8: Grammatical Relations.* New York/San Francisco/London: Academic Press.

Comrie, B.

1982 "Grammatical relations in Huichol". In Hopper & Thompson (eds., 1982), 95–115.

1989 *Language Universals and Linguistic Typology.* Oxford: Blackwell.

Conte, M.-E.

1977 "Introduzione". In Conte, M.-E. (ed.), *La linguistica testuale.* Milan: Feltrinelli, 11–50.

1988 *Condizioni di coerenza.* Firenze: La Nuova Italia.

1990 "Pronomi anaforici non-coreferenziali". In Conte, Giacalone Ramat & Ramat (eds., 1990), 201–215.

1996 "Anaphoric encapsulation". In De Mulder, W. & L. Tasmowski (eds.), *Coherence and Anaphora. Belgian Journal of Linguistics* 10, 1–10. Repr. in Conte (1999), 107–114.

1999 *Condizioni di coerenza.* New edition by Mortara Garavelli, B. Alessandria: Edizioni dell'Orso.

Conte, M.-E., A. Giacalone Ramat & P. Ramat (eds.)

1990 *Dimensioni della linguistica.* Milan: Franco Angeli.

Cornish, F.

1990 "Anaphore pragmatique, référence et modèles de discours". In Kleiber, G. & E. Tyvaert (eds.), *L'anaphore et ses domaines.* Metz: Centre d'Analyse Syntaxique, Université de Metz.

Coseriu, E.

1952 "Sistema, norma y habla". *Revista de la Facultad de Humanidades y Ciencias*, Montevideo, IX, 113–177. Repr. in Coseriu (1962), 11–113.

1962 *Teoría del lenguaje y lingüística general.* Madrid: Gredos.

1967 "Lexikalische Solidaritäten". *Poetica* I, 293–303.

1968 "Les structures lexématiques". *Zeitschrift für französische Sprache und Literatur, Beiheft* 1, 3–16.

1970 "Bedeutung und Bezeichnung im Lichte der strukturellen Semantik". In Hartmann, P. & H. Vernay (eds.), *Sprachwissenschaft und Übersetzung*. München, 104–121.

1982 "Les procédés sémantiques dans la formation des mots". *Cahiers Ferdinand de Saussure* 35, 3–16.

Cristofaro, S.

2003 *Subordination. A Typological Study*. Oxford: Oxford University Press.

Croft, W.

1990 *Typology and Universals*. Cambridge: Cambridge University Press.

1995 "Autonomy and functionalist linguistics". *Language* 71, 490–532.

1999 "Some contributions of typology to cognitive linguistics, and vice versa". In Janssen & Redeker (eds., 1999), 61–93.

2001 *Radical Construction Grammar*. Oxford: Oxford University Press.

Cruse, D. A.

1986 *Lexical Semantics*. Cambridge: Cambridge University Press.

1992 "Cognitive linguistics and word meaning: Taylor on linguistic categorization". *Journal of Linguistics* 28, 165–183.

2000 *Meaning in Language. An Introduction to Semantics and Pragmatics*. Oxford: Oxford University Press.

Cuzzolin, P.

1996 "I costrutti consecutivi". In Prandi (ed., 1996), 103–151.

D'Addio Colosimo, W.

1998 "Nominali anaforici incapsulatori: un aspetto della coesione lessicale". In De Mauro, T., S. Gensini & M. E. Piemontese (eds.), *Dalla parte del ricevente: percezione, comprensione, interpretazione*. Rome: Bulzoni, 143–151.

Daladier, A.

1978 *Problèmes d'analyse d'un type de nominalisation en français et de certains groupes nominaux complexes*. Thèse de 3e cycle. Paris: Université Paris VII, LADL.

D'Andrade, R.

1987 "A folk model of the mind". In Holland & Quinn (1987), 112–148.

Daneš, F.

1964 "A three-level approach to syntax". *Travaux Linguistiques de Prague* 1, 225–240.

1968 "Some thoughts on the semantic structure of the sentence". *Lingua* 21, 55–67.

1974 "Functional sentence perspective and the organization of the text". In Daneš (ed., 1974), 106–128.

1985 "Some remarks on causal relationships in language and text". *Recueil Linguistique de Bratislava*, 151–157.

Daneš, F. (ed.)

1974 *Papers in Functional Sentence Perspective*. Prague: Academia.

Danto, A. C.
1965(1968) "Basic Actions". *American Philosophical Quarterly* 2, 141–148. Repr. in White (ed., 1968), 43–58.
Dardano, M.
1991 *Manualetto di linguistica italiana*. Bologna: Zanichelli.
Darnell, M., E. Moravcsik, F. J. Newmeyer, M. Noonan & K. Wheatley (eds.)
1998 *Functionalism and Formalism in Linguistics, Vol. I: General Papers*. Amsterdam/Philadelphia: John Benjamins.
Dascal, M.
1987 "Defending literal meaning". *Cognitive Science* 11, 259–281.
Davidson, D.
1967 "Truth and meaning". *Synthèse* 17, 304–323.
1963(1968) "Actions, reasons and causes". *Journal of Philosophy* LX, 685–700. Repr. in White (ed., 1968): 79–94.
1970 "Semantics for natural languages". In Visentini, B. (ed.), *Linguaggi nella società e nella tecnica*. Milan: Edizioni di Comunità, 177–188.
1978(1984) "What metaphors mean". *Critical Inquiry* 5. Repr. in Davidson, D., *Inquiries into Truth and Interpretation*. Oxford: Clarendon Press, 245–263.
Davison, A.
1980 "Peculiar passives". *Language* 56, 42–66.
Dennett, D.
1969 *Content and Consciousness*. London/New York: Routledge & Kegan Paul.
1995 *Darwin's Dangerous Idea*. New York: Simon & Schuster.
Derrida, J.
1967 *De la grammatologie*. Paris: Les Editions de Minuit.
Dijk, T. A. van & W. Kintsch
1983 *Strategies of Discourse Comprehension*. New York/San Francisco/London: Academic Press.
Dik, S. C.
1968 *Co-ordination*. Amsterdam: North Holland.
1978 *Functional Grammar*. Amsterdam: North Holland.
1989(1997) *The Theory of Functional Grammar. Part I: The Structure of the Clause*. Dordrecht/Providence: Foris. 2nd revised edition Berlin/New York: Mouton de Gruyter.
1989(1997a) *The Theory of Functional Grammar. Part II: Complex and Derived Constructions*. Dordrecht/Providence: Foris. 2nd revised edition. Berlin/New York: Mouton de Gruyter.
Dik, S. C., K. Hengeveld, E. Vester & C. Vet
1990 "The hierarchical structure of the clause and the typology of adverbial satellites". In Nuyts, Bolkenstein & Vet (eds., 1990), 25–70.
Dirven, R.
1997 "Emotions as causes and the cause of emotions". In Niemeier, S. & R. Dirven (eds.), *The Language of Emotions*. Amsterdam/Philadelphia: John Benjamins, 55–83.

Dirven, R., & R. Pörings (eds.)
2002 *Metaphor and Metonymy in Comparison and Contrast.* Berlin/New York: Mouton De Gruyter.

Dixon, R. M. W.
1977 "Where have all adjectives gone?". *Studies in Language* I, 19–80.
1994 "Adjectives". In Asher (ed., 1994), 29–35.

Donnellan, K. S.
1966 "Reference and definite descriptions". *The Philosophical Review* 75, 281–304.

Duchacek, O.
1965 "Sur quelques problèmes de l'antonymie". *Cahiers de lexicologie* VI, 1, 55–66.

Ducrot, O.
1972(1980) *Dire et ne pas dire.* 2nd edition. Paris: Hermann.
1980 *Les mots du discours.* Paris: Les Editions de Minuit.

Dummett, M.
1988 "The Origins of Analytical Philosophy". *Lingua e stile* 23, 3–49; 171–210.

Durie, M.
1995 "Towards an understanding of linguistic evolution and the notion 'X has a function Y'". In Abraham, Givón & Thompson (eds., 1995), 275–308.

Eco, U.
1975 *A Theory of Semiotics.* Bloomington: Indiana University Press.
1990 *I limiti dell'interpretazione.* Milan: Bompiani.

Ehrliholzer, H. P.
1965 *Der sprachliche Ausdruck der Kausalität im Altitalienischen.* Winterthur.

Empson, W.
1930(1953) *Seven Types of Ambiguity.* 3th ed. London: Chatto and Windus.

Faarland, J. T.
1998 "L'actance dans les langues germaniques". In Feuillet (ed., 1998), 789–809.

Faral, E.
1924 *Les arts poétiques du XIIe et du XIIIe siècles.* Paris: Champion.

Feinberg, J.
1968 "Action and responsibility". In Black, M. (ed.), *Philosophy in America.* London: George Allen & Unwin Ltd, 134–60. Repr. in White (ed., 1968): 95–119.

Ferrari, A.
1995 *Connessioni. Uno studio integrato della subordinazione avverbiale.* Genève: Editions Slatkine.

Feuillet, J. (ed.)
1998 *Actance et Valence dans les Langues de l'Europe.* Berlin/New York: Mouton de Gruyter.

Fillmore, Ch. J.
1968 "The case for case". In Bach, E. & R. Harms (eds.). *Universals in Linguistic Theory.* New York: Holt, Rinehart & Winston, 1–88.

1975 "An alternative to checklist theories of meaning". In Cogen, C. et alii (eds.). *Proceedings of the First Annual Meeting of the Berkeley Linguistic Society.* Berkeley: Berkeley Linguistic Society, 123–131.

1977 "Topics in lexical semantics". In Cole, R. W. (ed.), *Current issues in Linguistic Theory.* Bloomington: Indiana University Press, 76–138.

1977a "The case for case reopened". In Cole & Sadock (eds., 1977), 59–81.

1985 "Syntactic intrusion and the notion of grammatical construction". In *Proceedings of the Eleventh Annual Meeting of the Berkeley Linguistic Society.* Berkeley: Berkeley Linguistic Society, 73–87.

1988 "The mechanism of 'construction grammar'". In *Proceedings of the Fourteenth Annual Meeting of the Berkeley Linguistic Society.* Berkeley: Berkeley Linguistic Society, 35–55.

Firbas, J.

1964 "On defining the theme in functional sentence analysis". *Travaux Linguistiques de Prague* I, 267–280.

1970 "On the interplay of means of FSP". In *Actes du Xe congrès international des linguistes.* Bucarest. Vol. II, 741–745.

1974 "Some aspects of the Czechoslovak approach to problems of FSP". In Daneš (ed., 1974).

1992 *Functional Sentence Perspective in Written and Spoken Discourse.* Cambridge: Cambridge University Press.

Firth, J. R.

1950(1957) "Personality and Language in Society". *The Sociological Review* XLII, 3. Repr. in Firth, J. R., *Papers in Linguistics.* London: Oxford University Press, 177–189.

Fish, S.

1980 "Interpretive Autority in the Classroom and in Literary Criticism". In Fish, S., *Is there a Text in this Class? The autority of Interpretive Communities.* Cambridge / Mass: Harvard College.

Fodor, J. A. & J. J. Katz (eds.)

1964 *The Structure of Language: Readings in the Philosophy of Language.* Englewood Cliffs: Prentice-Hall.

Foley, W. A. & R. D. Van Valin

1984 *Functional Syntax and Universal Grammar.* Cambridge: Cambridge University Press.

Fónagy, I.

1975 "La structure sémantique des constructions possessives". In Kristeva, J., J.-C. Milner & N. Ruwet (eds.), *Langue, discours, société.* Paris: Editions du Seuil, 44–84.

Fontanier, P.

1968 *Les figures du discours.* Paris: Flammarion. Contains: *Manuel classique pour l'étude des tropes* (1821. 4th edition, 1830) and *Traité général des figures de discours autres que les tropes* (1827).

Fourquet, J.
1959 "Strukturelle Syntax und inhaltbezogene Grammatik". In *Sprache: Schlüssel zur Welt. Festschrift für Leo Weisgerber*. Düsseldorf: Schwann, 134–145.

Fraser, B.
1988 "Motor oil is motor oil". *Journal of Pragmatics* 12, 215–220.

Frege, G.
1891 *Funktion und Begriff*. Jena. Engl. transl.: "Function and Concept", in Geach, P. & M. Black (eds. 1960), *Translations from the Philosophical Writings of Gottlob Frege*. Oxford: Blackwell.

Freud, S.
1920 *Jenseits des Lustprinzips*. Leipzig/Wien/Zürich: Internationaler Psychoanalitischer Verlag.

Fuchs, C.
1982 *La paraphrase*. Paris: Presses Universitaires de France.

Garcia-Murga, F.
1999 "A conceptual analysis of linguistic presuppositions". *Quaderni di semantica* XX, 107–130.

Geeraerts, D.
1988 "On necessary and sufficient conditions". *Journal of Semantics* 5, 275–291.
1991 "La grammaire cognitive et l'histoire de la sémantique lexicale". *Communications* 53, 17–50.

Geis, M. L., & A. M. Zwicky
1971 "On invited inferences". *Linguistic Inquiry* 2, 561–566.

Genette, G.
1966 *Figures*. Paris: Editions du Seuil.
1968 "Introduction". In Fontanier, P., *Les figures du discours*. Paris: Flammarion, 5–17.

Gernsbacher, M. A. & T. Givón (eds.)
1994 *Coherence in Spontaneous Text*. Amsterdam/Philadelphia: John Benjamins.

Gibbs, R. W.
1994 *The Poetics of Mind*. Cambridge: Cambridge University Press.

Gile, D.
1995 *Basic concepts and models for interpreter and translator training*. Amsterdam/Philadelphia: John Benjamins.

Giorgi, A. & F. Pianesi
1997 *Tense and Aspect. From Semantics to Morphosyntax*. New York-Oxford: Oxford University Press.

Giry-Schneider, J.
1987 *Les prédicats nominaux en français. Les phrases simples à verbe support*. Geneva: Droz.

Givón, T.
1983 *Topic Continuity in Discourse. A Quantitative Cross-Linguistic Study*. Amsterdam/Philadelphia: John Benjamins.
1984 *Syntax. A Functional-Typological Introduction*, Amsterdam/Philadelphia: John Benjamins.

1984a "Direct object and dative shifting: Semantic and pragmatic case". In Plank (ed., 1984), 151–182.
1995 *Functionalism and Grammar.* Amsterdam/Philadelphia: John Benjamins.
1997 "Grammatical relations: an introduction". In T. Givón (ed.), *Grammatical Relations. A functionalist perspective.* Amsterdam/Philadelphia: John Benjamins, 1–84.

Gleason, H. A.
1961 *An Introduction to Descriptive Linguistics.* New York: Holt, Rinehart & Winston.

Goddard, C.
1991 "Testing the Translatability of Semantic Primitives into an Australian Aboriginal Language". *Anthropological Linguistics* 33/1, 31–56.

Goldberg, A. E.
1995 *Constructions. A Construction Grammar Approach to Argument Structure.* Chicago/London: The University of Chicago Press.

Goodenough, W. H.
1951 *Property, Kin, and Community on Truck.* Yale: Yale University Publications in Anthropology.
1956 "Componential analysis and the study of meaning". *Language* 32, 195–216.

Goodman, N.
1968 *The Languages of Art.* Indianapolis/New York: Bobbs-Merril.

Goodwin, Ch.
1981 *Conversational Organization Interaction between Speakers and Hearers.* New York/San Francisco/London: Academic Press.

Goossens, L.
1990 "Metaphtonymy: the interaction of metaphor and metonymy in expressions for linguistic actions". *Cognitive Linguistics* 1, 323–340.

Graffi, G.
1975 "Equivalenti o inconciliabili? Su alcuni sviluppi recenti della linguistica trasformazionale". In Vignuzzi, U., G. Ruggiero & R. Simone (eds.), *Teoria e storia degli studi linguistici.* Rome: Bulzoni, 281–338.

Grandi, N.
2002 *Morfologie in contatto.* Milan: Franco Angeli.

Greenberg, J. H.
1966 "Some universals of grammar with particular reference to the order of meaningful elements". In Greenberg, J. H. (ed), *Universals of Grammar.* Cambridge/Mass.: MIT Press, 73–113.

Grice, H. P.
1957 (1967) "Meaning". *Philosophical Review* 66, 377–88. Repr. in Strawson (ed., 1967), 39–48.
1975 "Logic and conversation". In Cole & Morgan (eds. 1975), 41–58.

Gross, G.
1987 *Les constructions converses du français.* Geneva/Paris: Droz.
1992 "Syntaxe du complément de nom". *Linguisticae Investigationes* XV, 2, 255–284.

1992a "Forme d'un dictionnaire électronique". In Clas, A. & H. Safar (eds), *L'environnement traductionnel.* Sillery (Canada): Presses de l'Université du Québec, 255–271.
1993 "Trois applications de la notion de verbe support". *L'information grammaticale* 59, 16–23.
1994 "Classes d'objets et description des verbes". *Langages* 115, 15–30.
1996 *Les expressions figées en français.* Gap, Paris: Ophrys.
1998 "Pour une typologie des prédicats nominaux". In Kronning, H., C. Norén, B. Novén, G. Ransbo, L.-G. Sundell & B. Svane (eds.), *Langage et référence. Mélanges offerts à Kerstin Jonasson à l'occasion de ses soixante ans.* Uppsala: Acta Universitatis Uppsaliensis, 221–230.
Forthcom. "De quelques perspectives dans l'étude du sens". In Bersani Berselli, G. & F. Frasnedi (eds.), *Le Semantiche. Approcci interdisciplinari al problema del significato.* Bologna: CLUEB.

Gross, G. & M. Prandi
2004 *La finalité: Fondements conceptuels et genèse linguistique.* Louvain-La-Neuve: De Boek Université.

Groupe λ-l
1975 "Car, parce que, puisque". *Revue Romane* 10, 248–280.

Groupe μ
1970 *Rhétorique générale.* Larousse: Paris.

Habermas, J.
1986 "Moralität und Sittlichkeit. Treffen Hegel's Einwände gegen Kant auch auf die Diskursethik zu?". In *Moralität und Sittlichkeit.* Frankfurt am Main: Suhrkamp, 16–37.

Haiman, J.
1980 "Dictionaries and encyclopaedias". *Lingua* 50, 329–357.

Haiman, J. & S. A. Thompson (eds)
1988 *Clause Combining in Grammar and Discourse.* Amsterdam/Philadelphia: John Benjamins.

Haiman, L. M. & A. Duranti
1982 "On the object relation in Bantu". In Hopper & Thompson (eds., 1982), 217–239.

Halliday, M. A. K.
1967 "Notes on transitivity and theme in English". Part I. *Journal of Linguistics* 3, 37–81.
1967a "Notes on transitivity and theme in English". Part II. *Journal of Linguistics* 3, 199–244.
1968 "Notes on transitivity and theme in English". Part III. *Journal of Linguistics* 4, 179–215.
1970 "Language structure and language function". In Lyons (ed., 1970), 140–165.
1976 "A brief sketch of systemic grammar". In Kress, G. (ed.), *Halliday: System and Function in Language.* Oxford: Oxford University Press, 3–6.
1978 *Language as Social Semiotic.* London: Arnold.

Halliday, M. A. K. & R. Hasan
1976 *Cohesion in English.* London/New York: Longman.
Harder, P.
1999 "Partial autonomy. Ontology and methodology in cognitive linguistics". In Janssen & Redeker (eds., 1999), 195–222.
Harris, Z.
1946 "From morpheme to utterance". *Language* 22, 161–183.
1970 *Papers in Structural and Transformational Linguistics.* Dordrecht: Reidel.
1976 *Notes du cours de syntaxe.* Paris: Editions du Seuil.
Hanks, W.
1992 "The indexical ground of deictic reference". In Duranti, A. & Ch. Goodwin (eds.), *Rethinking Context.* Cambridge: Cambridge University Press, 43–76.
Hartman, J.
1970 *Beyond Formalism.* New Haven/London: Yale University Press.
Haspelmath, M.
1995 "The converb as a cross-linguistic valid category", in Haspelmath, M. & E. König (eds.), *Converbs in Cross-Linguistic Perspective.* Berlin/New York: Mouton de Gruyter, 1–56.
Hawkins, J. A.
1986 *A Comparative Typology of English and German. Unifying the contrasts.* London/Sydney: Croom Helm.
Hegel, G. W. F.
1812–1813(1969) *Wissenschaft der Logik. Erster Band: Die Objective Logik.* Nürnberg, 1812–1813. Repr. in Hegel, G. W. F., *Gesammelte Werke,* Band XI. Hamburg: Felix Meiner Verlag, 1978. Engl. transl.: *Hegel's Science of Logic.* London: George Allen & Unwin Ltd./New York: Humanities Press, 1969.
Helbig, G.
1971 "Theoretische und praktische Aspekte eines Valenzmodelles". In Helbig, G. (ed.), *Beiträge zur Valenztheorie.* The Hague: Mouton, 31–49.
1982 *Valenz, Satzglieder, semantische Kasus,* Satzmodelle. Leipzig: Verlag Enzyclopädie.
Hengeveld, K.
1990 "The hierarchical structure of utterances". In Nuyts, Bolkenstein & Vet (eds., 1990), 1–23.
Herman, J.
1963 *La formation du système roman des conjonctions de subordination.* Berlin: Akademie Verlag.
Hesse, M.
1965 *Models and Analogies in Science.* Notre Dame: Notre Dame University Press.
Hjelmslev, L.
1943(1961) *Omkring sprogteoriens grundlaeggelse.* Copenhagen. Engl. transl.: *Prolegomena to a Theory of Language.* Madison: The University of Wisconsin Press.

Hockett, Ch. F.
1958 *A Course in Modern Linguistics.* New York: McMillan.
Holland, D. & N. Quinn (eds.)
1987 *Cultural Models in Language and Thought.* Cambridge: Cambridge University Press.
Hopper, P. J.
1979 "Aspect and foregrounding in discourse". In Givón, T. (ed.), *Discourse and Syntax. Syntax and Semantics* 12. New York/San Francisco/London: Academic Press, 213–241.
1987 "Emergent grammar". In *Proceedings of the Thirteenth Annual Meeting of the Berkeley Linguistic Society.* Berkeley: Berkeley Linguistic Society, 213–241.
Hopper, P. J. & S. A. Thompson
1980 "Transitivity in grammar and discourse". *Language* 56, 251–299.
1982 "Introduction". In Hopper & Thompson (eds., 1982), xiii-xiv.
Hopper, P. J. & S. A. Thompson (eds.)
1982 *Sudies in Transitivity. Syntax and Semantics* 15. New York/San Francisco/London: Academic Press.
Hopper, P. J. & E. C. Traugott
1993 *Grammaticalization.* Cambridge: Cambridge University Press.
Hudson, R.
1992 "So-called 'double objects' and grammatical relations". *Language* 68, 251–276.
Humboldt, W. von
1836(1963) *Über die Verschiedenheit des menschlichen Sprachbaues und ihren Einfluss über die Geistliche Entwicklung des Menschengeschlechts*, Berlin. Repr. in Humboldt, W. von, *Werke in fünf Bänden*, Band III. Darmstadt: Cotta.
Hundius, H. & U. Kölver
1983 "Syntax and semantics of numeral classifiers in Thai". *Studies in Language* 7, 2, 164–214.
Husserl, E.
1901(1970) *Logische Untersuchungen.* Band 1: Halle 1900; Band II: Halle 1901. Rev. edition: Band 1 (*Prolegomena*); Band II, Part I (Res. I-V), Halle 1913; Band II, Part II (Res. VI), Halle 1921. Critical edition: *Husserliana* XVIII (1975) & XIX (1984). The Hague: Nijoff. Engl. transl.: *Logical Investigations.* London: Routledge & Kegan Paul.
1913(1931) *Ideen zu einer reinen Phänomenologie und phänomenologische Philosophie*, Buch I, *Allgemeine Einführung in die reine Phänomenologie*, Halle. Critical edition: *Husserliana*, vol. III. The Hague: Nijoff 1950. Engl. transl.: *Ideas: General Introduction to Pure Phenomenology.* London: G. Allen & Unwin Ltd./New York: The Macmillan Company, 1931.
Inwagen, P. van
1993 *Metaphysics.* Oxford: Oxford University Press.
Jakobs, R. & P. S. Rosenbaum (eds.)
1970 *Readings in English Transformational Grammar.* Waltham / Mass.: Blaisdell.

Jakobson, R.
1949 "The phonemic and grammatical aspects of language in their interrelations". In *Proceedings of the Sixth International Congress of Linguists.* Paris: Klincksieck, 5–18.
1960 "Closing statements: linguistics and poetics". In Sebeok, Th. A. (ed.), *Style in Language.* Cambridge / Mass.: The MIT Press, 350–377.
1953(1971) "Results of the conference of anthropologists and linguists". *International Journal of American Linguistics* 19. Repr. in Jakobson (1971), 554–567.
1959(1971) "Boas' view of grammatical meaning". In *The Anthropology of Franz Boas: Essays on the Centennial of his Birth, Memoir LXXX.* Stanford: American Anthropological Association. Repr. in Jakobson (1971), 489–496.
1966 "A la recherche de l'essence du langage". *Diogène* 51, 22–38.
1976(1988) *Six leçons sur le son et sur le sens.* Paris: Les Editions de Minuit. Repr. in Jakobson (1988): 319–390.
1971 *Selected Writings. Vol. II: Word and Language.* The Hague/Paris: Mouton.
1988 *Selected Writings. Vol. VIII: Major Works,* 1976–1980. The Hague/Paris: Mouton.

Jakobson, R. & L. R. Waugh
1979(1988) *The Sound Shape of Language.* Bloomington/London: Indiana University Press. Repr. in Jakobson (1988): 1–315.

Janssen, T. & G. Redeker (eds.)
1999 *Cognitive Linguistics: Foundations, Scope, and Methodology.* Berlin/New York: Mouton de Gruyter.

Jespersen, O.
1909(1954) *A Modern English Grammar on Historical Principles.* Copenhagen: Munksgaard. Repr.: London: George Allen & Unwin.
1924 *The Philosophy of Grammar.* London: George Allen & Unwin.
1933 *Essentials of English Grammar.* London: George Allen & Unwin.

Johnson, D. E.
1977 "On relationl constraints in grammar". In Cole & Sadock (eds., 1977), 151–178.

Kant, I.
1763(1992) *Versuch den Begriff der negativen Größen in die Weltweisheit zu führen,* Königsberg. Repr. in *Immanuel Kants Werke, Band II,* Berlin 1912. Engl. transl.: "Attempt to introduce the concept of negative magnitudes into philosophy". In *The Cambridge Edition of the Works of Immauel Kant, Theoretical Philosophy, 1755–1770.* Cambridge: Cambridge University Press, 1992.
1781(1963) *Kritik der reinen Vernunft,* I. Riga, 1781. II. Riga, 1787. Repr. in: *Immanuel Kants Werke, Band III,* Berlin, 1913. Engl. transl.: *Critique of Pure Reason.* London: Macmillan.

Karttunen, L.
1969 "Discourse Referents". *International Conference of Computational Linguistics.* Stockholm.

Katz, J. J.
1964 "Semi-sentences". In Fodor & Katz (eds. 1964), 400–416.
Katz, J. J., & J. A. Fodor
1963 "The structure of a semantic theory". *Language* 39, 170–210. Repr. in Fodor & Katz (eds., 1964), 479–518.
Keenan, E. L.
1976 "Towards a universal definition of 'subject'". In Li, Ch. N. (ed.), *Subject and Topic.* New York/San Francisco/London: Academic Press, 303–333.
Keenan, E. L. & B. Comrie
1977 "Noun phrase accessibility and universal grammar". *Linguistic Inquiry* 8, 63–99.
Kempson, R.
1977 *Semantic Theory.* Cambridge: Cambridge University Press.
Kirkwood, H. W.
1969 "Aspects of word order and its communicative function in English and German". *Journal of Linguistics* 5, 85–107.
Kittay, E. F.
1987 *Metaphor.* Oxford: Oxford University Press.
Kleiber, G.
1978 "Phrases et valeurs de vérité". In Martin (ed., 1978), 21–66.
1990 *La sémantique du prototype.* Paris: Presses Universitaires de France.
Kleiber, G. & M. Riegel
1978 "Les 'grammaires floues'". In Martin (ed., 1978), 67–123.
König, E.
1985 "On the history of concessive connectives in English. Diachronic and synchronic evidence". *Lingua* 66, 1–19.
König, E. & E. C. Traugott
1988 "Pragmatic strengthening and semantic change: the conventionalizing of conversational implicature". In Hüllen, W. & R. Schulze (eds.), *Understanding the Lexicon. Meaning, Sense and World Knowledge in Lexical Semantics.* Tübingen: Niemeyer, 110–124.
Kortmann, B.
1991 *Adverbial Subordinators in the Languages of Europe.* Eurotyp Working Paper V, 3. Strasbourg: European Science Foundation.
1997 *Adverbial Subordination.* Berlin/New York: Mouton de Gruyter.
Krier, F.
1986 "Die localdeiktischen Ausdrücke im Alemannischen des Kanton Wallis (Schweiz)". *Zeitschrift für Dialektologie und Linguistik* 53, 33–44.
Kuhn, T. S.
1962 *The Structure of Scientific Revolutions.* Chicago/London: The University of Chicago Press.
1979 "Metaphor in Science". In Ortony (ed. 1979).
Kuryłowicz, J.
1964 *The Inflectional Categories of Indo-European.* Heidelberg: Winter.

Labov, W.

1973 "The boundaries of words and their meaning". In Bailey, C. J. & R. Shuy (eds.), *New Ways of Analyzing Variation in English*. Washington: Georgetown University Press.

Lakoff, G.

1968 "Instrumental adverbs and the concept of deep structure". *Foundations of Language* 4, 4–29.

1971 "Presuppositions and relative well formedness". In Steinberg & Jakobovits (eds., 1971), 329–340.

1987 *Women, Fire and Dangerous Things*. Chicago/London: The University of Chicago Press.

Lakoff, G. & M. Johnson

1981 *Metaphors we Live by*. Chicago/London: The University of Chicago Press.

2003 "Afterword, 2003". In *Metaphors we Live by*. New edition. Chicago/London: The University of Chicago Press.

Lakoff, G. & M. Turner

1989 *More than Cool Reason*. Chicago/London: The University of Chicago Press.

Landheer, R.

1996 "Le paradoxe: un mécanisme de bascule". In Landheer, R. & P. J. Smith (eds.), *Le paradoxe en linguistique et en littérature*. Geneva: Droz, 91–116.

2002 "La métaphore, une question de vie ou de mort?". *Semen* 15, 25–40.

Langacker, R. W.

1987 *Foundations of Cognitive Grammar*, I. Stanford: Stanford University Press.

1991 *Foundations of Cognitive Grammar*, II. Stanford: Stanford University Press.

1993 "Clause structure in cognitive grammar". *Studi italiani di linguistica teorica e applicata* XXII, 465–508.

1999 "Assessing the cognitive linguistic enterprise". In Janssen & Redeker (eds., 1999), 13–59.

Lazard, G.

1998 "Définition des actants dans les langues européennes". In Feuillet (ed., 1998), 11–146.

Leech, J.

1974 *Semantics*. Harmondsworth: Penguin Books.

Lees, R. B.

1963 *The Grammar of English Nominalisation*. Bloomington: Indiana University Press/The Hague: Mouton.

Le Goff, J.

1978 "Documento/Monumento". In *Enciclopedia Einaudi*, Vol. V. Turin: Einaudi.

Lehmann, Ch.

1988 "Towards a typology of clause linkage". In Haiman & Thompson (eds., 1988), 181–225.

Le Guern, M.

1973 *Sémantique de la métaphore et de la métonymie*. Paris: Larousse.

Lehrer, A.
1974 *Semantic Fields and Lexical Structure.* Amsterdam: North Holland.

Leisi, E.
1953(1975) *Der Wortinhalt.* 2nd ed. Heidelberg: Winter.

Le Pesant, D.
1994 "Les compléments nominaux du verbe *lire*: une illustration de la notion de 'classe d'objets'". *Langages* 115, 31–46.

Le Pesant, D. & M. Mathieu-Colas (eds.)
1998 *Les classes d'objets. Langages* 131.

Lepschy, G. C.
1978 *Saggi di linguistica italiana.* Bologna: Il Mulino.

Lepschy, A. L. & G. C. Lepschy
1977 *The Italian Language Today.* London: Hutchinson.

Levin, S. R.
1977 *The Semantics of Metaphor.* Baltimora/London: John Hopkins Press.

Levinson, S. C.
1983 *Pragmatics.* Cambridge: Cambridge University Press.
1997 "From outer to inner space: linguistic categories and non-linguistic thinking". In Nuyts & Pederson (eds., 1997), 13–45.

Lévi-Strauss, C.
1962 *La pensée sauvage.* Paris: Librairie Plon.

Lichtenberk, F.
1982 "Individuation hierarchies in Manam". In Hopper & Thompson (eds., 1982), 261–276.

Longacre, R. E.
1985 "Sentences as combinations of clauses". In Shopen (ed., 1985), 235–286.

Lounsbury, F. L.
1956 "A semantic analysis of the Pawnee kinship usage". *Language* 32, 158–194.
1964 "The structural analysis of kinship semantics". In Lunt, H. G. (ed.), *Proceedings of the Ninth International Congress of Linguists.* The Hague: Mouton, 1073–1093.

Lucy, J.
1992 *Grammatical Categories and Cognition: A Case Study of the Linguistic Relativity Hypothesis.* Cambridge: Cambridge University Press.

Lyons, J.
1963 *Structural Semantics.* Oxford: Blackwell.
1966 "Towards a 'notional' theory of the 'parts of speech'". *Journal of Linguistics* 2, 209–236.
1968 *Introduction to Theoretical Linguistics.* Cambridge: Cambridge University Press.
1977 *Semantics.* Cambridge: Cambridge University Press.

Lyons, J. (ed.)
1970 *New Horizons in Linguistics.* Harmondsworth: Penguin Books.

Malinowski, B.
1923(1952) "The problem of meaning in primitive languages". In Ogden, C. K. & I. A. Richards, *The Meaning of Meaning*, 10th ed., London: Routledge & Kegan Paul, 296–336.

Manetti, G.
1987 *Le teorie del segno nell'antichità classica.* Milan: Bompiani.

Martin, R.
1976 *Inférence, antonymie et paraphrase.* Paris: Klincksieck.

Martin, R. (ed.)
1978 *La recevabilité en linguistique.* Paris: Klincksieck.

Martinet, A. (ed.)
1979 *Grammaire fonctionnelle du français.* Paris: Crédif.

Mathesius, V.
1928 "On linguistic characterology with illustration from modern English". In *Actes du Premier Congrès International des Linguistes.* The Hague: Mouton, 56–63. Repr. in Vachek, J. (ed.), *A Prague School Reader in Linguistics.* Bloomington: Indiana University Press, 1964, 59–67.
1975 *A functional Analysis of Present-day English on a General Linguistic Basis.* Prague: Academia.

Matoré, G.
1953 *La méthode en lexicologie.* Paris: Marcel Didier.

Matthews, P. H.
1981 *Syntax.* Cambridge: Cambridge University Press.

Matthiessen, Ch. & S. A. Thompson
1988 "The structure of discourse and 'subordination'". In Haiman & Thompson (eds., 1988), 275–317.

McCawley, J. D.
1970(1971) "Where do noun phrases come from?". In Jakobs & Rosenbaum (eds., 1970). Rev. version in Steinberg & Jakobovits (eds., 1971), 217–231.

Meisel, J.
1987 "Reference to past events and actions in the development of natural second language acquisition". In Pfaff, C. W. (ed.), *First and Second Language Acquisition Processes.* New York: Newbery House, 206–224.

Mellema, P.
1974 "A brief against Case Grammar". *Foundations of Language* 11, 39–76.

Merleau-Ponty, M.
1945 *Phénoménologie de la perception.* Paris: Gallimard.

Mithun, M.
1984 "The evolution of noun incorporation". *Language* 60, 846–894.

Molinié, G.
1992 *Dictionnaire de rhétorique.* Paris: Livres de Poche.

Moore, G. E.
1925(1959) "A defence of common sense". In Muirhead, J. H. (ed.), *Contemporary British Philosophy*. Repr. in Moore (1959), 32–59.

1939(1959) "Proof of an external world". *Proceedings of the British Academy* XXV. Repr. in Moore (1959), 127–150.

1959 *Philosophical Papers.* London: George Allen & Unwin LTD/New York: The Macmillan Company.

Morier, H.

1961 *Dictionnaire de poétique et de rhétorique.* Paris: Presses Universitaires de France.

Mortara Garavelli, B.

1985 *La parola d'altri. Prospettive di analisi del discorso riportato.* Palermo: Sellerio.

Mühlhäusler, P.

2001 "Universals and typology of space", in Haspelmath, M., E. König, W. Österreicher & W. Raible (eds.), *Language Typology and Language Universals. An International Handbook.* Berlin/New York: Mouton de Gruyter.

Newman, J.

1996 *Give. A Cognitive Linguistic Study.* Berlin/New York: Mouton de Gruyter.

Newmeyer, F. J.

1998 "Language Form and Language Function". Cambridge/Mass./London: The MIT Press.

Nida, E. A.

1959 "Principles of translation as exemplified by Bible translating". In Brower, R. A. (ed.), *On Translation.* Cambridge/Mass.: Harvard University Press, 11–31.

1975 *Componential Analysis of Meaning.* The Hague/Paris: Mouton.

Nillson-Ehle, H.

1947 *Les propositions complétives juxtaposées en italien moderne.* Lund: Lunds Universitets Årsskrift.

Noonan, M.

1985 "Complementation". In Shopen (ed., 1985), 42–140.

1992 *A Grammar of Lango.* Berlin/New York: Mouton de Gruyter.

Norman, R.

1989 "Respect for persons: autonomy and equality". *Revue Internationale de Philosophie* 170, 323–341.

Nuyts, J.

1990 "Linguistic representation and conceptual knowledge representation". In Nuyts, Bolkenstein & Vet (eds., 1990), 263–293.

Nuyts, J., A. M. Bolkenstein & C. Vet (eds.)

1990 *Layers and Levels of Representation in Language Theory.* Amsterdam/Philadelphia: John Benjamins.

Nuyts, J. & E. Pederson (eds.)

1997 *Language and Conceptualization.* Cambridge: Cambridge University Press.

O'Connor, J. D.

1973 *Phonetics.* Harmondsworth: Penguin Books.

Oreström, B.
1983 *Turn-Taking in English Conversation.* Lund: Liber Förlag.
Ortony, A. (ed.)
1979 *Metaphor and Thought.* Cambridge: Cambridge University Press.
Palmer, F. R.
1976 *Semantics.* Cambridge: Cambridge University Press.
1994 *Grammatical Roles and Relations.* Cambridge: Cambridge University Press.
Panther, K.-U. & G. Radden (eds.)
1999 *Metonymy in Language and Thought.* Amsterdam/Philadelphia: John Benjamins.
Payne, J. R.
1985 "Complex phrases and complex sentences". In Shopen (ed., 1985), 3–41.
Peirce, Ch. S.
1932 *Collected Papers,* Vol. II: *Elements of Logic, Book II: Speculative Grammar.* Cambridge/Mass.: Harvard University Press.
Perissinotto, L.
1992 *Logica e immagini del mondo.* Milan: Guerini e Associati.
Perlmutter, D.
1980 "Relational grammar". In Moravcsik, E. A. & J. Wirth (eds.,), *Current Approaches to Syntax. Sintax and Semantics* 13. New York/San Francisco/London: Academic Press, 195–229.
Perlmutter, D. (ed.)
1983 *Studies in Relational Grammar,* Vol. I. Chicago: The University of Chicago Press.
Perlmutter, D. & C. Rosen (eds.)
1984 *Studies in Relational Grammar,* Vol. II. Chicago: The University of Chicago Press.
Perrin, L.
1996 *L'ironie mise en trope.* Paris: Editions Kimé.
Pinkal, M.
1985 "Kontextabhängigkeit, Vagheit, Mehrdeutigkeit". In Schwarze, Ch. & D. Wunderlich (eds.), *Handbuch der Lexicologie.* Königstein: Athenäum Verlag, 27–63.
Plank, F. (ed.)
1984 *Objects. Towards a Theory of Grammatical Relations.* New York/San Francisco/London: Academic Press.
Porzig, W.
1934 "Wesenhafte Bedeutungsbeziehungen". *Beiträge zur deutschen Sprache und Literatur* 58, 70–97.
Poublanc, F.
1991 "Logique et métaphysique". *Revue de métaphysique et de morale* 2, 147–179.
Prandi, M.
1987 *Sémantique du contresens.* Paris: Les Editions de Minuit.

1988 "Modificazioni oblique nel *Partigiano Johnny*". *Strumenti critici* n.s. III, 1, 111–164.
1991 "Figures textuelles du silence: l'exemple de la réticence". In Parret, H. (ed.), *Le sens et ses hétérogénéités.* Paris: Editions du CNRS, 155–174.
1992 *Grammaire philosophique des tropes.* Paris: Les Editions de Minuit.
1999 "Dall'analogia all'inferenza: la motivazione delle espressioni idiomatiche". *Quaderni di semantica* XX, 1, 131–145.

Prandi, M. (ed.)
1996 *La subordinazione non completiva: un frammento di grammatica filosofica. Studi Italiani di Linguistica Teorica e Applicata* XXV, 1.

Putnam, H.
1973 "Meaning, reference and stereotypes". *The Journal of Philosophy* 70, 699–711.

Quasthoff, U. M.
1994 "Context". In Asher (ed., 1994), 730–737.

Quine, W. V. O.
1953(1961) *From a Logical Point of View*, 2nd edition. Cambridge/Mass.: Harvard University Press.

Quirk, R., S. Greenbaum, G. Leech & J. Svartvik
1984 *A comprehensive Grammar of the English Language.* London/New York: Longman.

Ramat, P.
1984 *Linguistica tipologica.* Bologna: Il Mulino.
1998 Review of Nuyts & Pederson 1997. *Archivio Glottologico Italiano* LXXXIII, 86–90.

Reichling, A.
1961 "Principles and methods of syntax". *Lingua* 10, 1–17.

Reinhart, T.
1984 "Principles of Gestalt perception in the temporal organization of narrative texts". *Linguistics* 22, 779–809.

Reiter, R.
1980 "A logic for default reasoning". *Artificial Intelligence* 13, 81–132.

Richards, I. A.
1936 *The Philosophy of Rhetoric.* Oxford: Oxford University Press.

Ricoeur, P.
1975 *La métaphore vive.* Paris: Editions du Seuil.
1977 "Le discours de l'action". In Tiffeneau, D. (ed.), *La Sémantique de l'action.* Paris: Editions du CNRS, 3–137.

Riemer, N.
2002 "Remetonymizing metaphor: Hypercategories in semantic extension". *Cognitive Linguistics* 12, 379–401.

Rijkhoff, J.
2002 *The Noun Phrase.* Oxford/New York: Oxford University Press.

Rosch, E.

1972 "Universals in Color Naming and Memory". *Journal of Experimental Psychology* 93, 10–20.

1973 "On the internal structure of perceptual and semantic categories". In Moore, T. E. (ed.), *Cognitive development and the Acquisition of Language*. New York/San Francisco/London: Academic Press, 111–144.

1975 "Cognitive reference points". *Cognitive Psychology* 7, 532–547).

1978 "Principles of categorization". In Rosch, E. & B. B. Lloyd (eds.), *Cognition and Categorization*. Hillsdale/N. J.: Lawrence Erlbaum Associates, 27–48.

Ross, J. R.

1970 "On declarative sentences". In Jakobs & Rosenbaum (eds., 1970), 222–272.

Ross, S.

1974 "Caricature". *The Monist*, 285–293.

Rumelhart, D. E.

1980 "Schemata: the building blocks of Cognition". In Spiro, R. J., B. C. Bruce & W. F. Brewer (eds.), *Theoretical Issues on Reading Comprehension*. Hillsdale/N. J.: Lawrence Erlbaum Associates, 35–58.

Russell, B.

1912 *The Problems of Philosophy*. London: William and Norgate. Repr.: Oxford: Oxford University Press, 1967; 1980.

Ruwet, N.

1975 "Synecdoques et métonymies". *Poétique* 23, 371–388.

Samuels, M. L.

1972 *Linguistic Evolution with Special Reference to English*. Cambridge: Cambridge University Press.

Sanford, J. & L. M. Moxey

1994 "Aspects of coherence in written language: a psychological perspective". In Gernsbacher & Givón (eds., 1994), 161–187.

Sapir, E.

1921 *Language. An Introduction to the Study of Speech*. New York: Harcourt, Brace & World, Inc.

1944 "On grading: a study in semantics". *Philosophy of Science* 2, 93–116. Repr. in E. Sapir, *Selected Writings in Language, Culture and Personality*, edited by D. G. Mandelbaum. Berkeley: The University of California Press, 1949, 122–149.

Saussure, F. de

1916 *Cours de linguistique générale*. Paris: Payot. Critical edition by T. de Mauro, Paris: Payot, 1972. Engl. transl.: *Course in General Linguistics*. London: Fontana / Collins, 1974.

Sayers, B. & M. Bain

1989 "A communication dilemma: contrasting orders of abstraction and the Asoiated logic". In *Papers Presented to the Interdisciplinary Research Workshop on Logical Connections*. Dallas: Summer Institute of Linguistics.

Schapira, Ch.
2000 "La phrase tautologique". *Linguisticae Investigationes* 23, 2, 269–286.
Searle, J.
1969 *Speech Acts. An Essay in the Philosophy of Language.* Cambridge: Cambridge University Press.
1975 "A taxinomy of illocutionary acts". In Gunderson, K. (ed.), *Language, Mind and Knowledge.* Minneapolis: Minnesota University Press, 344–369.
1978(1979) "Literal meaning". *Erkenntnis* 13, 1, 207–224. Repr. in Searle (1979a), 117–136.
1979 "Metaphor". In Ortony (ed., 1979). Repr. in Searle (1979a), 76–116.
1979a *Expression and Meaning.* Cambridge: Cambridge University Press.
1983 *Intentionality.* Cambridge: Cambridge University Press.
1995 *The Construction of Social Reality.* Harmondsworth: Penguin Books.
Sebeok, Th. A. (ed.)
1966 *Current Trends in Linguistics.* Vol. III: *Theoretical Foundations.* The Hague/Paris: Mouton.
1986 *Encyclopedic Dictionary of Semiotics.* Berlin/New York/Amsterdam: Mouton de Gruyter.
Segre, C.
1969 "Critica e strutturalismo". In *I segni e la critica.* Turin: Einaudi, 17–28.
1979 "Introduzione". In *I fioretti di S. Francesco.* Milan: Rizzoli, 5–21.
1985 *Avviamento all'analisi del testo letterario.* Turin: Einaudi.
Shank, R. C.
1975 "The structure of episodes in memory". In Bobrow, D. & A. Collins (eds.), *Representation and Understanding. Studies in Cognitive Science.* New York/San Francisco/London: Academic Press.
Shank, R. C. & R. P. Abelson
1977 *Scripts, Plans, Goals and Understanding. An Inquiry into Human Knowledge Structures.* Hillsdale/N. J.: Lawrence Erlbaum Associates
Shibatani, M.
1996 "Applicative and benefactive: a cognitive account". In Shibatani, M. & S. A. Thompson (eds.), *Grammatical Constructions. Their Form and Meaning.* Oxford: Clarendon Press, 157–194.
Schlick, M.
1936 "Meaning and verification". *The Philosophical Review* 45, 339–369.
Shopen, T. (ed.)
1985 *Language Typology and Syntactic Description.* Vol. II: *Complex Constructions.* Cambridge: Cambridge University Press.
Skorupsky, J.
1993 *English-Language Philosophy, 1750 to 1945.* Oxford/New York: Oxford University Press.
Skytte, G.
1983 *La sintassi dell'infinito in italiano moderno, Etudes romanes de l'Université de Copenhague. Revue Romane,* Suppl. 27.

Slobin, D.
1996 "From 'thought and language' to 'thinking for speaking'". In Gumperz, J. J. & S. C. Levinson (eds.), *Rethinking Linguistic Relativity*. Cambridge: Cambridge University Press, 70–96.

Sommers, F.
1963(1967) "Types and ontology". *The Philosophical Review* 72, 527–63. Repr. in Strawson (ed. 1967), 138–169.

Sosa, E.
1975 "Introduction". In Sosa (ed. 1975), 1–32.

Sosa, E. (ed.)
1975 *Causation and Conditionals*. Oxford: Oxford University Press.

Sperber, D. & D. Wilson
1986 *Relevance. Communication and Cognition*. Oxford: Blackwell.
1986a "Façons de parler". *Cahiers de linguistique française* 7, 9–41.

Stalnaker, R. C.
1970 "Pragmatics". *Synthèse* 22, 272–289.
1973 "Presuppositions". *Journal of Philosophical Logic* 2, 447–457.
1974 "Pragmatic presuppositions". In Munitz, M. K. & P. K. Unger (eds.), *Semantics and Philosophy*. New York: New York University Press, 197–214.

Steinberg, D. D. & L. A. Jakobovits (eds.)
1971 *Semantics*. Cambridge: Cambridge University Press.

Steinitz, R.
1969 *Adverbial-Syntax*. Berlin: Akademie Verlag.

Stewart, D.
2002 "Il congiuntivo italiano: modo della realtà? Uno sguardo al congiuntivo nelle grammatiche italiane moderne". In Schena, L., M. Prandi & M. Mazzoleni (eds.), *Intorno al congiuntivo*. Bologna: CLUEB, 105–122.

Strawson, P. F.
1952 *Introduction to Logical Theory*. London: Methuen & Co.
1959(1964) *Individuals. An essay in Descriptive Metaphysics*. London: Methuen & Co. New paperback edition.
1992 *Metaphysics and Analysis*. Oxford: Oxford University Press.

Strawson, P. F. (ed.)
1967 *Philosophical Logic*. Oxford: Oxford University Press.

Svoboda, A.
1974 "On two communicative dynamisms". In Daneš (ed., 1974), 38–42.

Swan, M.
1980 *Practical English Usage*. Oxford: Oxford University Press.

Sweet, H.
1891–1898 *A New English Grammar: Logical and Historical*. London: Clarendon Press.

Sweetster, E.
1990 *From Etymology to Pragmatics*. Cambridge: Cambridge University Press.

Talmy, L.
1978 "Figure and ground in complex sentences". In Greenberg, J. H., C. A. Ferguson & E. A. Moravcsick (eds.), *Universals of Human Language.* Vol. 4: *Syntax.* Stanford: Stanford University Press, 625–652.
2000 *Toward a Cognitive Semantics.* Vol. I: *Concept Structuring Systems.* Cambridge / Mass: The MIT Press.
Taylor, Ch.
1964 *The Explanation of Behaviour.* London: Routledge & Kegan Paul/New York: The Humanities Press.
Taylor, J. R.
1989 *Linguistic Categorization: Prototypes in Linguistic Theory.* Oxford: Clarendon Press.
Tesnière, L.
1959(1966) *Eléments de syntaxe structurale.* 2nd edition. Paris: Klincksieck.
Thompson, S. A.
1987 "Subordination and narrative event structure". In Tomlin, R. (ed.), *Coherence and Grounding in Discourse.* Amsterdam/Philadelphia: John Benjamins, 435–454.
Thompson, S. A. & R. E. Longacre
1985 "Adverbial clauses". In Shopen (ed., 1985), 171–234.
Todorov, T.
1966 "Les anomalies sémantiques". *Langages* 1, 100–128.
1970 "Synecdoques". *Communications* 16. Repr. in Todorov, T., W. Empson, J. Cohen, G. Hartman & F. Rigolot (eds.), *Sémantique de la poésie.* Paris: Editions du Seuil, 1979, 7–26.
Tomlin, R.
1985 "Foreground-background information and the syntax of subordination". *Text* 5, 85–122.
Trier, J.
1931(1973) *Der deutsche Wortschatz im Sinnbezirk des Verstandes. Die Geschichte eines sprachlichen Feldes.* Part I: *Von den Anfangen bis zum Beginn des 13. Jahrhunderts.* Heidelberg: Winter. Repr. in Trier (1973), 40–65.
1932(1973) "Sprachliche Felder". *Zeitschrift für Deutsche Bildung* 8. Repr. in Trier (1973), 93–109.
1934(1973) "Das sprachliche Feld. Eine Auseinandersetzung". *Neue Jahrbücher für Wissenschaft und Jugendbildung* 10. Repr. in Trier (1973), 145–178.
1973 *Aussätze und Vorträge zur Wortfeldtheorie.* Herausgegeben von Lee, A. van der, & O. Reichmann. The Hague/Paris: Mouton.
Troubetzkoy, N. S.
1939 *Grundzüge der Phonologie.* Prague: Travaux du Cercle Linguistique de Prague.
Urmson, J. O.
1952(1968) "Motives and causes". *Proceedings of the Aristotelian Society* XXVI, 179–94. Repr. in White (ed., 1968), 153–165.

Velde, R. G. van de

1984 *Prolegomena to Inferential Discourse Processing.* Amsterdam/Philadelphia: John Benjamins.

Vater, H.

1978 "On the possibility of distinguishing between complements and adjuncts". In Abraham, W. (ed.), *Valence, Semantic Case and Grammatical Relations*, Amsterdam, 21–45.

Vendler, Z.

1967 *Linguistics in Philosophy.* Ithaca / N.Y: Cornell University Press.

1970 "Say what you think". In Cown, J. (ed.), *Studies in Thought and Language.* Tucson: The University of Arizona Press, 79–97.

Verstraete, J.-C.

1998 "A semiotic model for the description of levels in conjunction: external, internal-modal and internal-speech functional". *Functions of Language* 5, 179–211.

1999 "The distinction between epistemic and speech act conjunction". *Belgian Essays in Linguistics and Literature*, 119–130.

2002 "The functional value of non-integration in clause combining: interpersonal versus discursive independence". *Word* 53, 37–65.

Vinsauf, G. de

"Poetria Nova", in Faral (1924).

Waisman, F.

1945(1968) "Verifiability". *Proceedings of the Aristotelian Society*, Suppl. Vol. 19. Repr. in Parkinson, G. H. R. (ed.), *The Theory of Meaning.* Oxford: Oxford University Press, 35–60.

Walsh, M.

1995 "Body parts in Murrinh-Patha: incorporation, grammar and metaphor". In Chappell, H. & W. McGregor (eds.), *The Grammar of Inalienability: a Typological Perspective on Body Parts Terms and The Part Whole Relation.* Berlin/New York: Mouton de Gruyter, 327–380.

Waltereit, R.

1999 "Grammatical constraints on metonymic reference". In Panther & Radden (eds., 1999), 233–253.

Wandruszka, U.

1991(2001) "Frasi subordinate al congiuntivo". In Renzi, L., G. Salvi & A. Cardinaletti (eds.), *Grande grammatica italiana di consultazione.* Vol. II, 2nd ed. Bologna: Il Mulino, 415–481.

Weber, M.

1922 *Wirtschaft und Gesellschaft.* Tübingen: Mohr.

Weinreich, U.

1966 "Explorations in semantic theory". In Sebeok, Th. A. (ed., 1966).

1975 "Lexicographic definitions in descriptive semantics". In Householder, F. H. & S. Saporta (eds.), *Problems in Lexicography.* Bloomington: Indiana University Press, 25–44.

Weinrich, H.
1958 "Münze und Wort. Untersuchungen an einem Bildfeld". In *Romanica. Festschrift Rohlfs.* Halle: Niemeyer, 508–521.
1963 "Semantik der kühnen Metapher". *Deutsche Vierteljahrs-schrift für Literaturwissenschaft and Geistesgeschichte* 37, 325–344.
1964 *Tempus. Besprochene und erzählte Welt.* Stuttgart: Kohlhammer.
1964a "Typen der Gedächtnismetaphorik". *Archiv für Begriffsgeschichte* IX, 23–26.

Wells, R.
1947 "Immediate constituents". *Language* 23, 81–117.

Wetzer, H.
1996 *The typology of adjectival predication.* Berlin/New York: Mouton de Gruyter.

White, A. R.
1968 "Introduction". In White (ed., 1968), 1–18.

White, A. R. (ed.)
1968 *The Philosophy of Action.* Oxford: Oxford University Press.

Whitman-Linsen, C.
1992 *Through the Dubbing Glass. The Synchronization of American Motion Pictures into German, French and Spanish.* Bern/Frankfurt am Main: Peter Lang.

Whorf, B. L.
1941(1956) "The relation of habitual thought and behaviour to language". In Spier, L. (ed.), *Language, Culture and Personality, Essays in Memory of Edward Sapir.* Menasha/Wis: Sapir Memorial Publication Found, 75–93. Repr. in Whorf (1956).
1956 *Language, Thought and Reality: Selected Writings of Benjamin Lee Whorf.* New York: Wiley.

Wierzbicka, A.
1972 *Semantic Primitives.* Frankfurt a. M.: Athenäum Verlag.
1980 *Lingua Mentalis.* Sidney/New York: Academic Press.
1985 *Lexicography and Conceptual Analysis.* Ann Arbor: Karoma.
1987 "Boys will be boys: 'Radical Semantics' vs 'Radical Pragmatics'". *Language* 63, 95–114.
1988 *The Semantics of Grammar.* Amsterdam/Philadelphia: John Benjamins.
1988a "Boys will be boys: a rejoinder to Bruce Fraser". *Journal of Pragmatics* 12, 221–224.
1995 "A semantic basis for grammatical typology". In Abraham, Givón & Thompson (eds., 1995), 179–209.
1996 *Semantics. Primes and Universals.* Oxford/New York: Oxford University Press.

Wilmet, M.
1986 *La détermination nominale.* Paris: Presses Universitaires de France.

Windelband, W.
1894 "Geschichte und Naturwissenschaft". In *Das Stiftungsfest der Kaiser-Wilhelms-Universität.* Strasbourg: Universitätsbuchdruckerei Heitz & Mündel.

Wittgenstein, L.

1922(1961) *Tractatus Logico-Philosophicus. German Text with English Translation.* London: Routledge & Kegan Paul. *German Text with a New English Translation* by Pears, D. F. & B. F. McGuinness. London: Routledge & Kegan Paul.

1929 "Some remarks on logical form". *Proceedings of the Aristotelian Society.* Suppl. Vol. IX, 162–171.

1953(1968) *Philosophische Untersuchungen.* Oxford: Blackwell. Engl. transl.: *Philosophical Investigations.* Oxford: Blackwell.

1961 *Notebooks 1914–1916.* Oxford: Blackwell.

1969 *Über Gewissheit — On Certainty.* Oxford: Blackwell.

Wright, G. H. von

1971 *Explanation and Understanding.* Ithaca-New York: Cornell University Press.

Zgusta, L.

1971 *Manual of Lexicography.* Prague: Academia. The Hague/Paris: Mouton.

Dictionaries

Collins Cobuild English Language Dictionary. London: Harper Collins Publishers, 1989.

Webster's Third New International Dictionary of the English Language. London: Bell & Sons LTD, 1961.

Index

In the series *Human Cognitive Processing* the following titles have been published thus far or are scheduled for publication:

1 **YU, Ning:** The Contemporary Theory of Metaphor. A perspective from Chinese. 1998. x, 278 pp.
2 **COOPER, David L.:** Linguistic Attractors. The cognitive dynamics of language acquisition and change. 1999. xv, 375 pp.
3 **FUCHS, Catherine and Stéphane ROBERT (eds.):** Language Diversity and Cognitive Representations. 1999. x, 229 pp.
4 **PANTHER, Klaus-Uwe and Günter RADDEN (eds.):** Metonymy in Language and Thought. 1999. vii, 410 pp.
5 **NUYTS, Jan:** Epistemic Modality, Language, and Conceptualization. A cognitive-pragmatic perspective. 2001. xx, 429 pp.
6 **FORTESCUE, Michael:** Pattern and Process. A Whiteheadian perspective on linguistics. 2001. viii, 312 pp.
7 **SCHLESINGER, Izchak M., Tamar KEREN-PORTNOY and Tamar PARUSH:** The Structure of Arguments. 2001. xx, 264 pp.
8 **SANDERS, Ted J.M., Joost SCHILPEROORD and Wilbert SPOOREN (eds.):** Text Representation. Linguistic and psycholinguistic aspects. 2001. viii, 364 pp.
9 **GRAUMANN, Carl Friedrich and Werner KALLMEYER (eds.):** Perspective and Perspectivation in Discourse. 2002. vi, 401 pp.
10 **SKOUSEN, Royal, Deryle LONSDALE and Dilworth B. PARKINSON (eds.):** Analogical Modeling. An exemplar-based approach to language. 2002. x, 417 pp.
11 **SHELLEY, Cameron:** Multiple Analogies in Science and Philosophy. 2003. xvi, 168 pp.
12 **EVANS, Vyvyan:** The Structure of Time. Language, meaning and temporal cognition. 2004. x, 287 pp.
13 **PRANDI, Michele:** The Building Blocks of Meaning. Ideas for a Philosophical grammar. 2004. xviii, 511 pp. + index.